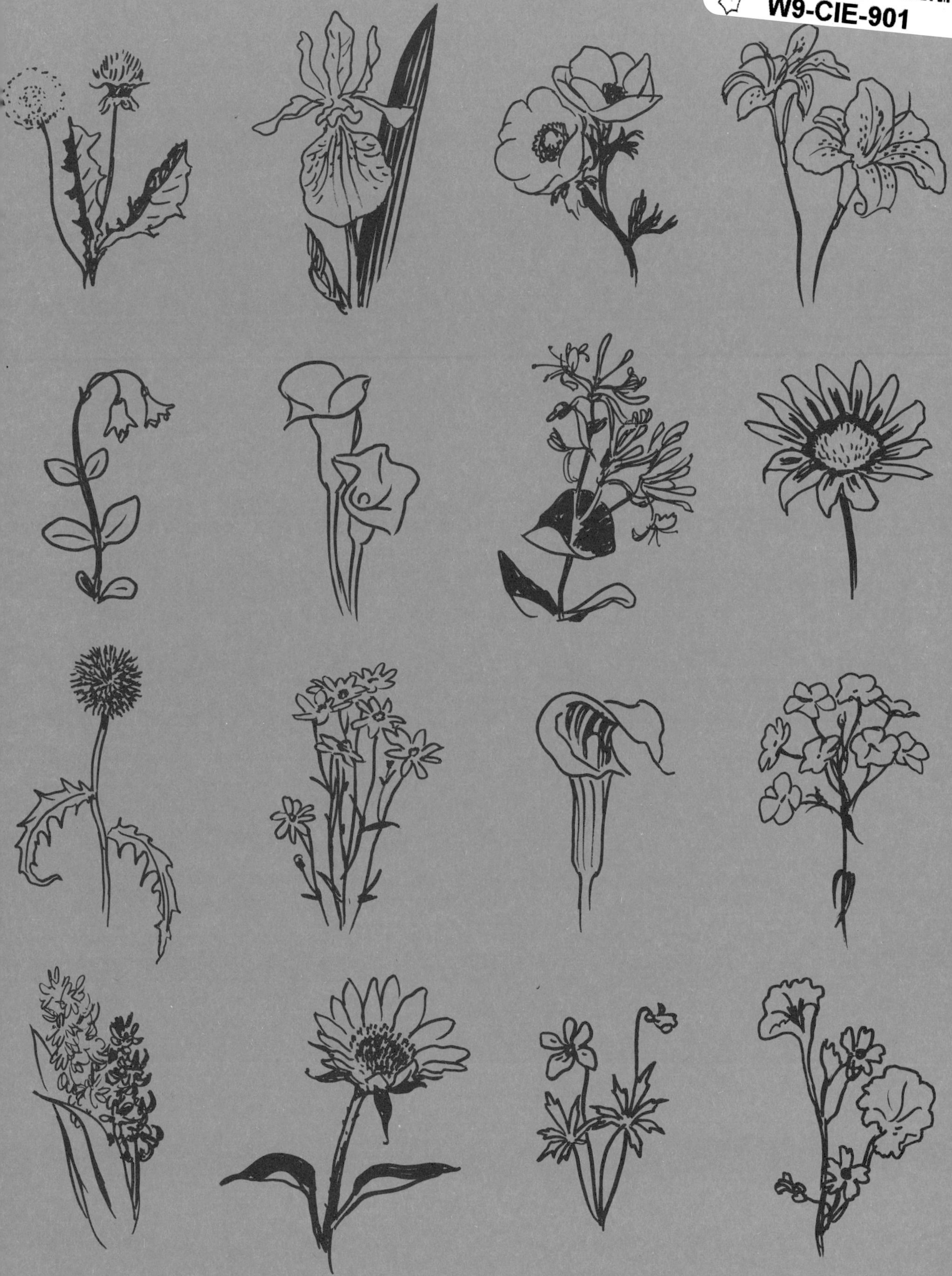

Asterios

DAVID MAZZUCCHELLI

PANTHEON BOOKS
NEW YORK

Polyp

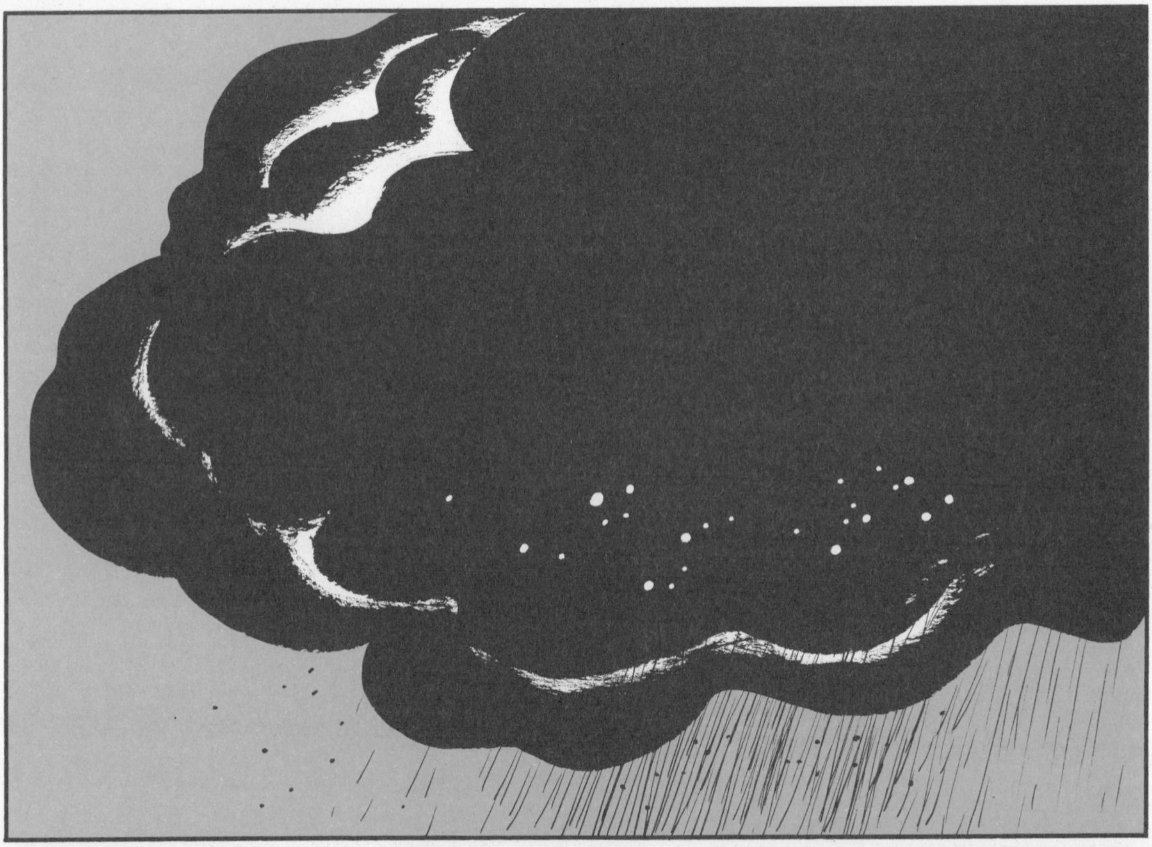
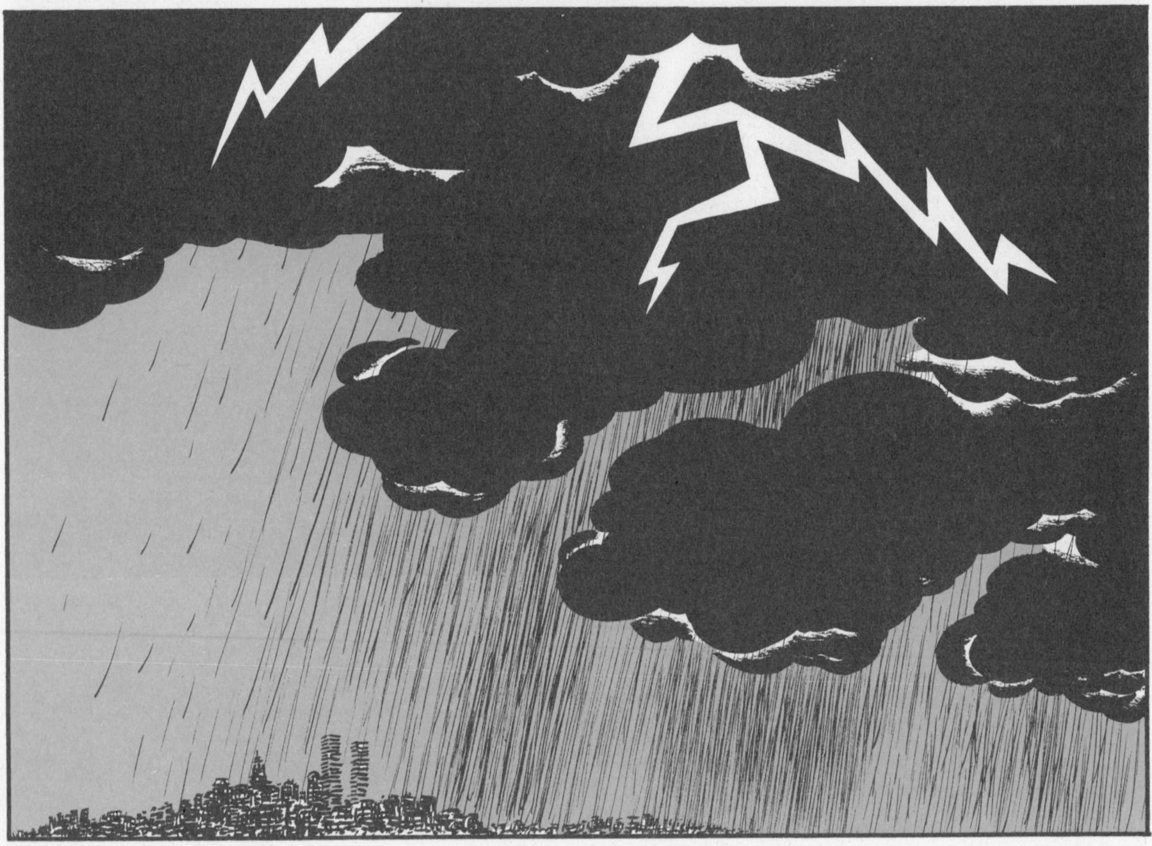

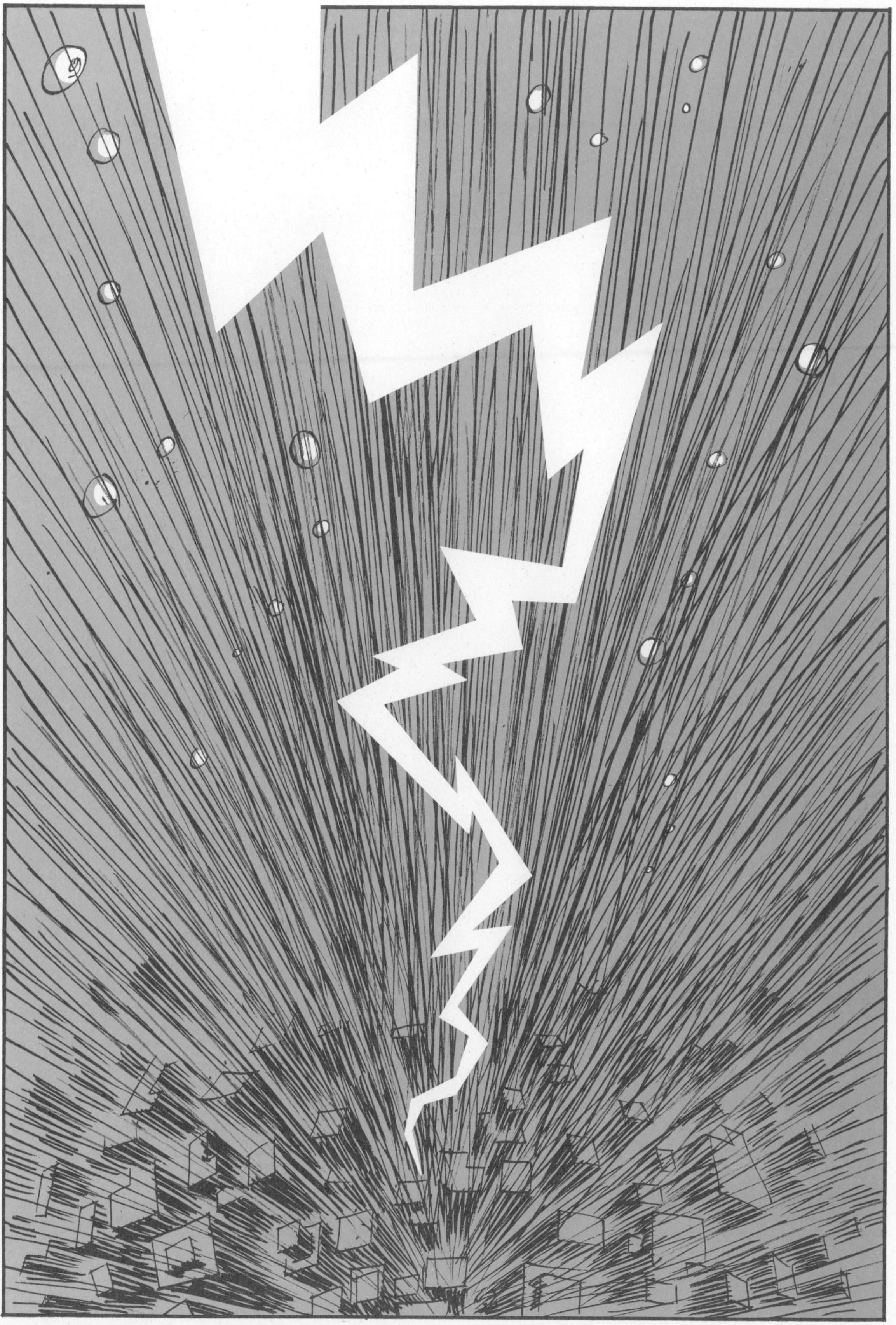

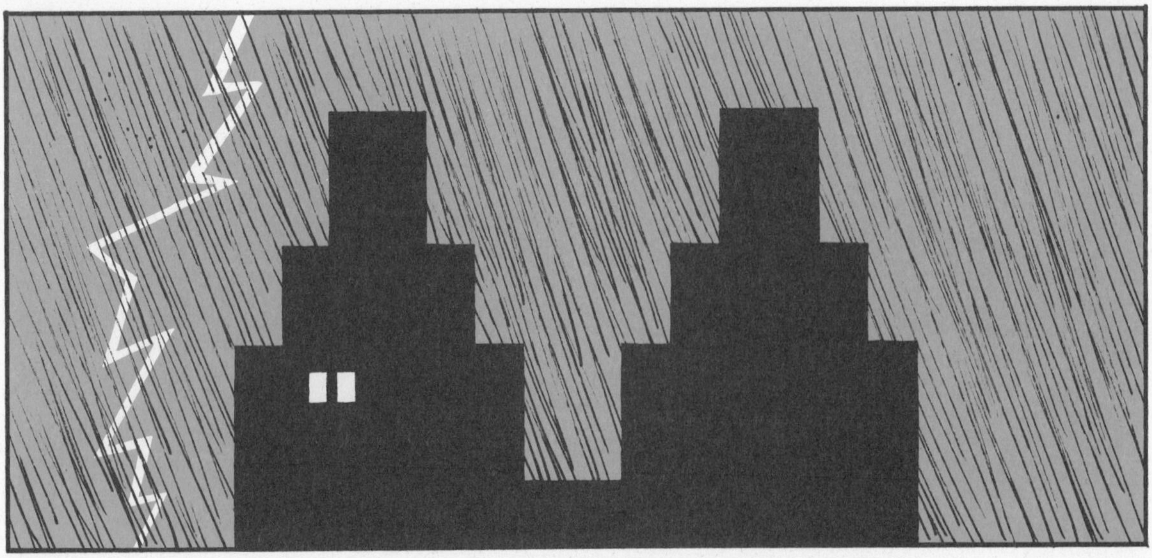

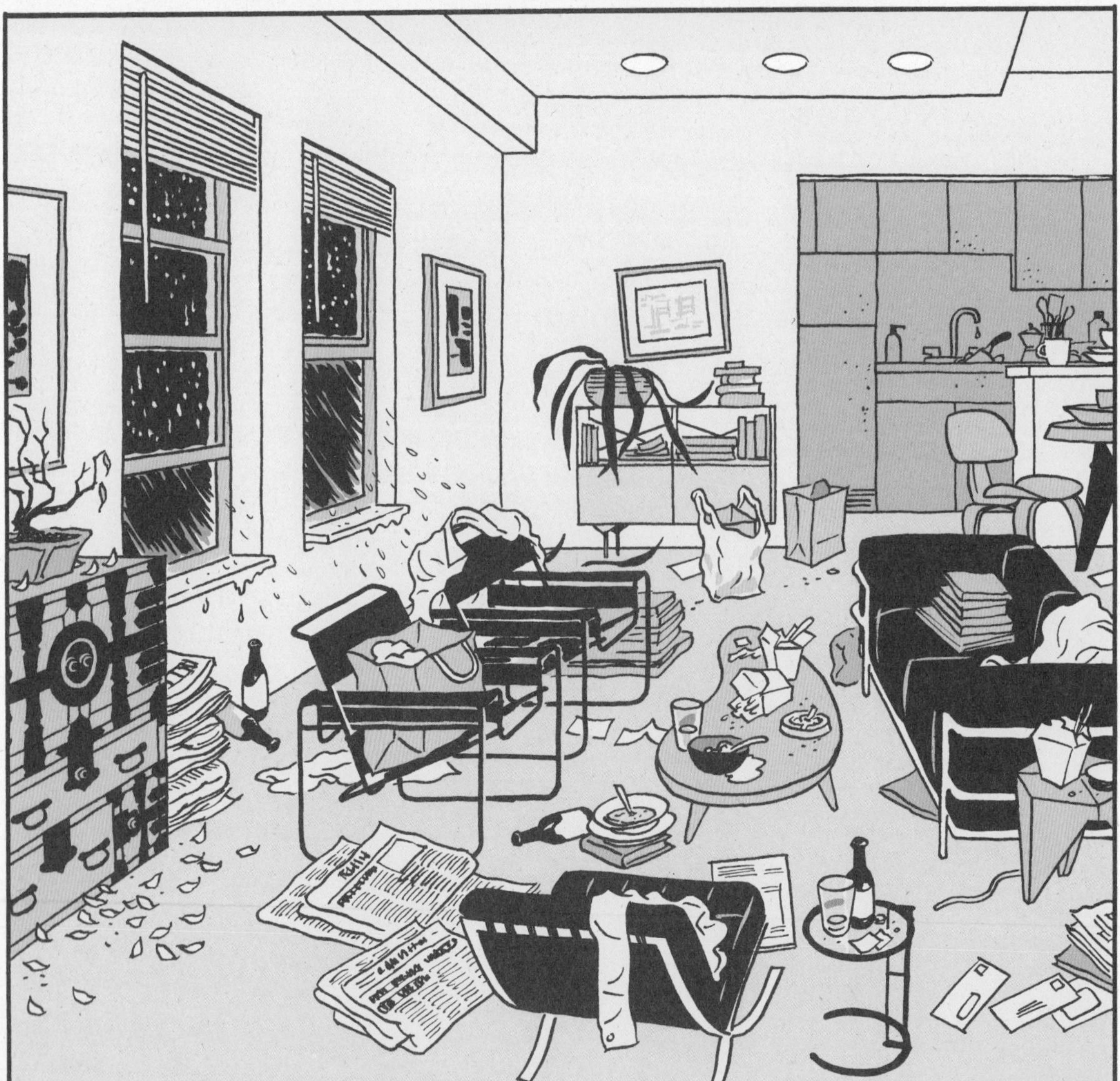

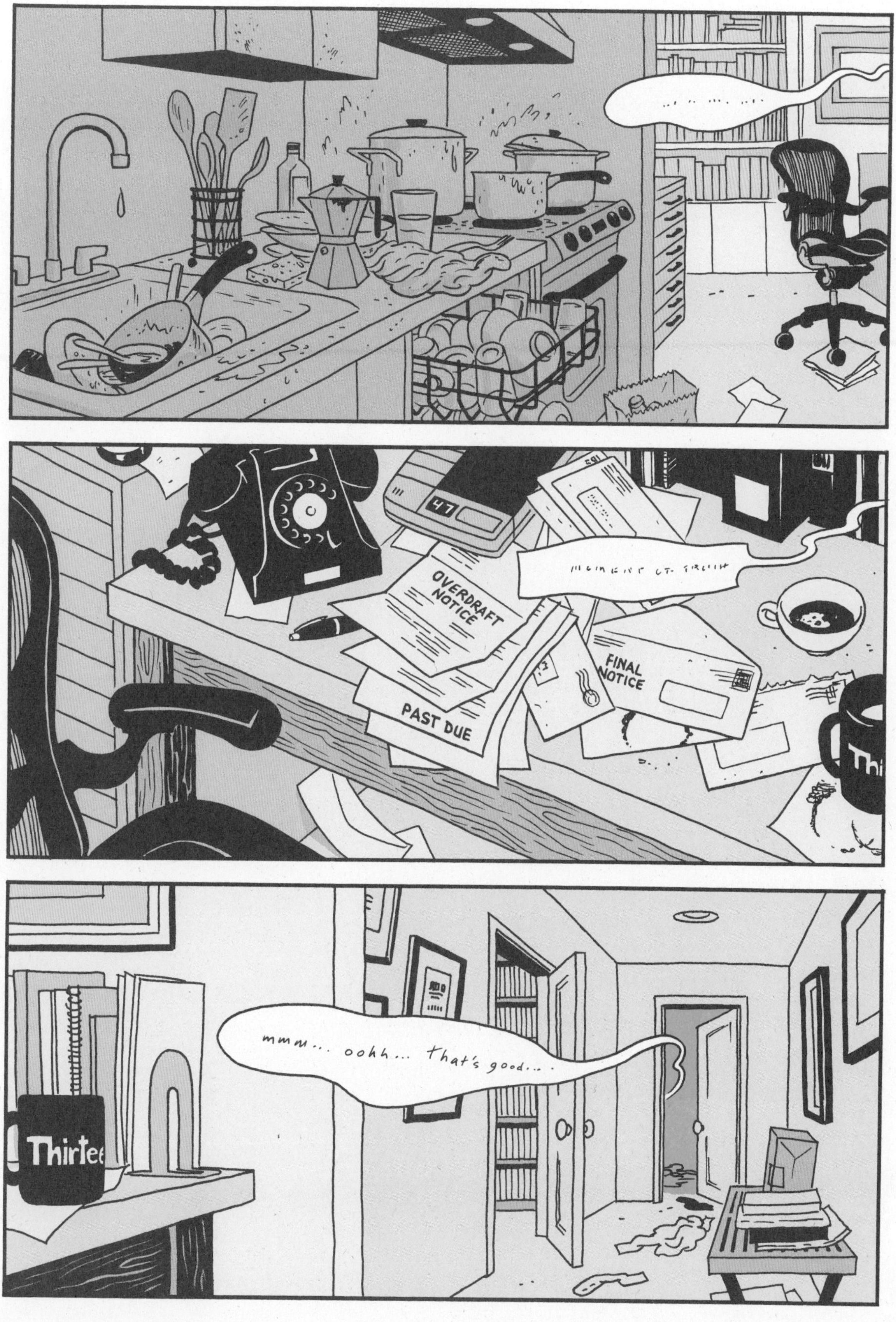
OVERDRAFT NOTICE
FINAL NOTICE
PAST DUE
Thir
Thirtee
mmm... oohh... that's good...

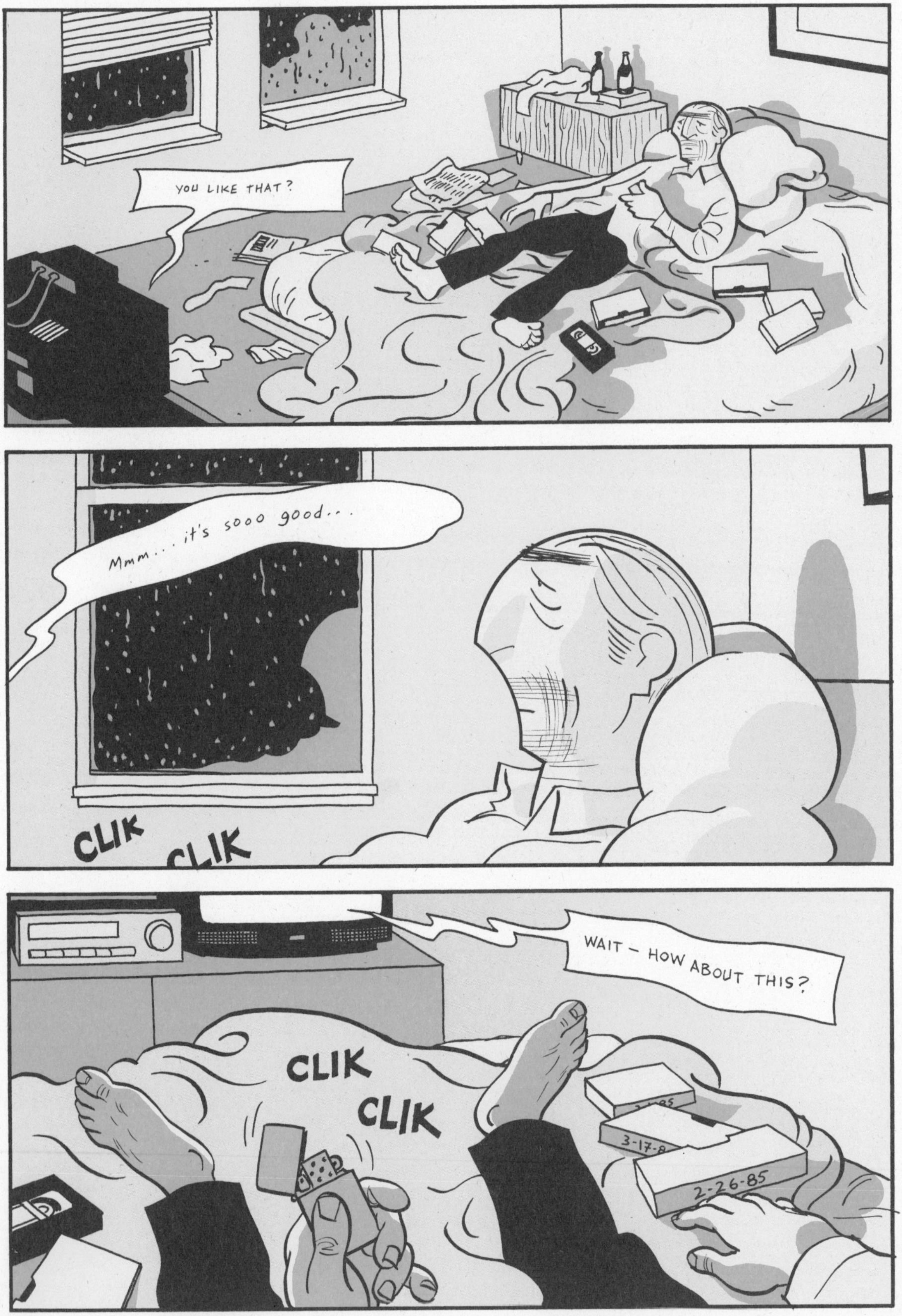
YOU LIKE THAT?
Mmm... it's sooo good...
CLIK
CLIK
WAIT – HOW ABOUT THIS?
CLIK
CLIK
3-17-8
2-26-85

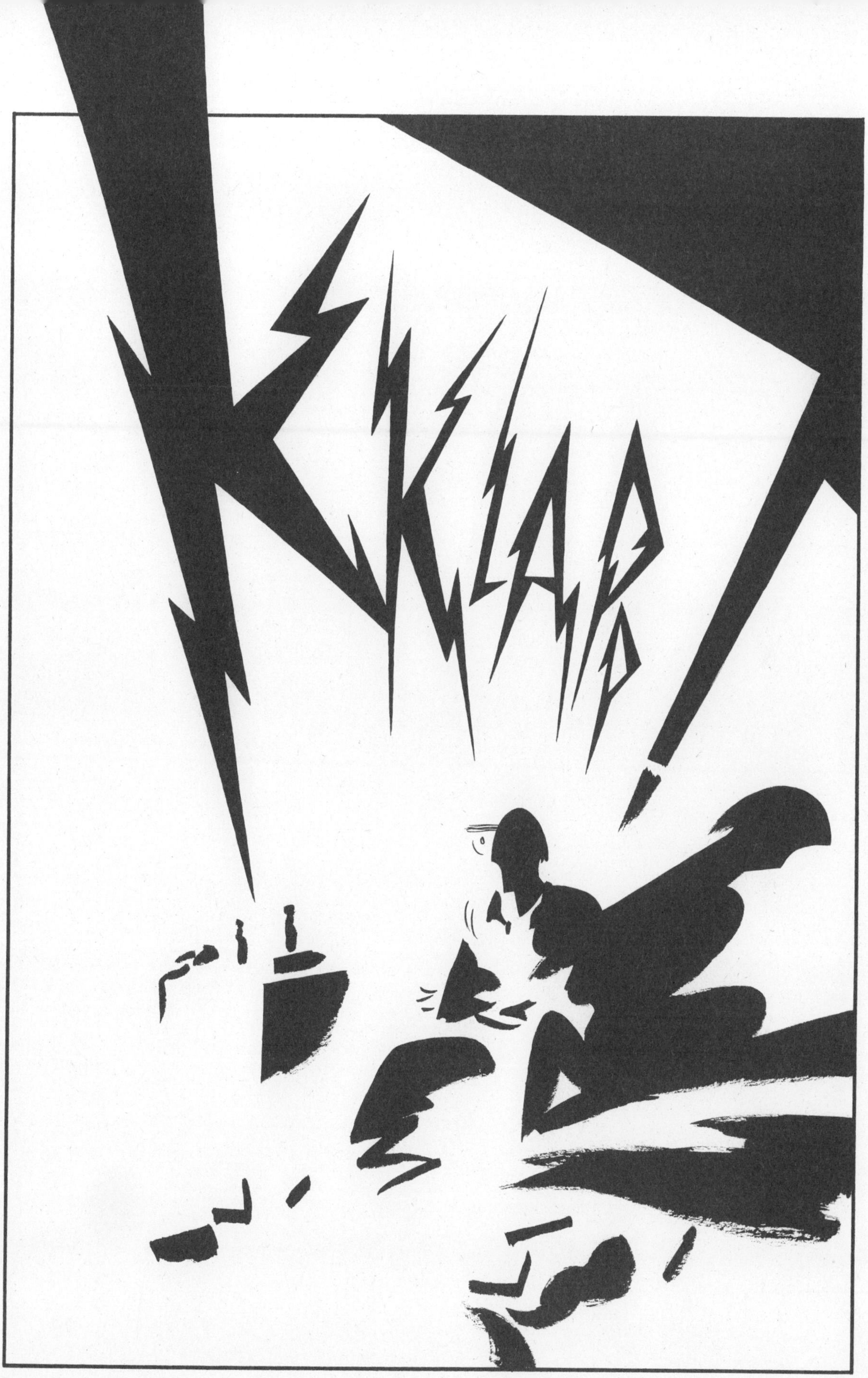
KKLABP!

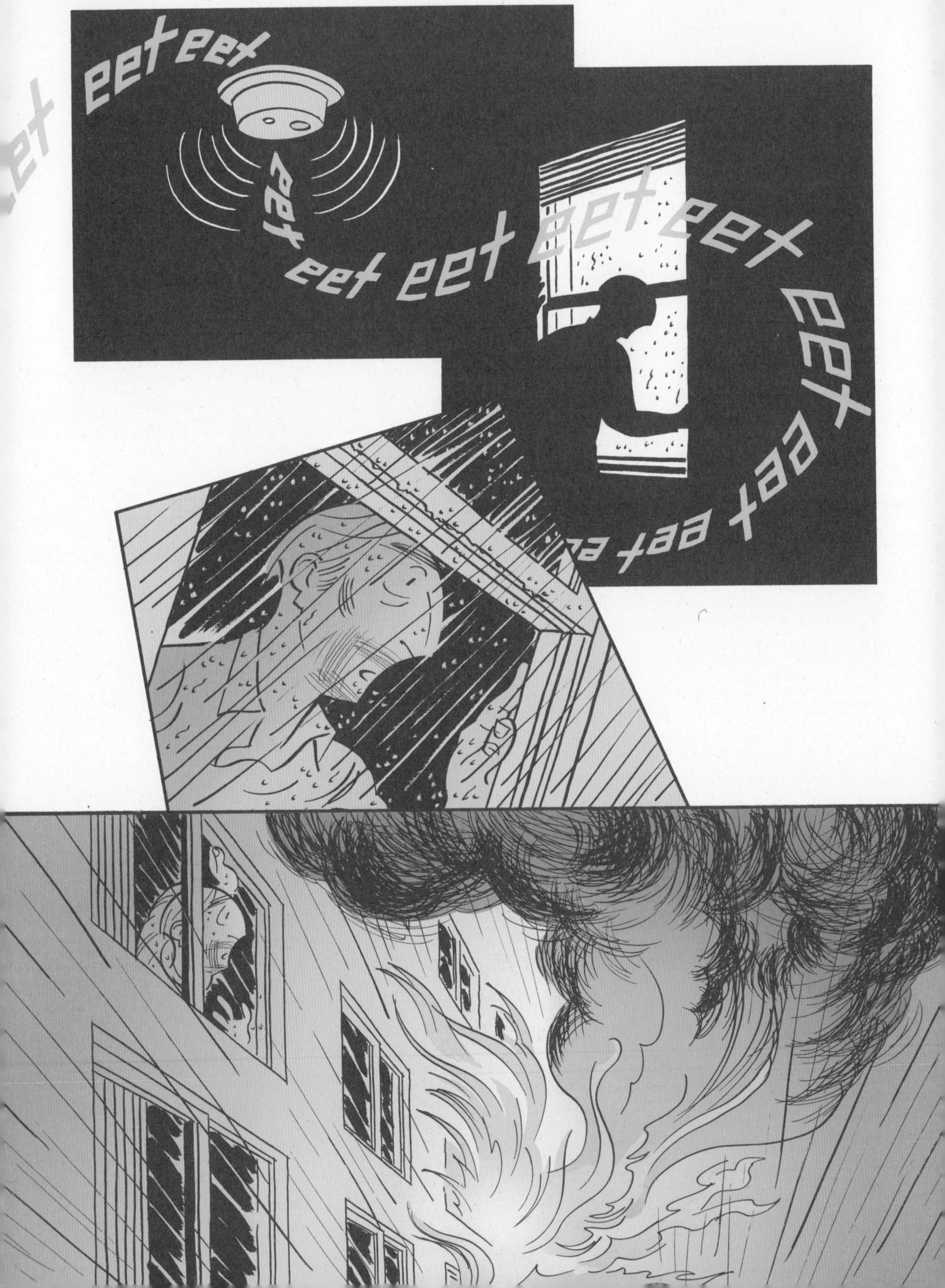
eet eet
eet eet eet eet eet
eet eet eet

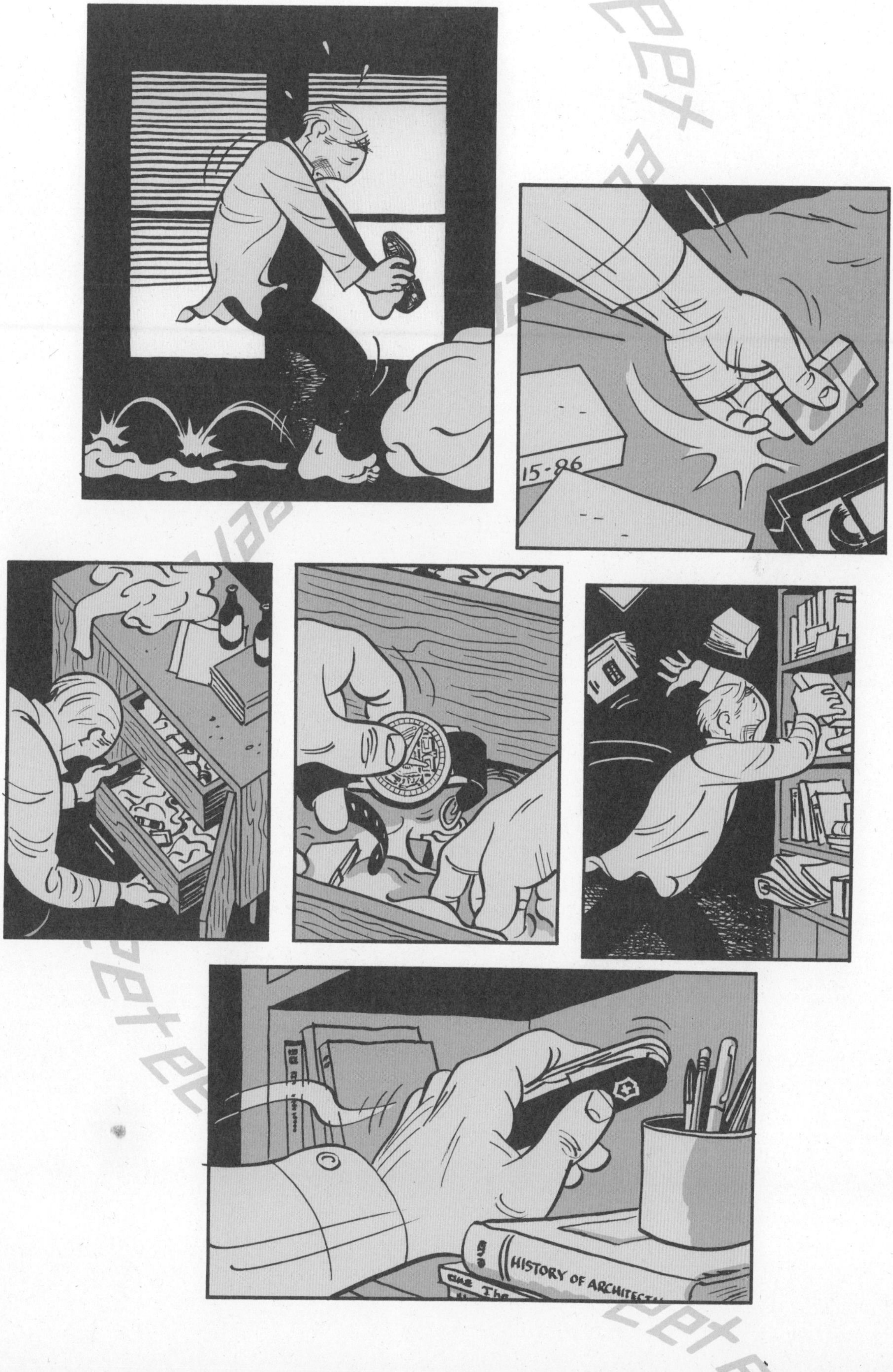
15-86
HISTORY OF ARCHITECT

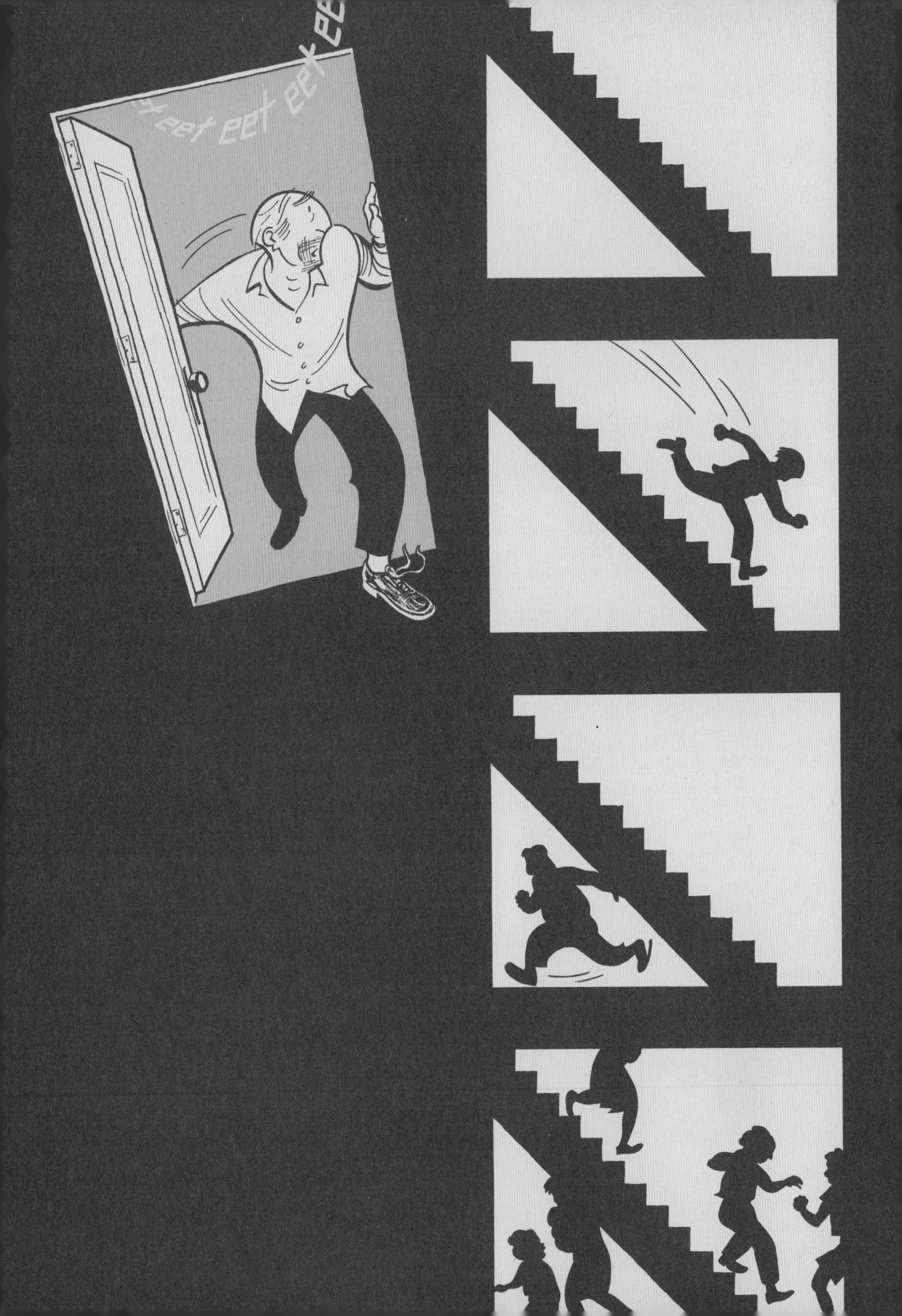
eet eet eet

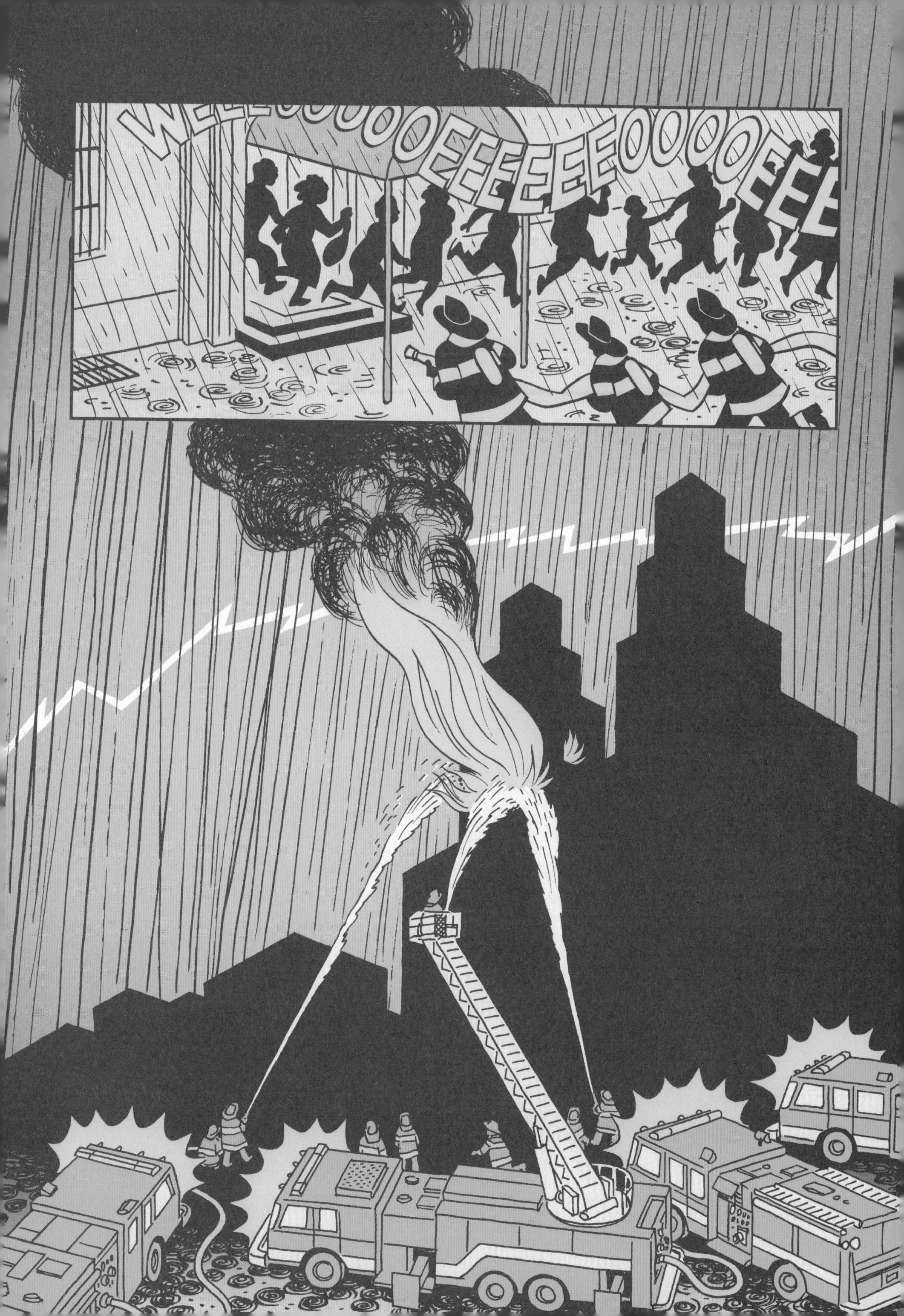
WEEEOOOOOOEEEEEEEOOOOOEEE

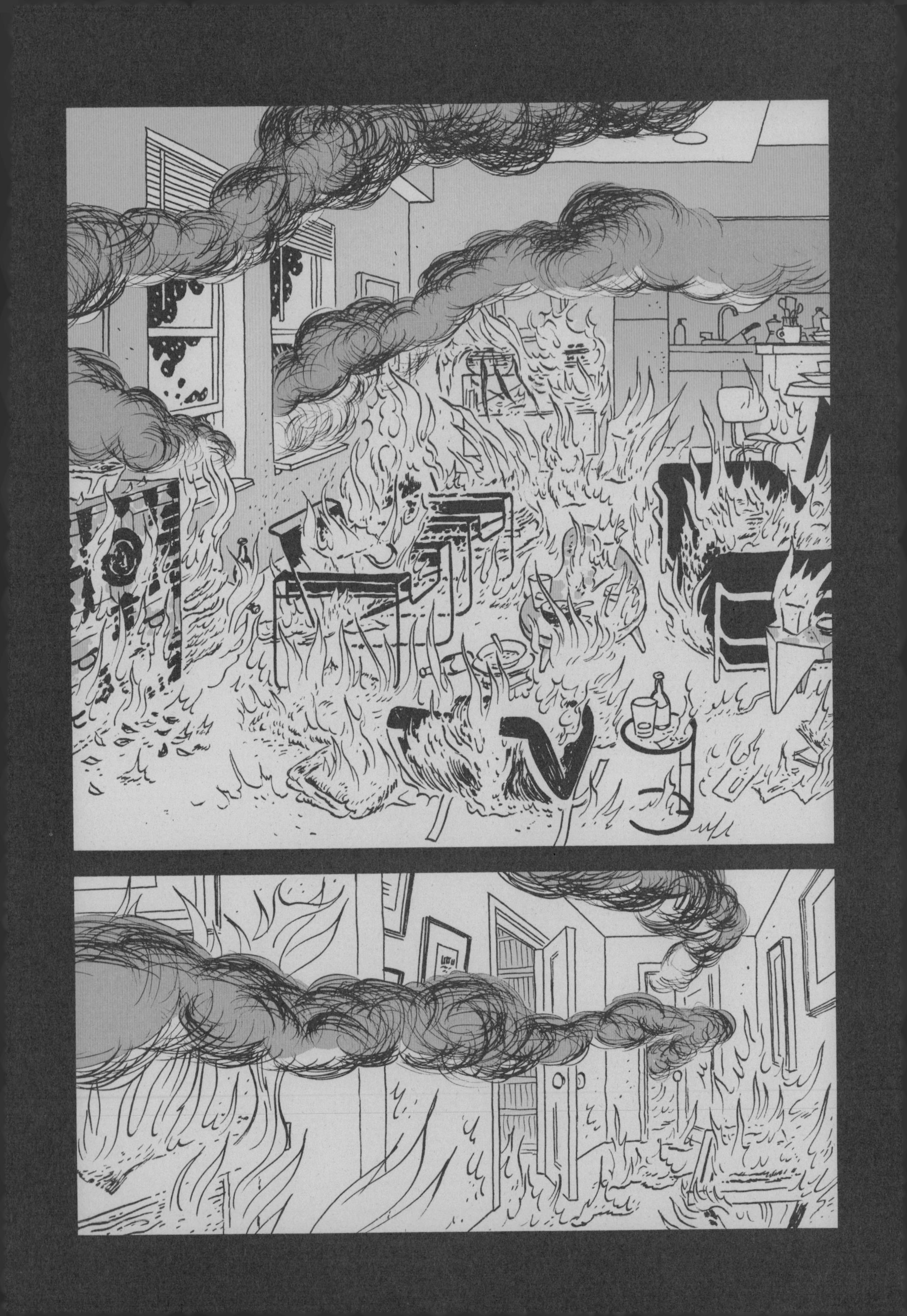

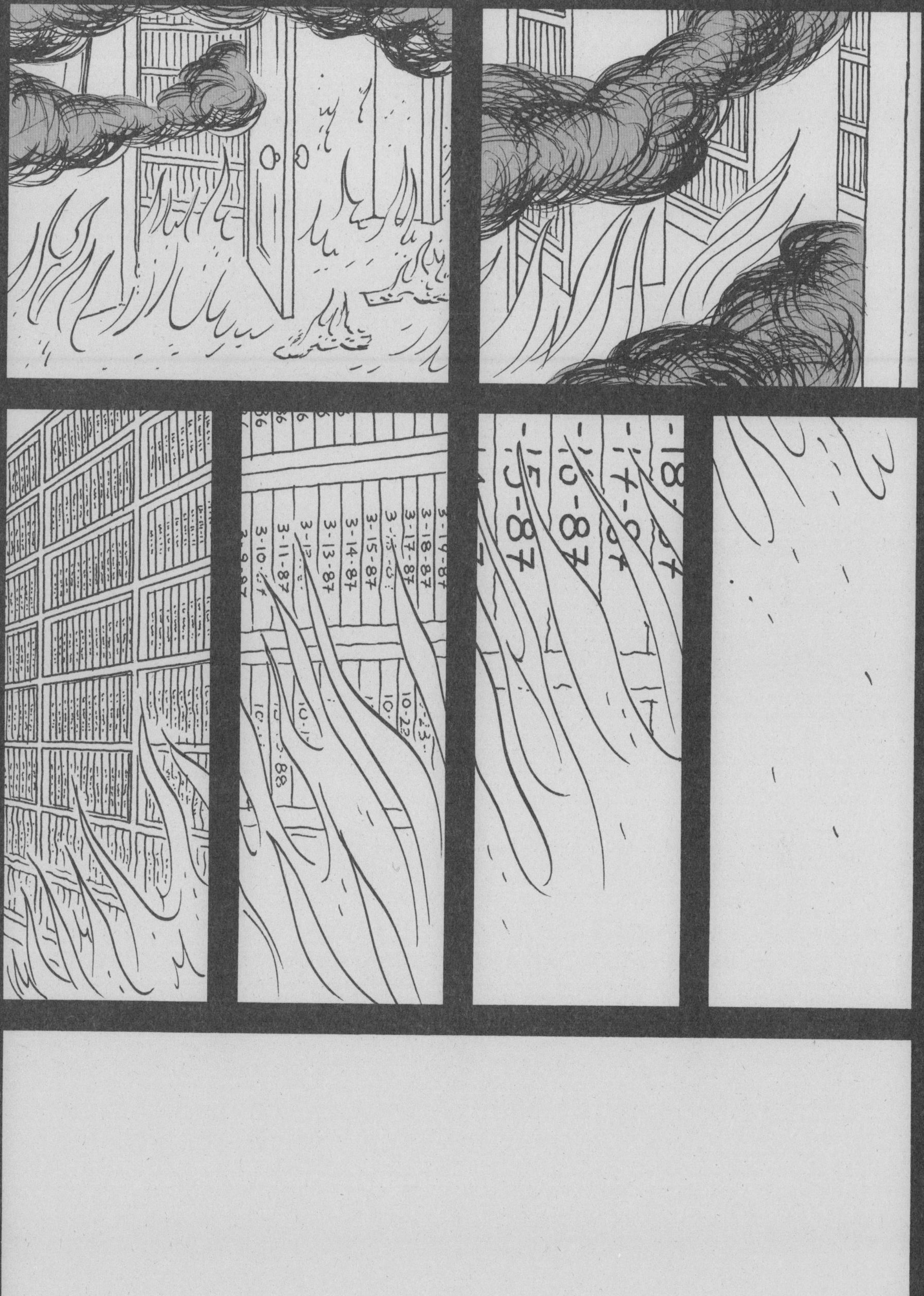

3-19-87
3-18-87
3-17-87
3-15-87
3-14-87
3-13-87
3-11-87
3-9-87

THIS IS ASTERIOS POLYP.

IF IT WERE POSSIBLE FOR ME TO NARRATE THIS STORY, I'D BEGIN HERE.

RIGHT NOW, HE'S WATCHING HIS HOME BURN UP.

TODAY — COINCIDENTALLY — ALSO HAPPENS TO BE HIS FIFTIETH BIRTHDAY.

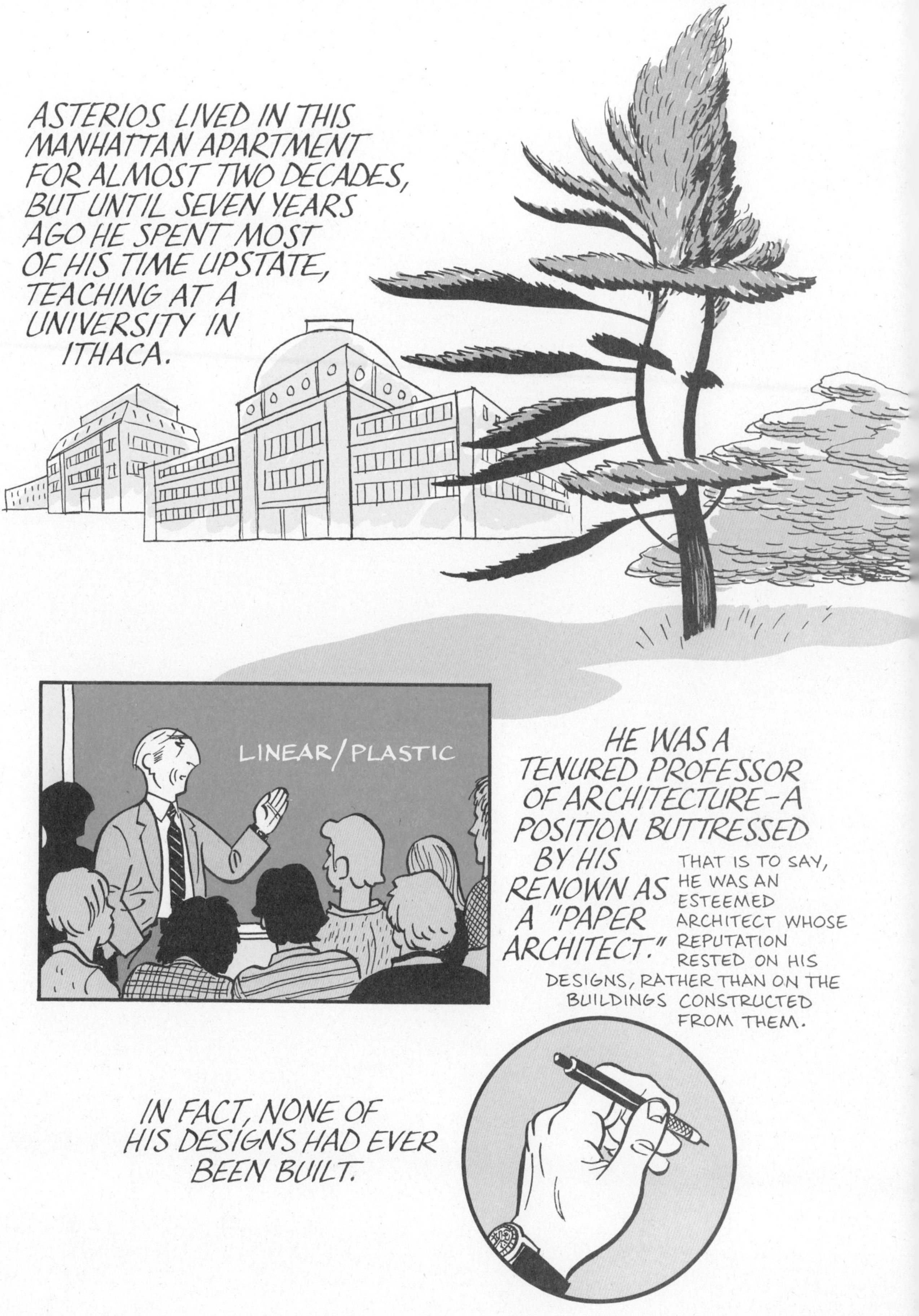
ASTERIOS LIVED IN THIS MANHATTAN APARTMENT FOR ALMOST TWO DECADES, BUT UNTIL SEVEN YEARS AGO HE SPENT MOST OF HIS TIME UPSTATE, TEACHING AT A UNIVERSITY IN ITHACA.
LINEAR/PLASTIC
HE WAS A TENURED PROFESSOR OF ARCHITECTURE—A POSITION BUTTRESSED BY HIS RENOWN AS A "PAPER ARCHITECT."
THAT IS TO SAY, HE WAS AN ESTEEMED ARCHITECT WHOSE REPUTATION RESTED ON HIS DESIGNS, RATHER THAN ON THE BUILDINGS CONSTRUCTED FROM THEM.
IN FACT, NONE OF HIS DESIGNS HAD EVER BEEN BUILT.

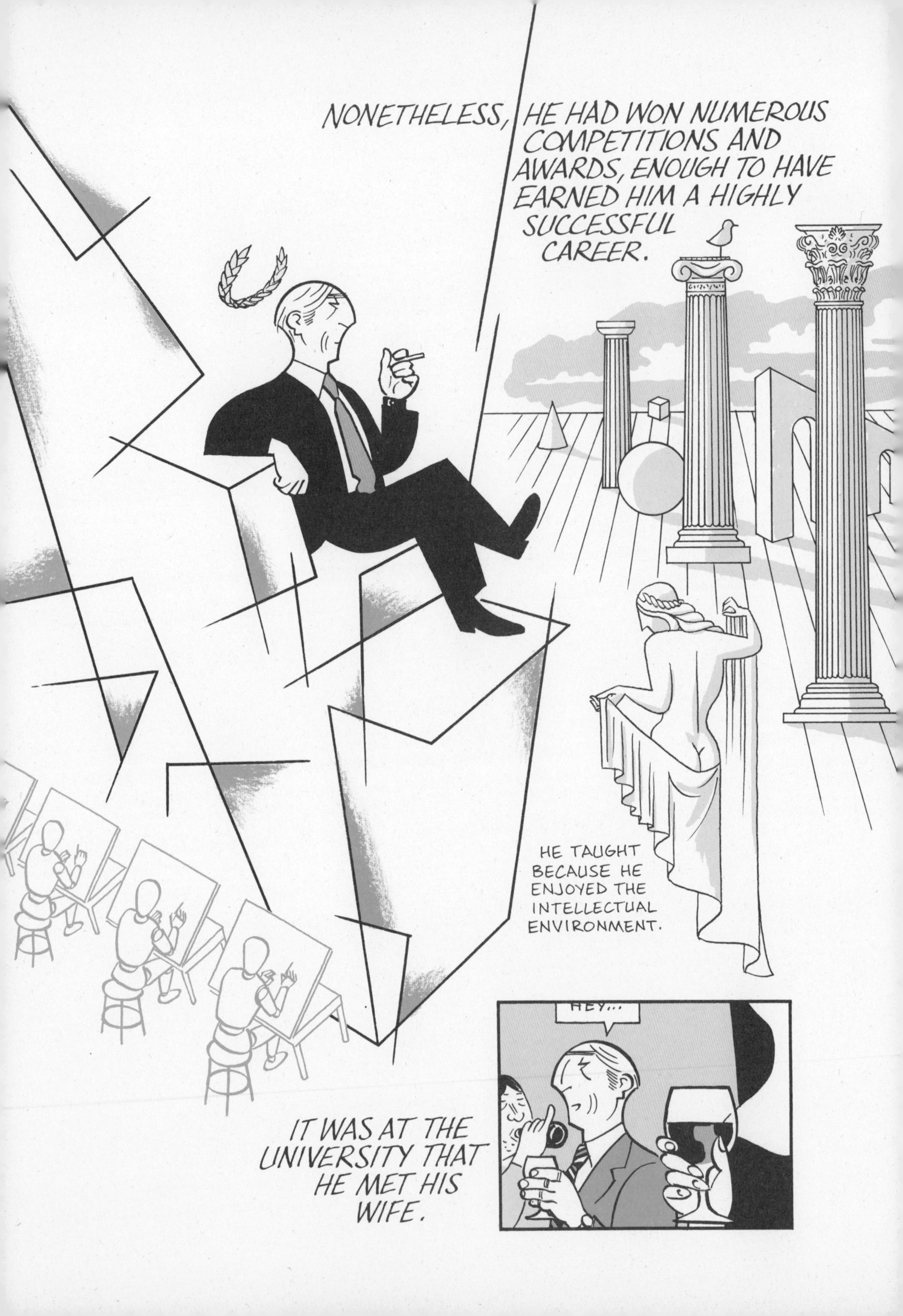
NONETHELESS, HE HAD WON NUMEROUS COMPETITIONS AND AWARDS, ENOUGH TO HAVE EARNED HIM A HIGHLY SUCCESSFUL CAREER.
HE TAUGHT BECAUSE HE ENJOYED THE INTELLECTUAL ENVIRONMENT.
IT WAS AT THE UNIVERSITY THAT HE MET HIS WIFE.
HEY...

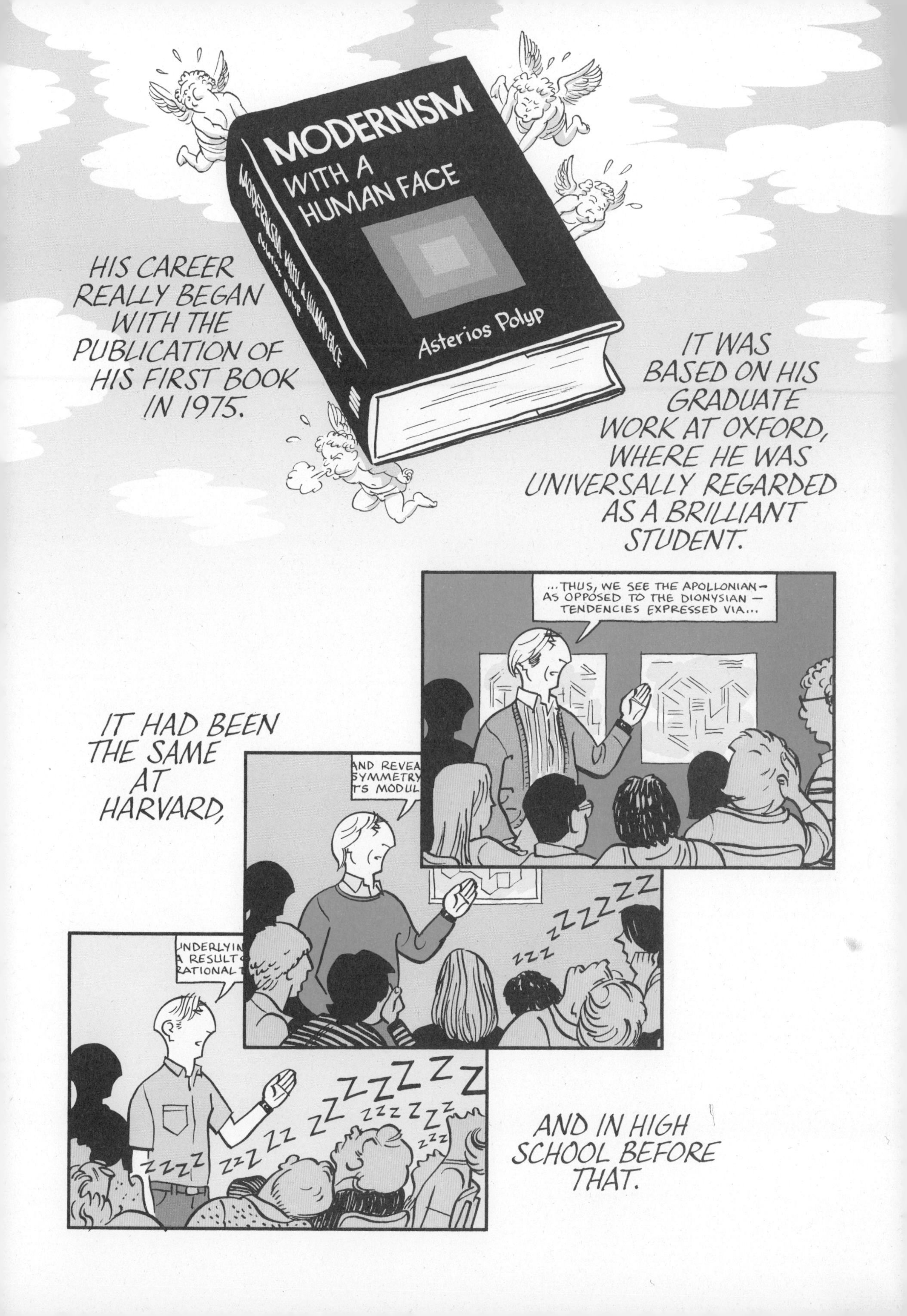
MODERNISM WITH A HUMAN FACE
Asterios Polyp
HIS CAREER REALLY BEGAN WITH THE PUBLICATION OF HIS FIRST BOOK IN 1975.
IT WAS BASED ON HIS GRADUATE WORK AT OXFORD, WHERE HE WAS UNIVERSALLY REGARDED AS A BRILLIANT STUDENT.
...THUS, WE SEE THE APOLLONIAN— AS OPPOSED TO THE DIONYSIAN— TENDENCIES EXPRESSED VIA...
IT HAD BEEN THE SAME AT HARVARD,
AND REVEA
SYMMETRY
TS MODUL
Z Z Z Z Z Z Z Z Z
UNDERLYIN
A RESULT
RATIONAL
Z Z Z Z Z Z Z Z Z Z Z Z Z Z Z Z
AND IN HIGH SCHOOL BEFORE THAT.

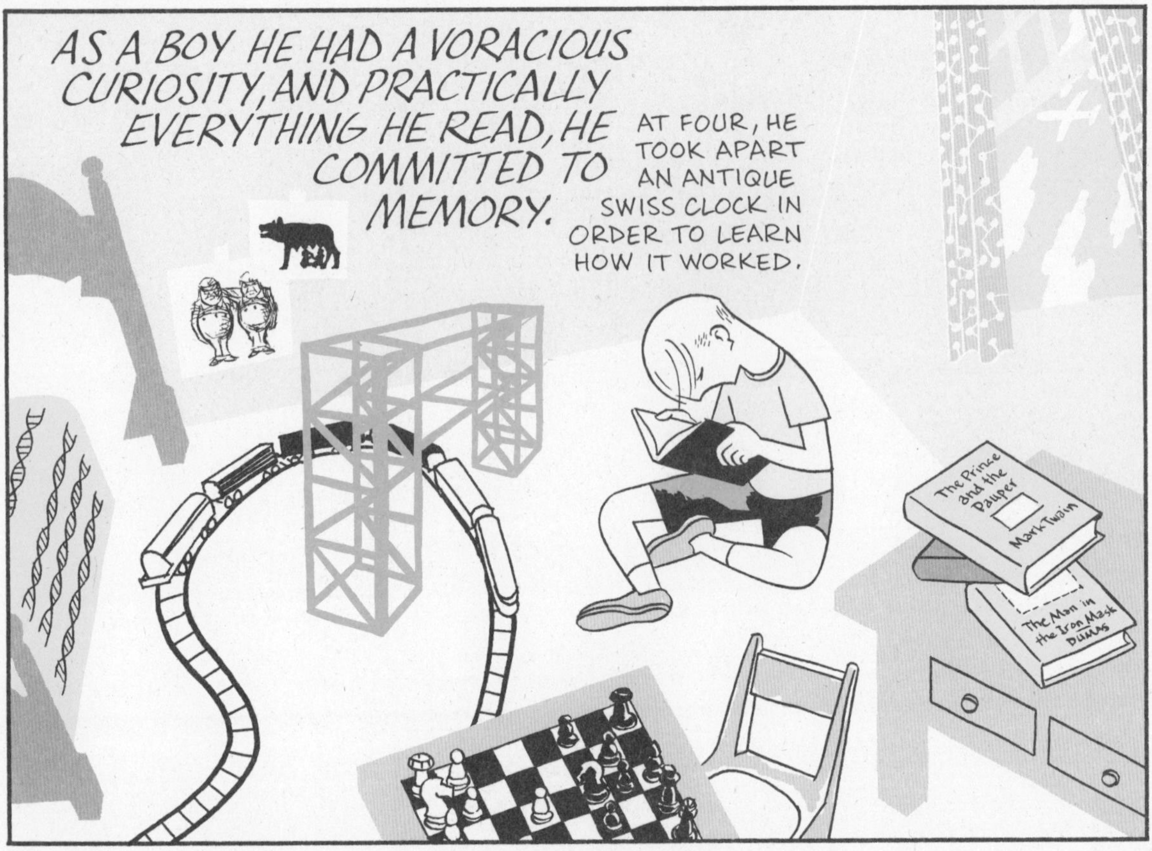
AS A BOY HE HAD A VORACIOUS CURIOSITY, AND PRACTICALLY EVERYTHING HE READ, HE COMMITTED TO MEMORY.
AT FOUR, HE TOOK APART AN ANTIQUE SWISS CLOCK IN ORDER TO LEARN HOW IT WORKED.
The Prince and the Pauper
Mark Twain
The Man in the Iron Mask
Dumas

HIS FATHER, DR. EUGENIOS POLYP, HAD IMMIGRATED AS A CHILD WITH HIS FAMILY IN 1919.

AN EXASPERATED ELLIS ISLAND OFFICIAL HAD CUT THE FAMILY NAME IN HALF, LEAVING ONLY THE FIRST FIVE LETTERS.

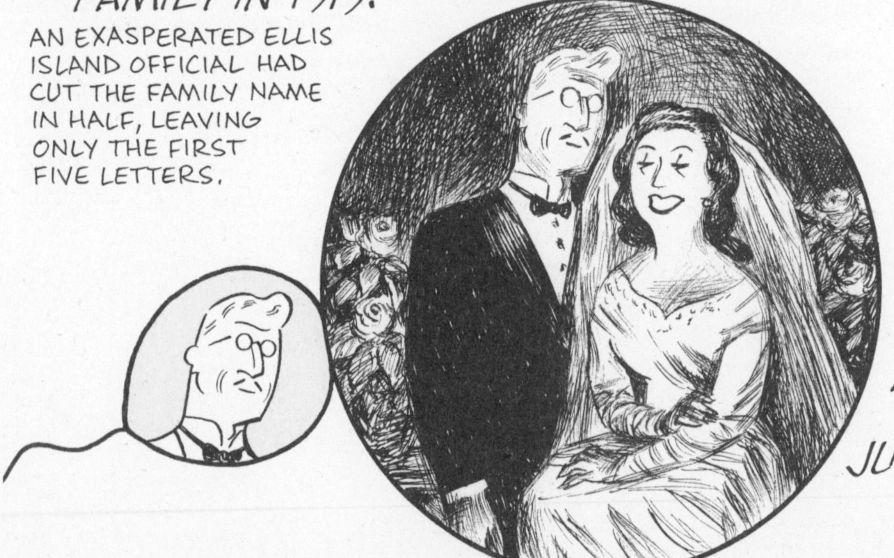

EUGENIOS MARRIED A HOPEFUL YOUNG GIRL NAMED AGLIA OLIO, AND ON JUNE 22, 1950,

AFTER A PAINFUL, THIRTY-THREE-HOUR LABOR, AGLIA GAVE BIRTH BY CESAREAN SECTION TO IDENTICAL TWINS.

HER HUSBAND DEFERRED TO THE EXPERT IN OBSTETRICS.

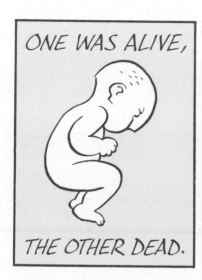

ONE WAS ALIVE, THE OTHER DEAD.

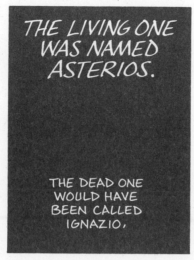

THE LIVING ONE WAS NAMED ASTERIOS.

THE DEAD ONE WOULD HAVE BEEN CALLED IGNAZIO,

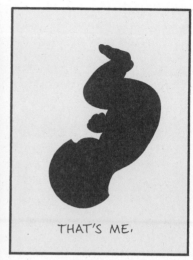

THAT'S ME.

AND NOW
(FIFTY YEARS LATER),
ASTERIOS IS STANDING
IN THE RAIN, WATCHING HIS
HOME BURN UP,
THINKING ONE
THING:

NOT AGAIN.

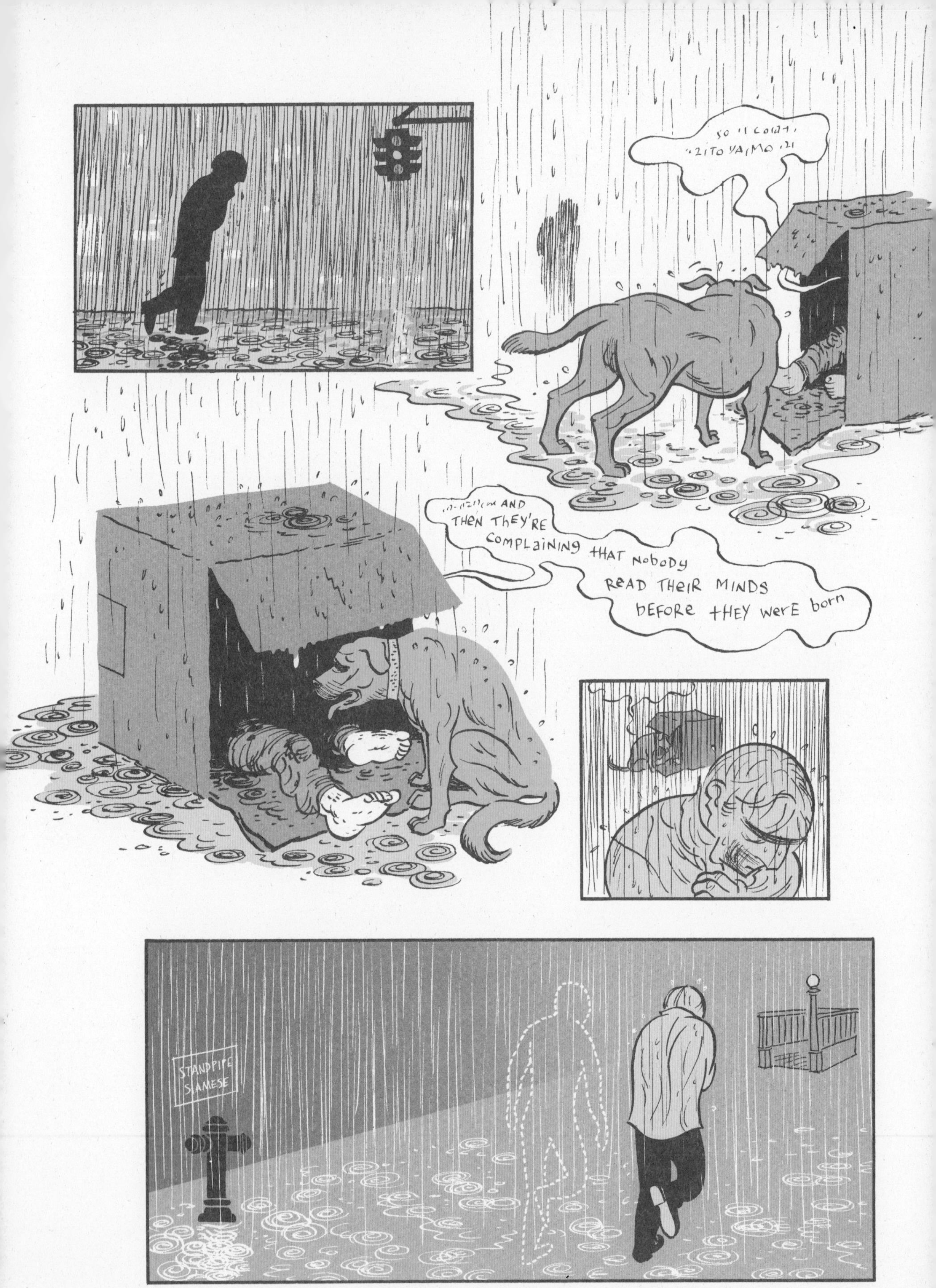
AND THEN THEY'RE COMPLAINING THAT NOBODY READ THEIR MINDS BEFORE THEY WERE BORN
STANDPIPE SIAMESE

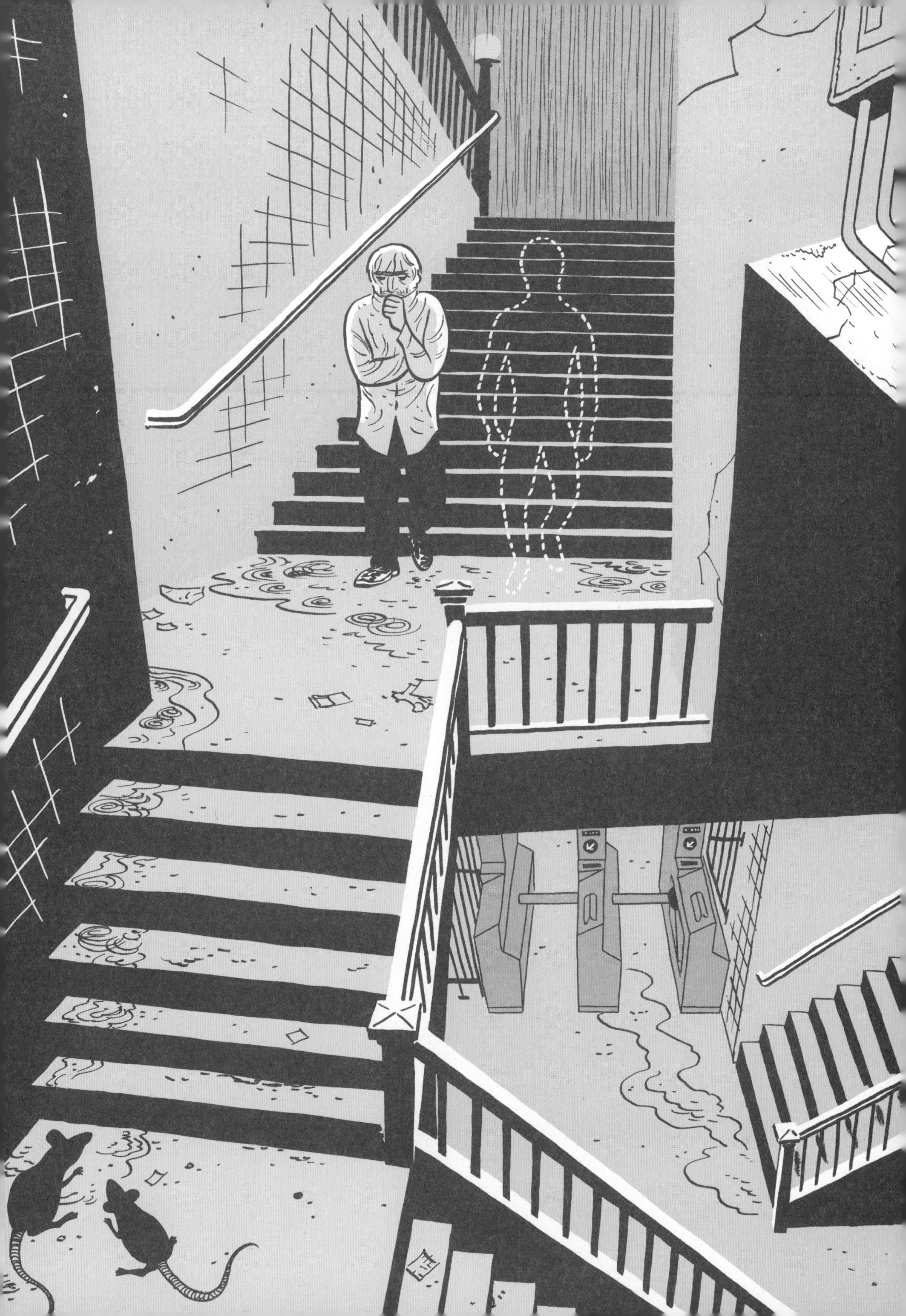

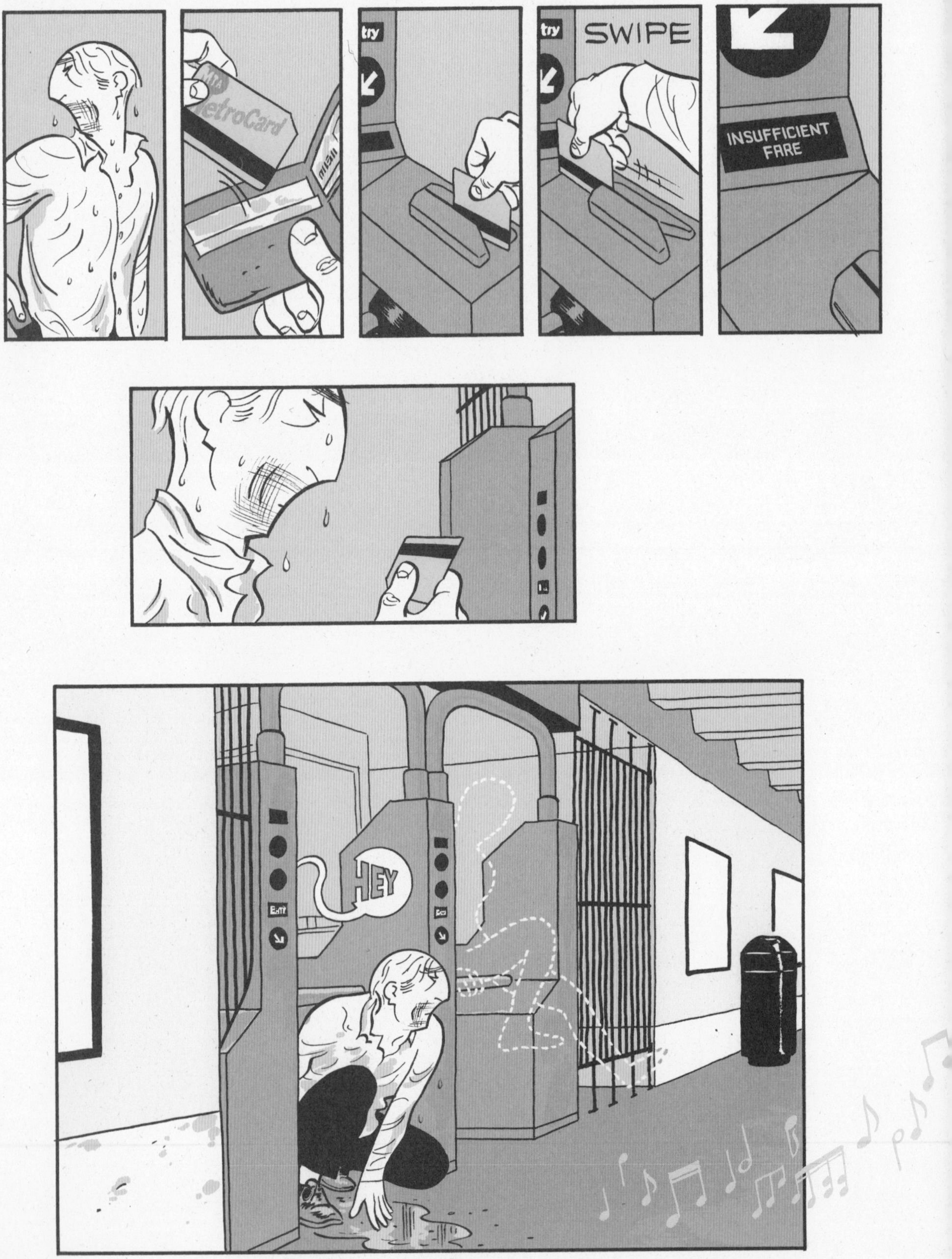
try
try
SWIPE
INSUFFICIENT FARE
HEY

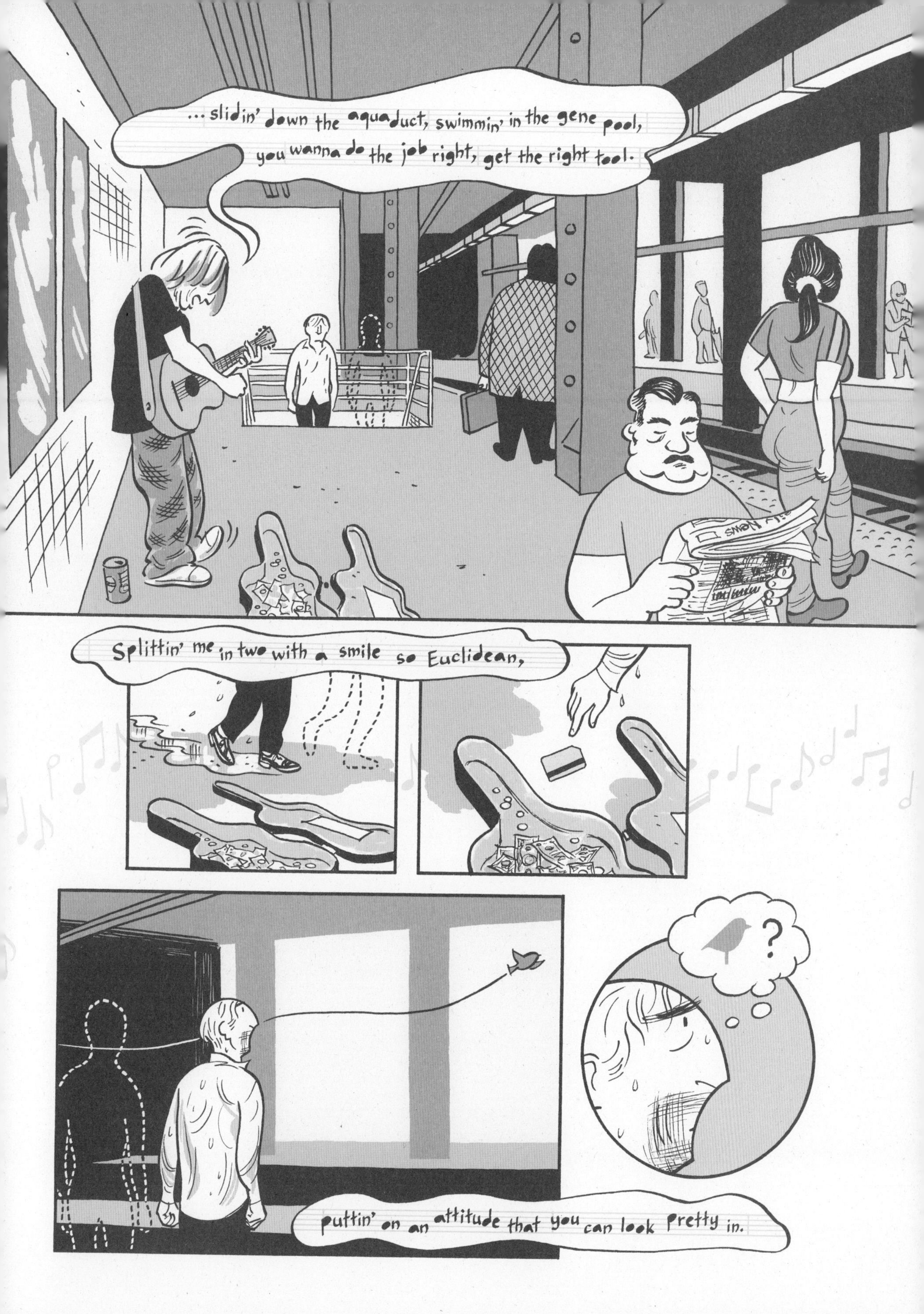
...slidin' down the aquaduct, swimmin' in the gene pool, you wanna do the job right, get the right tool.
Splittin' me in two with a smile so Euclidean,
puttin' on an attitude that you can look pretty in.

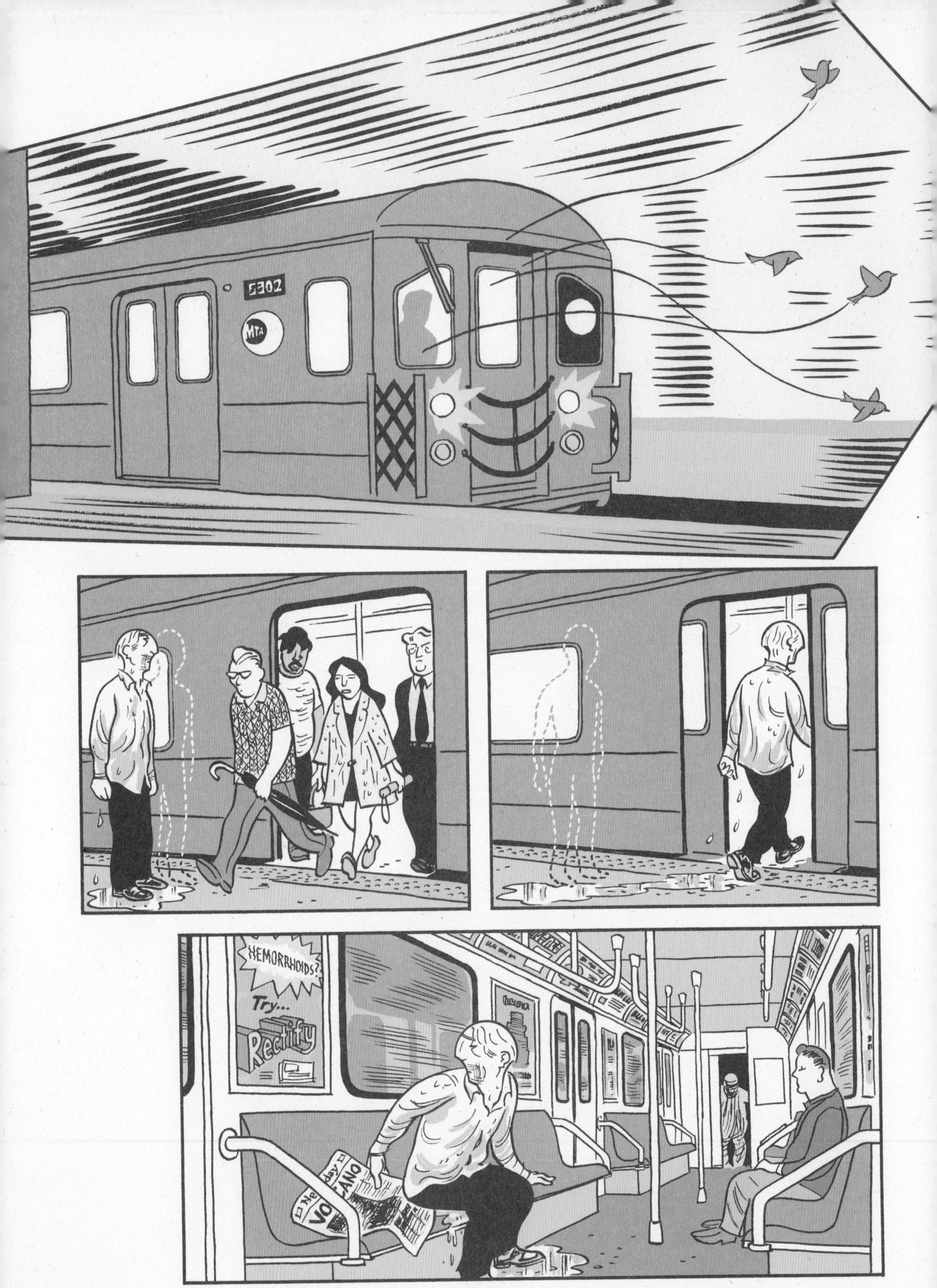
5302
MTA
HEMORRHOIDS?
Try...
Rectify

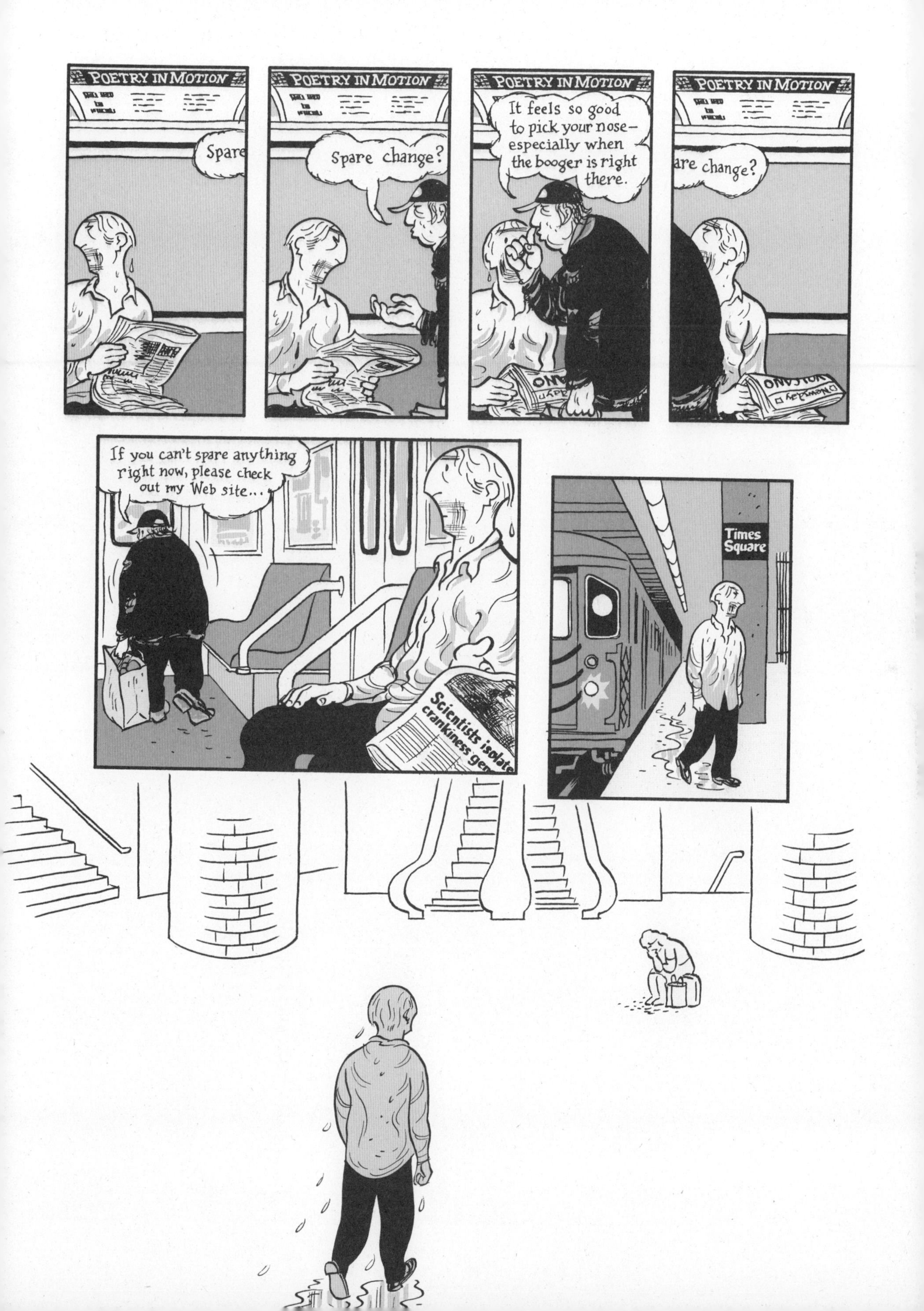
POETRY IN MOTION
Spare
POETRY IN MOTION
Spare change?
POETRY IN MOTION
It feels so good to pick your nose—especially when the booger is right there.
POETRY IN MOTION
are change?
Newsday
VOLCANO
If you can't spare anything right now, please check out my Web site...
Scientists isolate crankiness gen
Times Square

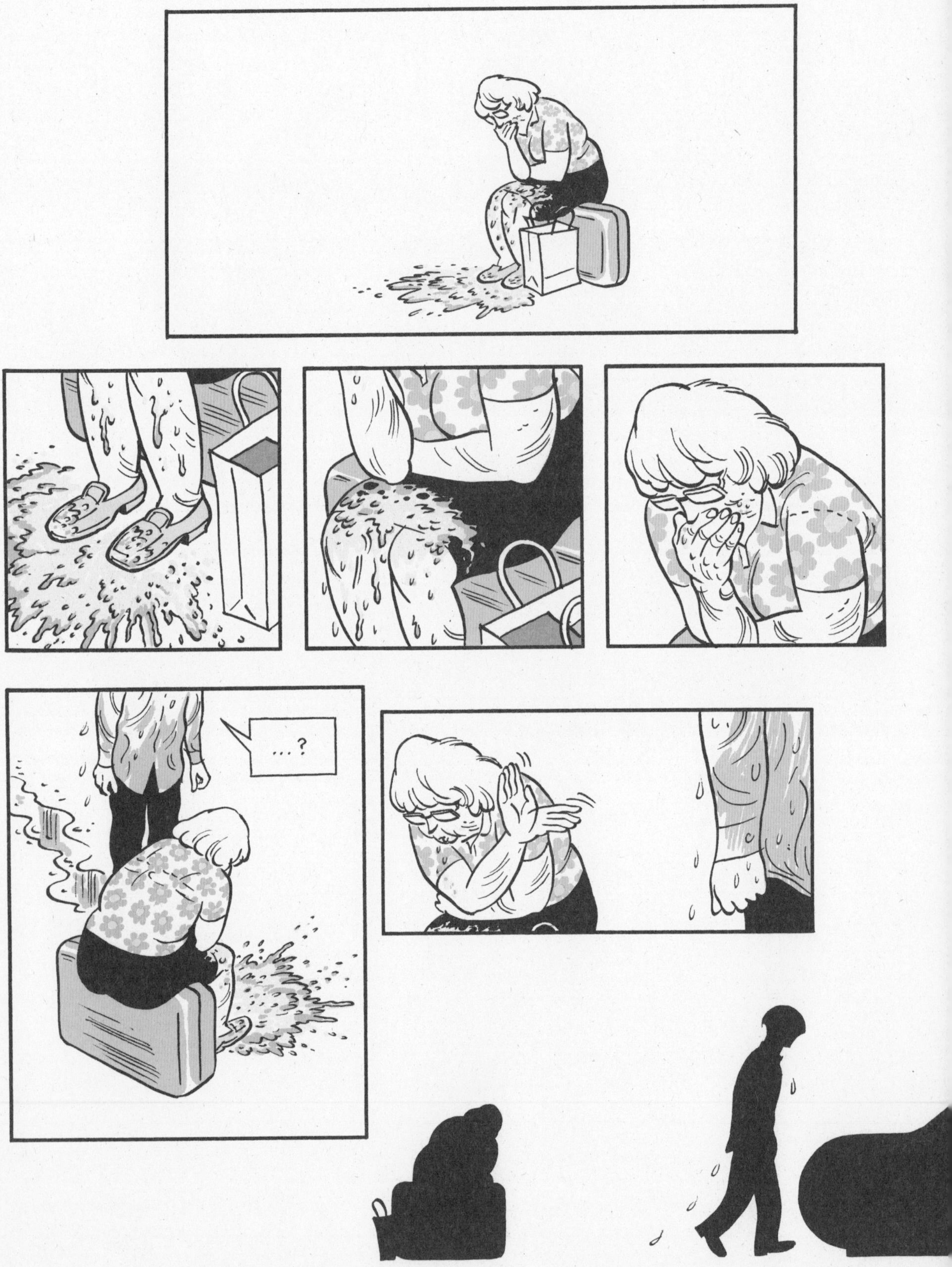
...?

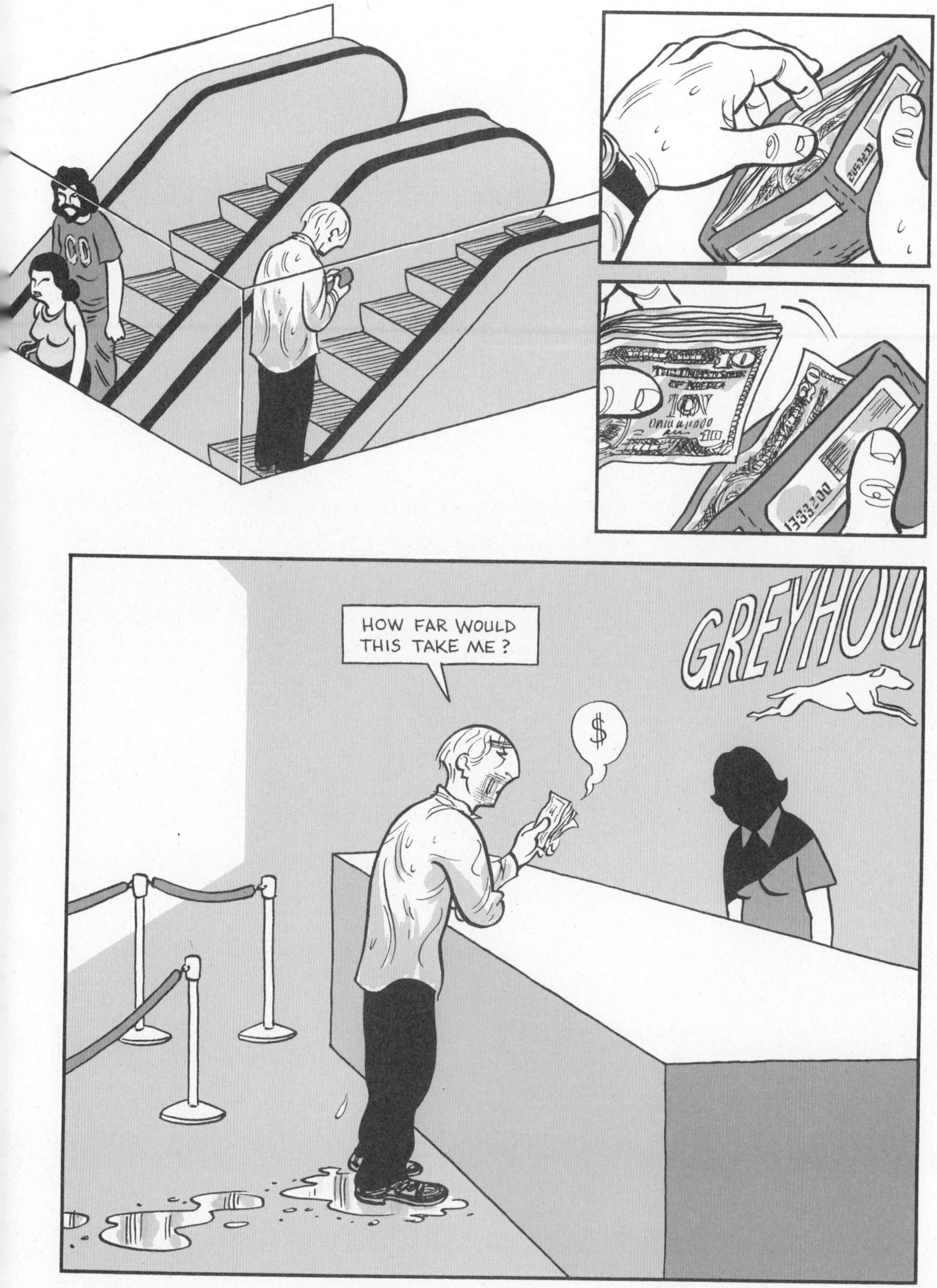
HOW FAR WOULD
THIS TAKE ME?
$
GREYHOU

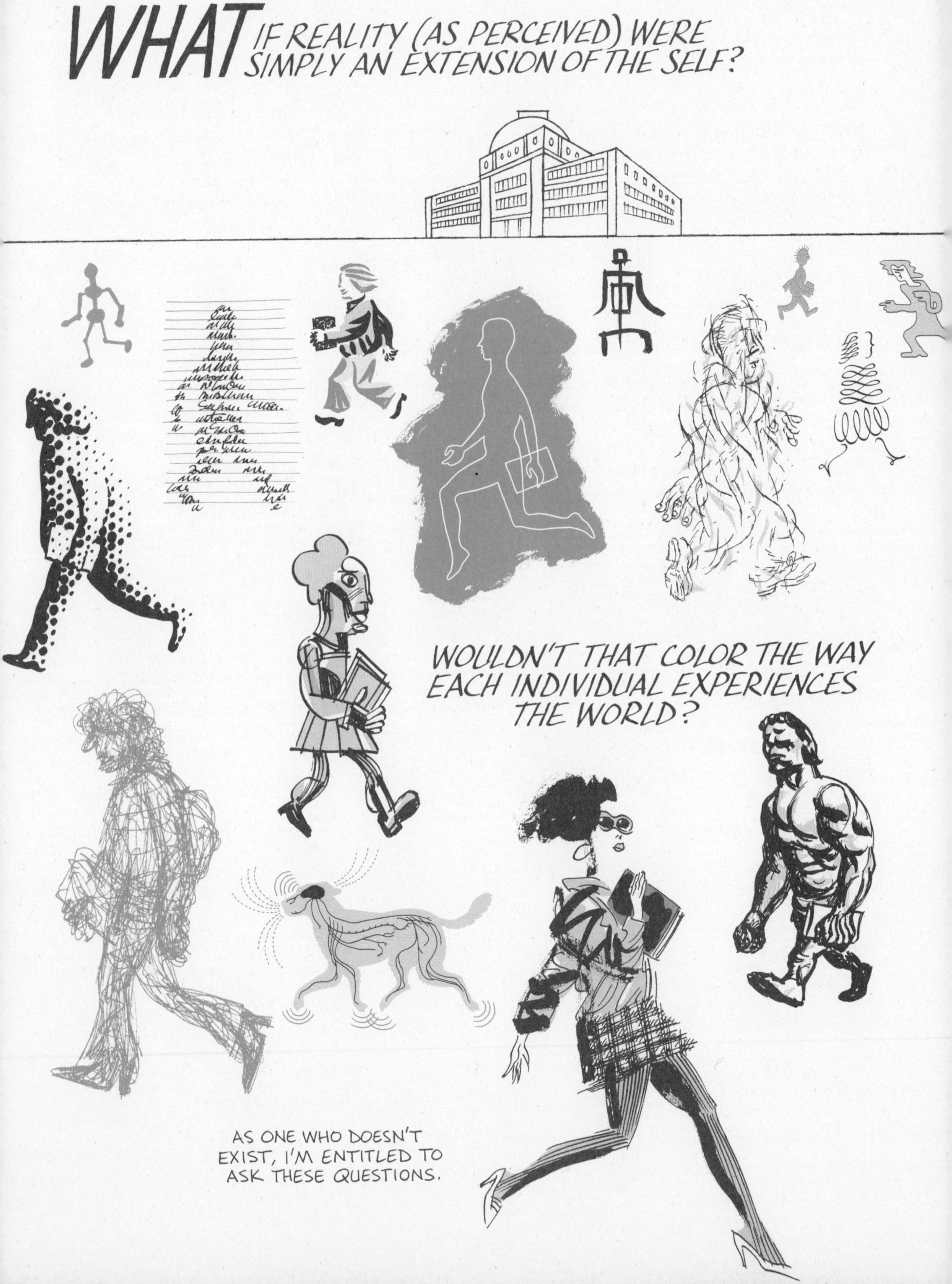
WHAT IF REALITY (AS PERCEIVED) WERE SIMPLY AN EXTENSION OF THE SELF?
WOULDN'T THAT COLOR THE WAY EACH INDIVIDUAL EXPERIENCES THE WORLD?
AS ONE WHO DOESN'T EXIST, I'M ENTITLED TO ASK THESE QUESTIONS.

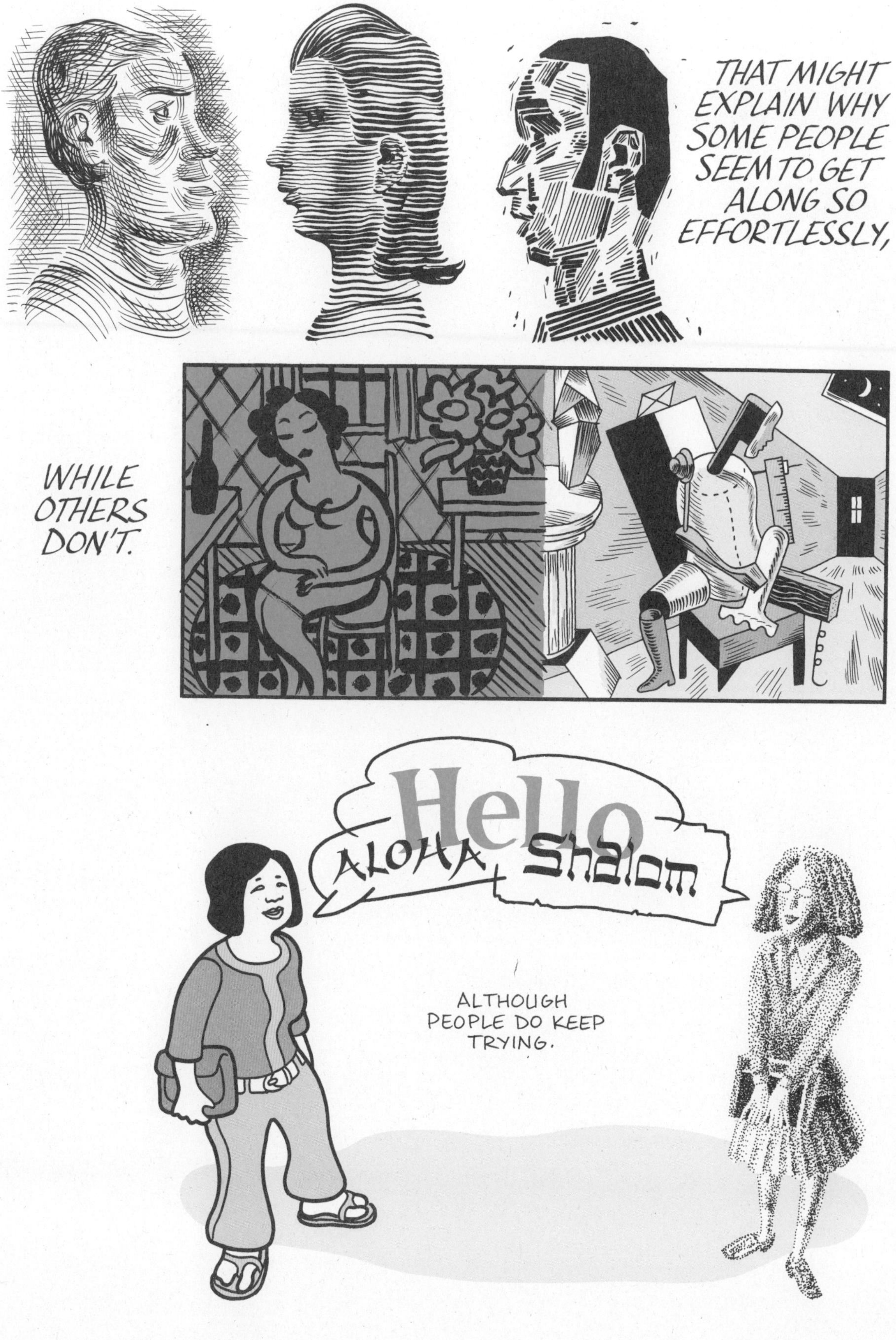
THAT MIGHT EXPLAIN WHY SOME PEOPLE SEEM TO GET ALONG SO EFFORTLESSLY,
WHILE OTHERS DON'T.
Hello
ALOHA
Shalom
ALTHOUGH PEOPLE DO KEEP TRYING.

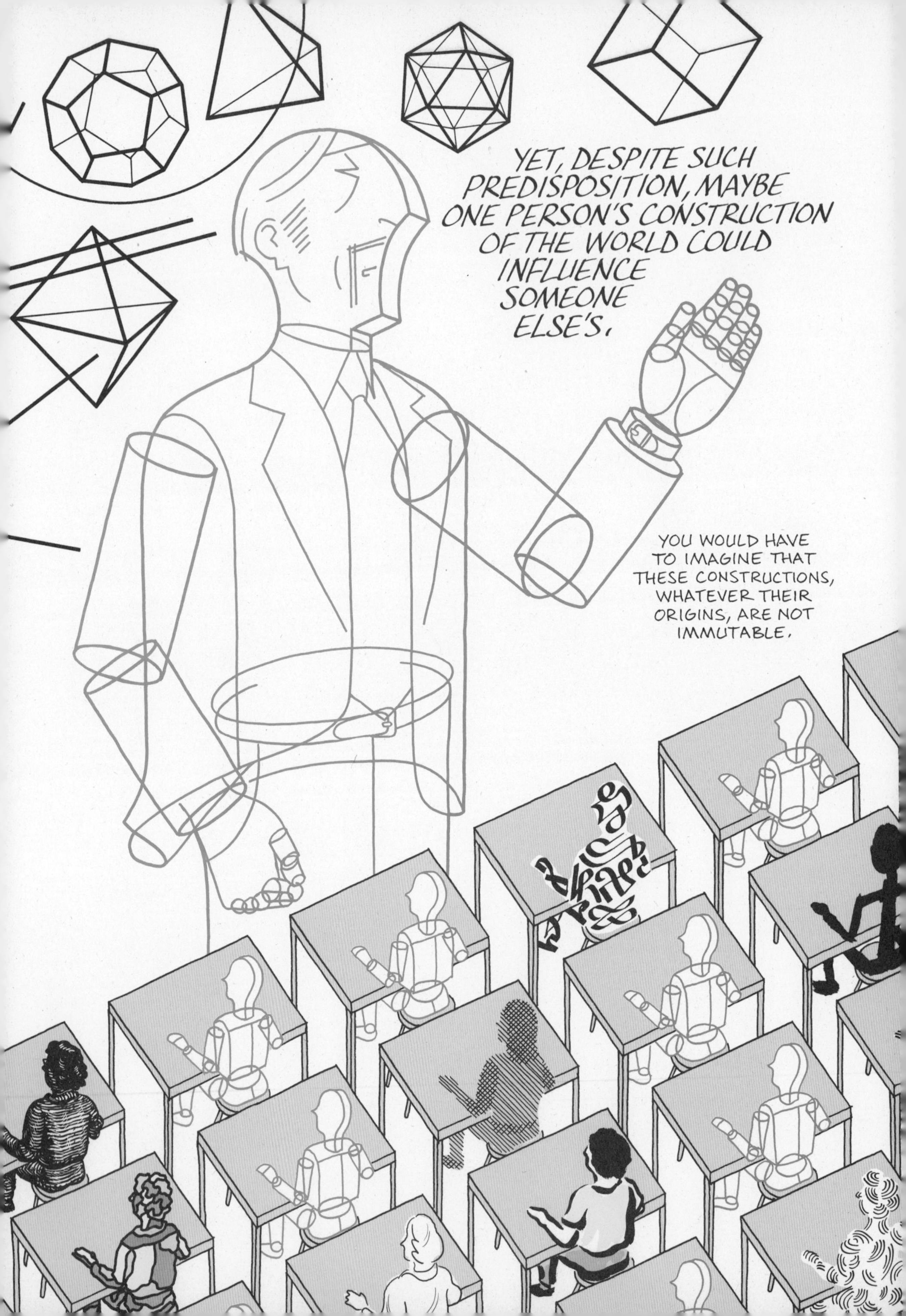
YET, DESPITE SUCH PREDISPOSITION, MAYBE ONE PERSON'S CONSTRUCTION OF THE WORLD COULD INFLUENCE SOMEONE ELSE'S.
YOU WOULD HAVE TO IMAGINE THAT THESE CONSTRUCTIONS, WHATEVER THEIR ORIGINS, ARE NOT IMMUTABLE.

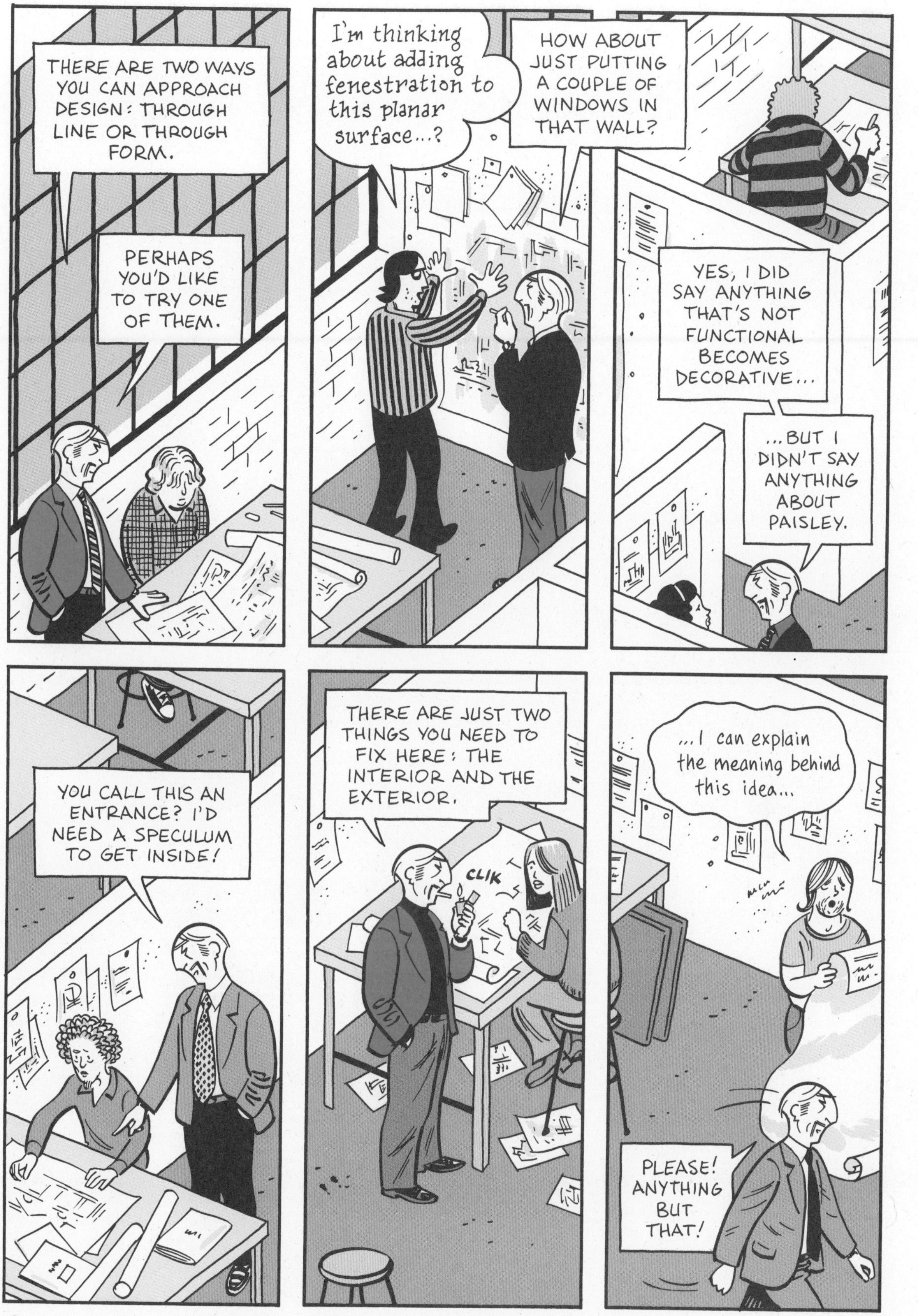
THERE ARE TWO WAYS YOU CAN APPROACH DESIGN: THROUGH LINE OR THROUGH FORM.
PERHAPS YOU'D LIKE TO TRY ONE OF THEM.
I'm thinking about adding fenestration to this planar surface...?
HOW ABOUT JUST PUTTING A COUPLE OF WINDOWS IN THAT WALL?
YES, I DID SAY ANYTHING THAT'S NOT FUNCTIONAL BECOMES DECORATIVE...
...BUT I DIDN'T SAY ANYTHING ABOUT PAISLEY.
YOU CALL THIS AN ENTRANCE? I'D NEED A SPECULUM TO GET INSIDE!
THERE ARE JUST TWO THINGS YOU NEED TO FIX HERE: THE INTERIOR AND THE EXTERIOR.
CLIK
...I can explain the meaning behind this idea...
PLEASE! ANYTHING BUT THAT!

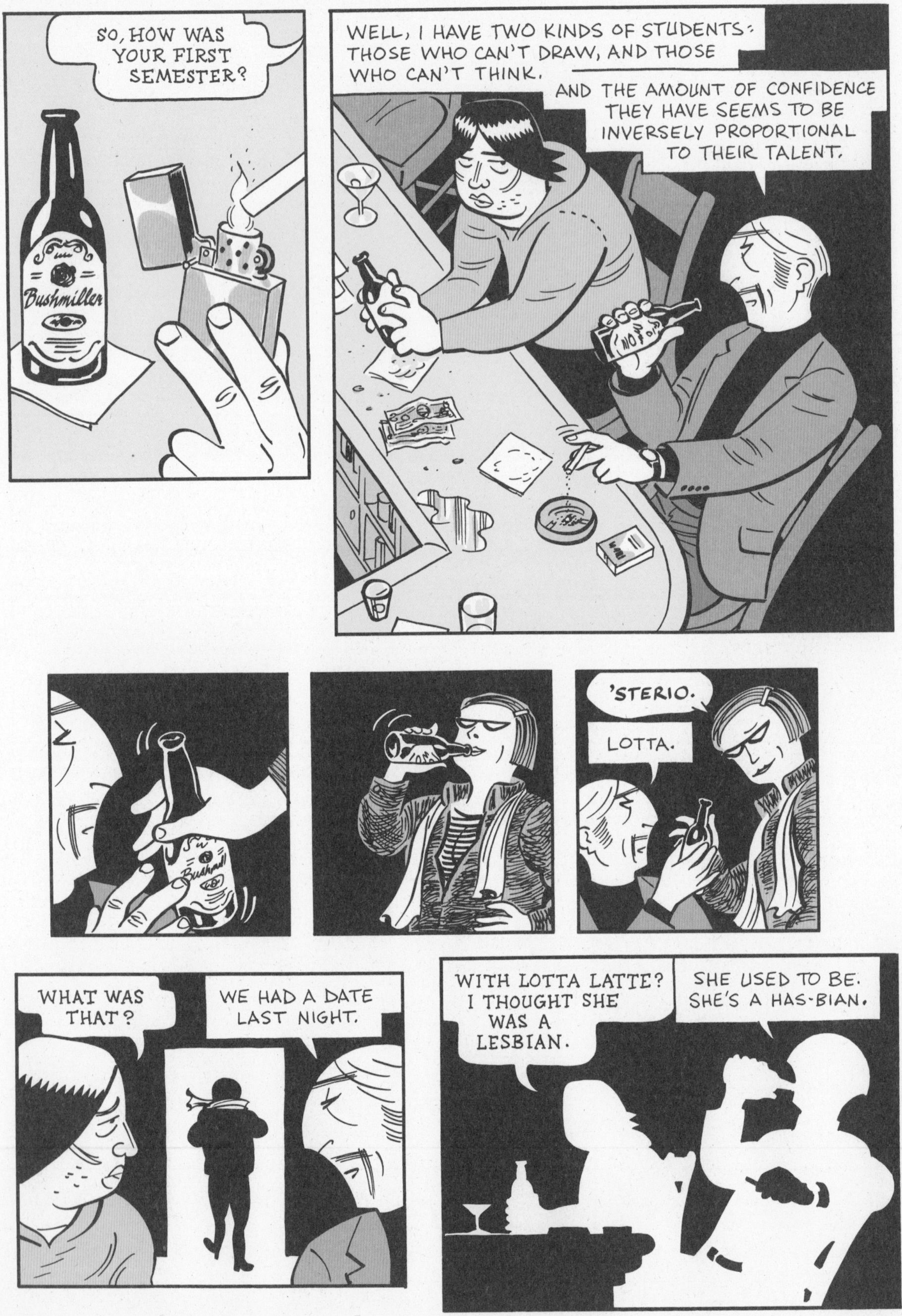
SO, HOW WAS YOUR FIRST SEMESTER?
Bushmiller
WELL, I HAVE TWO KINDS OF STUDENTS: THOSE WHO CAN'T DRAW, AND THOSE WHO CAN'T THINK.
AND THE AMOUNT OF CONFIDENCE THEY HAVE SEEMS TO BE INVERSELY PROPORTIONAL TO THEIR TALENT.
'STERIO.
LOTTA.
WHAT WAS THAT?
WE HAD A DATE LAST NIGHT.
WITH LOTTA LATTE? I THOUGHT SHE WAS A LESBIAN.
SHE USED TO BE. SHE'S A HAS-BIAN.

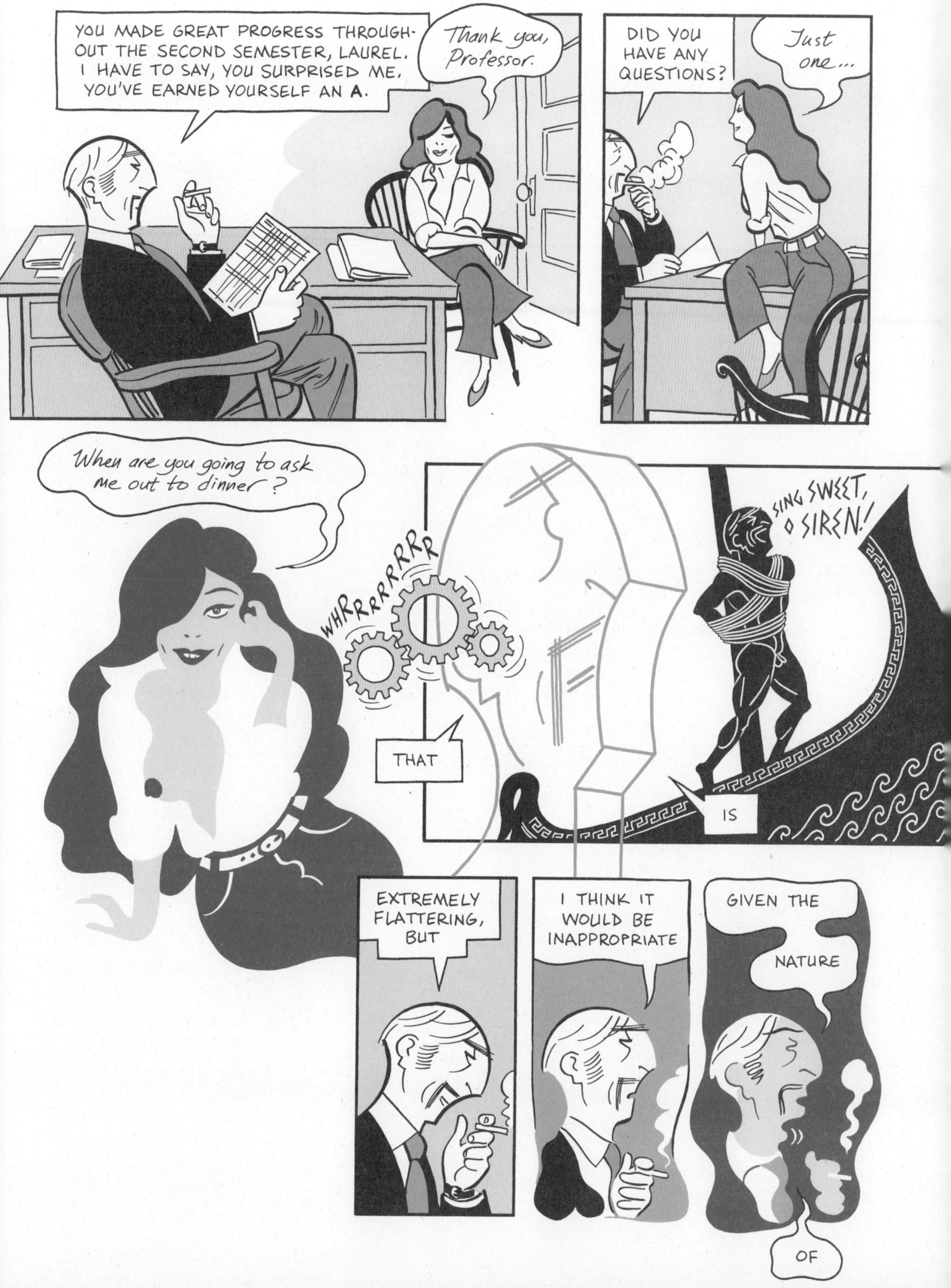

YOU MADE GREAT PROGRESS THROUGH-OUT THE SECOND SEMESTER, LAUREL. I HAVE TO SAY, YOU SURPRISED ME. YOU'VE EARNED YOURSELF AN A.
Thank you, Professor.
DID YOU HAVE ANY QUESTIONS?
Just one...
When are you going to ask me out to dinner?
WHRRRRRRRRR
SING SWEET, O SIREN!
THAT
IS
EXTREMELY FLATTERING, BUT
I THINK IT WOULD BE INAPPROPRIATE
GIVEN THE
NATURE
OF

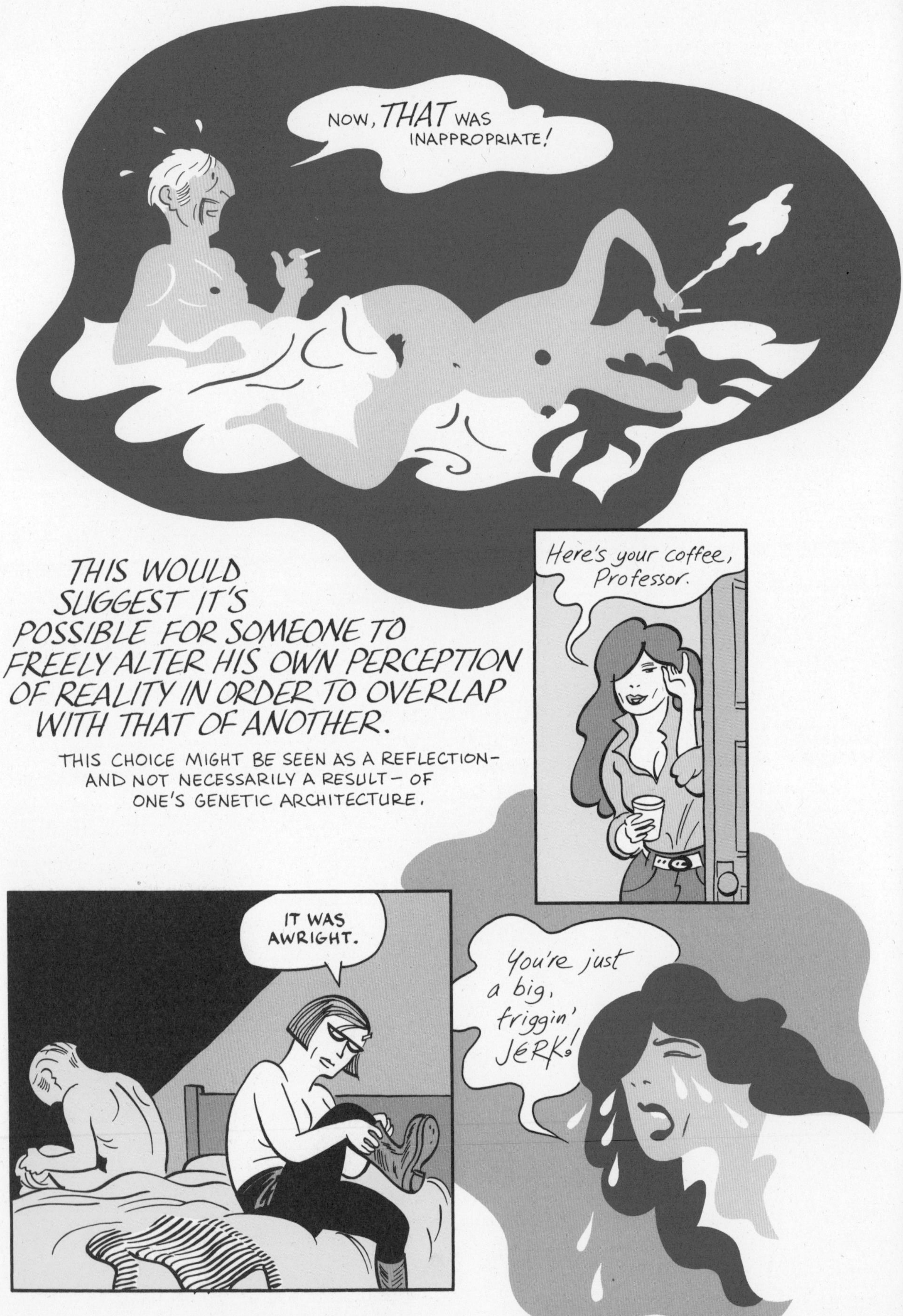
NOW, THAT WAS INAPPROPRIATE!
THIS WOULD SUGGEST IT'S POSSIBLE FOR SOMEONE TO FREELY ALTER HIS OWN PERCEPTION OF REALITY IN ORDER TO OVERLAP WITH THAT OF ANOTHER.
THIS CHOICE MIGHT BE SEEN AS A REFLECTION- AND NOT NECESSARILY A RESULT- OF ONE'S GENETIC ARCHITECTURE.
Here's your coffee, Professor.
IT WAS AWRIGHT.
You're just a big, friggin' JERK!

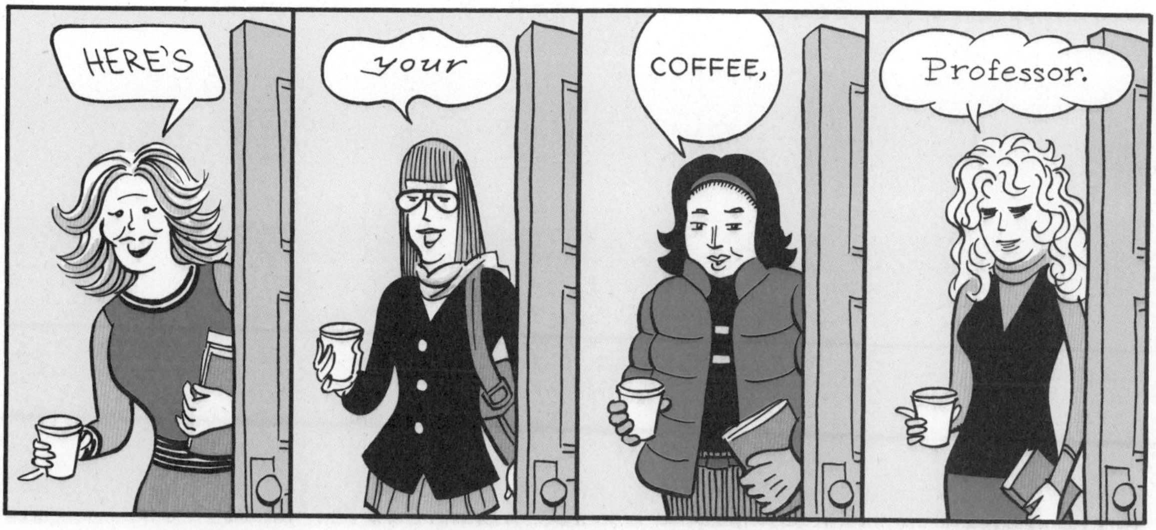
HERE'S
your
COFFEE,
Professor.

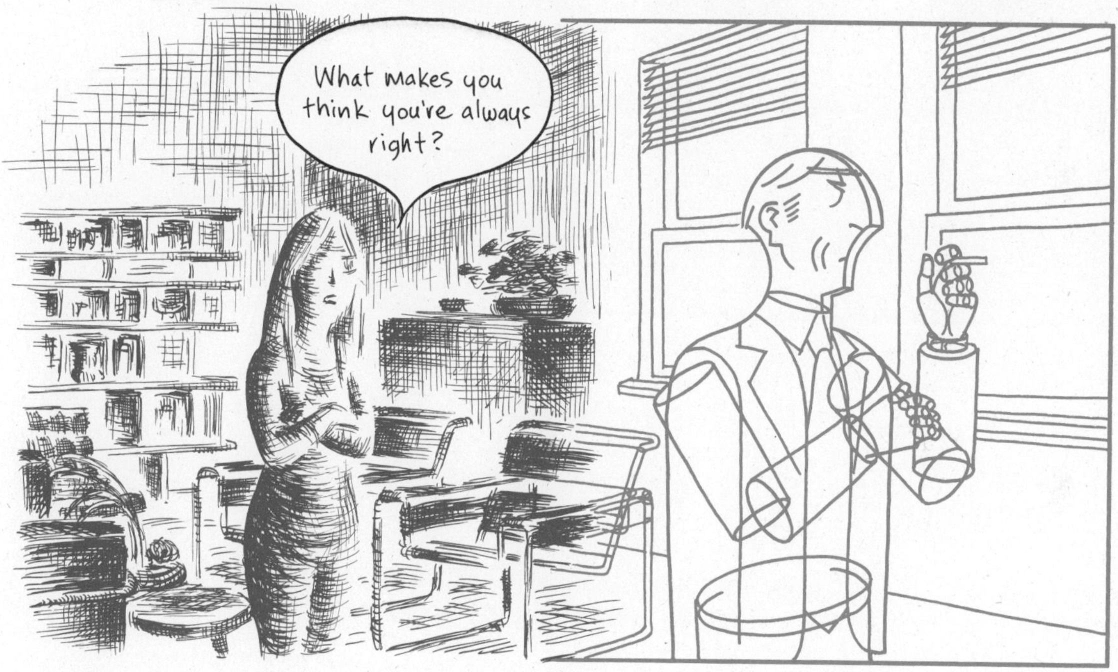
What makes you think you're always right?

WOULDN'T THAT BE NICE?

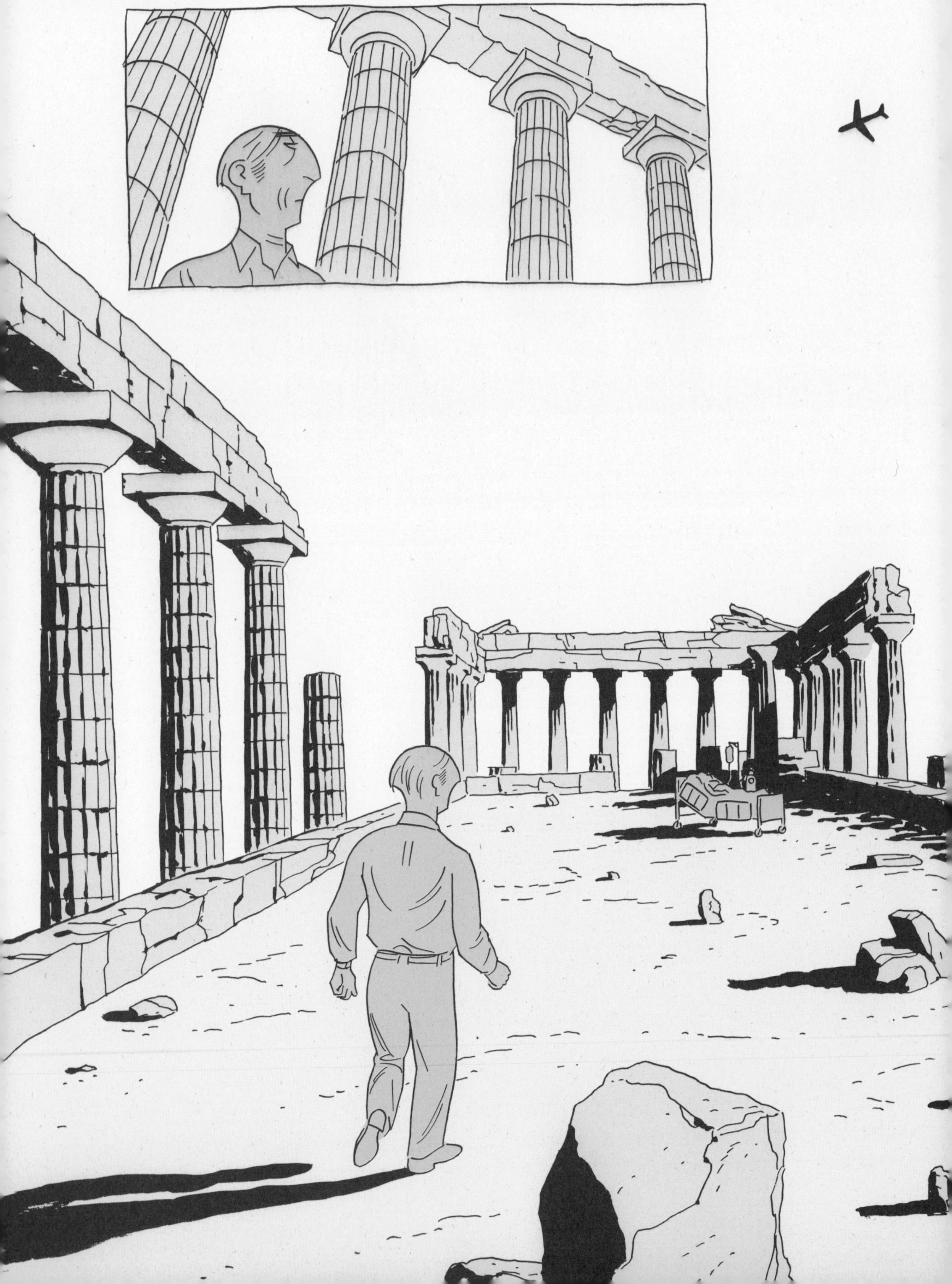

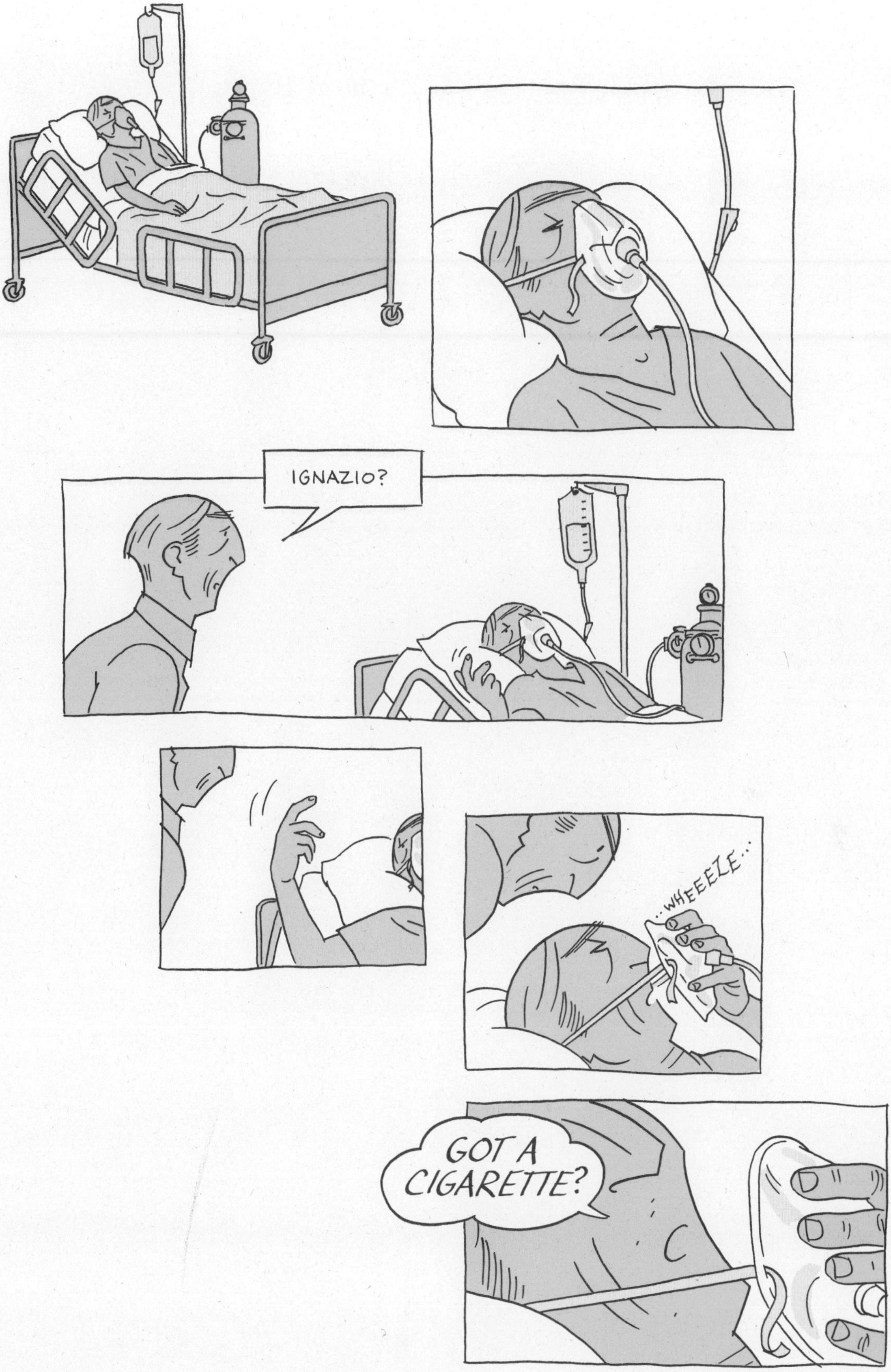
IGNAZIO?
...WHEEEZE...
GOT A CIGARETTE?

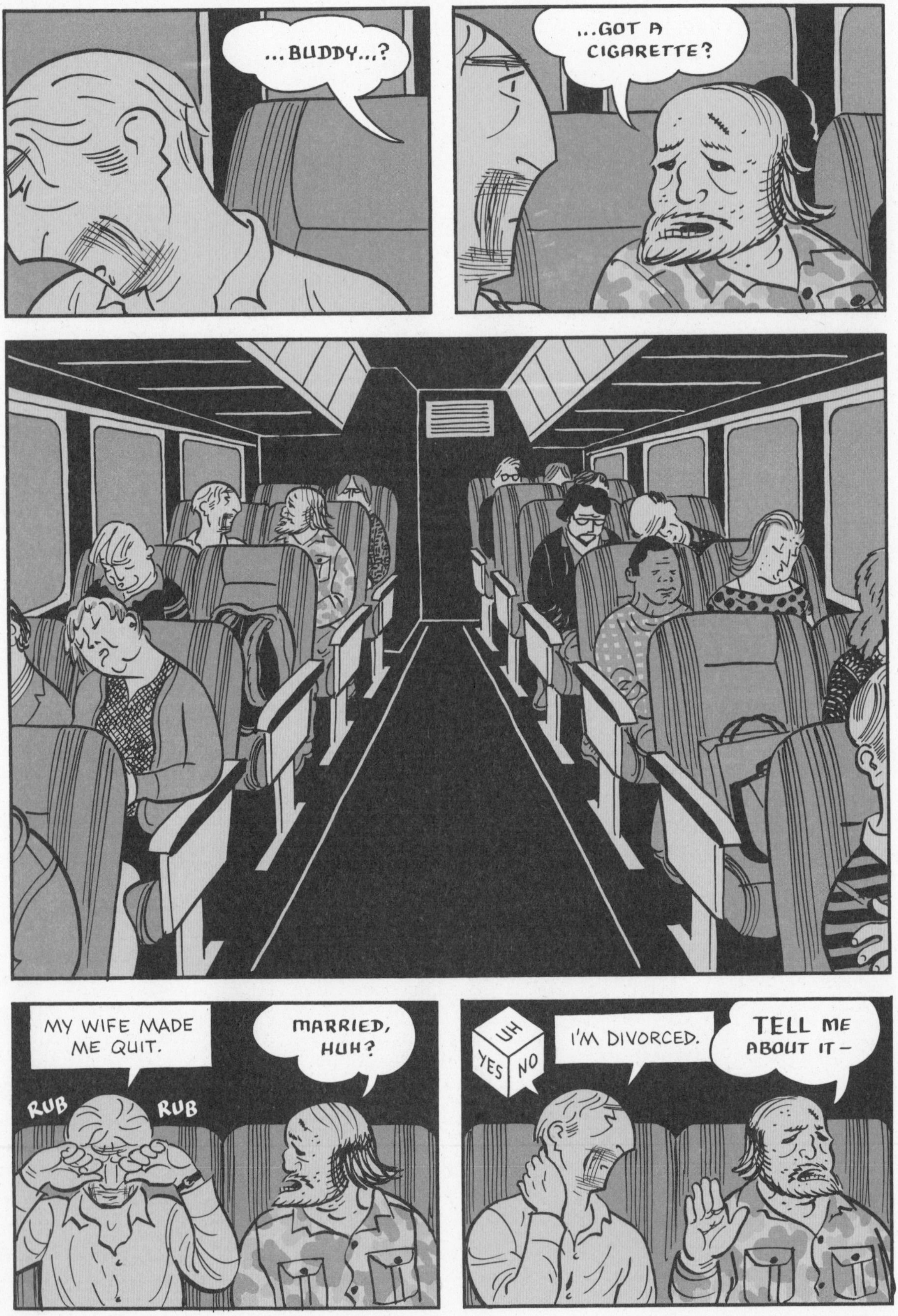
...BUDDY...?
...GOT A CIGARETTE?
MY WIFE MADE ME QUIT.
RUB
RUB
MARRIED, HUH?
UH
YES
NO
I'M DIVORCED.
TELL ME ABOUT IT–

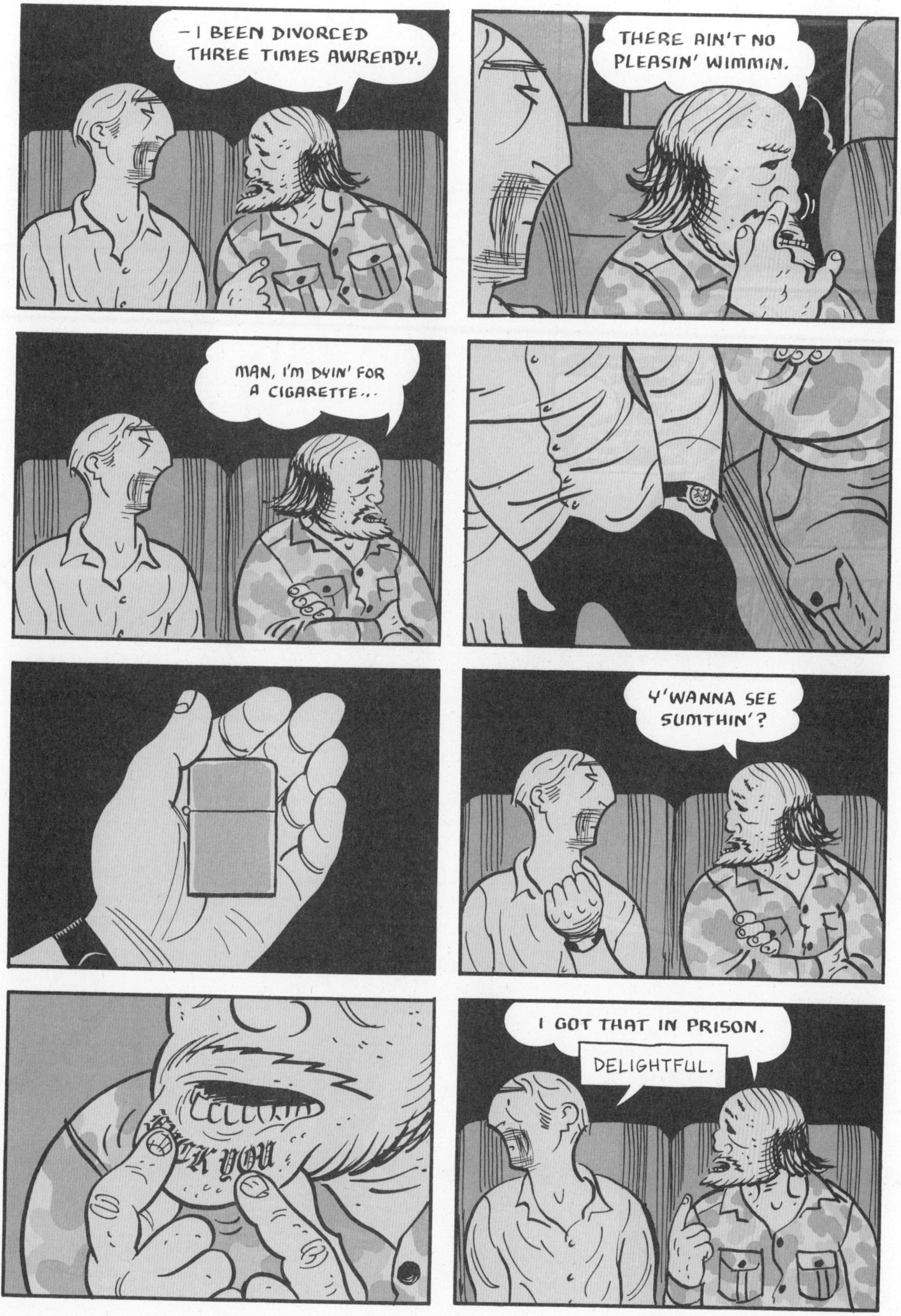

– I BEEN DIVORCED THREE TIMES AWREADY.
THERE AIN'T NO PLEASIN' WIMMIN.
MAN, I'M DYIN' FOR A CIGARETTE...
Y'WANNA SEE SUMTHIN'?
I GOT THAT IN PRISON.
DELIGHTFUL.

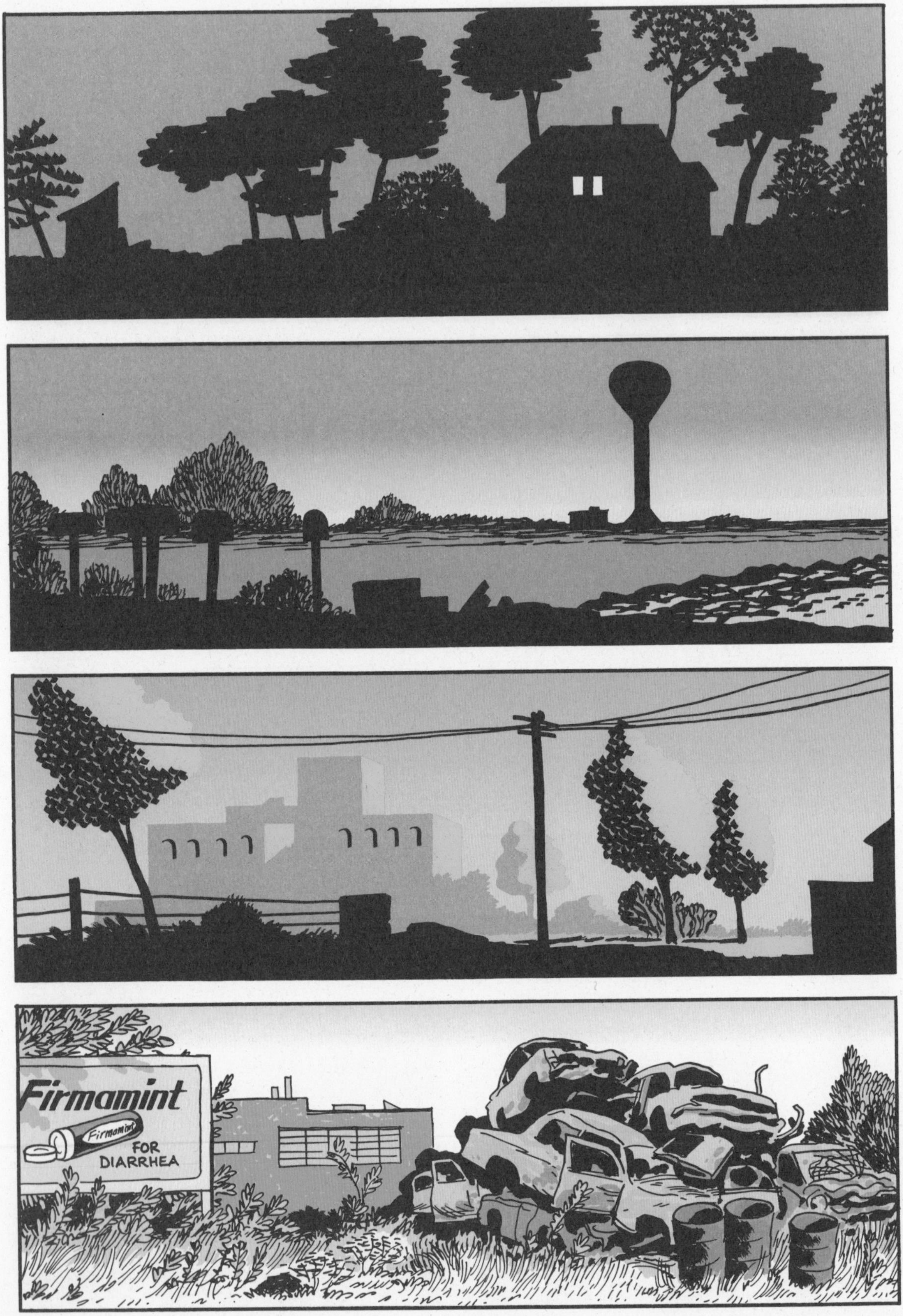
Firmamint
Firmamint
FOR
DIARRHEA

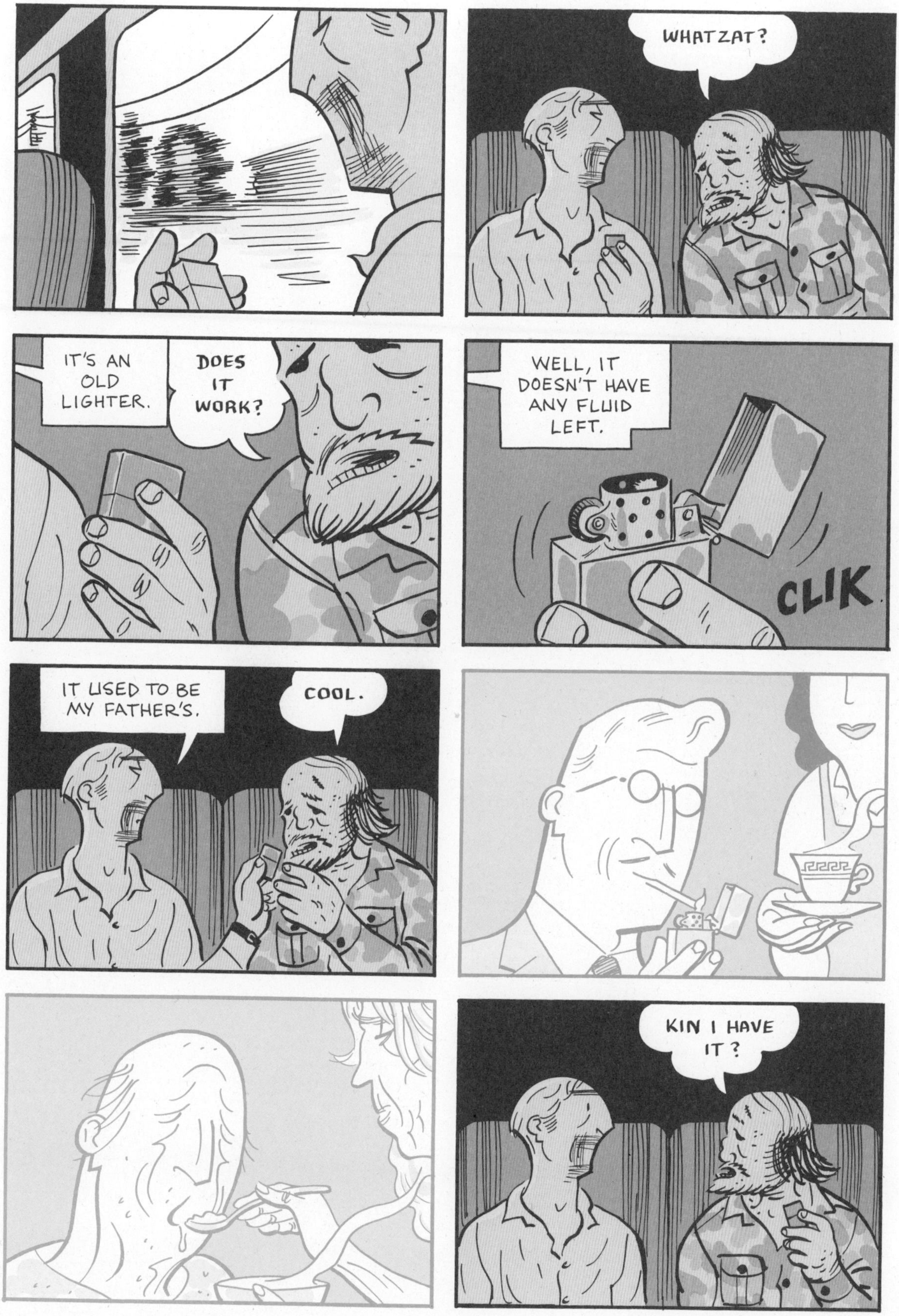
WHATZAT?
IT'S AN OLD LIGHTER.
DOES IT WORK?
WELL, IT DOESN'T HAVE ANY FLUID LEFT.
CLIK
IT USED TO BE MY FATHER'S.
COOL.
KIN I HAVE IT?

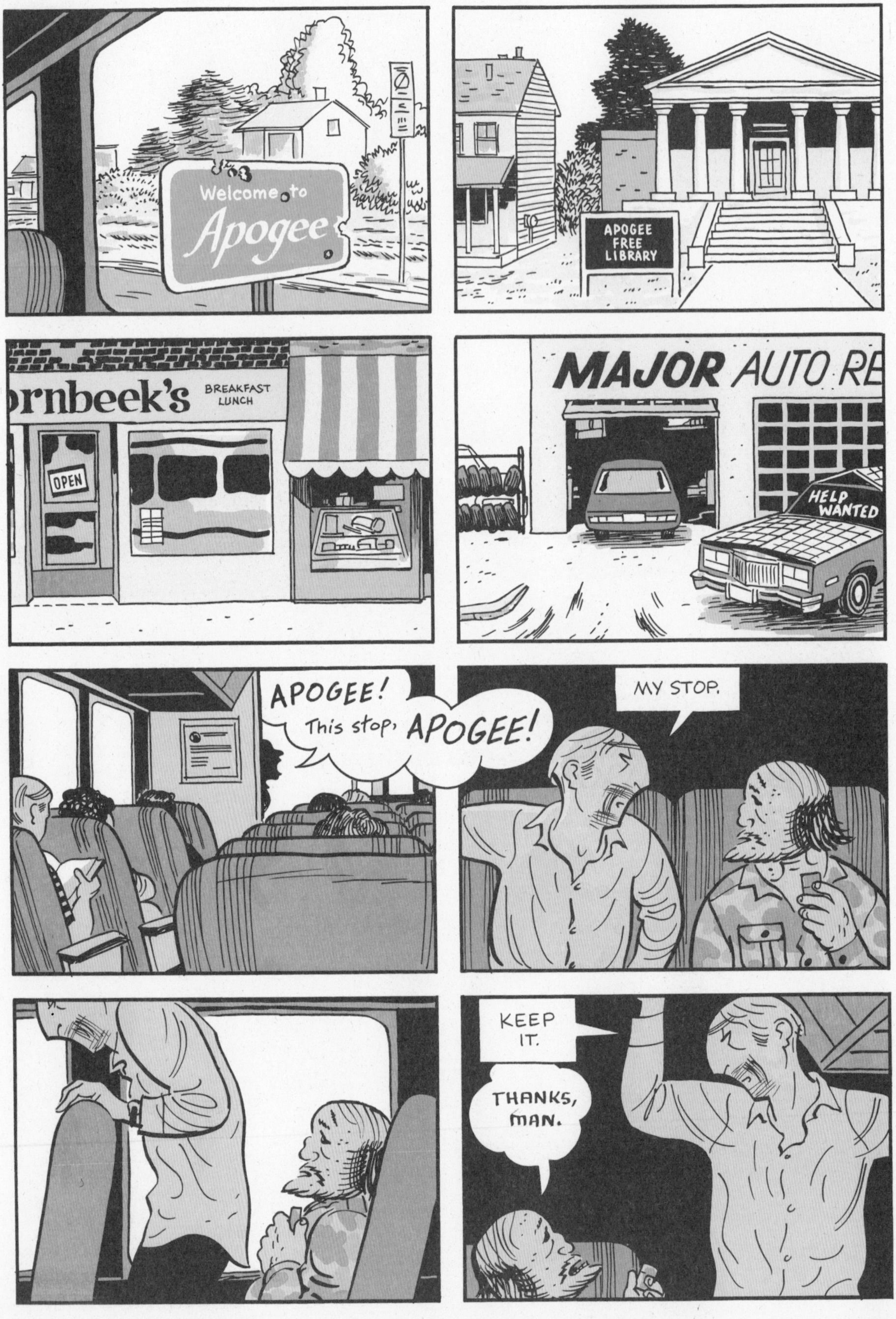
Welcome to
Apogee
APOGEE FREE LIBRARY
rnbeek's
BREAKFAST LUNCH
OPEN
MAJOR AUTO RE
HELP WANTED
APOGEE! This stop, APOGEE!
MY STOP.
KEEP IT.
THANKS, MAN.

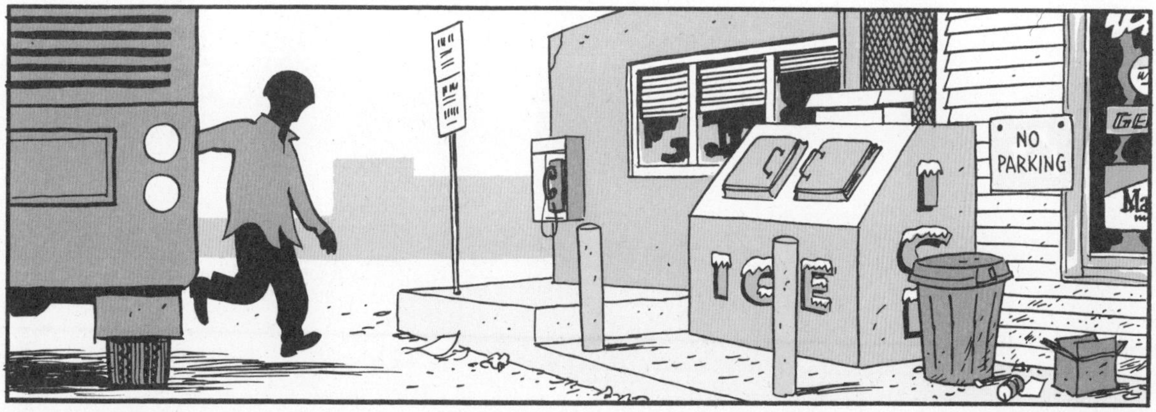
NO PARKING
ICE

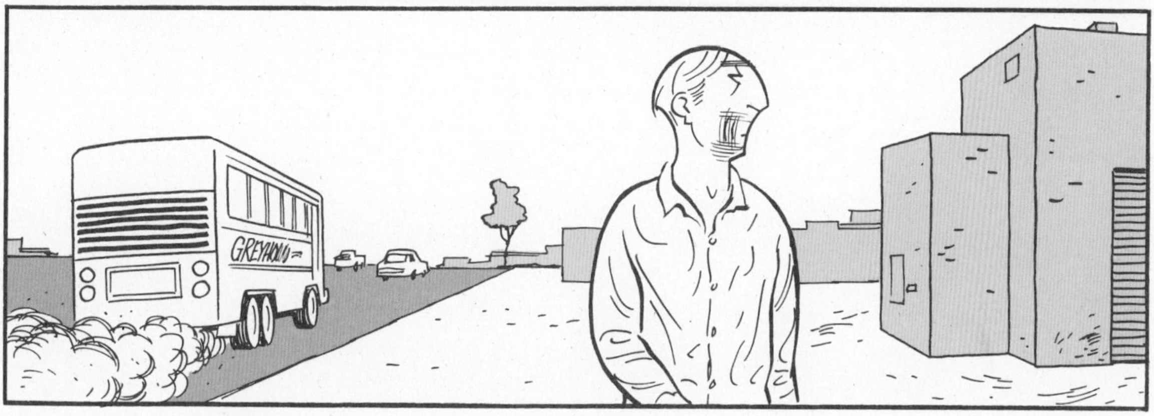

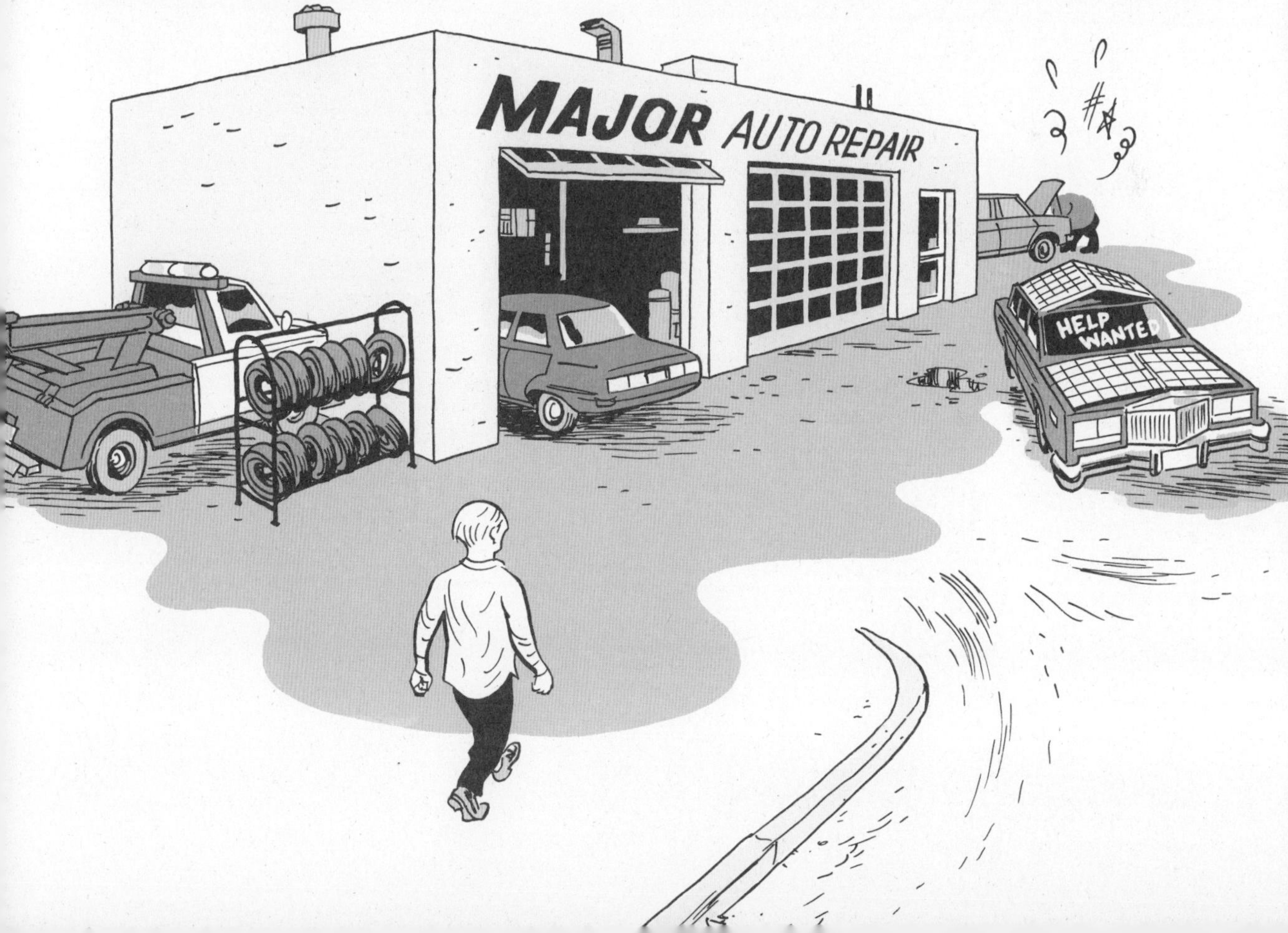
MAJOR AUTO REPAIR
HELP WANTED

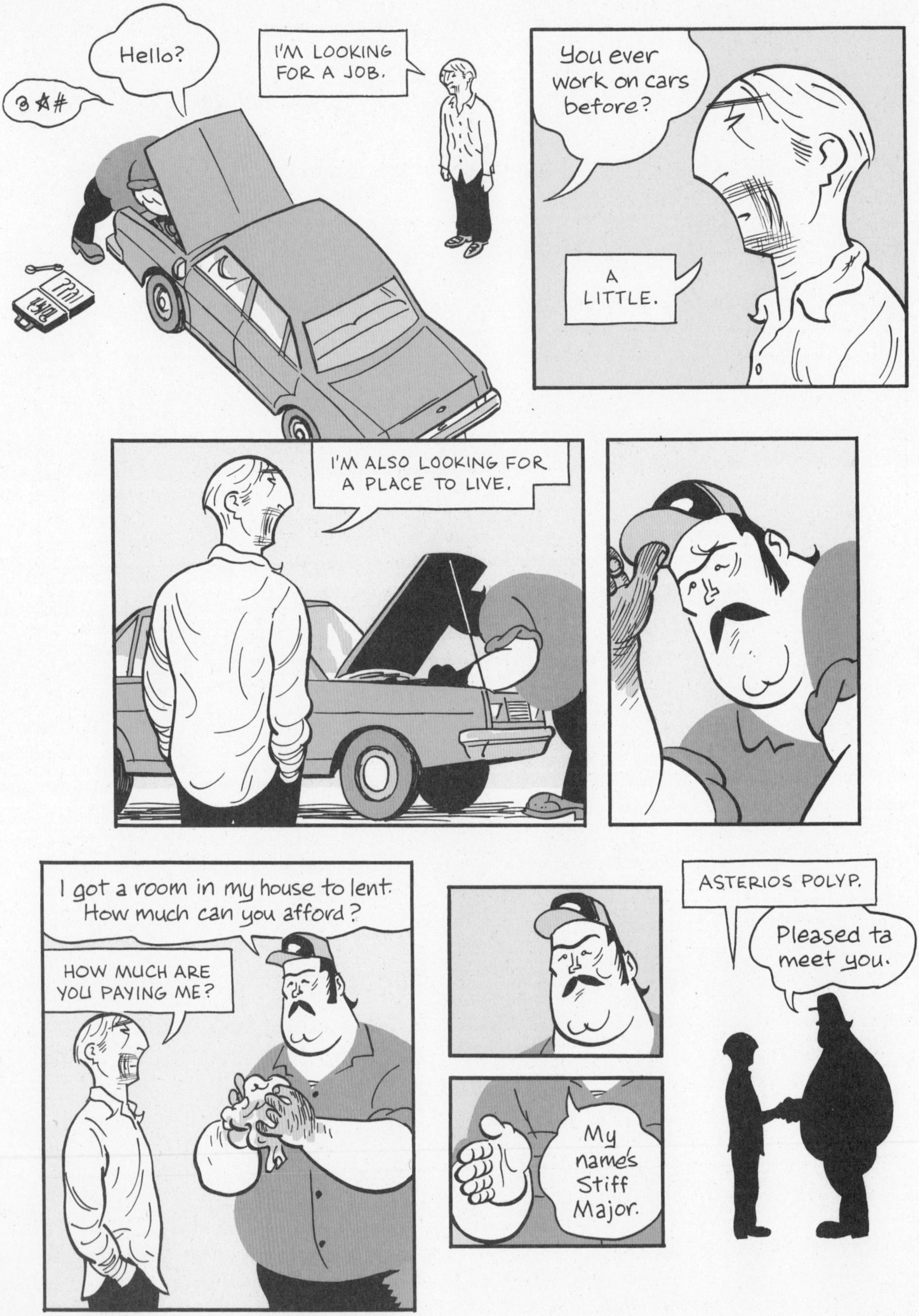

@☆#
Hello?
I'M LOOKING FOR A JOB.
You ever work on cars before?
A LITTLE.
I'M ALSO LOOKING FOR A PLACE TO LIVE.
I got a room in my house to lent. How much can you afford?
HOW MUCH ARE YOU PAYING ME?
My name's Stiff Major.
ASTERIOS POLYP.
Pleased ta meet you.

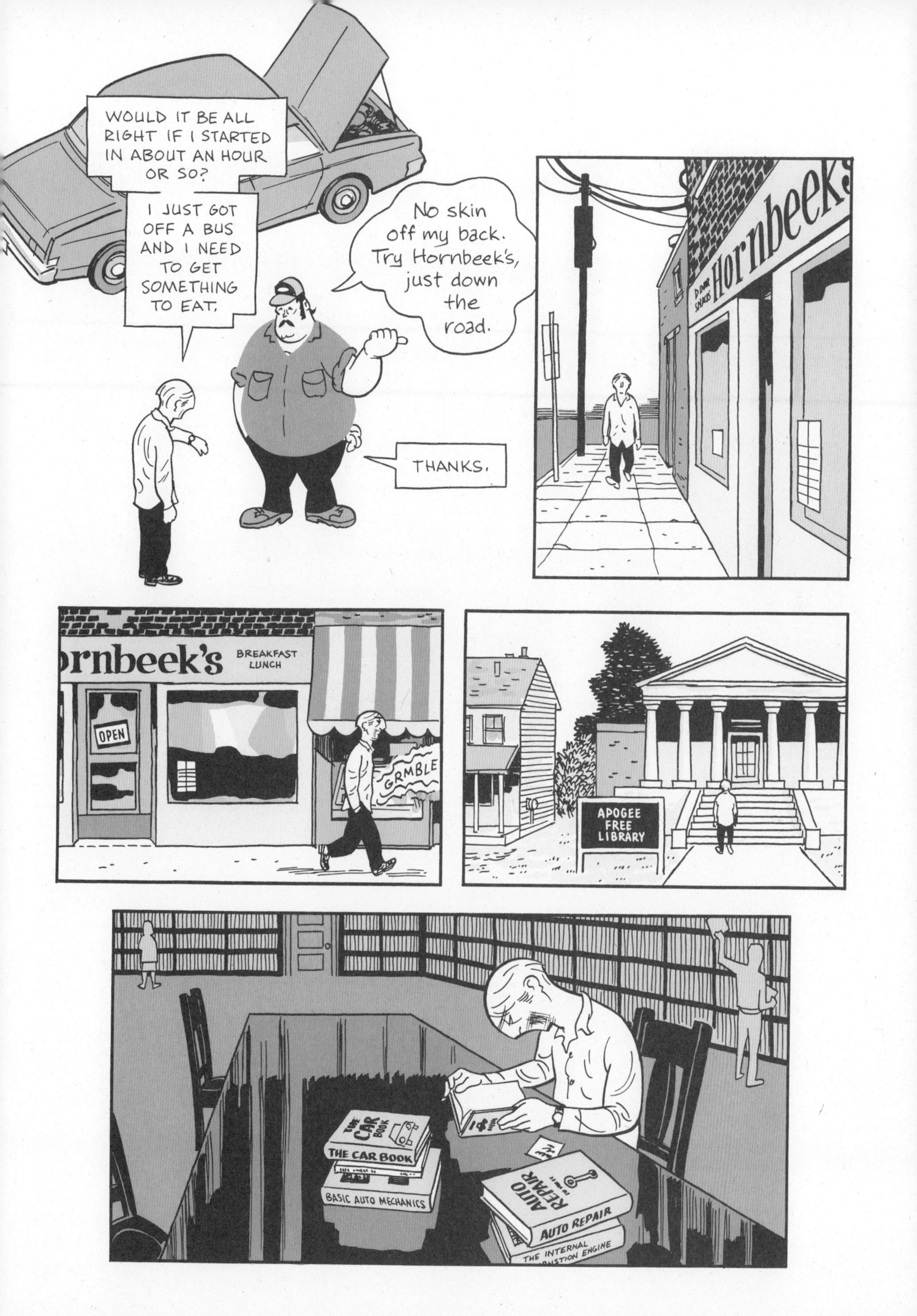
WOULD IT BE ALL RIGHT IF I STARTED IN ABOUT AN HOUR OR SO?
I JUST GOT OFF A BUS AND I NEED TO GET SOMETHING TO EAT.
No skin off my back. Try Hornbeek's, just down the road.
THANKS.
Hornbeek's
ornbeek's
BREAKFAST
LUNCH
OPEN
GRMBLE
APOGEE FREE LIBRARY
THE CAR BOOK
BASIC AUTO MECHANICS
AUTO REPAIR
AUTO REPAIR

AT A FACULTY PARTY IN 1984, ASTERIOS WAS REGALING THE ASSEMBLY WITH HIS INSIGHT INTO COMMUNICATION,

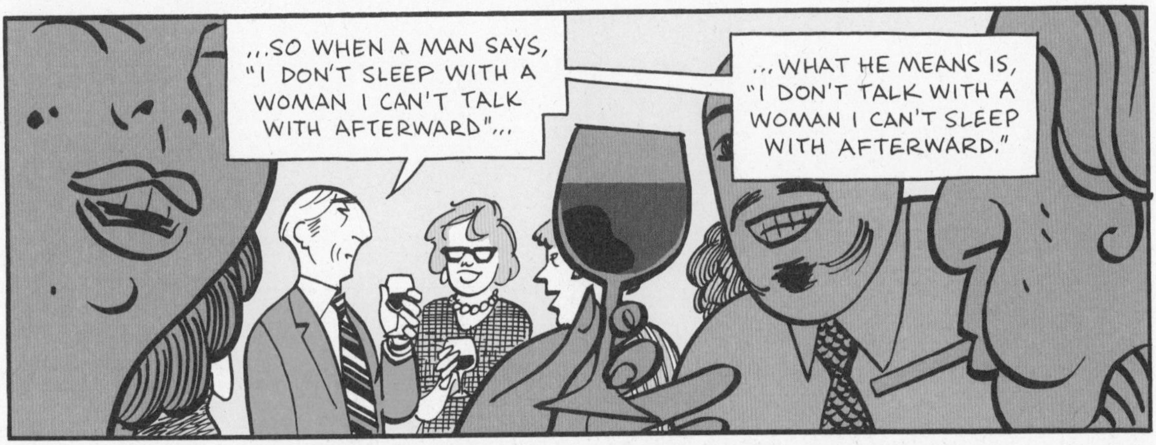
...SO WHEN A MAN SAYS, "I DON'T SLEEP WITH A WOMAN I CAN'T TALK WITH AFTERWARD"...
...WHAT HE MEANS IS, "I DON'T TALK WITH A WOMAN I CAN'T SLEEP WITH AFTERWARD."

HIS UNDERSTANDING OF HUMAN BEHAVIOR,

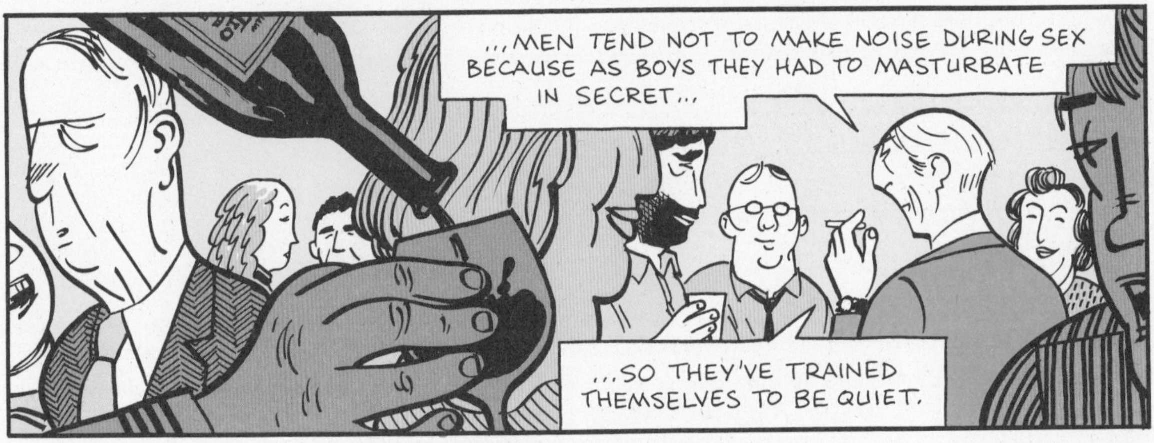
...MEN TEND NOT TO MAKE NOISE DURING SEX BECAUSE AS BOYS THEY HAD TO MASTURBATE IN SECRET...
...SO THEY'VE TRAINED THEMSELVES TO BE QUIET.

AND HIS SENSITIVITY.

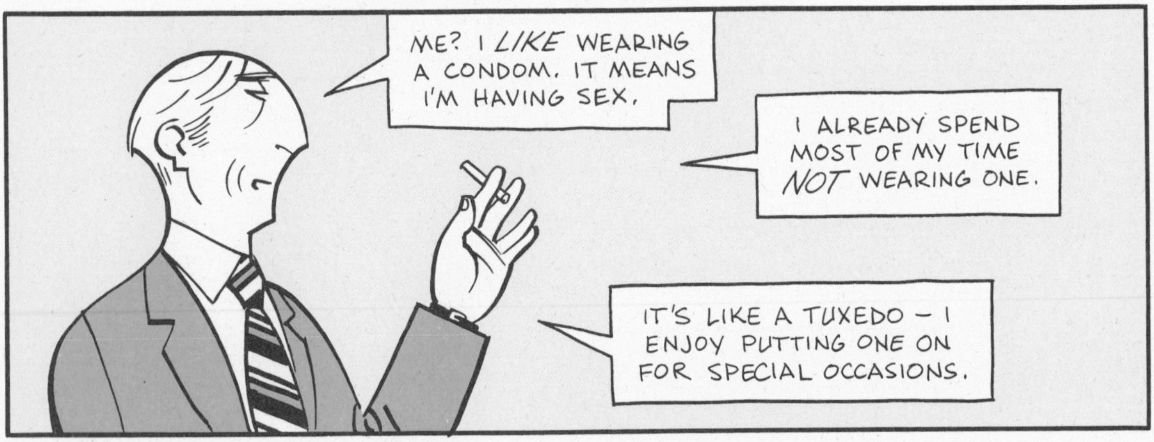
ME? I *LIKE* WEARING A CONDOM. IT MEANS I'M HAVING SEX.
I ALREADY SPEND MOST OF MY TIME *NOT* WEARING ONE.
IT'S LIKE A TUXEDO – I ENJOY PUTTING ONE ON FOR SPECIAL OCCASIONS.

HE WAS QUITE CAPABLE OF HOLDING FORTH ON A VARIETY OF TOPICS.

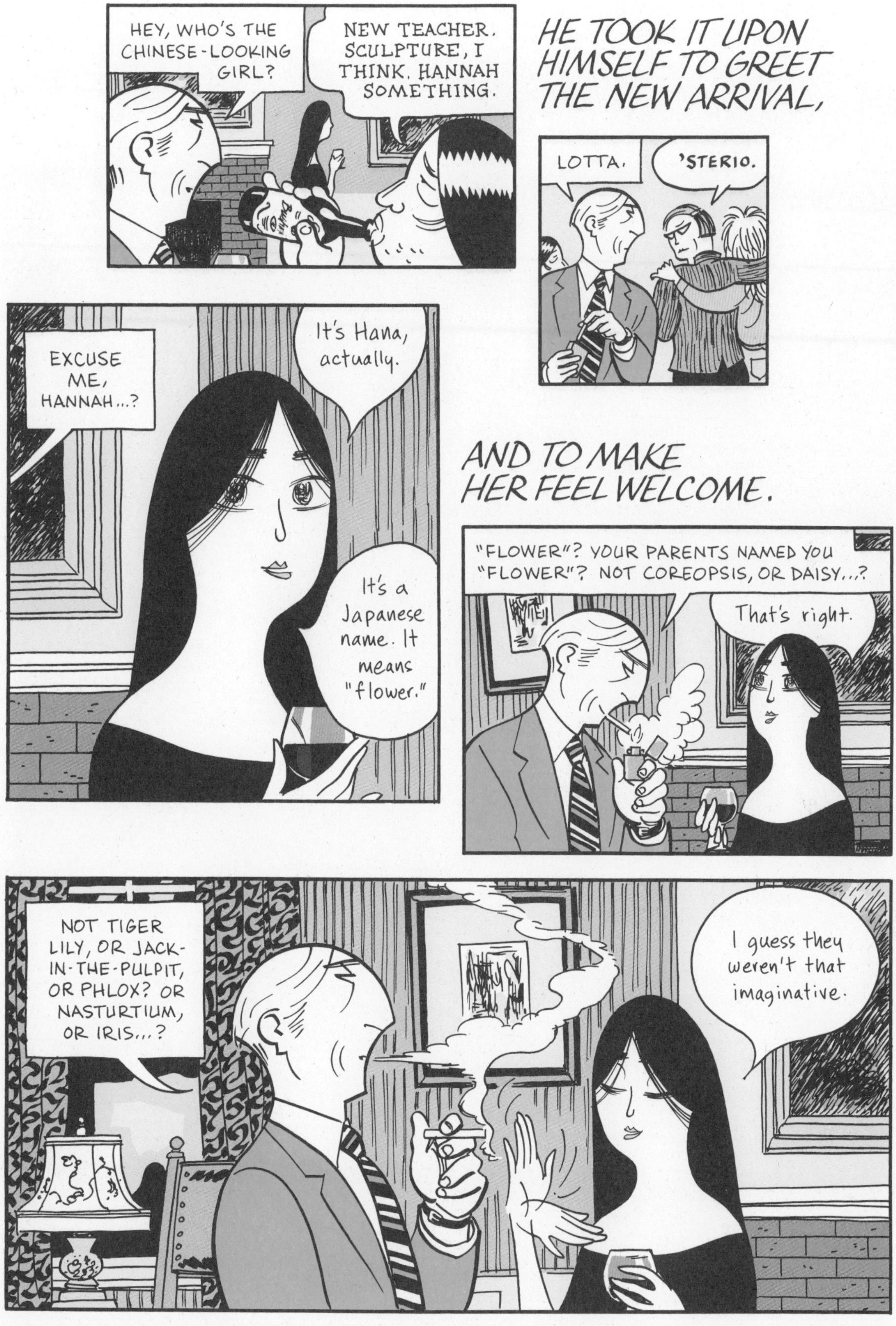
HEY, WHO'S THE CHINESE-LOOKING GIRL?
NEW TEACHER. SCULPTURE, I THINK. HANNAH SOMETHING.
HE TOOK IT UPON HIMSELF TO GREET THE NEW ARRIVAL,
LOTTA.
'STERIO.
EXCUSE ME, HANNAH...?
It's Hana, actually.
It's a Japanese name. It means "flower."
AND TO MAKE HER FEEL WELCOME.
"FLOWER"? YOUR PARENTS NAMED YOU "FLOWER"? NOT COREOPSIS, OR DAISY...?
That's right.
NOT TIGER LILY, OR JACK-IN-THE-PULPIT, OR PHLOX? OR NASTURTIUM, OR IRIS...?
I guess they weren't that imaginative.

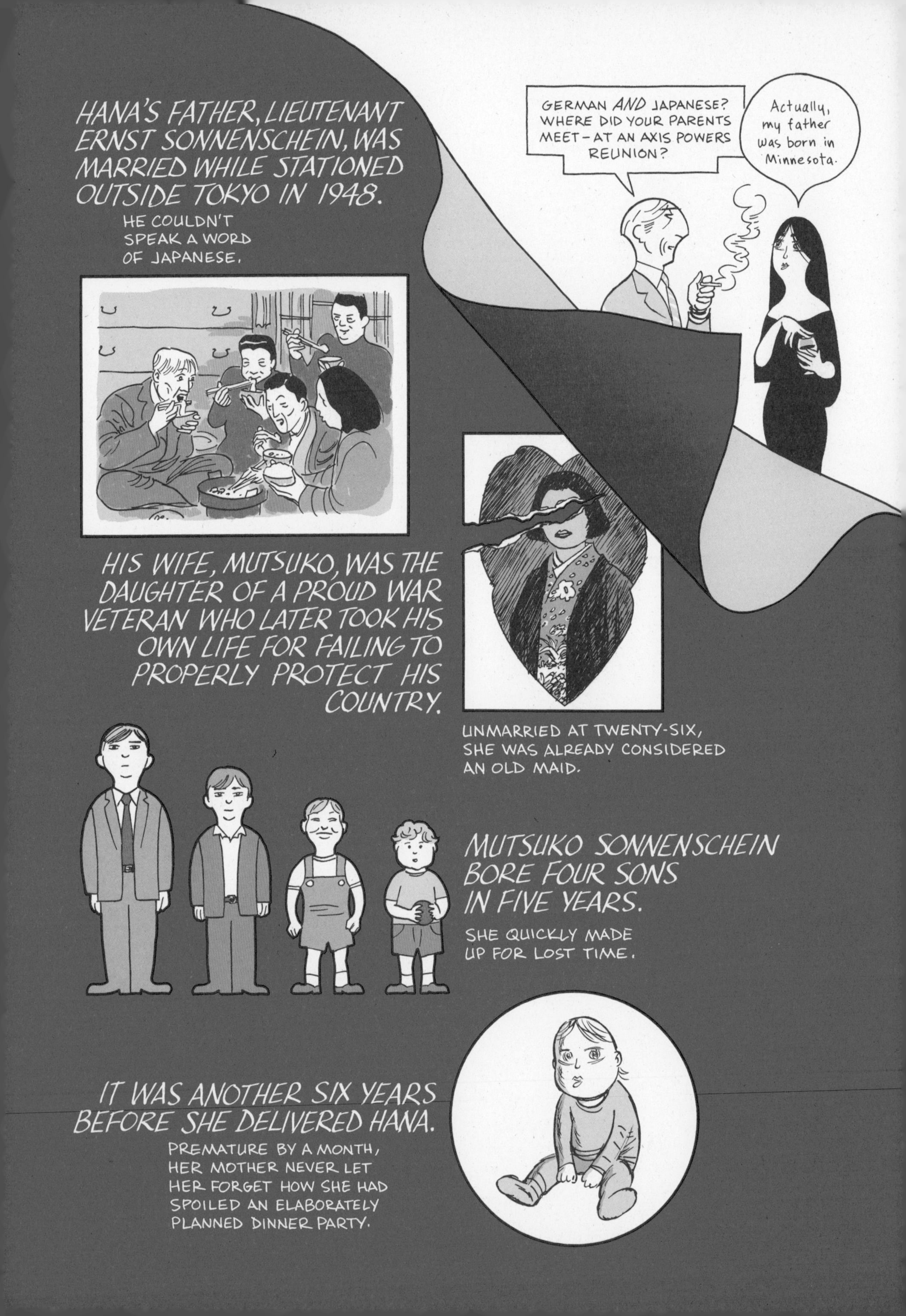
HANA'S FATHER, LIEUTENANT ERNST SONNENSCHEIN, WAS MARRIED WHILE STATIONED OUTSIDE TOKYO IN 1948.
HE COULDN'T SPEAK A WORD OF JAPANESE.
GERMAN *AND* JAPANESE? WHERE DID YOUR PARENTS MEET—AT AN AXIS POWERS REUNION?
Actually, my father was born in Minnesota.
HIS WIFE, MUTSUKO, WAS THE DAUGHTER OF A PROUD WAR VETERAN WHO LATER TOOK HIS OWN LIFE FOR FAILING TO PROPERLY PROTECT HIS COUNTRY.
UNMARRIED AT TWENTY-SIX, SHE WAS ALREADY CONSIDERED AN OLD MAID.
MUTSUKO SONNENSCHEIN BORE FOUR SONS IN FIVE YEARS.
SHE QUICKLY MADE UP FOR LOST TIME.
IT WAS ANOTHER SIX YEARS BEFORE SHE DELIVERED HANA.
PREMATURE BY A MONTH, HER MOTHER NEVER LET HER FORGET HOW SHE HAD SPOILED AN ELABORATELY PLANNED DINNER PARTY.

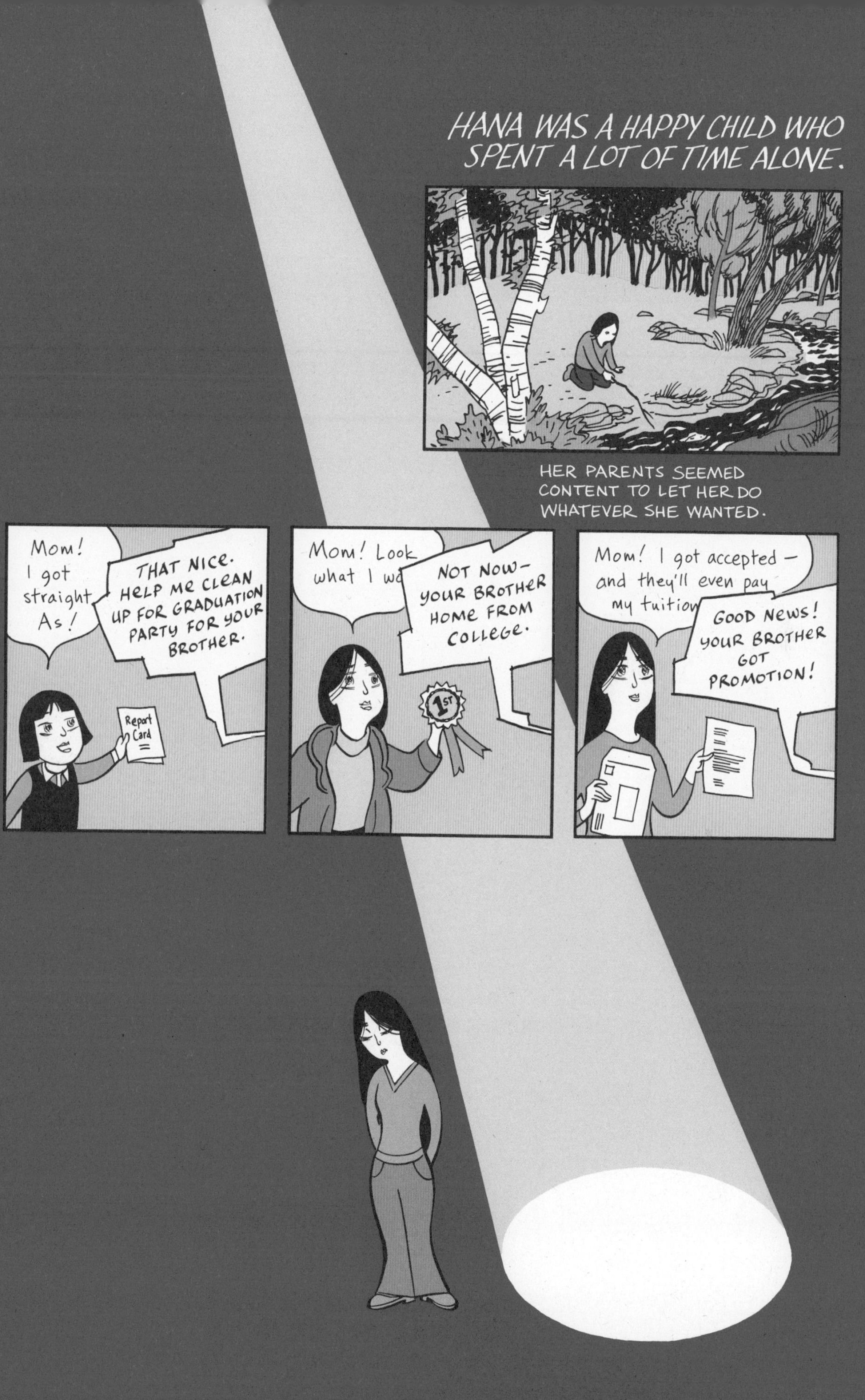
HANA WAS A HAPPY CHILD WHO SPENT A LOT OF TIME ALONE.
HER PARENTS SEEMED CONTENT TO LET HER DO WHATEVER SHE WANTED.
Mom! I got straight As!
THAT NICE. HELP ME CLEAN UP FOR GRADUATION PARTY FOR YOUR BROTHER.
Report Card
Mom! Look what I w
NOT NOW— YOUR BROTHER HOME FROM COLLEGE.
1ST
Mom! I got accepted — and they'll even pay my tuition
GOOD NEWS! YOUR BROTHER GOT PROMOTION!

HANA ATTENDED A
PRESTIGIOUS COLLEGE OF
ART IN RHODE ISLAND ON A
HER PARENTS, THINKING A COLLEGE **FULL**
EDUCATION UNNECESSARY
FOR A GIRL, ALLOWED **SCHOLAR-**
ONLY THIS COURSE OF STUDY... **SHIP.**

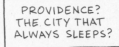
PROVIDENCE?
THE CITY THAT
ALWAYS SLEEPS?

I
liked
it.

ALTHOUGH SHE WAS AN
EXTRAORDINARY STUDENT,
SHE ALWAYS WORRIED
ABOUT BEING THE WORST
IN THE CLASS.

...NOT REALIZING THAT ART
WAS THE ONLY THING SHE
EVER WANTED TO STUDY.

*SHE HAD A FEW BOYFRIENDS,
BUT ONLY BECAUSE THEY
SOUGHT HER OUT.*
SHE WORKED SO HARD,
SHE HAD LITTLE TIME
FOR A SOCIAL LIFE.

AFTER FOUR OUTSTANDING
YEARS, SHE WAS CHOSEN
TO DELIVER THE
VALEDICTORY ADDRESS.
SHE DECLINED BECAUSE
SHE WAS TOO SHY TO
SPEAK IN THE
CROWDED AUDITORIUM.

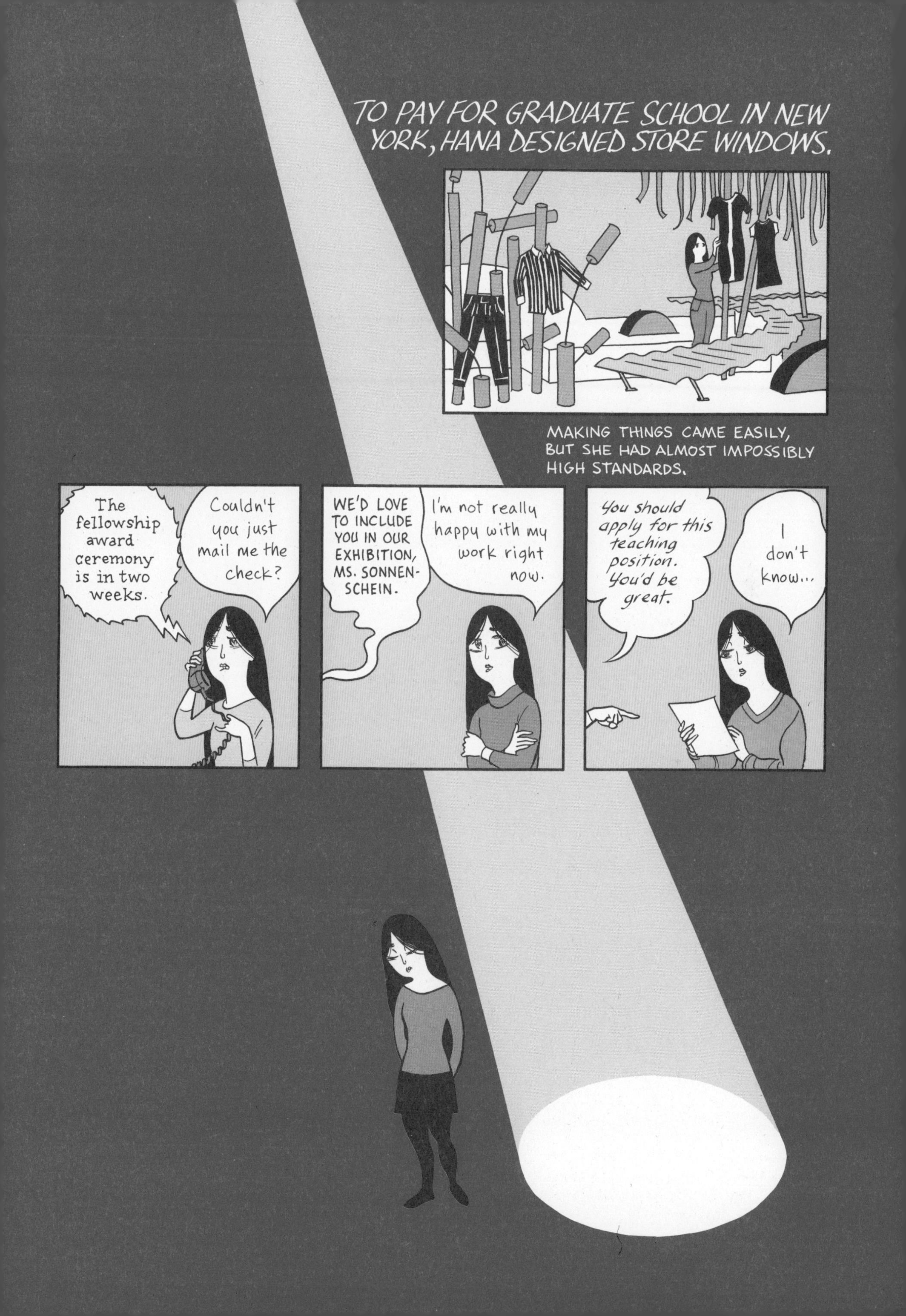
TO PAY FOR GRADUATE SCHOOL IN NEW YORK, HANA DESIGNED STORE WINDOWS.
MAKING THINGS CAME EASILY, BUT SHE HAD ALMOST IMPOSSIBLY HIGH STANDARDS.
The fellowship award ceremony is in two weeks.
Couldn't you just mail me the check?
WE'D LOVE TO INCLUDE YOU IN OUR EXHIBITION, MS. SONNENSCHEIN.
I'm not really happy with my work right now.
You should apply for this teaching position. You'd be great.
I don't know...

IN 1984, HANA SONNENSCHEIN ATTENDED HER FIRST FACULTY PARTY.

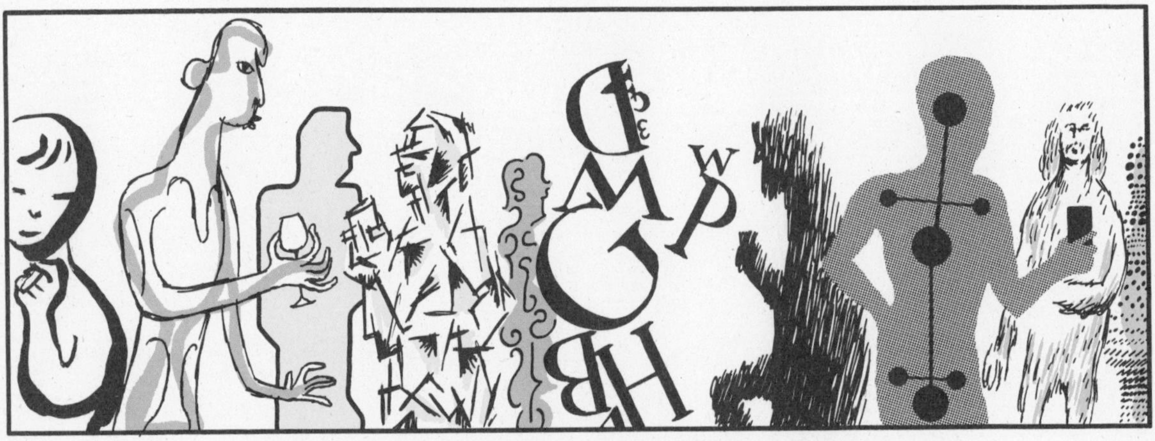

SHE DIDN'T KNOW ANYONE THERE,

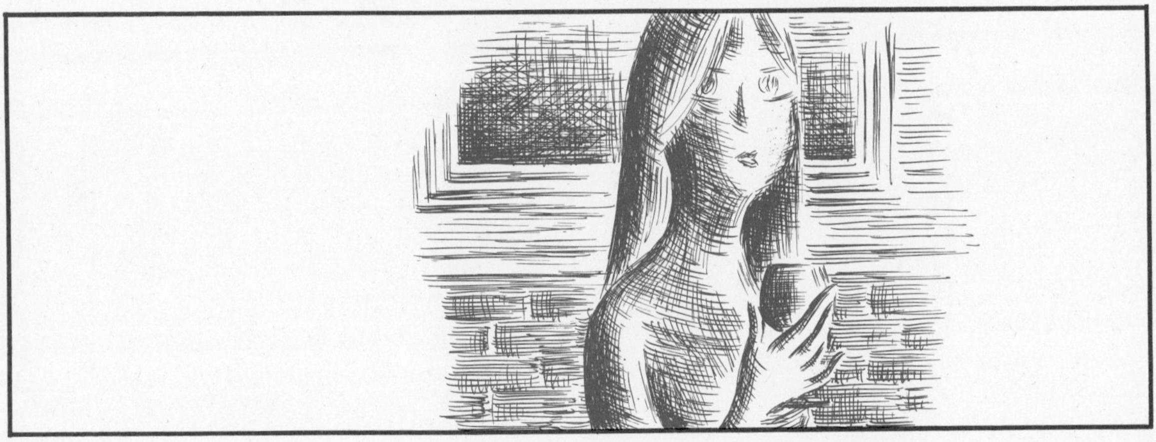

BUT ONE PERSON CAUGHT HER EYE.

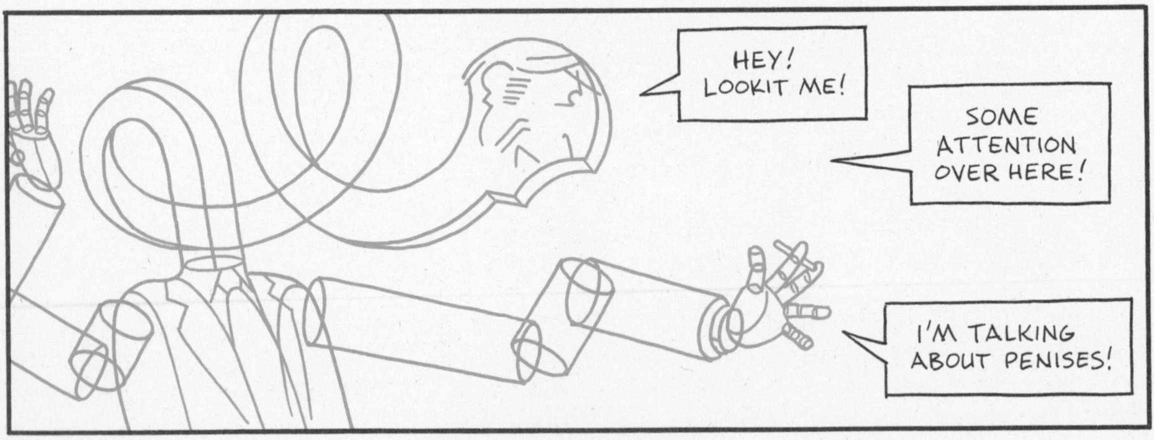
HEY! LOOKIT ME!
SOME ATTENTION OVER HERE!
I'M TALKING ABOUT PENISES!

DON'T ASK ME TO EXPLAIN THESE THINGS.

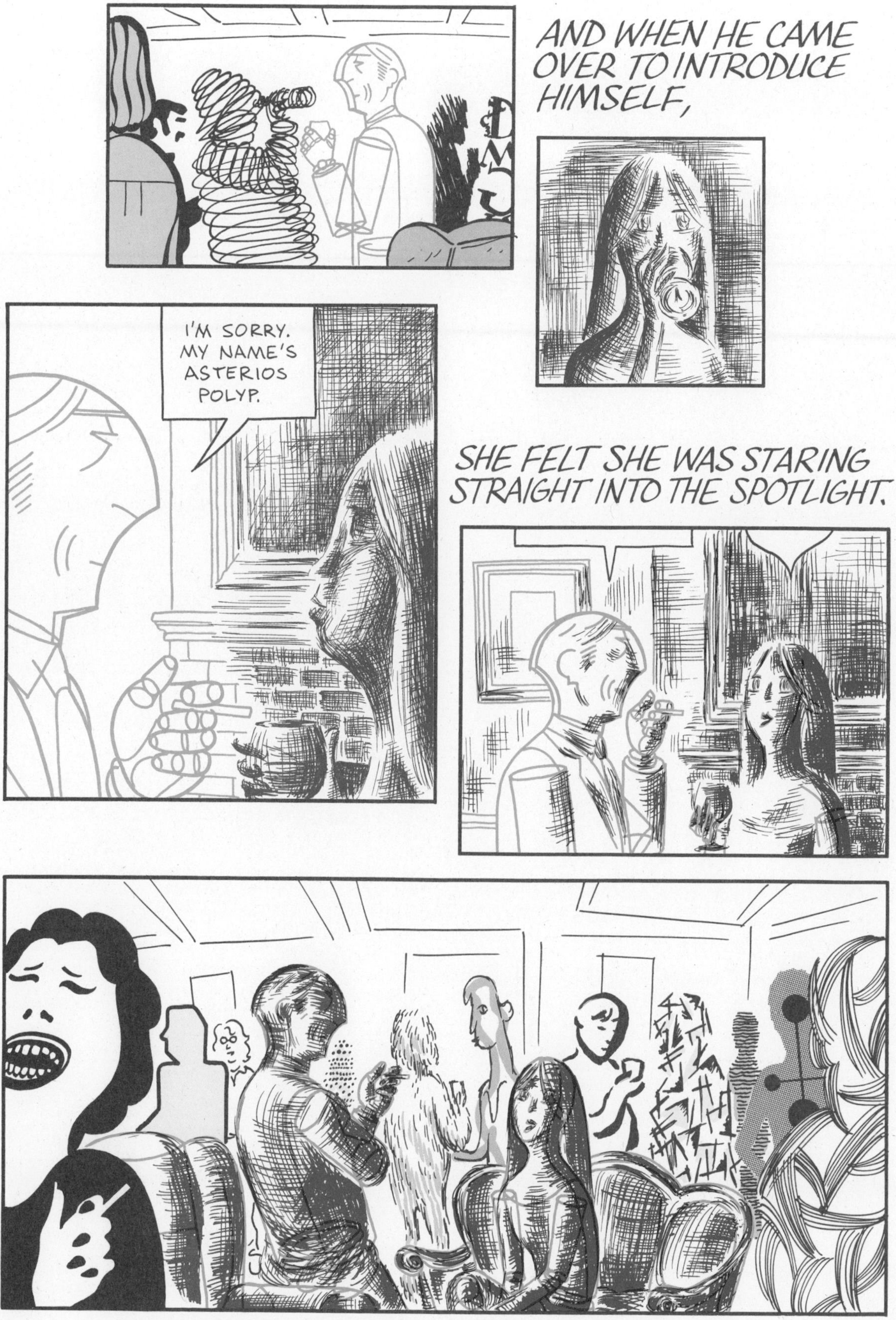
AND WHEN HE CAME OVER TO INTRODUCE HIMSELF,
I'M SORRY. MY NAME'S ASTERIOS POLYP.
SHE FELT SHE WAS STARING STRAIGHT INTO THE SPOTLIGHT.

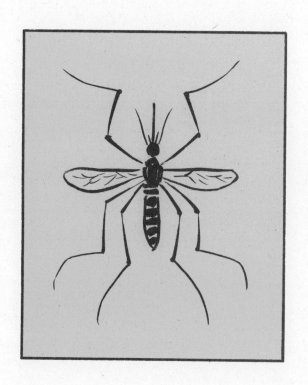

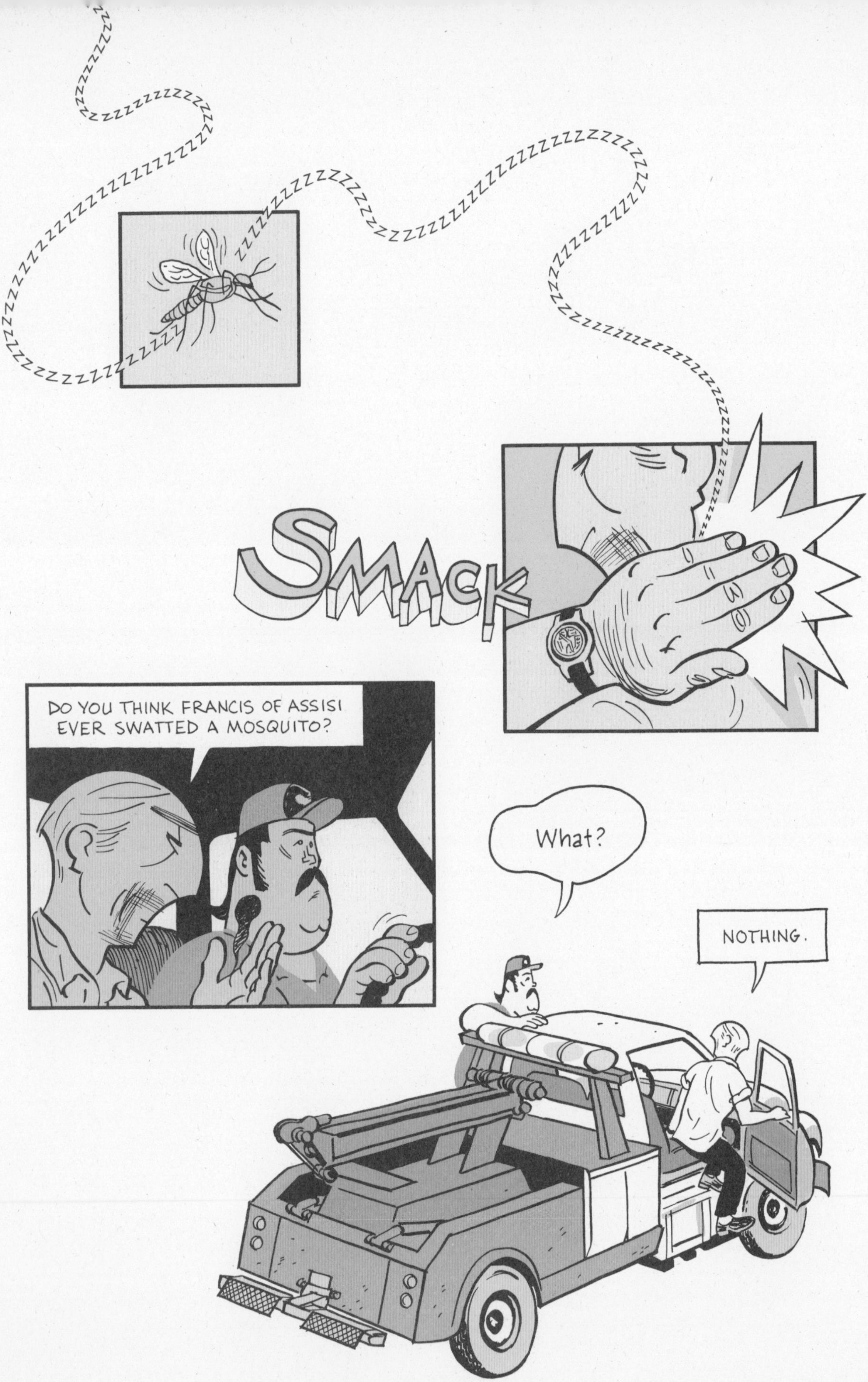
SMACK
DO YOU THINK FRANCIS OF ASSISI EVER SWATTED A MOSQUITO?
What?
NOTHING.

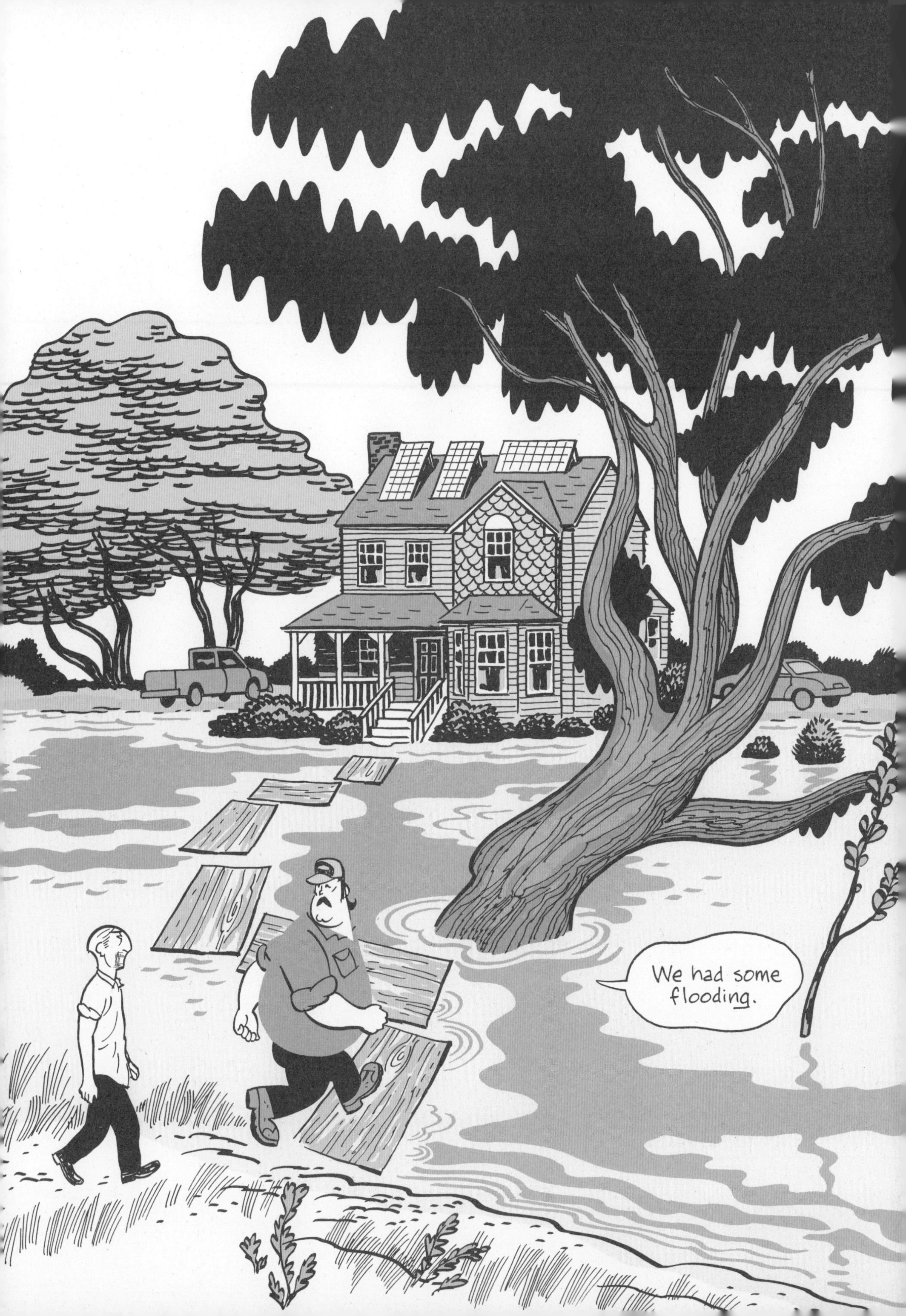
We had some flooding.

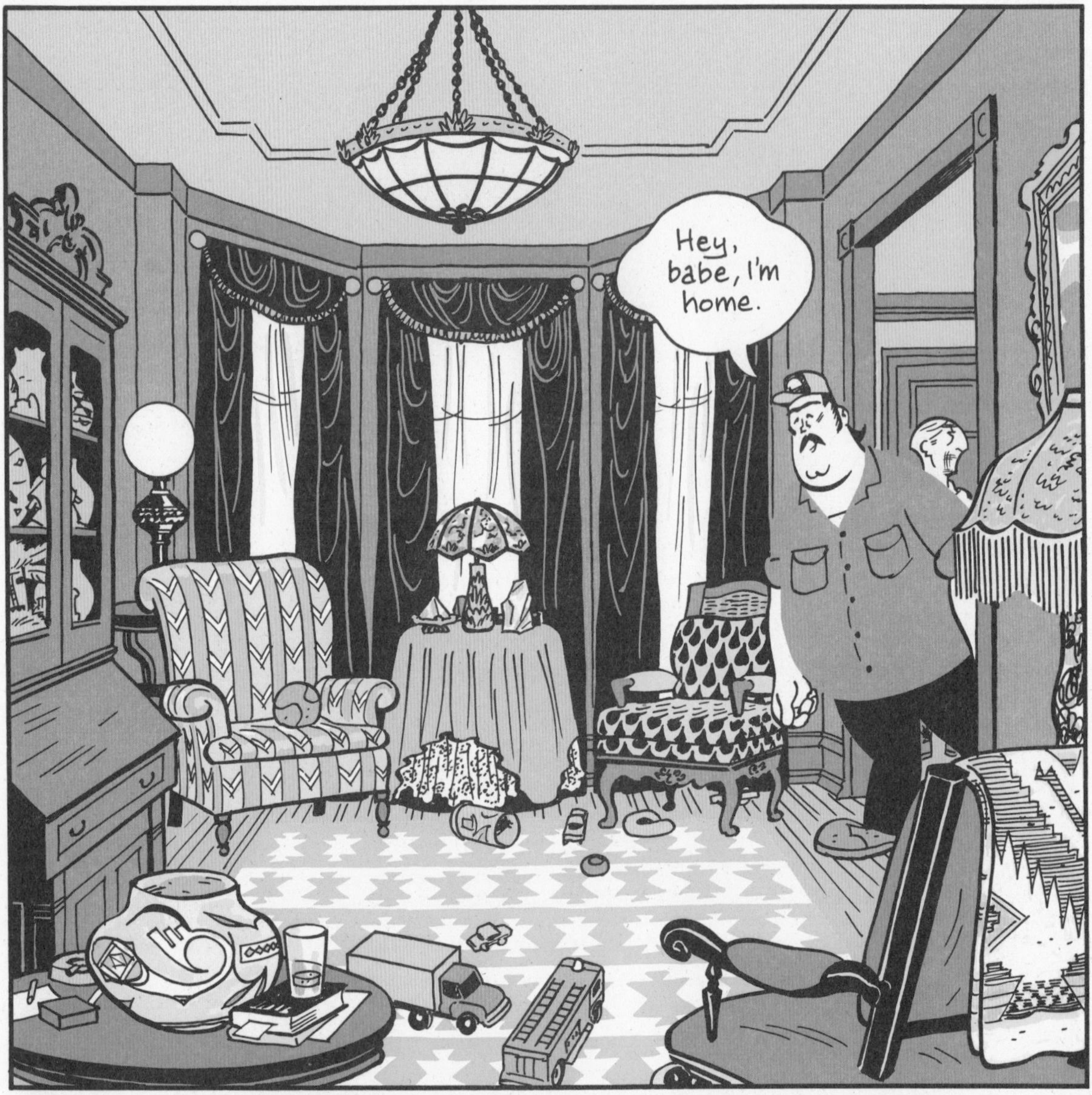
Hey, babe, I'm home.

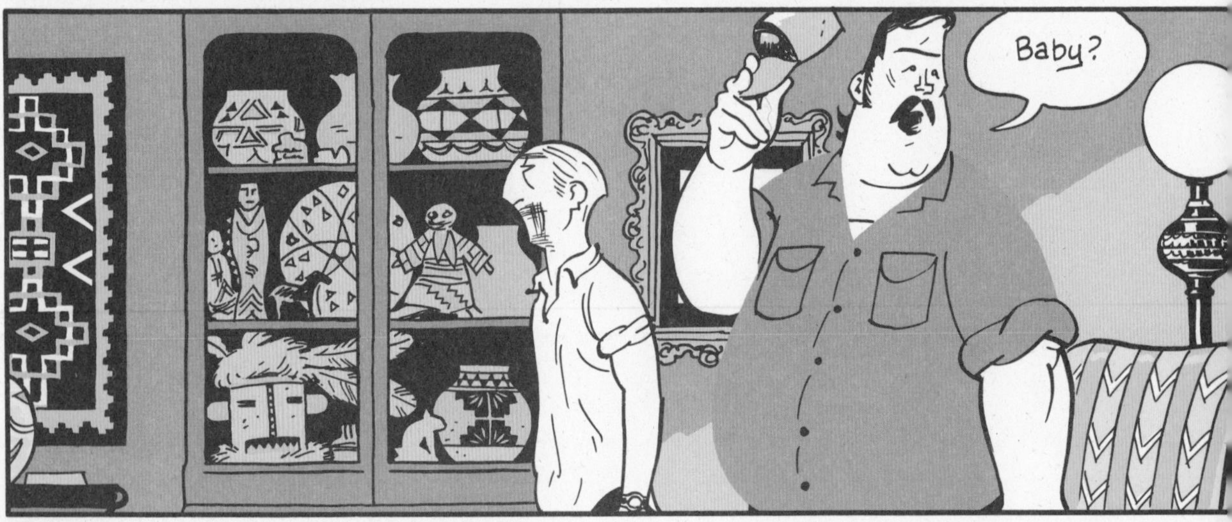
Baby?

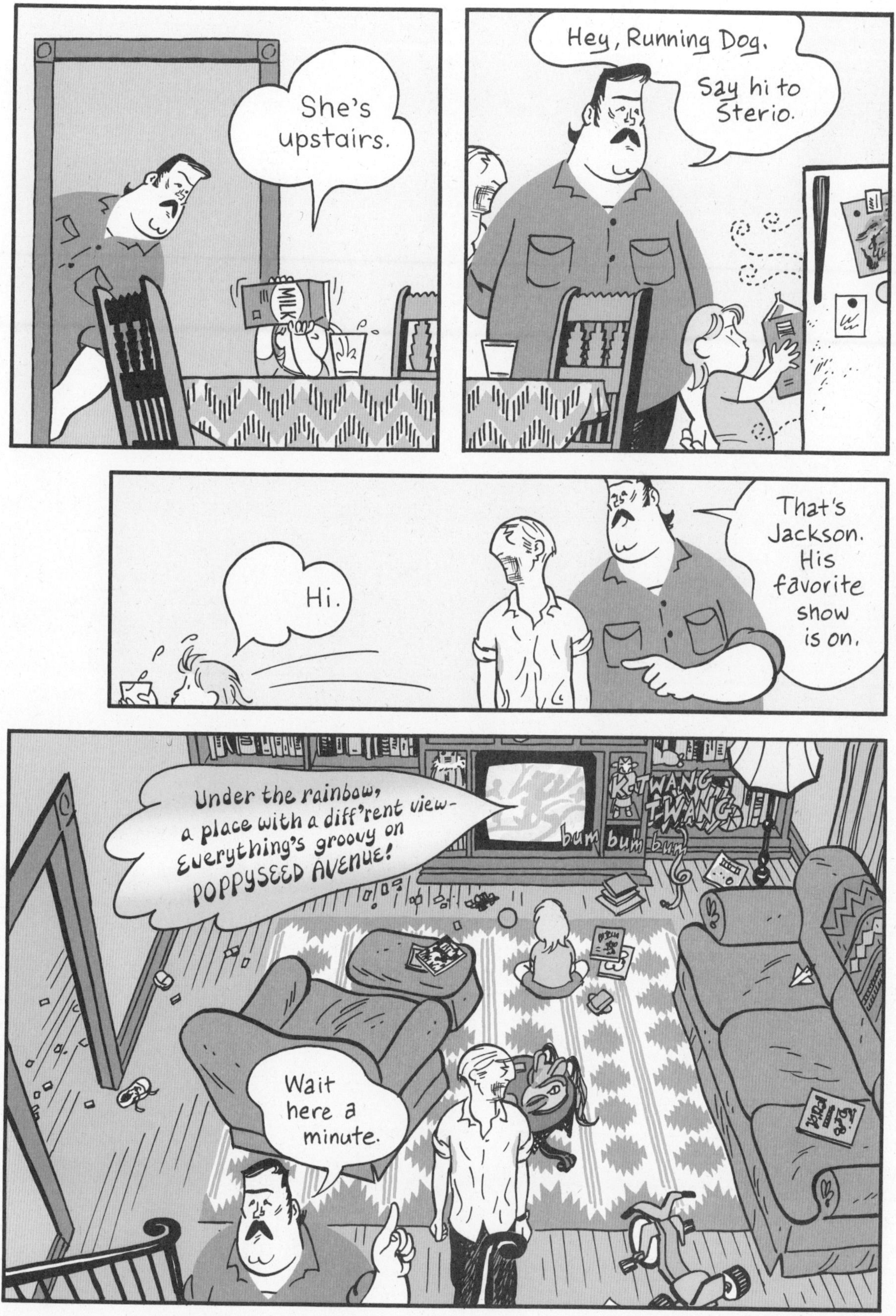

She's upstairs.
Hey, Running Dog.
Say hi to Sterio.
That's Jackson. His favorite show is on.
Hi.
Under the rainbow, a place with a diff'rent view-Everything's groovy on POPPYSEED AVENUE!
K-TWANG TWANG
bum bum bum
Wait here a minute.

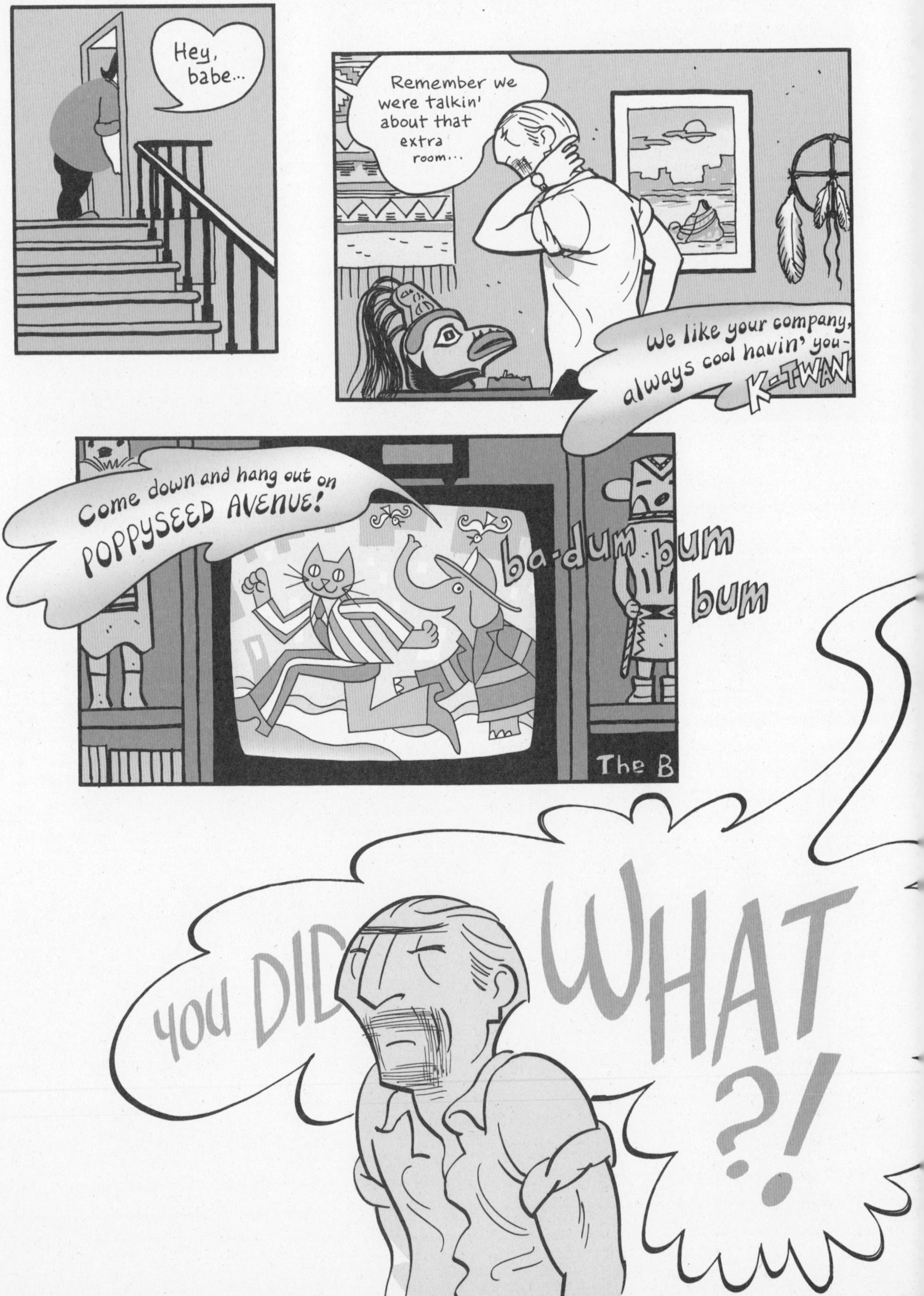

Hey, babe...
Remember we were talkin' about that extra room...
We like your company, always cool havin' you-
K-TWAN
Come down and hang out on POPPYSEED AVENUE!
ba-dum bum bum
The B
YOU DID WHAT ?!

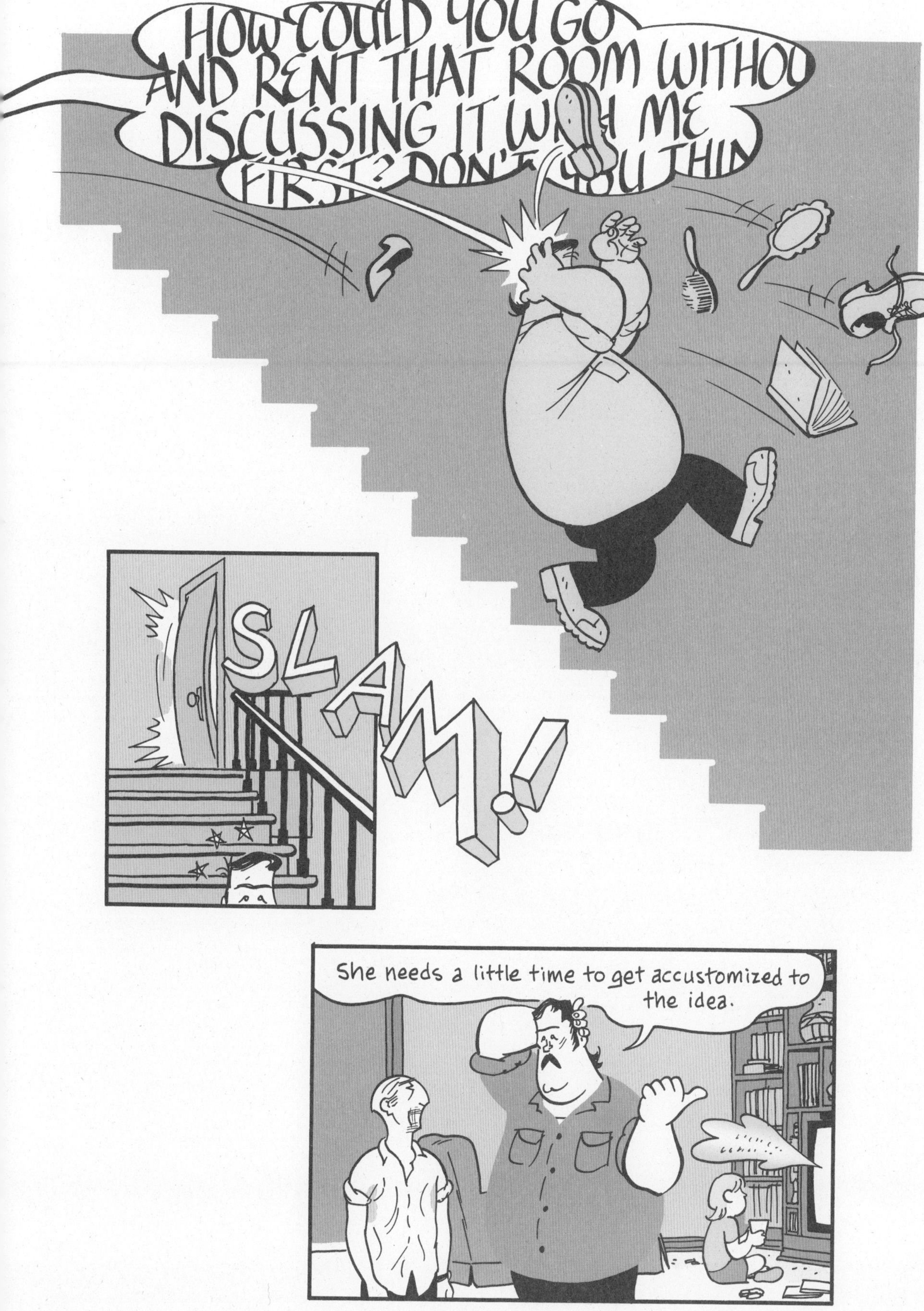
HOW COULD YOU GO AND RENT THAT ROOM WITHOU DISCUSSING IT W H ME FIRST? DON'T YOU THIN
SLAM!!
She needs a little time to get accustomized to the idea.

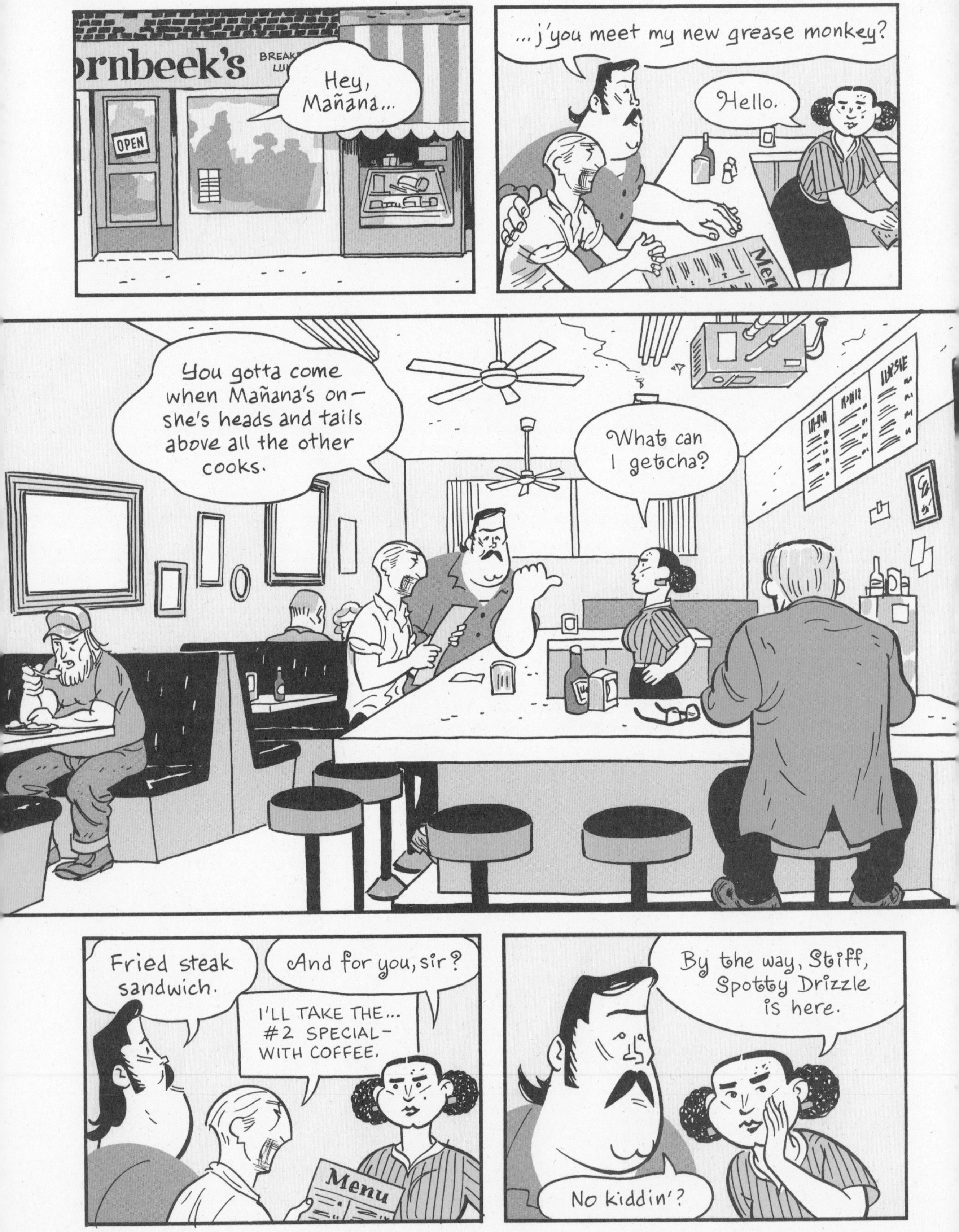

ornbeek's
BREAK
LU
OPEN
Hey, Mañana...
...j'you meet my new grease monkey?
Hello.
Men
You gotta come when Mañana's on— she's heads and tails above all the other cooks.
What can I getcha?
Fried steak sandwich.
And for you, sir?
I'LL TAKE THE... #2 SPECIAL— WITH COFFEE.
Menu
By the way, Stiff, Spotty Drizzle is here.
No kiddin'?

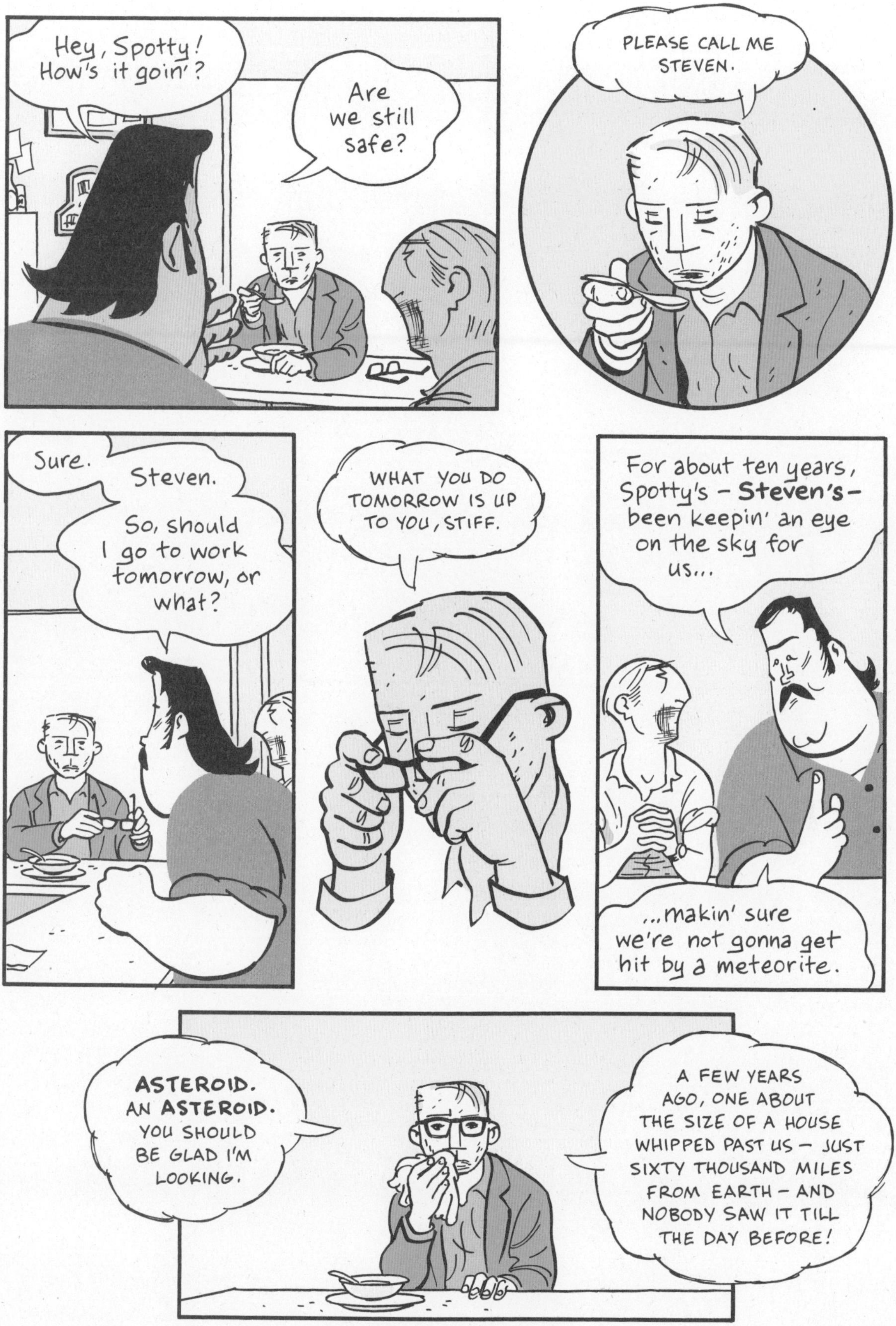
Hey, Spotty! How's it goin'?
Are we still safe?
PLEASE CALL ME STEVEN.
Sure.
Steven.
So, should I go to work tomorrow, or what?
WHAT YOU DO TOMORROW IS UP TO YOU, STIFF.
For about ten years, Spotty's – **Steven's** – been keepin' an eye on the sky for us...
...makin' sure we're not gonna get hit by a meteorite.
ASTEROID. AN **ASTEROID.** YOU SHOULD BE GLAD I'M LOOKING.
A FEW YEARS AGO, ONE ABOUT THE SIZE OF A HOUSE WHIPPED PAST US – JUST SIXTY THOUSAND MILES FROM EARTH – AND NOBODY SAW IT TILL THE DAY BEFORE!

ALL THE OBSERVATORIES, THEY HAVE THEIR TELESCOPES FOCUSED ON DEEP SPACE — THEY'RE NOT PAYING ATTENTION TO WHAT'S HAPPENING RIGHT HERE!

SOMEBODY'S GOTTA BE PREPARED. SOMEBODY'S GOTTA BE ON THE LOOKOUT. WE DON'T WANNA END UP JUST LIKE THE DINOSAURS!

The dinosaurs?

MR. DRIZZLE IS REFERRING TO THE ALVAREZ HYPOTHESIS, FIRST PROPOSED IN 1980, AND NOW RATHER WIDELY ACCEPTED.

IT SUPPOSES THAT A COMET — OR AN ASTEROID — ABOUT FIVE MILES WIDE STRUCK NEAR YUCATÁN SIXTY-FIVE MILLION YEARS AGO.

THE EXPLOSIVE IMPACT SENT ENOUGH DUST AND SOOT INTO THE ATMOSPHERE TO BLOCK OUT THE SUN AND CREATE A TOXIC ACID RAIN...

...A DEADLY COMBINATION FOR PLANT LIFE, AS WELL AS EVERYTHING ELSE UP THE FOOD CHAIN.

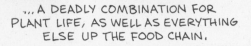

FORTUNATELY FOR US, A COMET THAT SIZE COLLIDES WITH THE EARTH MAYBE ONCE IN A HUNDRED MILLION YEARS.

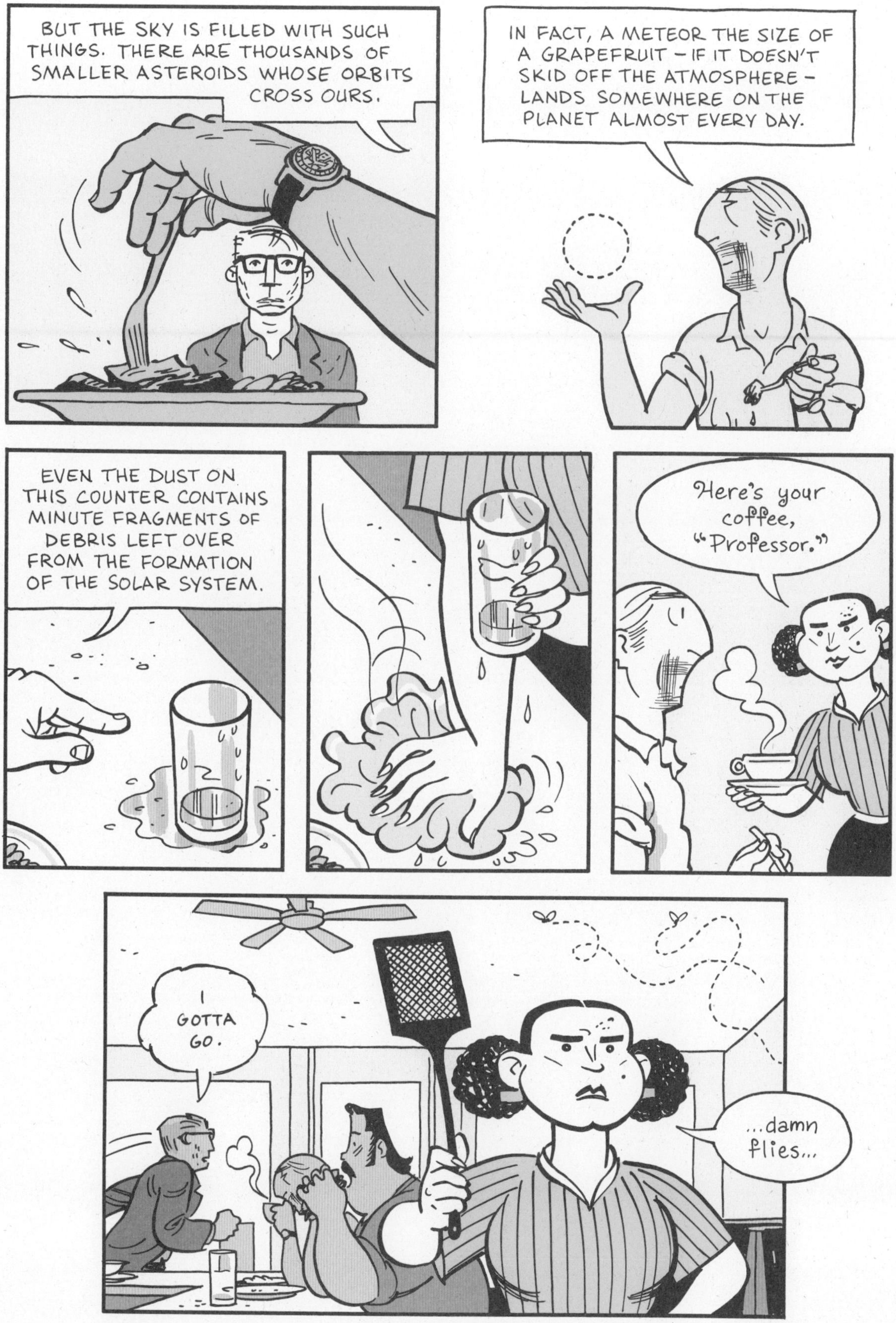
BUT THE SKY IS FILLED WITH SUCH THINGS. THERE ARE THOUSANDS OF SMALLER ASTEROIDS WHOSE ORBITS CROSS OURS.
IN FACT, A METEOR THE SIZE OF A GRAPEFRUIT – IF IT DOESN'T SKID OFF THE ATMOSPHERE – LANDS SOMEWHERE ON THE PLANET ALMOST EVERY DAY.
EVEN THE DUST ON THIS COUNTER CONTAINS MINUTE FRAGMENTS OF DEBRIS LEFT OVER FROM THE FORMATION OF THE SOLAR SYSTEM.
Here's your coffee, "Professor."
I GOTTA GO.
...damn flies...

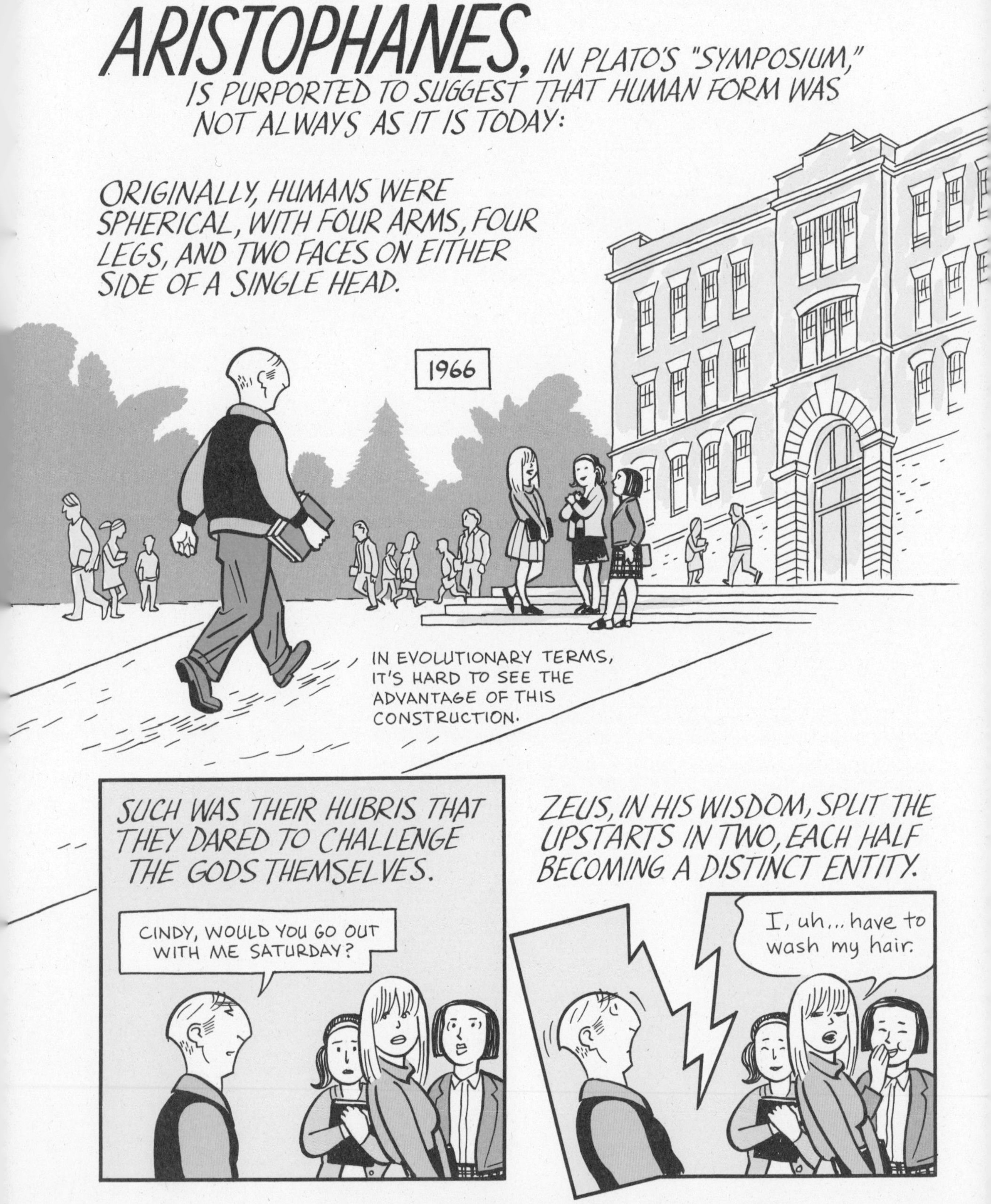
ARISTOPHANES, IN PLATO'S "SYMPOSIUM," IS PURPORTED TO SUGGEST THAT HUMAN FORM WAS NOT ALWAYS AS IT IS TODAY:
ORIGINALLY, HUMANS WERE SPHERICAL, WITH FOUR ARMS, FOUR LEGS, AND TWO FACES ON EITHER SIDE OF A SINGLE HEAD.
1966
IN EVOLUTIONARY TERMS, IT'S HARD TO SEE THE ADVANTAGE OF THIS CONSTRUCTION.
SUCH WAS THEIR HUBRIS THAT THEY DARED TO CHALLENGE THE GODS THEMSELVES.
CINDY, WOULD YOU GO OUT WITH ME SATURDAY?
ZEUS, IN HIS WISDOM, SPLIT THE UPSTARTS IN TWO, EACH HALF BECOMING A DISTINCT ENTITY.
I, uh... have to wash my hair.
PLATO MAKES CLEAR WHAT HE THINKS OF THIS THEORY BY HAVING SOCRATES CASUALLY DISMISS IT.

SINCE THEN, MEN AND WOMEN HAVE BEEN RUNNING AROUND IN A PANIC, SEARCHING FOR THEIR LOST COUNTERPARTS, IN A DESIRE TO BE WHOLE AGAIN.

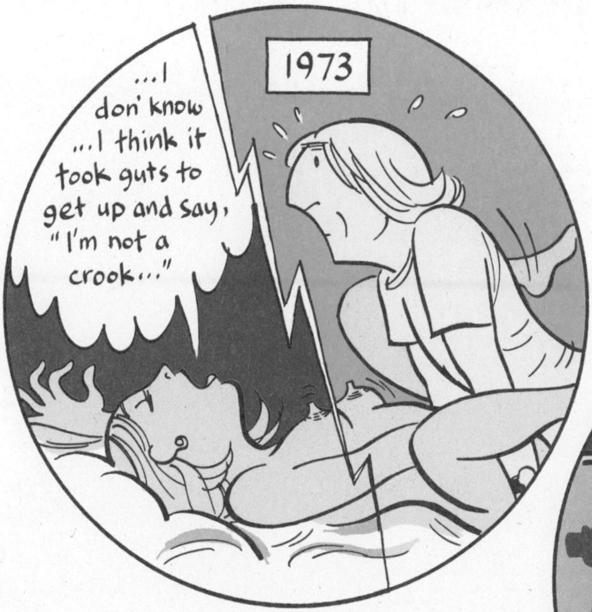
1973
...I don' know ...I think it took guts to get up and say, "I'm not a crook..."

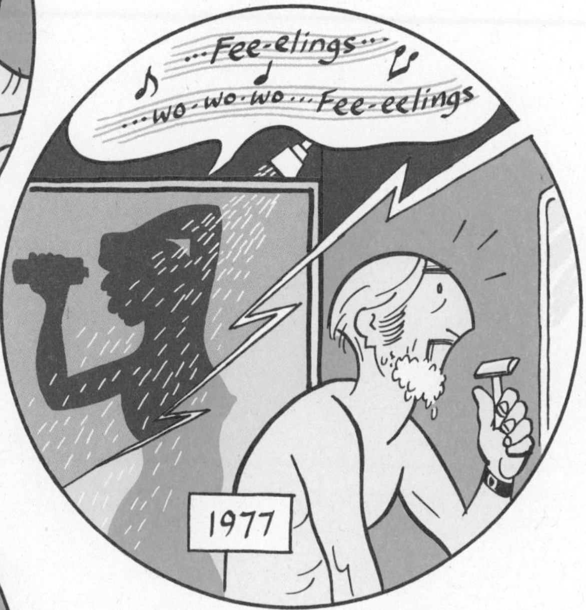
...Fee-elings... ...wo-wo-wo...Fee-eelings
1977

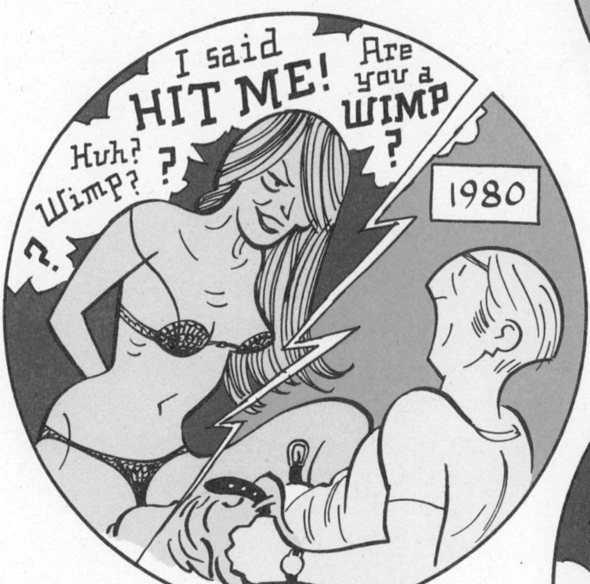
I said HIT ME!
Are you a WIMP?
Huh? Wimp? ? ?
1980

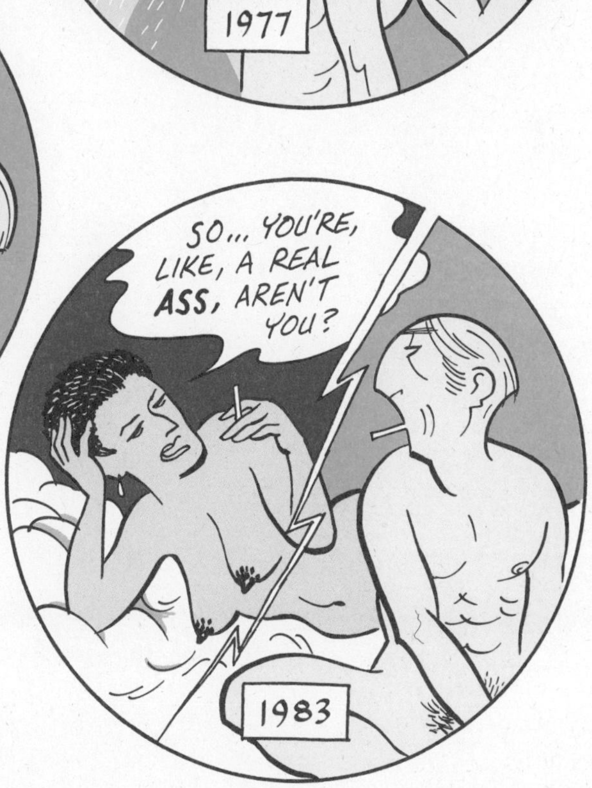
SO... YOU'RE, LIKE, A REAL **ASS**, AREN'T YOU?
1983

WE SHOULD AT LEAST GIVE SOME CREDIT TO ARISTOPHANES FOR ORIGINALITY.

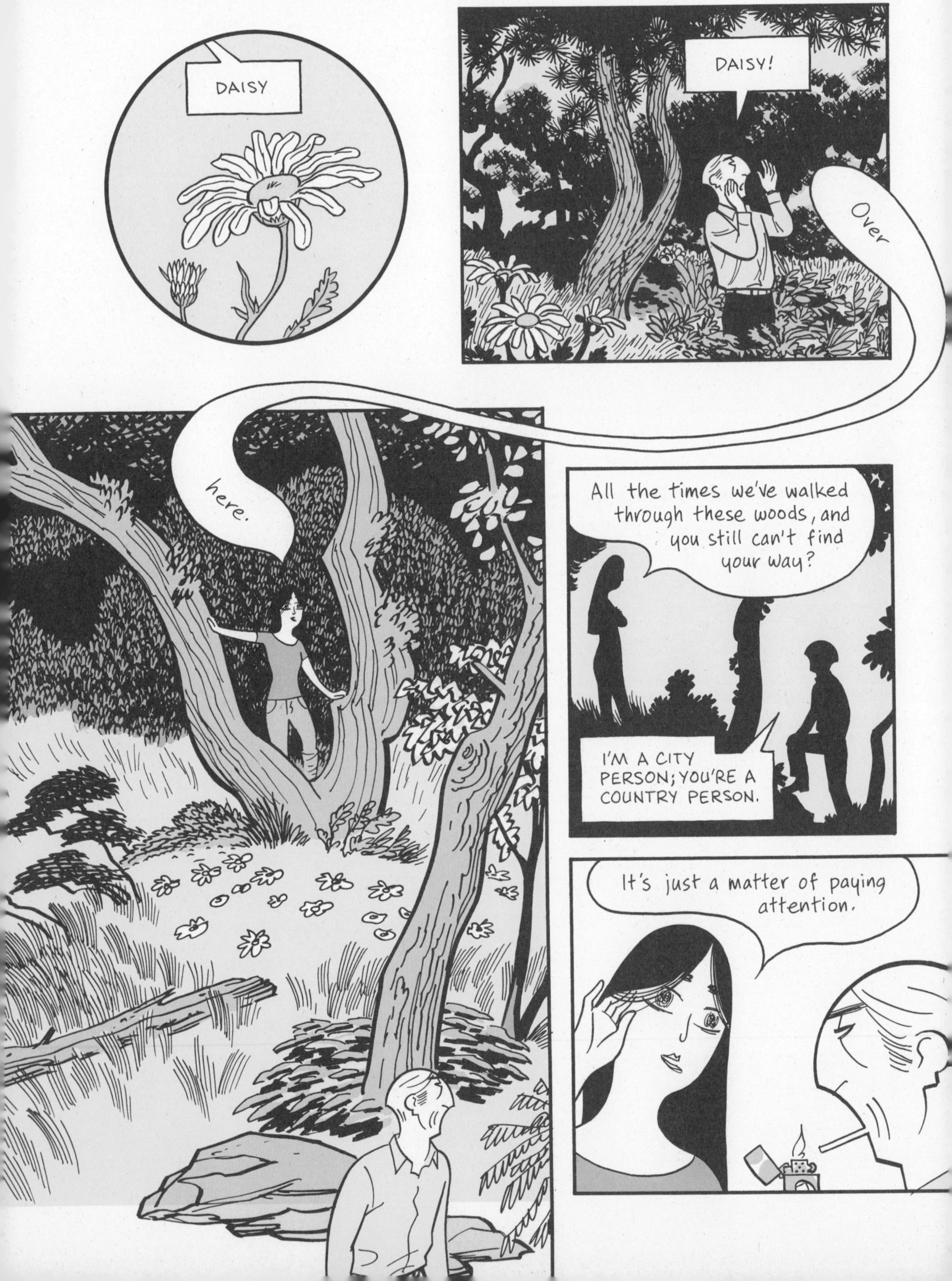
DAISY
DAISY!
Over
here.
All the times we've walked through these woods, and you still can't find your way?
I'M A CITY PERSON; YOU'RE A COUNTRY PERSON.
It's just a matter of paying attention.

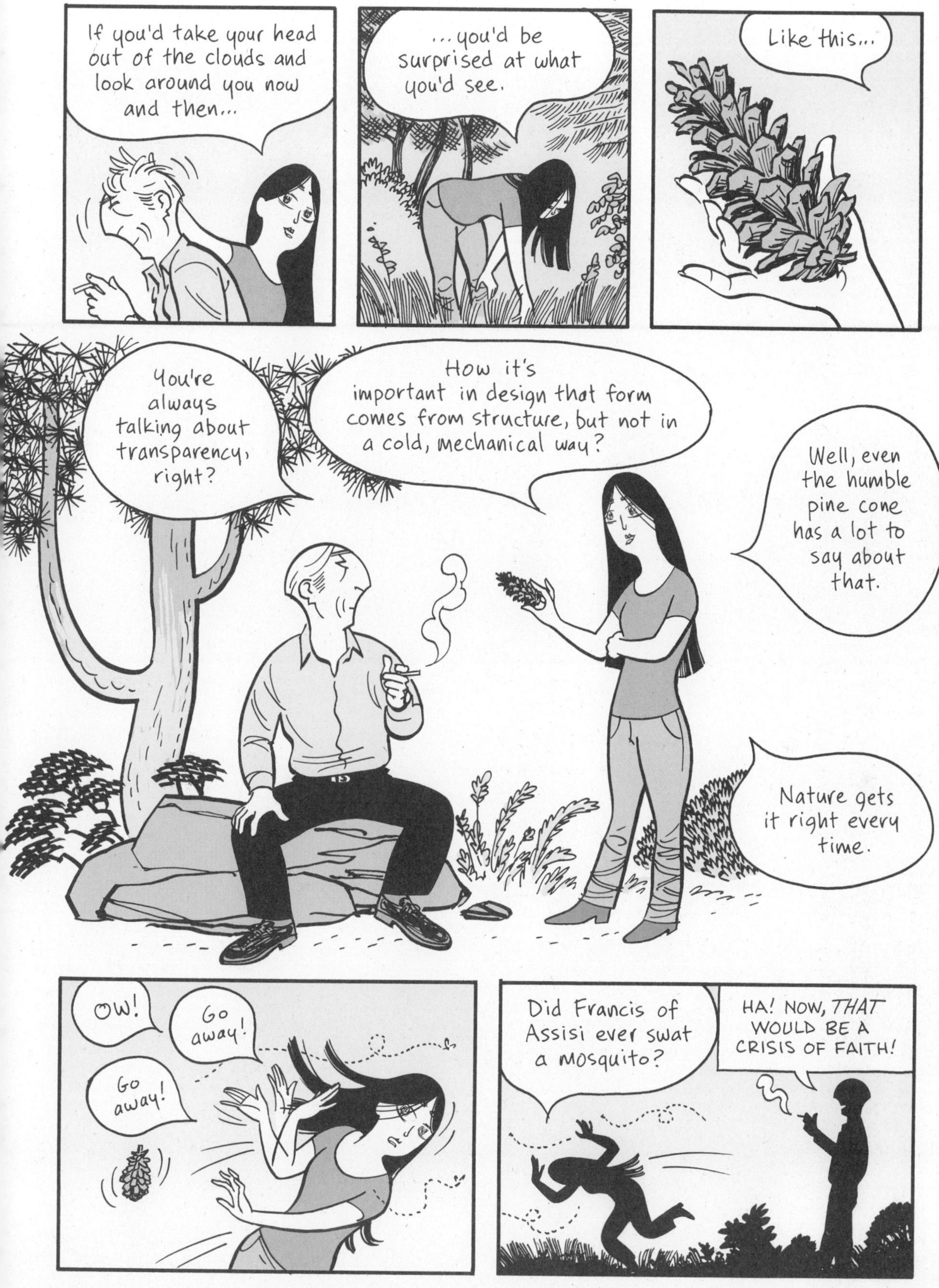
If you'd take your head out of the clouds and look around you now and then...
...you'd be surprised at what you'd see.
Like this...
You're always talking about transparency, right?
How it's important in design that form comes from structure, but not in a cold, mechanical way?
Well, even the humble pine cone has a lot to say about that.
Nature gets it right every time.
OW!
Go away!
Go away!
Did Francis of Assisi ever swat a mosquito?
HA! NOW, *THAT* WOULD BE A CRISIS OF FAITH!

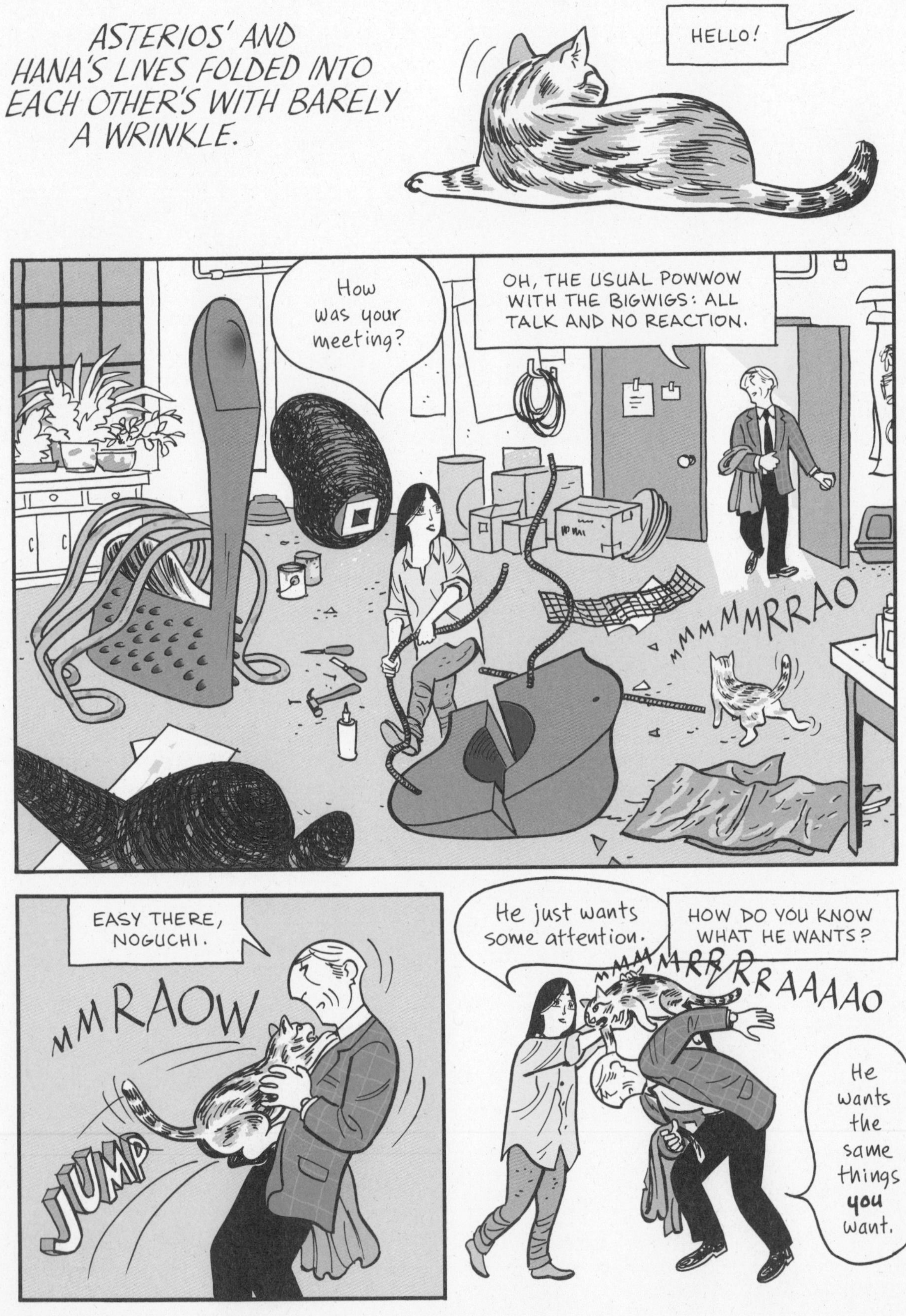
ASTERIOS' AND HANA'S LIVES FOLDED INTO EACH OTHER'S WITH BARELY A WRINKLE.
HELLO!
How was your meeting?
OH, THE USUAL POWWOW WITH THE BIGWIGS: ALL TALK AND NO REACTION.
MMMMMRRAO
EASY THERE, NOGUCHI.
MMRAOW
JUMP
He just wants some attention.
HOW DO YOU KNOW WHAT HE WANTS?
MMMMRRRRAAAAO
He wants the same things **you** want.

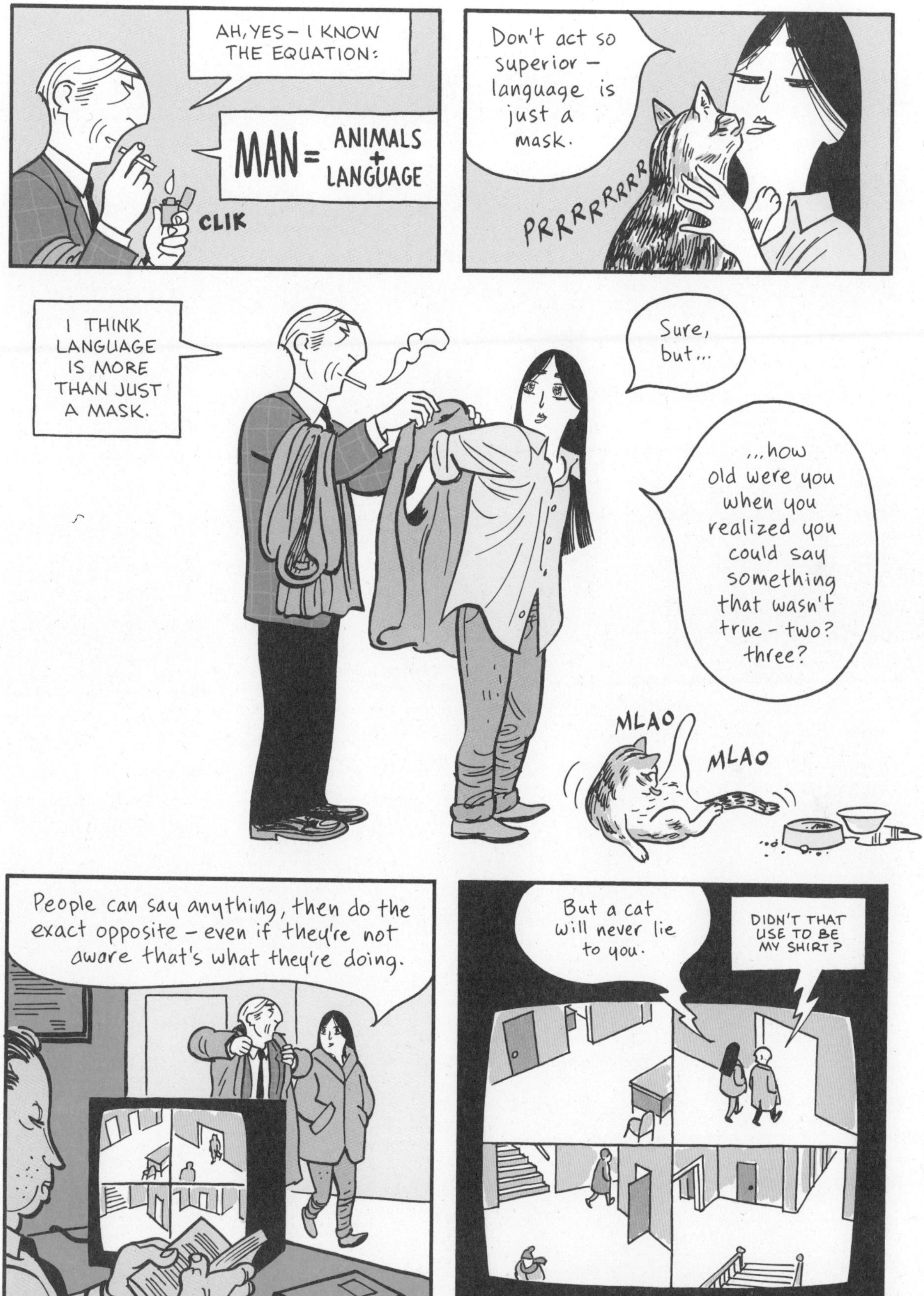
AH, YES– I KNOW THE EQUATION:
MAN = ANIMALS + LANGUAGE
CLIK
Don't act so superior – language is just a mask.
PRRRRRRRR
I THINK LANGUAGE IS MORE THAN JUST A MASK.
Sure, but...
...how old were you when you realized you could say something that wasn't true – two? three?
MLAO
MLAO
People can say anything, then do the exact opposite – even if they're not aware that's what they're doing.
But a cat will never lie to you.
DIDN'T THAT USE TO BE MY SHIRT?

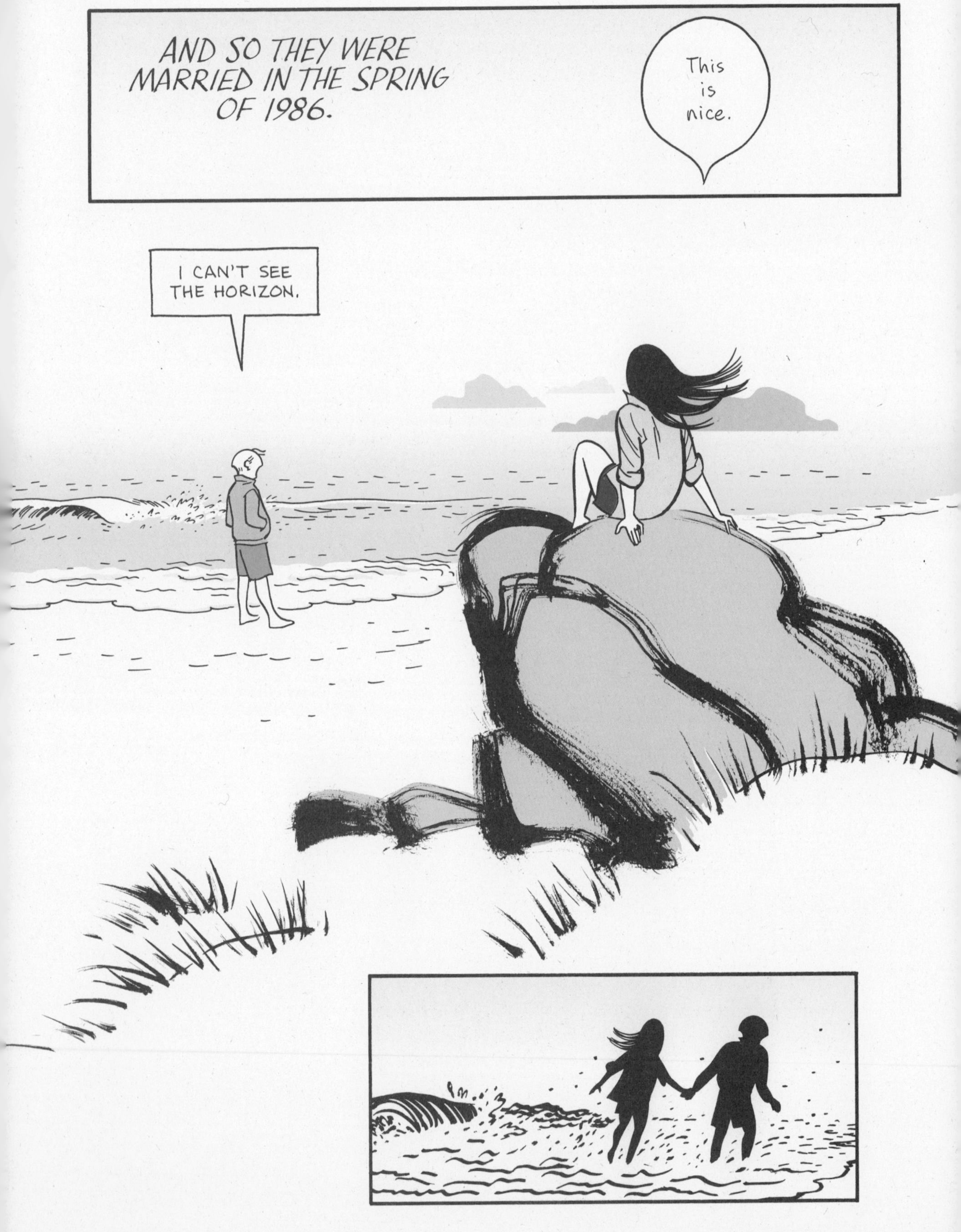
AND SO THEY WERE MARRIED IN THE SPRING OF 1986.
This is nice.
I CAN'T SEE THE HORIZON.

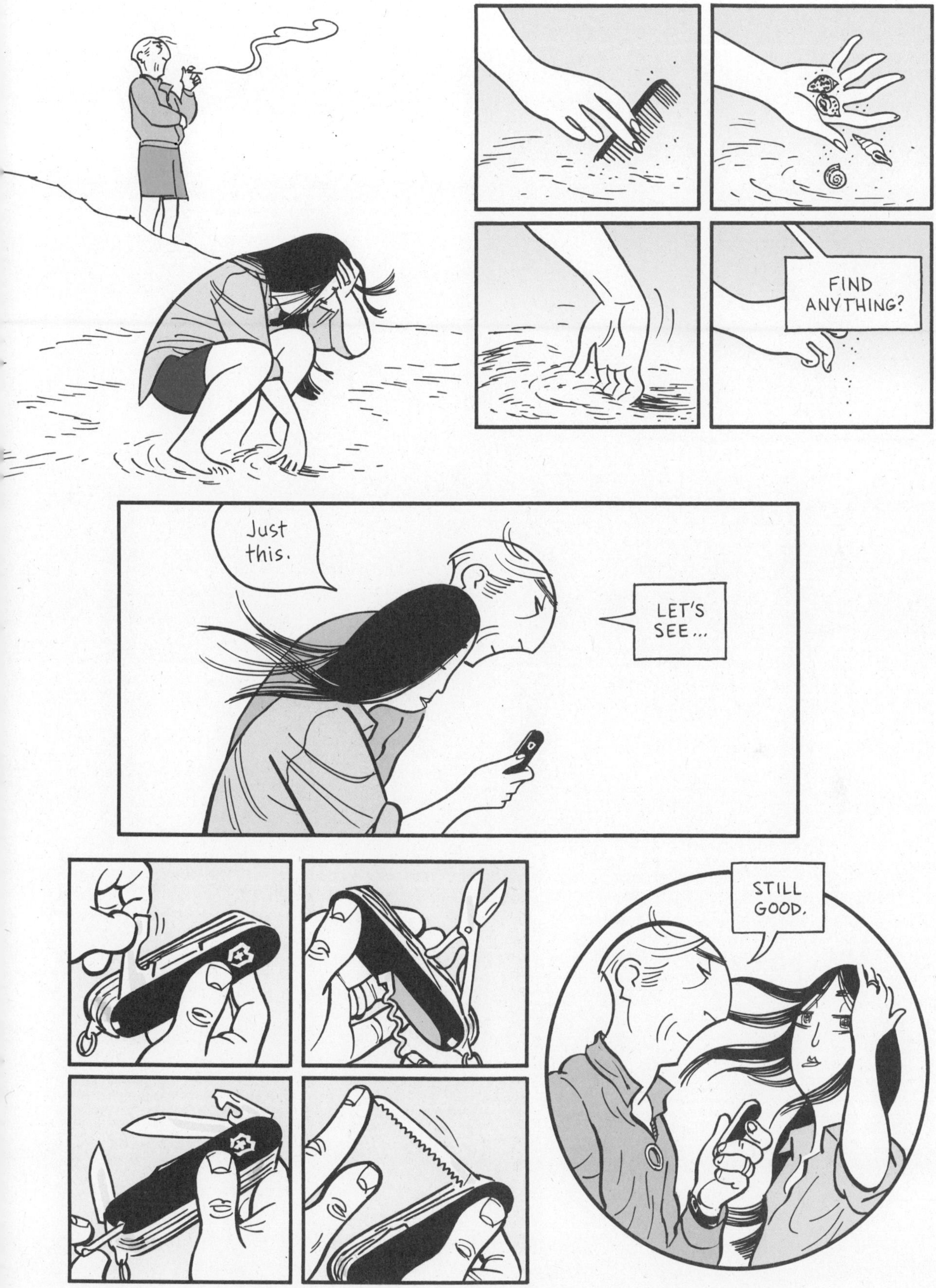
FIND ANYTHING?
Just this.
LET'S SEE...
STILL GOOD.

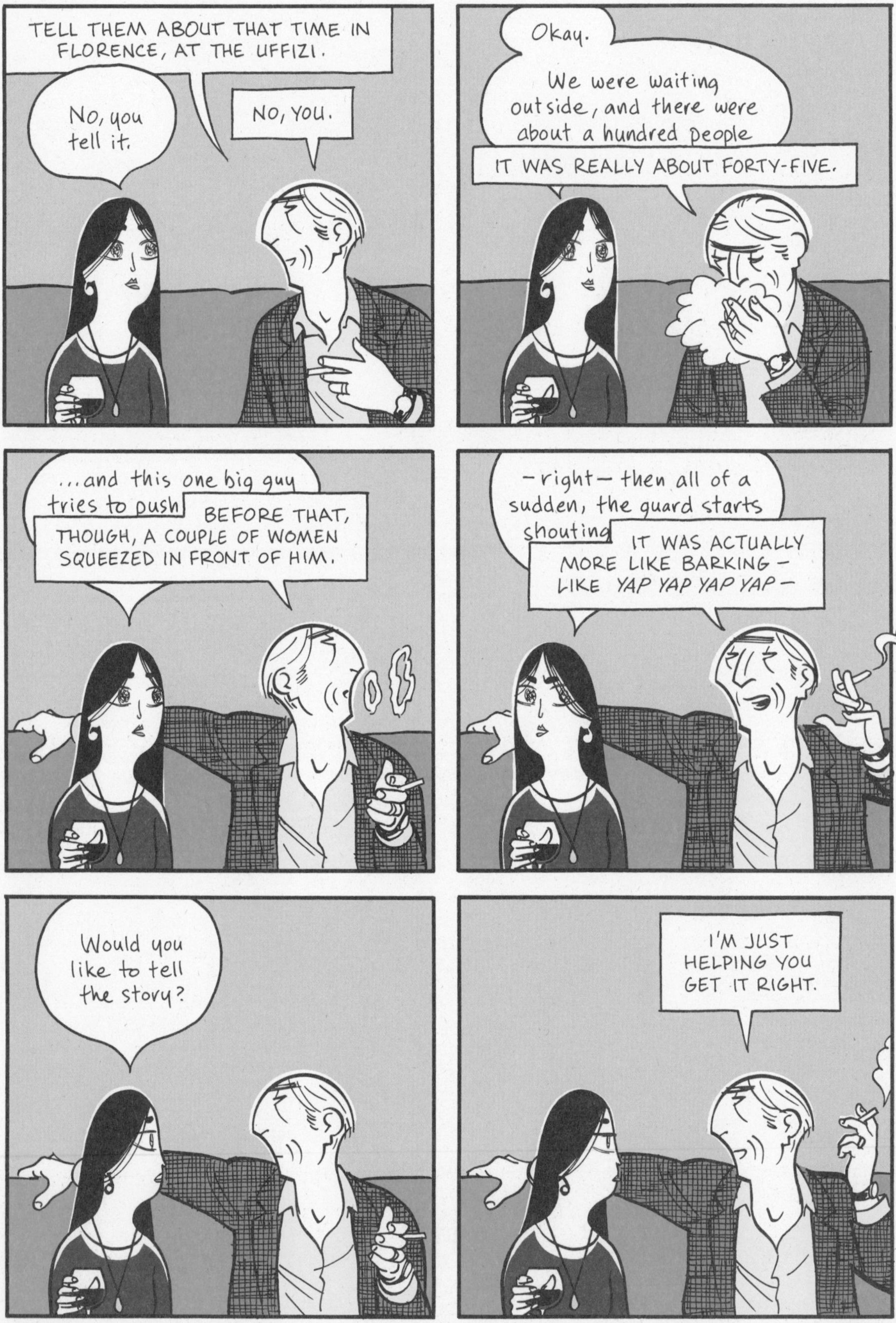

TELL THEM ABOUT THAT TIME IN FLORENCE, AT THE UFFIZI.
No, you tell it.
NO, YOU.
Okay.
We were waiting outside, and there were about a hundred people
IT WAS REALLY ABOUT FORTY-FIVE.
...and this one big guy tries to push
BEFORE THAT, THOUGH, A COUPLE OF WOMEN SQUEEZED IN FRONT OF HIM.
—right— then all of a sudden, the guard starts shouting
IT WAS ACTUALLY MORE LIKE BARKING— LIKE *YAP YAP YAP YAP*—
Would you like to tell the story?
I'M JUST HELPING YOU GET IT RIGHT.

THE FIRST TIME HANA VISITED ASTERIOS IN NEW YORK WAS SOON AFTER THEY MET, IN 1985.

SHE HAD TO COME TO MANHATTAN TO DISCUSS AN EXHIBITION WITH A SOHO GALLERY, SO HE INVITED HER TO DINNER.

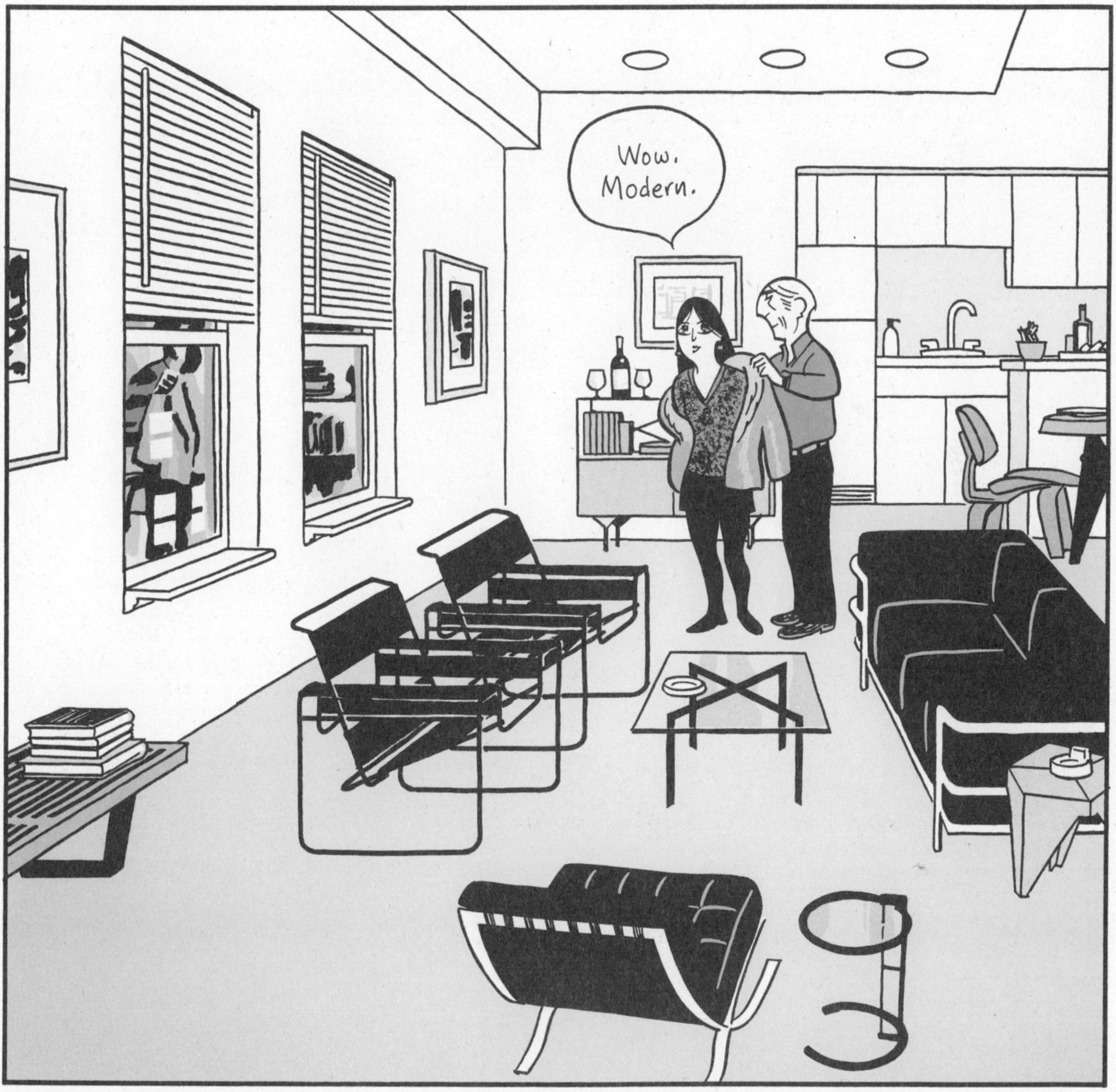
Wow. Modern.

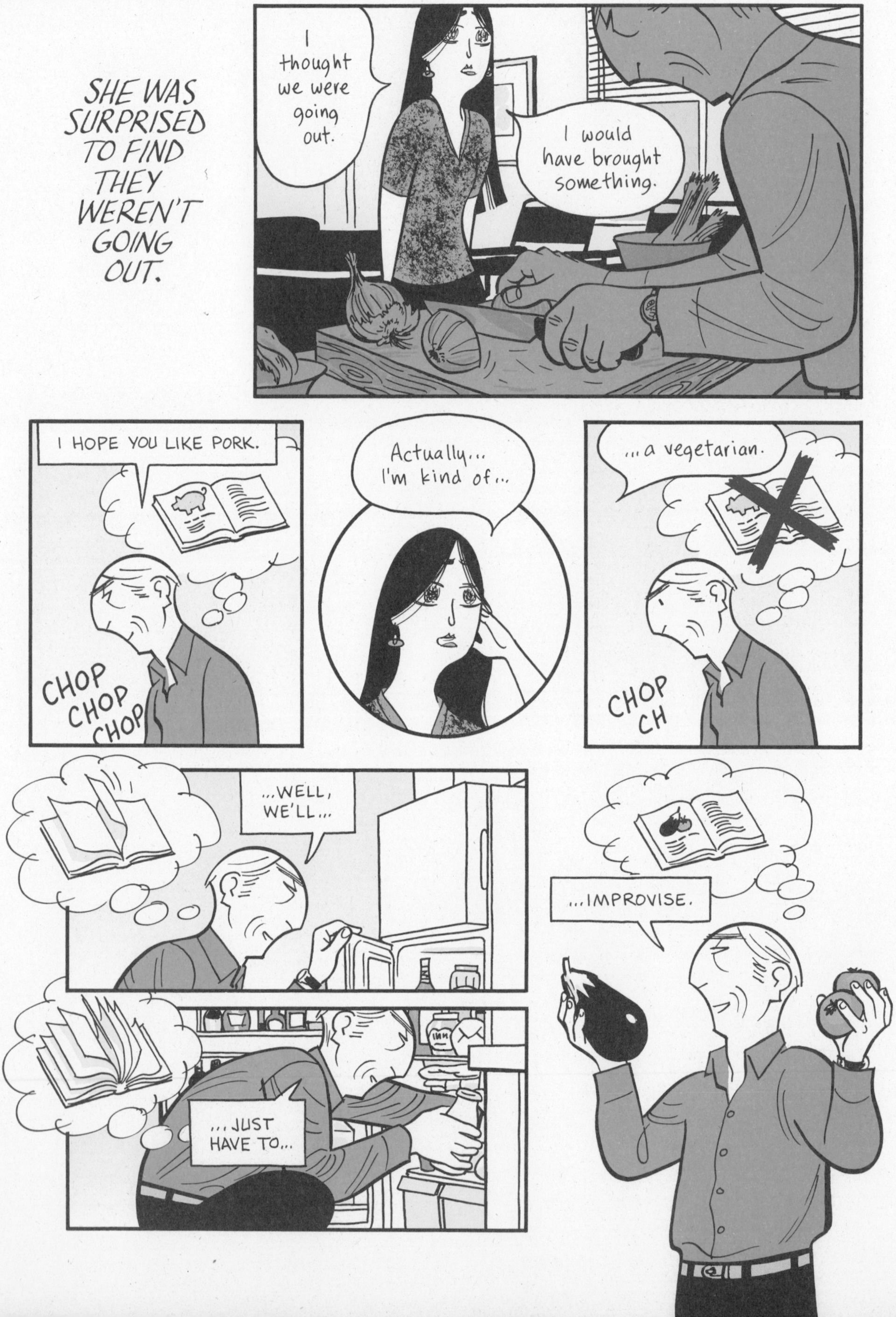
SHE WAS SURPRISED TO FIND THEY WEREN'T GOING OUT.
I thought we were going out.
I would have brought something.
I HOPE YOU LIKE PORK.
CHOP CHOP CHOP
Actually... I'm kind of...
...a vegetarian.
CHOP CH
...WELL, WE'LL...
...JUST HAVE TO...
...IMPROVISE.

ASTERIOS TOOK GREAT PRIDE IN COOKING—
IN MAKING DINING A CELEBRATION OF HUMAN INVENTION.

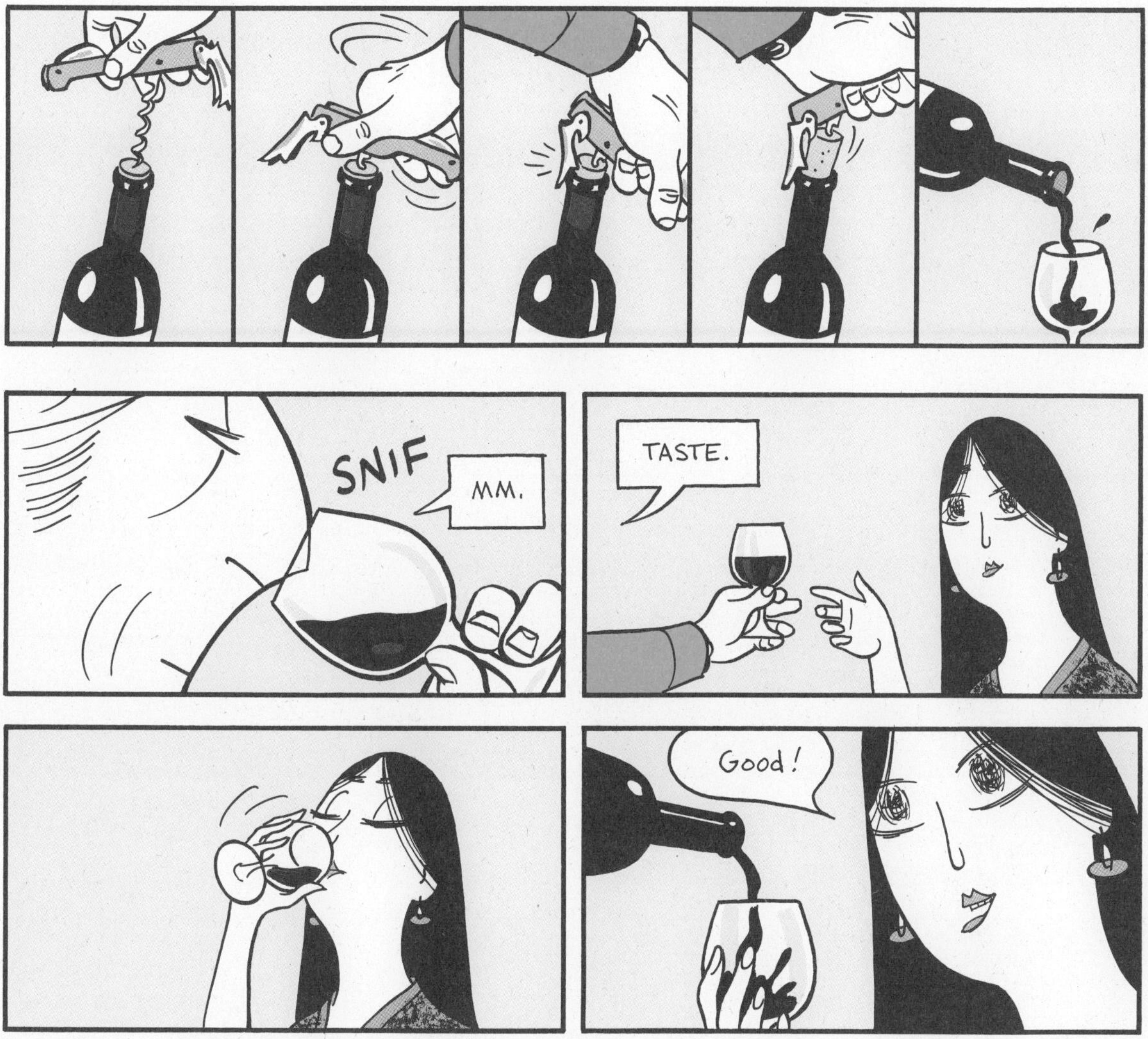
SNIF
MM.
TASTE.
Good!

IT WAS OF A PIECE WITH HIS VIEW OF ARCHITECTURE: FOUR WALLS AND A ROOF MAKE A SHELTER, BUT EXQUISITE DESIGN IS TRANSPORTING.

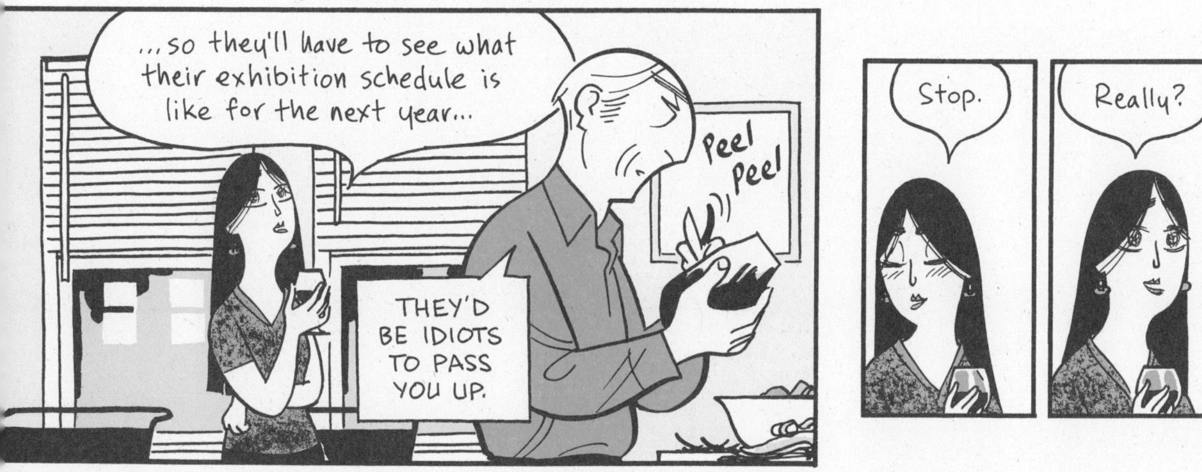
...so they'll have to see what their exhibition schedule is like for the next year...
Peel Peel
THEY'D BE IDIOTS TO PASS YOU UP.
Stop.
Really?

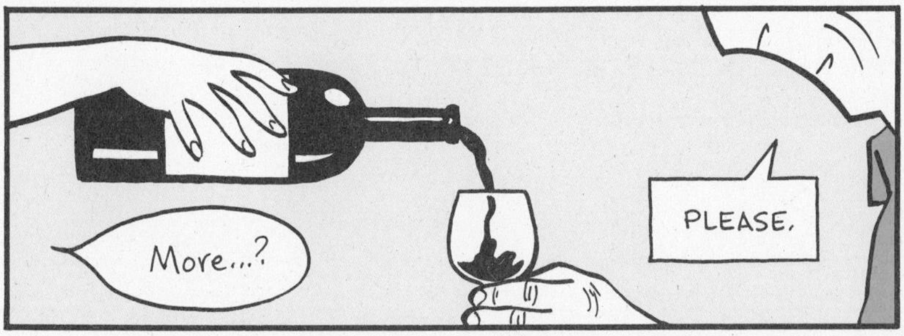
More...?
PLEASE.

NO INGREDIENT WAS INSIGNIFICANT, AND HE WOULD TRAVEL OUT OF HIS WAY TO PROCURE THE FRESHEST PRODUCE OR THE FINEST SPICES.

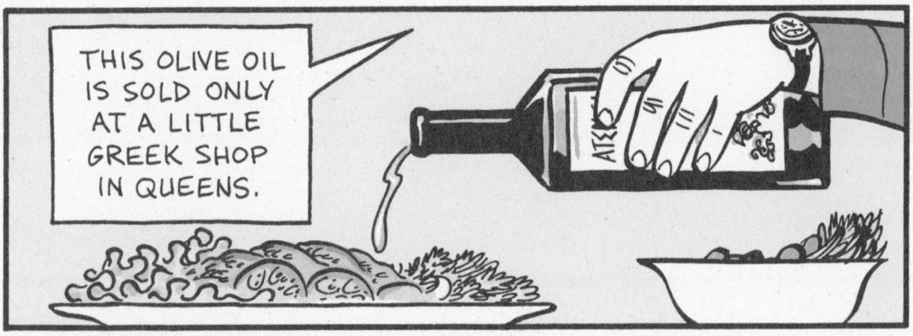
THIS OLIVE OIL IS SOLD ONLY AT A LITTLE GREEK SHOP IN QUEENS.

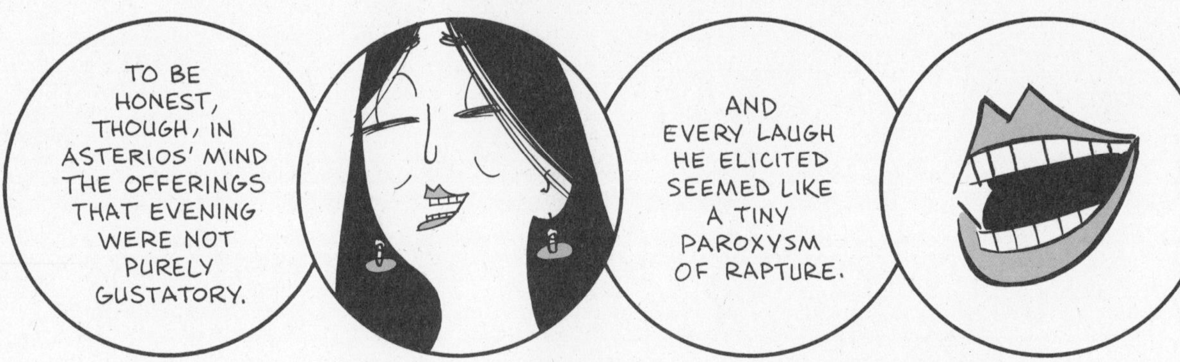
TO BE HONEST, THOUGH, IN ASTERIOS' MIND THE OFFERINGS THAT EVENING WERE NOT PURELY GUSTATORY.
AND EVERY LAUGH HE ELICITED SEEMED LIKE A TINY PAROXYSM OF RAPTURE.

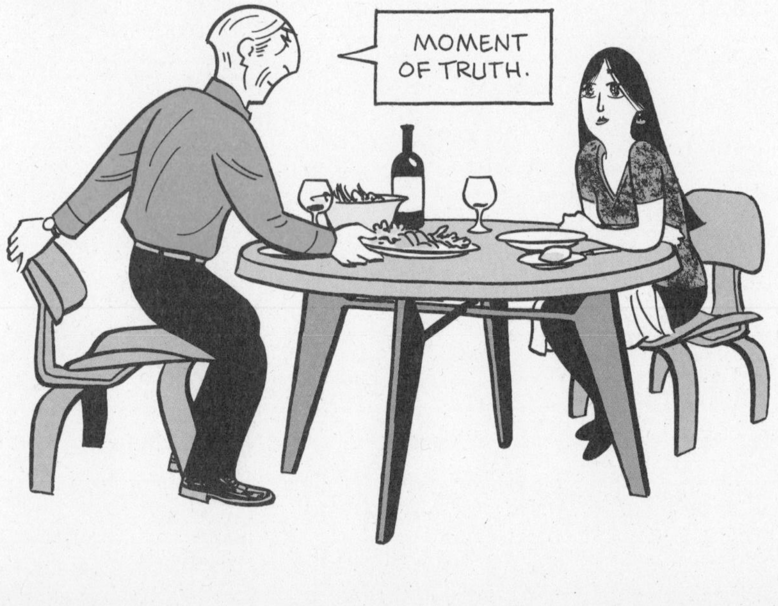
MOMENT OF TRUTH.

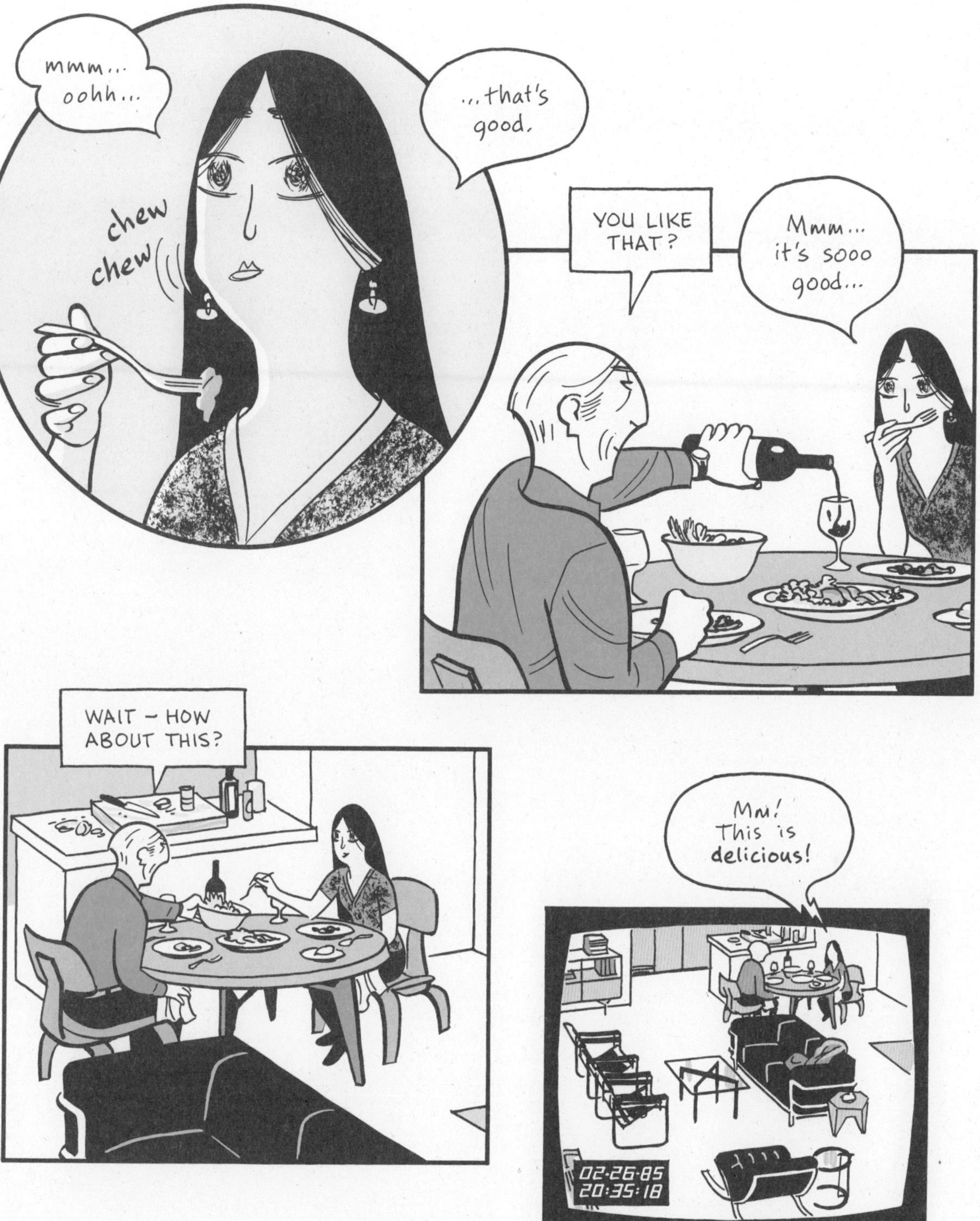
mmm... oohh...
chew chew
...that's good.
YOU LIKE THAT?
Mmm... it's sooo good...
WAIT – HOW ABOUT THIS?
Mm! This is delicious!
02-26-85
20:35:18

THAT WAS A NIGHT HE WOULD NEVER FORGET.

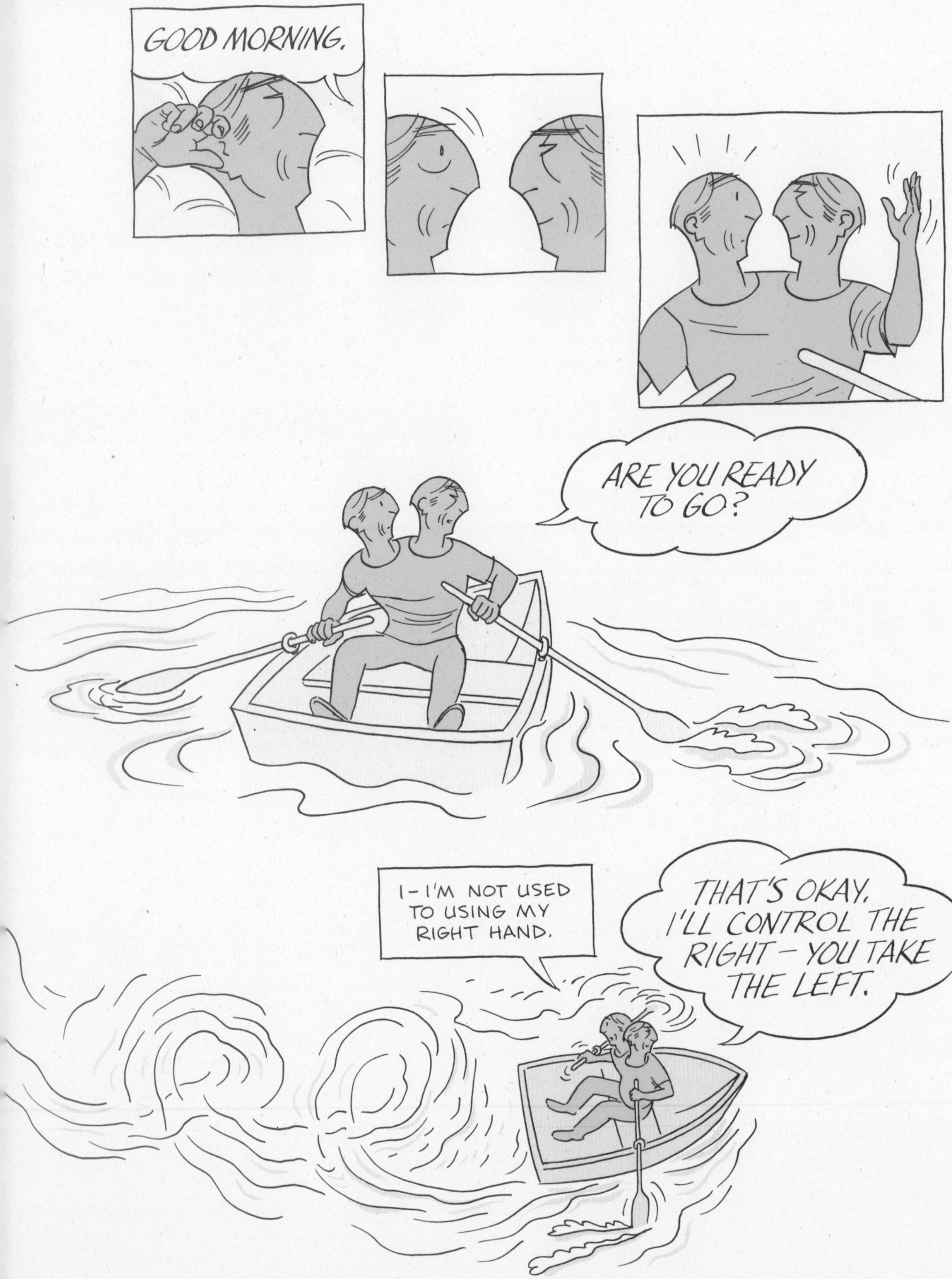
GOOD MORNING.
ARE YOU READY TO GO?
I-I'M NOT USED TO USING MY RIGHT HAND.
THAT'S OKAY. I'LL CONTROL THE RIGHT—YOU TAKE THE LEFT.

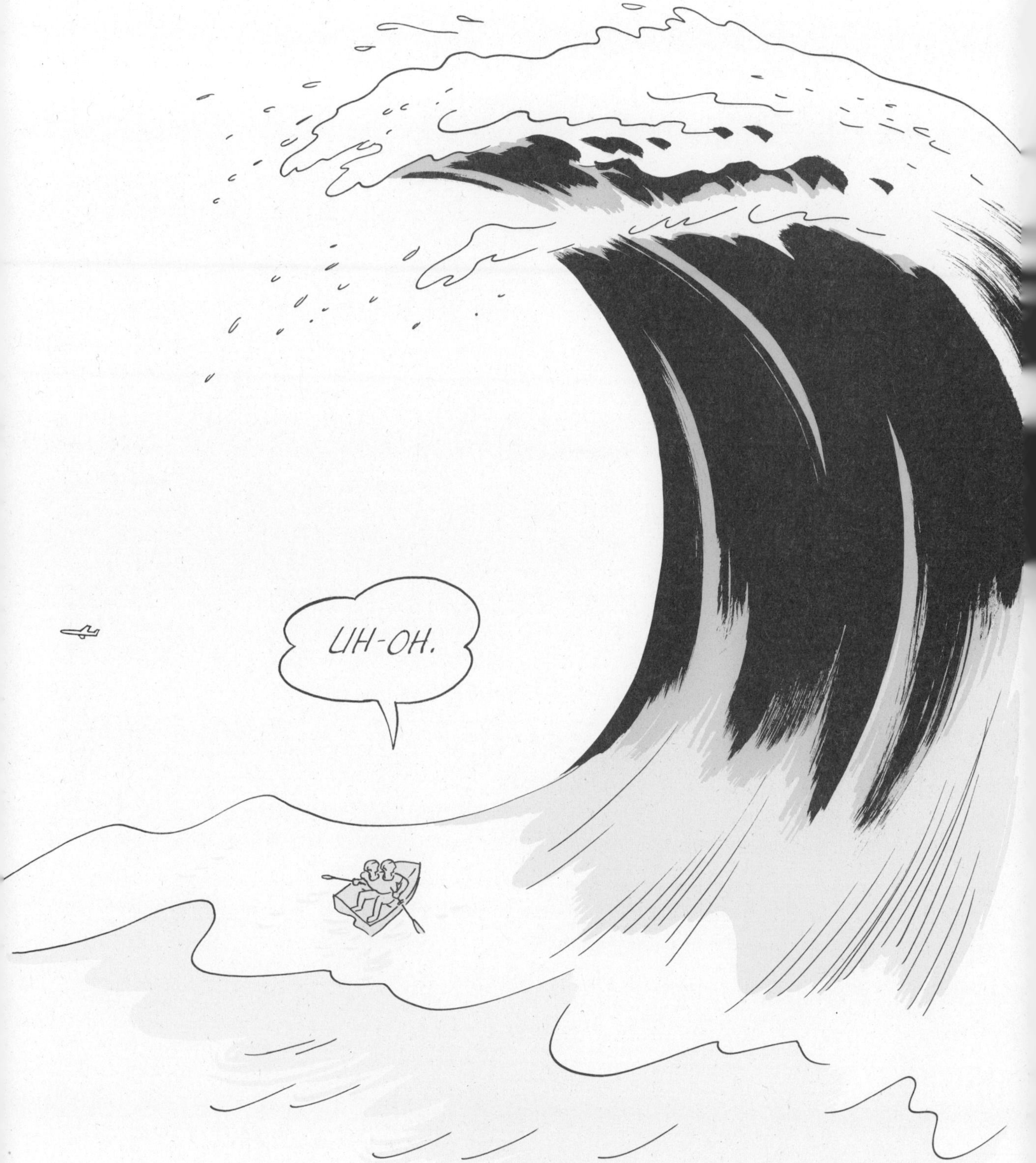
UH-OH.

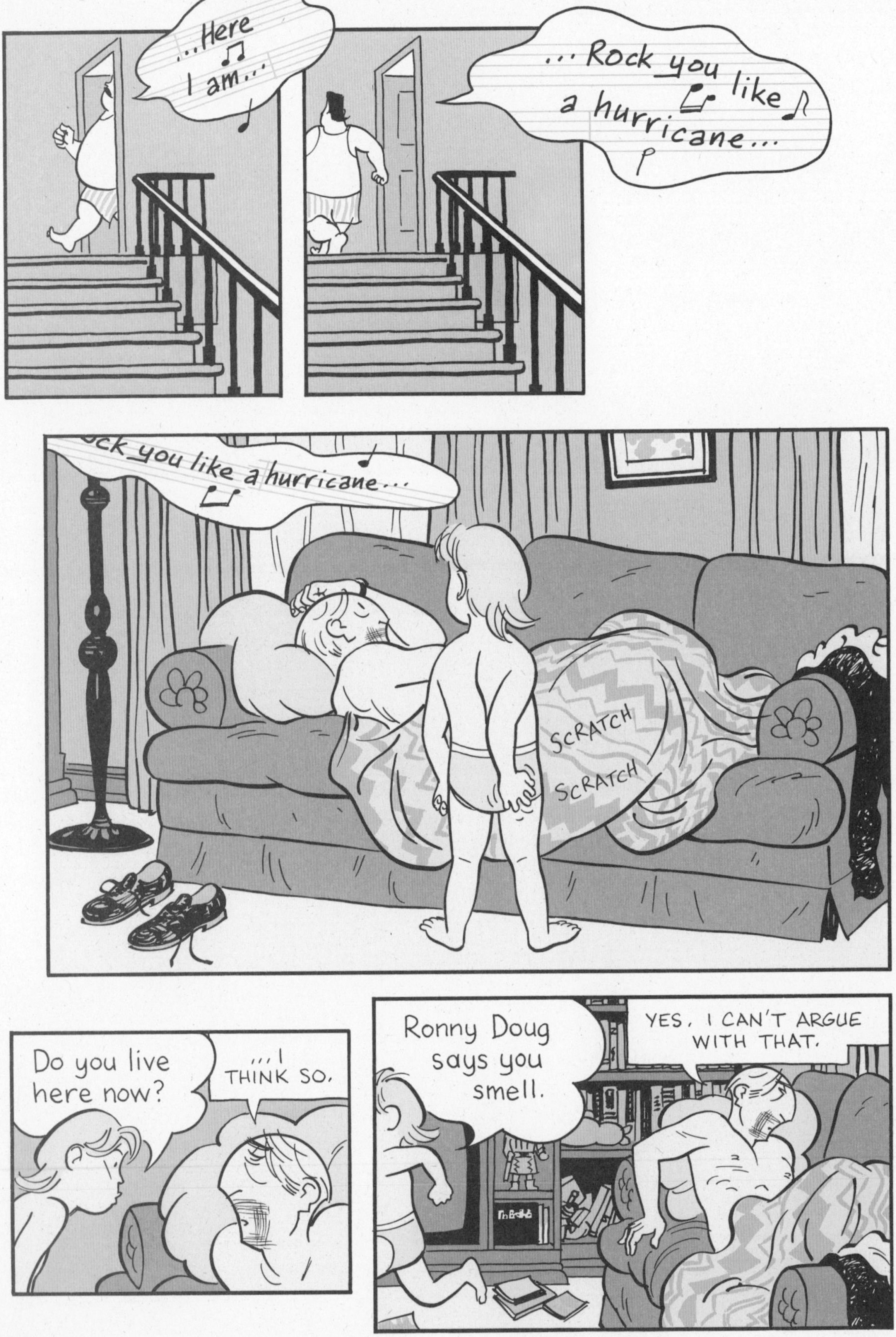
...Here I am...
...Rock you like a hurricane...
ck you like a hurricane...
SCRATCH
SCRATCH
Do you live here now?
...I THINK SO.
Ronny Doug says you smell.
YES. I CAN'T ARGUE WITH THAT.

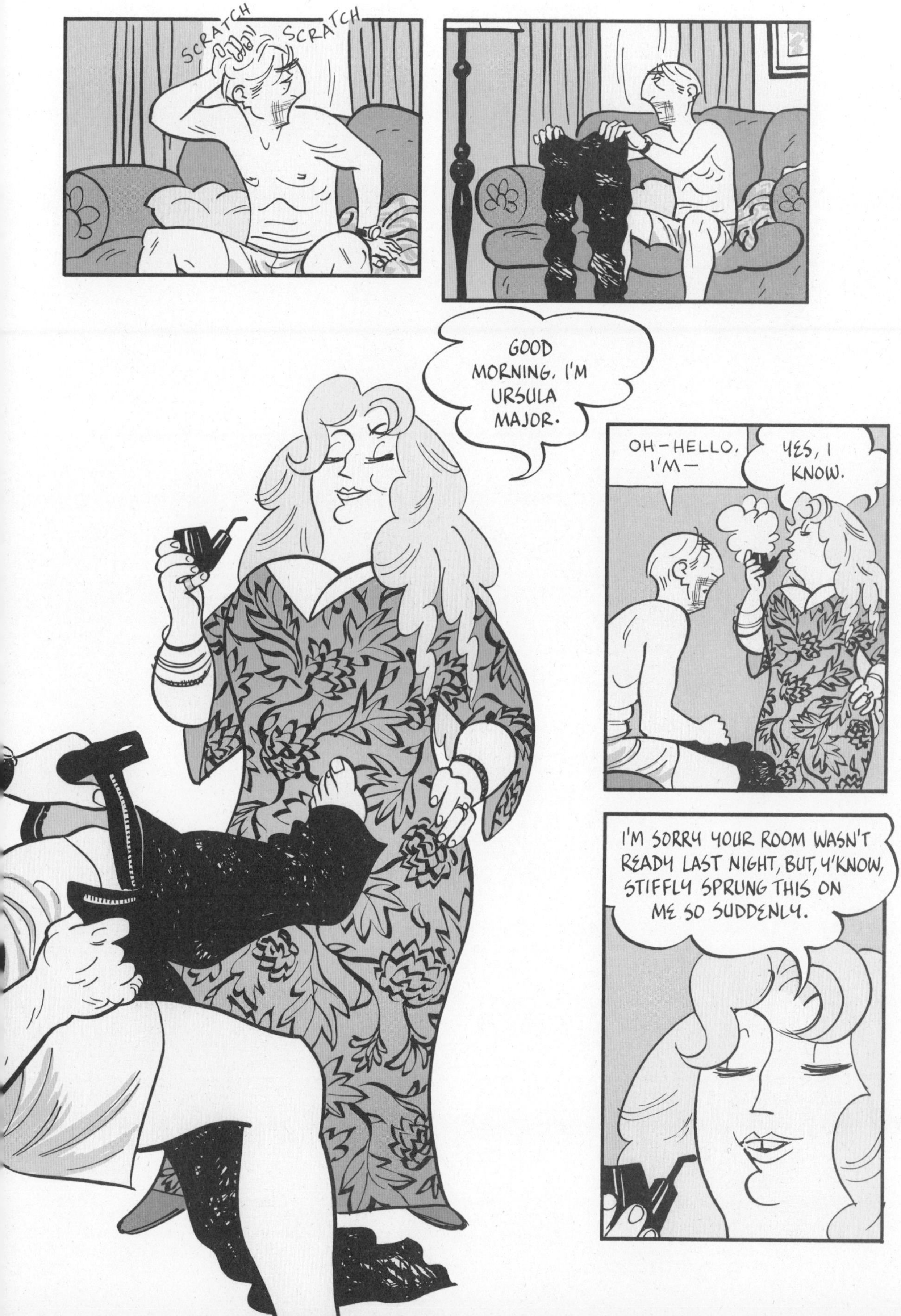
SCRATCH SCRATCH
GOOD MORNING. I'M URSULA MAJOR.
OH—HELLO. I'M—
YES, I KNOW.
I'M SORRY YOUR ROOM WASN'T READY LAST NIGHT, BUT, Y'KNOW, STIFFLY SPRUNG THIS ON ME SO SUDDENLY.

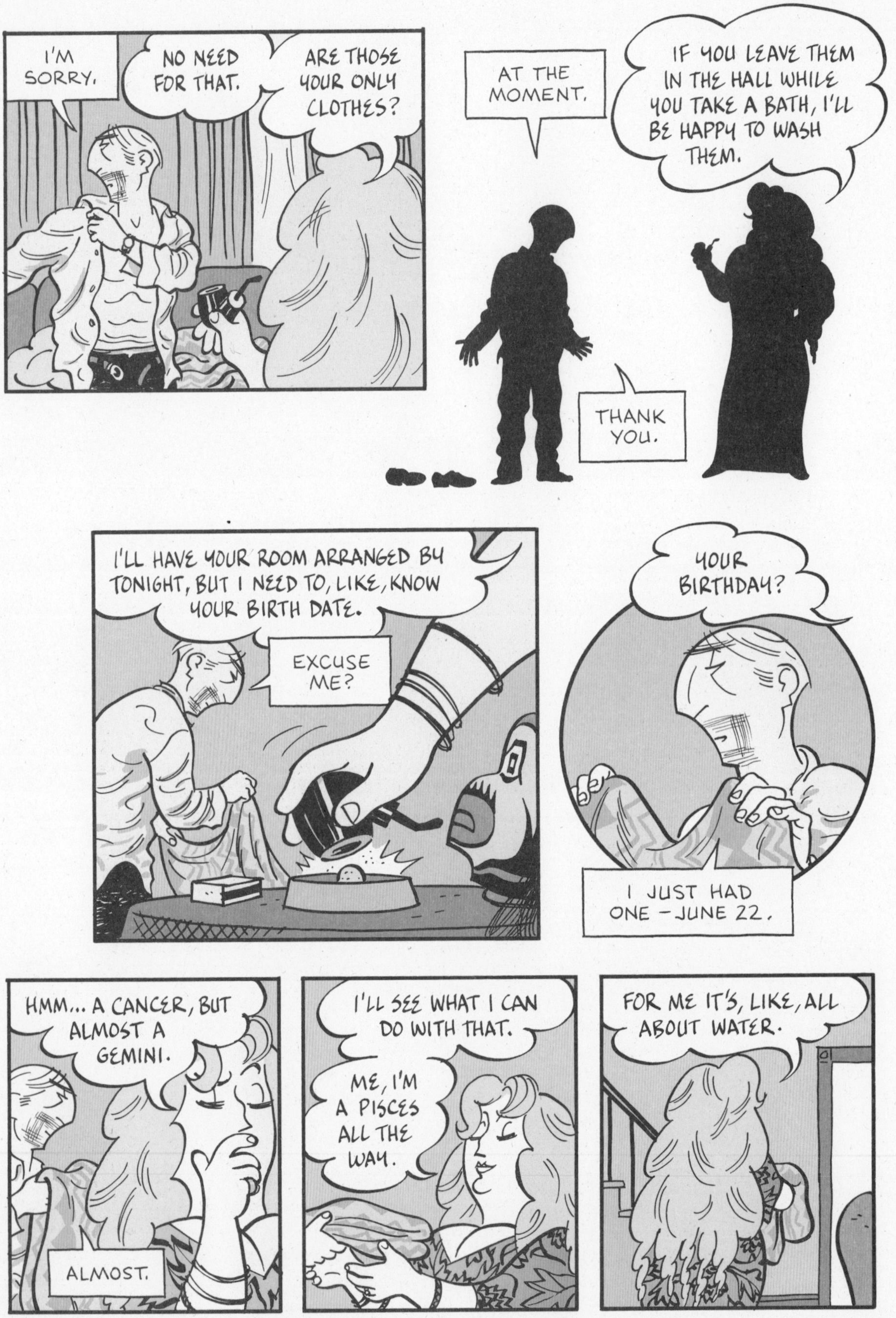
I'M SORRY.
NO NEED FOR THAT.
ARE THOSE YOUR ONLY CLOTHES?
AT THE MOMENT.
IF YOU LEAVE THEM IN THE HALL WHILE YOU TAKE A BATH, I'LL BE HAPPY TO WASH THEM.
THANK YOU.
I'LL HAVE YOUR ROOM ARRANGED BY TONIGHT, BUT I NEED TO, LIKE, KNOW YOUR BIRTH DATE.
EXCUSE ME?
YOUR BIRTHDAY?
I JUST HAD ONE – JUNE 22.
HMM... A CANCER, BUT ALMOST A GEMINI.
ALMOST.
I'LL SEE WHAT I CAN DO WITH THAT.
ME, I'M A PISCES ALL THE WAY.
FOR ME IT'S, LIKE, ALL ABOUT WATER.

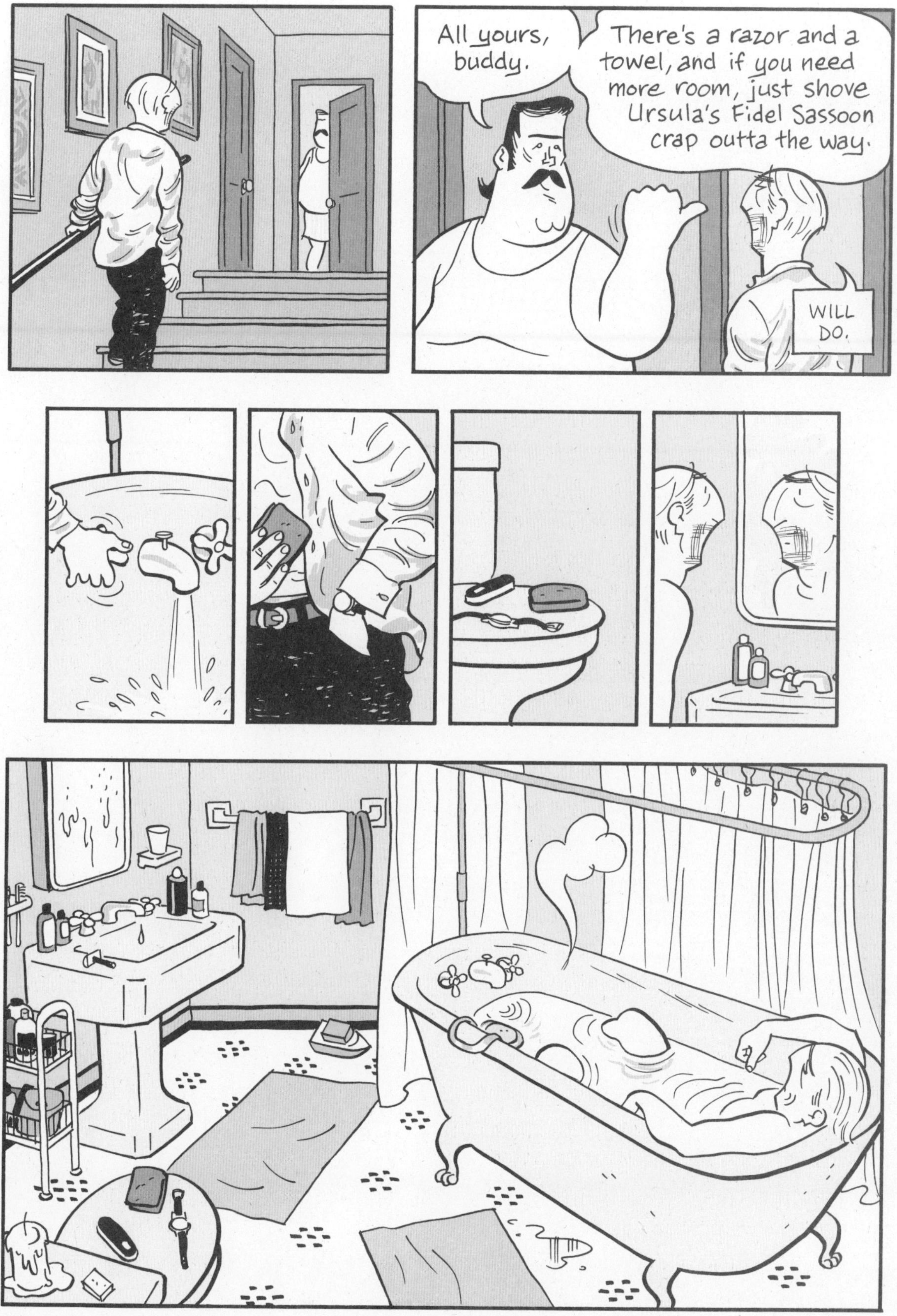
All yours, buddy.
There's a razor and a towel, and if you need more room, just shove Ursula's Fidel Sassoon crap outta the way.
WILL DO.

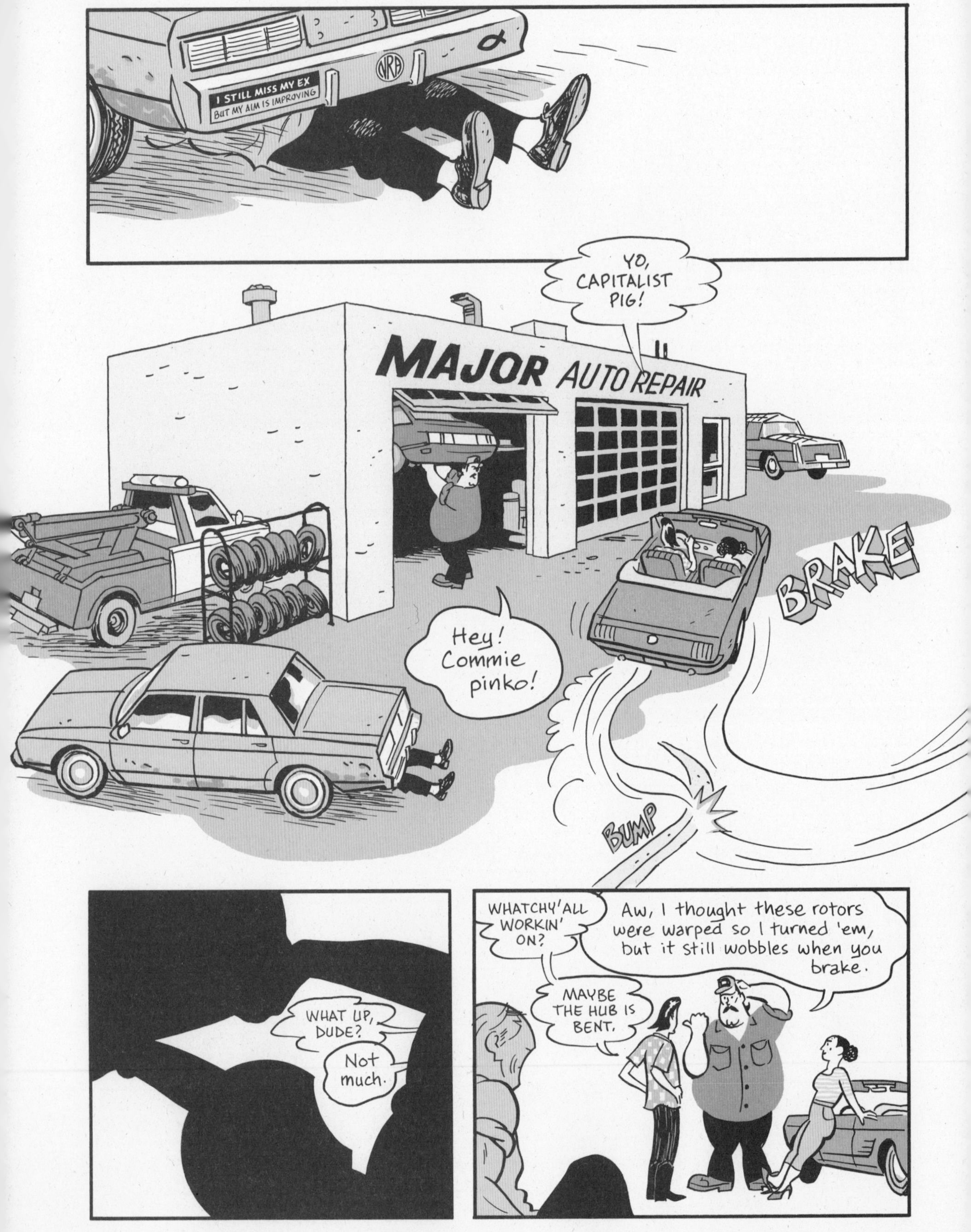
I STILL MISS MY EX
BUT MY AIM IS IMPROVING
NRA
YO, CAPITALIST PIG!
MAJOR AUTO REPAIR
BRAKE
Hey! Commie pinko!
BUMP
WHAT UP, DUDE?
Not much.
WHATCHY'ALL WORKIN' ON?
Aw, I thought these rotors were warped so I turned 'em, but it still wobbles when you brake.
MAYBE THE HUB IS BENT.

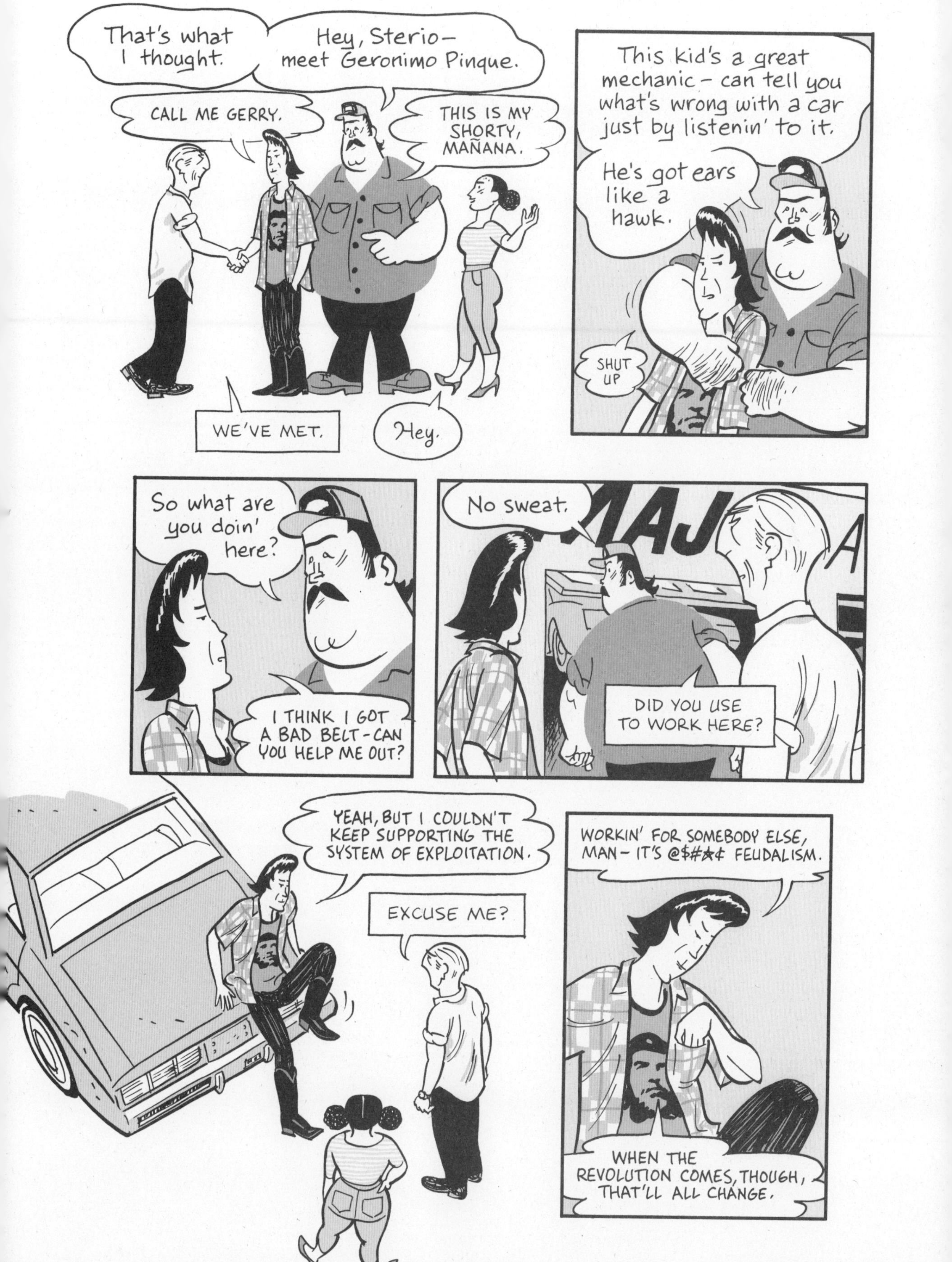
That's what I thought.
Hey, Sterio— meet Geronimo Pinque.
CALL ME GERRY.
THIS IS MY SHORTY, MAÑANA.
WE'VE MET.
Hey.
This kid's a great mechanic - can tell you what's wrong with a car just by listenin' to it.
He's got ears like a hawk.
SHUT UP
So what are you doin' here?
I THINK I GOT A BAD BELT - CAN YOU HELP ME OUT?
No sweat.
MAJ
A
DID YOU USE TO WORK HERE?
YEAH, BUT I COULDN'T KEEP SUPPORTING THE SYSTEM OF EXPLOITATION.
EXCUSE ME?
WORKIN' FOR SOMEBODY ELSE, MAN - IT'S @$#★¢ FEUDALISM.
WHEN THE REVOLUTION COMES, THOUGH, THAT'LL ALL CHANGE.

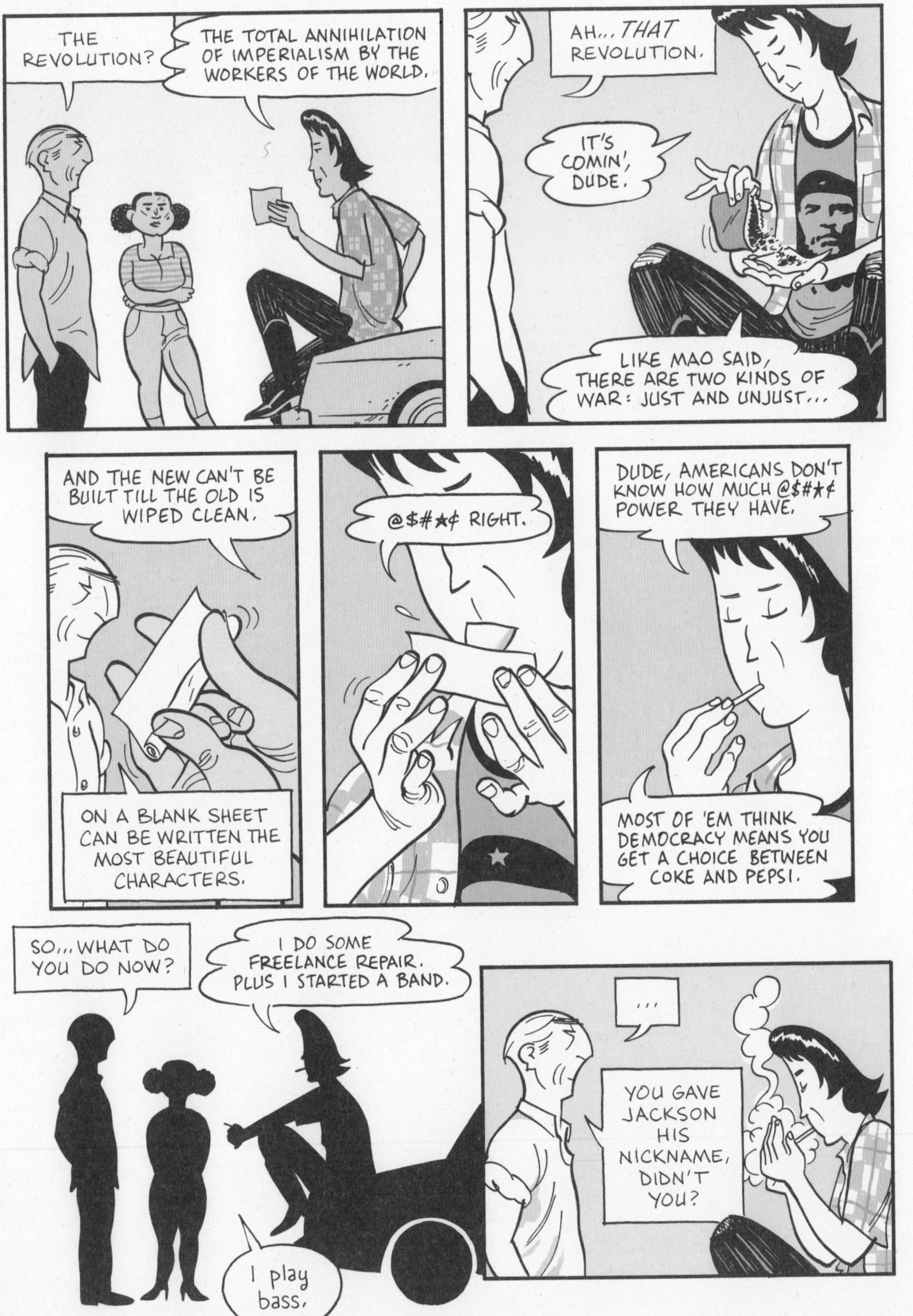
THE REVOLUTION?
THE TOTAL ANNIHILATION OF IMPERIALISM BY THE WORKERS OF THE WORLD.
AH... *THAT* REVOLUTION.
IT'S COMIN', DUDE.
LIKE MAO SAID, THERE ARE TWO KINDS OF WAR: JUST AND UNJUST...
AND THE NEW CAN'T BE BUILT TILL THE OLD IS WIPED CLEAN.
ON A BLANK SHEET CAN BE WRITTEN THE MOST BEAUTIFUL CHARACTERS.
@$#★¢ RIGHT.
DUDE, AMERICANS DON'T KNOW HOW MUCH @$#★¢ POWER THEY HAVE.
MOST OF 'EM THINK DEMOCRACY MEANS YOU GET A CHOICE BETWEEN COKE AND PEPSI.
SO... WHAT DO YOU DO NOW?
I DO SOME FREELANCE REPAIR. PLUS I STARTED A BAND.
I play bass.
...
YOU GAVE JACKSON HIS NICKNAME, DIDN'T YOU?

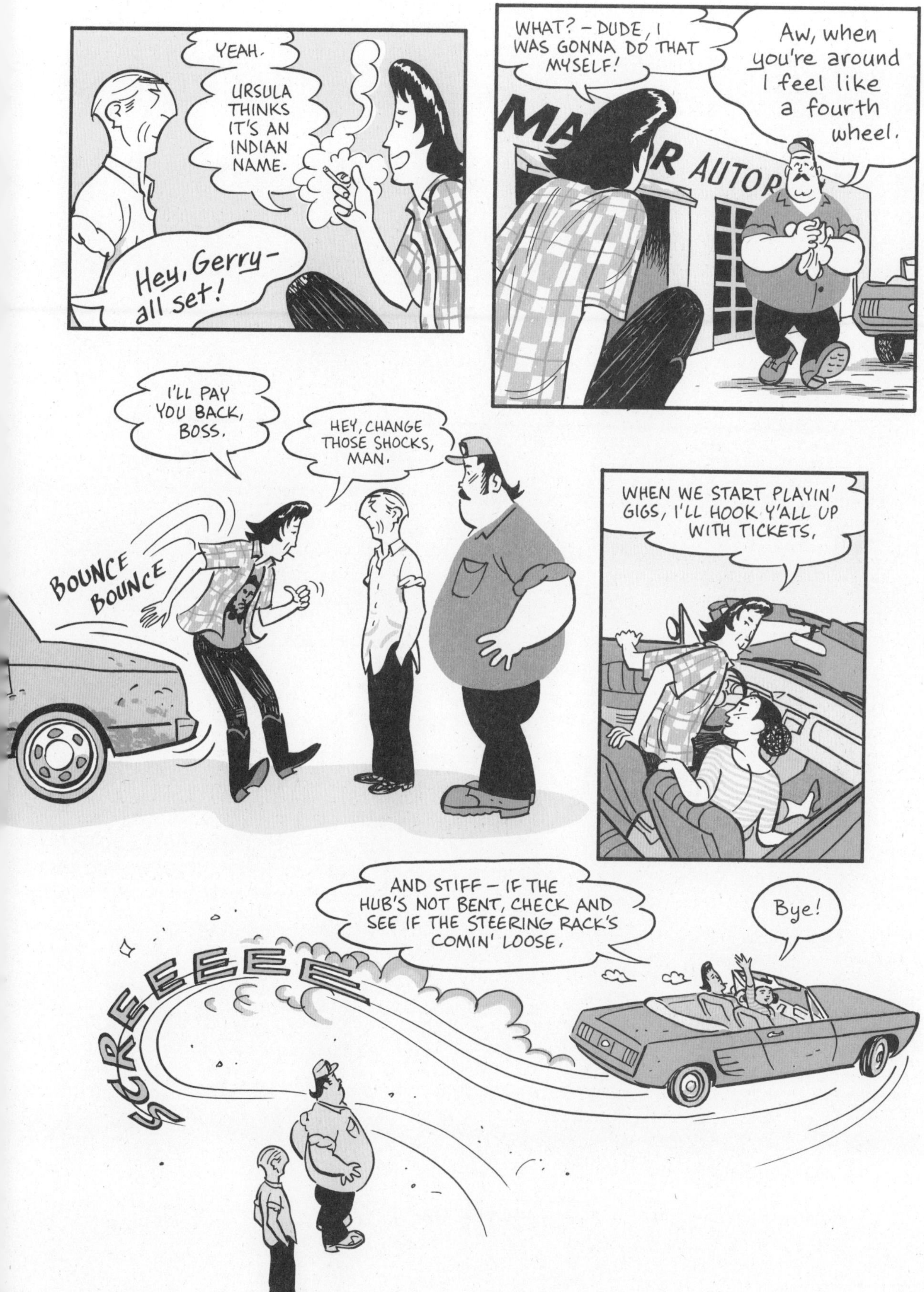
YEAH.
URSULA THINKS IT'S AN INDIAN NAME.
Hey, Gerry-all set!
WHAT? - DUDE, I WAS GONNA DO THAT MYSELF!
Aw, when you're around I feel like a fourth wheel.
I'LL PAY YOU BACK, BOSS.
HEY, CHANGE THOSE SHOCKS, MAN.
BOUNCE BOUNCE
WHEN WE START PLAYIN' GIGS, I'LL HOOK Y'ALL UP WITH TICKETS.
AND STIFF - IF THE HUB'S NOT BENT, CHECK AND SEE IF THE STEERING RACK'S COMIN' LOOSE.
Bye!
SCREEEEE

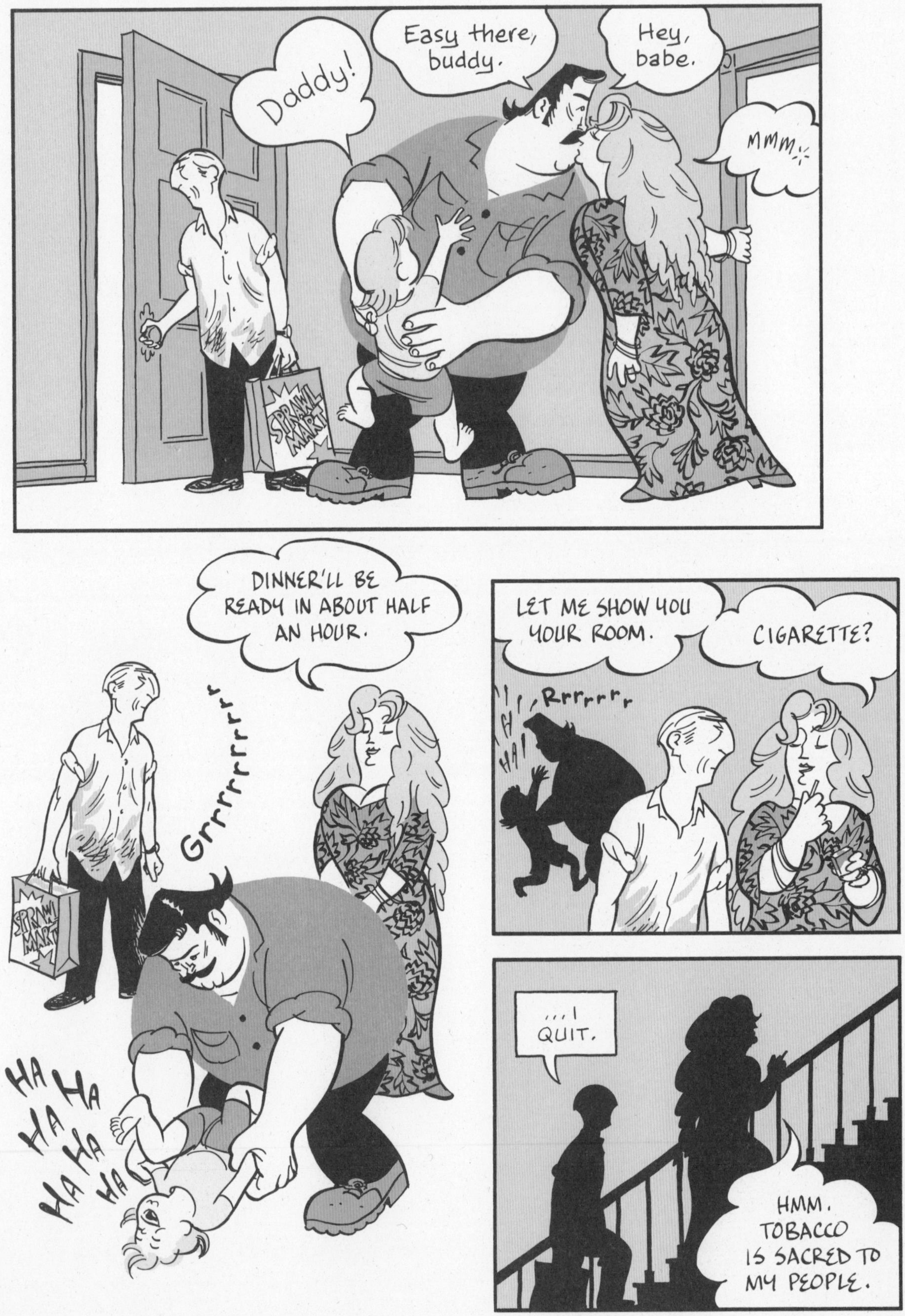
Daddy!
Easy there, buddy.
Hey, babe.
MMM
DINNER'LL BE READY IN ABOUT HALF AN HOUR.
Grrrrrrrrrr
HA HA HA HA HA HA HA
LET ME SHOW YOU YOUR ROOM.
CIGARETTE?
Rrrrrrr
...I QUIT.
HMM. TOBACCO IS SACRED TO MY PEOPLE.

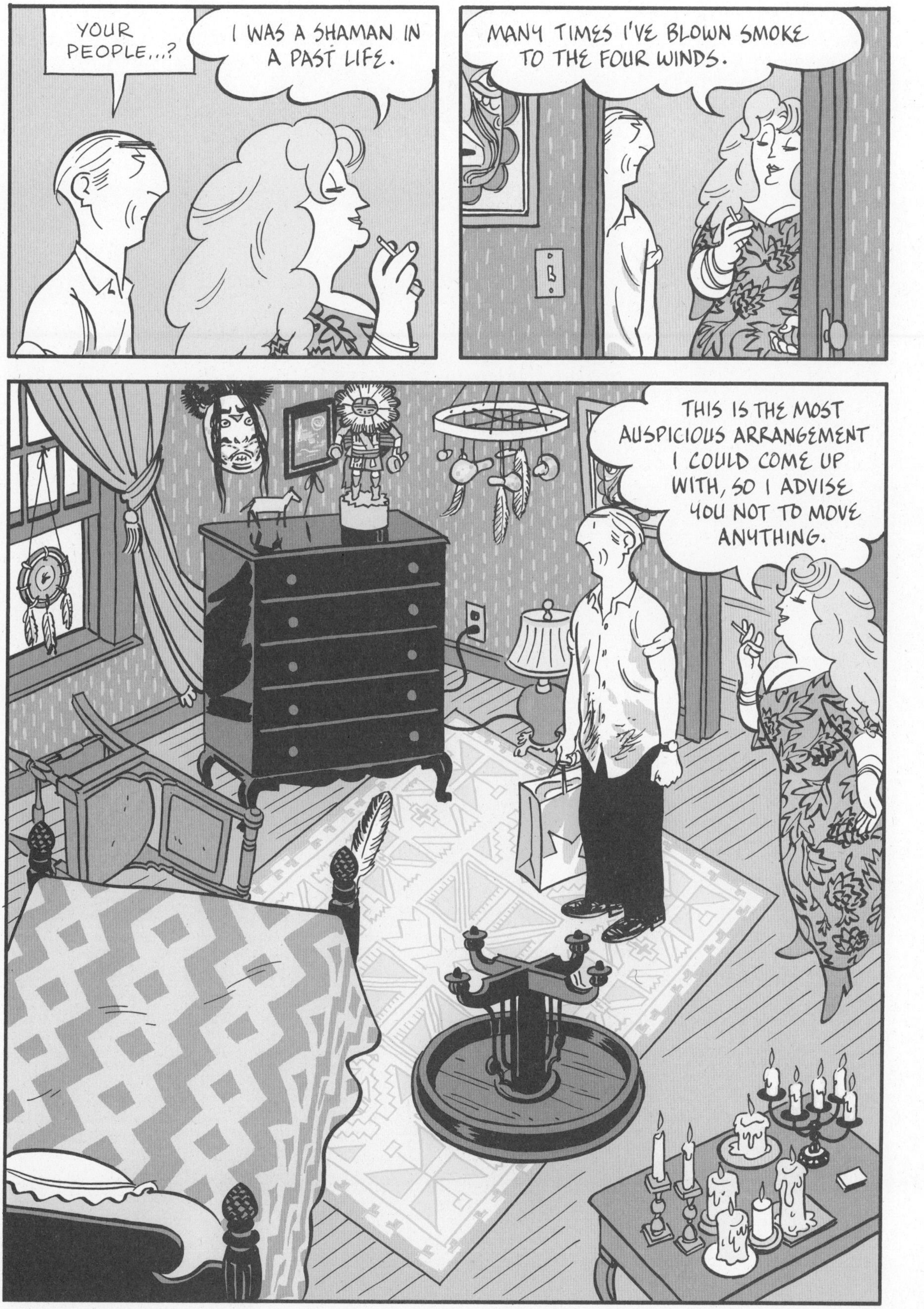
YOUR PEOPLE...?
I WAS A SHAMAN IN A PAST LIFE.
MANY TIMES I'VE BLOWN SMOKE TO THE FOUR WINDS.
THIS IS THE MOST AUSPICIOUS ARRANGEMENT I COULD COME UP WITH, SO I ADVISE YOU NOT TO MOVE ANYTHING.

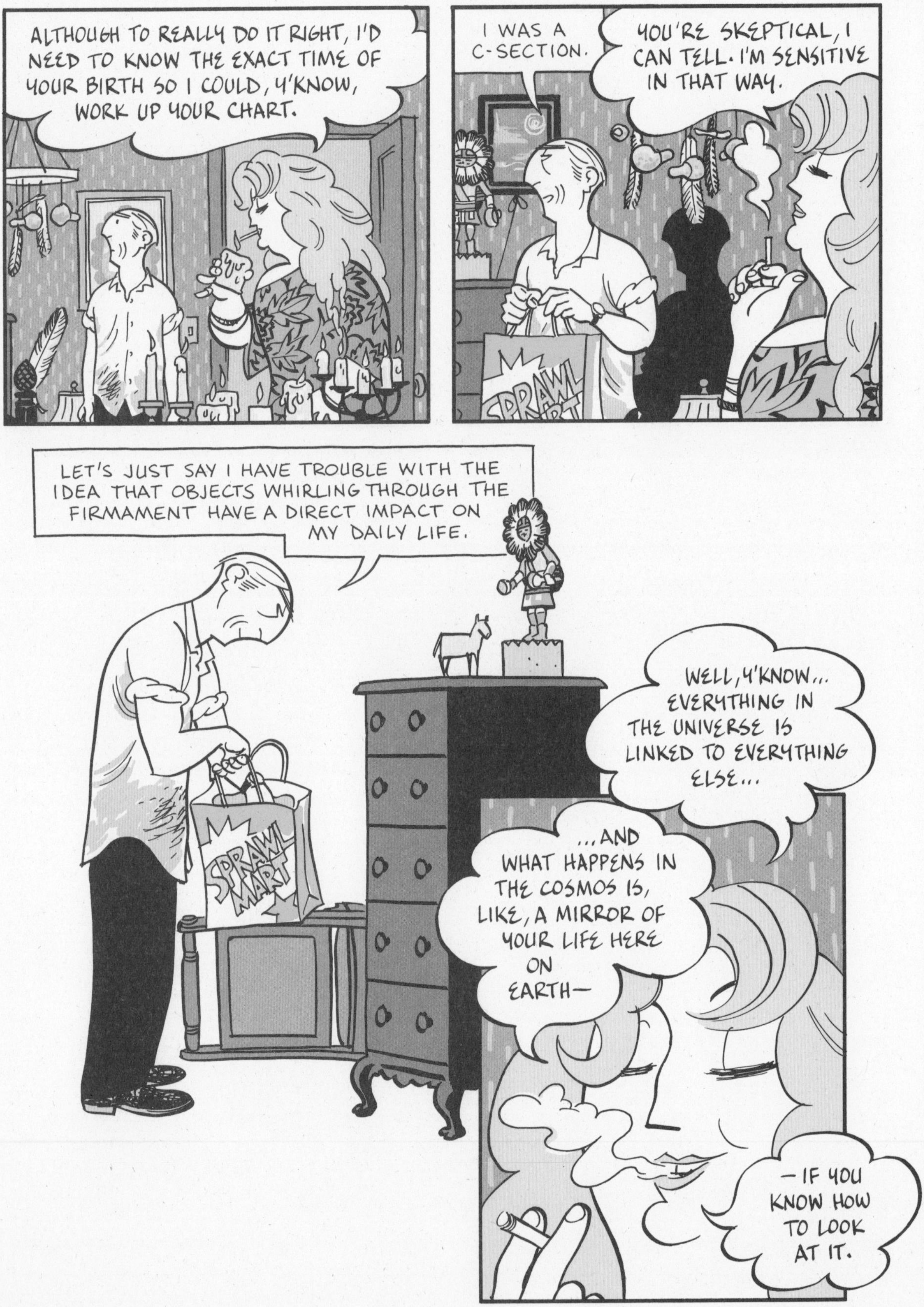
ALTHOUGH TO REALLY DO IT RIGHT, I'D NEED TO KNOW THE EXACT TIME OF YOUR BIRTH SO I COULD, Y'KNOW, WORK UP YOUR CHART.
I WAS A C-SECTION.
YOU'RE SKEPTICAL, I CAN TELL. I'M SENSITIVE IN THAT WAY.
SPRAWL MART
LET'S JUST SAY I HAVE TROUBLE WITH THE IDEA THAT OBJECTS WHIRLING THROUGH THE FIRMAMENT HAVE A DIRECT IMPACT ON MY DAILY LIFE.
WELL, Y'KNOW... EVERYTHING IN THE UNIVERSE IS LINKED TO EVERYTHING ELSE...
...AND WHAT HAPPENS IN THE COSMOS IS, LIKE, A MIRROR OF YOUR LIFE HERE ON EARTH—
—IF YOU KNOW HOW TO LOOK AT IT.

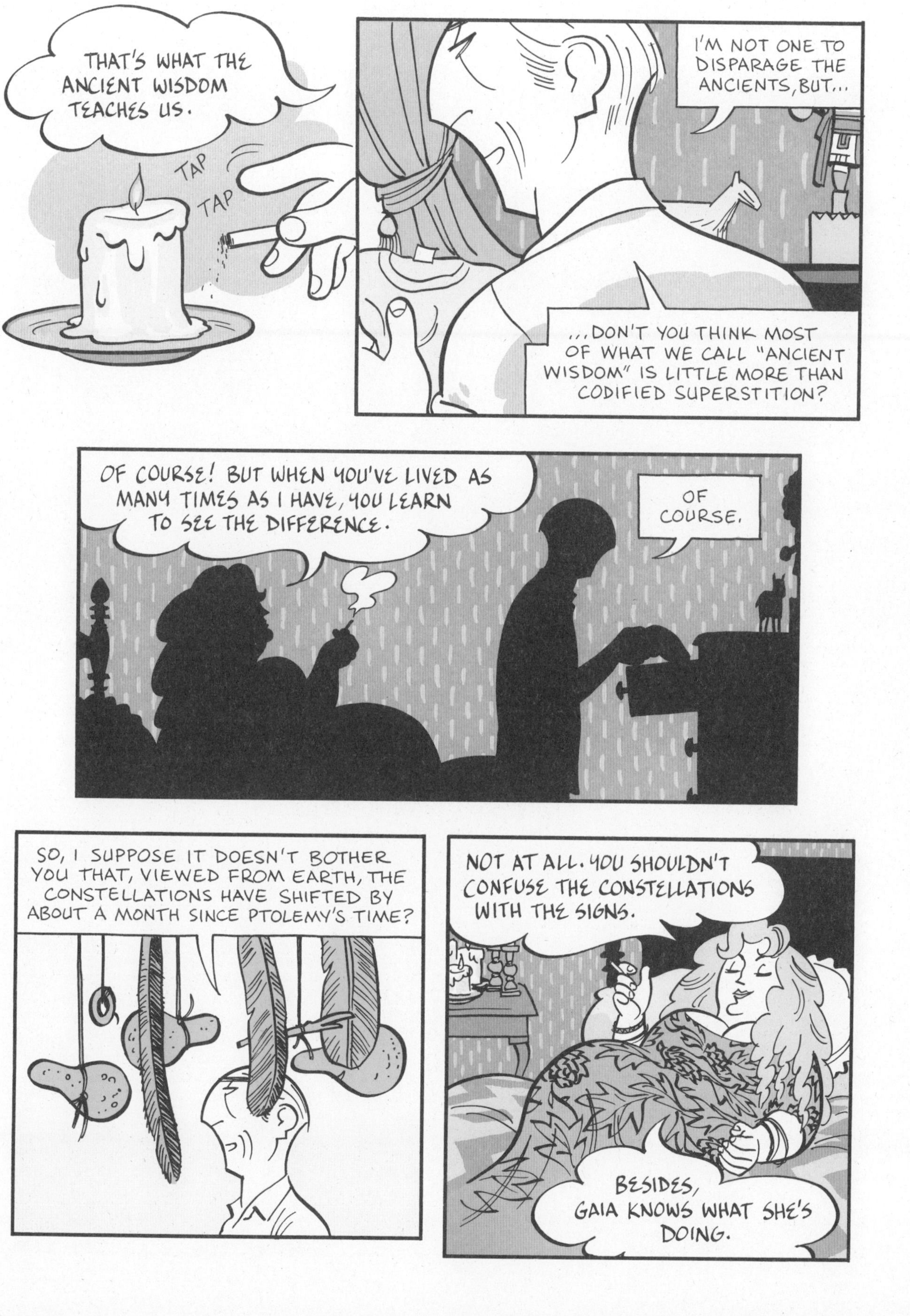
THAT'S WHAT THE ANCIENT WISDOM TEACHES US.
TAP TAP
I'M NOT ONE TO DISPARAGE THE ANCIENTS, BUT...
...DON'T YOU THINK MOST OF WHAT WE CALL "ANCIENT WISDOM" IS LITTLE MORE THAN CODIFIED SUPERSTITION?
OF COURSE! BUT WHEN YOU'VE LIVED AS MANY TIMES AS I HAVE, YOU LEARN TO SEE THE DIFFERENCE.
OF COURSE.
SO, I SUPPOSE IT DOESN'T BOTHER YOU THAT, VIEWED FROM EARTH, THE CONSTELLATIONS HAVE SHIFTED BY ABOUT A MONTH SINCE PTOLEMY'S TIME?
NOT AT ALL. YOU SHOULDN'T CONFUSE THE CONSTELLATIONS WITH THE SIGNS.
BESIDES, GAIA KNOWS WHAT SHE'S DOING.

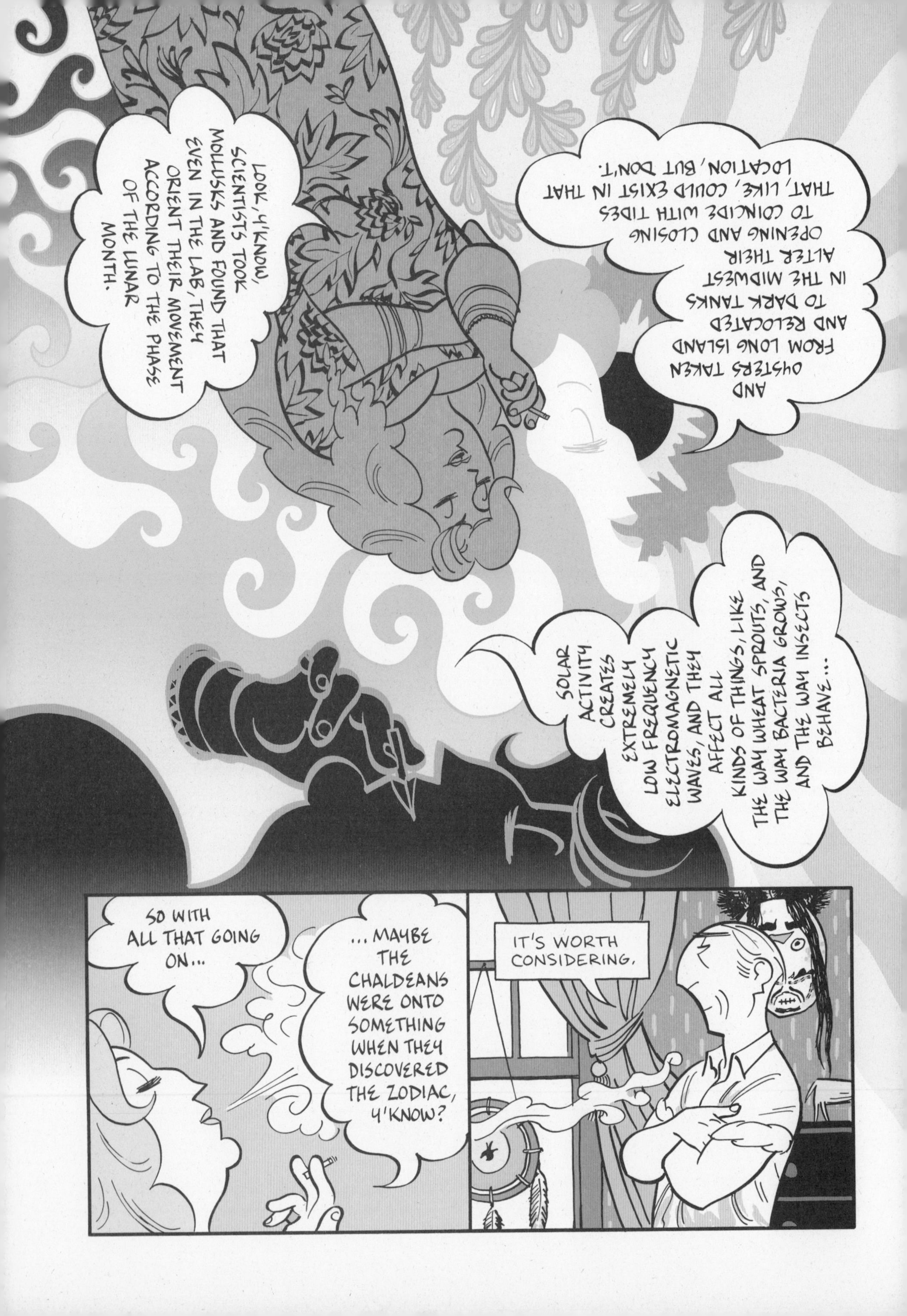
LOOK, Y'KNOW, SCIENTISTS TOOK MOLLUSKS AND FOUND THAT EVEN IN THE LAB, THEY ORIENT THEIR MOVEMENT ACCORDING TO THE PHASE OF THE LUNAR MONTH.
AND OYSTERS TAKEN FROM LONG ISLAND AND RELOCATED TO DARK TANKS IN THE MIDWEST ALTER THEIR OPENING AND CLOSING TO COINCIDE WITH TIDES THAT, LIKE, COULD EXIST IN THAT LOCATION, BUT DON'T.
SOLAR ACTIVITY CREATES EXTREMELY LOW FREQUENCY ELECTROMAGNETIC WAVES, AND THEY AFFECT ALL KINDS OF THINGS, LIKE THE WAY WHEAT SPROUTS, AND THE WAY BACTERIA GROWS, AND THE WAY INSECTS BEHAVE...
SO WITH ALL THAT GOING ON...
... MAYBE THE CHALDEANS WERE ONTO SOMETHING WHEN THEY DISCOVERED THE ZODIAC, Y'KNOW?
IT'S WORTH CONSIDERING.

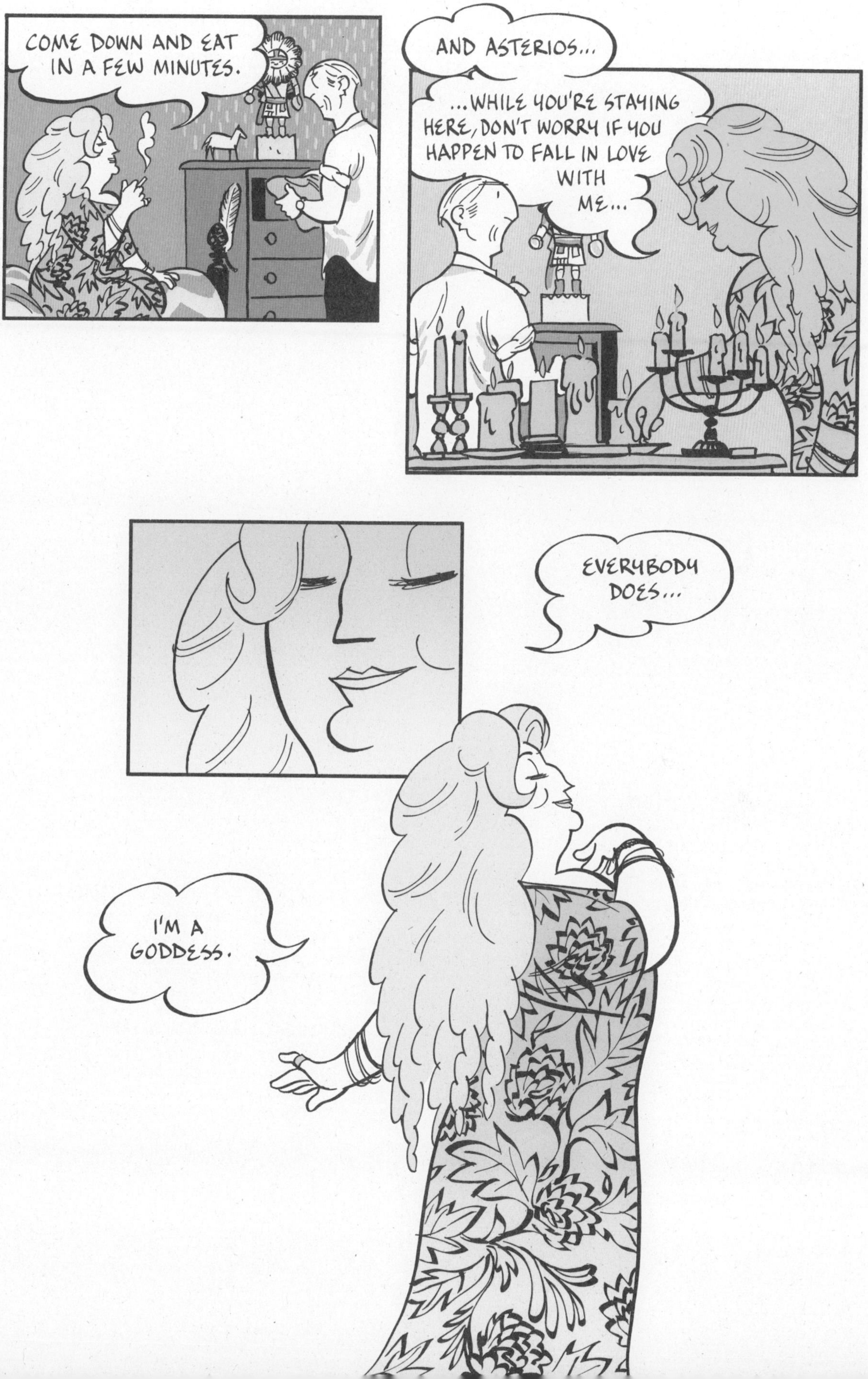
COME DOWN AND EAT IN A FEW MINUTES.
AND ASTERIOS...
...WHILE YOU'RE STAYING HERE, DON'T WORRY IF YOU HAPPEN TO FALL IN LOVE WITH ME...
EVERYBODY DOES...
I'M A GODDESS.

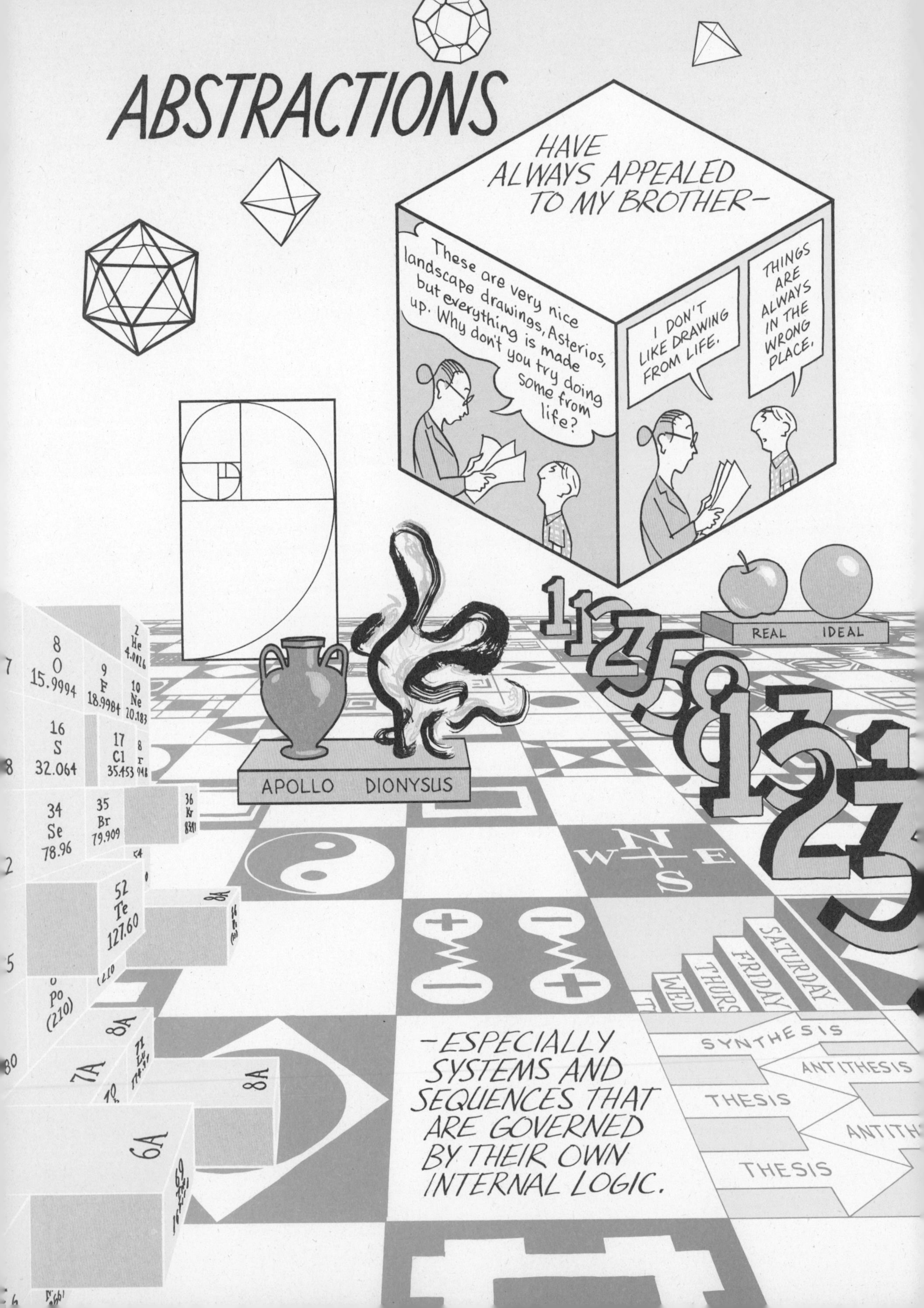
ABSTRACTIONS
HAVE ALWAYS APPEALED TO MY BROTHER—
These are very nice landscape drawings, Asterios, but everything is made up. Why don't you try doing some from life?
I DON'T LIKE DRAWING FROM LIFE.
THINGS ARE ALWAYS IN THE WRONG PLACE.
REAL
IDEAL
APOLLO
DIONYSUS
SATURDAY
FRIDAY
THURS
WED
—ESPECIALLY SYSTEMS AND SEQUENCES THAT ARE GOVERNED BY THEIR OWN INTERNAL LOGIC.
SYNTHESIS
ANTITHESIS
THESIS
THESIS

IN ADDITION, HE'S ALWAYS BEEN FOND OF ANALOGUES AND METAPHORS – SUCH AS THE DIVISION OF AN HOUR INTO WEDGES OF A CIRCLE –

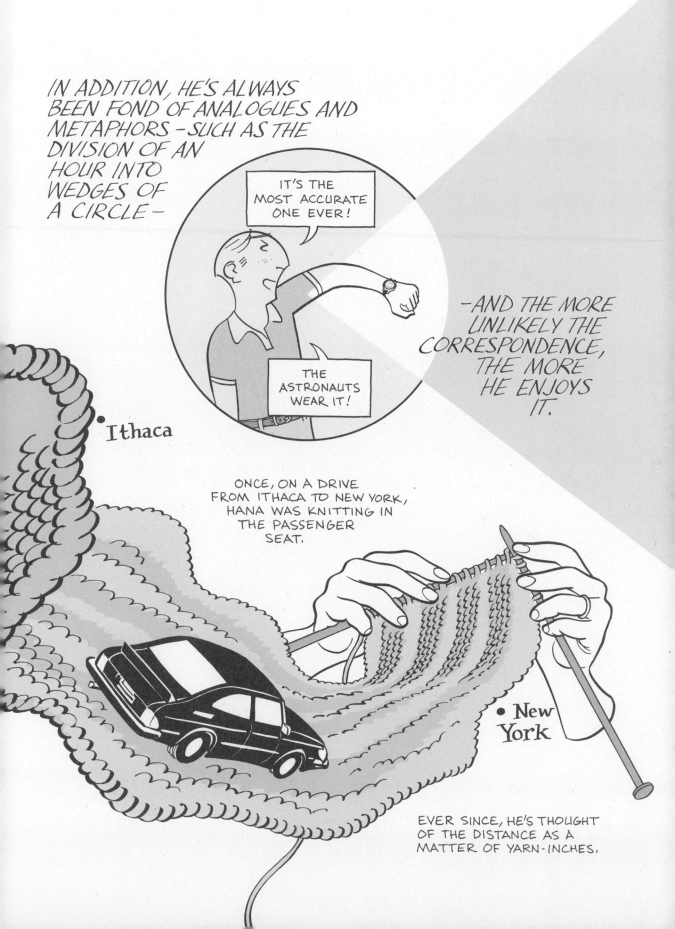

IT'S THE MOST ACCURATE ONE EVER!

THE ASTRONAUTS WEAR IT!

– AND THE MORE UNLIKELY THE CORRESPONDENCE, THE MORE HE ENJOYS IT.

Ithaca

ONCE, ON A DRIVE FROM ITHACA TO NEW YORK, HANA WAS KNITTING IN THE PASSENGER SEAT.

New York

EVER SINCE, HE'S THOUGHT OF THE DISTANCE AS A MATTER OF YARN-INCHES.

THIS DESIRE TO VIEW THE WORLD THROUGH A FILTER—TO SUPERIMPOSE A RATIONAL SYSTEM ON TO ITS SEEMING RANDOMNESS—IS REVEALED IN HIS OWN FAVORITE IDEATION.

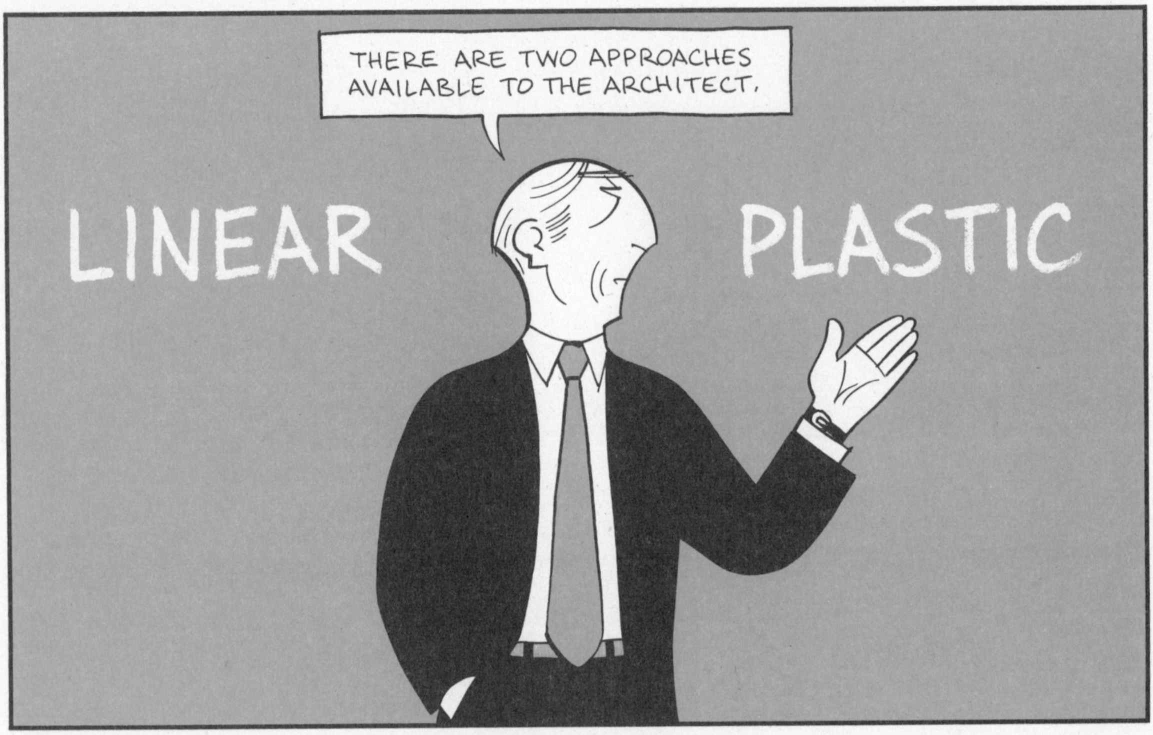
THERE ARE TWO APPROACHES AVAILABLE TO THE ARCHITECT.
LINEAR
PLASTIC

IT IS A FORMULATION THAT IS APPLIED WITH PRISMATIC VARIETY.

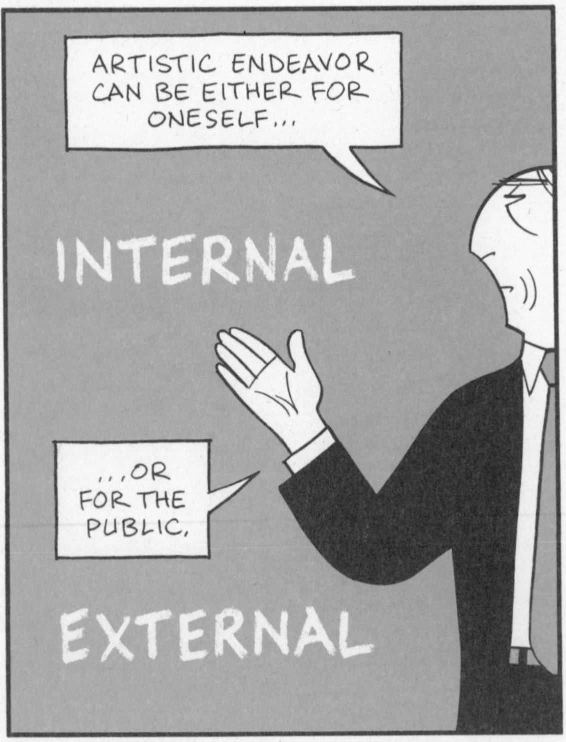
ARTISTIC ENDEAVOR CAN BE EITHER FOR ONESELF...
INTERNAL
...OR FOR THE PUBLIC.
EXTERNAL

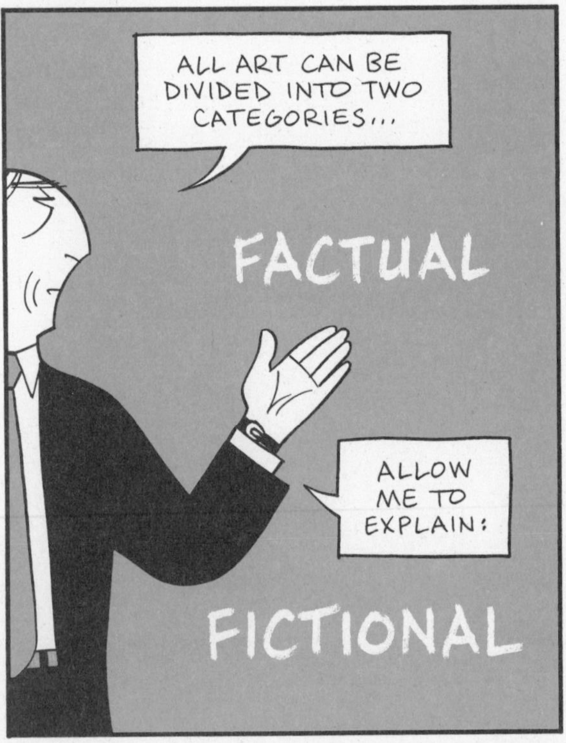
ALL ART CAN BE DIVIDED INTO TWO CATEGORIES...
FACTUAL
ALLOW ME TO EXPLAIN:
FICTIONAL

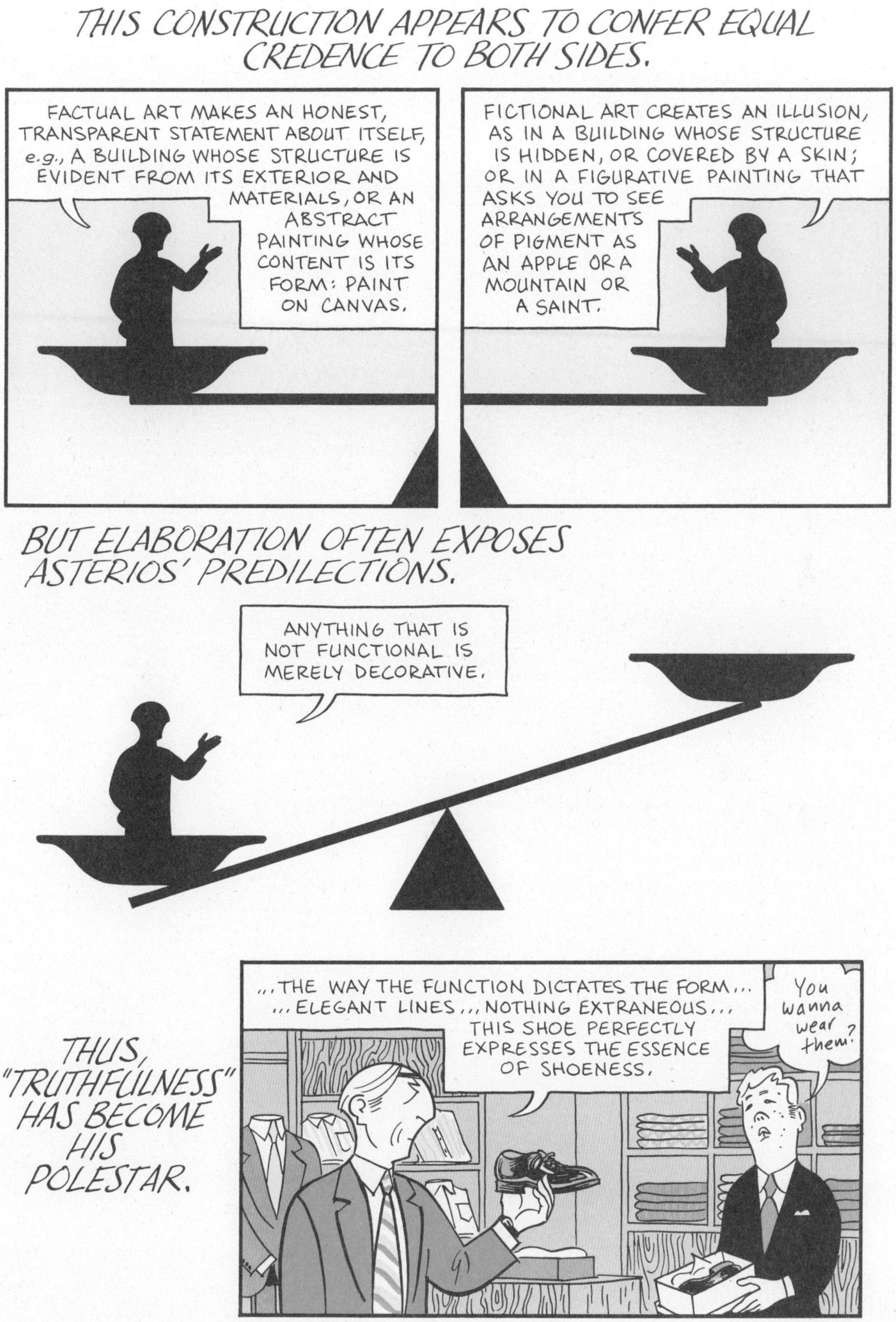
THIS CONSTRUCTION APPEARS TO CONFER EQUAL CREDENCE TO BOTH SIDES.
FACTUAL ART MAKES AN HONEST, TRANSPARENT STATEMENT ABOUT ITSELF, e.g., A BUILDING WHOSE STRUCTURE IS EVIDENT FROM ITS EXTERIOR AND MATERIALS, OR AN ABSTRACT PAINTING WHOSE CONTENT IS ITS FORM: PAINT ON CANVAS.
FICTIONAL ART CREATES AN ILLUSION, AS IN A BUILDING WHOSE STRUCTURE IS HIDDEN, OR COVERED BY A SKIN; OR IN A FIGURATIVE PAINTING THAT ASKS YOU TO SEE ARRANGEMENTS OF PIGMENT AS AN APPLE OR A MOUNTAIN OR A SAINT.
BUT ELABORATION OFTEN EXPOSES ASTERIOS' PREDILECTIONS.
ANYTHING THAT IS NOT FUNCTIONAL IS MERELY DECORATIVE.
THUS, "TRUTHFULNESS" HAS BECOME HIS POLESTAR.
...THE WAY THE FUNCTION DICTATES THE FORM... ...ELEGANT LINES... NOTHING EXTRANEOUS... THIS SHOE PERFECTLY EXPRESSES THE ESSENCE OF SHOENESS.
You wanna wear them?

HIS ASPIRATION TOWARD THE TRUE MANIFESTS ITSELF IN OTHER WAYS AS WELL.

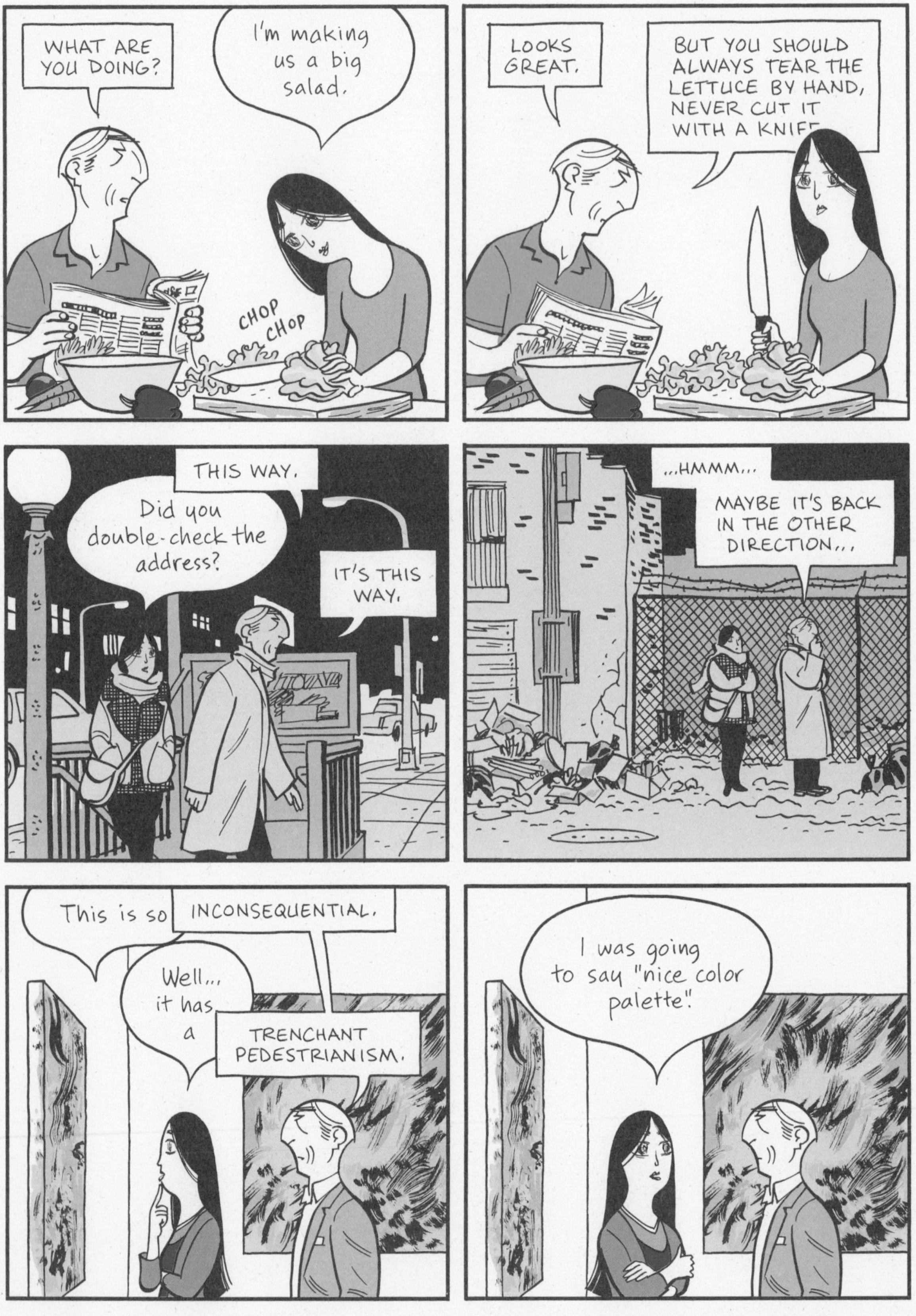
WHAT ARE YOU DOING?
I'm making us a big salad.
CHOP CHOP
LOOKS GREAT.
BUT YOU SHOULD ALWAYS TEAR THE LETTUCE BY HAND, NEVER CUT IT WITH A KNIF
THIS WAY.
Did you double-check the address?
IT'S THIS WAY.
...HMMM...
MAYBE IT'S BACK IN THE OTHER DIRECTION...
This is so
INCONSEQUENTIAL.
Well... it has a
TRENCHANT PEDESTRIANISM.
I was going to say "nice color palette."

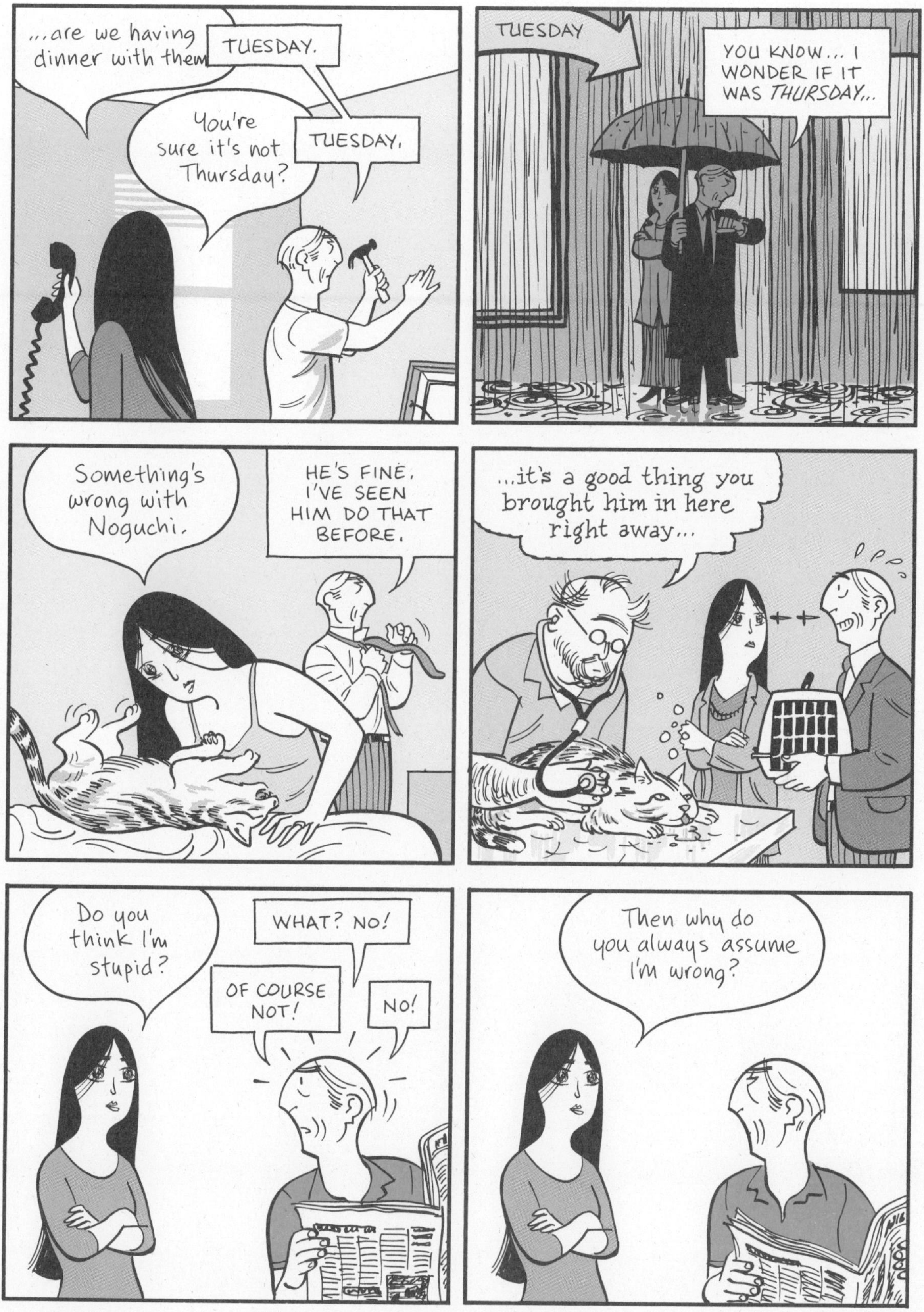
...are we having dinner with them
TUESDAY.
You're sure it's not Thursday?
TUESDAY.
TUESDAY
YOU KNOW... I WONDER IF IT WAS *THURSDAY*...
Something's wrong with Noguchi.
HE'S FINE. I'VE SEEN HIM DO THAT BEFORE.
...it's a good thing you brought him in here right away...
Do you think I'm stupid?
WHAT? NO!
OF COURSE NOT!
NO!
Then why do you always assume I'm wrong?

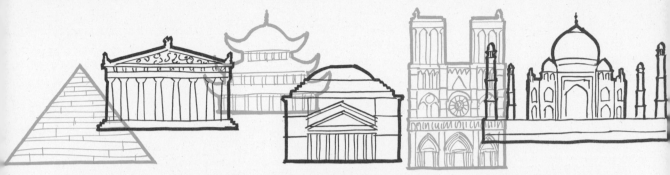

IN THE CERTITUDE OF SYMMETRY, THE CONSONENCE OF COUNTERPOISE, ASTERIOS FOUND A MEASURE OF SOLACE.

HE WAS AN EARLY DEFENDER OF THE MUCH-MALIGNED WORLD TRADE TOWERS.

DON'T YOU SEE? THE BRILLIANCE OF IT IS THAT THERE ARE *TWO* OF THEM.

HIS OWN DESIGNS ECHOED THIS ELOQUENT EQUILIBRIUM.

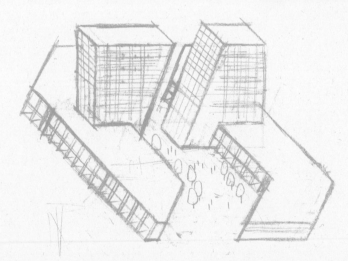

PARALLEL PARK
MIXED-USE COMPLEX, 1981
(FUNDING WITHDRAWN)

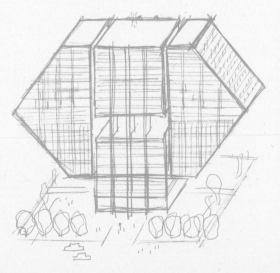

THE AKIMBO ARMS
APARTMENT BUILDING, 1983
(NEVER BUILT)

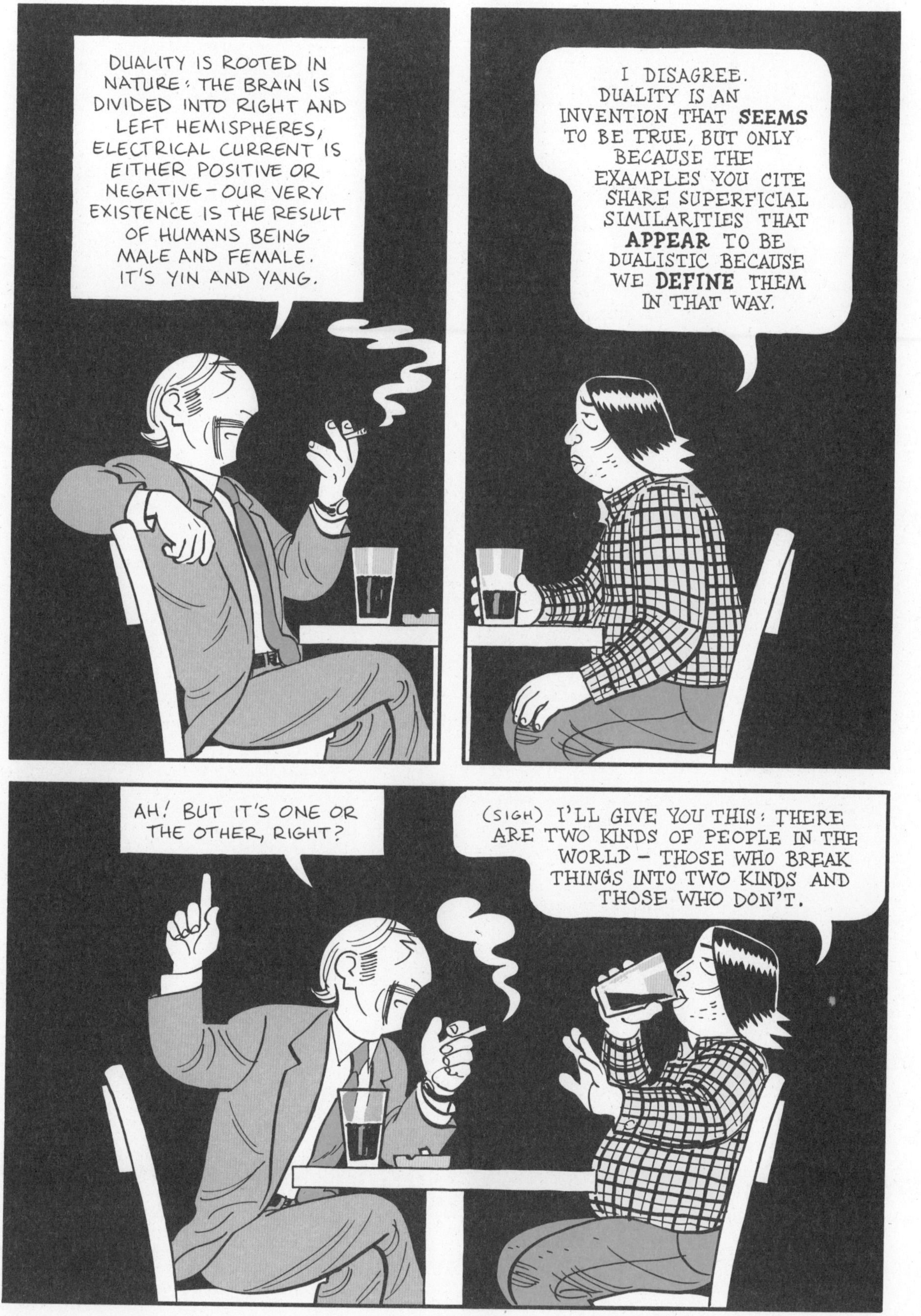
DUALITY IS ROOTED IN NATURE: THE BRAIN IS DIVIDED INTO RIGHT AND LEFT HEMISPHERES, ELECTRICAL CURRENT IS EITHER POSITIVE OR NEGATIVE - OUR VERY EXISTENCE IS THE RESULT OF HUMANS BEING MALE AND FEMALE. IT'S YIN AND YANG.
I DISAGREE. DUALITY IS AN INVENTION THAT **SEEMS** TO BE TRUE, BUT ONLY BECAUSE THE EXAMPLES YOU CITE SHARE SUPERFICIAL SIMILARITIES THAT **APPEAR** TO BE DUALISTIC BECAUSE WE **DEFINE** THEM IN THAT WAY.
AH! BUT IT'S ONE OR THE OTHER, RIGHT?
(SIGH) I'LL GIVE YOU THIS: THERE ARE TWO KINDS OF PEOPLE IN THE WORLD - THOSE WHO BREAK THINGS INTO TWO KINDS AND THOSE WHO DON'T.

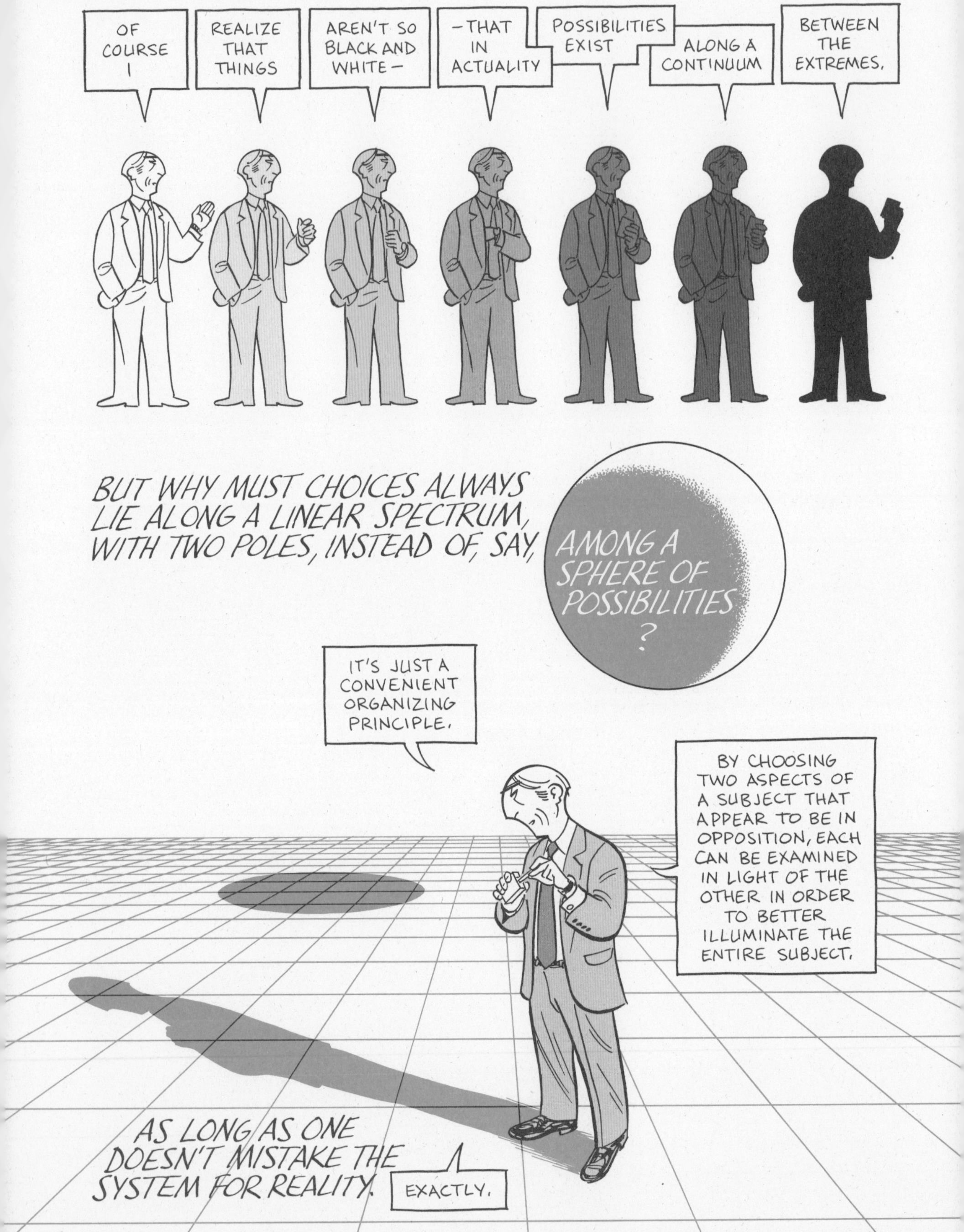
OF COURSE I
REALIZE THAT THINGS
AREN'T SO BLACK AND WHITE—
—THAT IN ACTUALITY
POSSIBILITIES EXIST
ALONG A CONTINUUM
BETWEEN THE EXTREMES.
BUT WHY MUST CHOICES ALWAYS LIE ALONG A LINEAR SPECTRUM, WITH TWO POLES, INSTEAD OF, SAY,
AMONG A SPHERE OF POSSIBILITIES ?
IT'S JUST A CONVENIENT ORGANIZING PRINCIPLE.
BY CHOOSING TWO ASPECTS OF A SUBJECT THAT APPEAR TO BE IN OPPOSITION, EACH CAN BE EXAMINED IN LIGHT OF THE OTHER IN ORDER TO BETTER ILLUMINATE THE ENTIRE SUBJECT.
AS LONG AS ONE DOESN'T MISTAKE THE SYSTEM FOR REALITY.
EXACTLY.

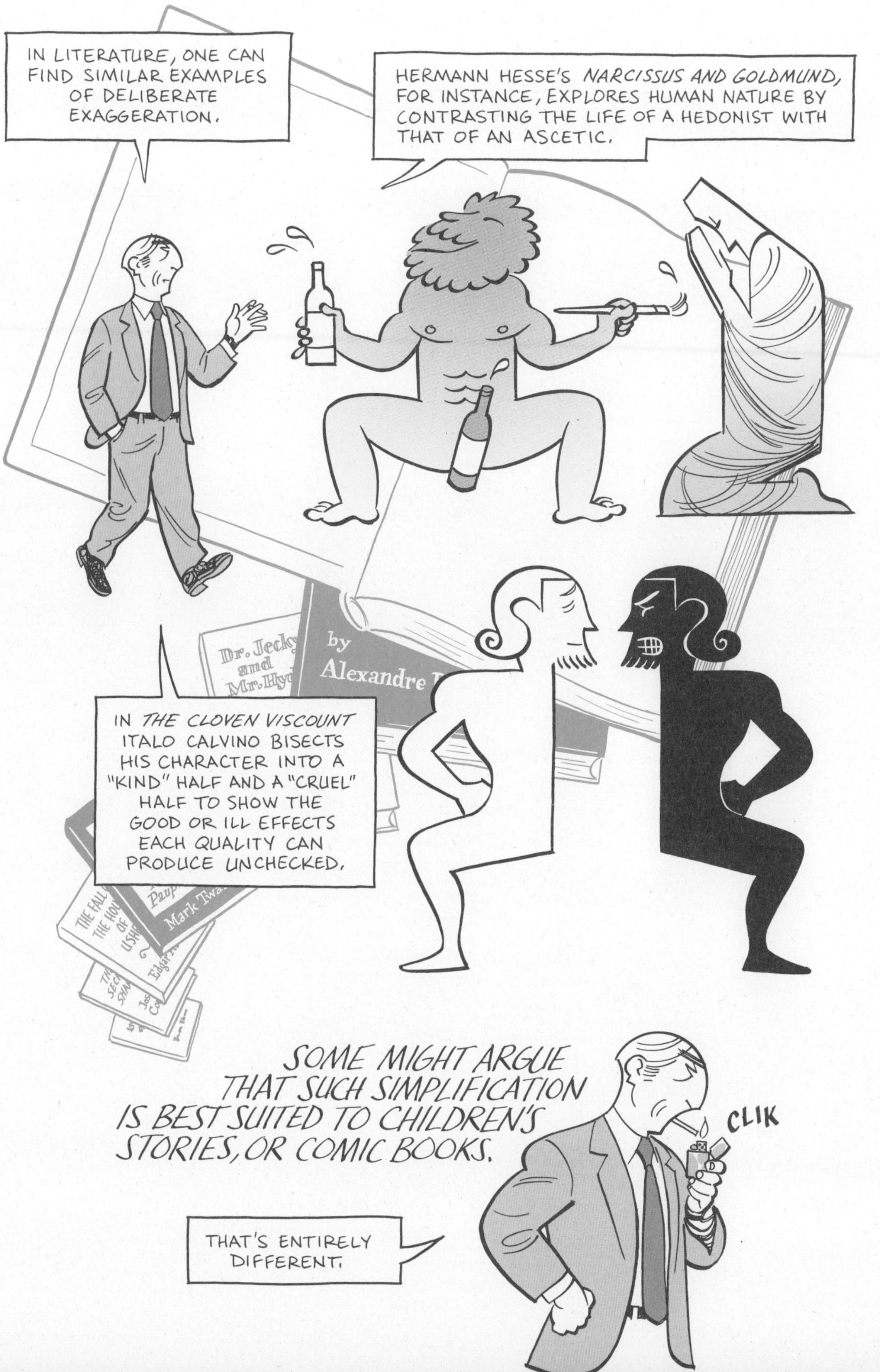
IN LITERATURE, ONE CAN FIND SIMILAR EXAMPLES OF DELIBERATE EXAGGERATION.
HERMANN HESSE'S *NARCISSUS AND GOLDMUND*, FOR INSTANCE, EXPLORES HUMAN NATURE BY CONTRASTING THE LIFE OF A HEDONIST WITH THAT OF AN ASCETIC.
Dr. Jecky and Mr. Hyd
by Alexandre
IN *THE CLOVEN VISCOUNT* ITALO CALVINO BISECTS HIS CHARACTER INTO A "KIND" HALF AND A "CRUEL" HALF TO SHOW THE GOOD OR ILL EFFECTS EACH QUALITY CAN PRODUCE UNCHECKED.
Mark Twa
SOME MIGHT ARGUE THAT SUCH SIMPLIFICATION IS BEST SUITED TO CHILDREN'S STORIES, OR COMIC BOOKS.
CLIK
THAT'S ENTIRELY DIFFERENT.

WHEN ALL IS SAID AND DONE, MAYBE ASTERIOS' PARTICULAR VISION HAS A MORE SPECIFIC SOURCE.

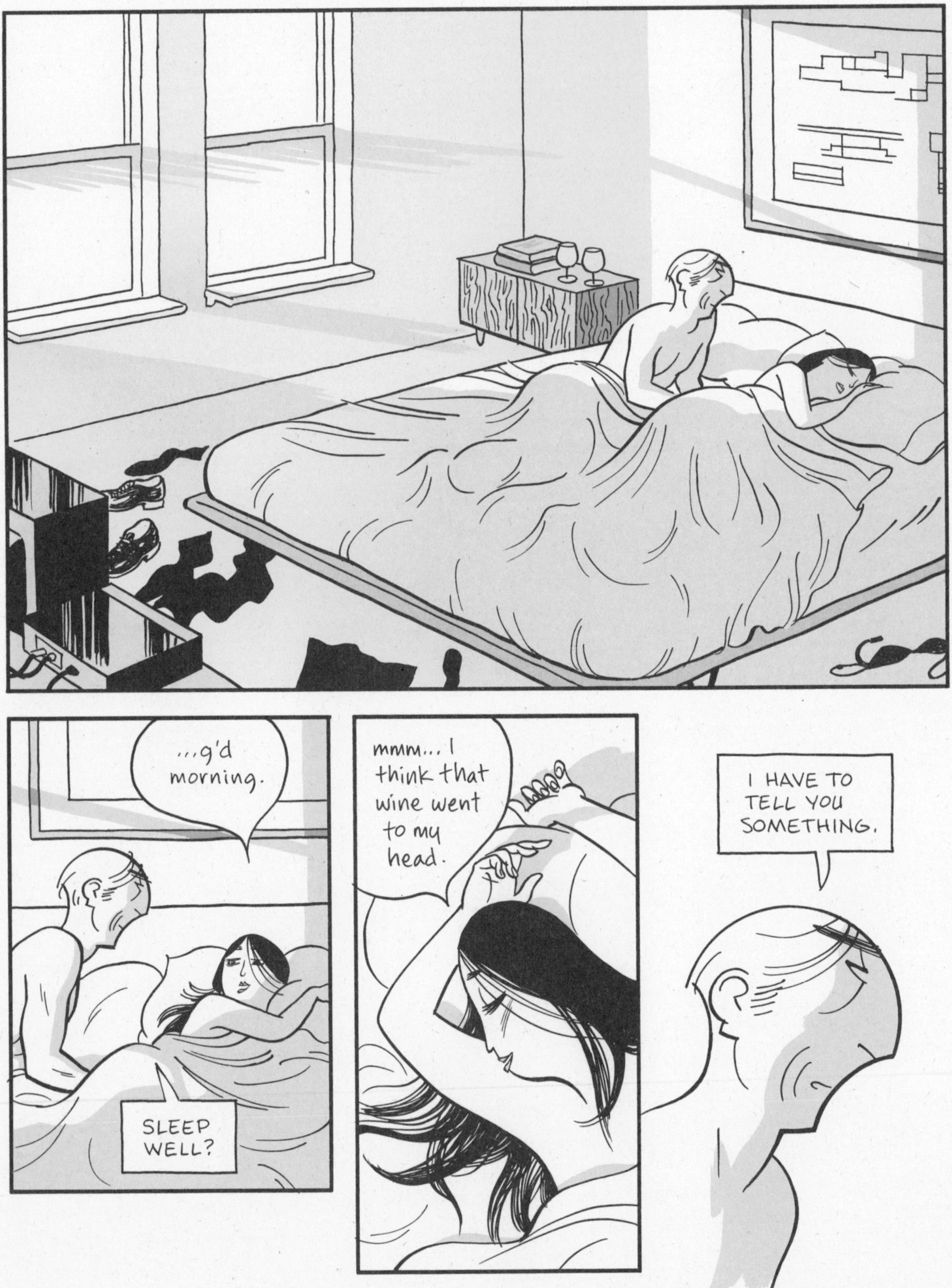
...g'd morning.
SLEEP WELL?
mmm... I think that wine went to my head.
I HAVE TO TELL YOU SOMETHING.

SEE THAT SMALL FIXTURE IN THE CORNER?

Yes.

IT'S A VIDEO CAMERA.

!

LET ME—

SLAP

You put a **video** camera in your bedroom?

ACTUALLY, THERE'S ONE IN EVERY ROOM.

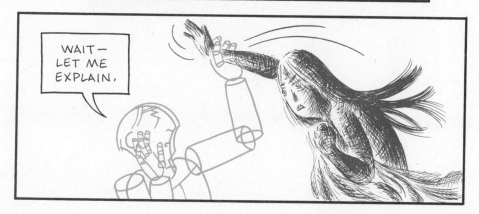

WAIT— LET ME EXPLAIN.

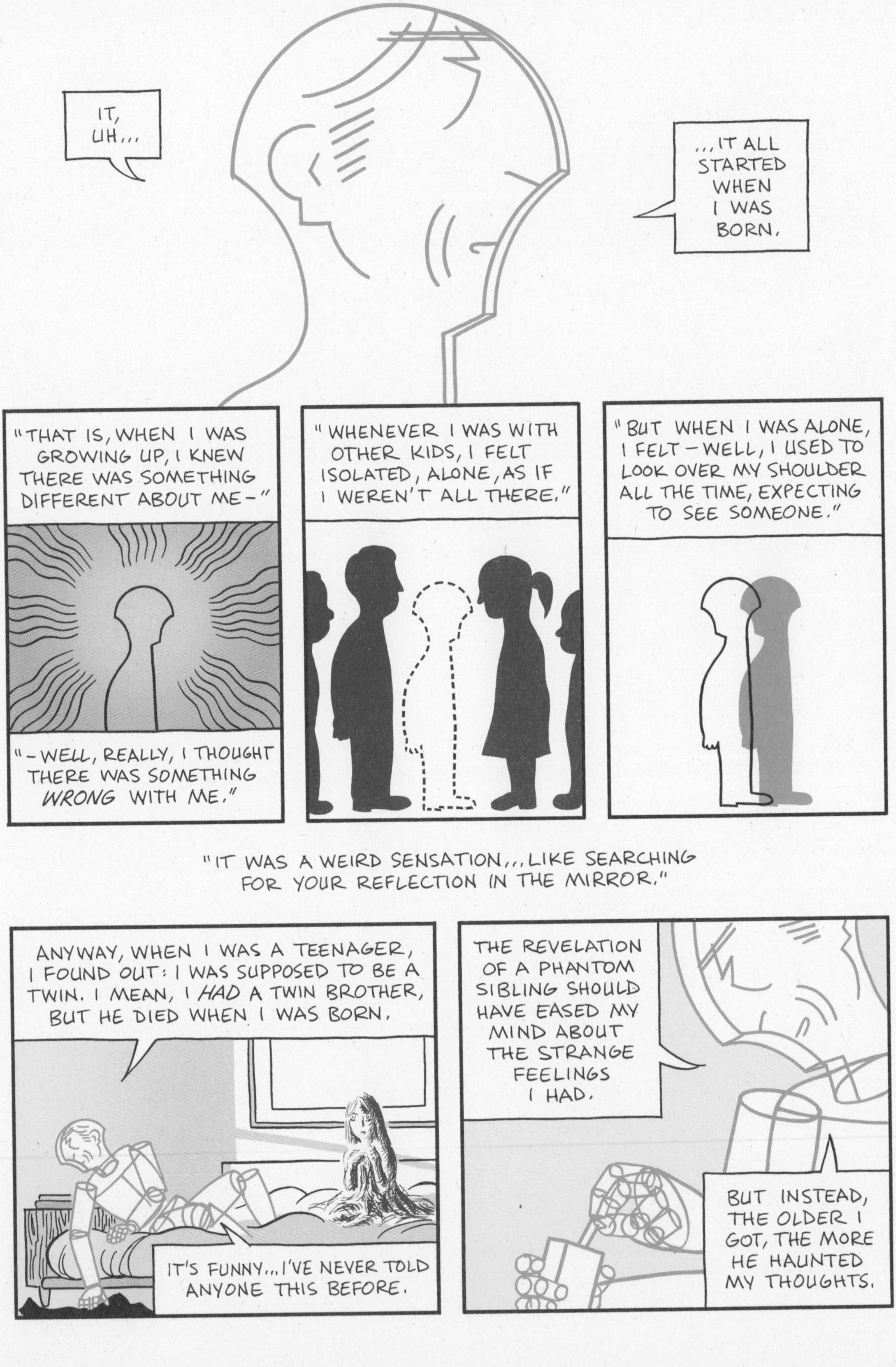
IT, UH...
...IT ALL STARTED WHEN I WAS BORN.
"THAT IS, WHEN I WAS GROWING UP, I KNEW THERE WAS SOMETHING DIFFERENT ABOUT ME–"
"–WELL, REALLY, I THOUGHT THERE WAS SOMETHING *WRONG* WITH ME."
"WHENEVER I WAS WITH OTHER KIDS, I FELT ISOLATED, ALONE, AS IF I WEREN'T ALL THERE."
"BUT WHEN I WAS ALONE, I FELT—WELL, I USED TO LOOK OVER MY SHOULDER ALL THE TIME, EXPECTING TO SEE SOMEONE."
"IT WAS A WEIRD SENSATION... LIKE SEARCHING FOR YOUR REFLECTION IN THE MIRROR."
ANYWAY, WHEN I WAS A TEENAGER, I FOUND OUT: I WAS SUPPOSED TO BE A TWIN. I MEAN, I *HAD* A TWIN BROTHER, BUT HE DIED WHEN I WAS BORN.
IT'S FUNNY... I'VE NEVER TOLD ANYONE THIS BEFORE.
THE REVELATION OF A PHANTOM SIBLING SHOULD HAVE EASED MY MIND ABOUT THE STRANGE FEELINGS I HAD.
BUT INSTEAD, THE OLDER I GOT, THE MORE HE HAUNTED MY THOUGHTS.

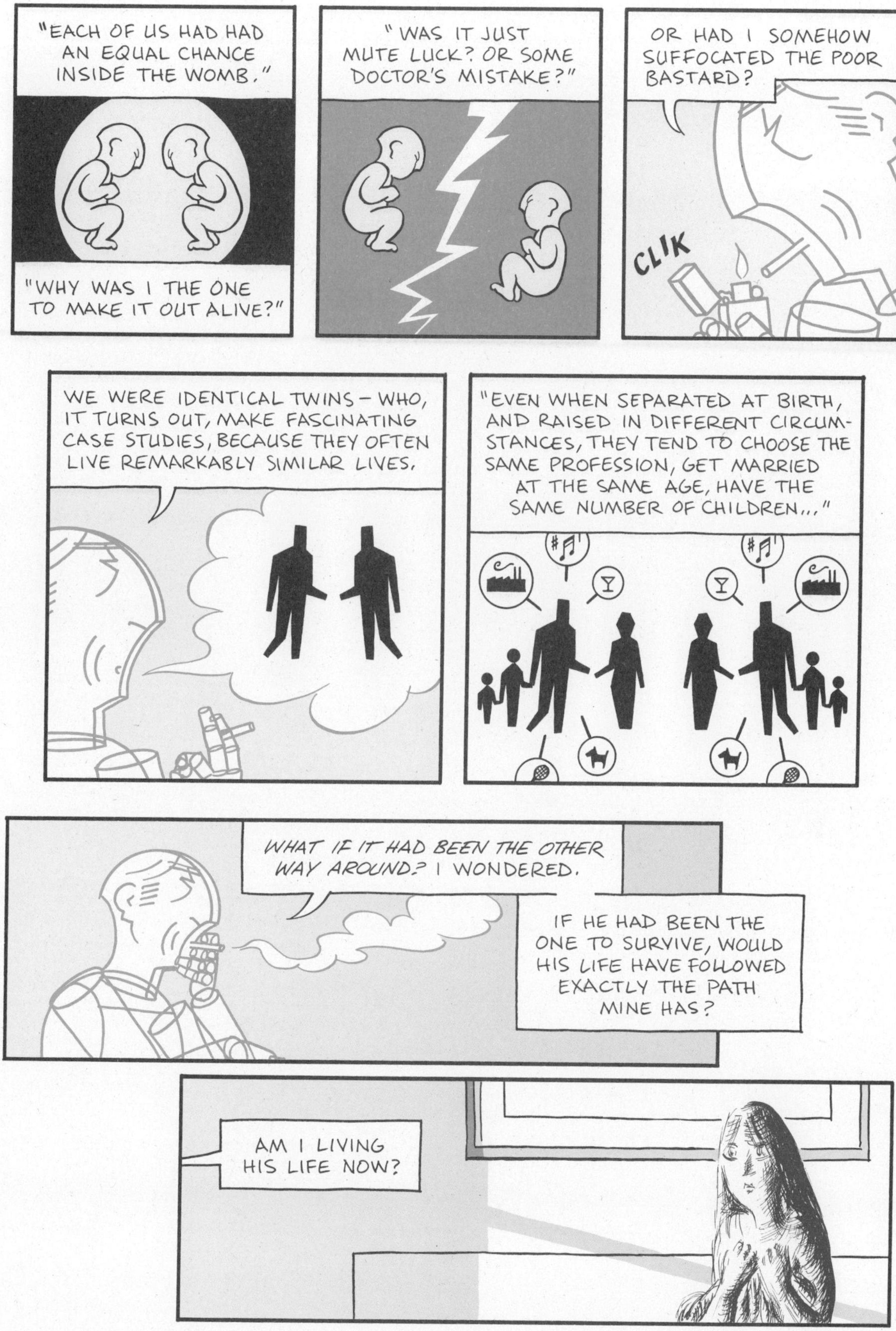
"EACH OF US HAD HAD AN EQUAL CHANCE INSIDE THE WOMB."
"WHY WAS I THE ONE TO MAKE IT OUT ALIVE?"
"WAS IT JUST MUTE LUCK? OR SOME DOCTOR'S MISTAKE?"
OR HAD I SOMEHOW SUFFOCATED THE POOR BASTARD?
CLIK
WE WERE IDENTICAL TWINS — WHO, IT TURNS OUT, MAKE FASCINATING CASE STUDIES, BECAUSE THEY OFTEN LIVE REMARKABLY SIMILAR LIVES.
"EVEN WHEN SEPARATED AT BIRTH, AND RAISED IN DIFFERENT CIRCUMSTANCES, THEY TEND TO CHOOSE THE SAME PROFESSION, GET MARRIED AT THE SAME AGE, HAVE THE SAME NUMBER OF CHILDREN..."
WHAT IF IT HAD BEEN THE OTHER WAY AROUND? I WONDERED.
IF HE HAD BEEN THE ONE TO SURVIVE, WOULD HIS LIFE HAVE FOLLOWED EXACTLY THE PATH MINE HAS?
AM I LIVING HIS LIFE NOW?

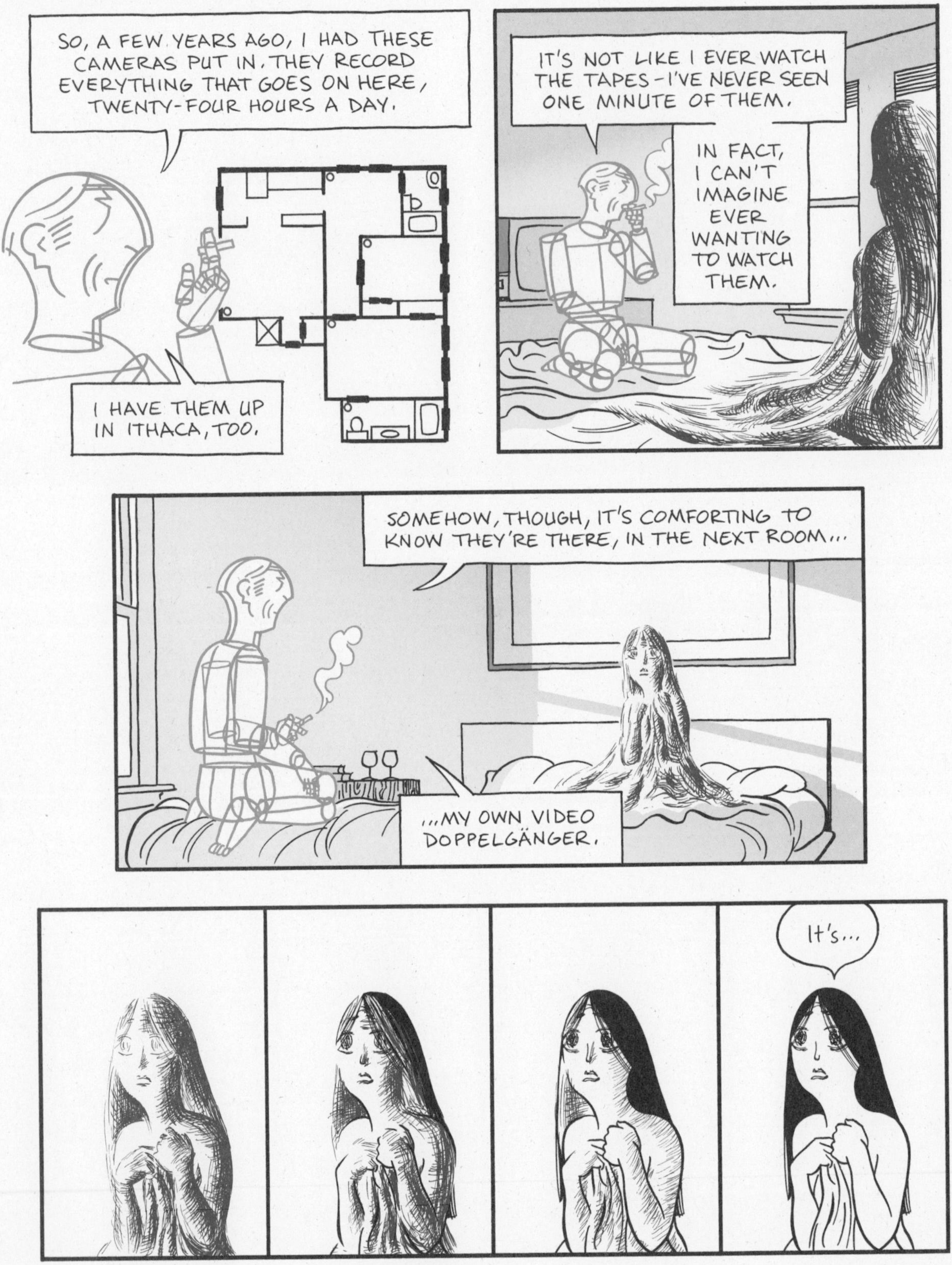
SO, A FEW YEARS AGO, I HAD THESE CAMERAS PUT IN. THEY RECORD EVERYTHING THAT GOES ON HERE, TWENTY-FOUR HOURS A DAY.
I HAVE THEM UP IN ITHACA, TOO.
IT'S NOT LIKE I EVER WATCH THE TAPES—I'VE NEVER SEEN ONE MINUTE OF THEM.
IN FACT, I CAN'T IMAGINE EVER WANTING TO WATCH THEM.
SOMEHOW, THOUGH, IT'S COMFORTING TO KNOW THEY'RE THERE, IN THE NEXT ROOM...
...MY OWN VIDEO DOPPELGÄNGER.
It's...

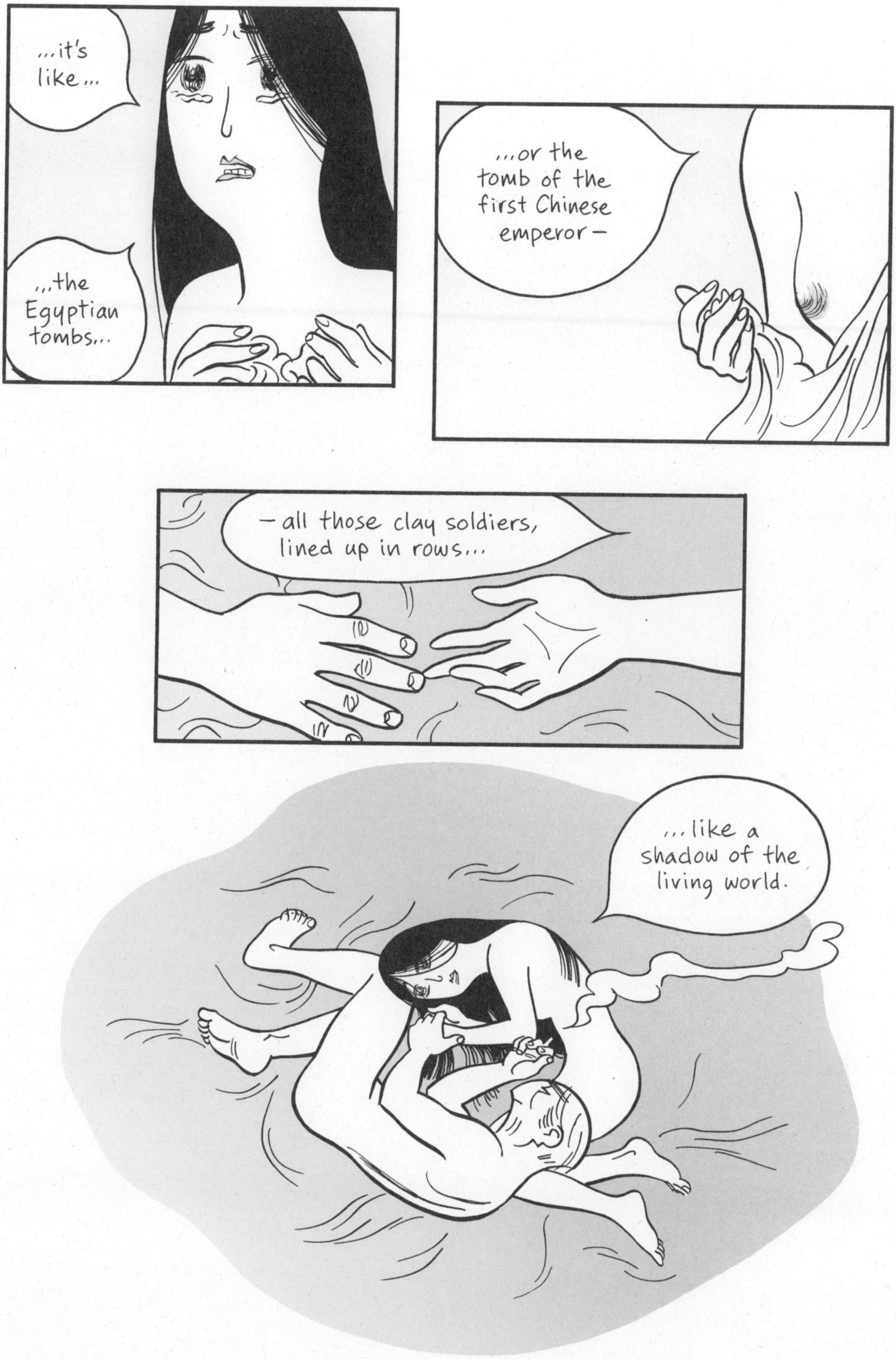
...it's like...
...the Egyptian tombs...
...or the tomb of the first Chinese emperor—
—all those clay soldiers, lined up in rows...
...like a shadow of the living world.

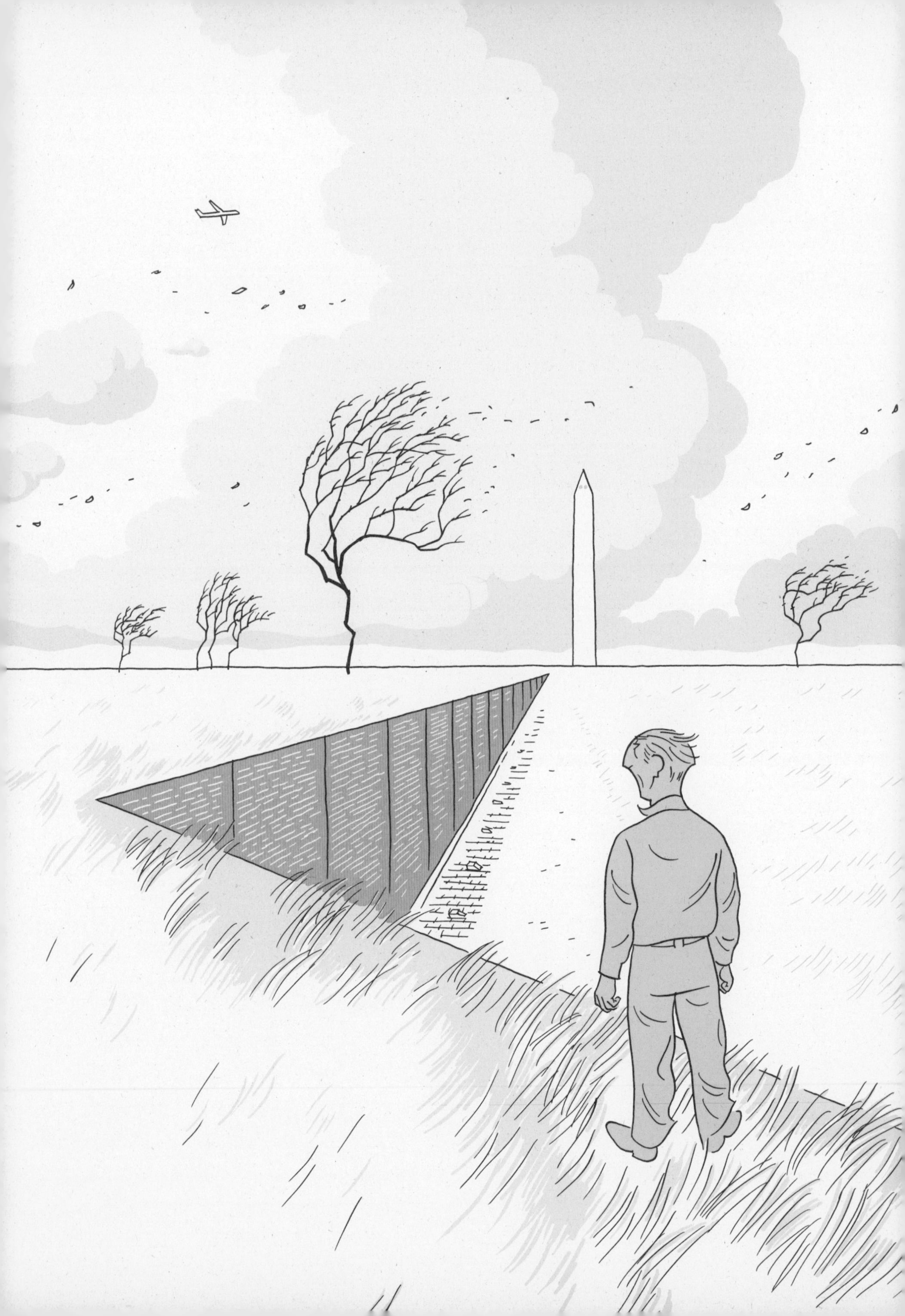

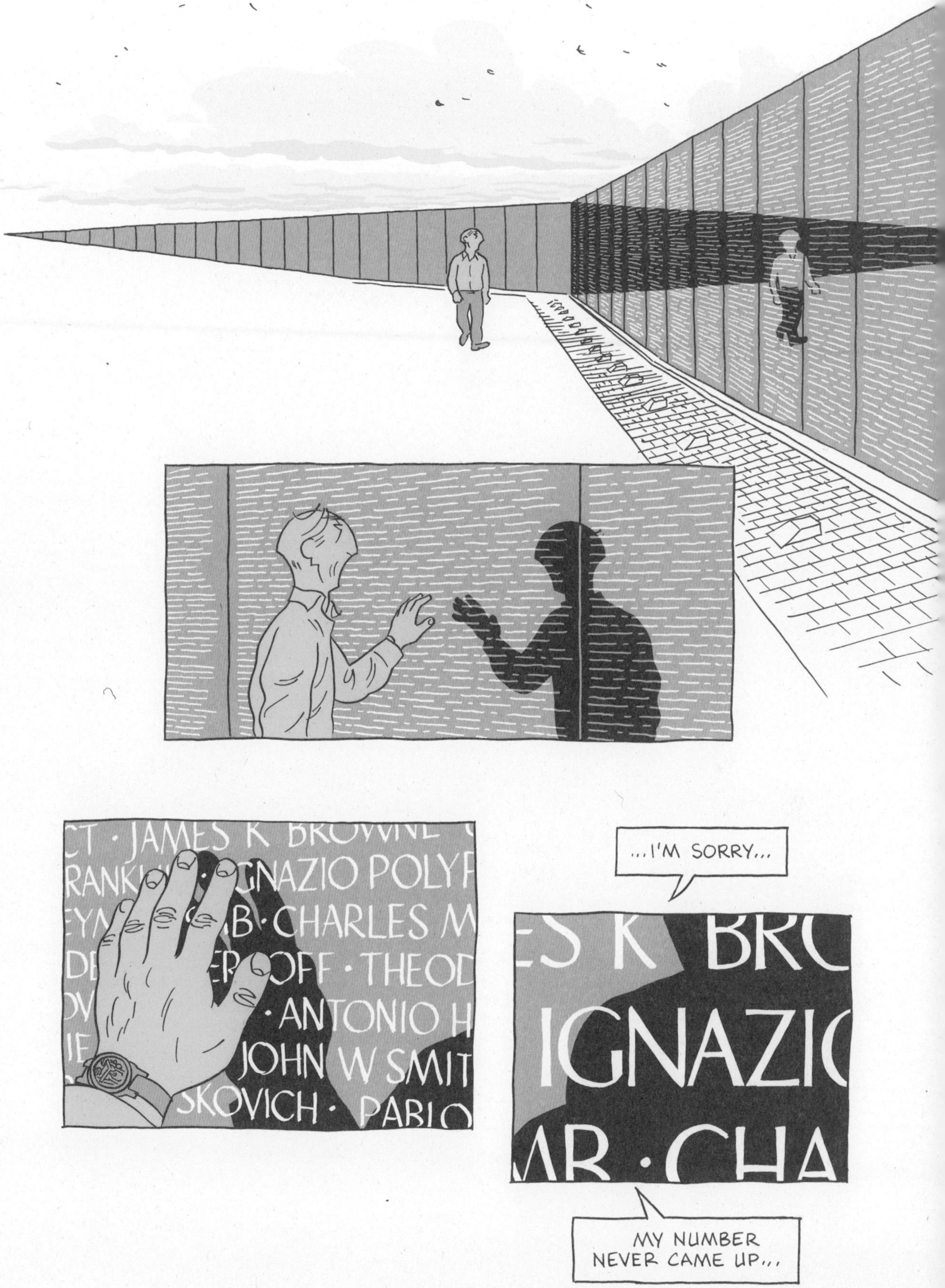
CT · JAMES K BROWNE
RANK GNAZIO POLY
B · CHARLES M
OFF · THEOD
· ANTONIO H
JOHN W SMIT
SKOVICH · PABLO
...I'M SORRY...
ES K BRO
IGNAZIO
MR · CHA
MY NUMBER NEVER CAME UP...

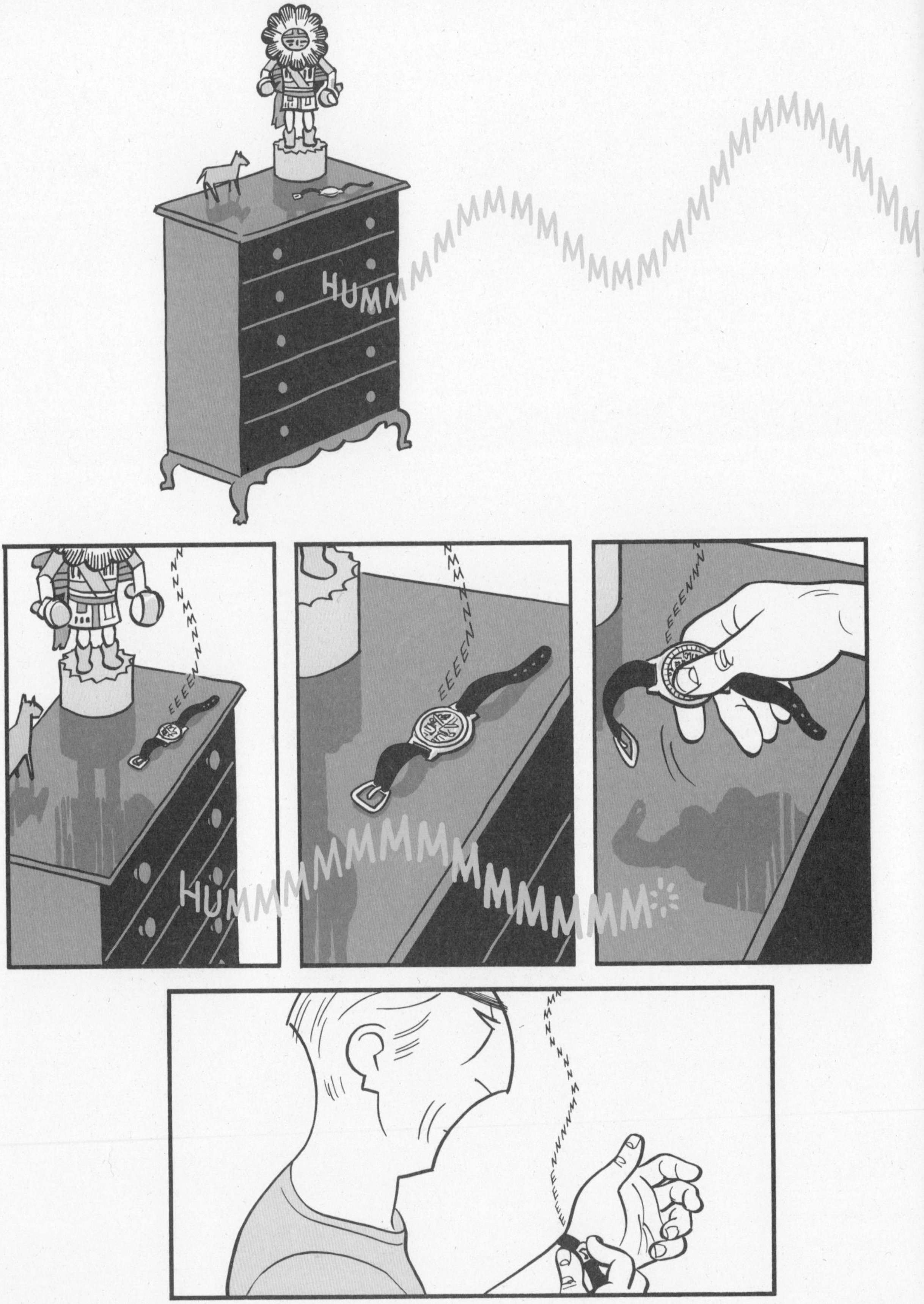
HUMMMMMMMMMMMMMMMMMMMMMMMMMMMMMMMMMMMMM
EEEENNNNNNN
EEEENNNNNNN
EEEENNNN
HUMMMMMMMMMMMMMMMMMMM
EEEEENNNNNNNNNNNM

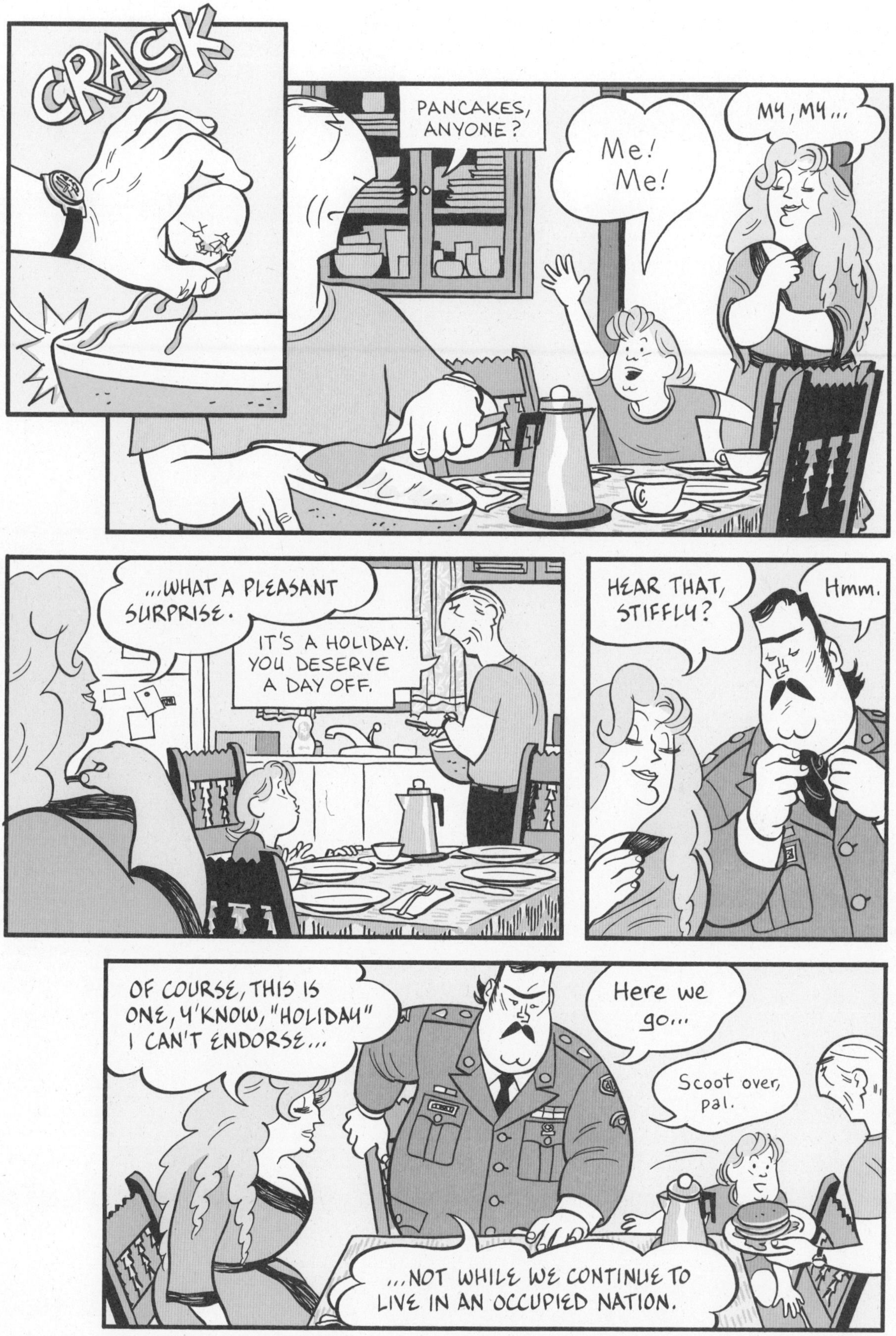
CRACK
PANCAKES, ANYONE?
Me! Me!
MY, MY...
...WHAT A PLEASANT SURPRISE.
IT'S A HOLIDAY. YOU DESERVE A DAY OFF.
HEAR THAT, STIFFLY?
Hmm.
OF COURSE, THIS IS ONE, Y'KNOW, "HOLIDAY" I CAN'T ENDORSE...
Here we go...
Scoot over, pal.
...NOT WHILE WE CONTINUE TO LIVE IN AN OCCUPIED NATION.

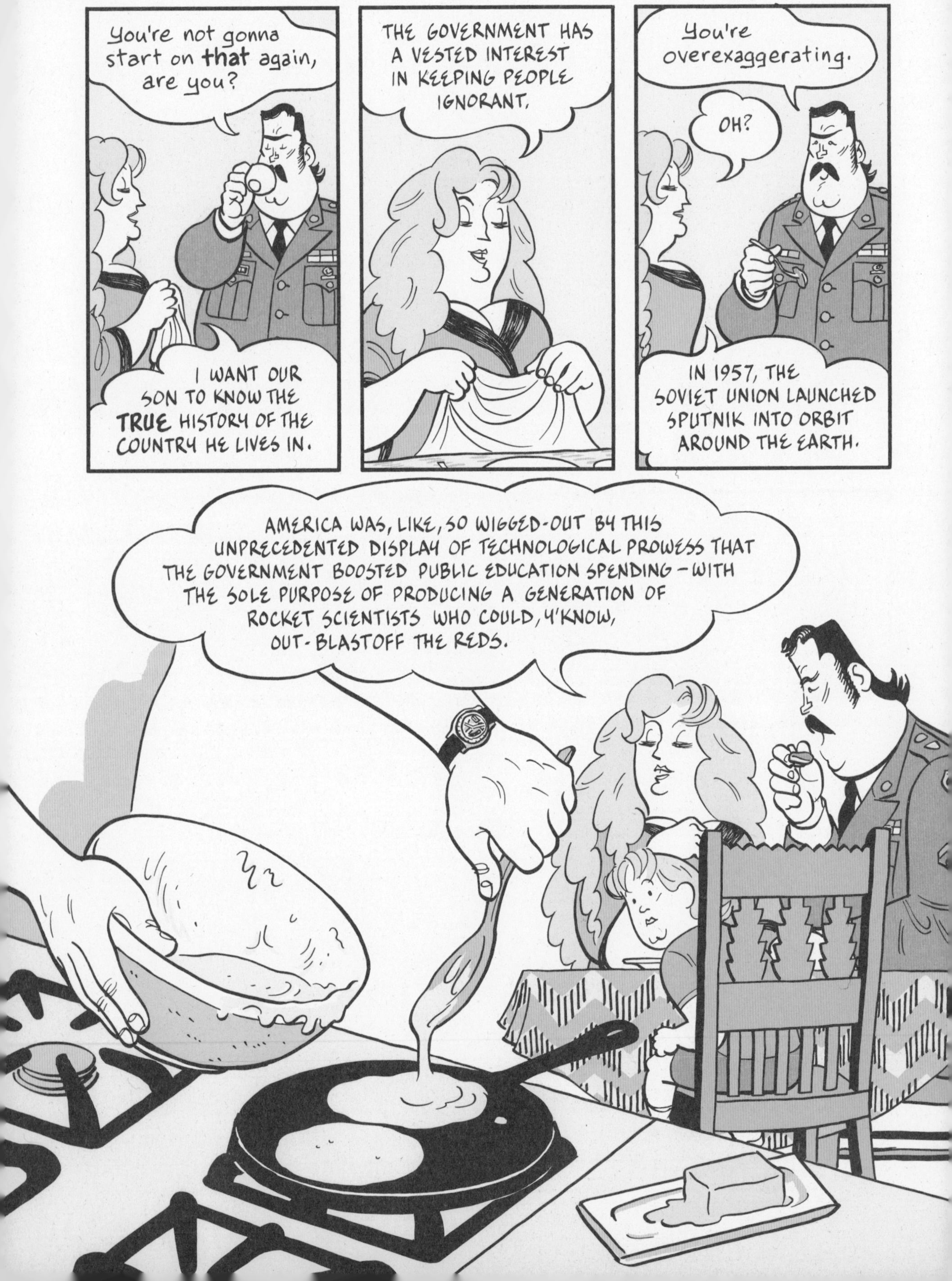
You're not gonna start on that again, are you?
I WANT OUR SON TO KNOW THE TRUE HISTORY OF THE COUNTRY HE LIVES IN.
THE GOVERNMENT HAS A VESTED INTEREST IN KEEPING PEOPLE IGNORANT.
You're overexaggerating.
OH?
IN 1957, THE SOVIET UNION LAUNCHED SPUTNIK INTO ORBIT AROUND THE EARTH.
AMERICA WAS, LIKE, SO WIGGED-OUT BY THIS UNPRECEDENTED DISPLAY OF TECHNOLOGICAL PROWESS THAT THE GOVERNMENT BOOSTED PUBLIC EDUCATION SPENDING—WITH THE SOLE PURPOSE OF PRODUCING A GENERATION OF ROCKET SCIENTISTS WHO COULD, Y'KNOW, OUT-BLASTOFF THE REDS.

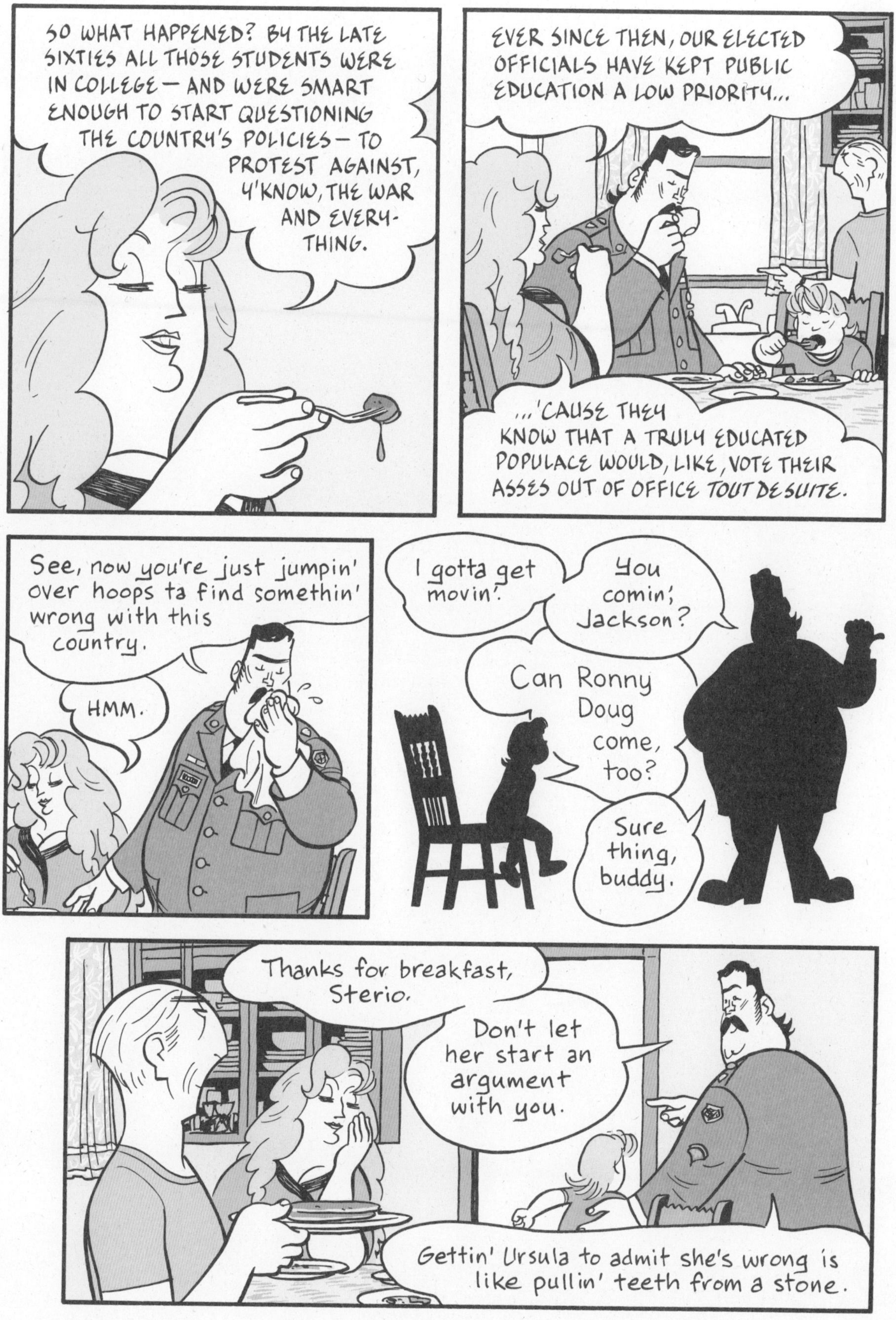
SO WHAT HAPPENED? BY THE LATE SIXTIES ALL THOSE STUDENTS WERE IN COLLEGE — AND WERE SMART ENOUGH TO START QUESTIONING THE COUNTRY'S POLICIES — TO PROTEST AGAINST, Y'KNOW, THE WAR AND EVERYTHING.
EVER SINCE THEN, OUR ELECTED OFFICIALS HAVE KEPT PUBLIC EDUCATION A LOW PRIORITY...
...'CAUSE THEY KNOW THAT A TRULY EDUCATED POPULACE WOULD, LIKE, VOTE THEIR ASSES OUT OF OFFICE *TOUT DE SUITE*.
See, now you're just jumpin' over hoops ta find somethin' wrong with this country.
HMM.
I gotta get movin'.
You comin', Jackson?
Can Ronny Doug come, too?
Sure thing, buddy.
Thanks for breakfast, Sterio.
Don't let her start an argument with you.
Gettin' Ursula to admit she's wrong is like pullin' teeth from a stone.

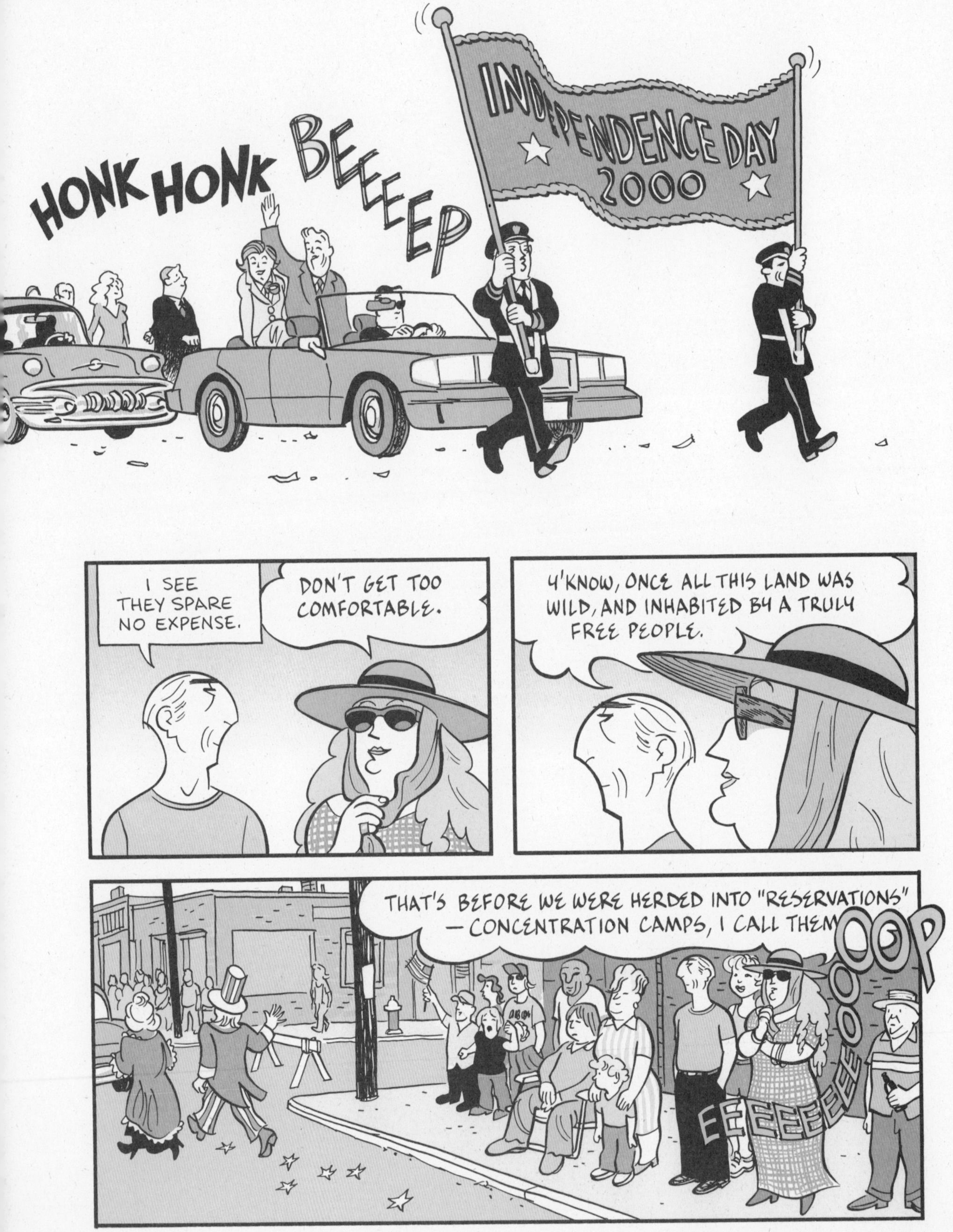
HONK HONK
BEEEEEP
INDEPENDENCE DAY 2000
I SEE THEY SPARE NO EXPENSE.
DON'T GET TOO COMFORTABLE.
Y'KNOW, ONCE ALL THIS LAND WAS WILD, AND INHABITED BY A TRULY FREE PEOPLE.
THAT'S BEFORE WE WERE HERDED INTO "RESERVATIONS" — CONCENTRATION CAMPS, I CALL THEM
EEEEEEEEOOOOOP

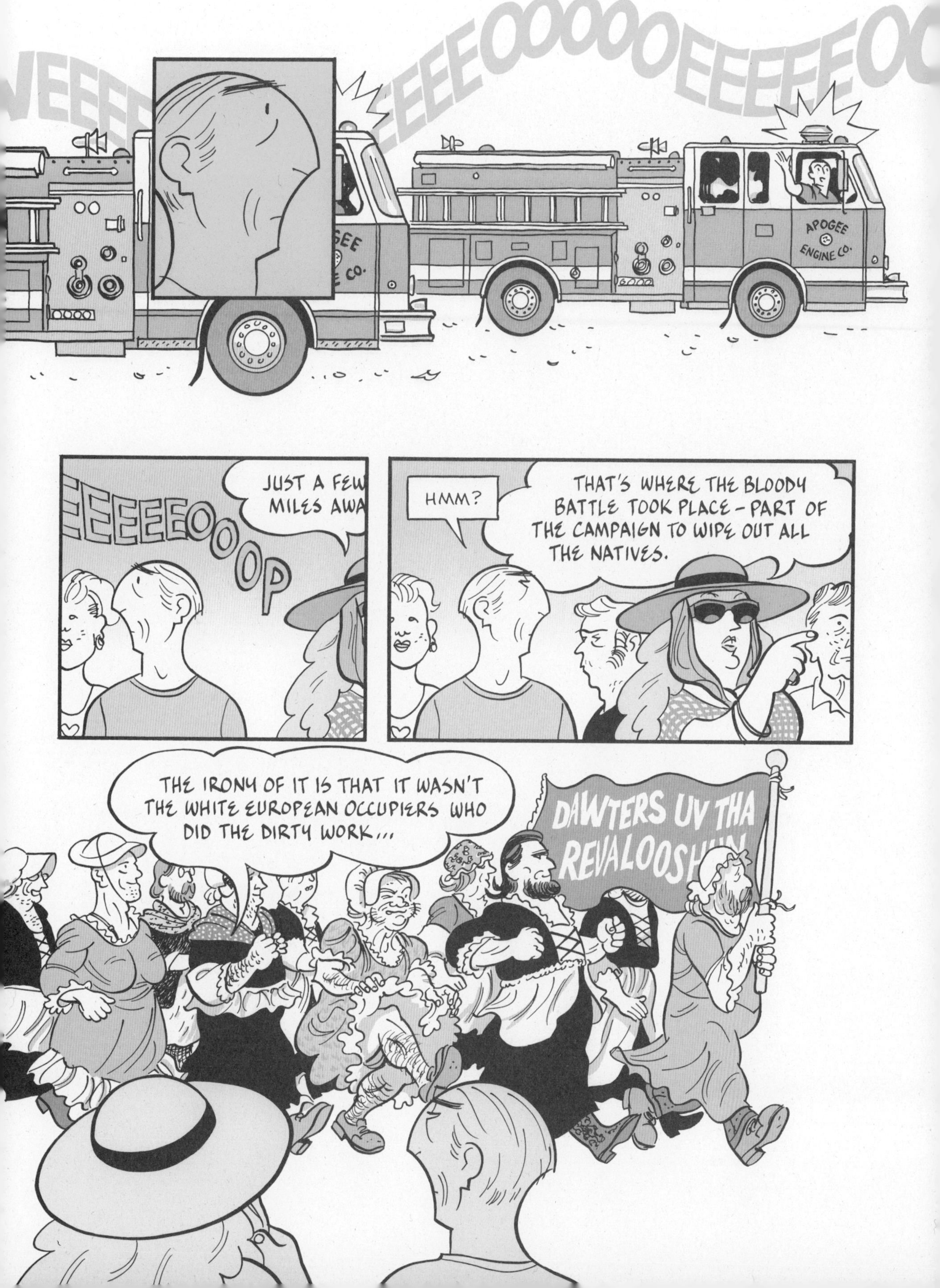
WEEEEEEEEEOOOOOOEEEEEEO
APOGEE ENGINE CO.
EEEEEEOOOP
JUST A FEW MILES AWA
HMM?
THAT'S WHERE THE BLOODY BATTLE TOOK PLACE - PART OF THE CAMPAIGN TO WIPE OUT ALL THE NATIVES.
THE IRONY OF IT IS THAT IT WASN'T THE WHITE EUROPEAN OCCUPIERS WHO DID THE DIRTY WORK...
DAWTERS UV THA REVALOOSH

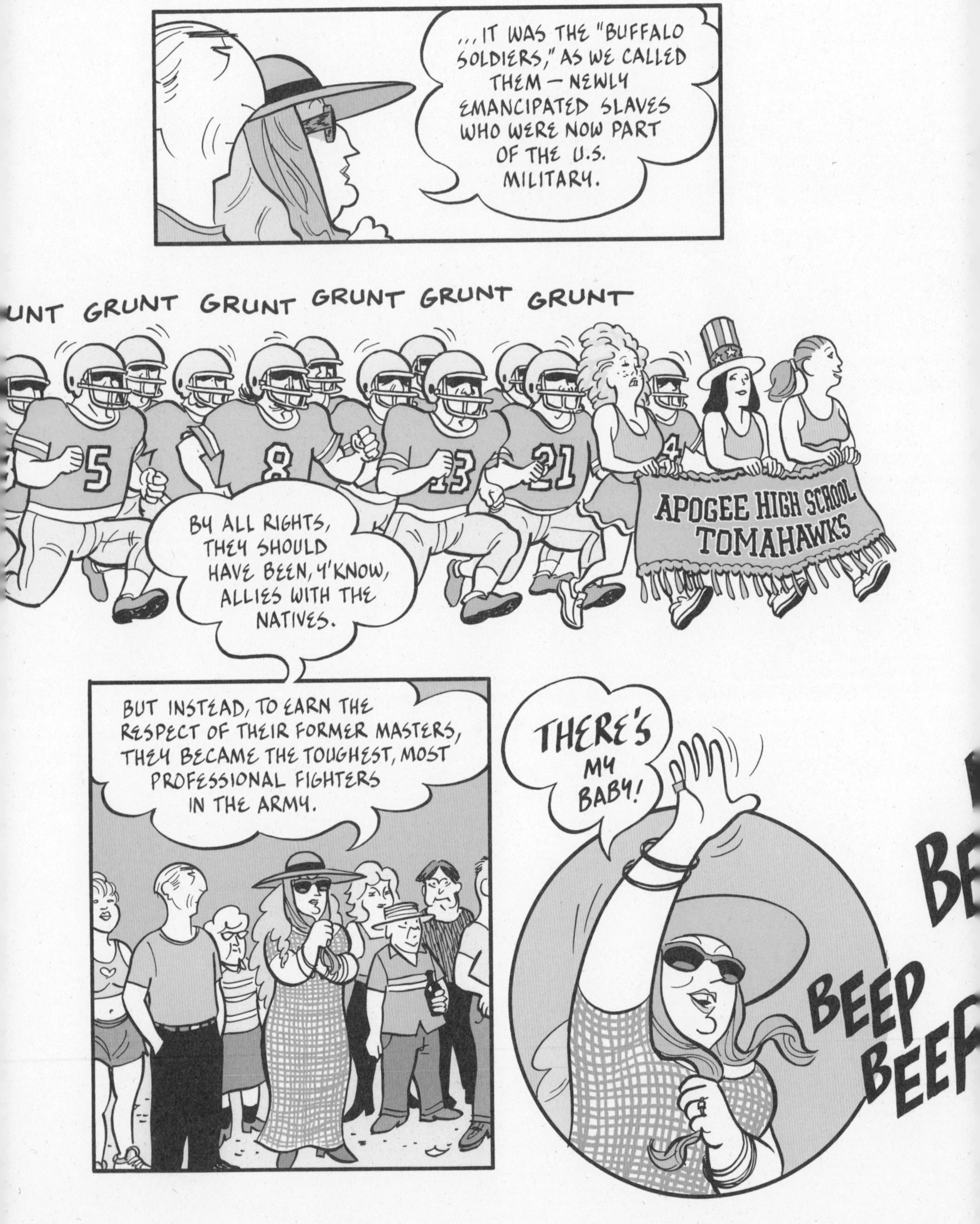

...IT WAS THE "BUFFALO SOLDIERS," AS WE CALLED THEM — NEWLY EMANCIPATED SLAVES WHO WERE NOW PART OF THE U.S. MILITARY.
UNT GRUNT GRUNT GRUNT GRUNT GRUNT
APOGEE HIGH SCHOOL TOMAHAWKS
BY ALL RIGHTS, THEY SHOULD HAVE BEEN, Y'KNOW, ALLIES WITH THE NATIVES.
BUT INSTEAD, TO EARN THE RESPECT OF THEIR FORMER MASTERS, THEY BECAME THE TOUGHEST, MOST PROFESSIONAL FIGHTERS IN THE ARMY.
THERE'S MY BABY!
BEEP

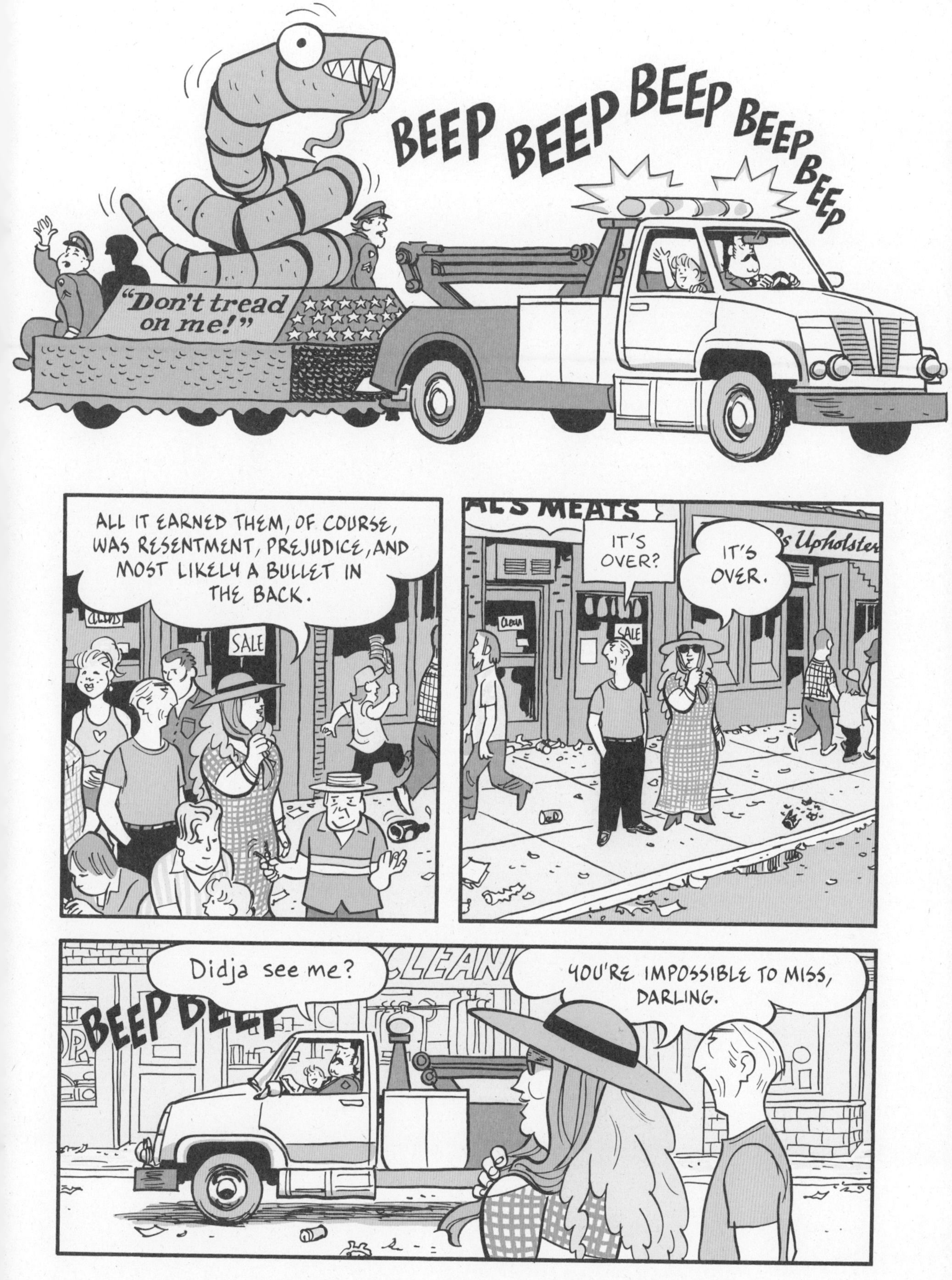

"Don't tread on me!"
BEEP BEEP BEEP BEEP BEEP
ALL IT EARNED THEM, OF COURSE, WAS RESENTMENT, PREJUDICE, AND MOST LIKELY A BULLET IN THE BACK.
SALE
AL'S MEATS
Upholster
IT'S OVER?
IT'S OVER.
SALE
Didja see me?
BEEP BEEP
CLEAN
YOU'RE IMPOSSIBLE TO MISS, DARLING.

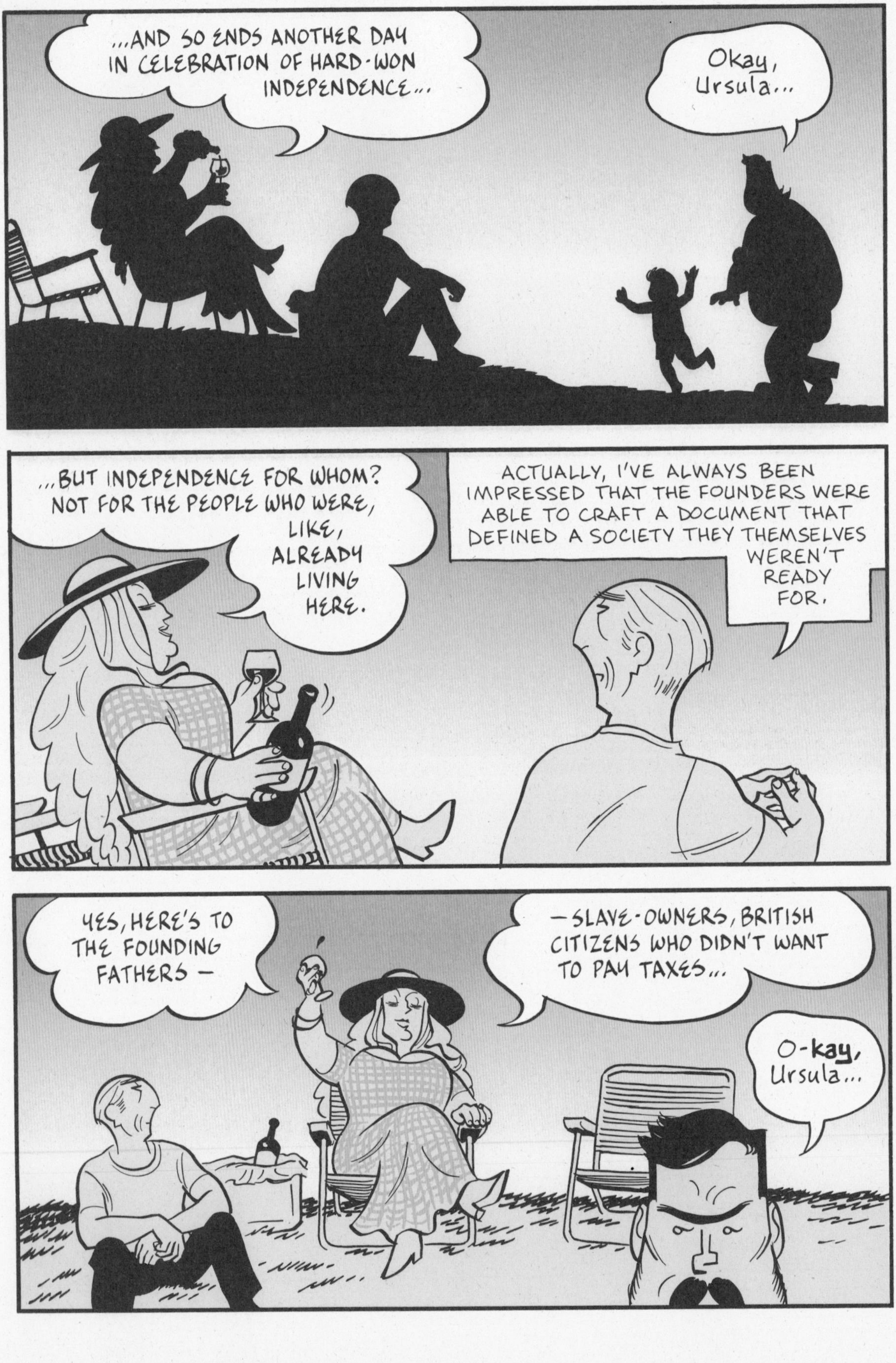
...AND SO ENDS ANOTHER DAY IN CELEBRATION OF HARD-WON INDEPENDENCE...
Okay, Ursula...
...BUT INDEPENDENCE FOR WHOM? NOT FOR THE PEOPLE WHO WERE, LIKE, ALREADY LIVING HERE.
ACTUALLY, I'VE ALWAYS BEEN IMPRESSED THAT THE FOUNDERS WERE ABLE TO CRAFT A DOCUMENT THAT DEFINED A SOCIETY THEY THEMSELVES WEREN'T READY FOR.
YES, HERE'S TO THE FOUNDING FATHERS —
— SLAVE-OWNERS, BRITISH CITIZENS WHO DIDN'T WANT TO PAY TAXES...
O-**kay**, Ursula...

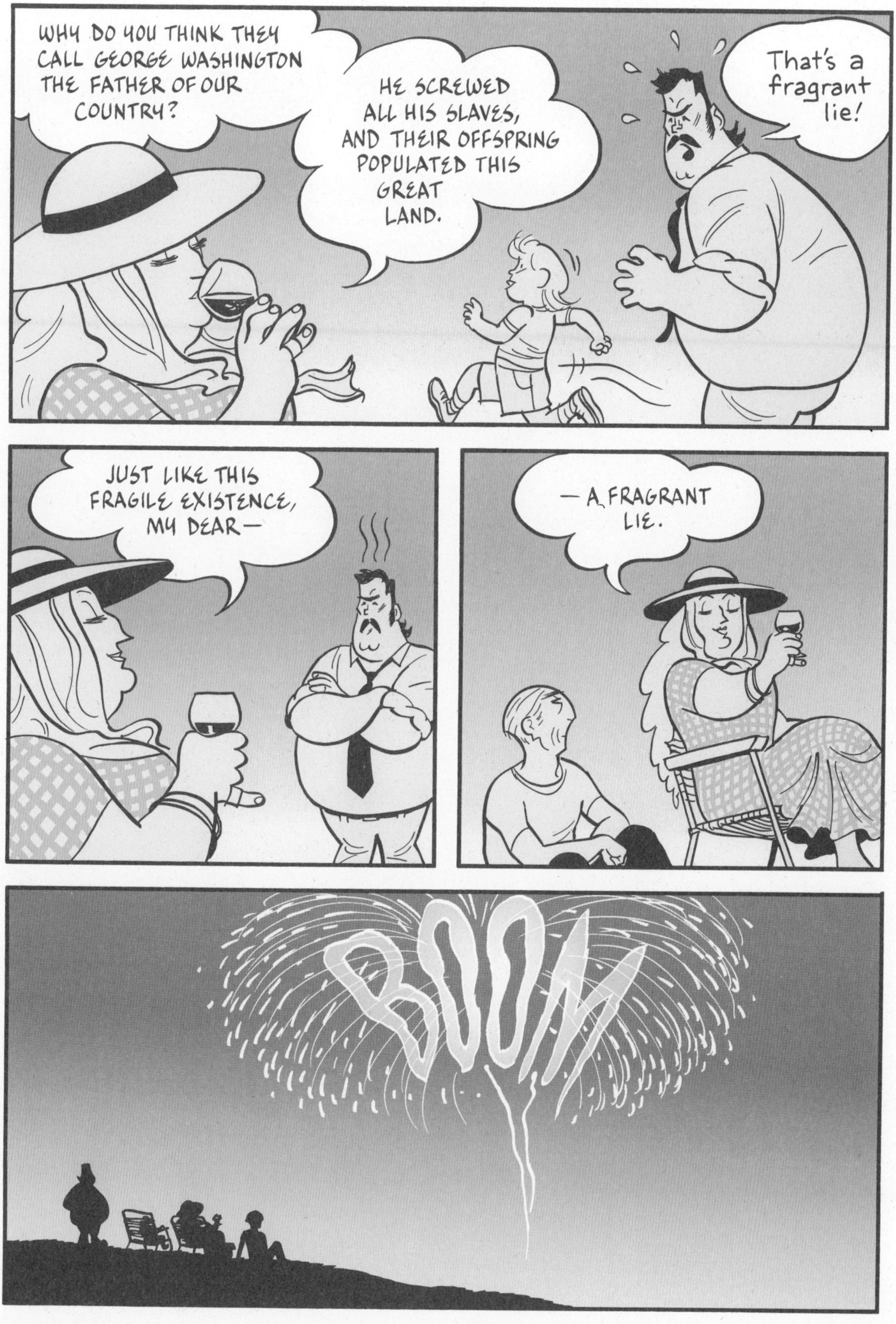
WHY DO YOU THINK THEY CALL GEORGE WASHINGTON THE FATHER OF OUR COUNTRY?
HE SCREWED ALL HIS SLAVES, AND THEIR OFFSPRING POPULATED THIS GREAT LAND.
That's a fragrant lie!
JUST LIKE THIS FRAGILE EXISTENCE, MY DEAR—
—A FRAGRANT LIE.
BOOM

OUR FATHER, EUGENIOS (THE DOCTOR), THOUGHT LITTLE ABOUT RELIGION.

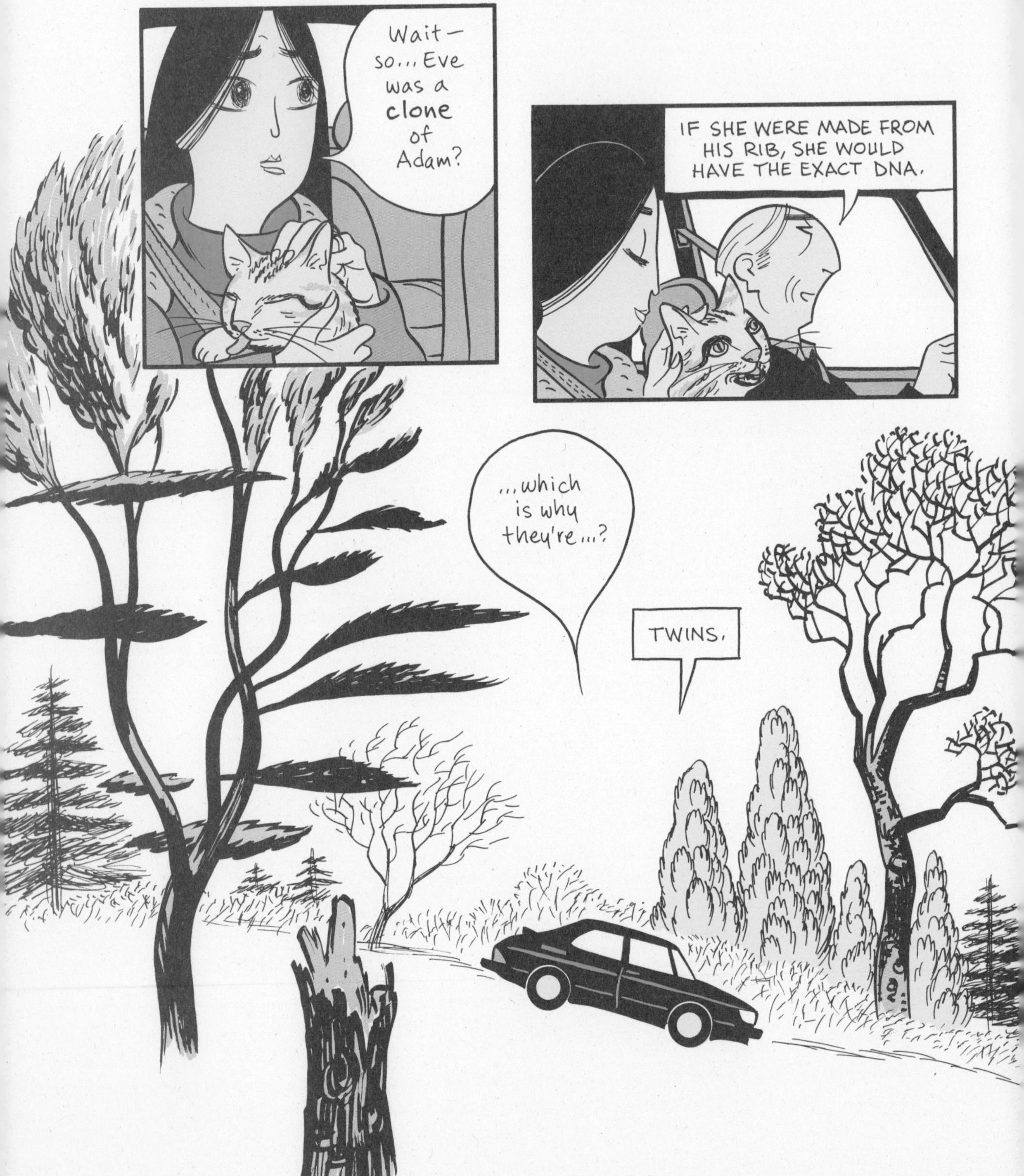

Wait— so... Eve was a **clone** of Adam?
IF SHE WERE MADE FROM HIS RIB, SHE WOULD HAVE THE EXACT DNA.
...which is why they're...?
TWINS.

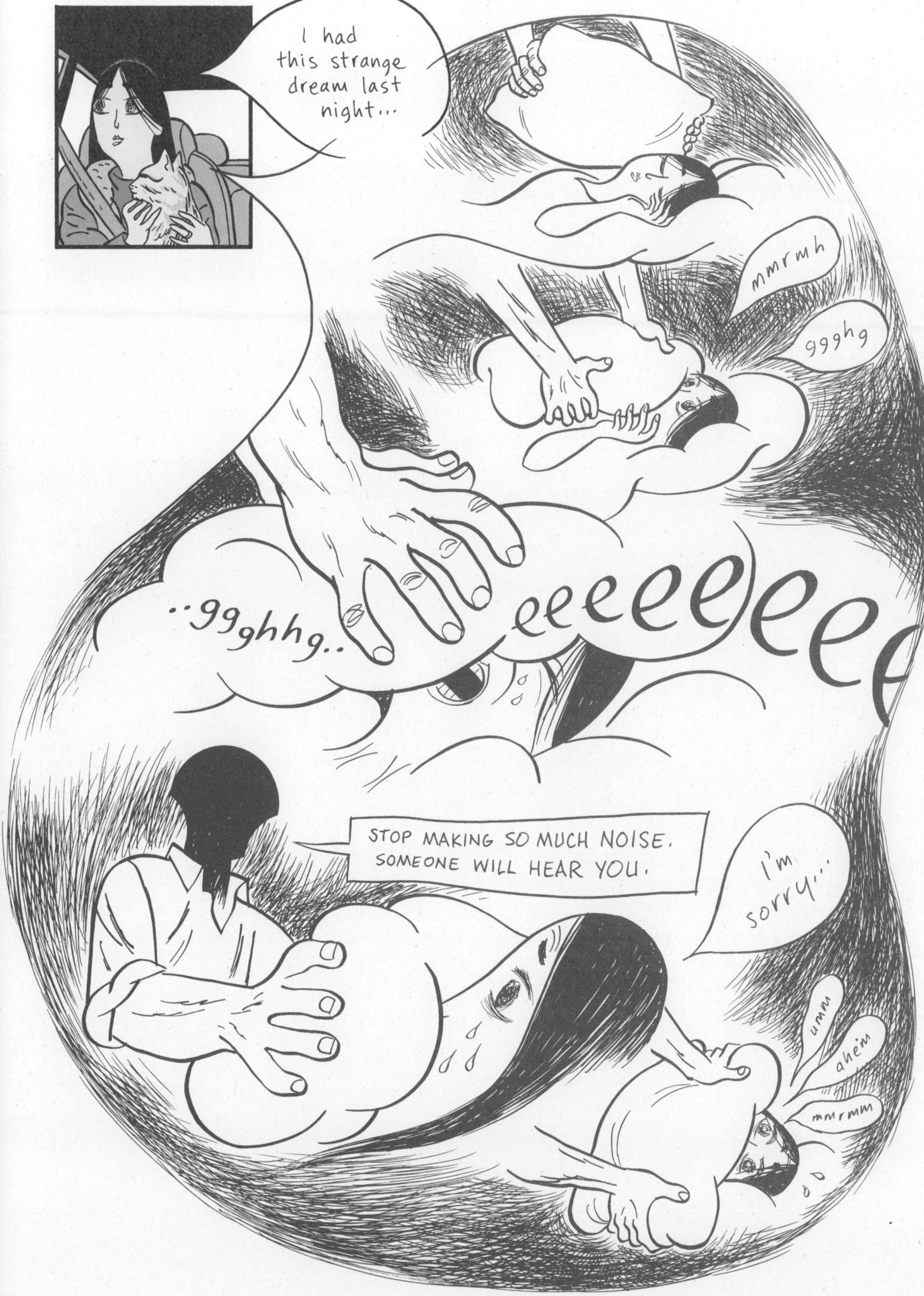
I had this strange dream last night...
mmrmh
ggghg
..gghhg..
eeeeeeee
STOP MAKING SO MUCH NOISE. SOMEONE WILL HEAR YOU.
i'm sorry...
umm
ahem
mmrmm

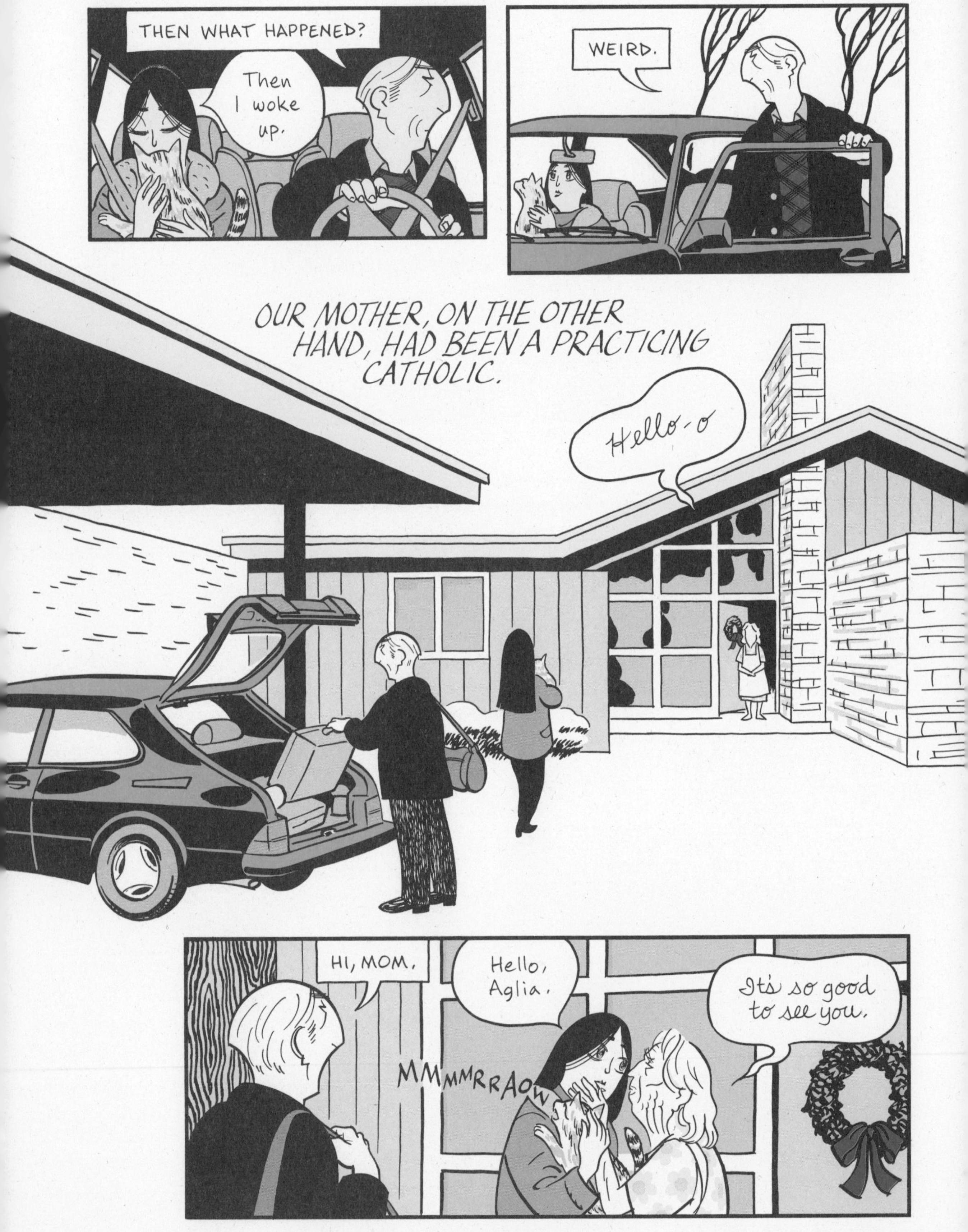
THEN WHAT HAPPENED?
Then I woke up.
WEIRD.
OUR MOTHER, ON THE OTHER HAND, HAD BEEN A PRACTICING CATHOLIC.
Hello-o
HI, MOM.
Hello, Aglia.
It's so good to see you.
MMMMRRAOW

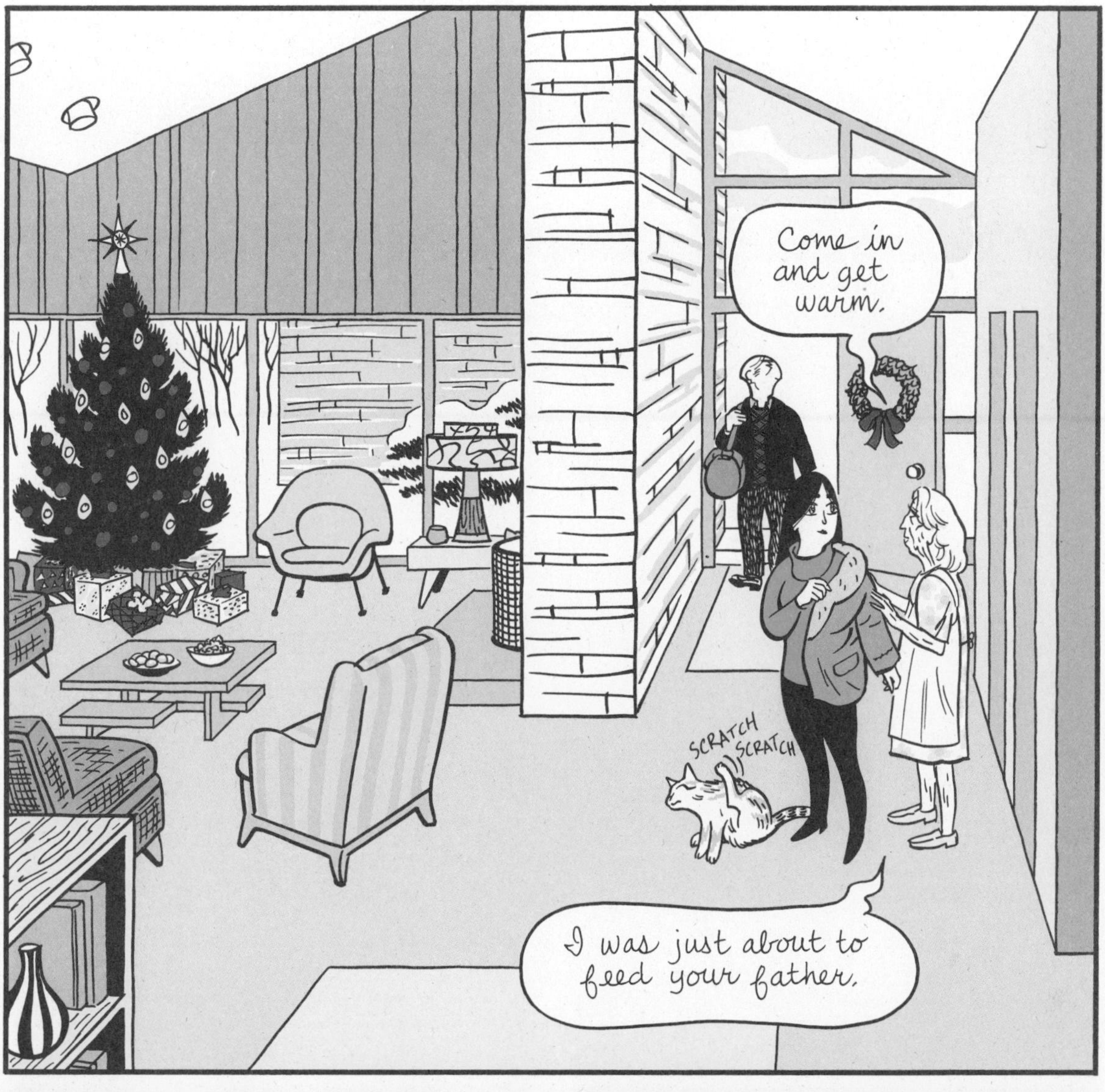
Come in and get warm.
SCRATCH SCRATCH
I was just about to feed your father.

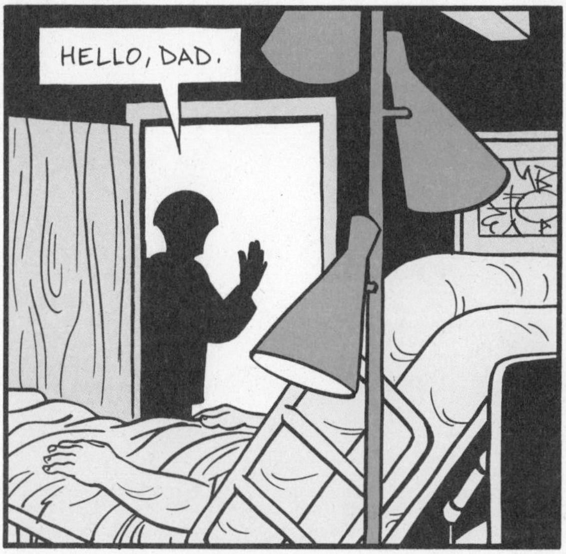
HELLO, DAD.

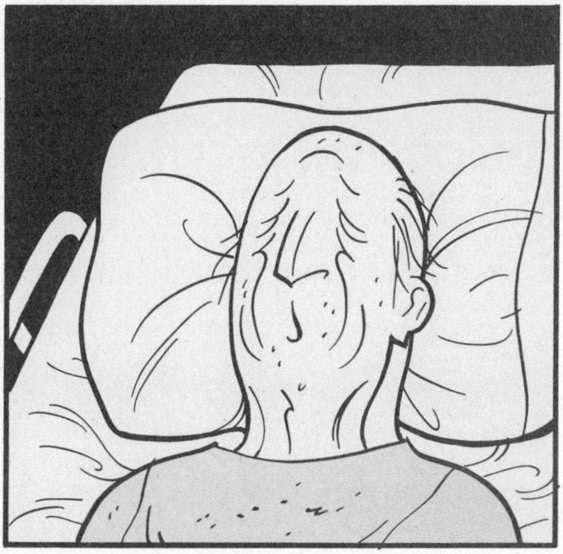

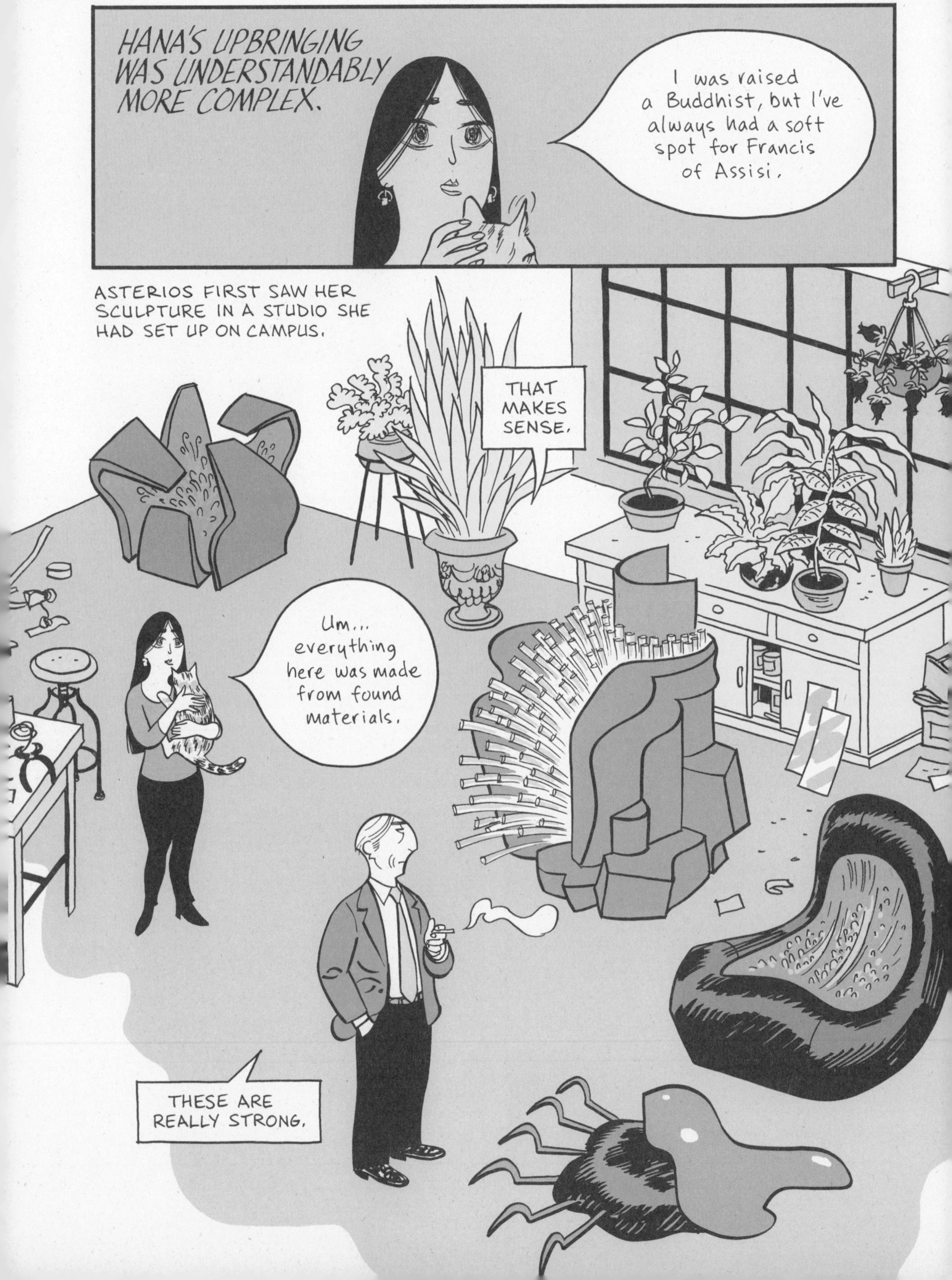
HANA'S UPBRINGING WAS UNDERSTANDABLY MORE COMPLEX.
I was raised a Buddhist, but I've always had a soft spot for Francis of Assisi.
ASTERIOS FIRST SAW HER SCULPTURE IN A STUDIO SHE HAD SET UP ON CAMPUS.
THAT MAKES SENSE.
Um... everything here was made from found materials.
THESE ARE REALLY STRONG.

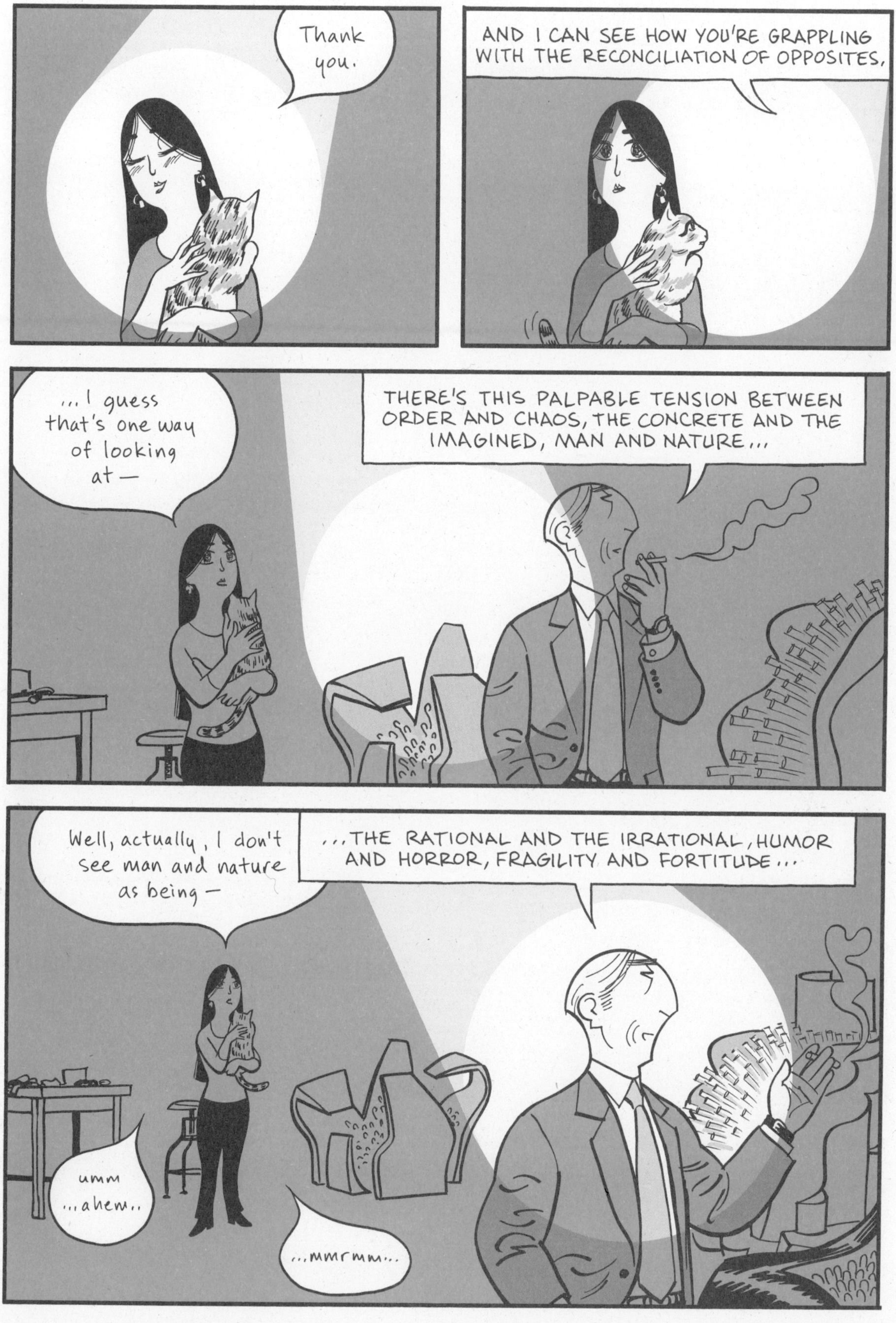
Thank you.
AND I CAN SEE HOW YOU'RE GRAPPLING WITH THE RECONCILIATION OF OPPOSITES,
...I guess that's one way of looking at—
THERE'S THIS PALPABLE TENSION BETWEEN ORDER AND CHAOS, THE CONCRETE AND THE IMAGINED, MAN AND NATURE...
Well, actually, I don't see man and nature as being—
...THE RATIONAL AND THE IRRATIONAL, HUMOR AND HORROR, FRAGILITY AND FORTITUDE...
umm ...ahem..
...mmrmm...

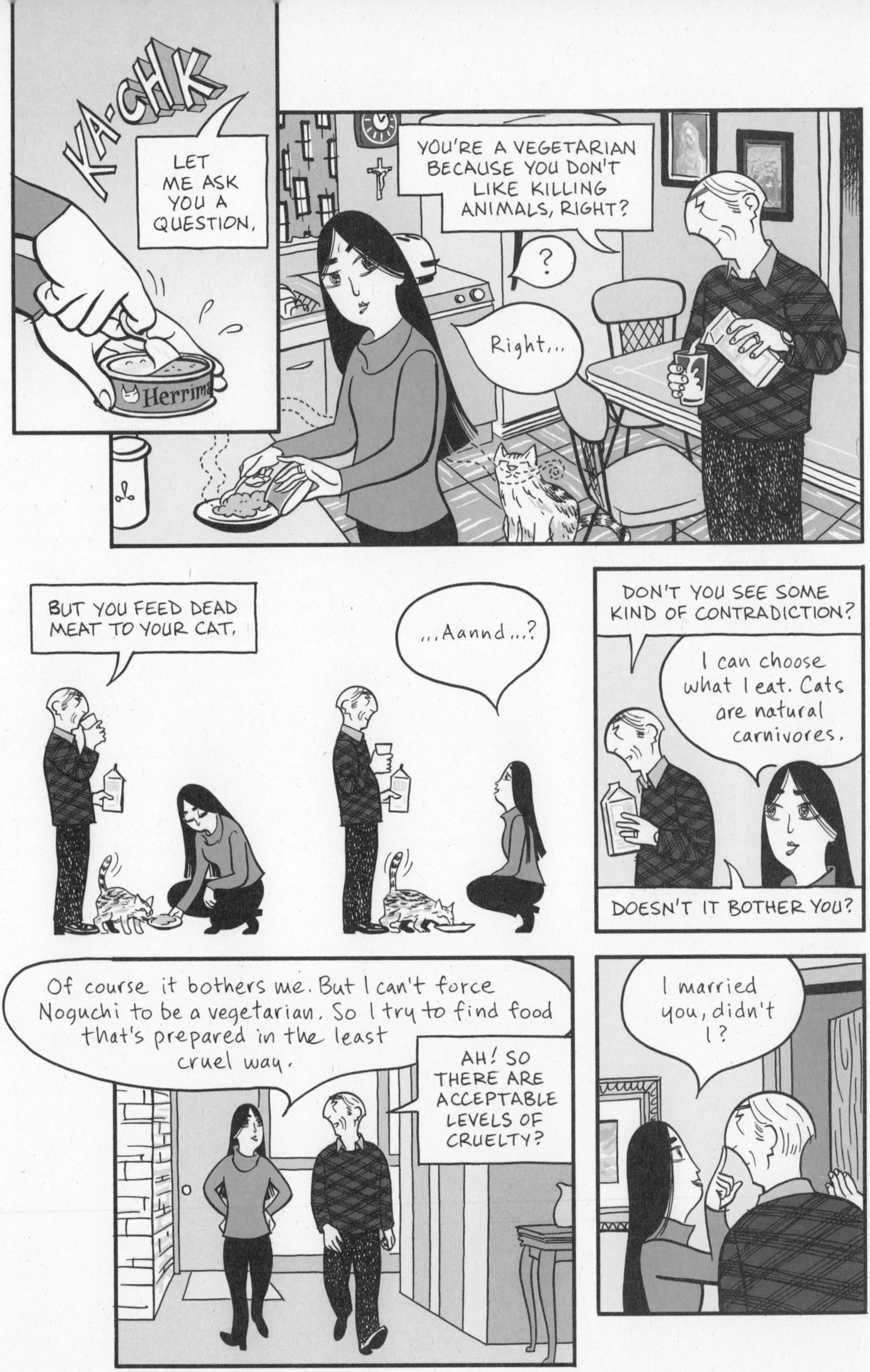
KA-CHK
LET ME ASK YOU A QUESTION.
Herrima
YOU'RE A VEGETARIAN BECAUSE YOU DON'T LIKE KILLING ANIMALS, RIGHT?
?
Right...
BUT YOU FEED DEAD MEAT TO YOUR CAT.
...Aannd...?
DON'T YOU SEE SOME KIND OF CONTRADICTION?
I can choose what I eat. Cats are natural carnivores.
DOESN'T IT BOTHER YOU?
Of course it bothers me. But I can't force Noguchi to be a vegetarian. So I try to find food that's prepared in the least cruel way.
AH! SO THERE ARE ACCEPTABLE LEVELS OF CRUELTY?
I married you, didn't I?

One last bite.

All done.

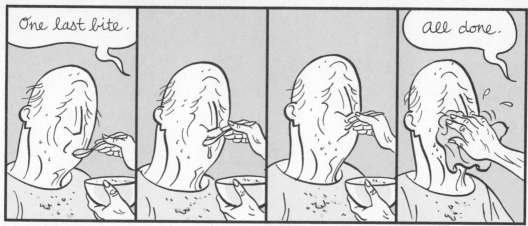

Is there any change?

No. There's never any change.

It must be very stressful.

Life is stressful, dear. That's why they say "rest in peace."

I'll never forget the day Gene had his stroke. Asterios was in school, and I was here at the sink when the phone rang—

YES, YOU'VE TOLD US THIS, MOM.

SEVERAL TIMES.

Well, I'm sorry I don't have any new stories. As you can see, I don't get out much.

But I'm not complaining...

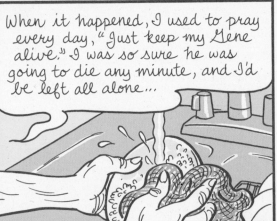

When it happened, I used to pray every day, "Just keep my Gene alive." I was so sure he was going to die any minute, and I'd be left all alone...

But your father didn't die.

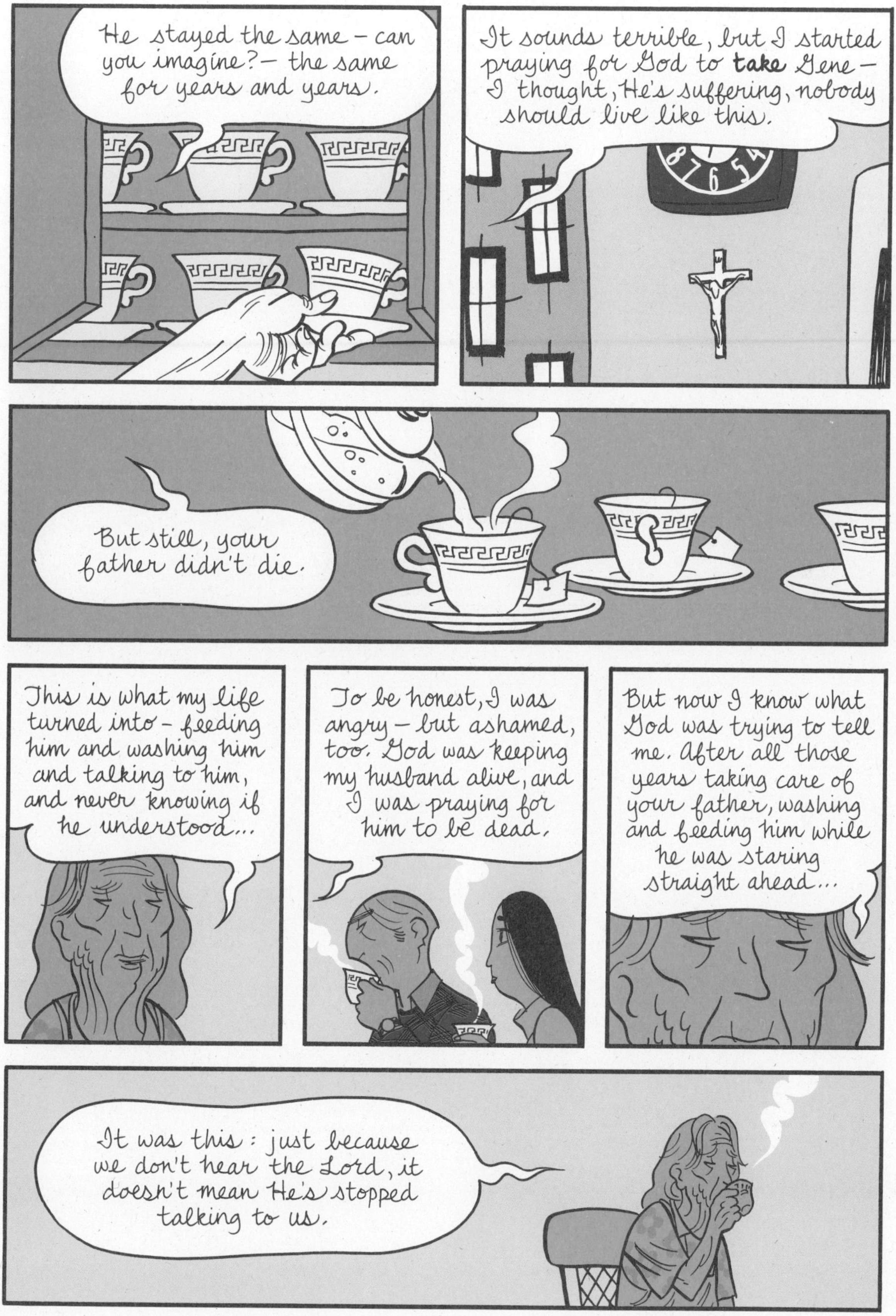
He stayed the same – can you imagine?– the same for years and years.
It sounds terrible, but I started praying for God to **take** Gene– I thought, He's suffering, nobody should live like this.
But still, your father didn't die.
This is what my life turned into– feeding him and washing him and talking to him, and never knowing if he understood...
To be honest, I was angry – but ashamed, too. God was keeping my husband alive, and I was praying for him to be dead.
But now I know what God was trying to tell me. After all those years taking care of your father, washing and feeding him while he was staring straight ahead...
It was this : just because we don't hear the Lord, it doesn't mean He's stopped talking to us.

ASTERIOS, OF COURSE, HAD A DIFFERENT THEORY.

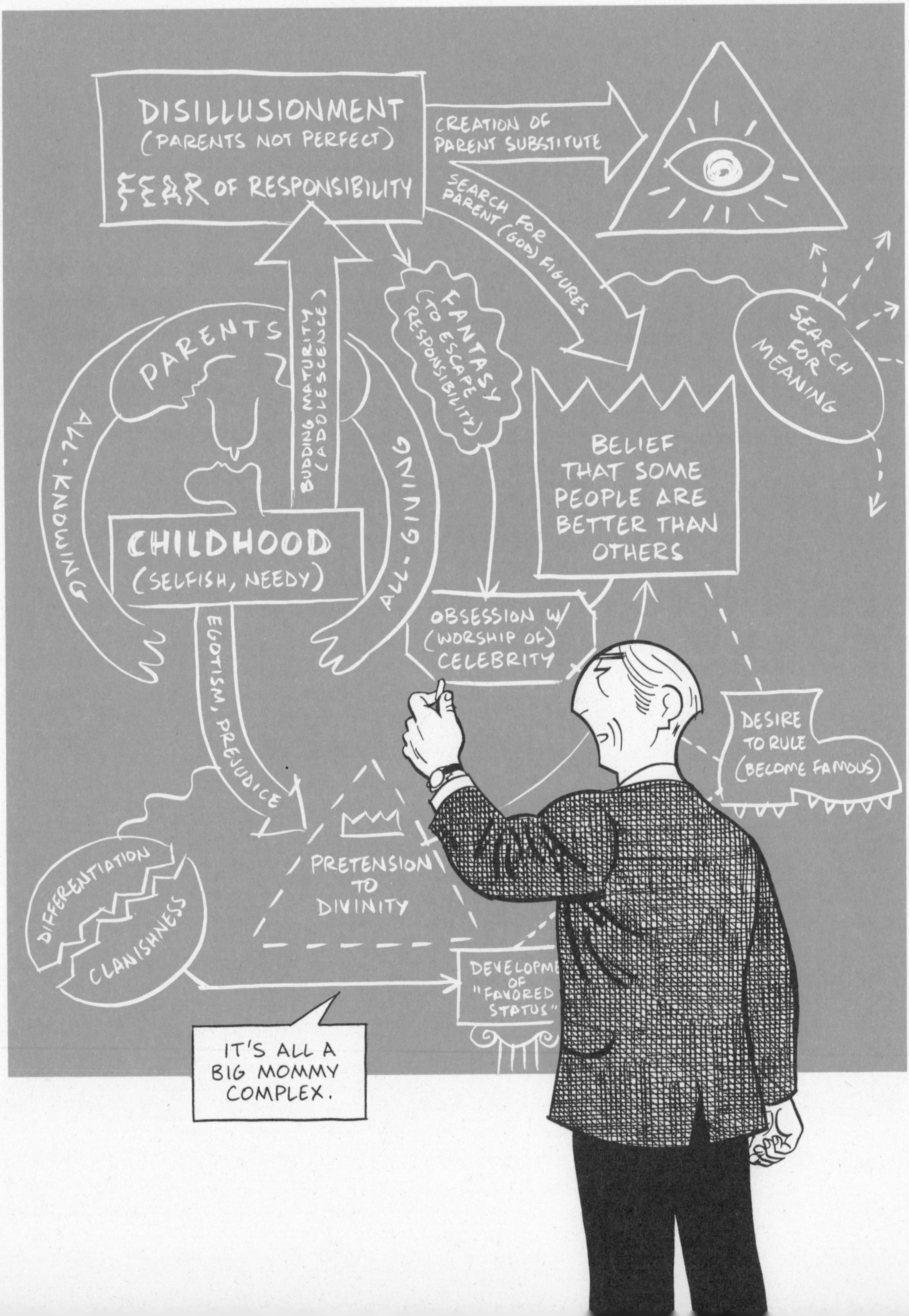
DISILLUSIONMENT (PARENTS NOT PERFECT)
FEAR OF RESPONSIBILITY
CREATION OF PARENT SUBSTITUTE
SEARCH FOR PARENT (GOD) FIGURES
FANTASY (TO ESCAPE RESPONSIBILITY)
BUDDING MATURITY (ADOLESCENCE)
PARENTS
ALL-KNOWING
ALL-GIVING
SEARCH FOR MEANING
BELIEF THAT SOME PEOPLE ARE BETTER THAN OTHERS
CHILDHOOD (SELFISH, NEEDY)
OBSESSION W/ (WORSHIP OF) CELEBRITY
EGOTISM, PREJUDICE
DESIRE TO RULE (BECOME FAMOUS)
PRETENSION TO DIVINITY
DIFFERENTIATION
CLANISHNESS
DEVELOPME OF "FAVORED STATUS"
IT'S ALL A BIG MOMMY COMPLEX.

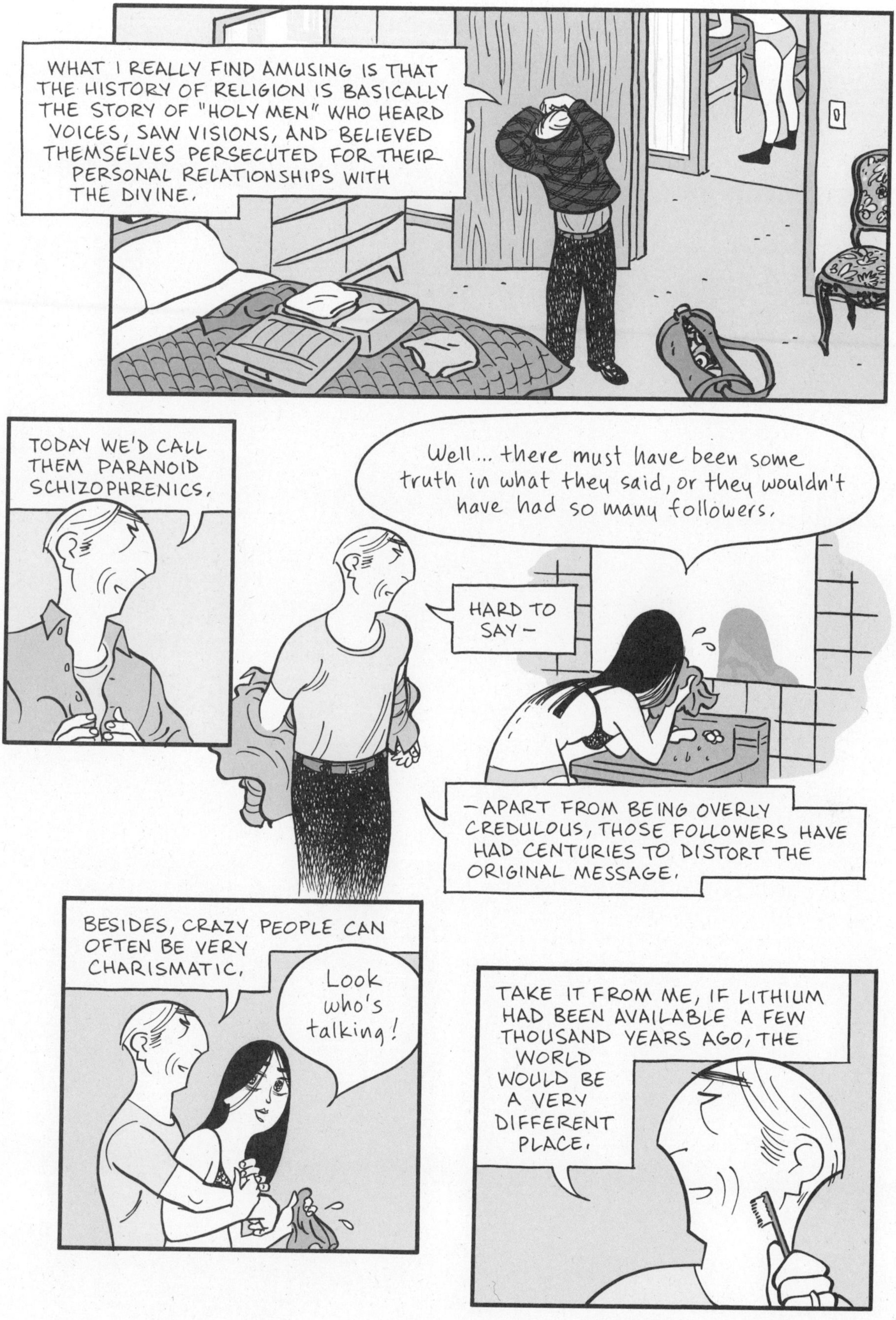
WHAT I REALLY FIND AMUSING IS THAT THE HISTORY OF RELIGION IS BASICALLY THE STORY OF "HOLY MEN" WHO HEARD VOICES, SAW VISIONS, AND BELIEVED THEMSELVES PERSECUTED FOR THEIR PERSONAL RELATIONSHIPS WITH THE DIVINE.
TODAY WE'D CALL THEM PARANOID SCHIZOPHRENICS.
Well... there must have been some truth in what they said, or they wouldn't have had so many followers.
HARD TO SAY—
—APART FROM BEING OVERLY CREDULOUS, THOSE FOLLOWERS HAVE HAD CENTURIES TO DISTORT THE ORIGINAL MESSAGE.
BESIDES, CRAZY PEOPLE CAN OFTEN BE VERY CHARISMATIC.
Look who's talking!
TAKE IT FROM ME, IF LITHIUM HAD BEEN AVAILABLE A FEW THOUSAND YEARS AGO, THE WORLD WOULD BE A VERY DIFFERENT PLACE.

ACCORDING TO HANA, THOUGH, ASTERIOS PRACTICED HIS OWN RITUALS OF DEVOTION.

MONTHS BEFORE THEY WERE MARRIED, SHE MOVED MOST OF HER BELONGINGS INTO HIS APARTMENT.
FOR ME?
It's a tansu.
Kitchen
Books
Shoes +
It's the trunk my parents used to carry their things on the ship from Japan.
IT'S BEAUTIFUL. THANK YOU.
Maybe it could go over there.
WAIT A MINUTE...
...WHAT'S THIS?
Oh – there are so many straight lines in here, I thought this would be a nice change.

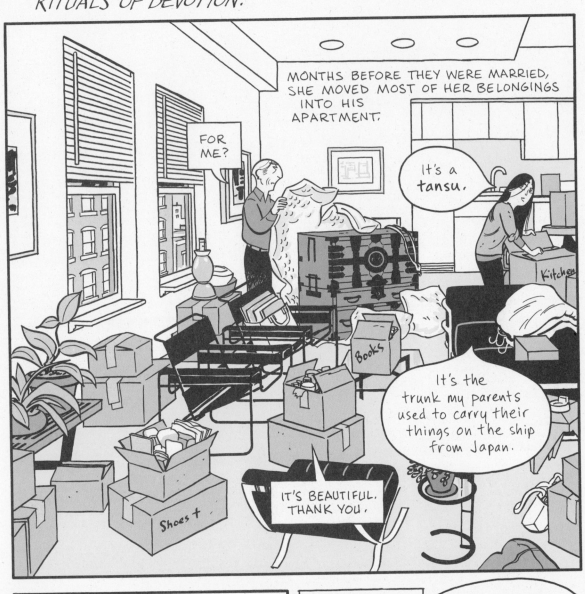

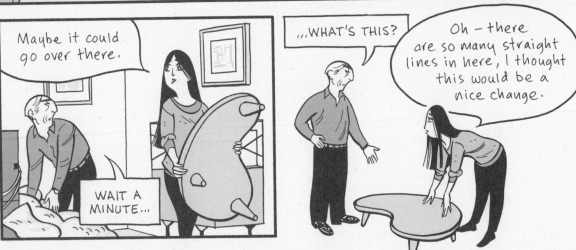

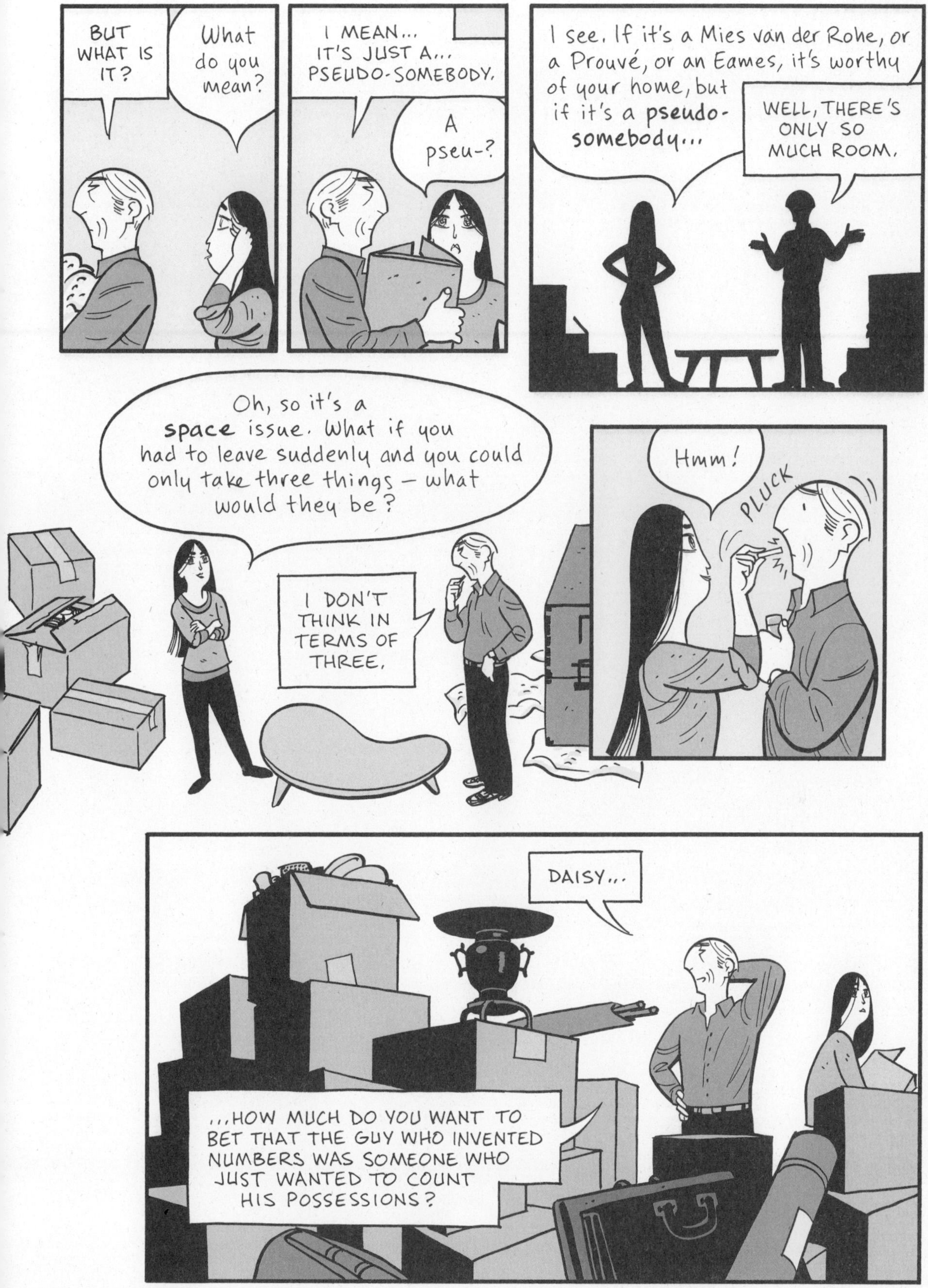
BUT WHAT IS IT?
What do you mean?
I MEAN... IT'S JUST A... PSEUDO-SOMEBODY.
A pseu-?
I see. If it's a Mies van der Rohe, or a Prouvé, or an Eames, it's worthy of your home, but if it's a **pseudo-somebody**...
WELL, THERE'S ONLY SO MUCH ROOM.
Oh, so it's a **space** issue. What if you had to leave suddenly and you could only take three things – what would they be?
I DON'T THINK IN TERMS OF THREE.
Hmm!
PLUCK
DAISY...
...HOW MUCH DO YOU WANT TO BET THAT THE GUY WHO INVENTED NUMBERS WAS SOMEONE WHO JUST WANTED TO COUNT HIS POSSESSIONS?

STILL, DESPITE HIS SKEPTICISM, ASTERIOS IS QUICK TO ADMIT THAT RELIGION ACCOUNTS FOR SOME OF THE MOST BEAUTIFUL WORKS OF ART IN MANKIND'S HISTORY.

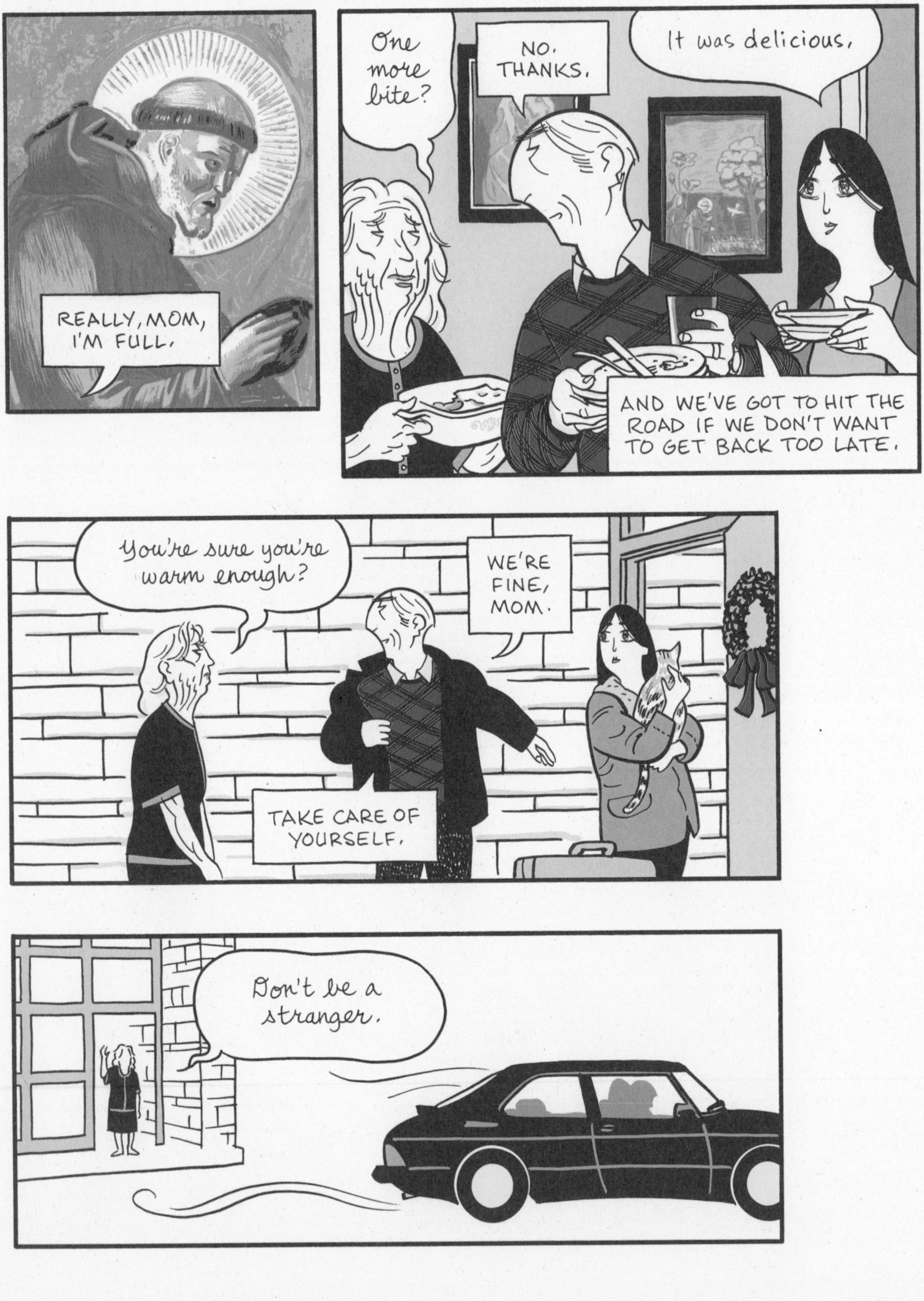
REALLY, MOM, I'M FULL.
One more bite?
NO. THANKS.
It was delicious.
AND WE'VE GOT TO HIT THE ROAD IF WE DON'T WANT TO GET BACK TOO LATE.
You're sure you're warm enough?
WE'RE FINE, MOM.
TAKE CARE OF YOURSELF.
Don't be a stranger.

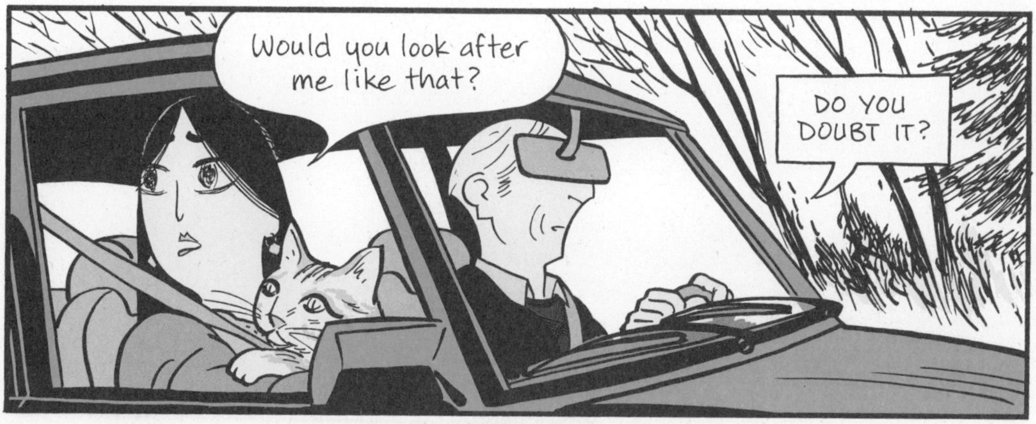
Would you look after me like that?
DO YOU DOUBT IT?

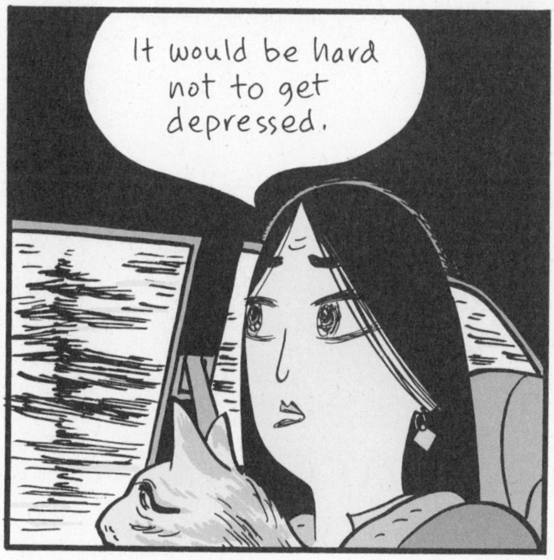
It would be hard not to get depressed.

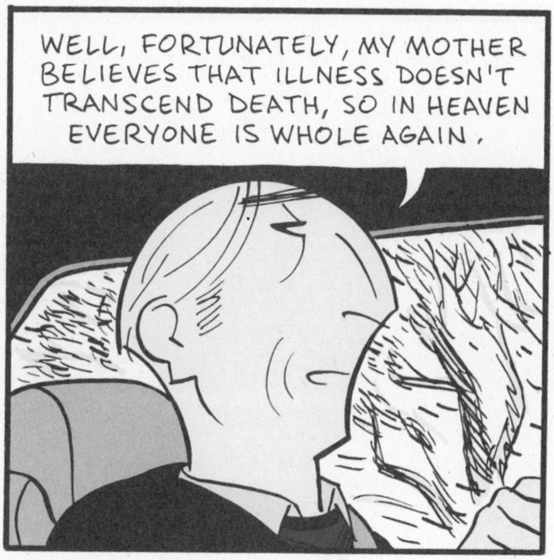
WELL, FORTUNATELY, MY MOTHER BELIEVES THAT ILLNESS DOESN'T TRANSCEND DEATH, SO IN HEAVEN EVERYONE IS WHOLE AGAIN.

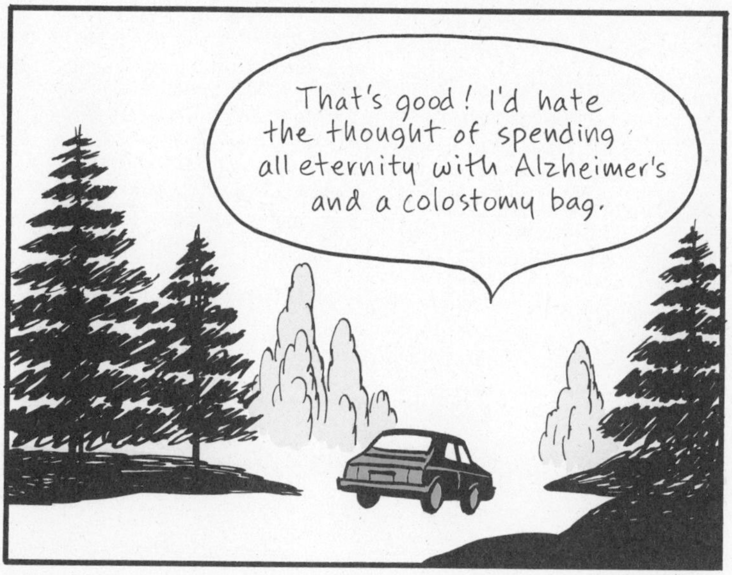
That's good! I'd hate the thought of spending all eternity with Alzheimer's and a colostomy bag.

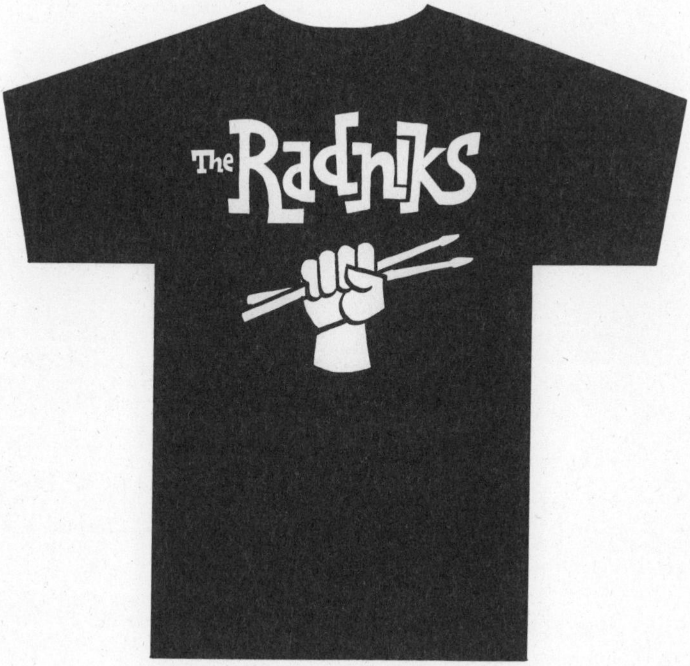
The Radniks

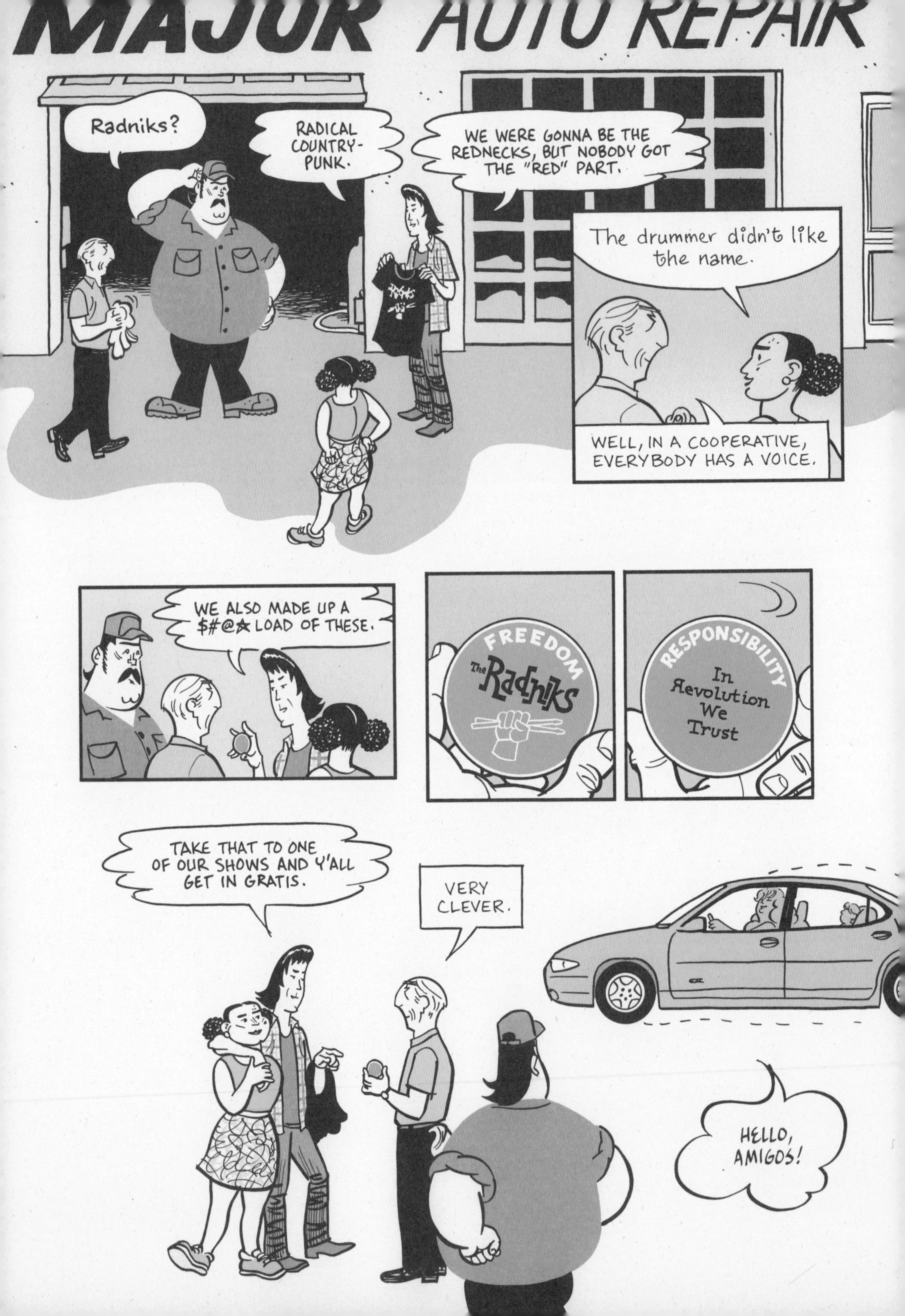
MAJOR AUTO REPAIR
Radniks?
RADICAL COUNTRY-PUNK.
WE WERE GONNA BE THE REDNECKS, BUT NOBODY GOT THE "RED" PART.
The drummer didn't like the name.
WELL, IN A COOPERATIVE, EVERYBODY HAS A VOICE.
WE ALSO MADE UP A $#@★ LOAD OF THESE.
FREEDOM
The Radniks
RESPONSIBILITY
In Revolution We Trust
TAKE THAT TO ONE OF OUR SHOWS AND Y'ALL GET IN GRATIS.
VERY CLEVER.
HELLO, AMIGOS!

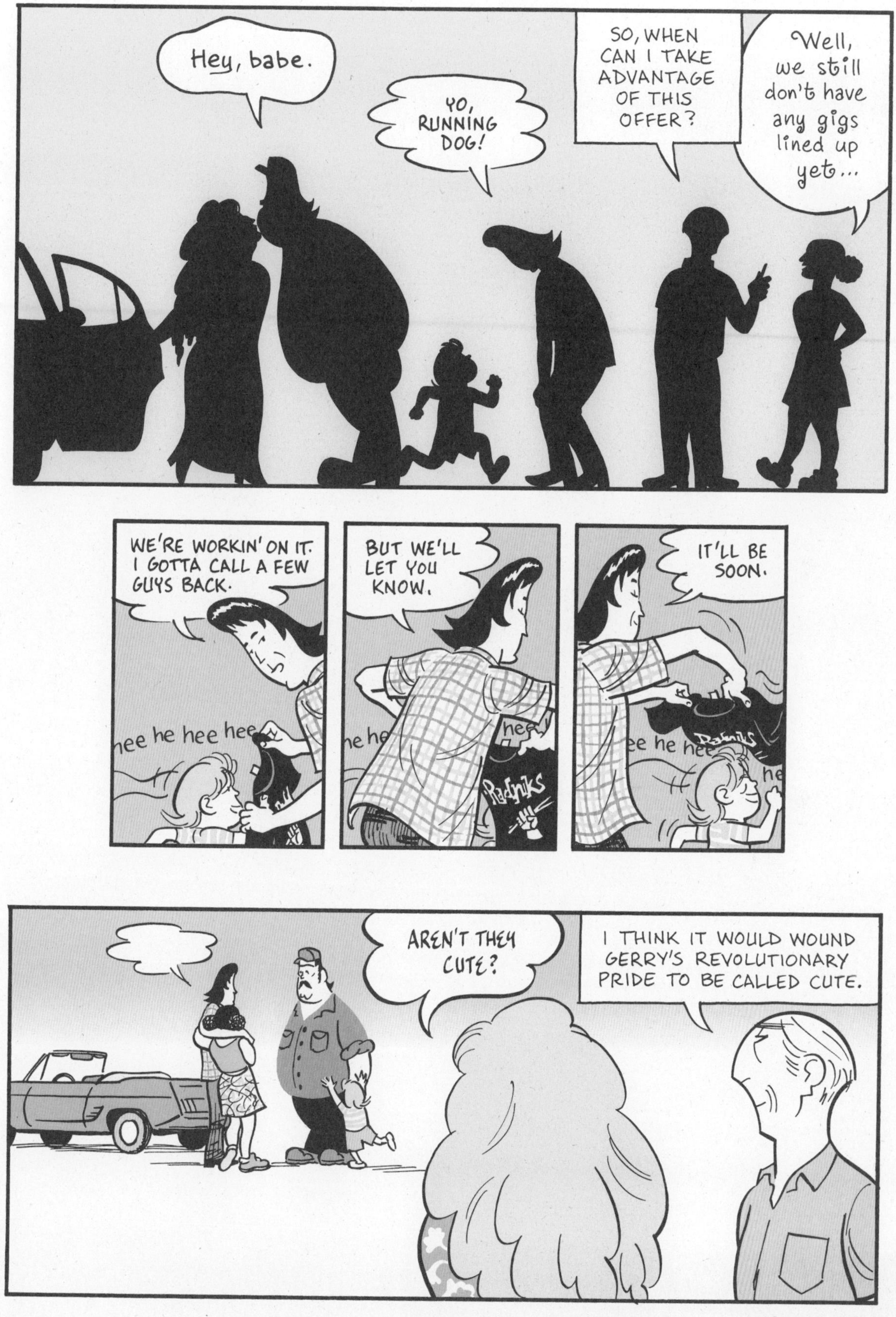
Hey, babe.
YO, RUNNING DOG!
SO, WHEN CAN I TAKE ADVANTAGE OF THIS OFFER?
Well, we still don't have any gigs lined up yet...
WE'RE WORKIN' ON IT. I GOTTA CALL A FEW GUYS BACK.
hee he hee hee
BUT WE'LL LET YOU KNOW.
Radniks
IT'LL BE SOON.
ARE'N'T THEY CUTE?
I THINK IT WOULD WOUND GERRY'S REVOLUTIONARY PRIDE TO BE CALLED CUTE.

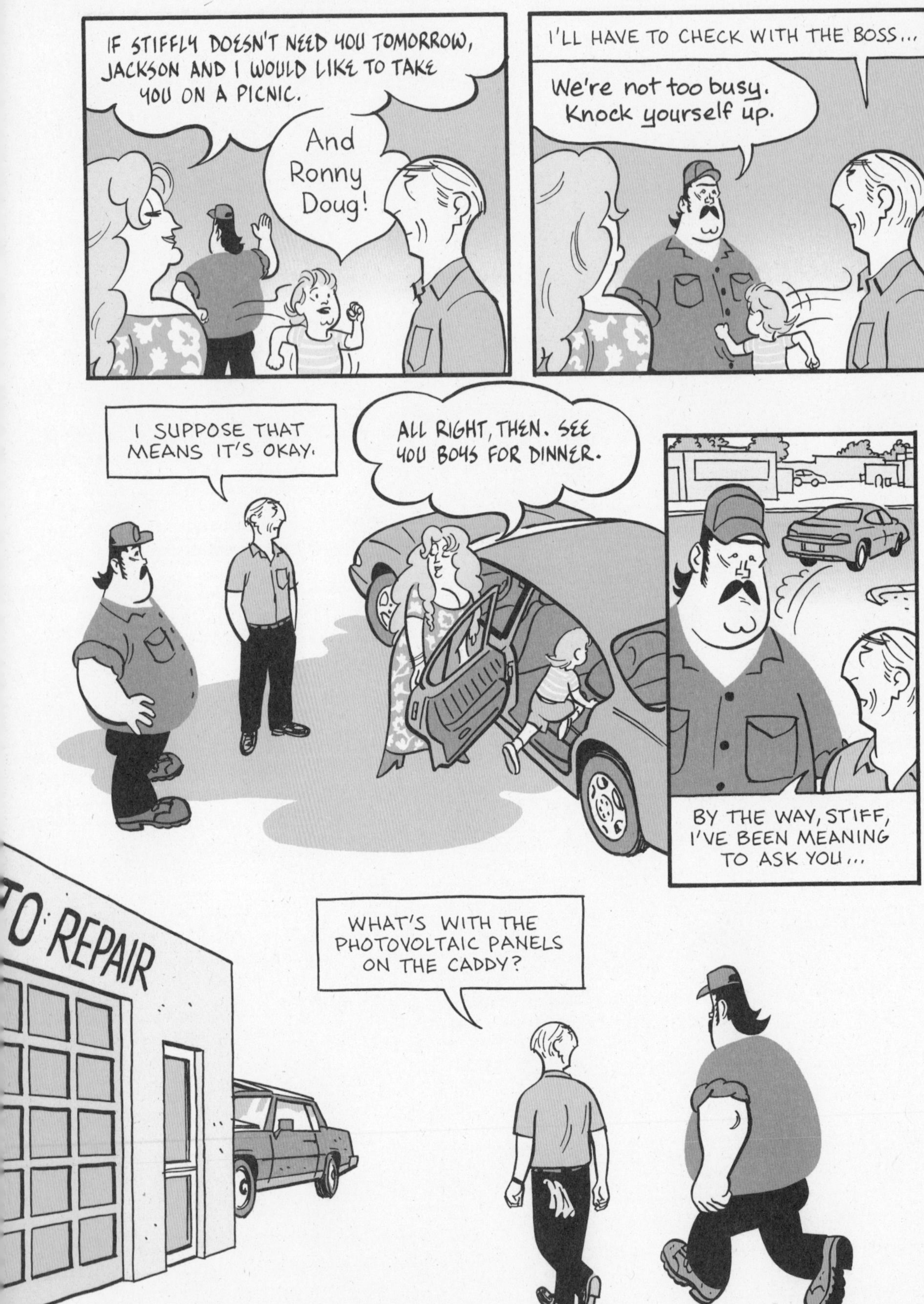
IF STIFFLY DOESN'T NEED YOU TOMORROW, JACKSON AND I WOULD LIKE TO TAKE YOU ON A PICNIC.
And Ronny Doug!
I'LL HAVE TO CHECK WITH THE BOSS...
We're not too busy. Knock yourself up.
I SUPPOSE THAT MEANS IT'S OKAY.
ALL RIGHT, THEN. SEE YOU BOYS FOR DINNER.
BY THE WAY, STIFF, I'VE BEEN MEANING TO ASK YOU...
TO REPAIR
WHAT'S WITH THE PHOTOVOLTAIC PANELS ON THE CADDY?

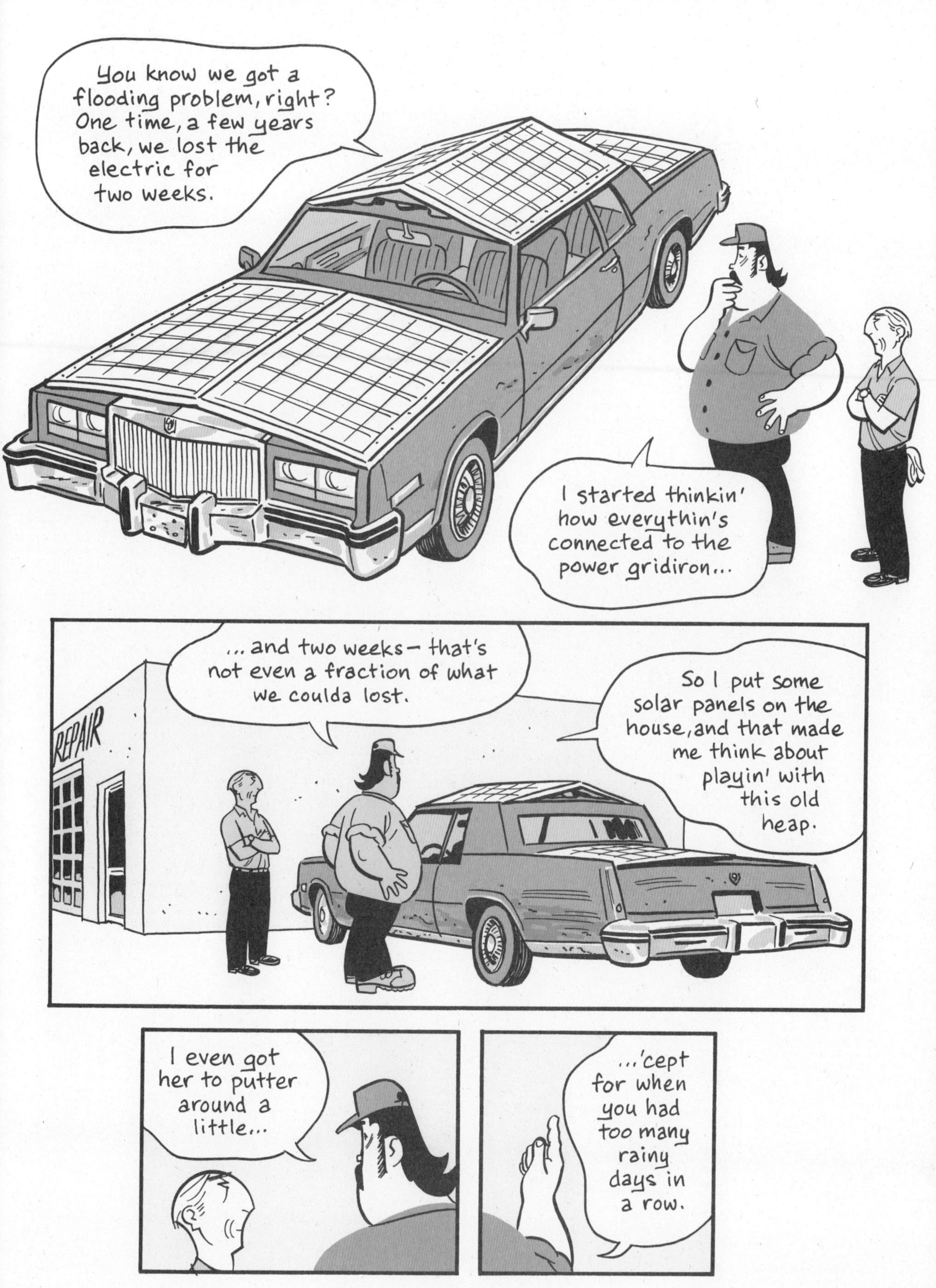
You know we got a flooding problem, right? One time, a few years back, we lost the electric for two weeks.
I started thinkin' how everythin's connected to the power gridiron...
...and two weeks— that's not even a fraction of what we coulda lost.
So I put some solar panels on the house, and that made me think about playin' with this old heap.
REPAIR
I even got her to putter around a little...
...'cept for when you had too many rainy days in a row.

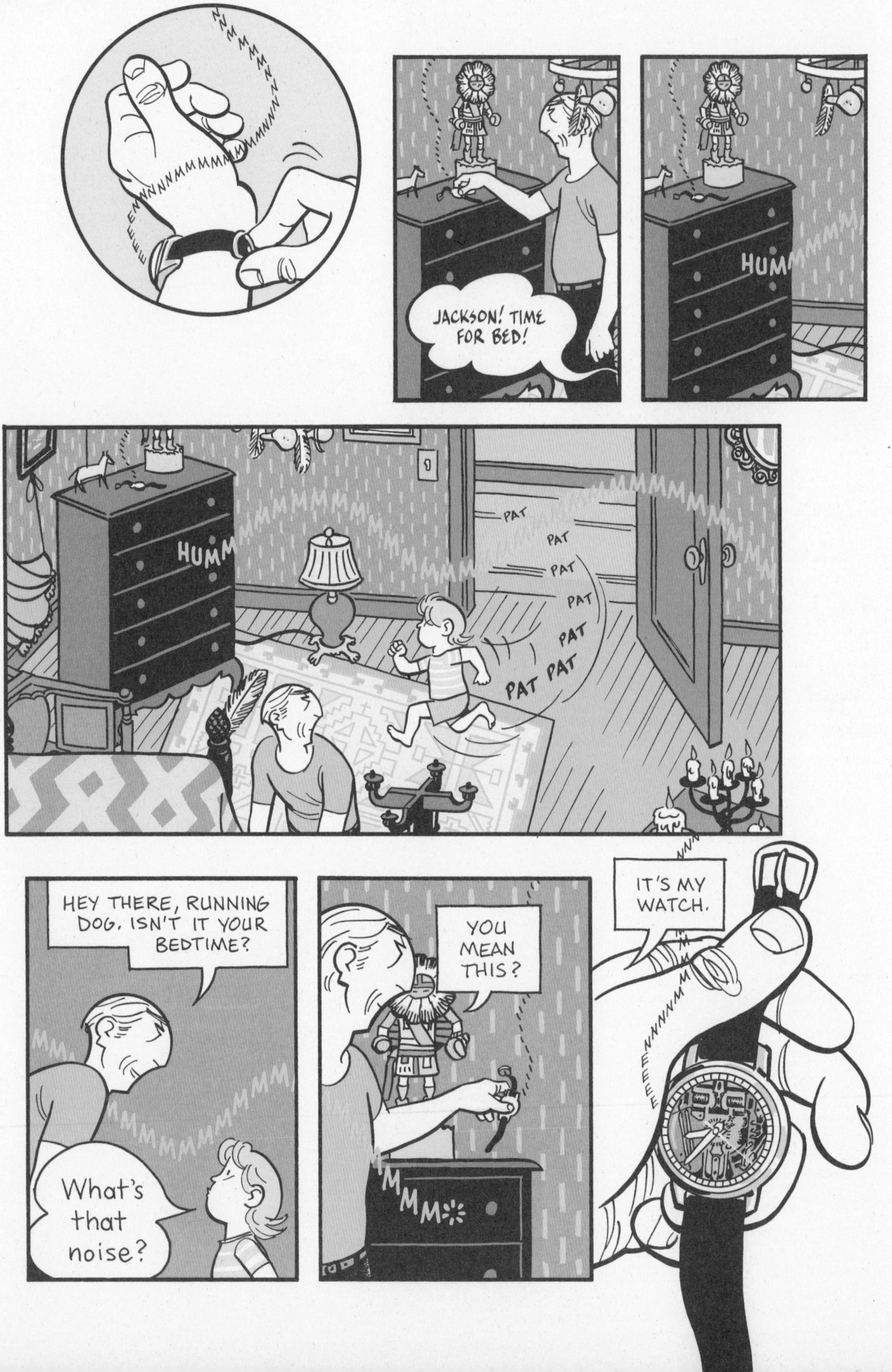
NNMMMNNNNMMMMNNNNMMMMMNNNNNEEEE
JACKSON! TIME FOR BED!
HUMMMMMM
HUMMMMMMMMMMMMMMMMMMMMMMMMMMM
PAT PAT PAT PAT PAT PAT PAT
HEY THERE, RUNNING DOG. ISN'T IT YOUR BEDTIME?
What's that noise?
YOU MEAN THIS?
IT'S MY WATCH.

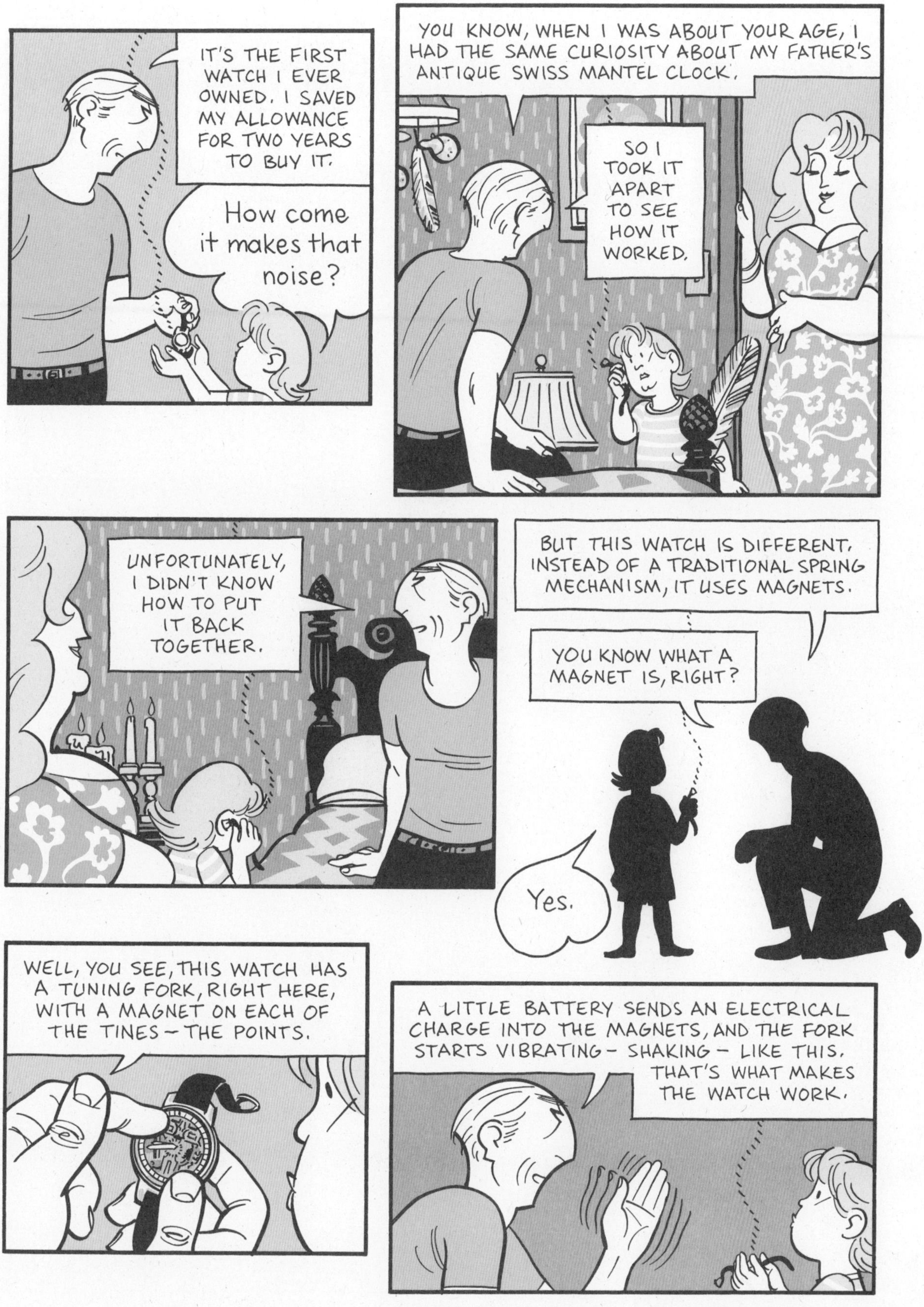
IT'S THE FIRST WATCH I EVER OWNED. I SAVED MY ALLOWANCE FOR TWO YEARS TO BUY IT.
How come it makes that noise?
YOU KNOW, WHEN I WAS ABOUT YOUR AGE, I HAD THE SAME CURIOSITY ABOUT MY FATHER'S ANTIQUE SWISS MANTEL CLOCK.
SO I TOOK IT APART TO SEE HOW IT WORKED.
UNFORTUNATELY, I DIDN'T KNOW HOW TO PUT IT BACK TOGETHER.
BUT THIS WATCH IS DIFFERENT. INSTEAD OF A TRADITIONAL SPRING MECHANISM, IT USES MAGNETS.
YOU KNOW WHAT A MAGNET IS, RIGHT?
Yes.
WELL, YOU SEE, THIS WATCH HAS A TUNING FORK, RIGHT HERE, WITH A MAGNET ON EACH OF THE TINES – THE POINTS.
A LITTLE BATTERY SENDS AN ELECTRICAL CHARGE INTO THE MAGNETS, AND THE FORK STARTS VIBRATING – SHAKING – LIKE THIS.
THAT'S WHAT MAKES THE WATCH WORK.

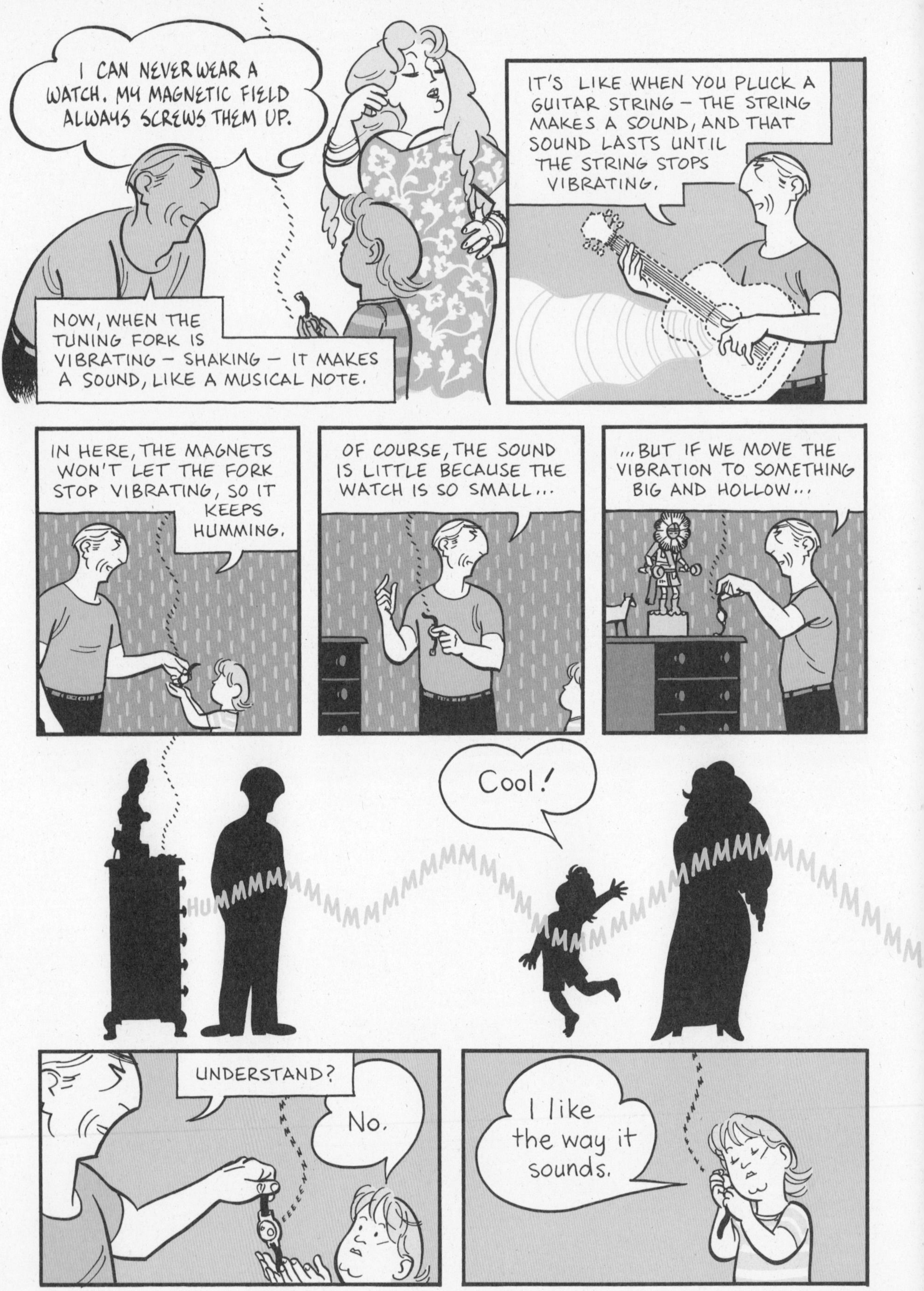
I CAN NEVER WEAR A WATCH. MY MAGNETIC FIELD ALWAYS SCREWS THEM UP.
NOW, WHEN THE TUNING FORK IS VIBRATING – SHAKING – IT MAKES A SOUND, LIKE A MUSICAL NOTE.
IT'S LIKE WHEN YOU PLUCK A GUITAR STRING – THE STRING MAKES A SOUND, AND THAT SOUND LASTS UNTIL THE STRING STOPS VIBRATING.
IN HERE, THE MAGNETS WON'T LET THE FORK STOP VIBRATING, SO IT KEEPS HUMMING.
OF COURSE, THE SOUND IS LITTLE BECAUSE THE WATCH IS SO SMALL...
...BUT IF WE MOVE THE VIBRATION TO SOMETHING BIG AND HOLLOW...
Cool!
HUMMMMMMMMMMMMMMMMMMMMMMMMMMMMMMMMMMMMMMMMMMMMMMMMMMM
UNDERSTAND?
No.
I like the way it sounds.

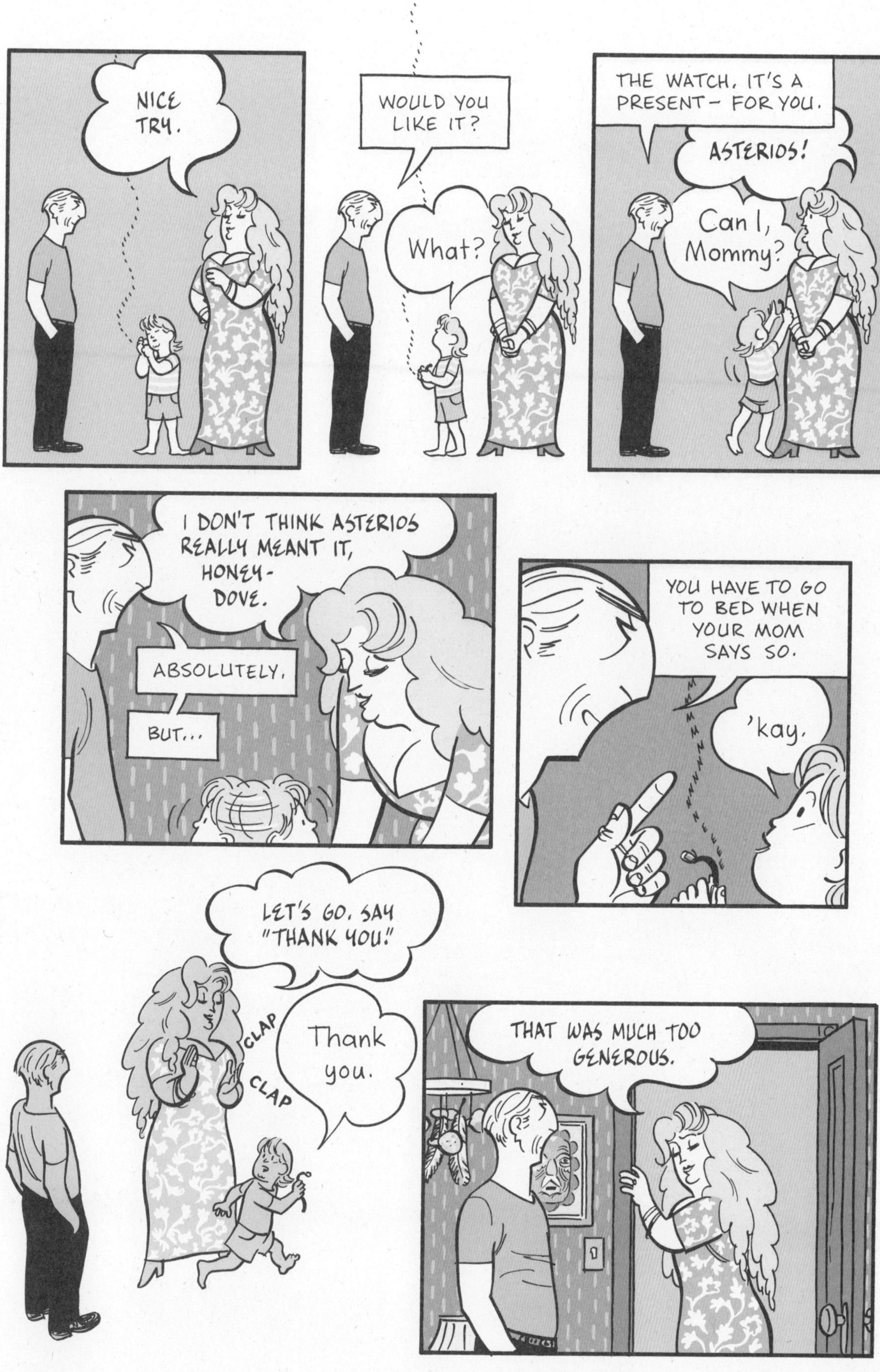

NICE TRY.
WOULD YOU LIKE IT?
What?
THE WATCH. IT'S A PRESENT– FOR YOU.
ASTERIOS!
Can I, Mommy?
I DON'T THINK ASTERIOS REALLY MEANT IT, HONEY-DOVE.
ABSOLUTELY.
BUT...
YOU HAVE TO GO TO BED WHEN YOUR MOM SAYS SO.
'kay.
LET'S GO. SAY "THANK YOU."
CLAP
CLAP
Thank you.
THAT WAS MUCH TOO GENEROUS.

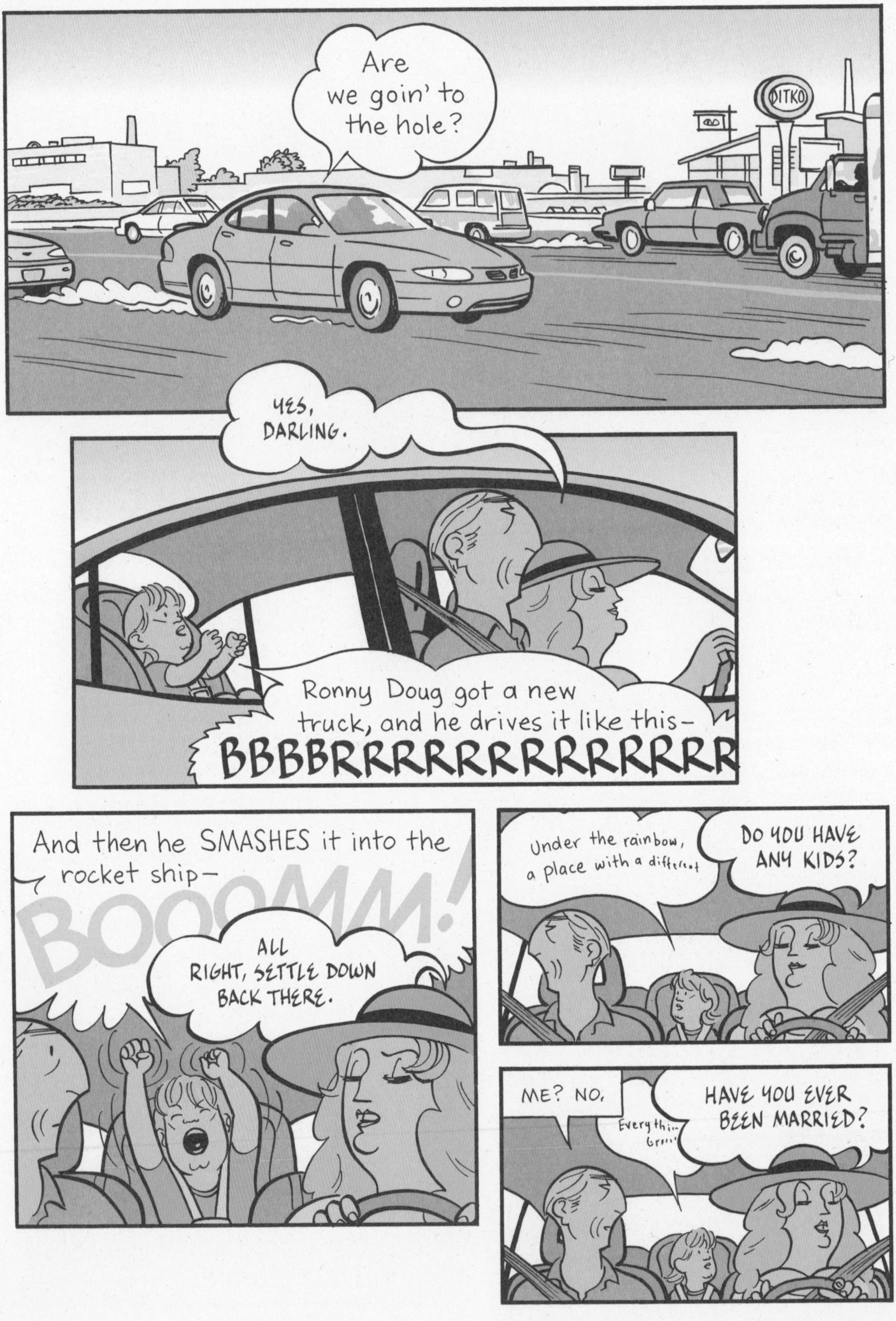

Are we goin' to the hole?
DITKO
YES, DARLING.
Ronny Doug got a new truck, and he drives it like this–
BBBBRRRRRRRRRRRRR
And then he SMASHES it into the rocket ship–
BOOOMM!
ALL RIGHT, SETTLE DOWN BACK THERE.
Under the rainbow, a place with a different
DO YOU HAVE ANY KIDS?
ME? NO.
Everythi–
HAVE YOU EVER BEEN MARRIED?

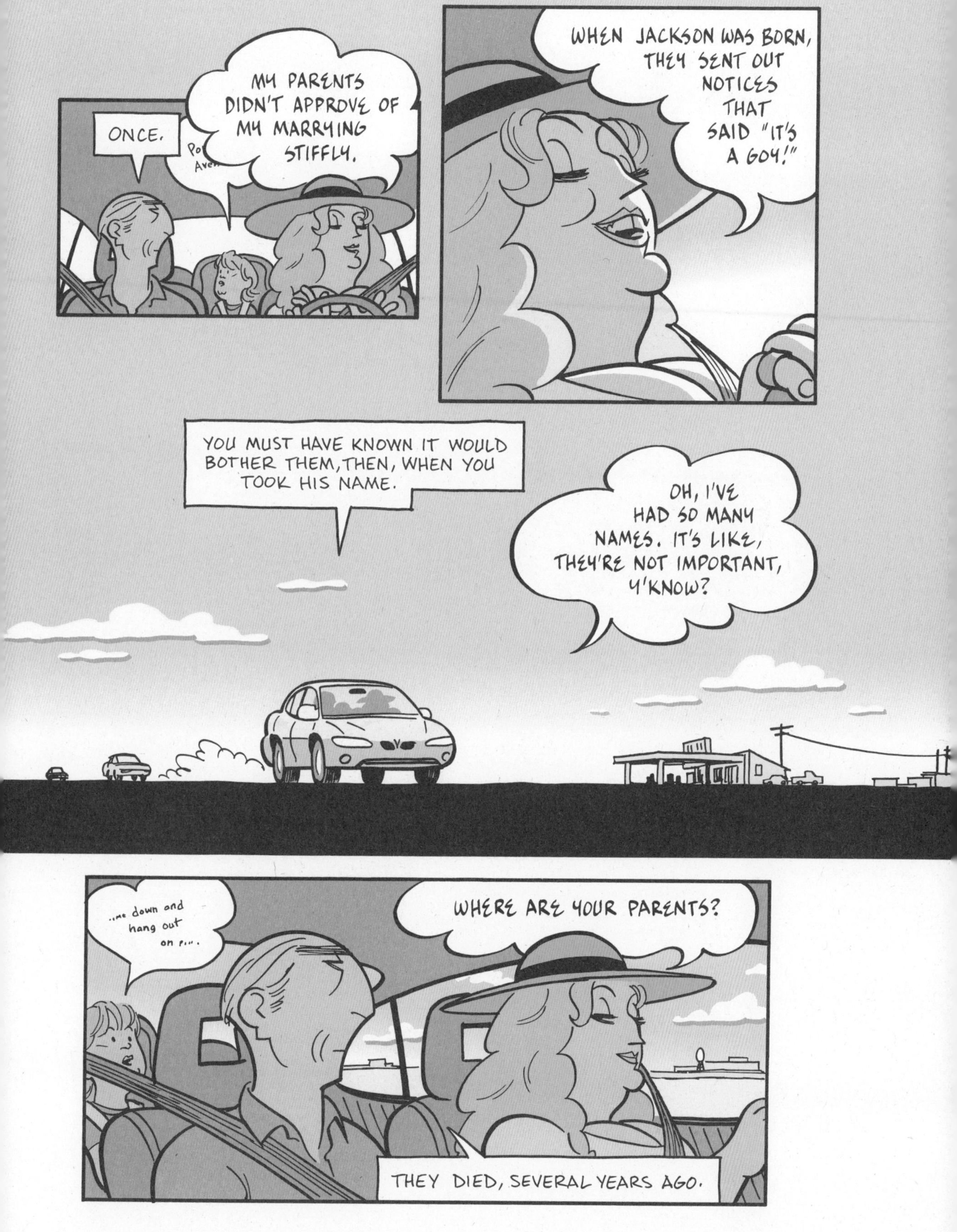
ONCE.
MY PARENTS DIDN'T APPROVE OF MY MARRYING STIFFLY.
WHEN JACKSON WAS BORN, THEY SENT OUT NOTICES THAT SAID "IT'S A GOY!"
YOU MUST HAVE KNOWN IT WOULD BOTHER THEM, THEN, WHEN YOU TOOK HIS NAME.
OH, I'VE HAD SO MANY NAMES. IT'S LIKE, THEY'RE NOT IMPORTANT, Y'KNOW?
..me down and hang out on r...
WHERE ARE YOUR PARENTS?
THEY DIED, SEVERAL YEARS AGO.

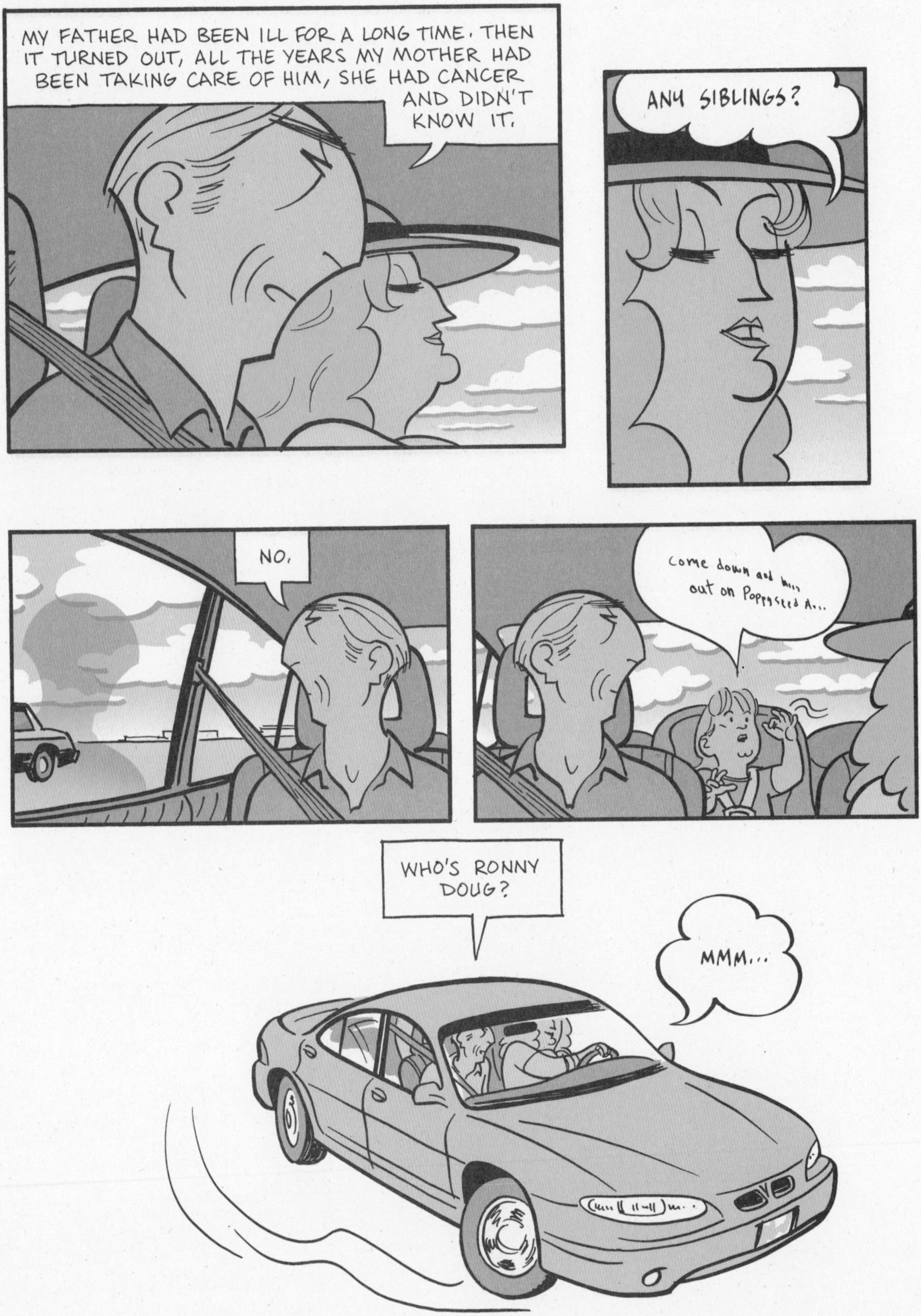
MY FATHER HAD BEEN ILL FOR A LONG TIME. THEN IT TURNED OUT, ALL THE YEARS MY MOTHER HAD BEEN TAKING CARE OF HIM, SHE HAD CANCER AND DIDN'T KNOW IT.
ANY SIBLINGS?
NO.
come down and
out on Poppyseed A...
WHO'S RONNY DOUG?
MMM...

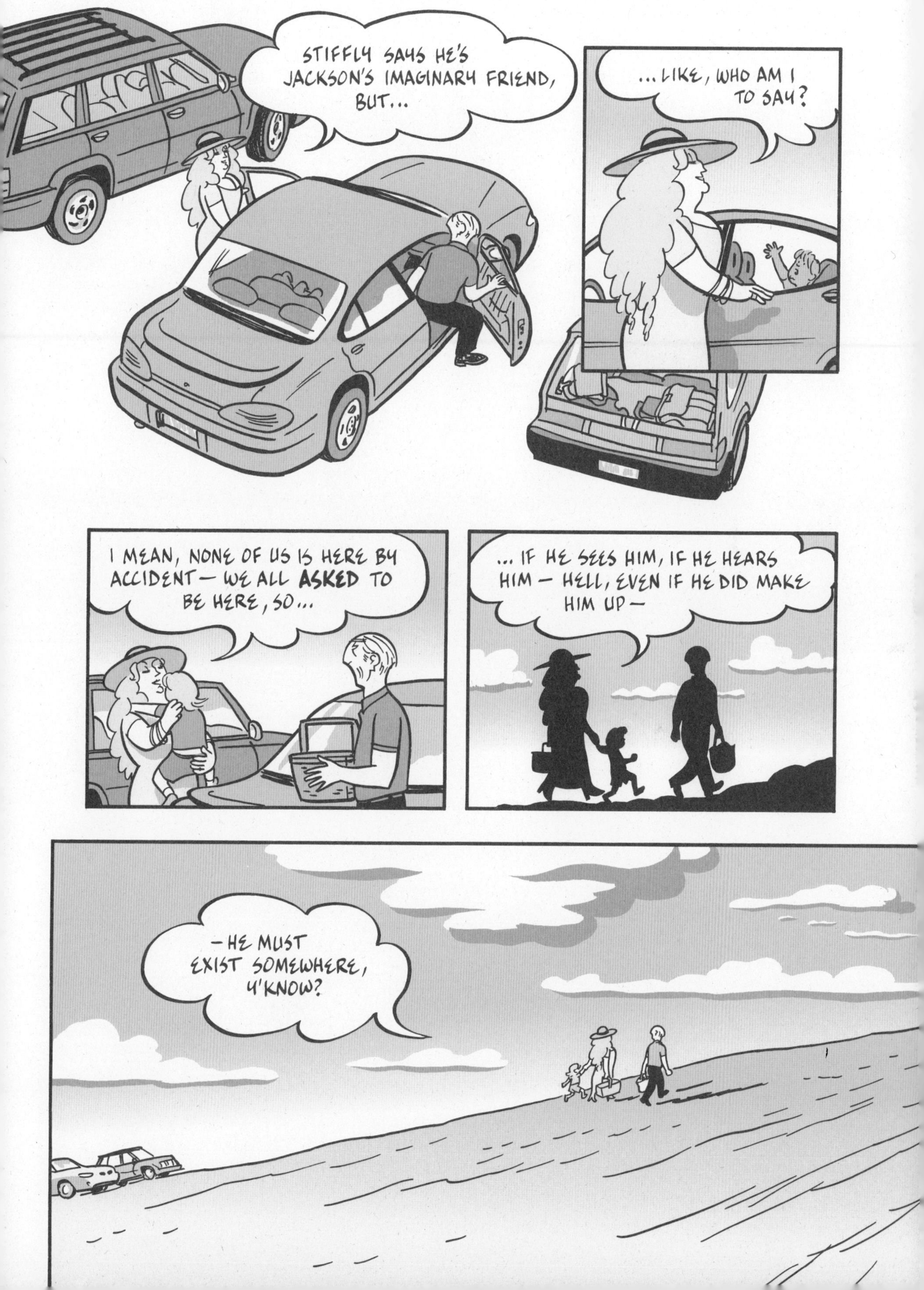
STIFFLY SAYS HE'S JACKSON'S IMAGINARY FRIEND, BUT...
...LIKE, WHO AM I TO SAY?
I MEAN, NONE OF US IS HERE BY ACCIDENT— WE ALL **ASKED** TO BE HERE, SO...
...IF HE SEES HIM, IF HE HEARS HIM — HELL, EVEN IF HE DID MAKE HIM UP—
—HE MUST EXIST SOMEWHERE, Y'KNOW?

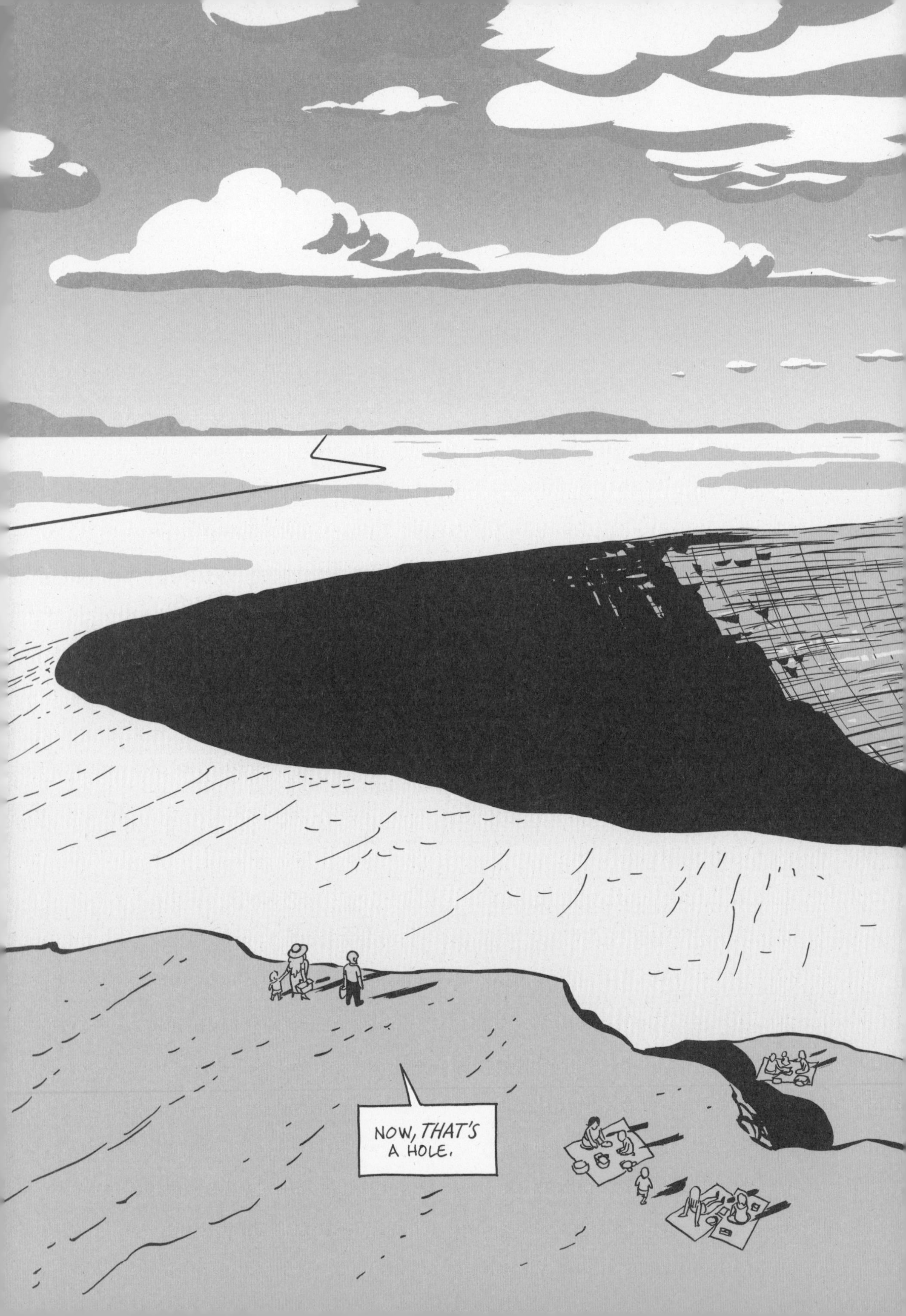
NOW, THAT'S A HOLE.

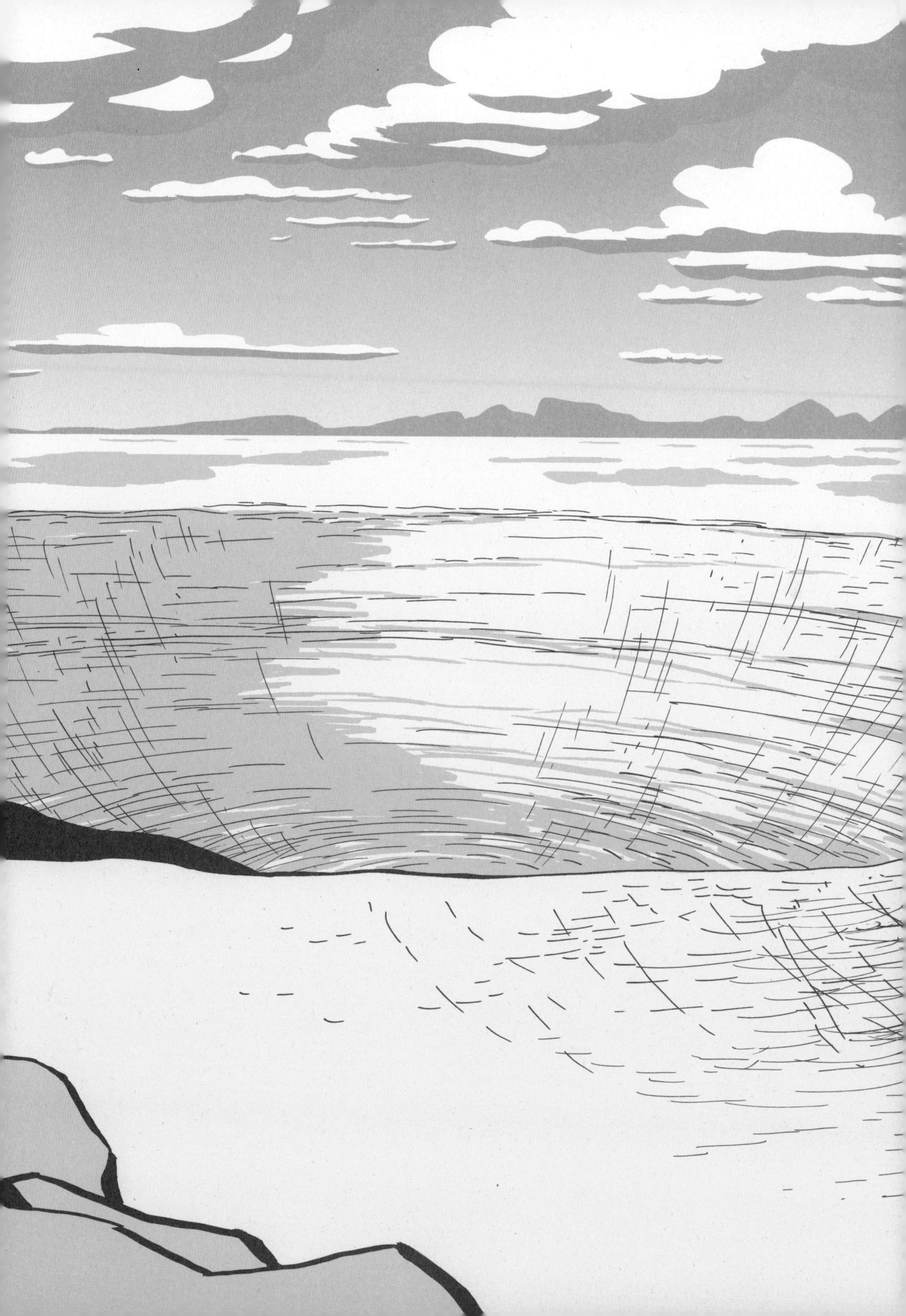

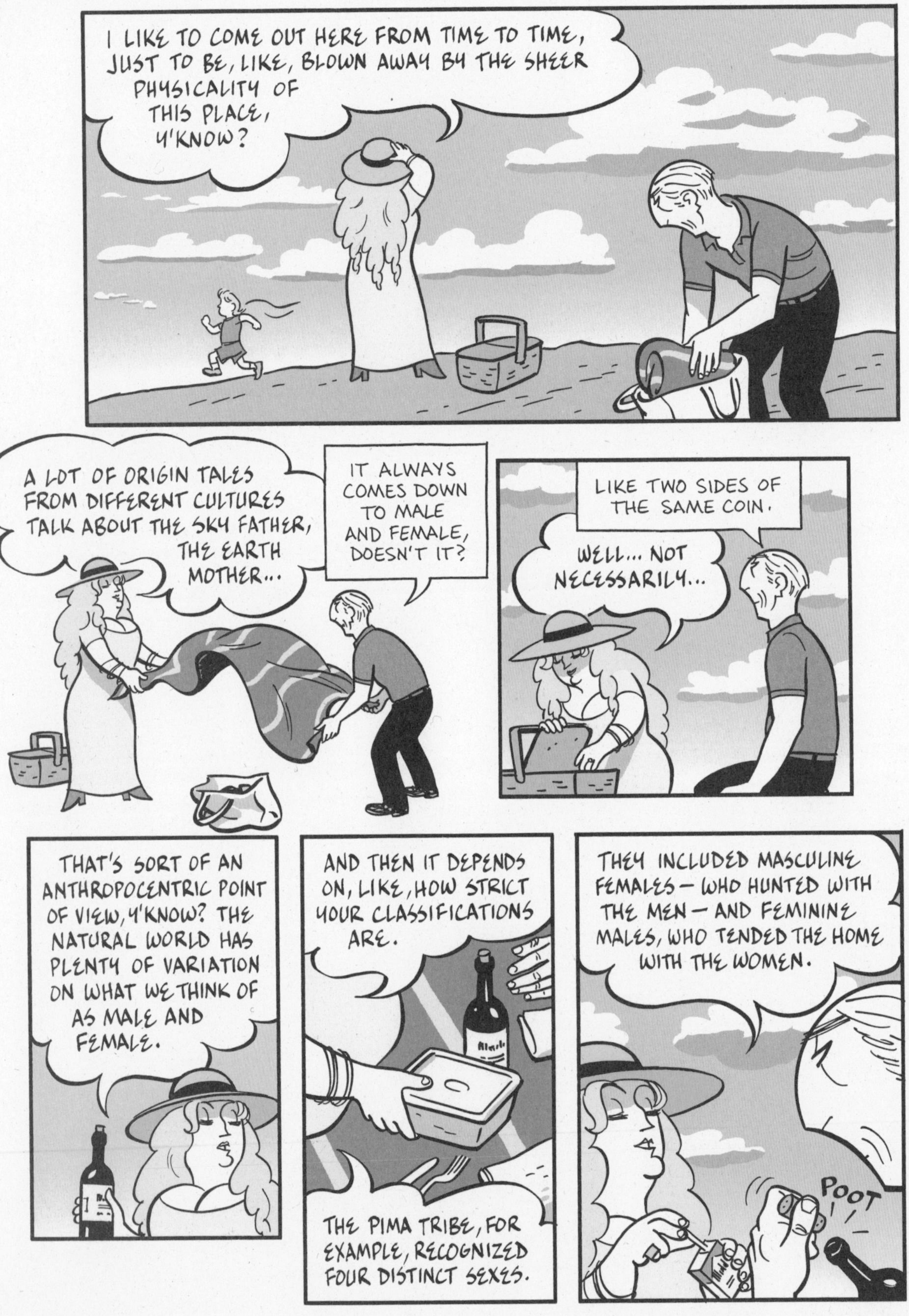
I LIKE TO COME OUT HERE FROM TIME TO TIME, JUST TO BE, LIKE, BLOWN AWAY BY THE SHEER PHYSICALITY OF THIS PLACE, Y'KNOW?
A LOT OF ORIGIN TALES FROM DIFFERENT CULTURES TALK ABOUT THE SKY FATHER, THE EARTH MOTHER...
IT ALWAYS COMES DOWN TO MALE AND FEMALE, DOESN'T IT?
LIKE TWO SIDES OF THE SAME COIN.
WELL... NOT NECESSARILY...
THAT'S SORT OF AN ANTHROPOCENTRIC POINT OF VIEW, Y'KNOW? THE NATURAL WORLD HAS PLENTY OF VARIATION ON WHAT WE THINK OF AS MALE AND FEMALE.
AND THEN IT DEPENDS ON, LIKE, HOW STRICT YOUR CLASSIFICATIONS ARE.
THE PIMA TRIBE, FOR EXAMPLE, RECOGNIZED FOUR DISTINCT SEXES.
THEY INCLUDED MASCULINE FEMALES — WHO HUNTED WITH THE MEN — AND FEMININE MALES, WHO TENDED THE HOME WITH THE WOMEN.
POOT

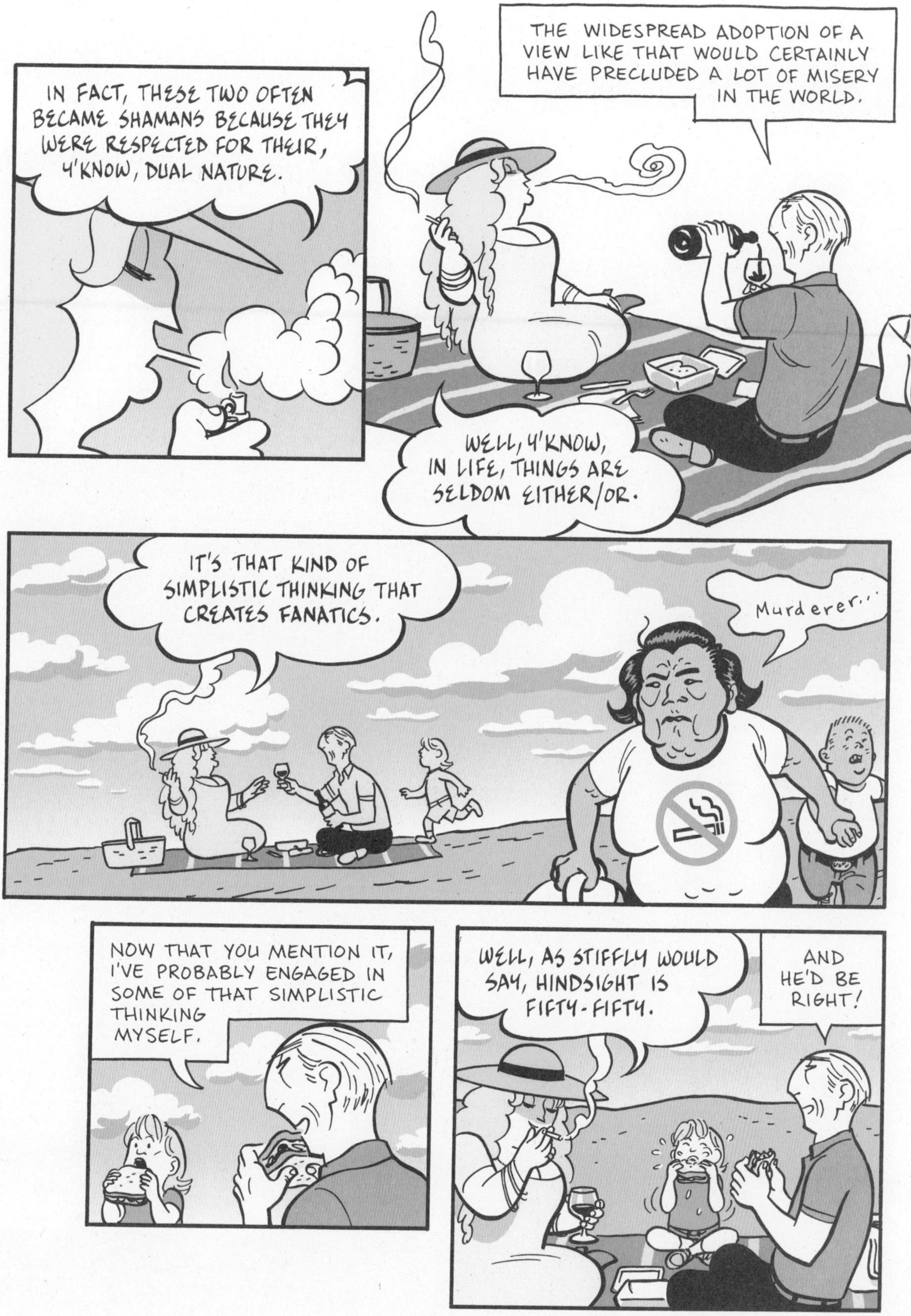
IN FACT, THESE TWO OFTEN BECAME SHAMANS BECAUSE THEY WERE RESPECTED FOR THEIR, Y'KNOW, DUAL NATURE.
THE WIDESPREAD ADOPTION OF A VIEW LIKE THAT WOULD CERTAINLY HAVE PRECLUDED A LOT OF MISERY IN THE WORLD.
WELL, Y'KNOW, IN LIFE, THINGS ARE SELDOM EITHER/OR.
IT'S THAT KIND OF SIMPLISTIC THINKING THAT CREATES FANATICS.
Murderer...
NOW THAT YOU MENTION IT, I'VE PROBABLY ENGAGED IN SOME OF THAT SIMPLISTIC THINKING MYSELF.
WELL, AS STIFFLY WOULD SAY, HINDSIGHT IS FIFTY-FIFTY.
AND HE'D BE RIGHT!

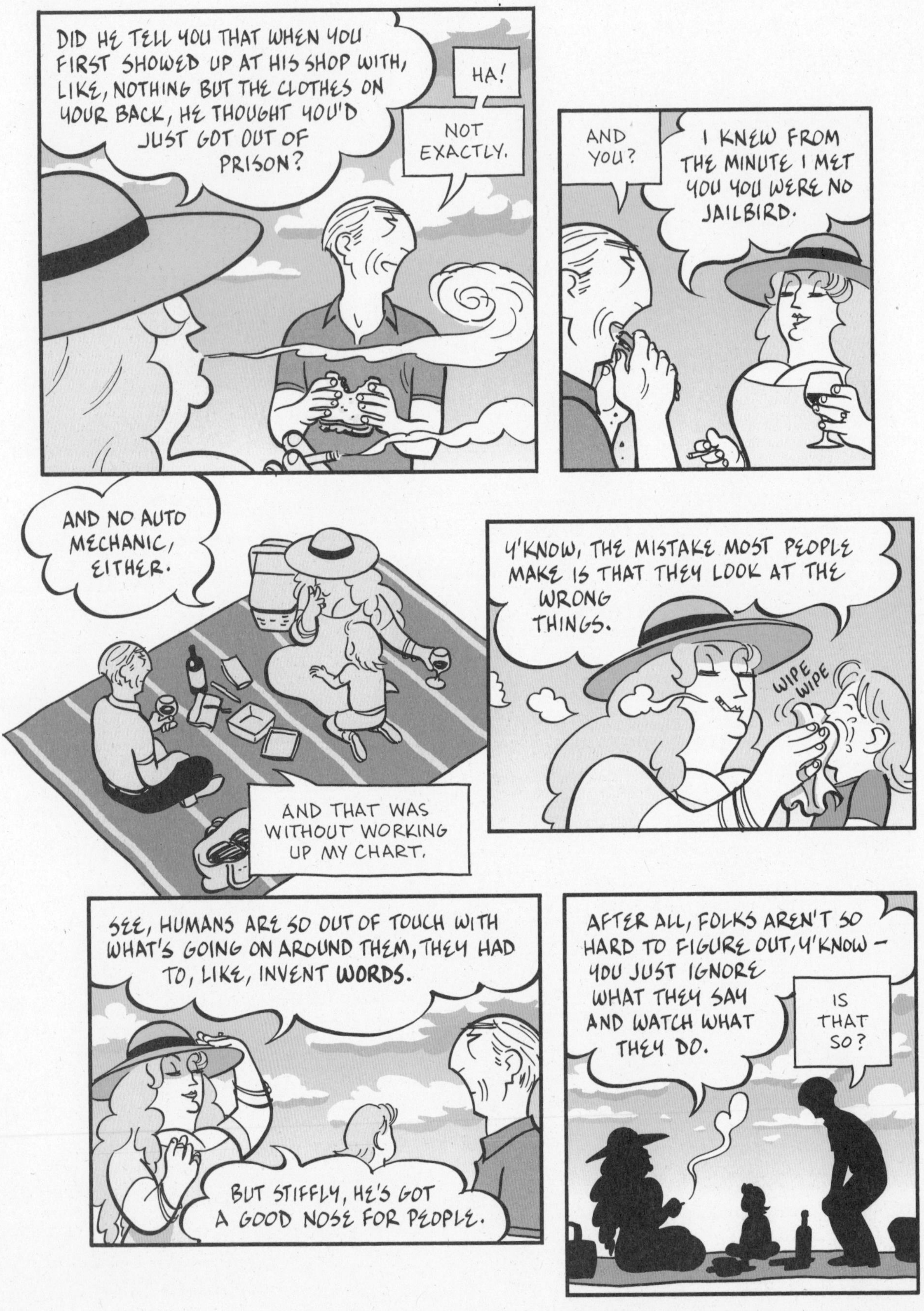
DID HE TELL YOU THAT WHEN YOU FIRST SHOWED UP AT HIS SHOP WITH, LIKE, NOTHING BUT THE CLOTHES ON YOUR BACK, HE THOUGHT YOU'D JUST GOT OUT OF PRISON?
HA!
NOT EXACTLY.
AND YOU?
I KNEW FROM THE MINUTE I MET YOU YOU WERE NO JAILBIRD.
AND NO AUTO MECHANIC, EITHER.
AND THAT WAS WITHOUT WORKING UP MY CHART.
Y'KNOW, THE MISTAKE MOST PEOPLE MAKE IS THAT THEY LOOK AT THE WRONG THINGS.
WIPE WIPE
SEE, HUMANS ARE SO OUT OF TOUCH WITH WHAT'S GOING ON AROUND THEM, THEY HAD TO, LIKE, INVENT **WORDS**.
BUT STIFFLY, HE'S GOT A GOOD NOSE FOR PEOPLE.
AFTER ALL, FOLKS AREN'T SO HARD TO FIGURE OUT, Y'KNOW — YOU JUST IGNORE WHAT THEY SAY AND WATCH WHAT THEY DO.
IS THAT SO?

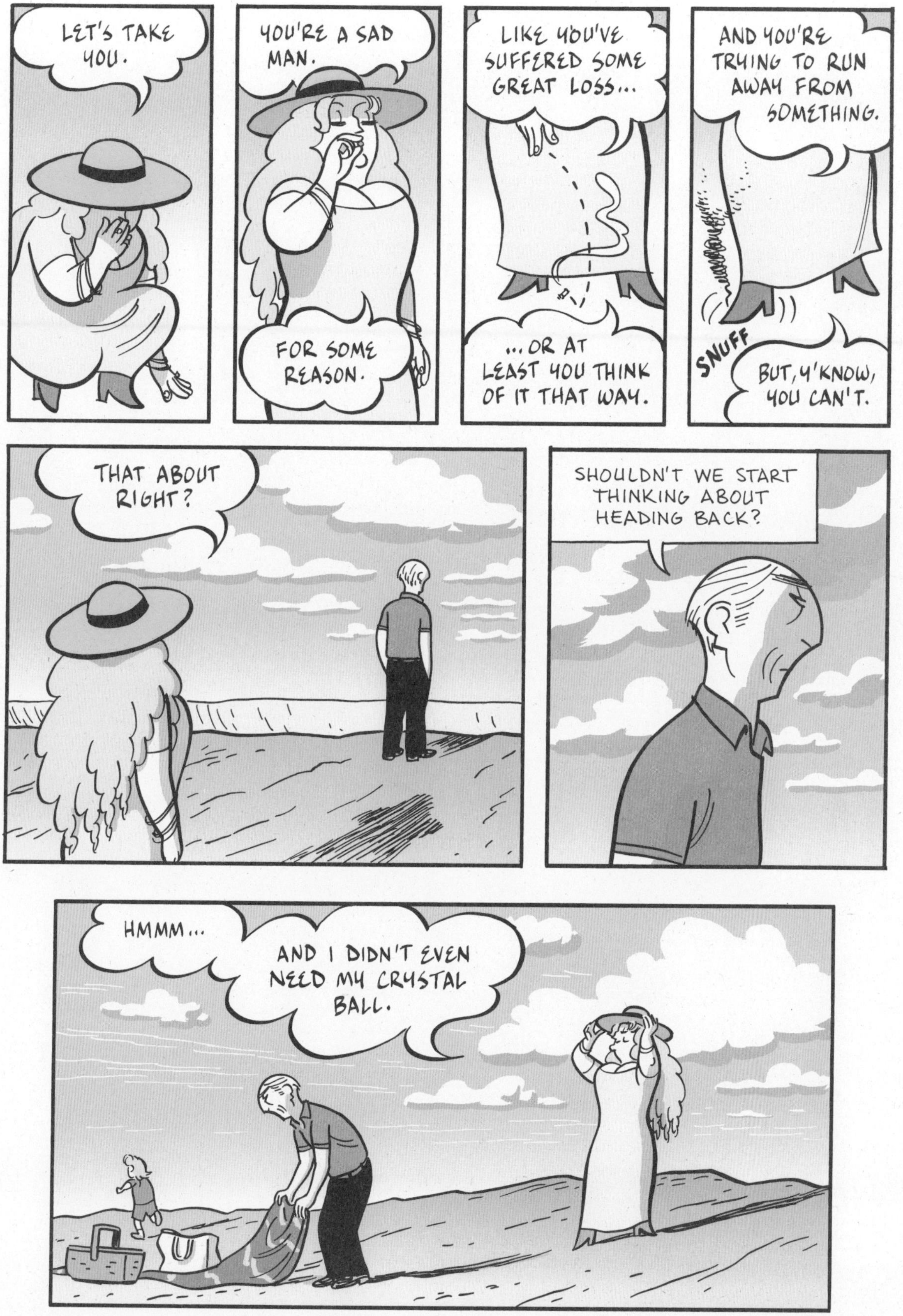
LET'S TAKE YOU.
YOU'RE A SAD MAN.
FOR SOME REASON.
LIKE YOU'VE SUFFERED SOME GREAT LOSS...
...OR AT LEAST YOU THINK OF IT THAT WAY.
AND YOU'RE TRYING TO RUN AWAY FROM SOMETHING.
SNUFF
BUT, Y'KNOW, YOU CAN'T.
THAT ABOUT RIGHT?
SHOULDN'T WE START THINKING ABOUT HEADING BACK?
HMMM...
AND I DIDN'T EVEN NEED MY CRYSTAL BALL.

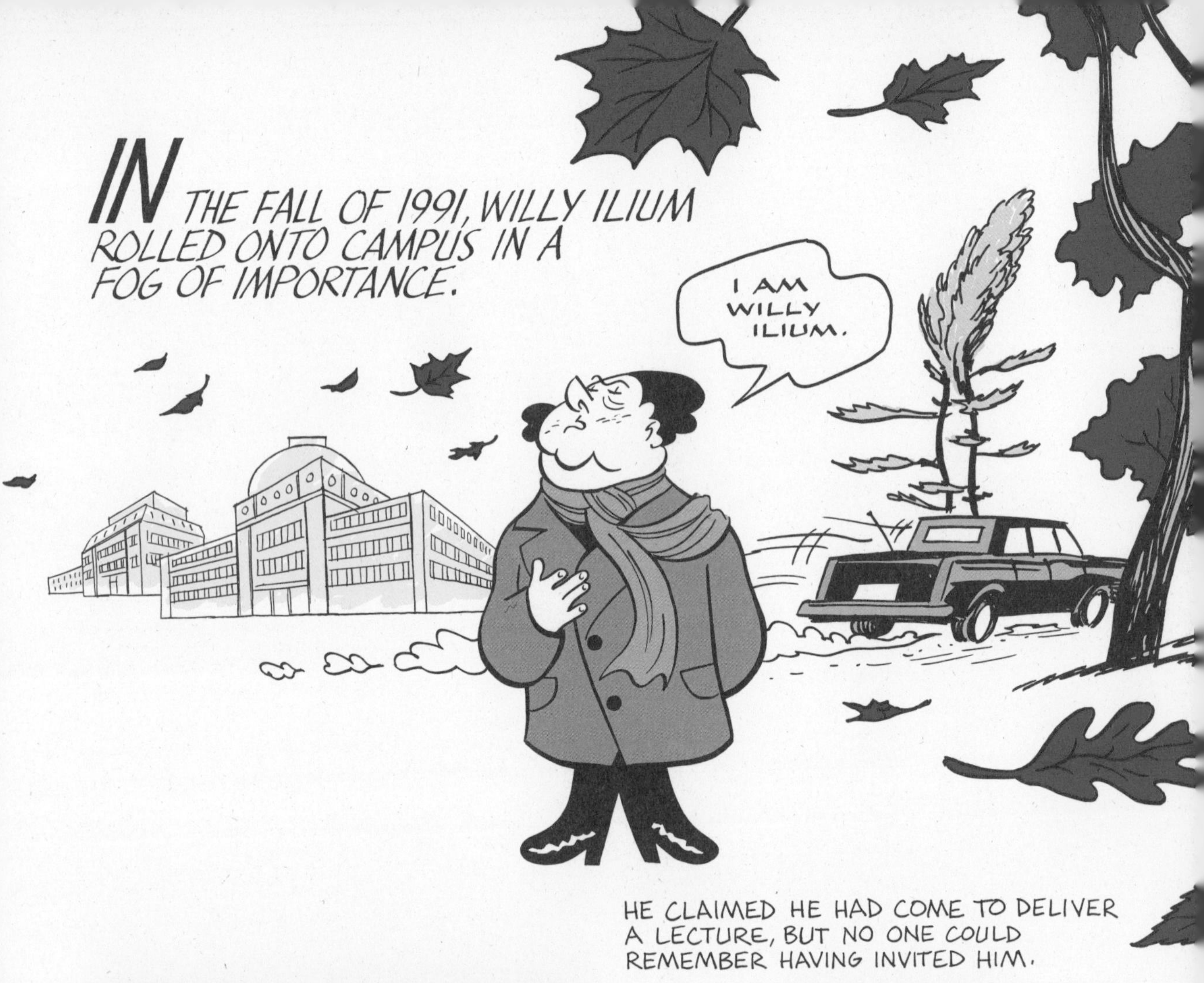
IN THE FALL OF 1991, WILLY ILIUM ROLLED ONTO CAMPUS IN A FOG OF IMPORTANCE.
I AM WILLY ILIUM.
HE CLAIMED HE HAD COME TO DELIVER A LECTURE, BUT NO ONE COULD REMEMBER HAVING INVITED HIM.

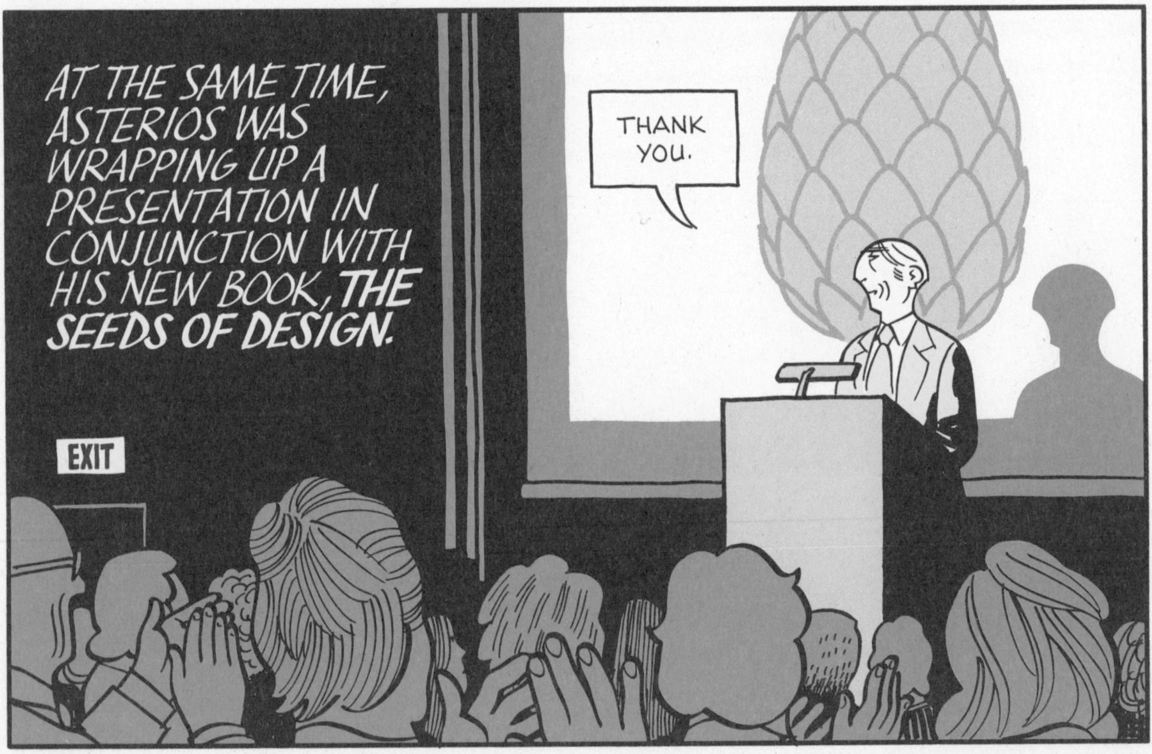
AT THE SAME TIME, ASTERIOS WAS WRAPPING UP A PRESENTATION IN CONJUNCTION WITH HIS NEW BOOK, THE SEEDS OF DESIGN.
THANK YOU.
EXIT

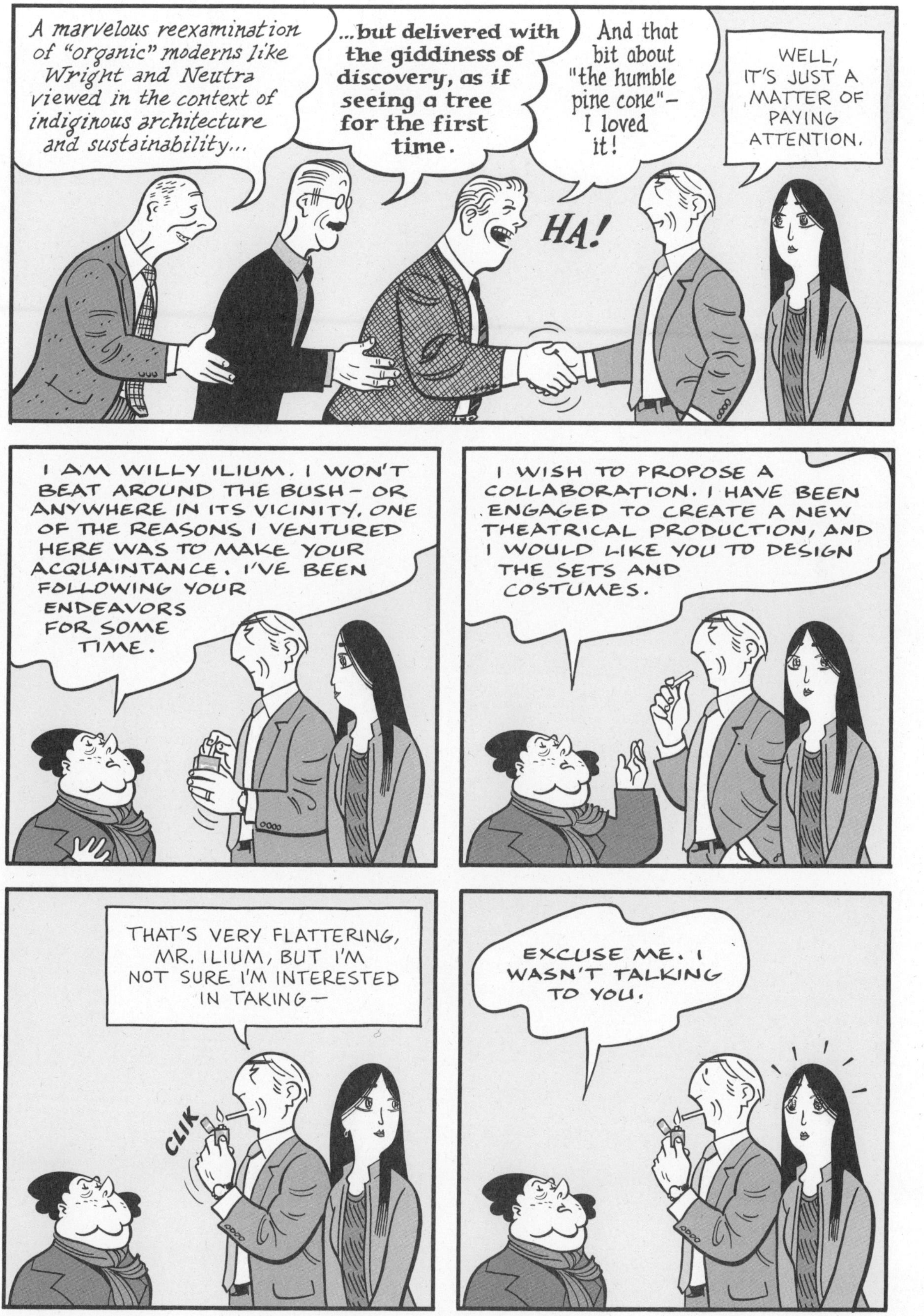

A marvelous reexamination of "organic" moderns like Wright and Neutra viewed in the context of indiginous architecture and sustainability...
...but delivered with the giddiness of discovery, as if seeing a tree for the first time.
And that bit about "the humble pine cone"— I loved it!
HA!
WELL, IT'S JUST A MATTER OF PAYING ATTENTION.
I AM WILLY ILIUM. I WON'T BEAT AROUND THE BUSH— OR ANYWHERE IN ITS VICINITY. ONE OF THE REASONS I VENTURED HERE WAS TO MAKE YOUR ACQUAINTANCE. I'VE BEEN FOLLOWING YOUR ENDEAVORS FOR SOME TIME.
I WISH TO PROPOSE A COLLABORATION. I HAVE BEEN ENGAGED TO CREATE A NEW THEATRICAL PRODUCTION, AND I WOULD LIKE YOU TO DESIGN THE SETS AND COSTUMES.
THAT'S VERY FLATTERING, MR. ILIUM, BUT I'M NOT SURE I'M INTERESTED IN TAKING—
CLIK
EXCUSE ME. I WASN'T TALKING TO YOU.

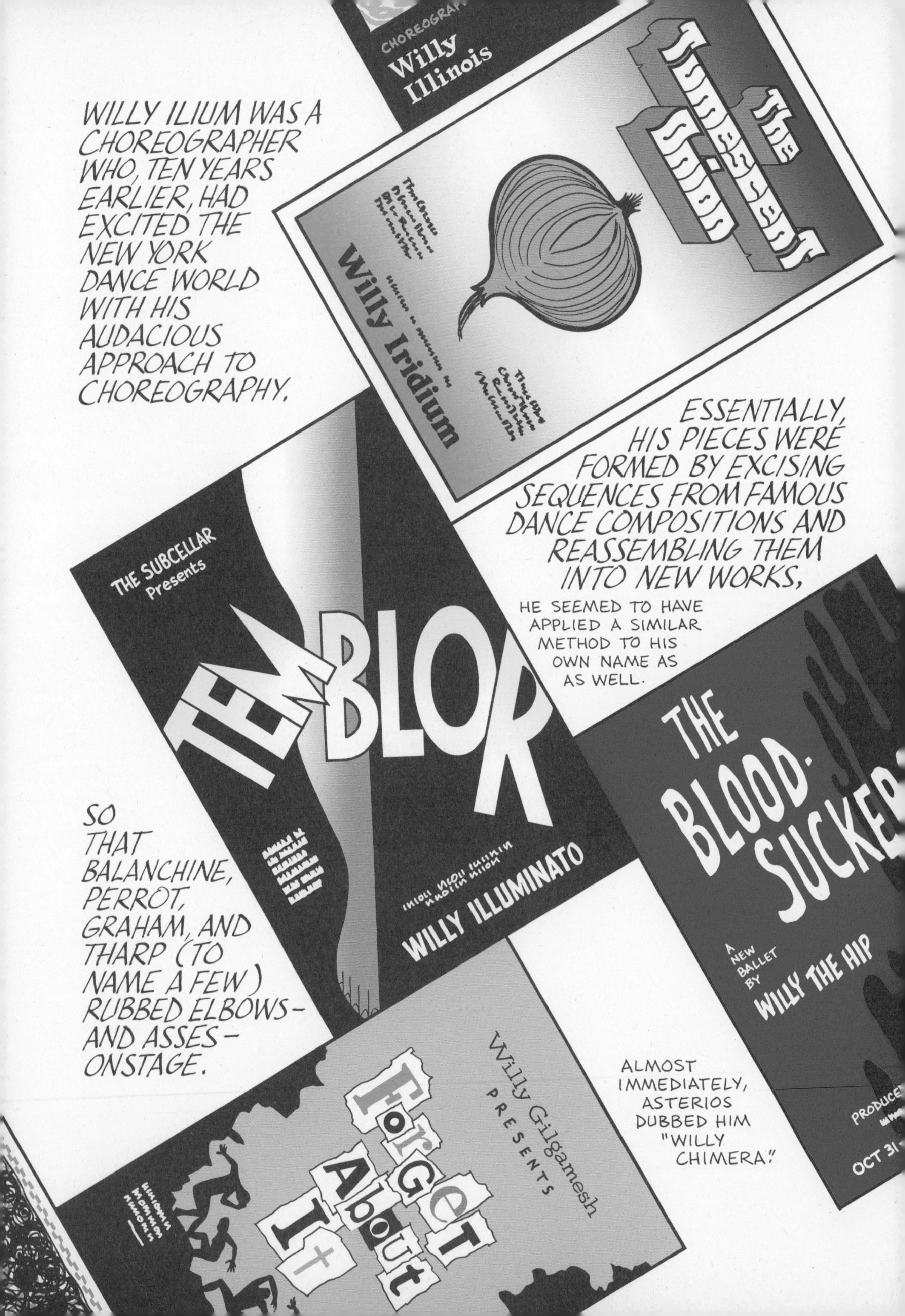
CHOREOGRAPHER
Willy Illinois
WILLY ILIUM WAS A CHOREOGRAPHER WHO, TEN YEARS EARLIER, HAD EXCITED THE NEW YORK DANCE WORLD WITH HIS AUDACIOUS APPROACH TO CHOREOGRAPHY.
Willy Iridium
ESSENTIALLY, HIS PIECES WERE FORMED BY EXCISING SEQUENCES FROM FAMOUS DANCE COMPOSITIONS AND REASSEMBLING THEM INTO NEW WORKS,
HE SEEMED TO HAVE APPLIED A SIMILAR METHOD TO HIS OWN NAME AS AS WELL.
THE SUBCELLAR Presents
TEMBLOR
WILLY ILLUMINATO
THE BLOOD. SUCKER
A NEW BALLET BY
WILLY THE HIP
PRODUCE
OCT 31
SO THAT BALANCHINE, PERROT, GRAHAM, AND THARP (TO NAME A FEW) RUBBED ELBOWS-AND ASSES-ONSTAGE.
Willy Gilgamesh PRESENTS
Forget About It
ALMOST IMMEDIATELY, ASTERIOS DUBBED HIM "WILLY CHIMERA."

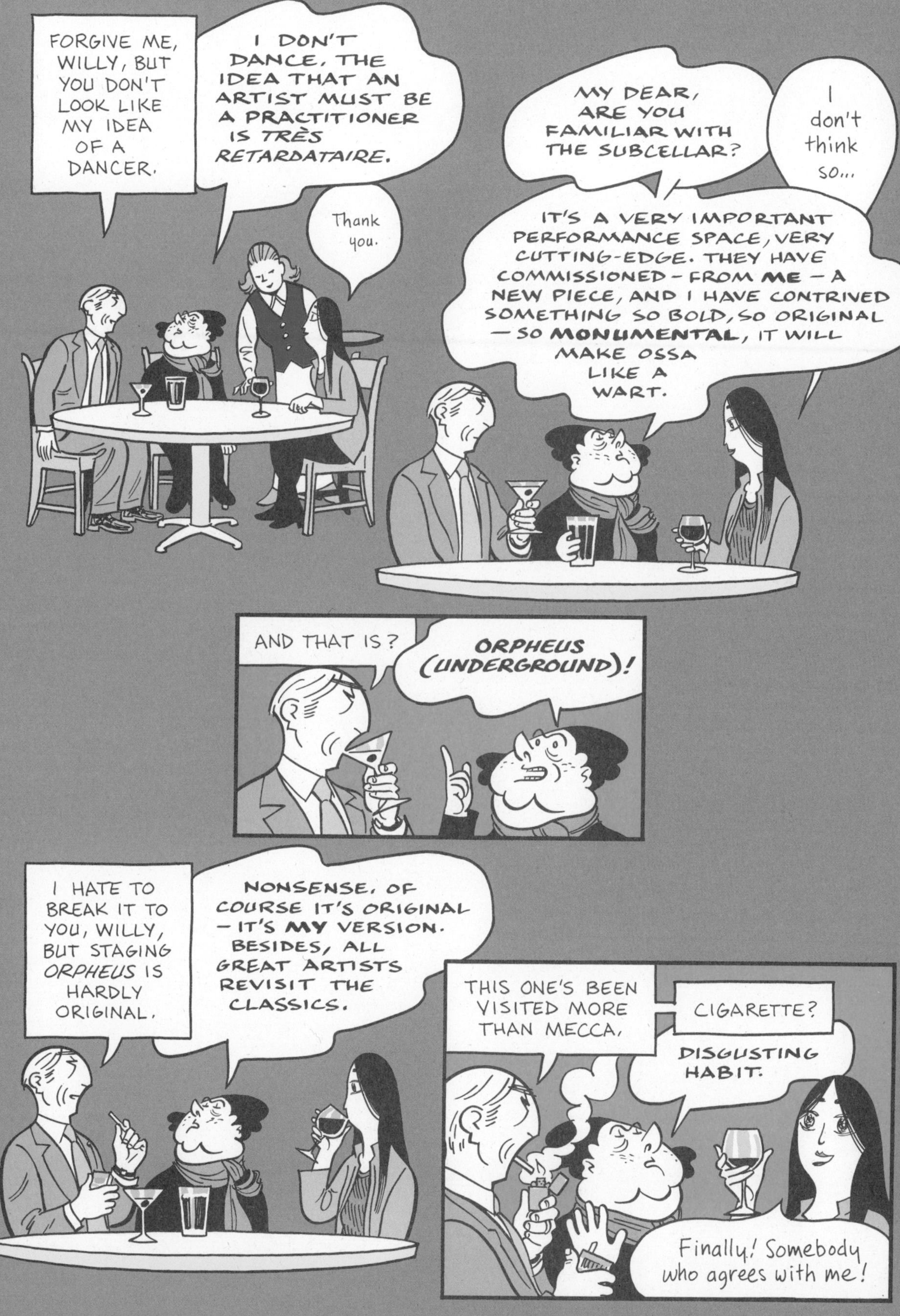
FORGIVE ME, WILLY, BUT YOU DON'T LOOK LIKE MY IDEA OF A DANCER.
I DON'T DANCE. THE IDEA THAT AN ARTIST MUST BE A PRACTITIONER IS *TRÈS RETARDATAIRE.*
Thank you.
MY DEAR, ARE YOU FAMILIAR WITH THE SUBCELLAR?
I don't think so...
IT'S A VERY IMPORTANT PERFORMANCE SPACE, VERY CUTTING-EDGE. THEY HAVE COMMISSIONED—FROM **ME**—A NEW PIECE, AND I HAVE CONTRIVED SOMETHING SO BOLD, SO ORIGINAL —SO **MONUMENTAL**, IT WILL MAKE OSSA LIKE A WART.
AND THAT IS?
ORPHEUS (UNDERGROUND)!
I HATE TO BREAK IT TO YOU, WILLY, BUT STAGING *ORPHEUS* IS HARDLY ORIGINAL.
NONSENSE. OF COURSE IT'S ORIGINAL —IT'S **MY** VERSION. BESIDES, ALL GREAT ARTISTS REVISIT THE CLASSICS.
THIS ONE'S BEEN VISITED MORE THAN MECCA.
CIGARETTE?
DISGUSTING HABIT.
Finally! Somebody who agrees with me!

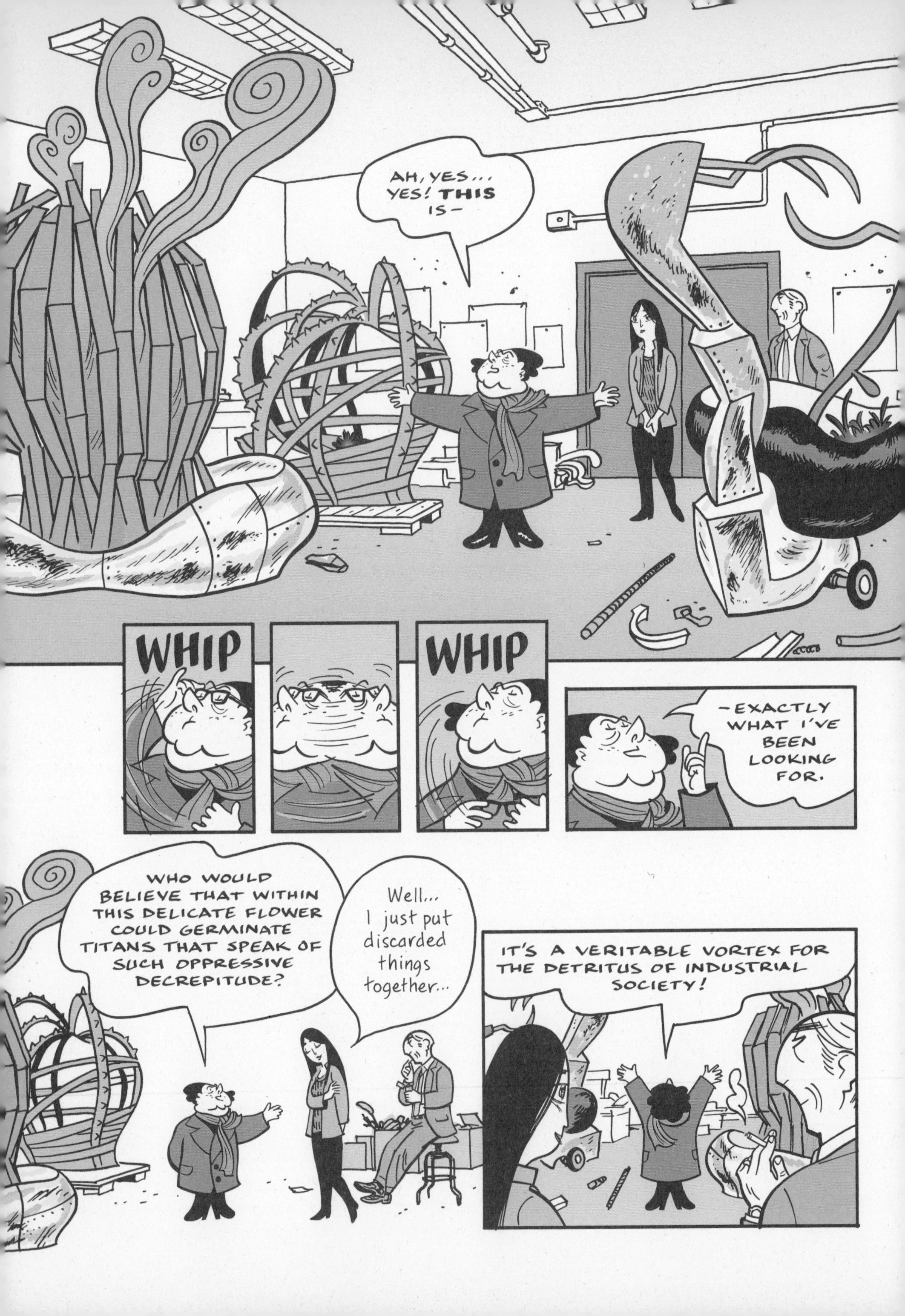
AH, YES...
YES! THIS
IS—
WHIP
WHIP
—EXACTLY WHAT I'VE BEEN LOOKING FOR.
WHO WOULD BELIEVE THAT WITHIN THIS DELICATE FLOWER COULD GERMINATE TITANS THAT SPEAK OF SUCH OPPRESSIVE DECREPITUDE?
Well... I just put discarded things together...
IT'S A VERITABLE VORTEX FOR THE DETRITUS OF INDUSTRIAL SOCIETY!

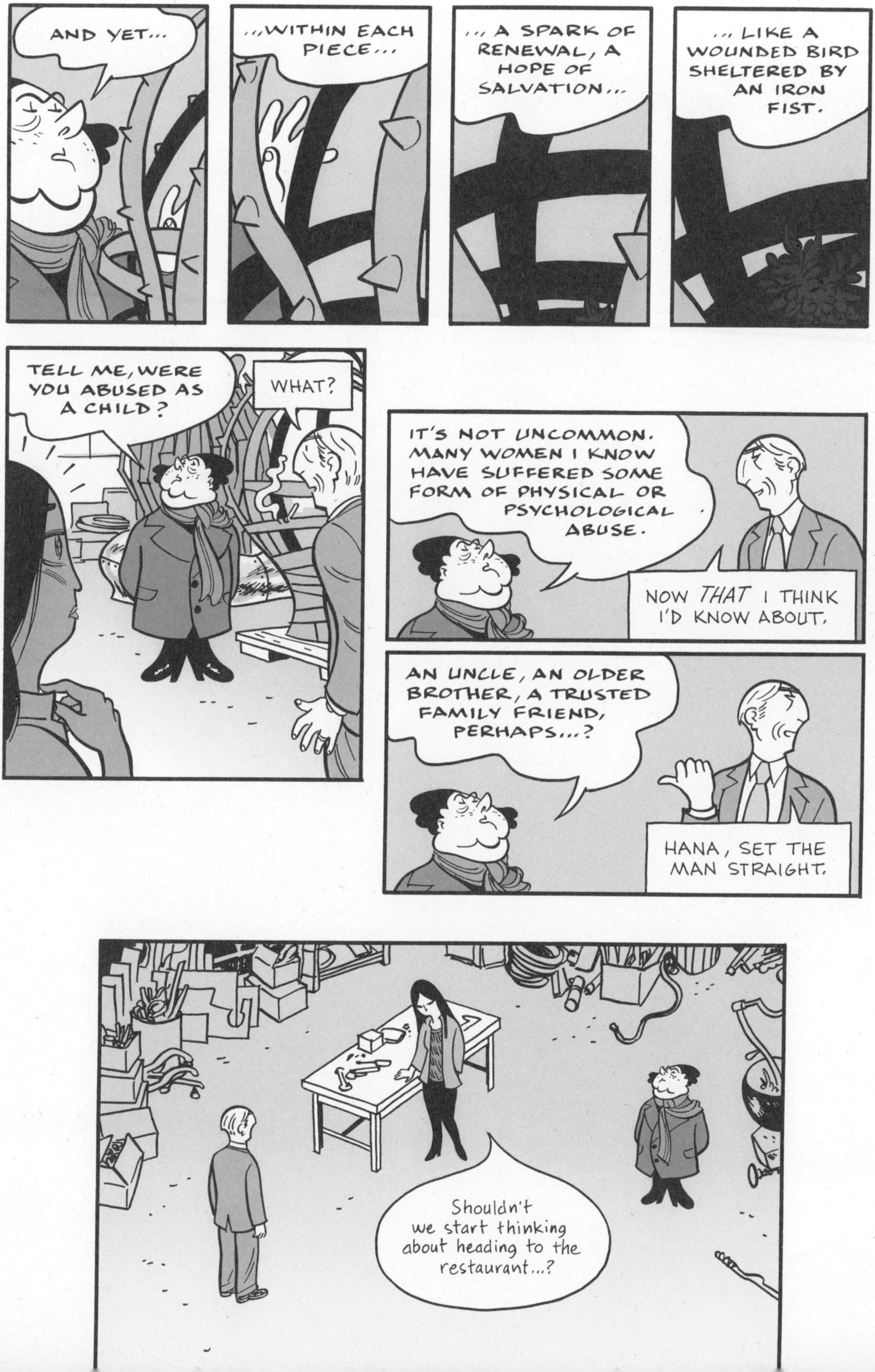
AND YET...
...WITHIN EACH PIECE...
... A SPARK OF RENEWAL, A HOPE OF SALVATION...
... LIKE A WOUNDED BIRD SHELTERED BY AN IRON FIST.
TELL ME, WERE YOU ABUSED AS A CHILD?
WHAT?
IT'S NOT UNCOMMON. MANY WOMEN I KNOW HAVE SUFFERED SOME FORM OF PHYSICAL OR PSYCHOLOGICAL ABUSE.
NOW *THAT* I THINK I'D KNOW ABOUT.
AN UNCLE, AN OLDER BROTHER, A TRUSTED FAMILY FRIEND, PERHAPS...?
HANA, SET THE MAN STRAIGHT.
Shouldn't we start thinking about heading to the restaurant...?

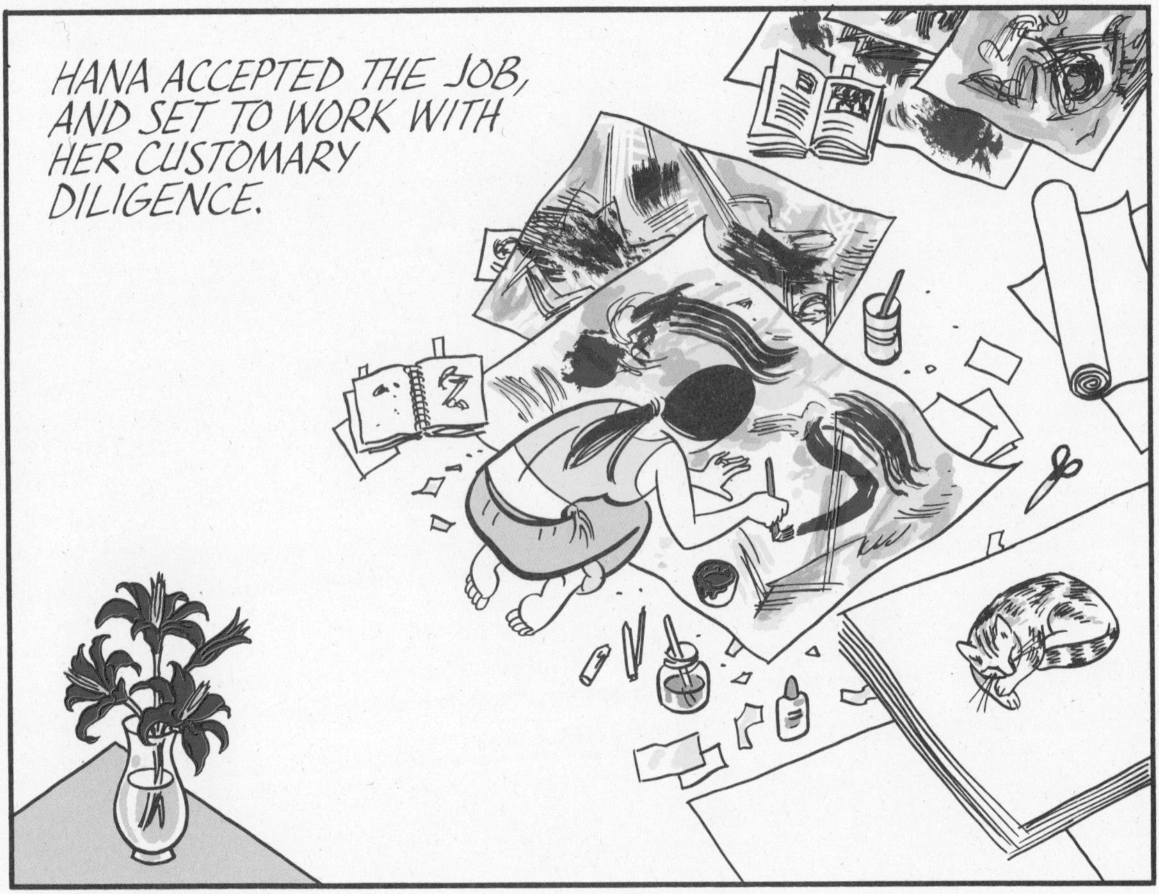
HANA ACCEPTED THE JOB, AND SET TO WORK WITH HER CUSTOMARY DILIGENCE.

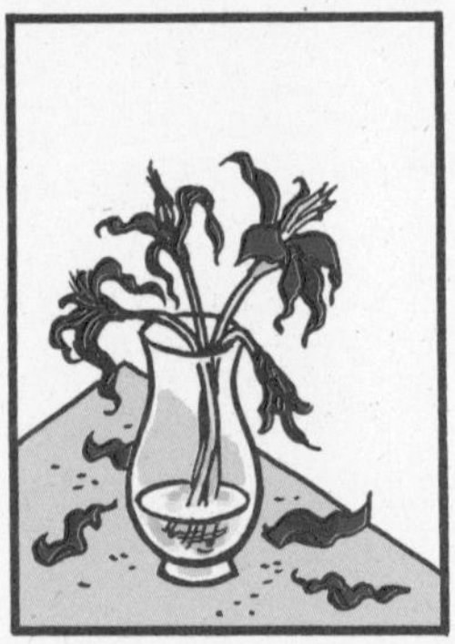

AND (AS USUAL), FEARING FAILURE, SHE OBSESSED OVER EVERY MARK IN EVERY DRAWING.

SHE ALSO BEGAN MAKING WEEKEND TRIPS TO NEW YORK FOR CONSULTATIONS WITH WILLY ILIUM.

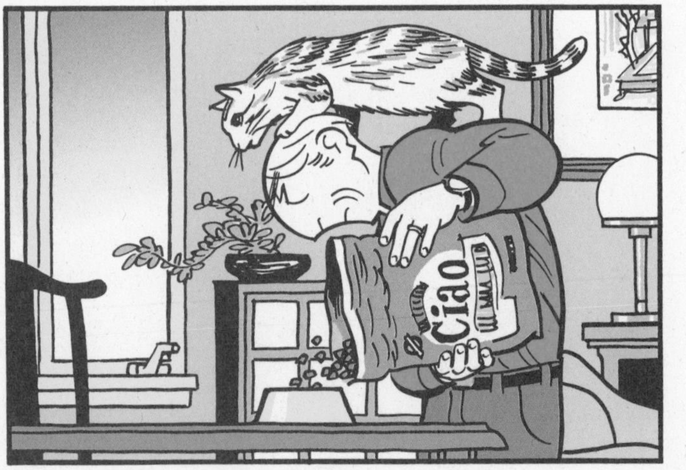
Ciao

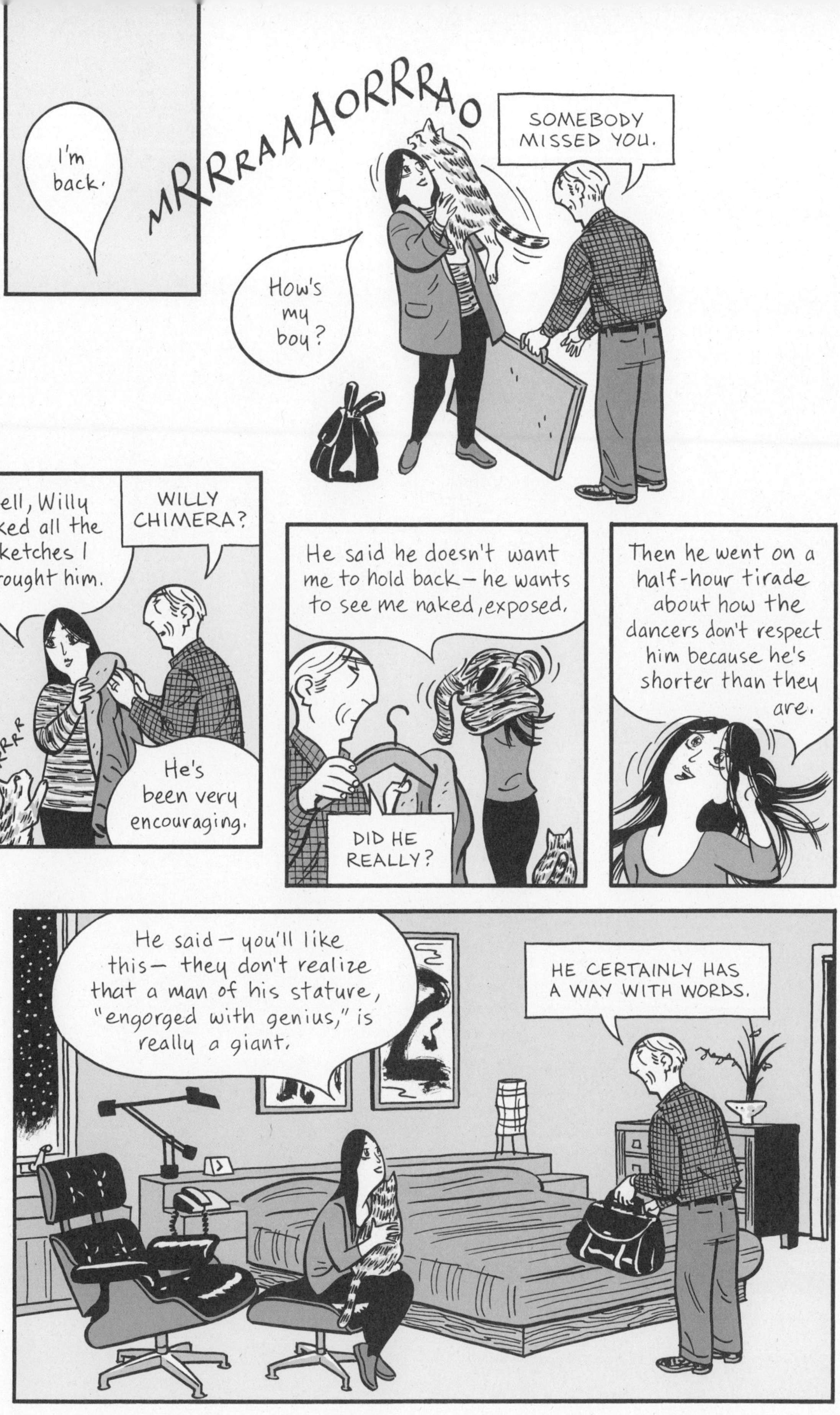
I'm back.
MRRRAAAORRRAO
SOMEBODY MISSED YOU.
How's my boy?
Well, Willy liked all the sketches I brought him.
WILLY CHIMERA?
PRRRRR
He's been very encouraging.
He said he doesn't want me to hold back—he wants to see me naked, exposed.
DID HE REALLY?
Then he went on a half-hour tirade about how the dancers don't respect him because he's shorter than they are.
He said—you'll like this—they don't realize that a man of his stature, "engorged with genius," is really a giant.
HE CERTAINLY HAS A WAY WITH WORDS.

OCCASIONALLY, ASTERIOS ACCOMPANIED HANA TO NEW YORK.

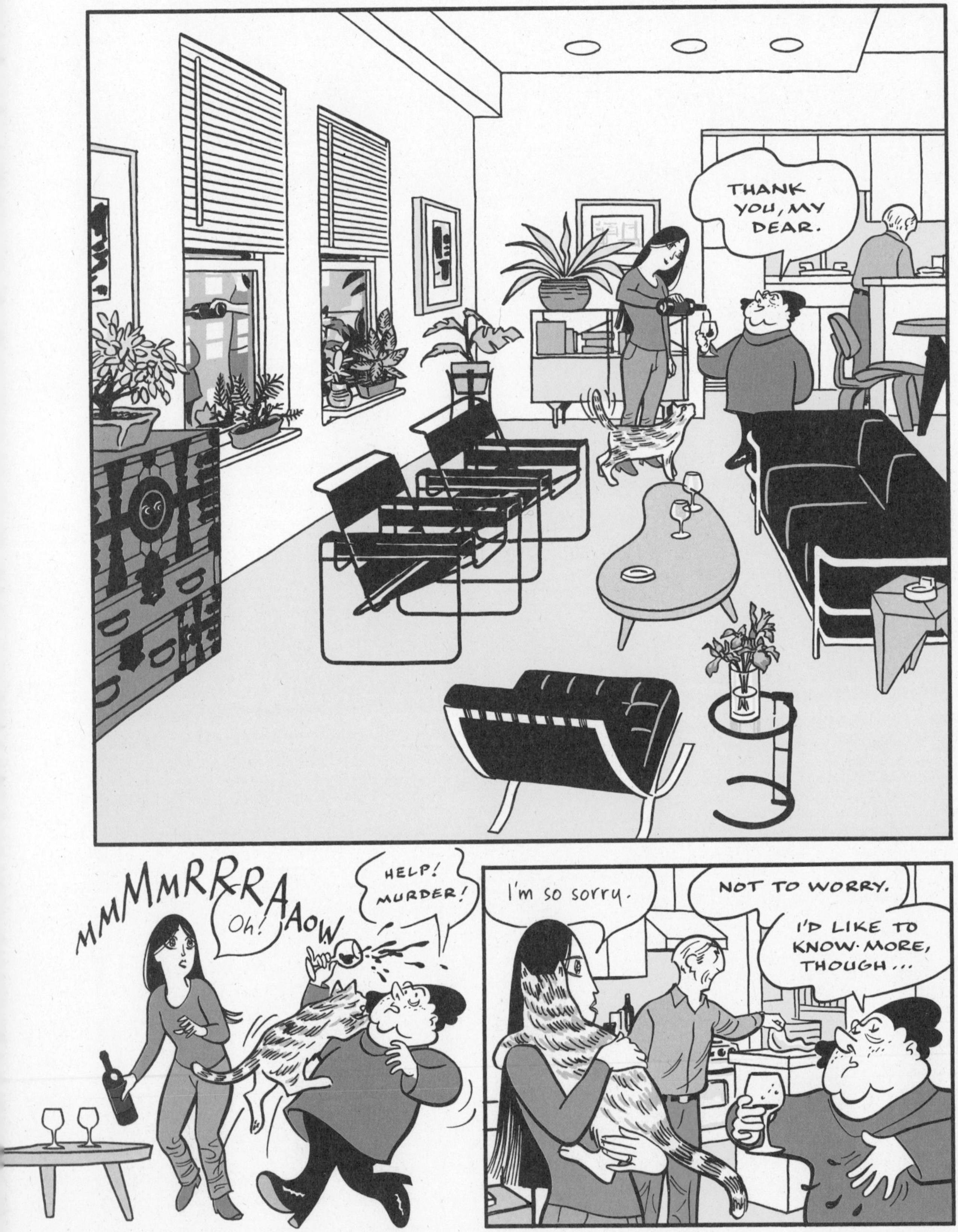
THANK YOU, MY DEAR.
MMMMRRRRAAOW
Oh!
HELP! MURDER!
I'm so sorry.
NOT TO WORRY.
I'D LIKE TO KNOW MORE, THOUGH...

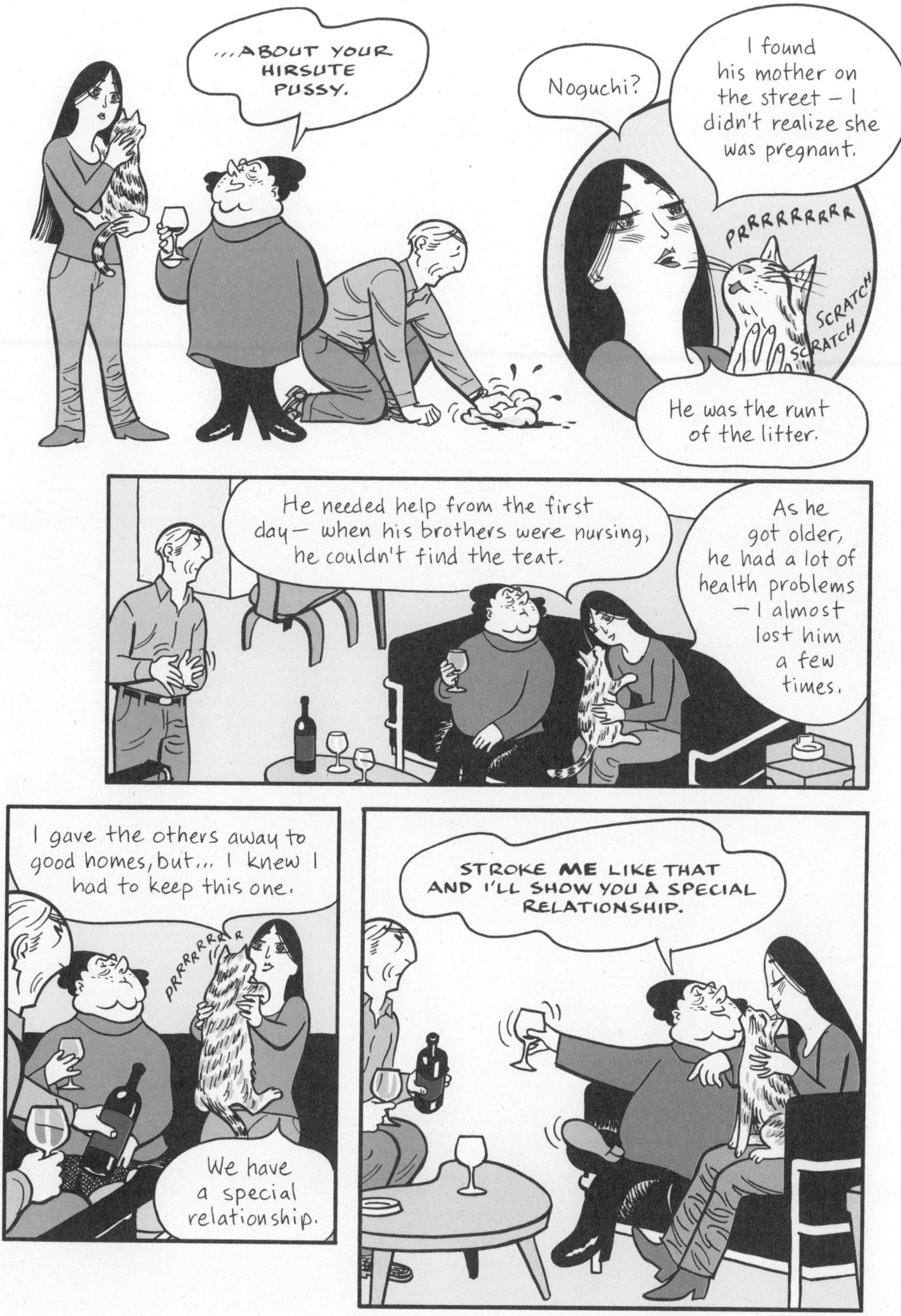
...ABOUT YOUR HIRSUTE PUSSY.
Noguchi?
I found his mother on the street – I didn't realize she was pregnant.
PRRRRRRRRR
SCRATCH SCRATCH
He was the runt of the litter.
He needed help from the first day– when his brothers were nursing, he couldn't find the teat.
As he got older, he had a lot of health problems – I almost lost him a few times.
I gave the others away to good homes, but... I knew I had to keep this one.
PRRRRRRRR
We have a special relationship.
STROKE ME LIKE THAT AND I'LL SHOW YOU A SPECIAL RELATIONSHIP.

SOON, ALMOST ALL OF HANA'S FREE TIME SEEMED TO BE DEVOTED TO **ORPHEUS (UNDERGROUND)**.

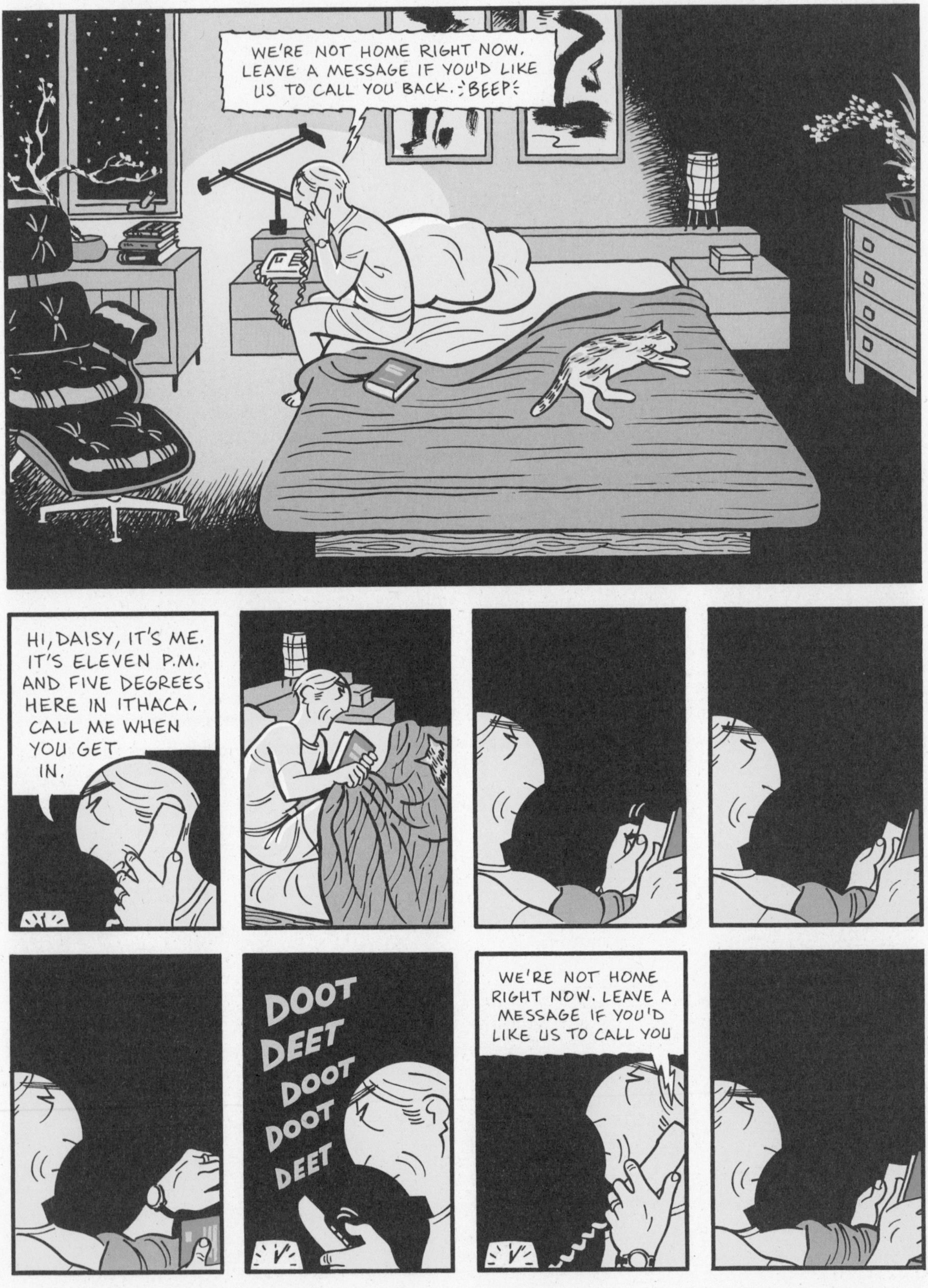
WE'RE NOT HOME RIGHT NOW. LEAVE A MESSAGE IF YOU'D LIKE US TO CALL YOU BACK. BEEP
HI, DAISY, IT'S ME. IT'S ELEVEN P.M. AND FIVE DEGREES HERE IN ITHACA. CALL ME WHEN YOU GET IN.
DOOT DEET DOOT DOOT DEET
WE'RE NOT HOME RIGHT NOW. LEAVE A MESSAGE IF YOU'D LIKE US TO CALL YOU

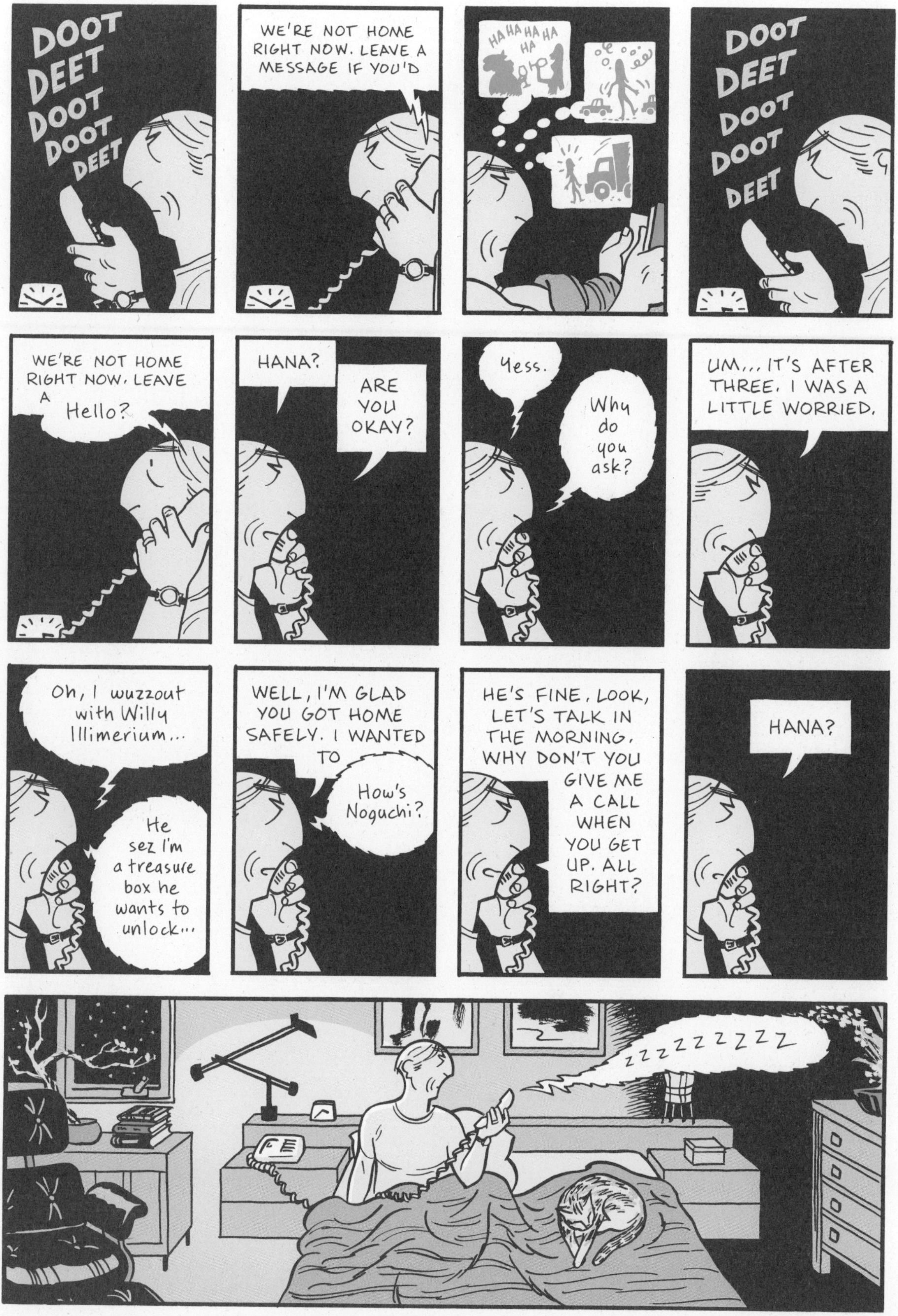
DOOT DEET DOOT DOOT DEET
WE'RE NOT HOME RIGHT NOW. LEAVE A MESSAGE IF YOU'D
HA HA HA HA HA
DOOT DEET DOOT DOOT DEET
WE'RE NOT HOME RIGHT NOW. LEAVE A
Hello?
HANA?
ARE YOU OKAY?
Yess.
Why do you ask?
UM... IT'S AFTER THREE. I WAS A LITTLE WORRIED.
Oh, I wuzzout with Willy Illimerium...
He sez I'm a treasure box he wants to unlock...
WELL, I'M GLAD YOU GOT HOME SAFELY. I WANTED TO
How's Noguchi?
HE'S FINE. LOOK, LET'S TALK IN THE MORNING. WHY DON'T YOU GIVE ME A CALL WHEN YOU GET UP. ALL RIGHT?
HANA?
ZZZZZZZZZ

THIS MEANT THAT ASTERIOS WAS TREATED TO THE WILLY CHIMERA EXPERIENCE A LITTLE MORE OFTEN THAN HE WOULD HAVE PREFERRED.

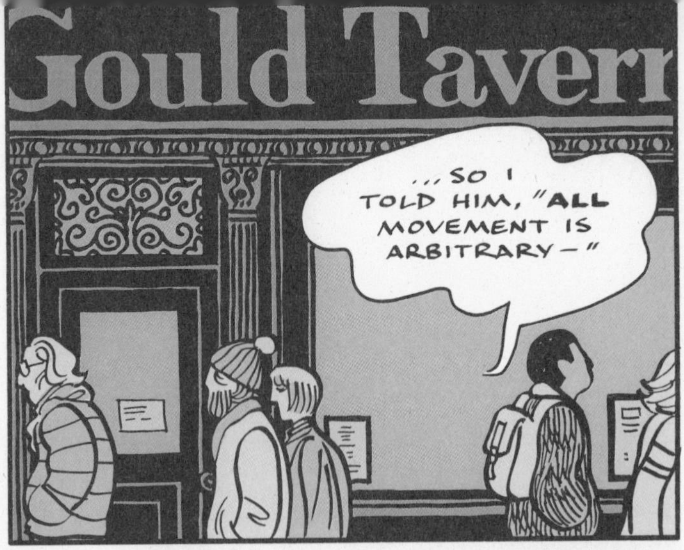
Gould Tavern
...SO I TOLD HIM, "ALL MOVEMENT IS ARBITRARY—"

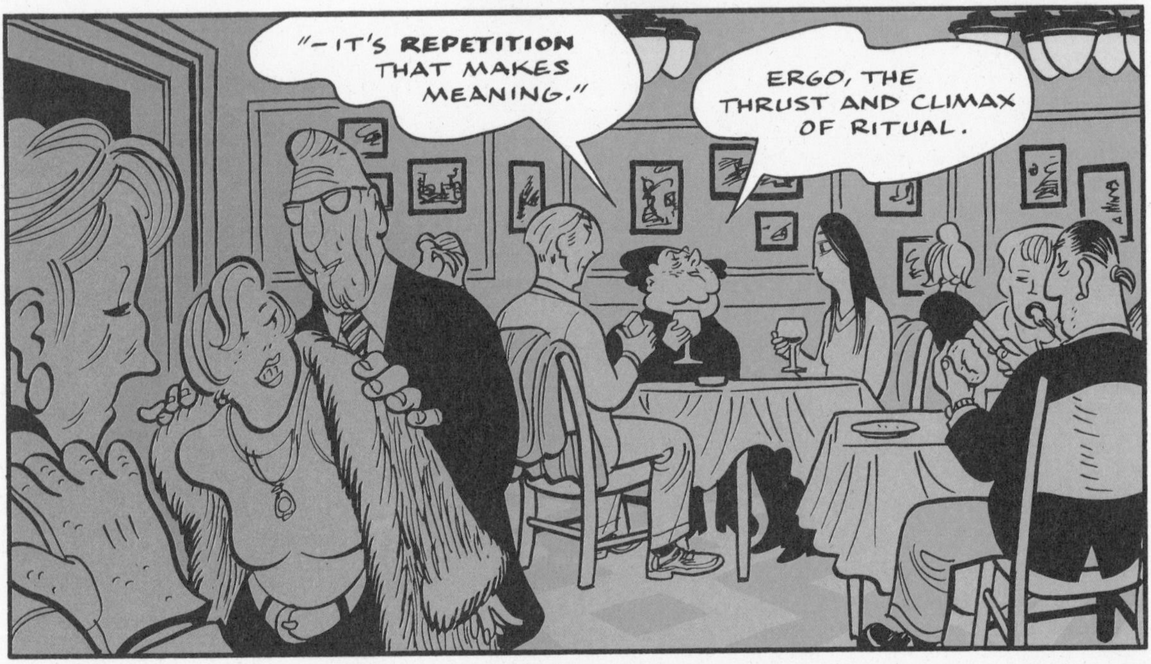
"—IT'S REPETITION THAT MAKES MEANING."
ERGO, THE THRUST AND CLIMAX OF RITUAL.

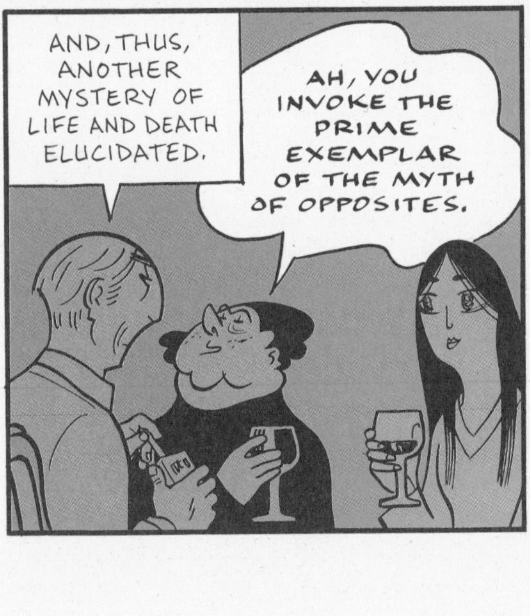
AND, THUS, ANOTHER MYSTERY OF LIFE AND DEATH ELUCIDATED.
AH, YOU INVOKE THE PRIME EXEMPLAR OF THE MYTH OF OPPOSITES.

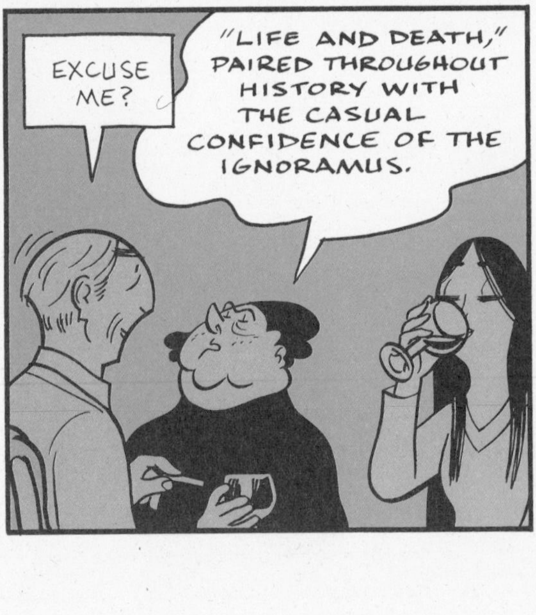
EXCUSE ME?
"LIFE AND DEATH," PAIRED THROUGHOUT HISTORY WITH THE CASUAL CONFIDENCE OF THE IGNORAMUS.

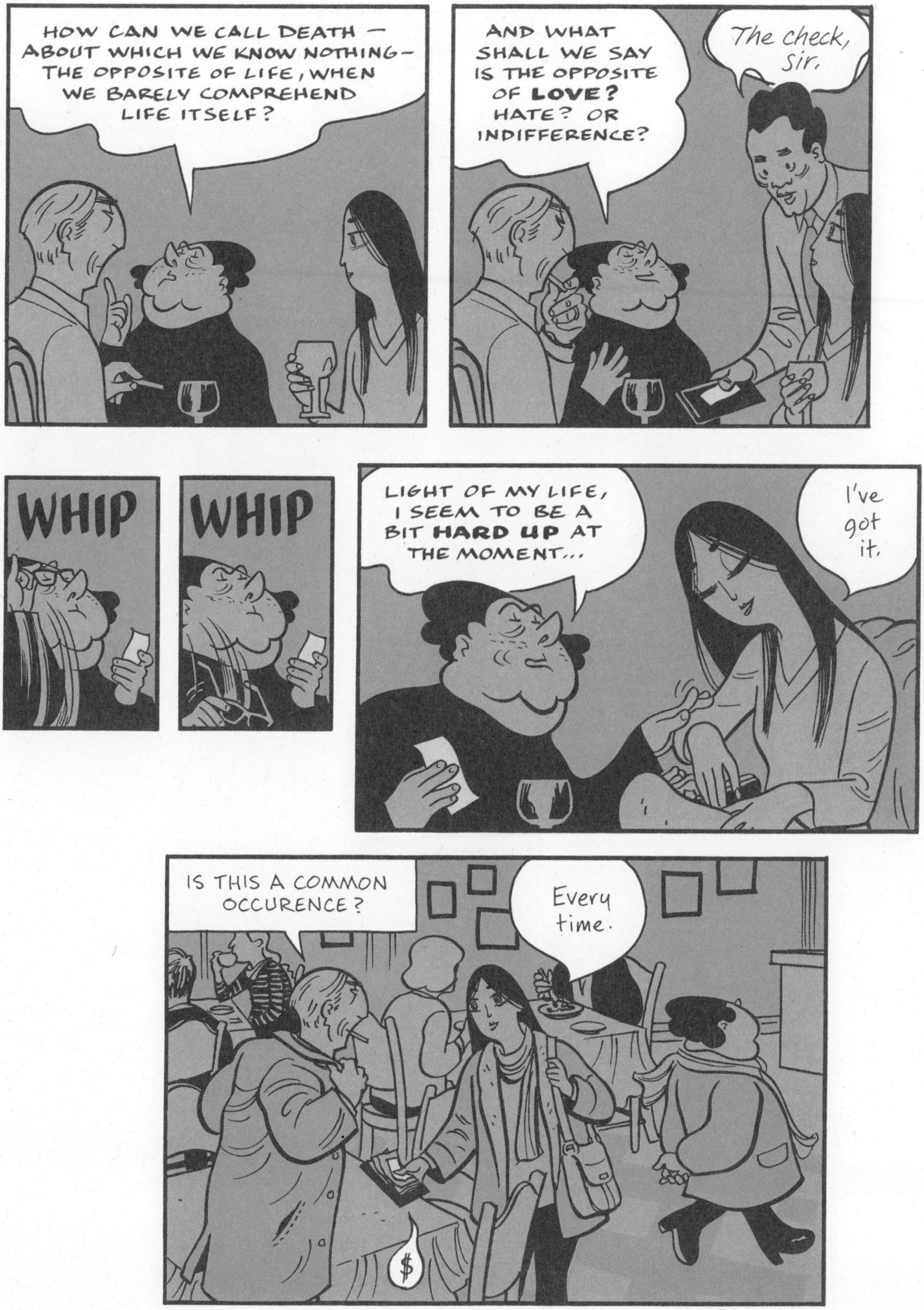
HOW CAN WE CALL DEATH — ABOUT WHICH WE KNOW NOTHING — THE OPPOSITE OF LIFE, WHEN WE BARELY COMPREHEND LIFE ITSELF?
AND WHAT SHALL WE SAY IS THE OPPOSITE OF **LOVE?** HATE? OR INDIFFERENCE?
The check, Sir.
WHIP
WHIP
LIGHT OF MY LIFE, I SEEM TO BE A BIT **HARD UP** AT THE MOMENT...
I've got it.
IS THIS A COMMON OCCURENCE?
Every time.
$

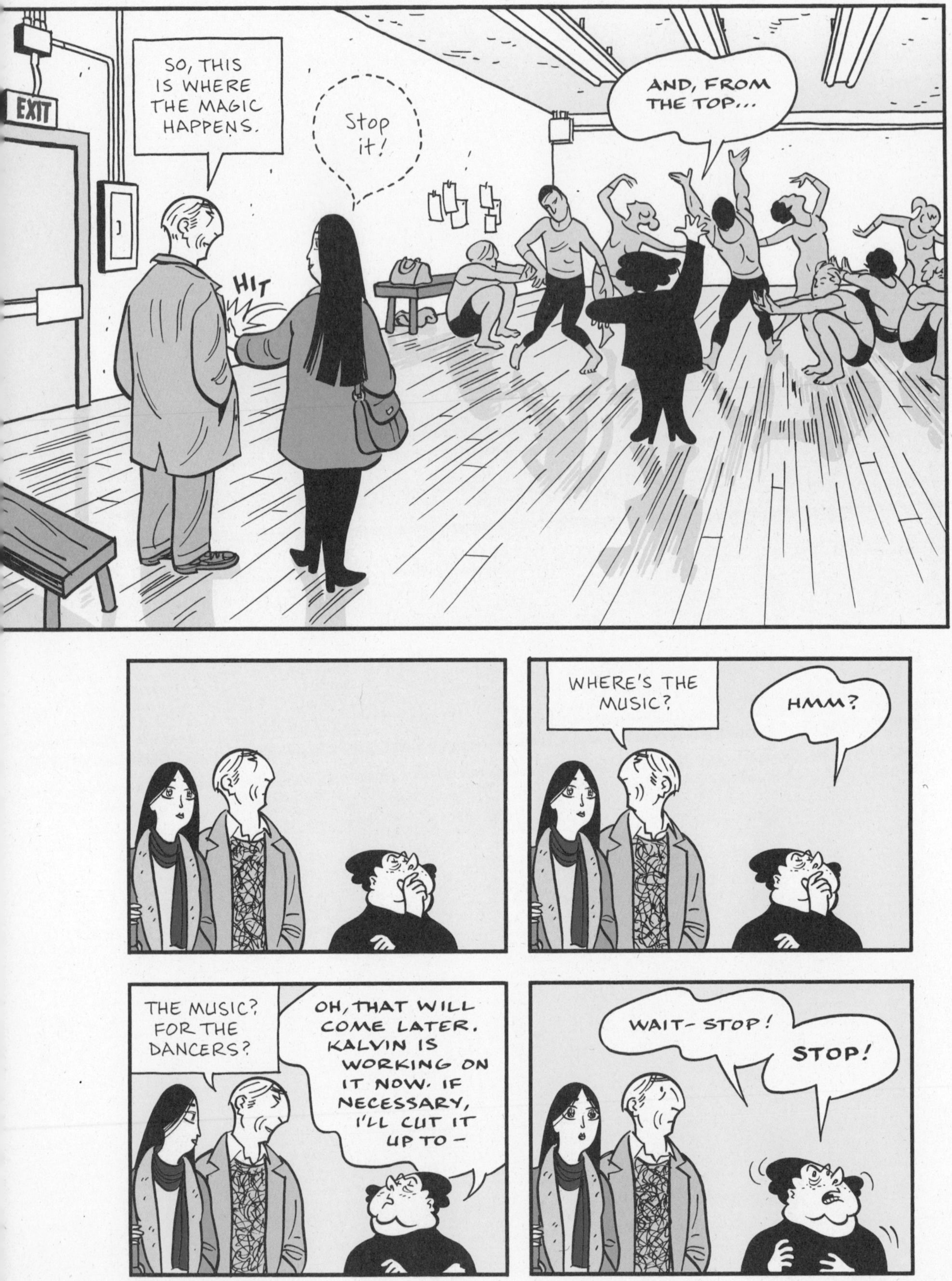
EXIT
SO, THIS IS WHERE THE MAGIC HAPPENS.
Stop it!
HIT
AND, FROM THE TOP...
WHERE'S THE MUSIC?
HMM?
THE MUSIC? FOR THE DANCERS?
OH, THAT WILL COME LATER. KALVIN IS WORKING ON IT NOW. IF NECESSARY, I'LL CUT IT UP TO -
WAIT- STOP!
STOP!

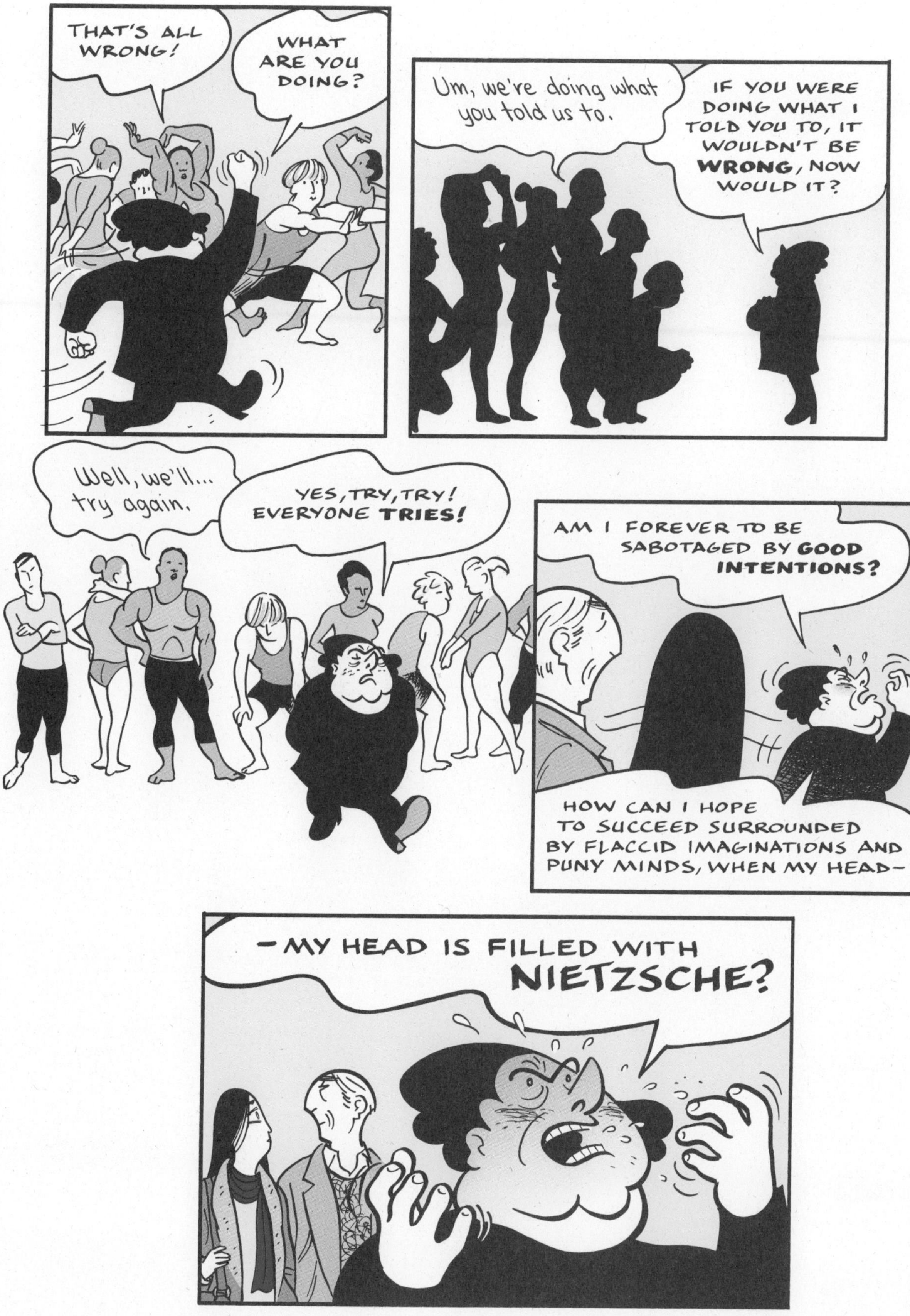
THAT'S ALL WRONG!
WHAT ARE YOU DOING?
Um, we're doing what you told us to.
IF YOU WERE DOING WHAT I TOLD YOU TO, IT WOULDN'T BE **WRONG**, NOW WOULD IT?
Well, we'll... try again.
YES, TRY, TRY! EVERYONE **TRIES!**
AM I FOREVER TO BE SABOTAGED BY **GOOD INTENTIONS?**
HOW CAN I HOPE TO SUCCEED SURROUNDED BY FLACCID IMAGINATIONS AND PUNY MINDS, WHEN MY HEAD—
—MY HEAD IS FILLED WITH **NIETZSCHE?**

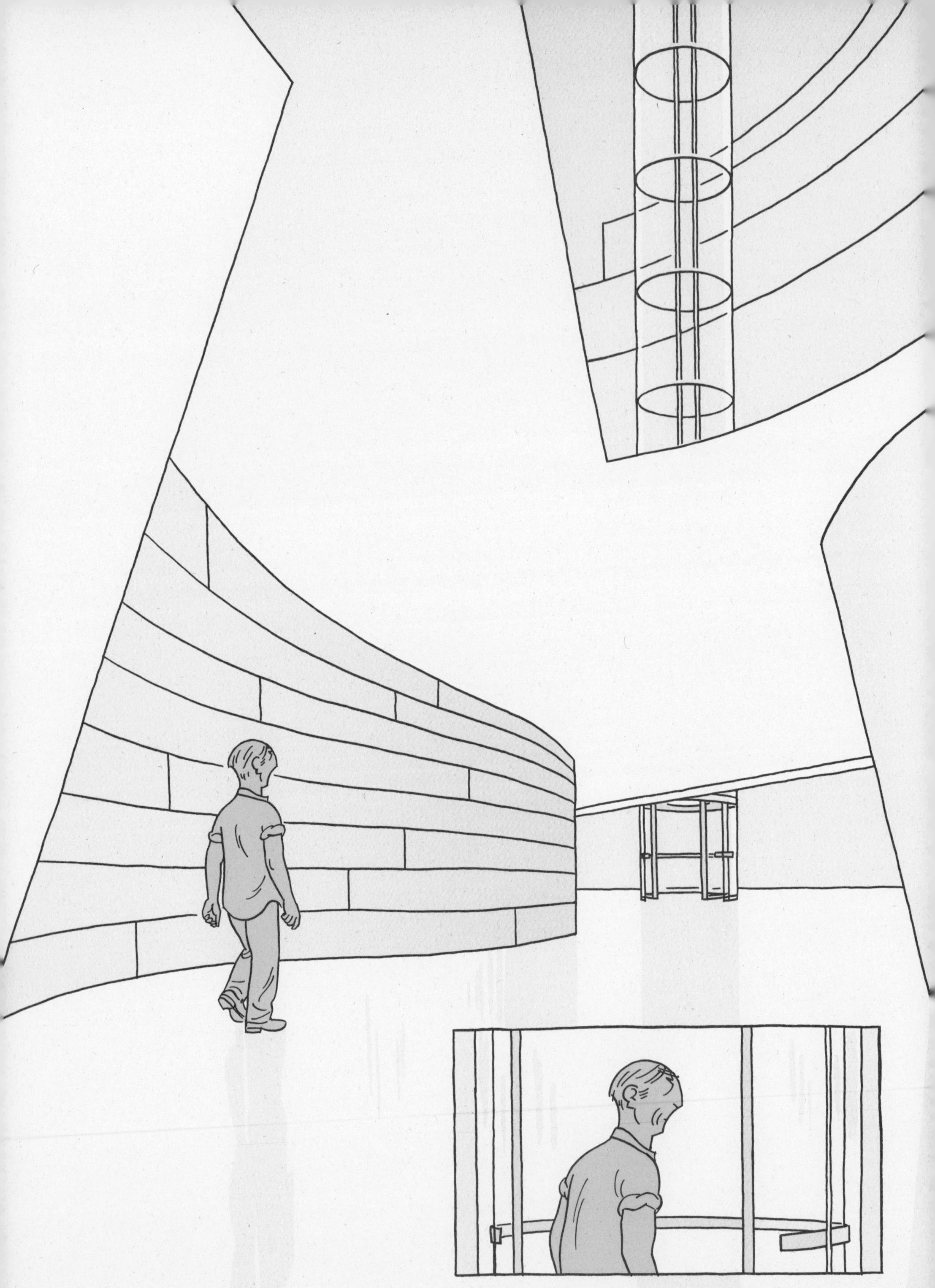

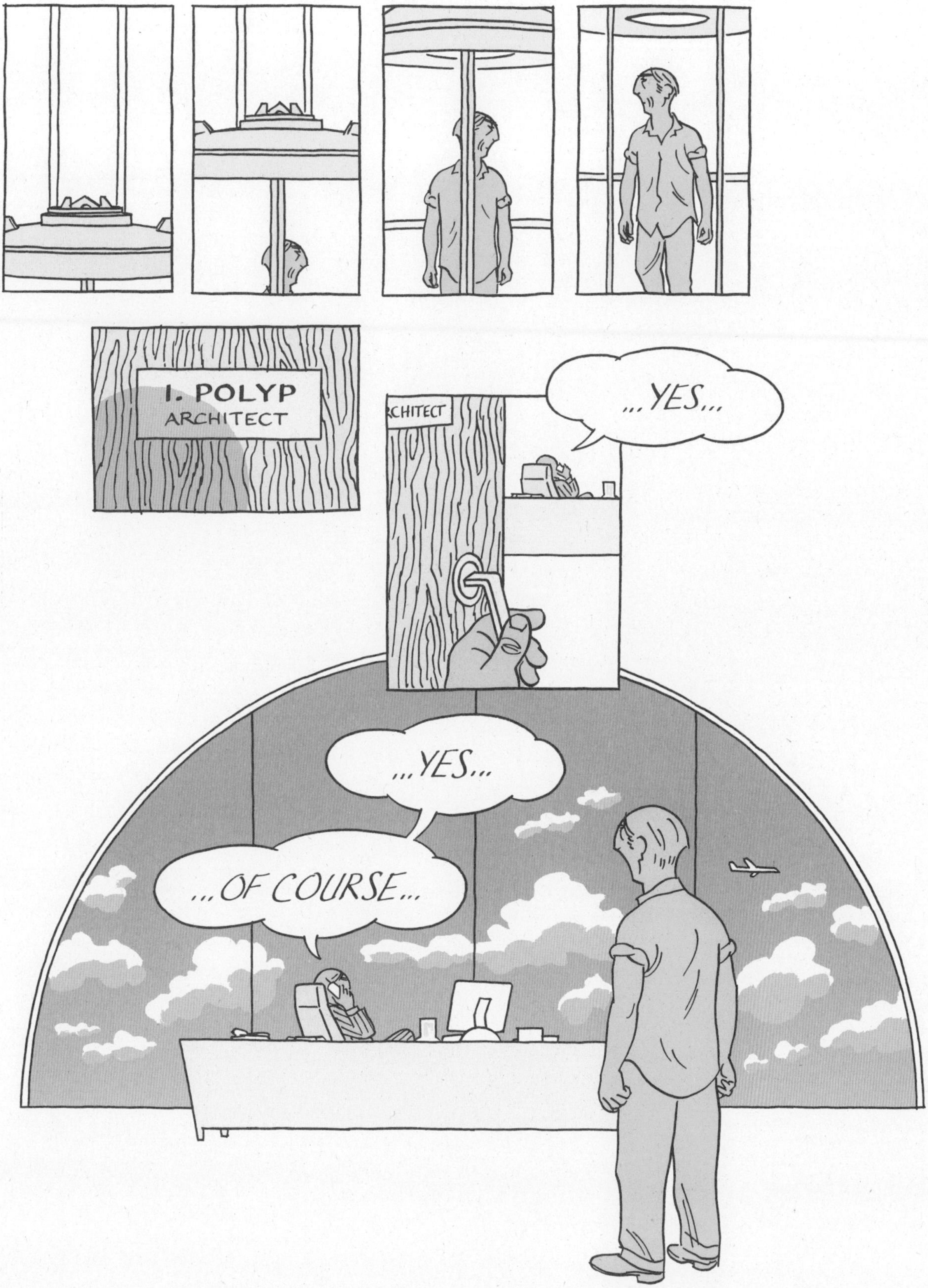
I. POLYP
ARCHITECT
ARCHITECT
...YES...
...YES...
...OF COURSE...

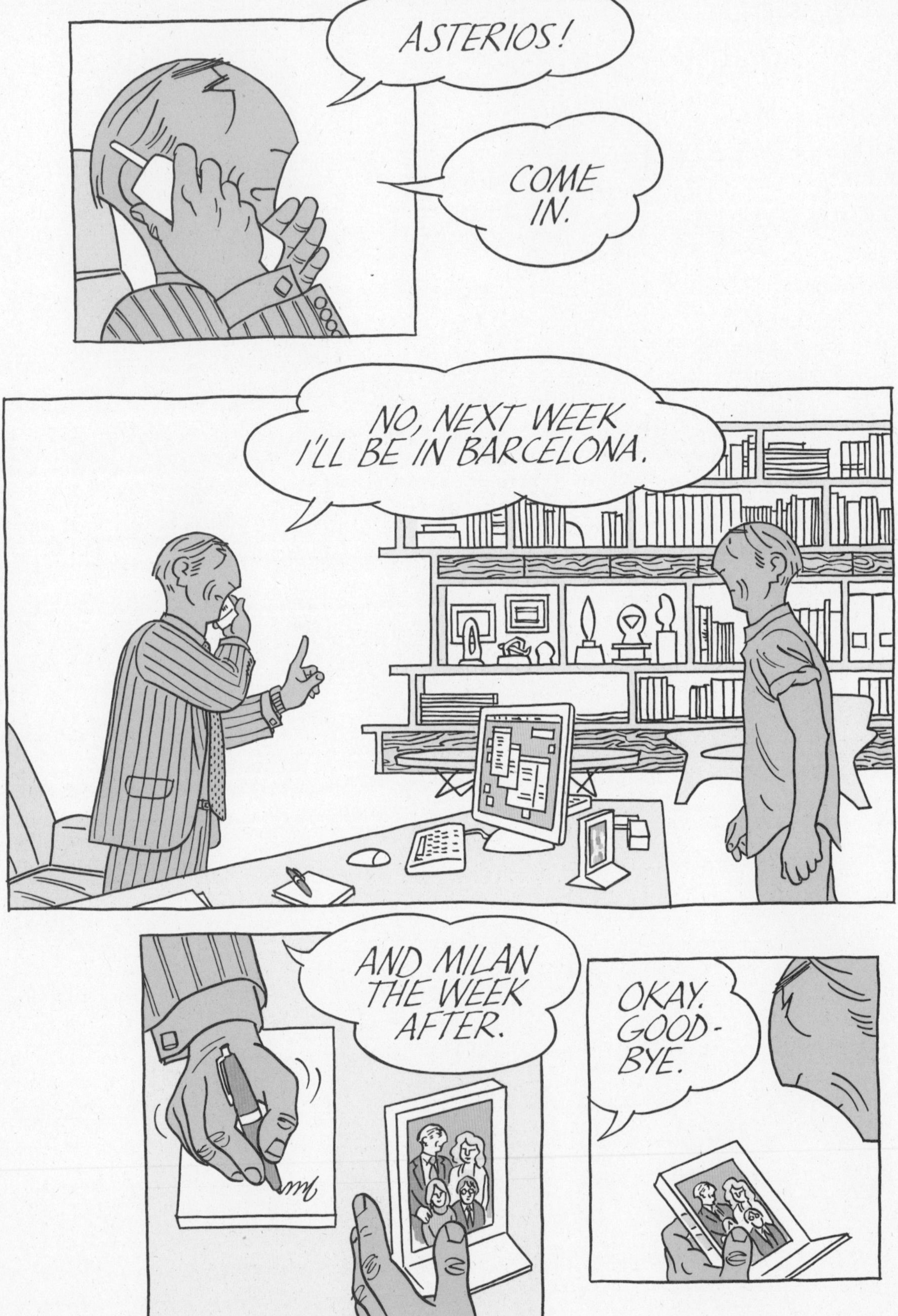
ASTERIOS!
COME IN.
NO, NEXT WEEK I'LL BE IN BARCELONA.
AND MILAN THE WEEK AFTER.
OKAY. GOOD-BYE.

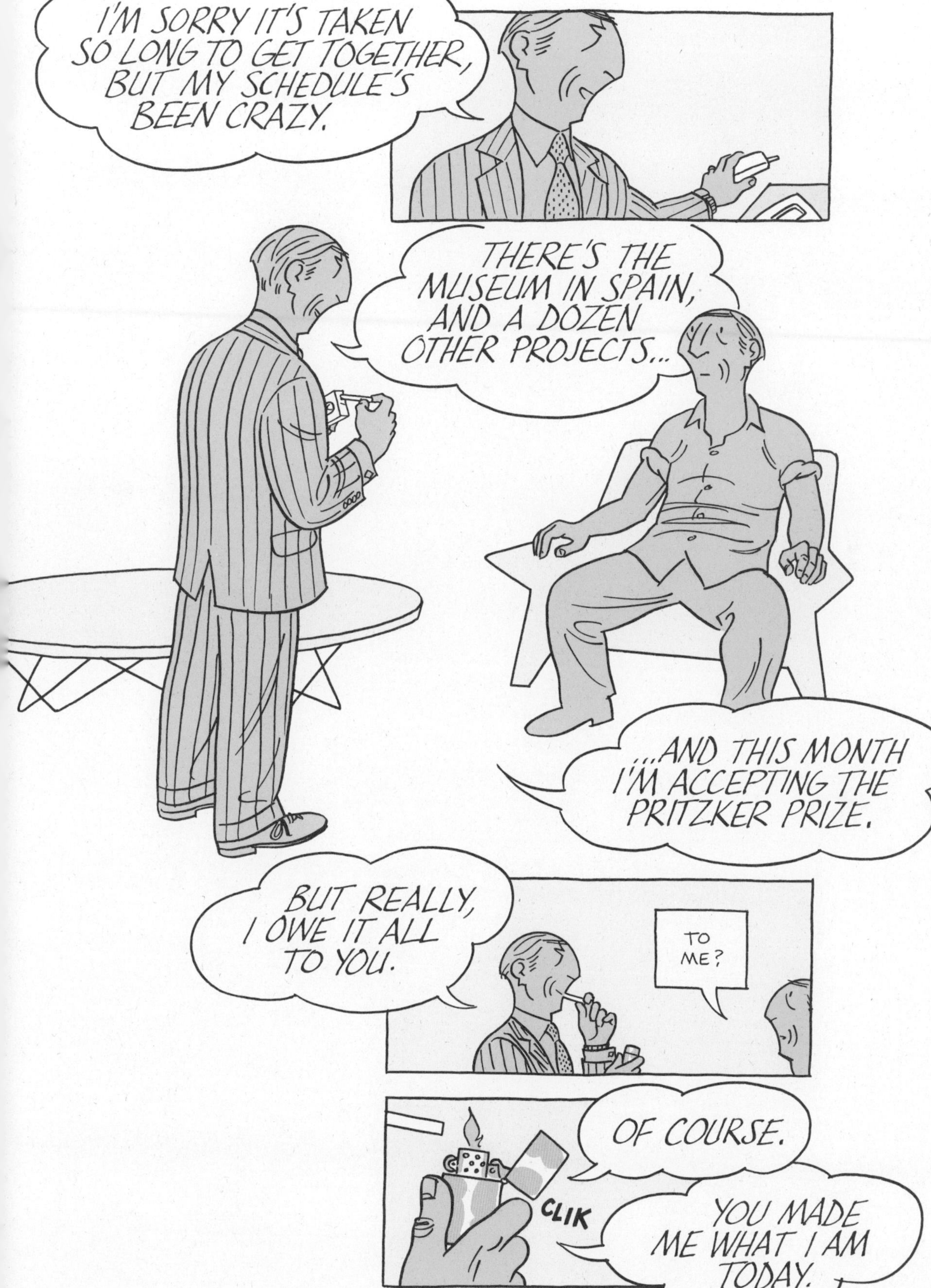
I'M SORRY IT'S TAKEN SO LONG TO GET TOGETHER, BUT MY SCHEDULE'S BEEN CRAZY.
THERE'S THE MUSEUM IN SPAIN, AND A DOZEN OTHER PROJECTS...
...AND THIS MONTH I'M ACCEPTING THE PRITZKER PRIZE.
BUT REALLY, I OWE IT ALL TO YOU.
TO ME?
OF COURSE.
CLIK
YOU MADE ME WHAT I AM TODAY.

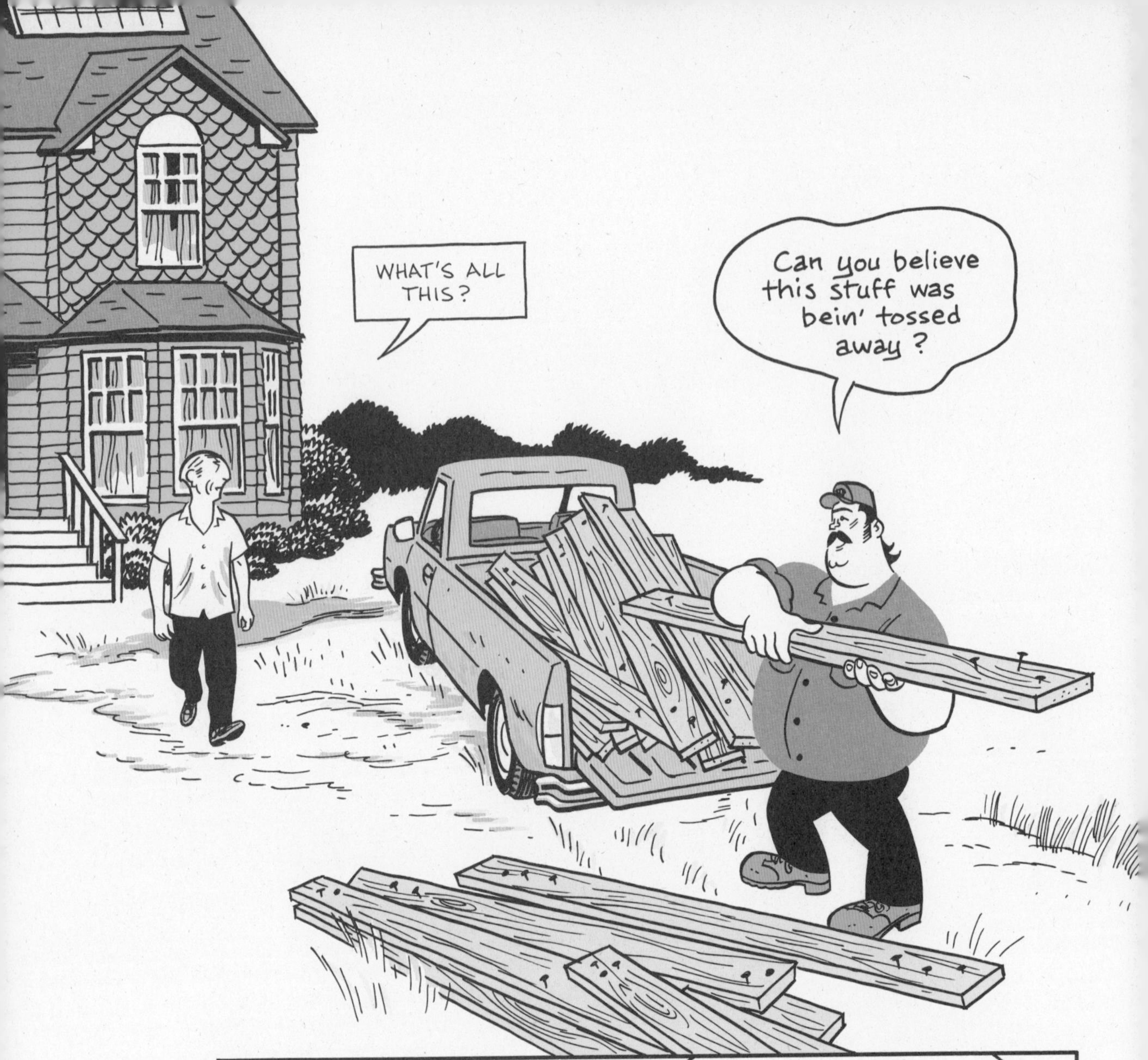
WHAT'S ALL THIS?
Can you believe this stuff was bein' tossed away?

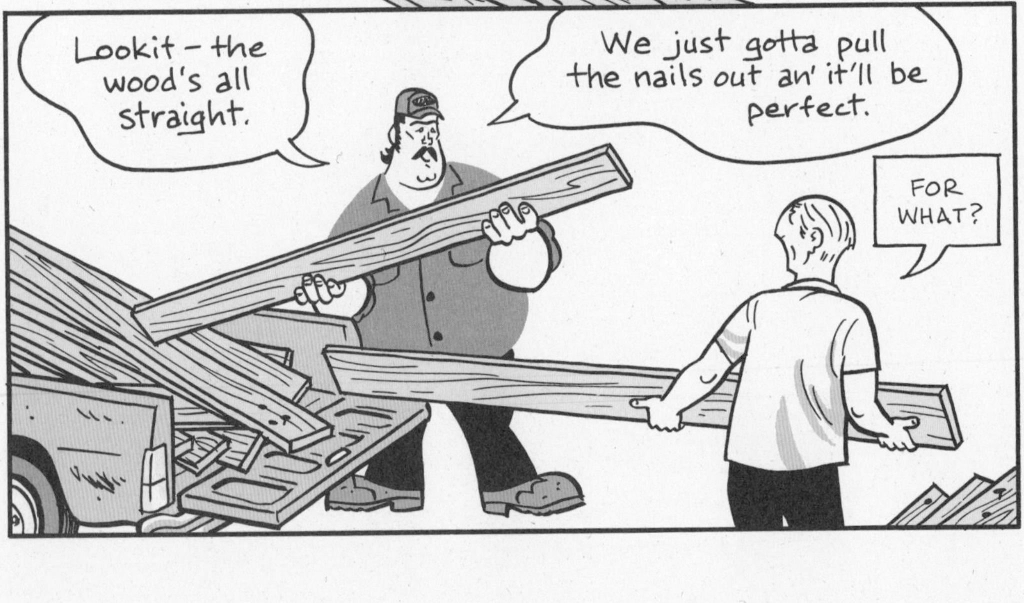
Lookit – the wood's all straight.
We just gotta pull the nails out an' it'll be perfect.
FOR WHAT?

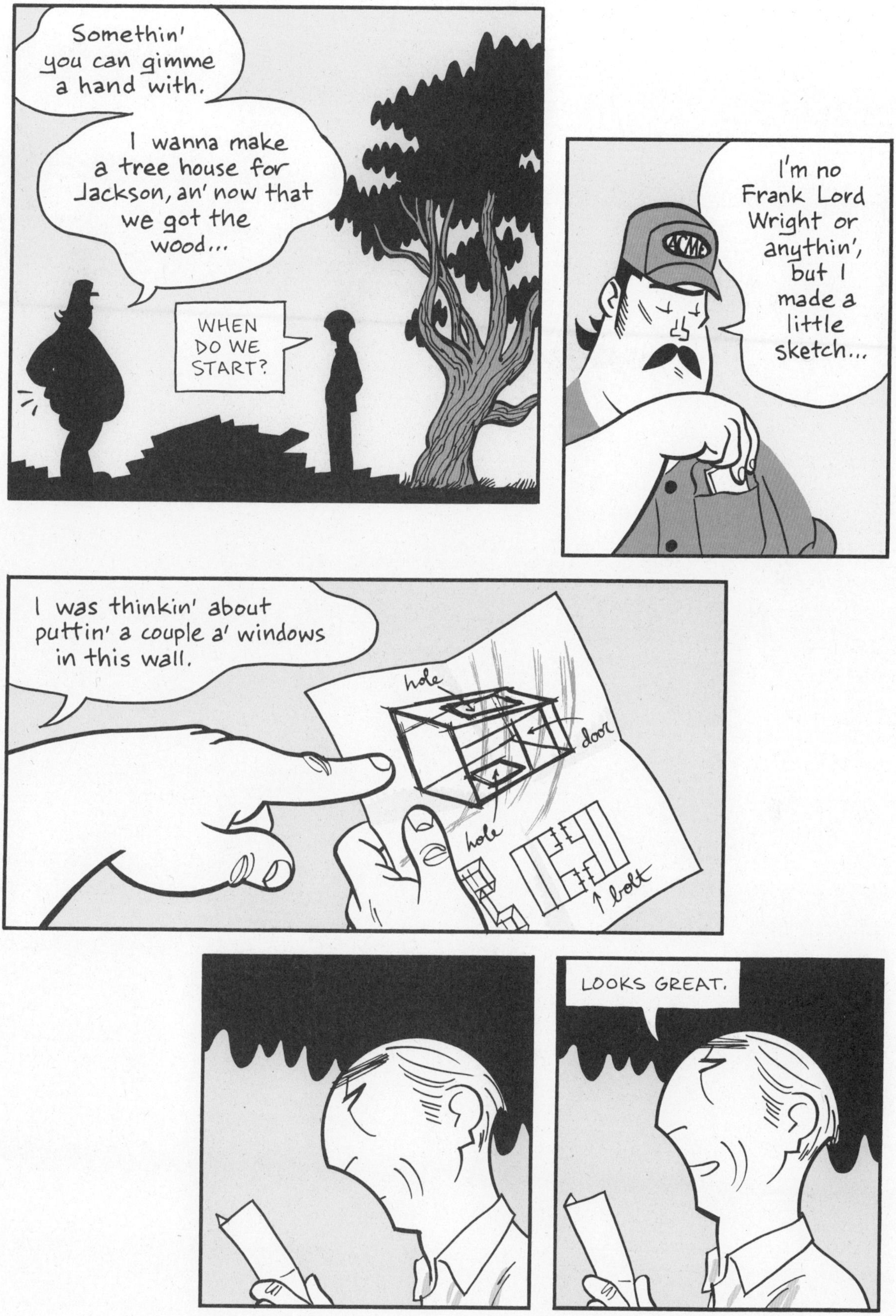
Somethin' you can gimme a hand with.
I wanna make a tree house for Jackson, an' now that we got the wood...
WHEN DO WE START?
I'm no Frank Lord Wright or anythin', but I made a little sketch...
I was thinkin' about puttin' a couple a' windows in this wall.
hole
door
hole
bolt
LOOKS GREAT.

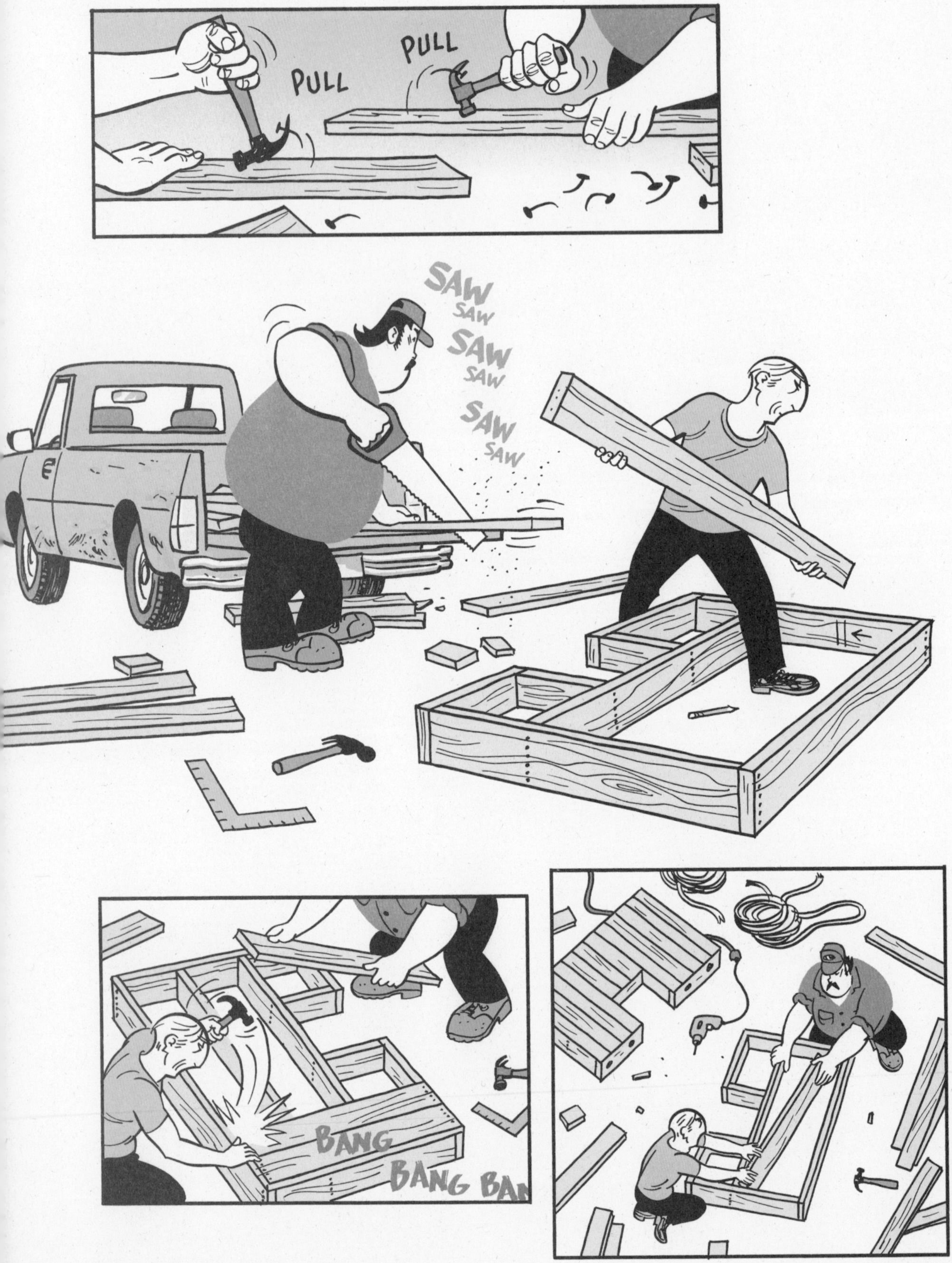

PULL
PULL
SAW
SAW
SAW
SAW
SAW
SAW
BANG
BANG BAN

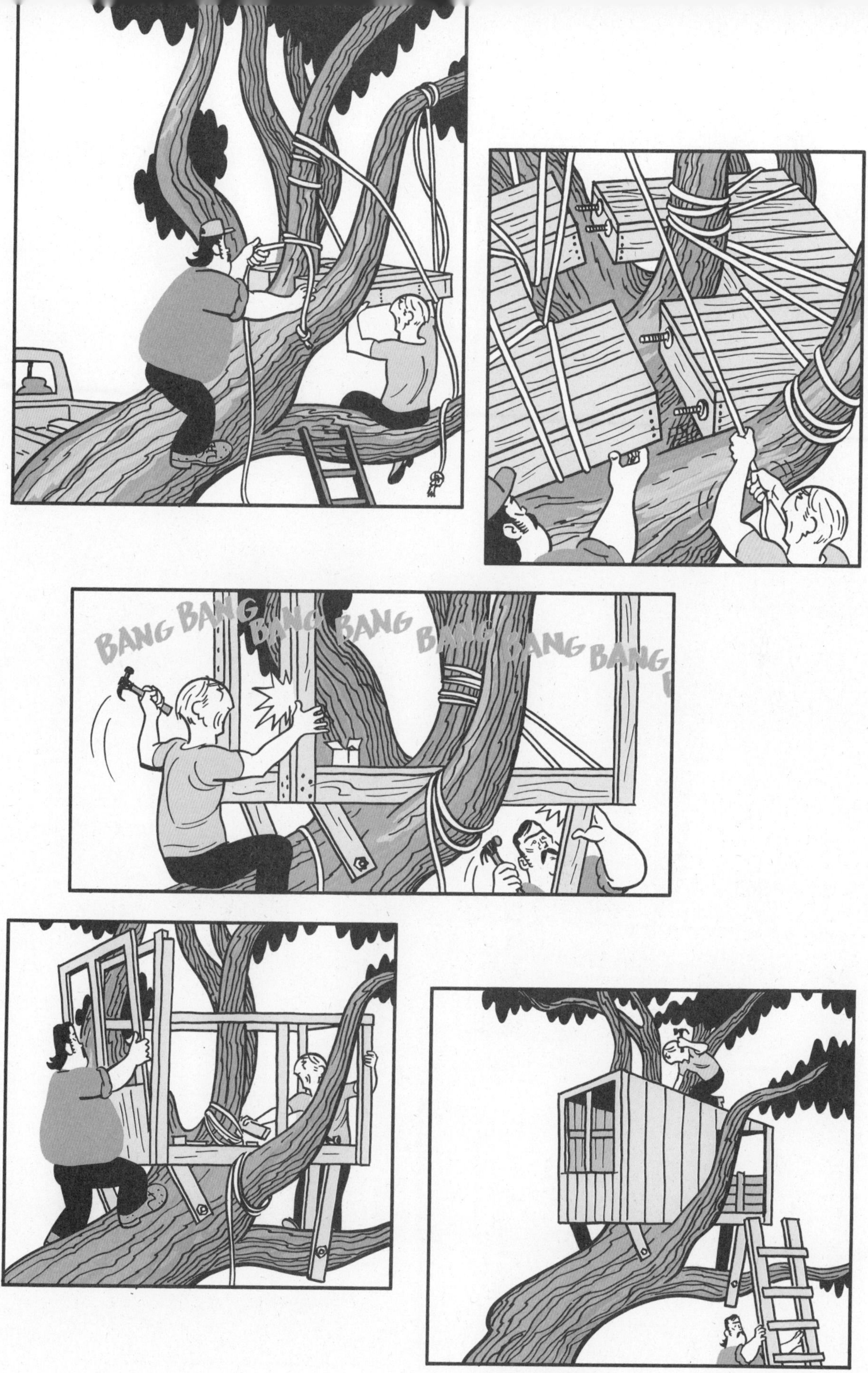
BANG BANG BANG BANG BANG BANG BANG

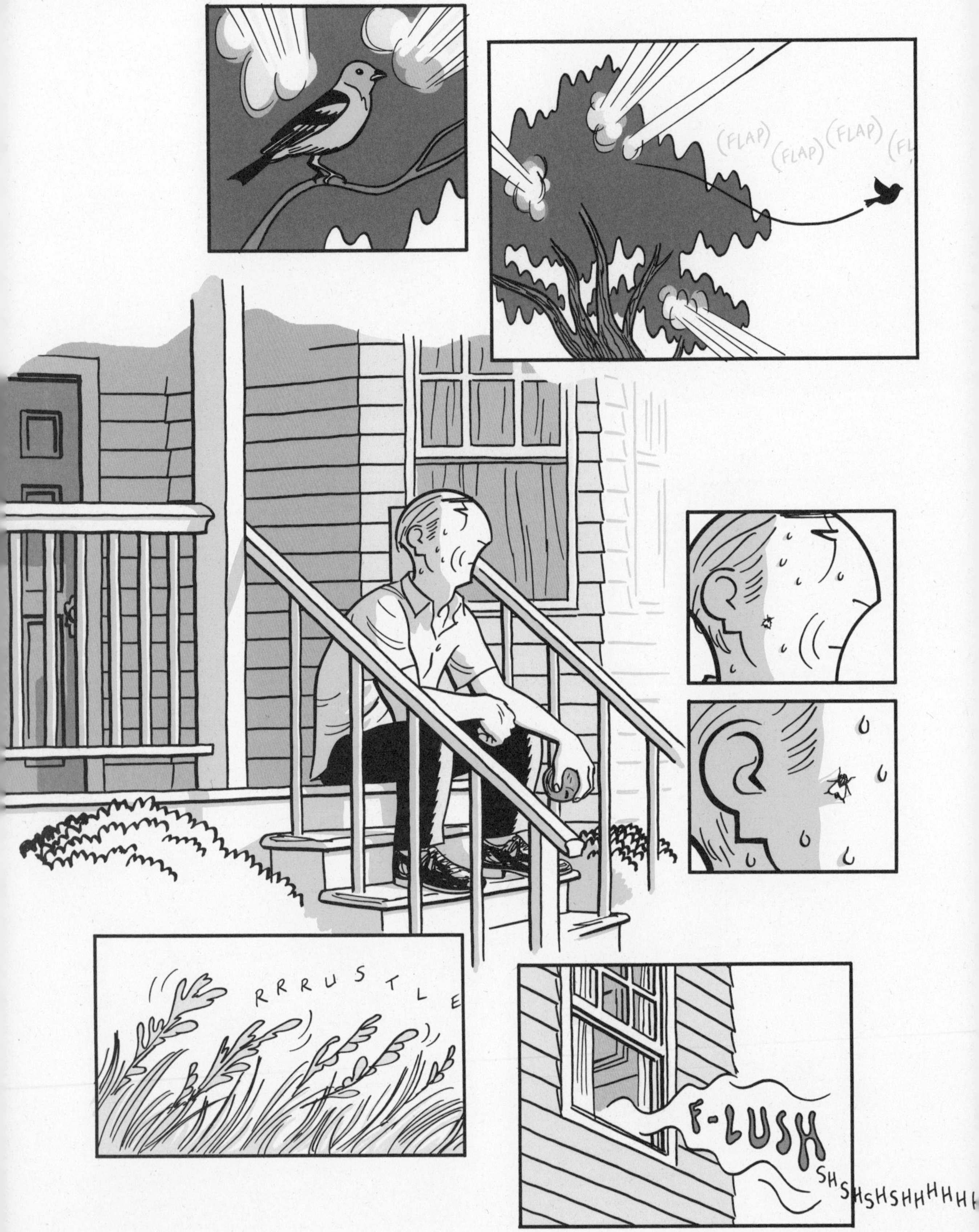

(FLAP) (FLAP) (FLAP) (FL
RRRUSTLE
F-LUSH
SHSHSHSHHHHH

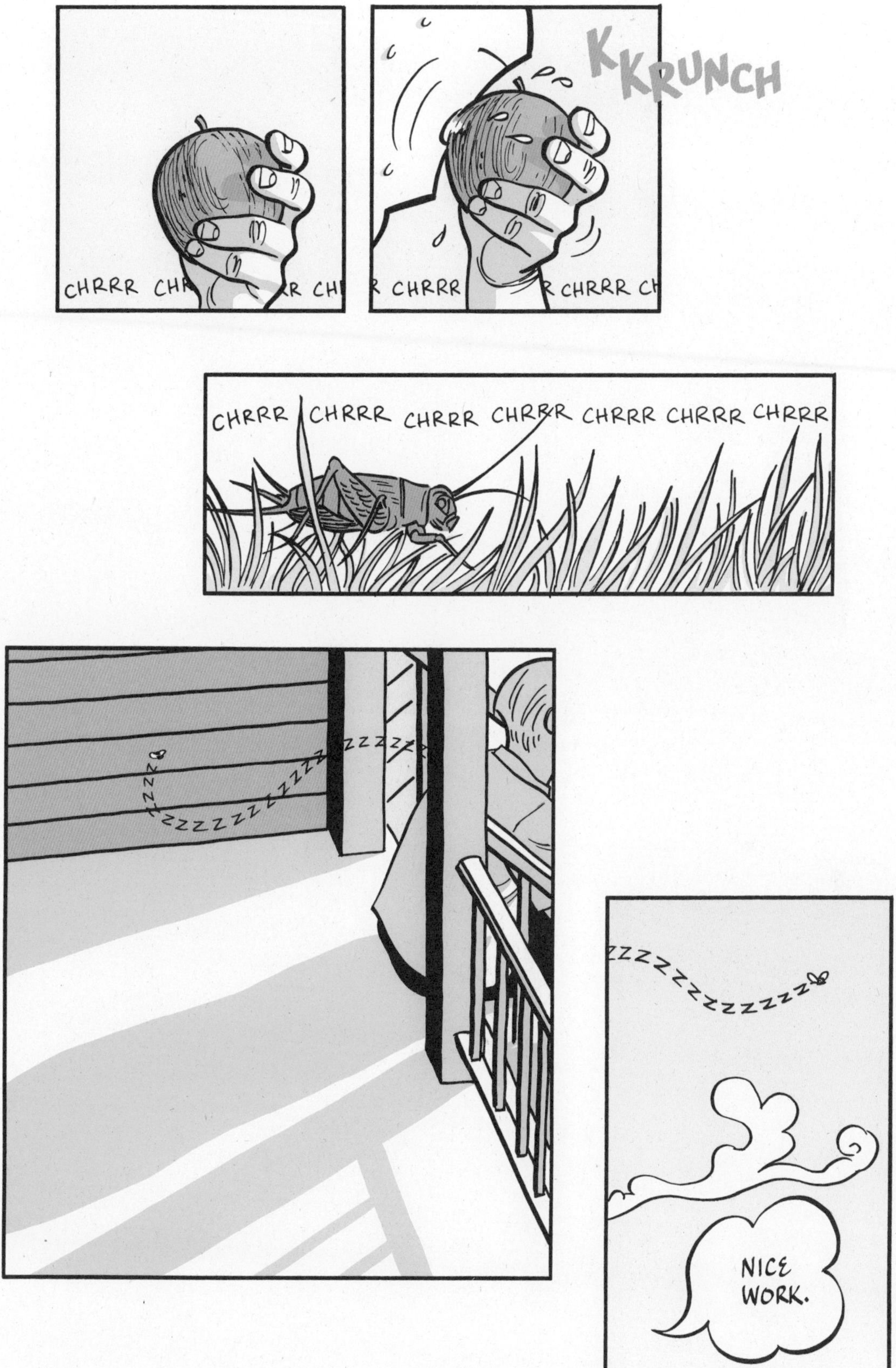
CHRRR CHR
R CH
R CHRRR
R CHRRR C
KKRUNCH
CHRRR CHRRR CHRRR CHRRR CHRRR CHRRR CHRRR
ZZZZZZZZZZZZZZZZZZZZZZZ
ZZZZZZZZZZZZZZ
NICE WORK.

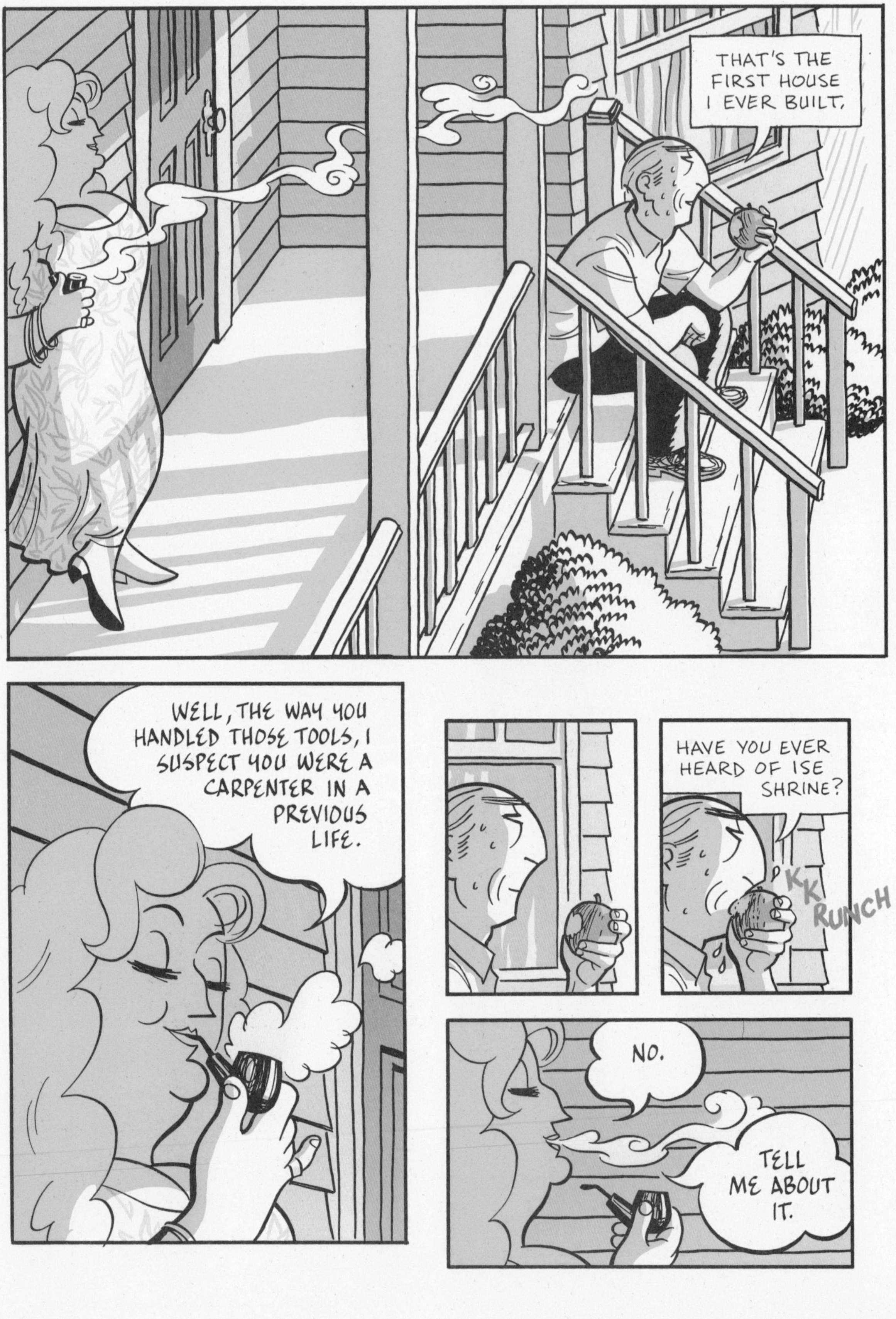
THAT'S THE FIRST HOUSE I EVER BUILT.
WELL, THE WAY YOU HANDLED THOSE TOOLS, I SUSPECT YOU WERE A CARPENTER IN A PREVIOUS LIFE.
HAVE YOU EVER HEARD OF ISE SHRINE?
KKRUNCH
NO.
TELL ME ABOUT IT.

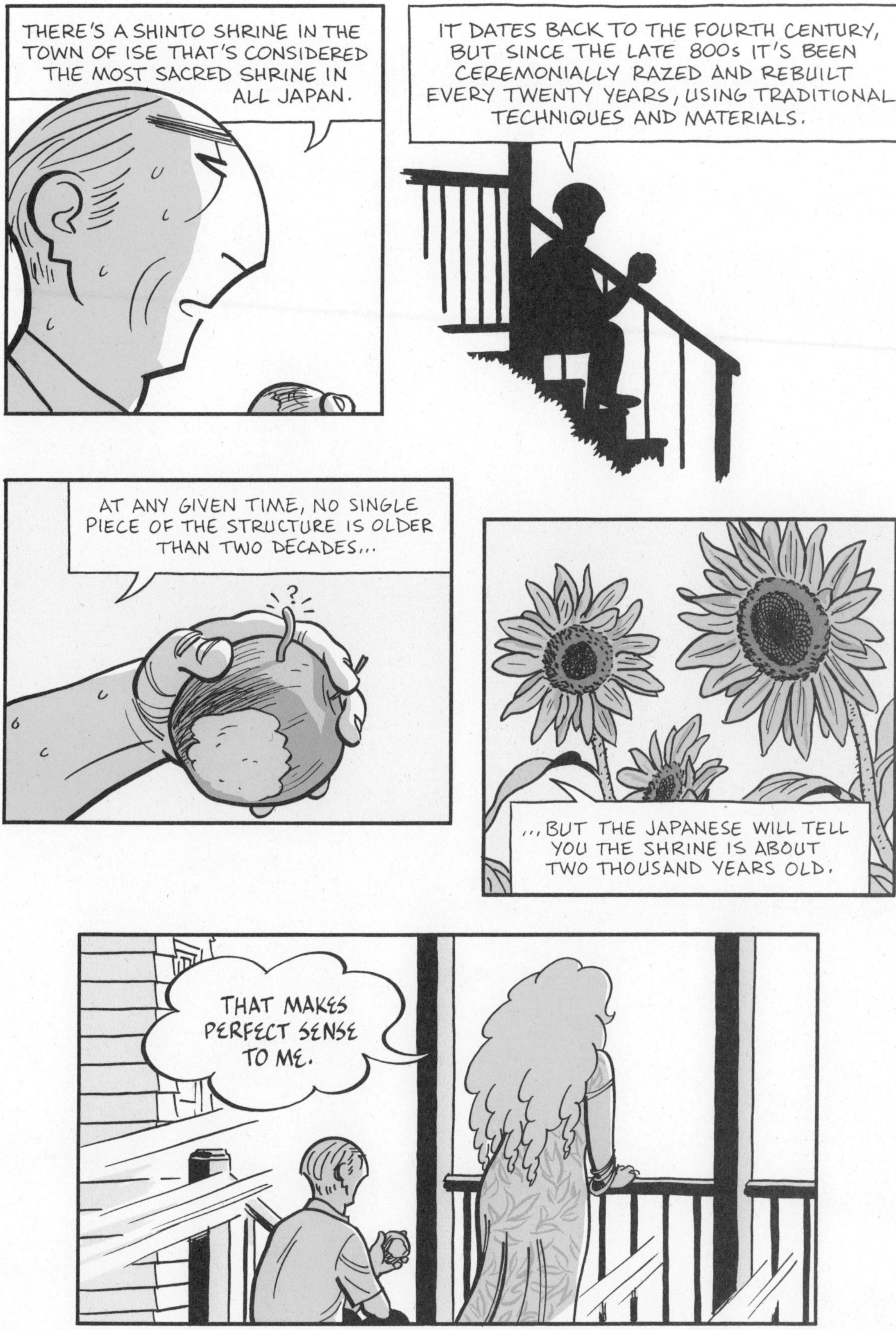
THERE'S A SHINTO SHRINE IN THE TOWN OF ISE THAT'S CONSIDERED THE MOST SACRED SHRINE IN ALL JAPAN.
IT DATES BACK TO THE FOURTH CENTURY, BUT SINCE THE LATE 800s IT'S BEEN CEREMONIALLY RAZED AND REBUILT EVERY TWENTY YEARS, USING TRADITIONAL TECHNIQUES AND MATERIALS.
AT ANY GIVEN TIME, NO SINGLE PIECE OF THE STRUCTURE IS OLDER THAN TWO DECADES...
?
...BUT THE JAPANESE WILL TELL YOU THE SHRINE IS ABOUT TWO THOUSAND YEARS OLD.
THAT MAKES PERFECT SENSE TO ME.

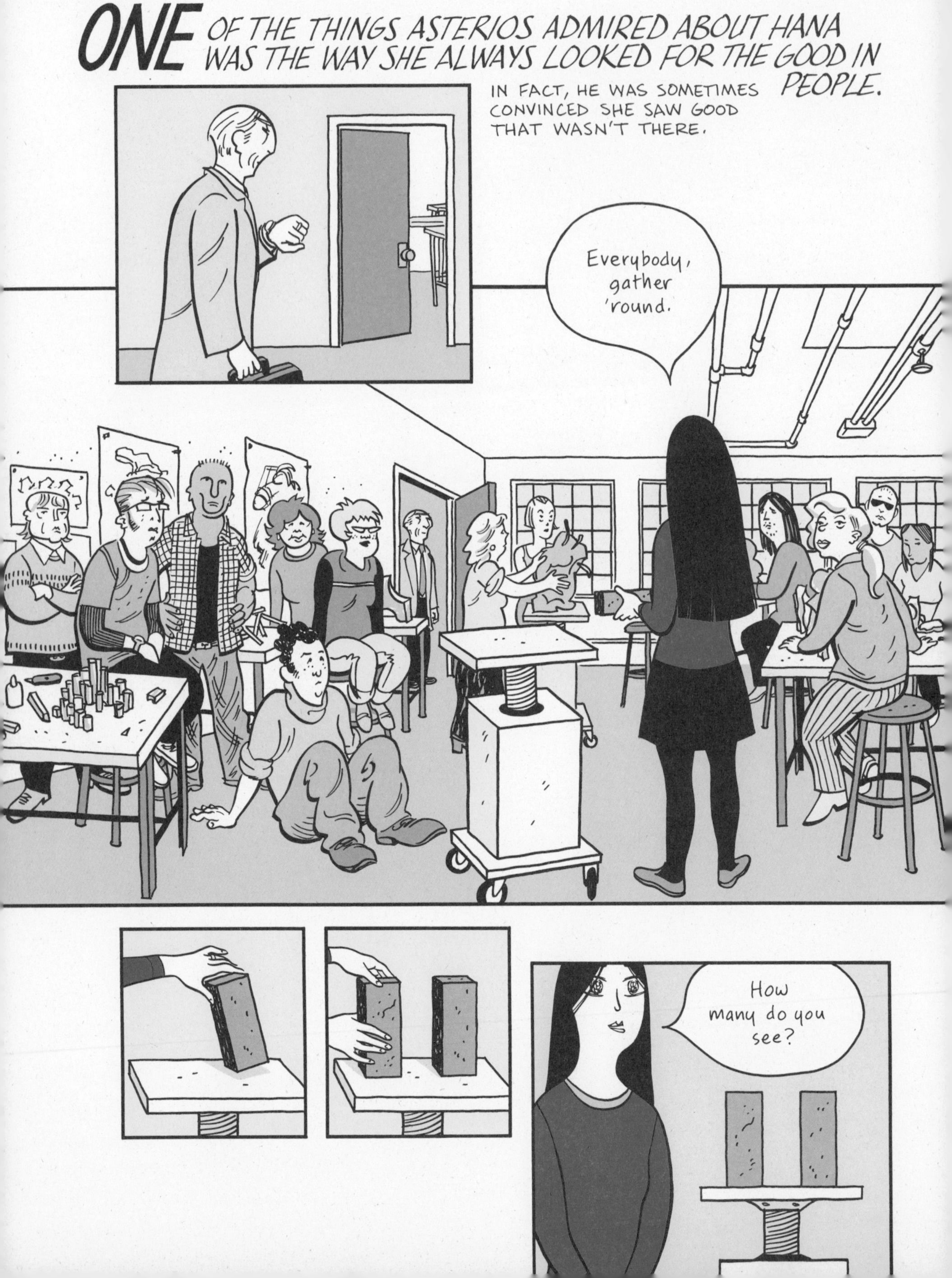
ONE OF THE THINGS ASTERIOS ADMIRED ABOUT HANA WAS THE WAY SHE ALWAYS LOOKED FOR THE GOOD IN PEOPLE.
IN FACT, HE WAS SOMETIMES CONVINCED SHE SAW GOOD THAT WASN'T THERE.
Everybody, gather 'round.
How many do you see?

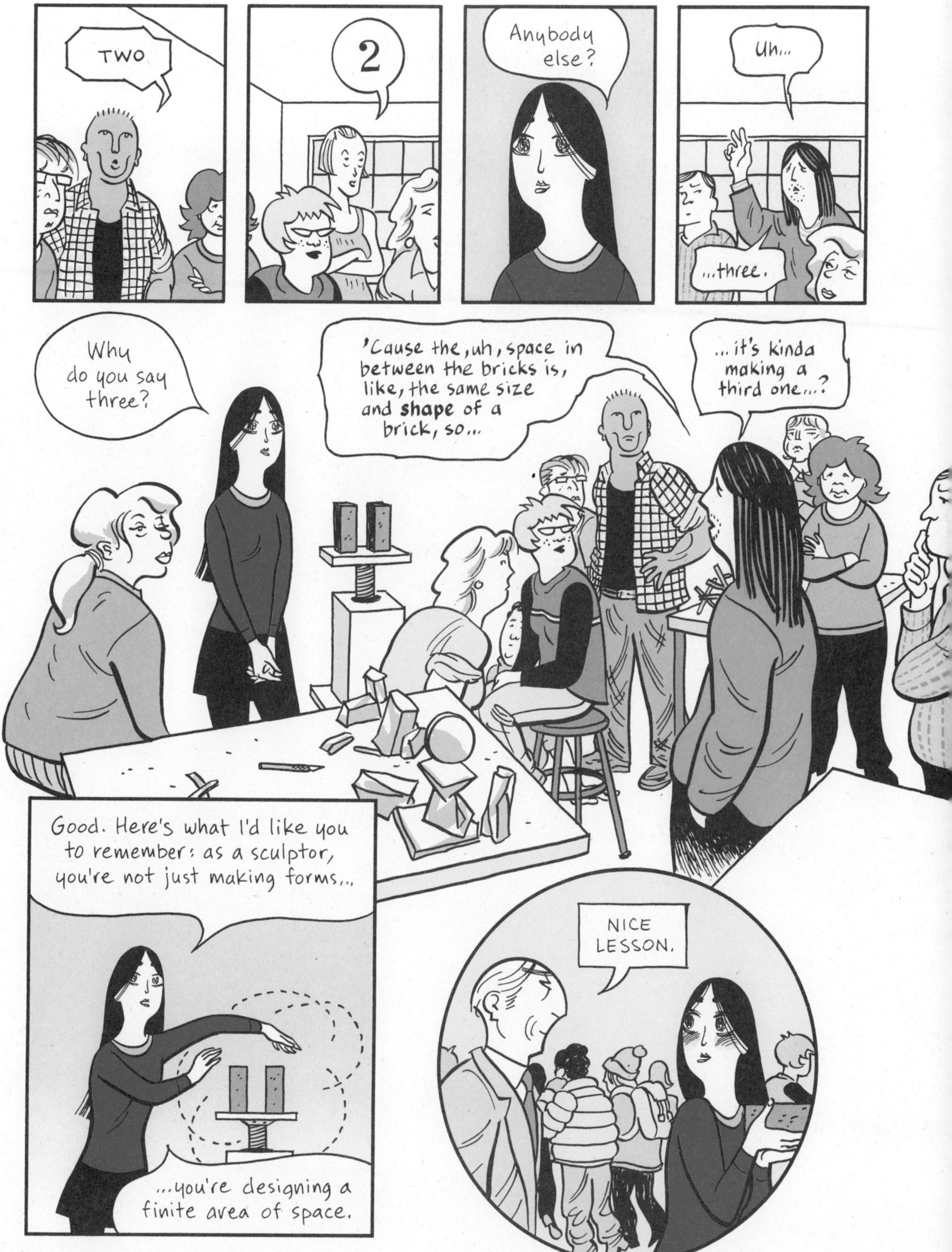
TWO
2
Anybody else?
Uh...
...three.
Why do you say three?
'Cause the, uh, space in between the bricks is, like, the same size and **shape** of a brick, so...
...it's kinda making a third one...?
Good. Here's what I'd like you to remember: as a sculptor, you're not just making forms...
...you're designing a finite area of space.
NICE LESSON.

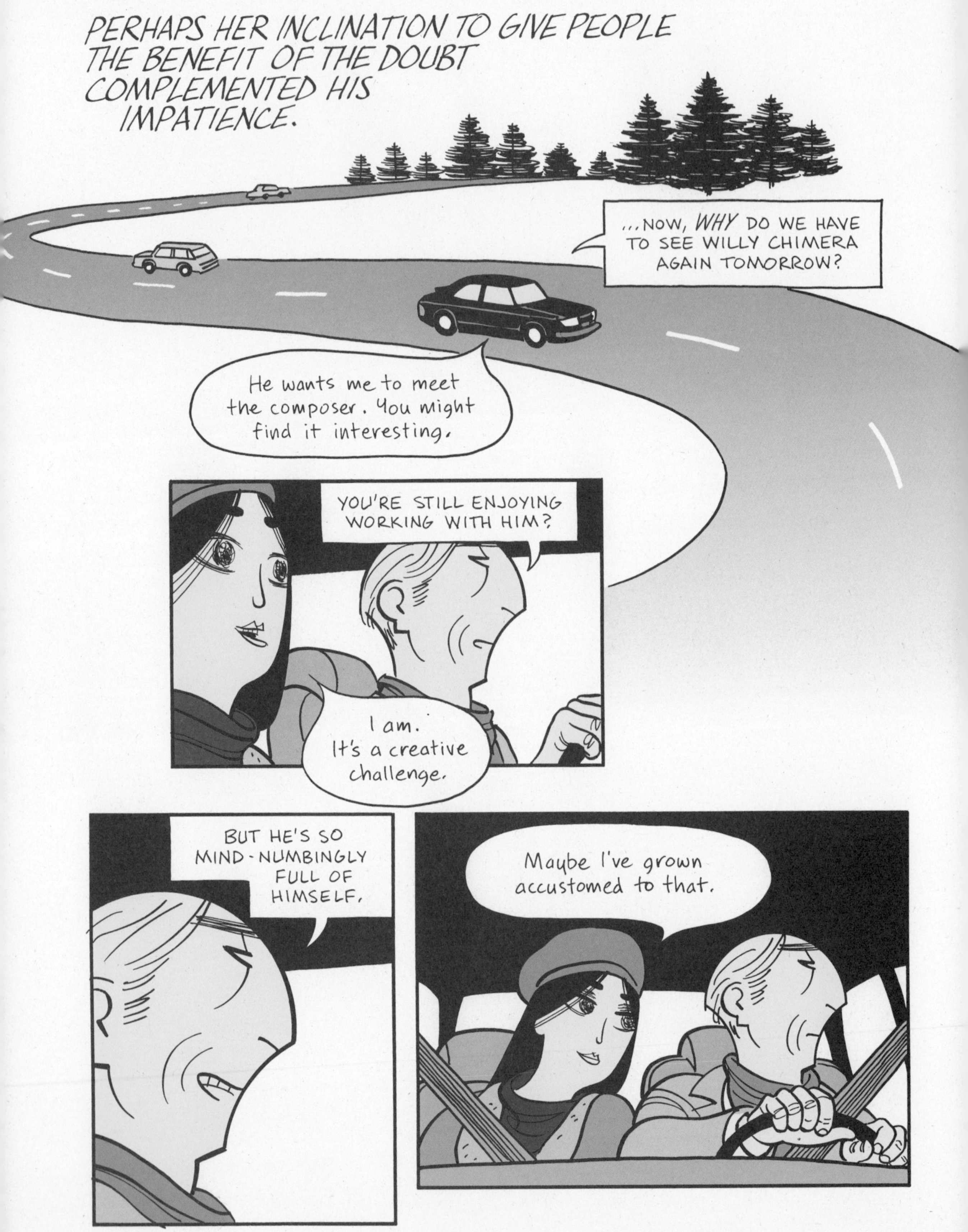
PERHAPS HER INCLINATION TO GIVE PEOPLE THE BENEFIT OF THE DOUBT COMPLEMENTED HIS IMPATIENCE.
...NOW, *WHY* DO WE HAVE TO SEE WILLY CHIMERA AGAIN TOMORROW?
He wants me to meet the composer. You might find it interesting.
YOU'RE STILL ENJOYING WORKING WITH HIM?
I am. It's a creative challenge.
BUT HE'S SO MIND-NUMBINGLY FULL OF HIMSELF.
Maybe I've grown accustomed to that.

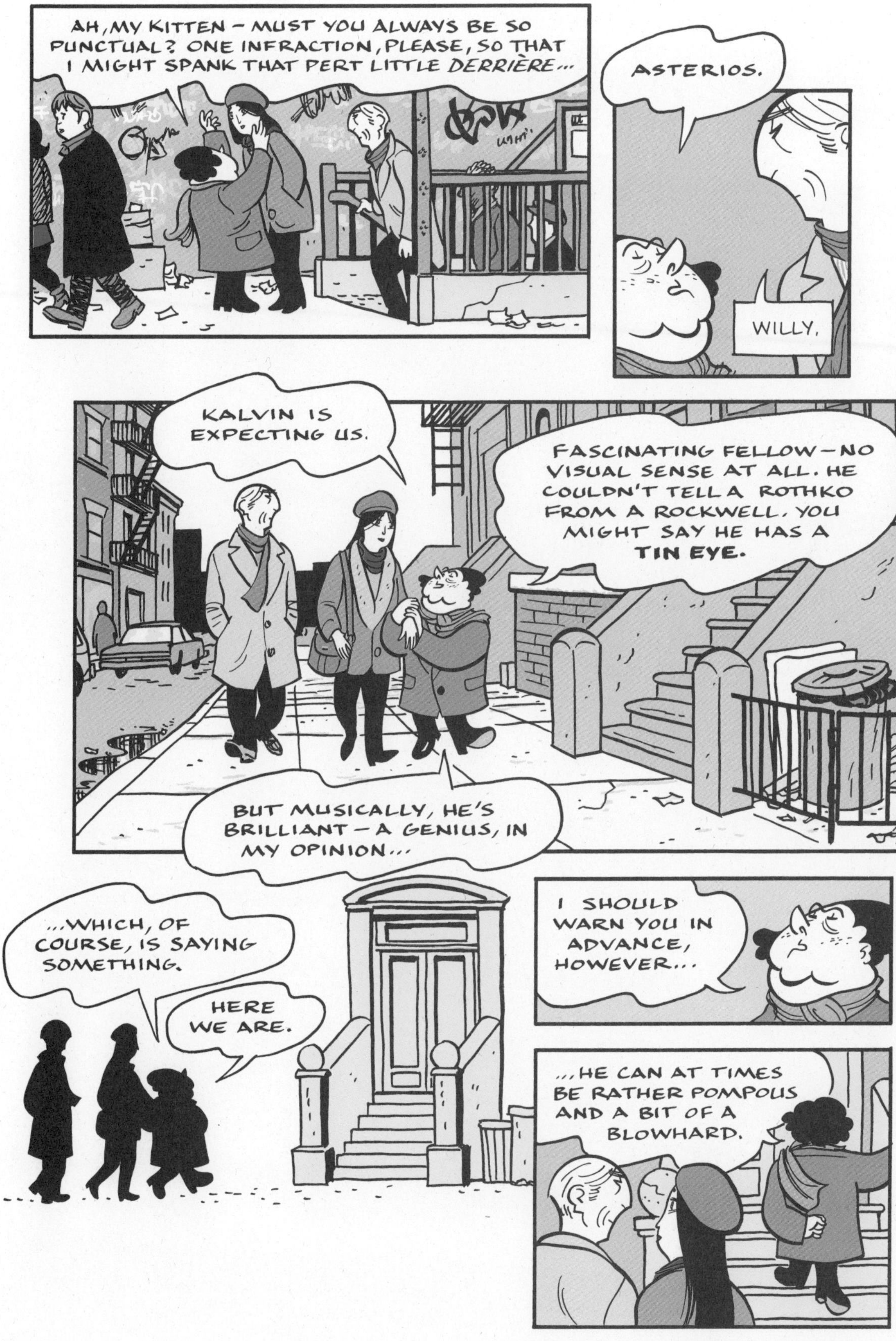
AH, MY KITTEN – MUST YOU ALWAYS BE SO PUNCTUAL? ONE INFRACTION, PLEASE, SO THAT I MIGHT SPANK THAT PERT LITTLE *DERRIÈRE*...
ASTERIOS.
WILLY.
KALVIN IS EXPECTING US.
FASCINATING FELLOW – NO VISUAL SENSE AT ALL. HE COULDN'T TELL A ROTHKO FROM A ROCKWELL. YOU MIGHT SAY HE HAS A **TIN EYE.**
BUT MUSICALLY, HE'S BRILLIANT – A GENIUS, IN MY OPINION...
...WHICH, OF COURSE, IS SAYING SOMETHING.
HERE WE ARE.
I SHOULD WARN YOU IN ADVANCE, HOWEVER...
...HE CAN AT TIMES BE RATHER POMPOUS AND A BIT OF A BLOWHARD.

KALVIN KOHOUTEK, ASTERIOS WONDERED BRIEFLY IF THAT WAS NOT HIS GIVEN NAME.
A COMPOSER KNOWN FOR HIS ECLECTIC AND EXPERIMENTAL MUSICAL EXPLORATIONS, CALLED HIS STYLE OF LIVING "BOHEGEOIS."

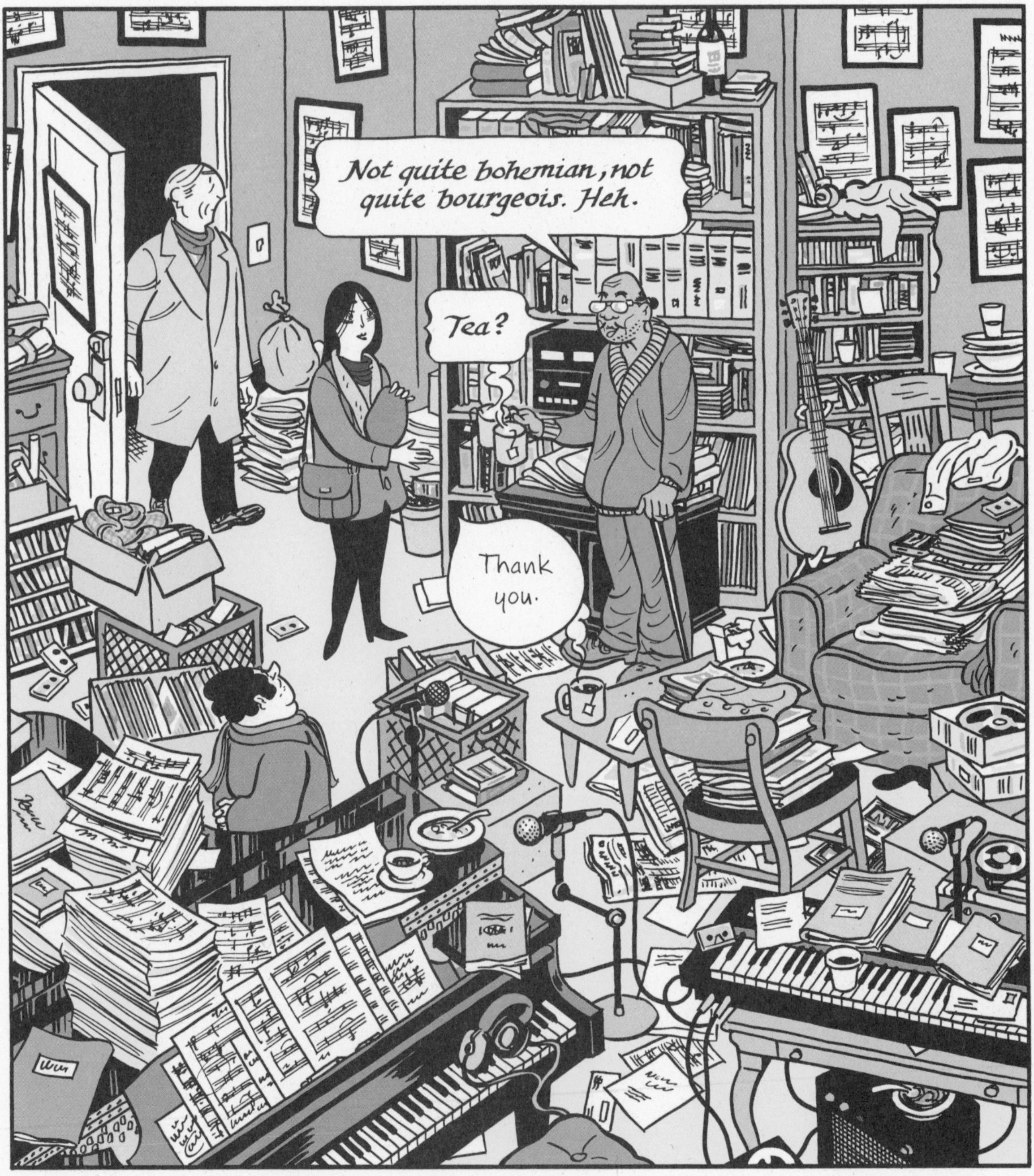

Not quite bohemian, not quite bourgeois. Heh.
Tea?
Thank you.

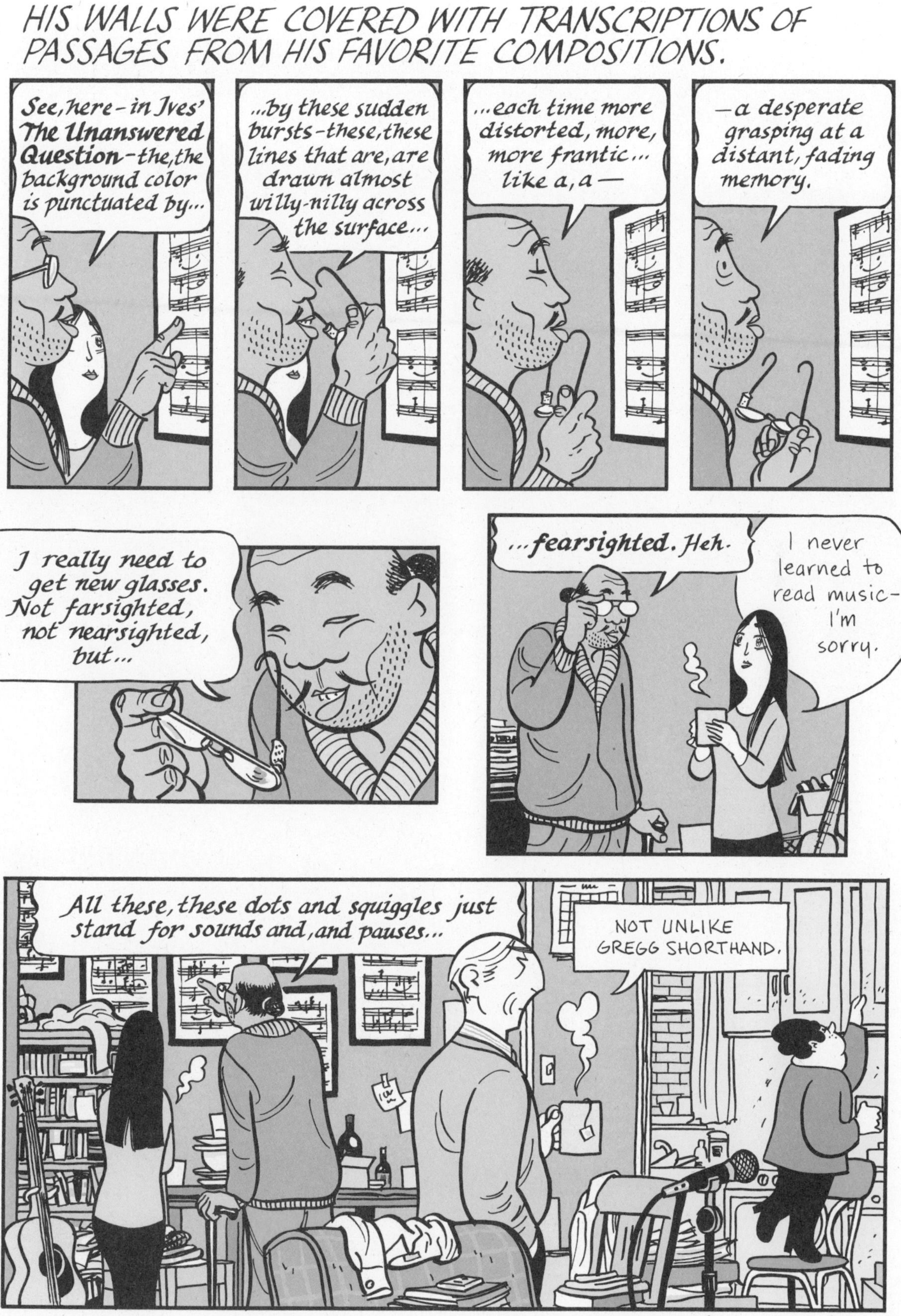
HIS WALLS WERE COVERED WITH TRANSCRIPTIONS OF PASSAGES FROM HIS FAVORITE COMPOSITIONS.
See, here - in Ives' **The Unanswered Question** - the, the background color is punctuated by...
...by these sudden bursts - these, these lines that are, are drawn almost willy-nilly across the surface...
...each time more distorted, more, more frantic... like a, a —
— a desperate grasping at a distant, fading memory.
I really need to get new glasses. Not farsighted, not nearsighted, but...
...**fearsighted**. Heh.
I never learned to read music - I'm sorry.
All these, these dots and squiggles just stand for sounds and, and pauses...
NOT UNLIKE GREGG SHORTHAND.

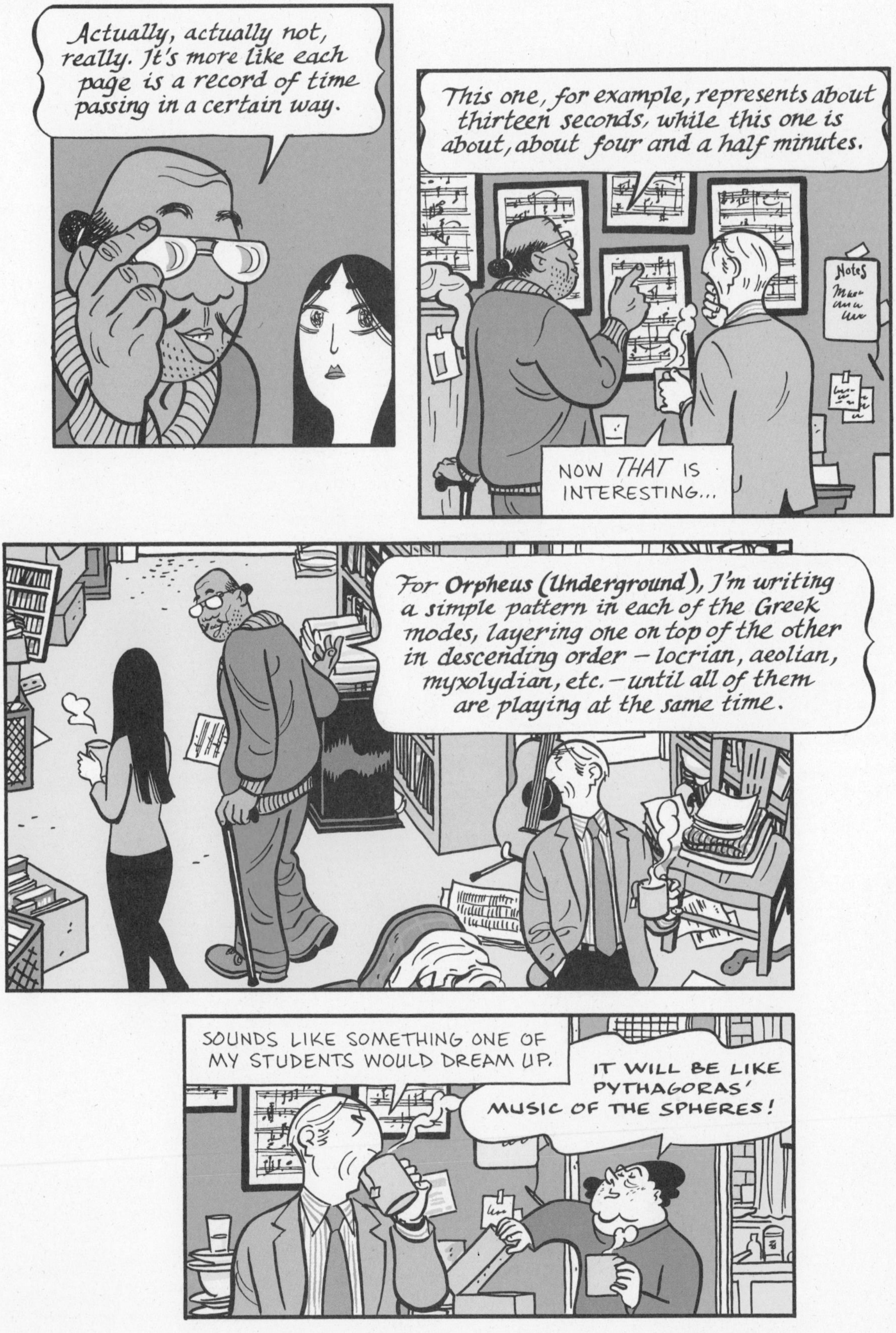
Actually, actually not, really. It's more like each page is a record of time passing in a certain way.
This one, for example, represents about thirteen seconds, while this one is about, about four and a half minutes.
NOW THAT IS INTERESTING...
For Orpheus (Underground), I'm writing a simple pattern in each of the Greek modes, layering one on top of the other in descending order – locrian, aeolian, myxolydian, etc. – until all of them are playing at the same time.
SOUNDS LIKE SOMETHING ONE OF MY STUDENTS WOULD DREAM UP.
IT WILL BE LIKE PYTHAGORAS' MUSIC OF THE SPHERES!
Notes

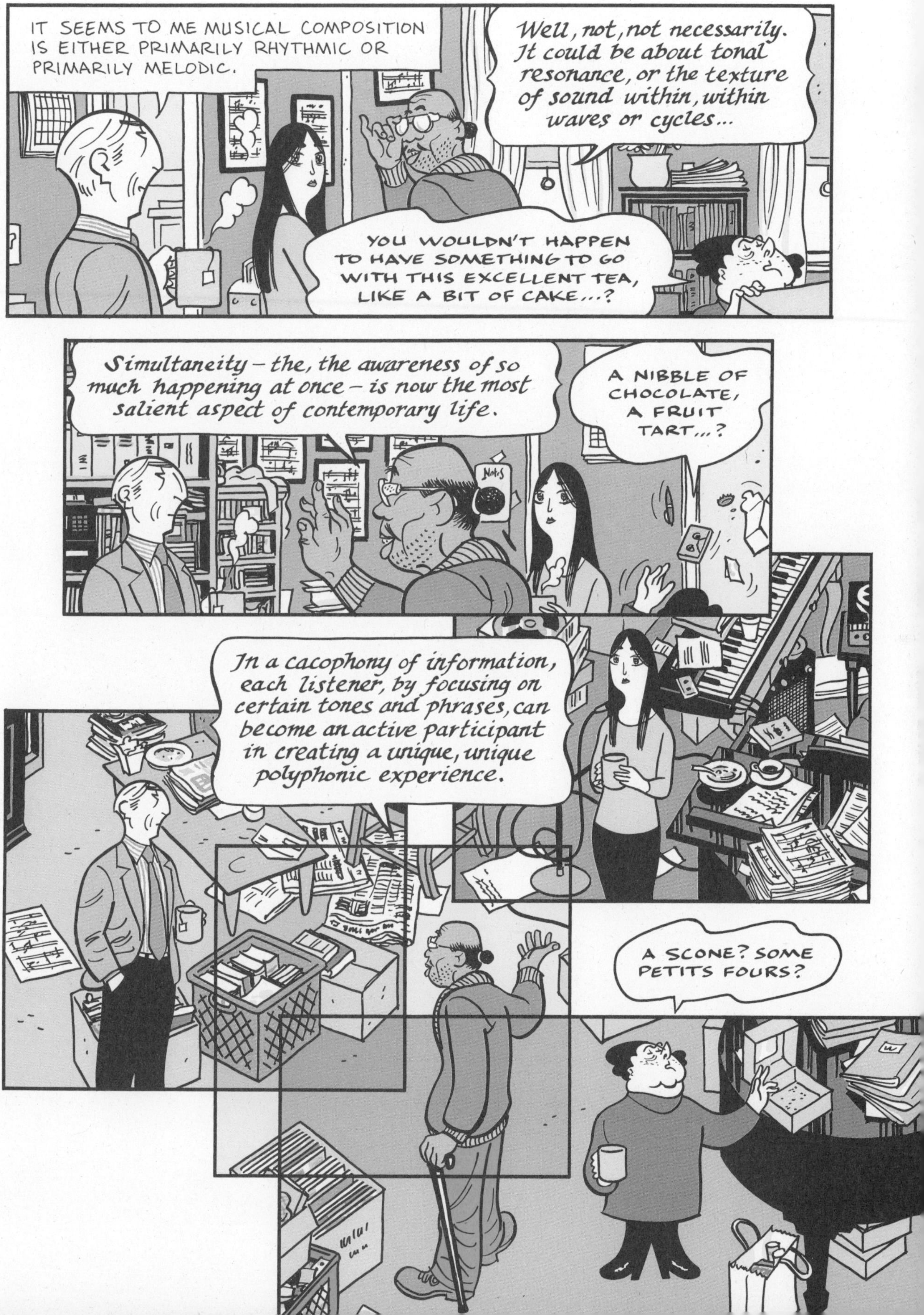
IT SEEMS TO ME MUSICAL COMPOSITION IS EITHER PRIMARILY RHYTHMIC OR PRIMARILY MELODIC.
Well, not, not necessarily. It could be about tonal resonance, or the texture of sound within, within waves or cycles...
YOU WOULDN'T HAPPEN TO HAVE SOMETHING TO GO WITH THIS EXCELLENT TEA, LIKE A BIT OF CAKE...?
Simultaneity – the, the awareness of so much happening at once – is now the most salient aspect of contemporary life.
A NIBBLE OF CHOCOLATE, A FRUIT TART...?
Notes
In a cacophony of information, each listener, by focusing on certain tones and phrases, can become an active participant in creating a unique, unique polyphonic experience.
A SCONE? SOME PETITS FOURS?

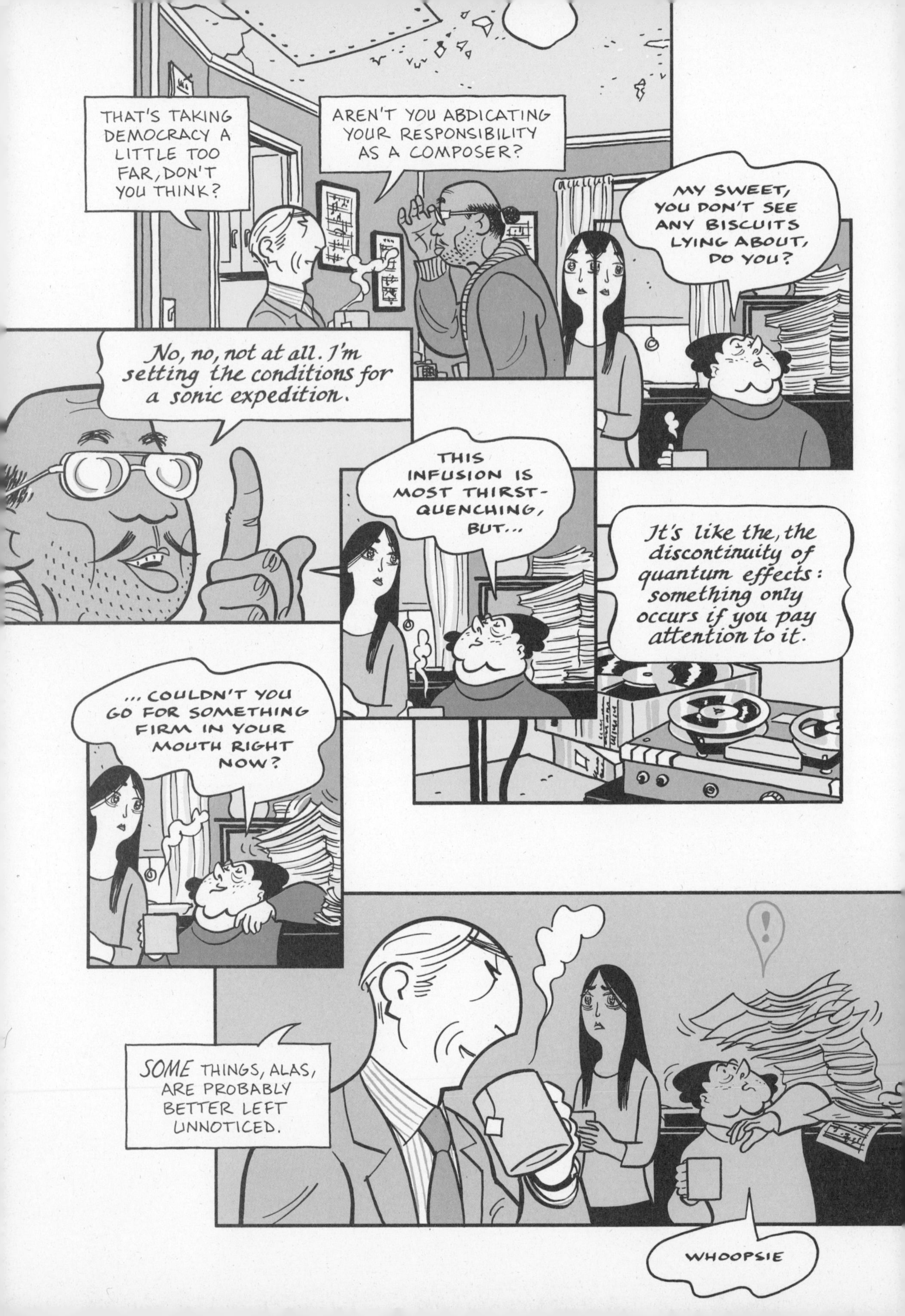
THAT'S TAKING DEMOCRACY A LITTLE TOO FAR, DON'T YOU THINK?
AREN'T YOU ABDICATING YOUR RESPONSIBILITY AS A COMPOSER?
MY SWEET, YOU DON'T SEE ANY BISCUITS LYING ABOUT, DO YOU?
No, no, not at all. I'm setting the conditions for a sonic expedition.
THIS INFUSION IS MOST THIRST-QUENCHING, BUT...
It's like the, the discontinuity of quantum effects: something only occurs if you pay attention to it.
... COULDN'T YOU GO FOR SOMETHING FIRM IN YOUR MOUTH RIGHT NOW?
SOME THINGS, ALAS, ARE PROBABLY BETTER LEFT UNNOTICED.
!
WHOOPSIE

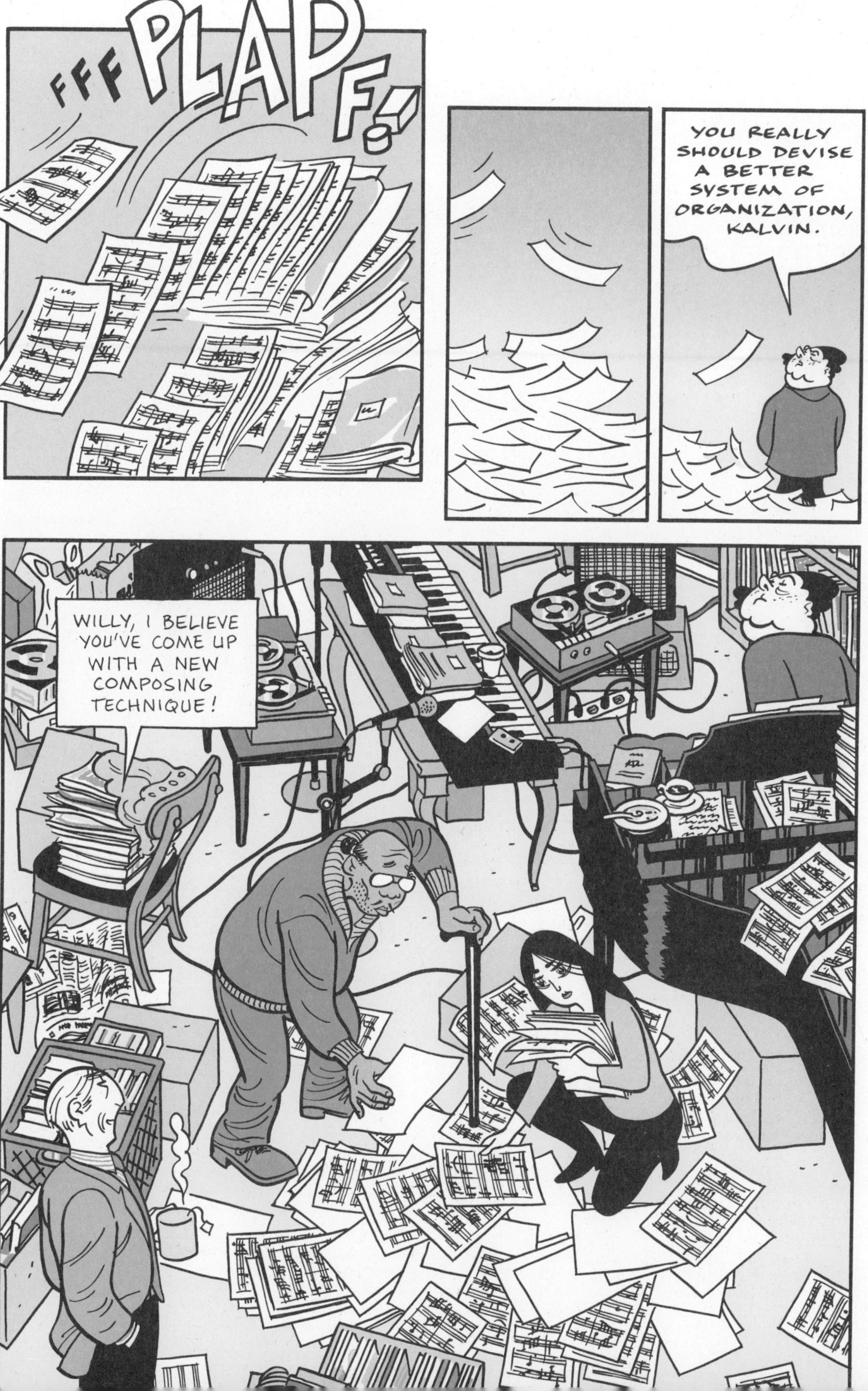
FFF PLAPF
YOU REALLY SHOULD DEVISE A BETTER SYSTEM OF ORGANIZATION, KALVIN.
WILLY, I BELIEVE YOU'VE COME UP WITH A NEW COMPOSING TECHNIQUE!

ASTERIOS CAN'T RECALL IF HANA HAD ANYTHING TO SAY ON THE WAY HOME. HE WAS TOO BUSY THINKING UP NEW REJOINDERS TO KOHOUTEK'S COMMENTS.

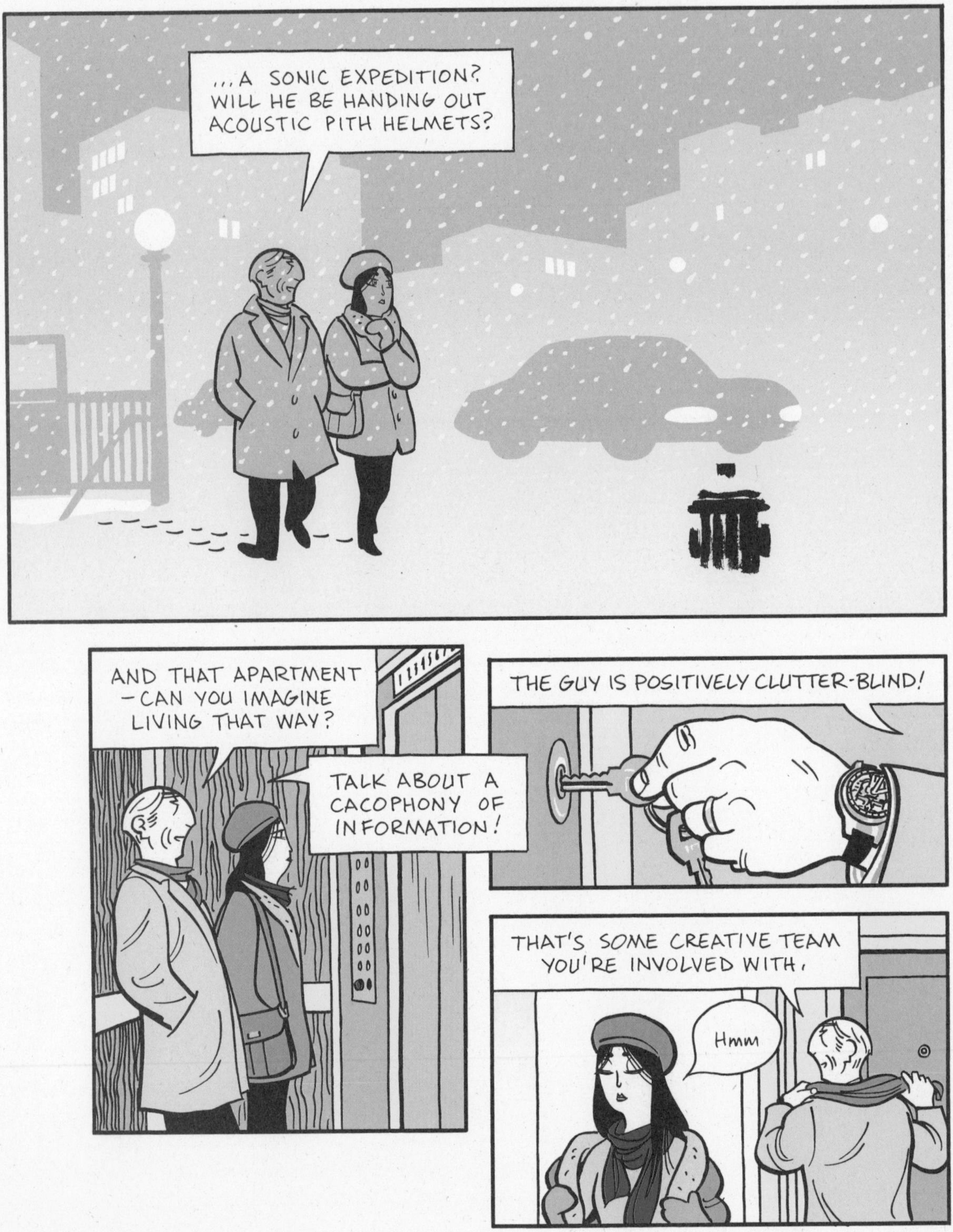
...A SONIC EXPEDITION? WILL HE BE HANDING OUT ACOUSTIC PITH HELMETS?
AND THAT APARTMENT —CAN YOU IMAGINE LIVING THAT WAY?
TALK ABOUT A CACOPHONY OF INFORMATION!
THE GUY IS POSITIVELY CLUTTER-BLIND!
THAT'S SOME CREATIVE TEAM YOU'RE INVOLVED WITH.
Hmm

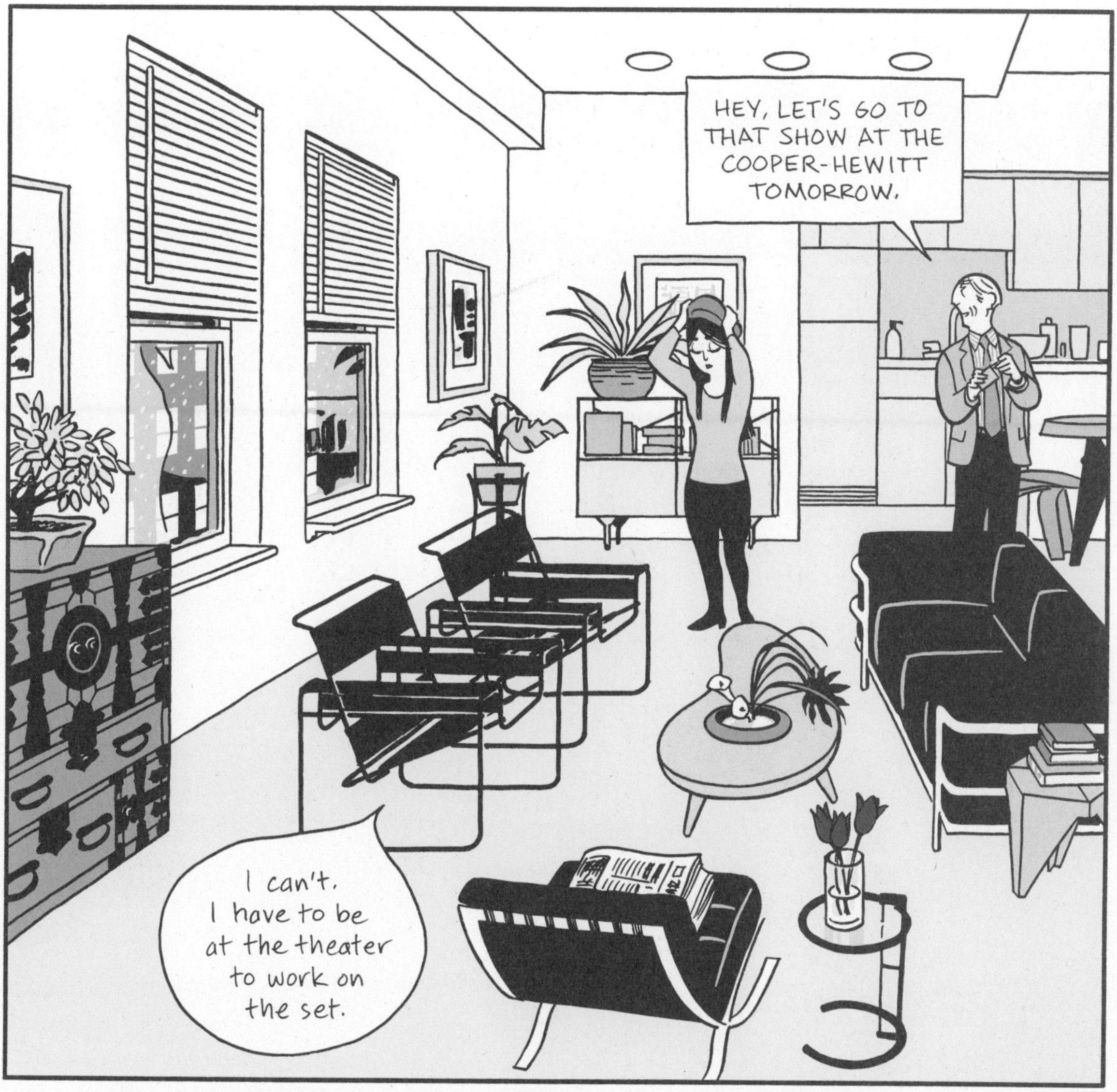
HEY, LET'S GO TO THAT SHOW AT THE COOPER-HEWITT TOMORROW.
I can't. I have to be at the theater to work on the set.

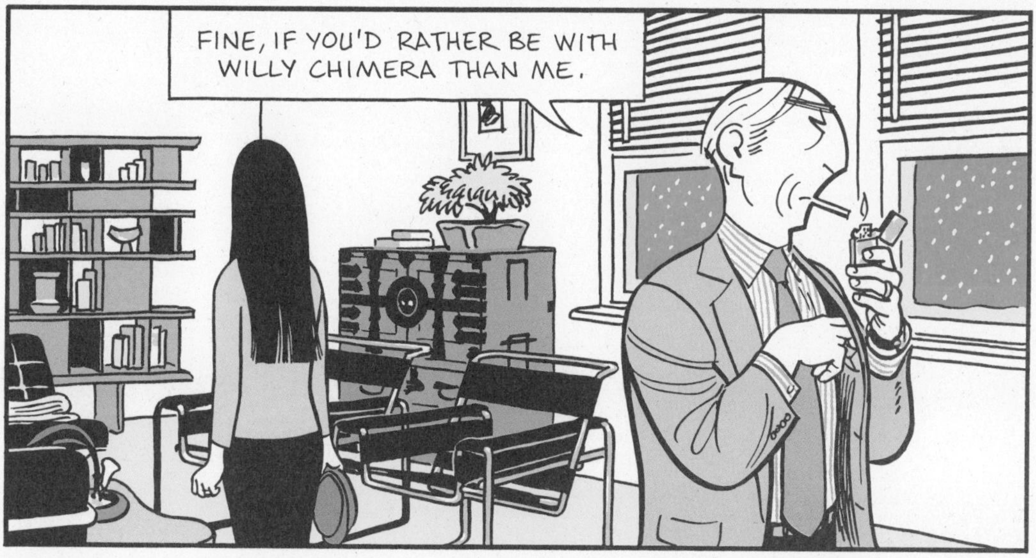
FINE, IF YOU'D RATHER BE WITH WILLY CHIMERA THAN ME.

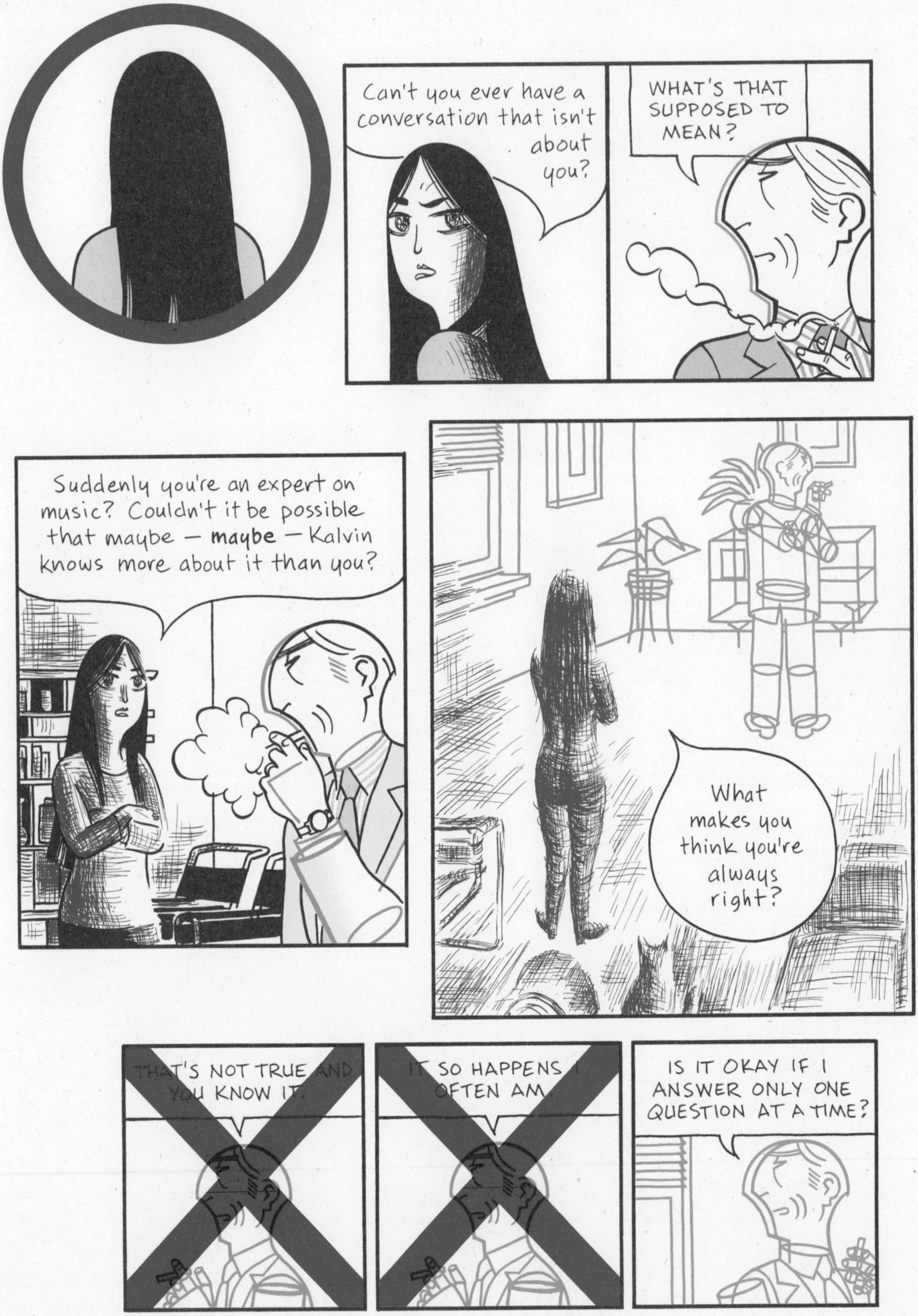
Can't you ever have a conversation that isn't about you?
WHAT'S THAT SUPPOSED TO MEAN?
Suddenly you're an expert on music? Couldn't it be possible that maybe — **maybe** — Kalvin knows more about it than you?
What makes you think you're always right?
THAT'S NOT TRUE AND YOU KNOW IT.
IT SO HAPPENS I OFTEN AM.
IS IT OKAY IF I ANSWER ONLY ONE QUESTION AT A TIME?

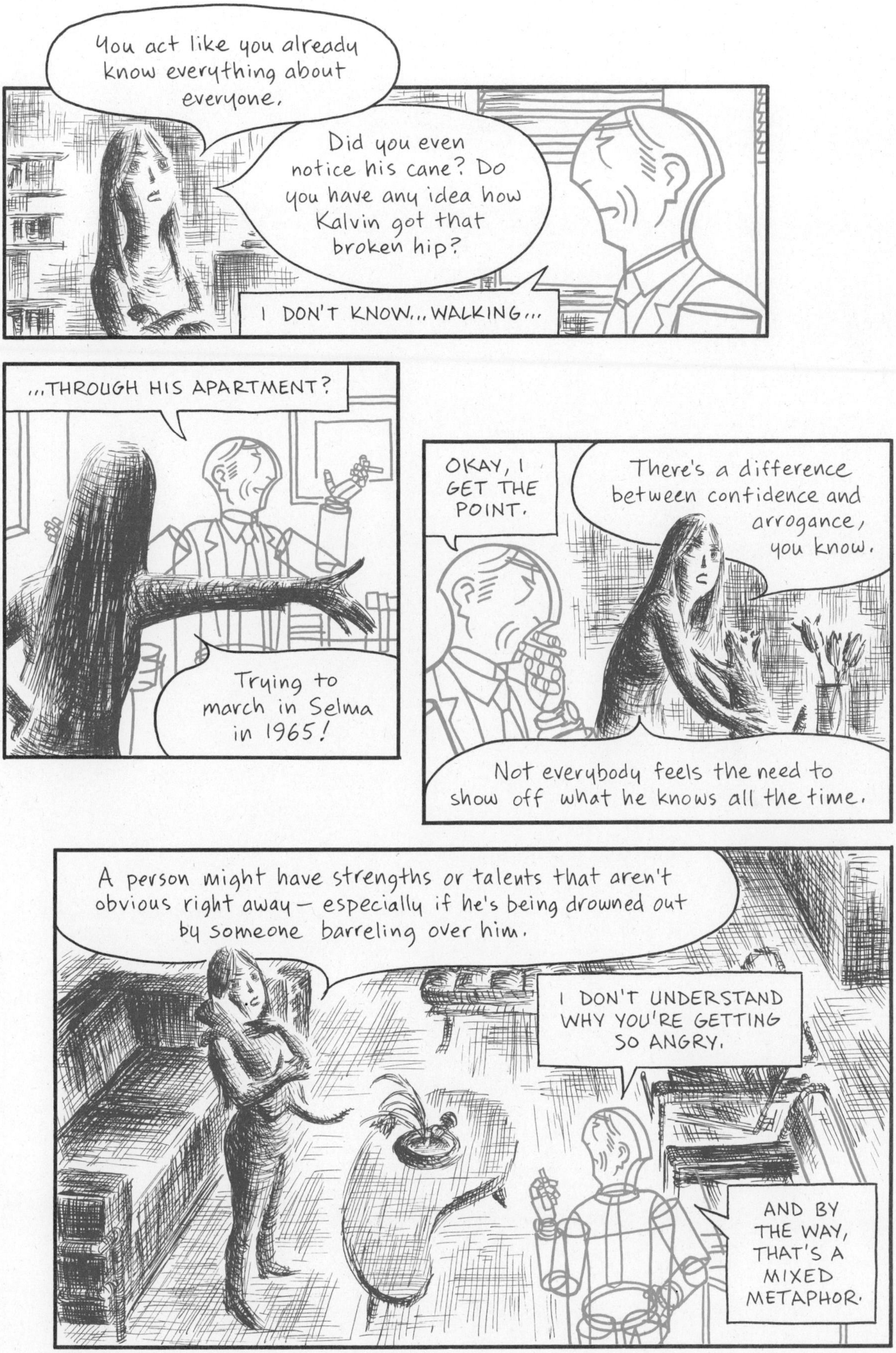
You act like you already know everything about everyone.
Did you even notice his cane? Do you have any idea how Kalvin got that broken hip?
I DON'T KNOW... WALKING...
...THROUGH HIS APARTMENT?
Trying to march in Selma in 1965!
OKAY, I GET THE POINT.
There's a difference between confidence and arrogance, you know.
Not everybody feels the need to show off what he knows all the time.
A person might have strengths or talents that aren't obvious right away— especially if he's being drowned out by someone barreling over him.
I DON'T UNDERSTAND WHY YOU'RE GETTING SO ANGRY.
AND BY THE WAY, THAT'S A MIXED METAPHOR.

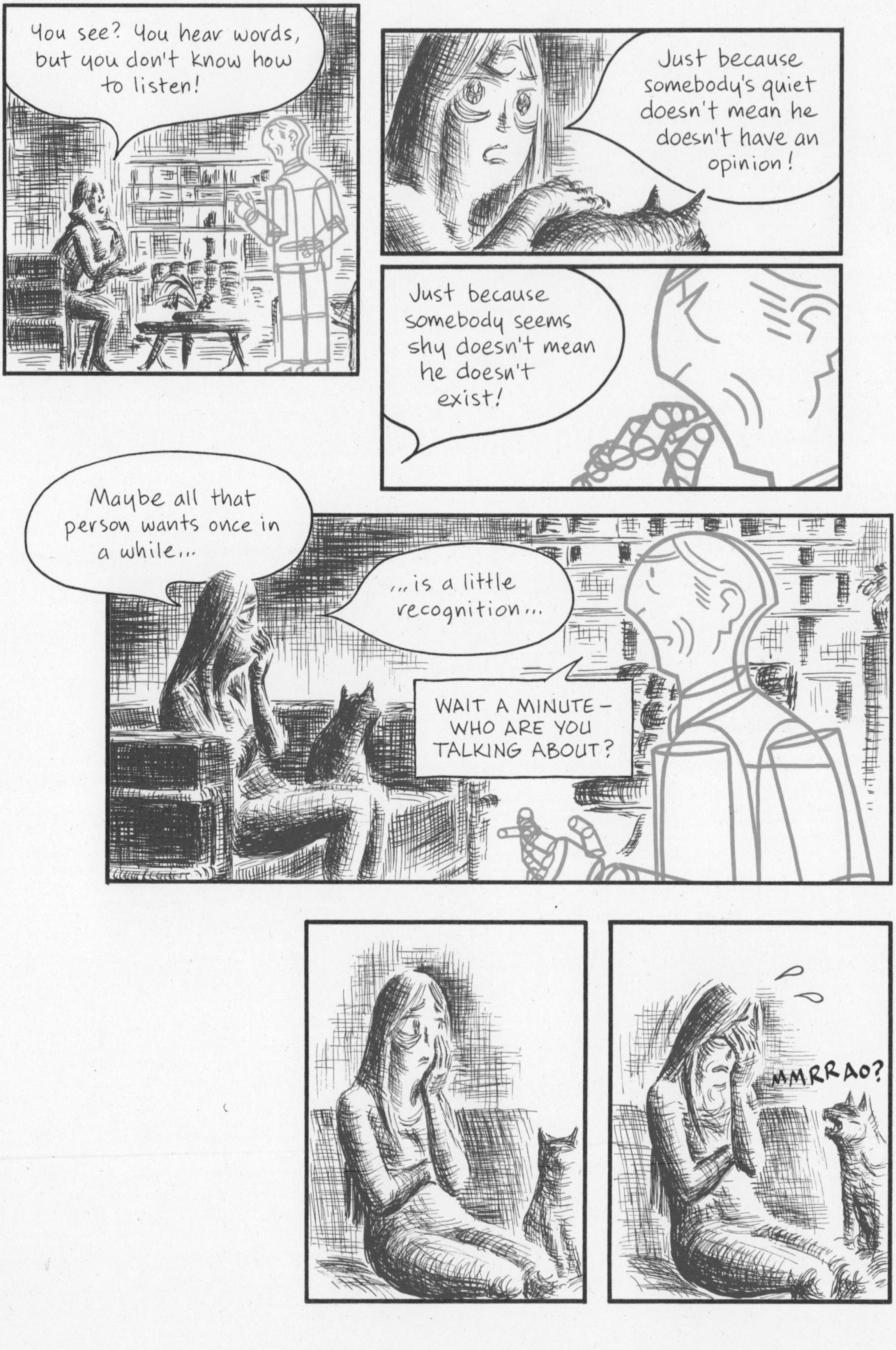
You see? You hear words, but you don't know how to listen!
Just because somebody's quiet doesn't mean he doesn't have an opinion!
Just because somebody seems shy doesn't mean he doesn't exist!
Maybe all that person wants once in a while...
...is a little recognition...
WAIT A MINUTE— WHO ARE YOU TALKING ABOUT?
MMRRAO?

Why do you always let him talk to me like that?

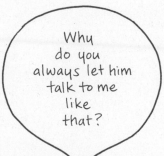

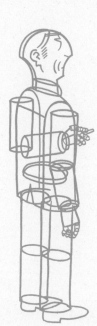

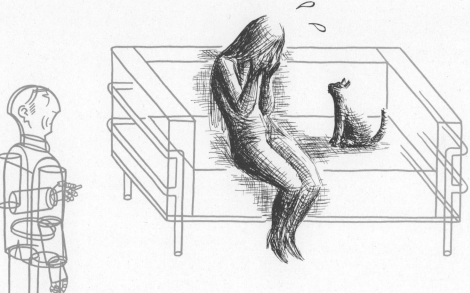

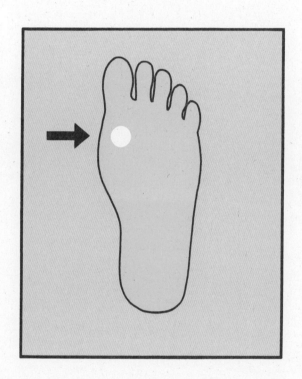

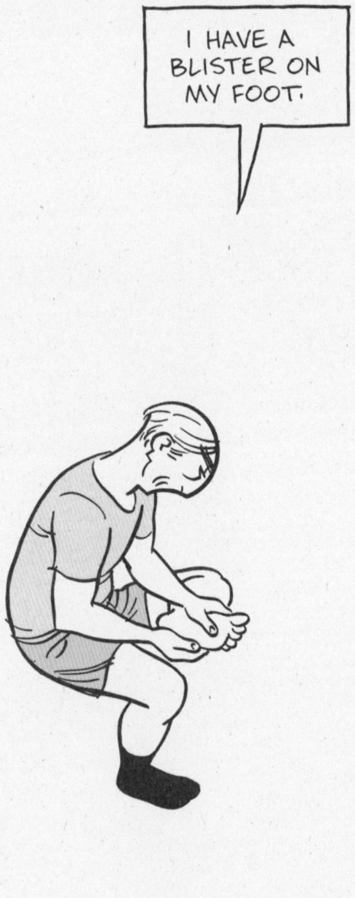
I HAVE A BLISTER ON MY FOOT.

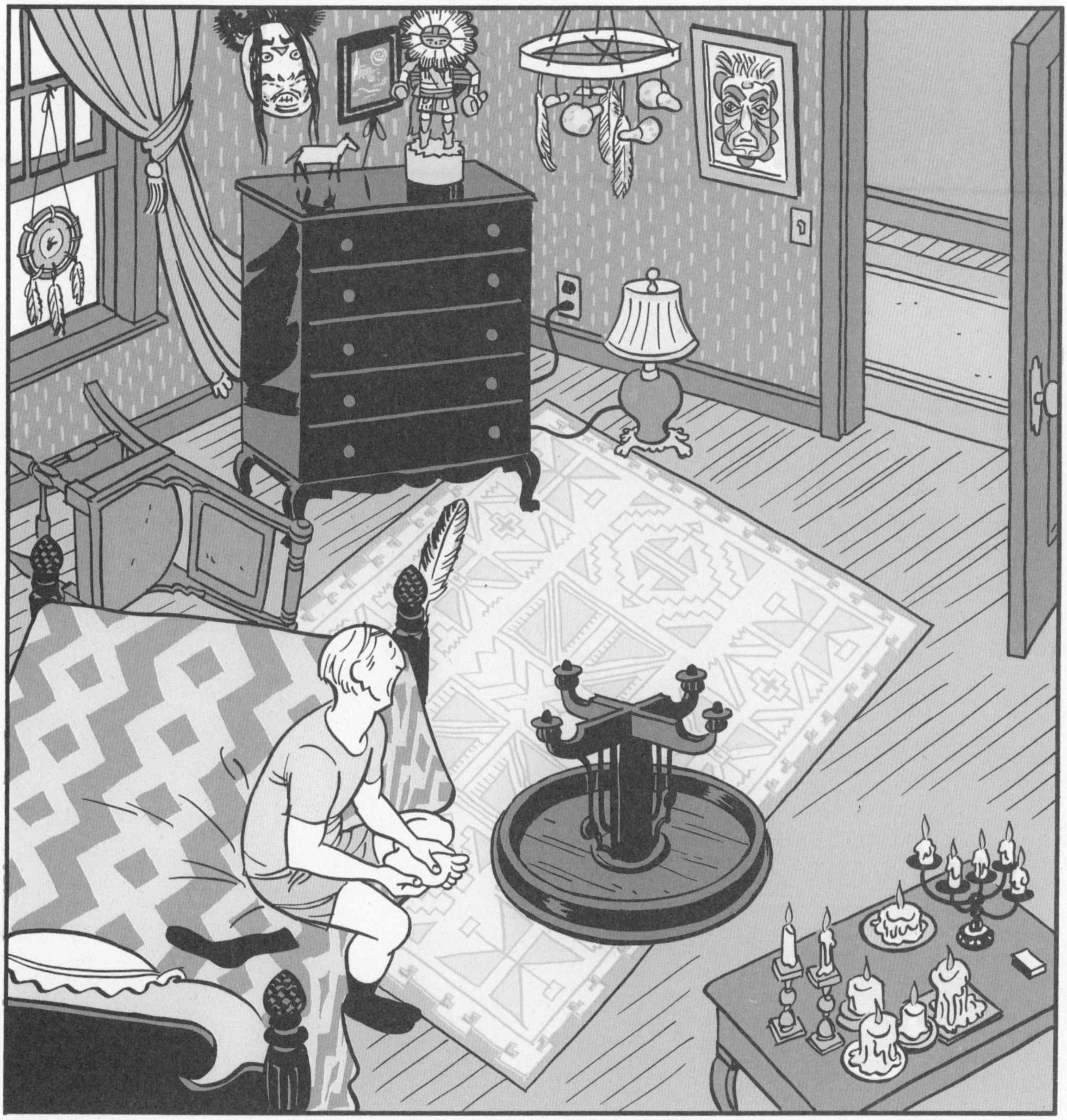

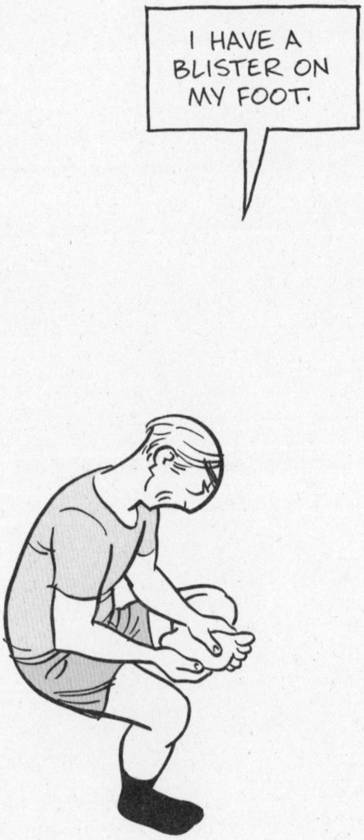
I HAVE A BLISTER ON MY FOOT.

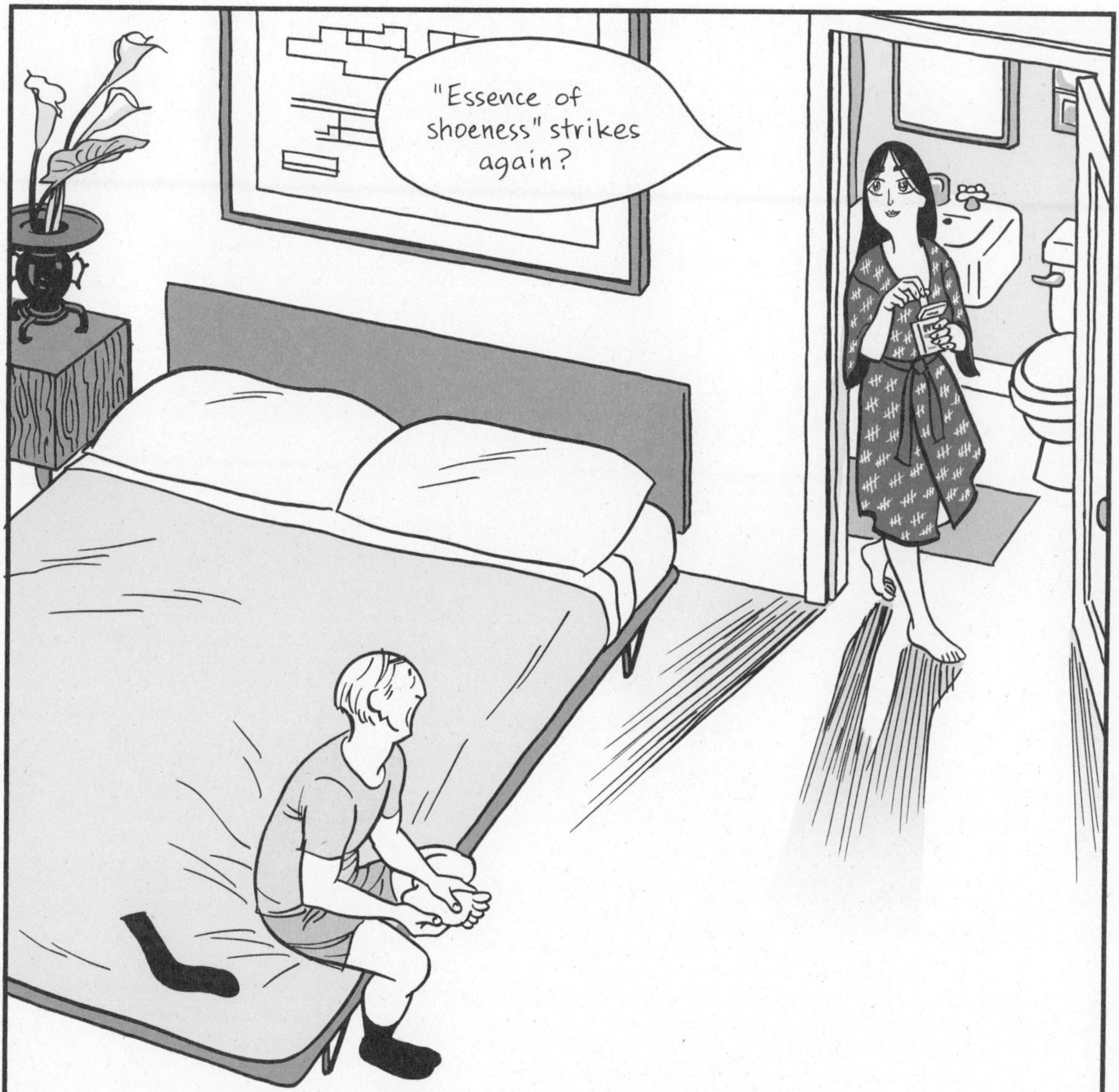
"Essence of shoeness" strikes again?

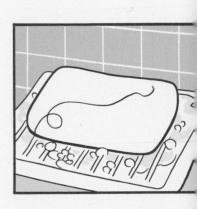

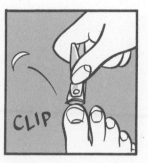

CLIP

Oh, no.

Oh, no.

WHAT?

SSSLURP!

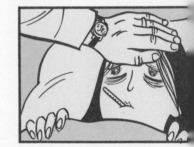

Get it out! Get it out!

HOLD ON...

WAIT A MINUTE...

Hurry!

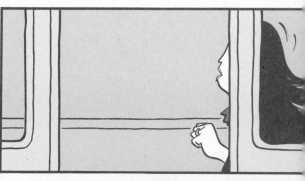

...WHERE'S THAT THING YOU FOUND TODAY?

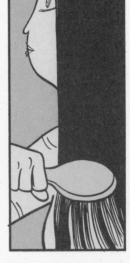

OKAY....HOLD STILL....

Wait—wait— Be careful!

TRUST ME?

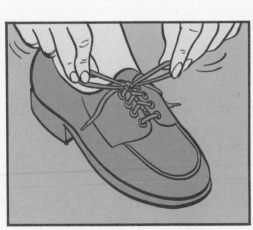

BITE
BU-URP
SNIFF
SNIFF
SCRATCH
SNIFF
ZZZ
ZZ

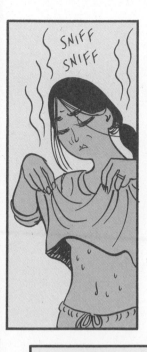

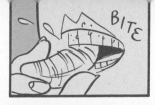

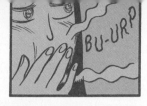

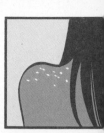

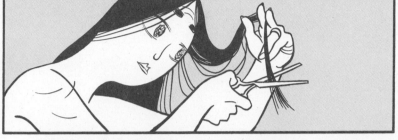

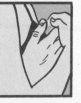

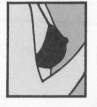

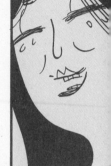

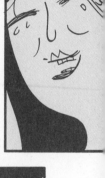

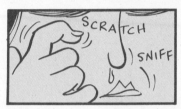

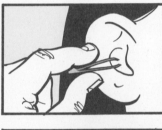

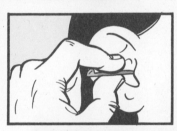

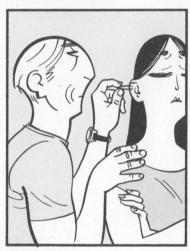

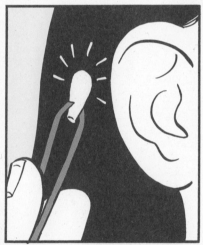

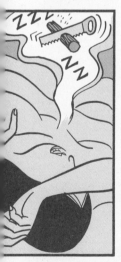

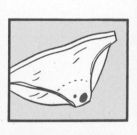

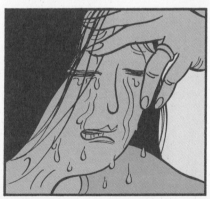

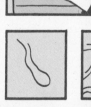

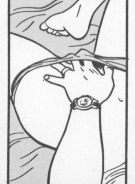

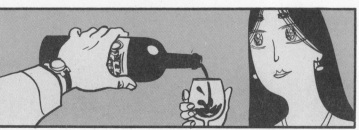

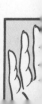

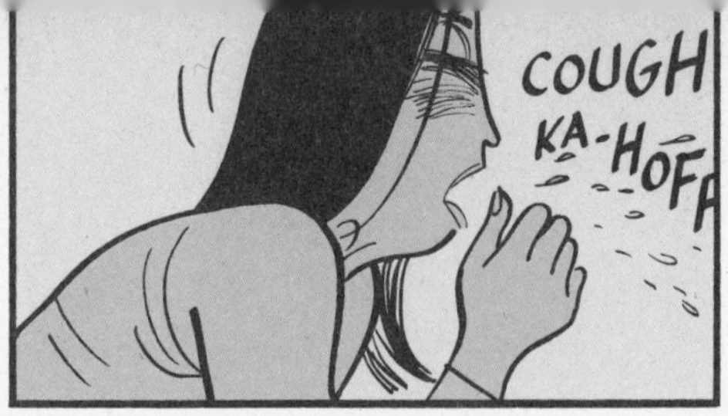
COUGH
KA-HOFF

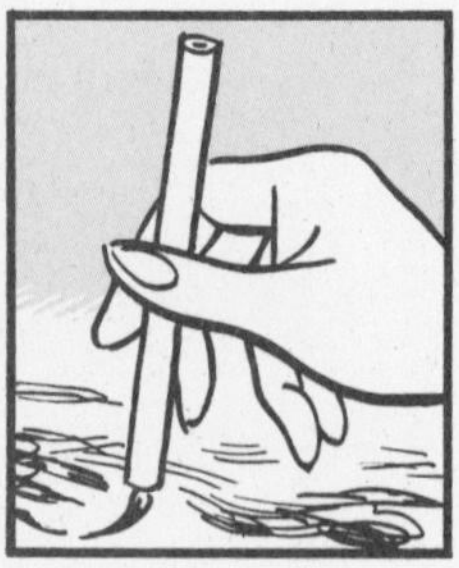

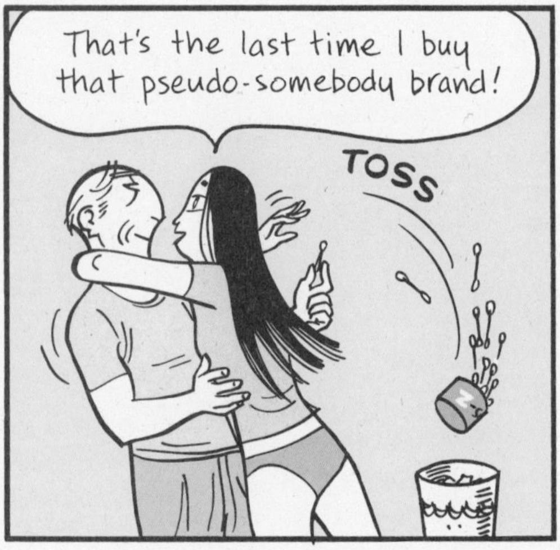
That's the last time I buy that pseudo-somebody brand!
TOSS

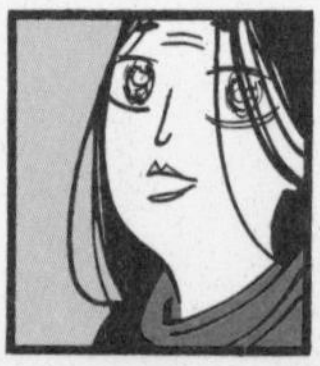

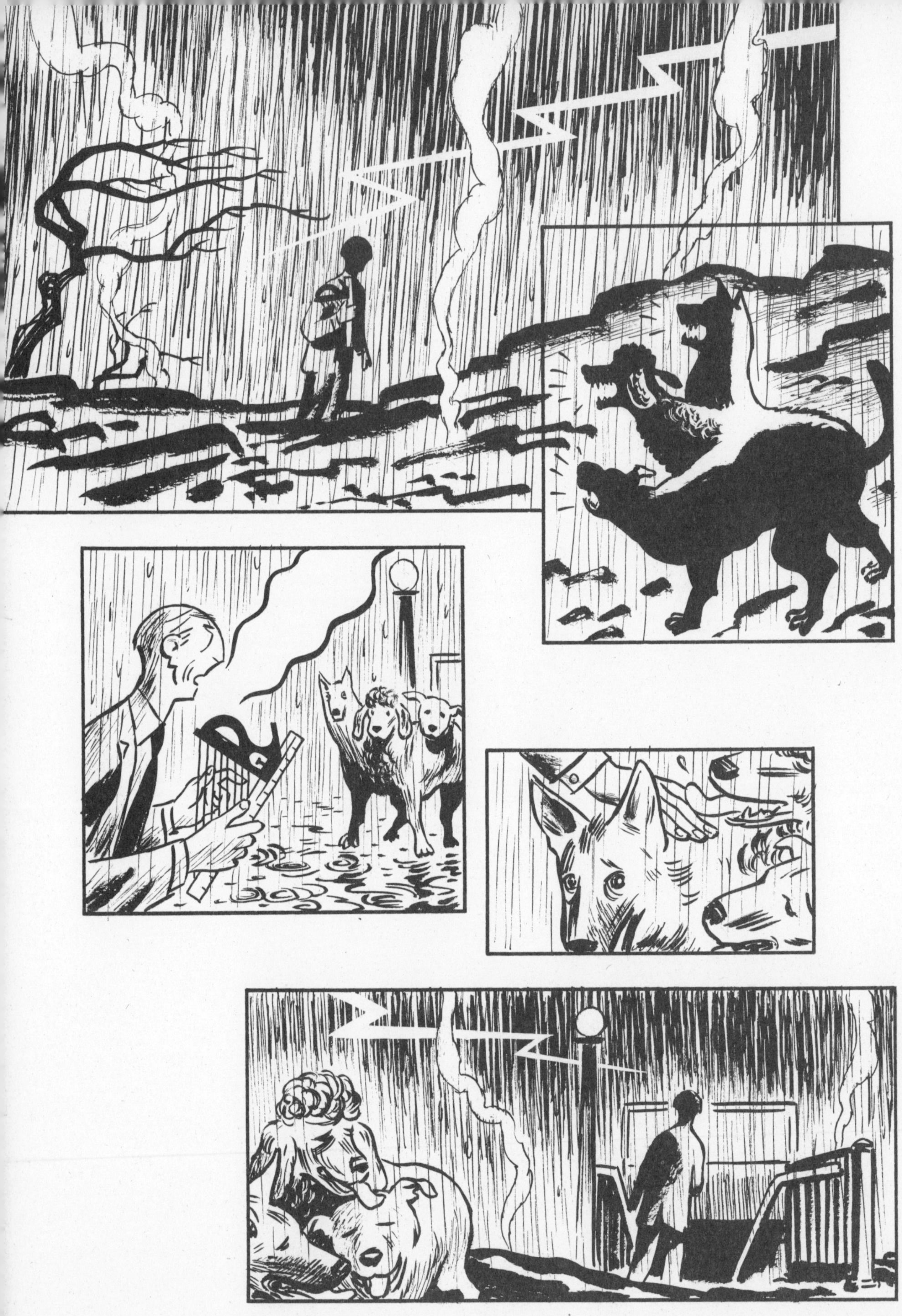

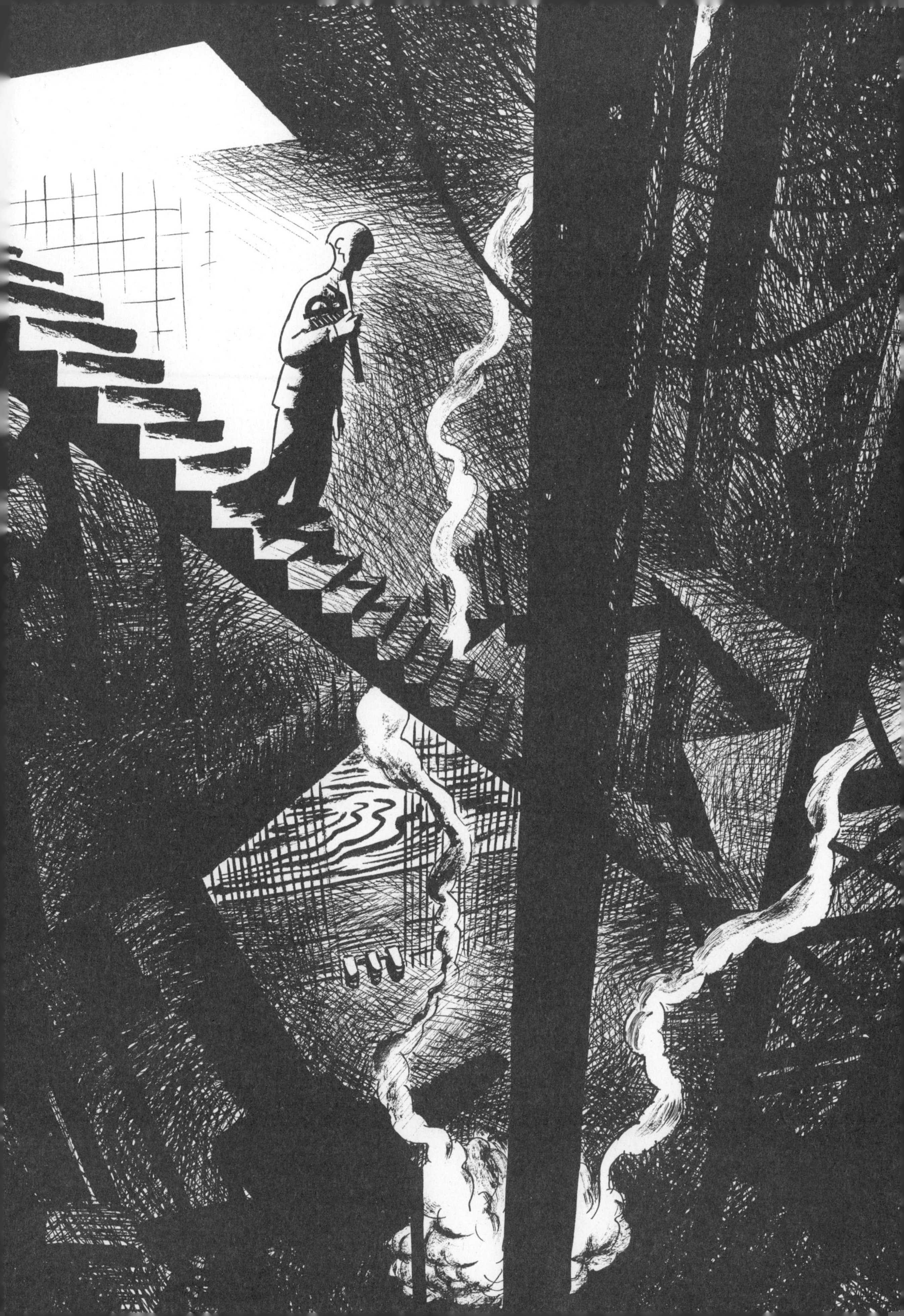

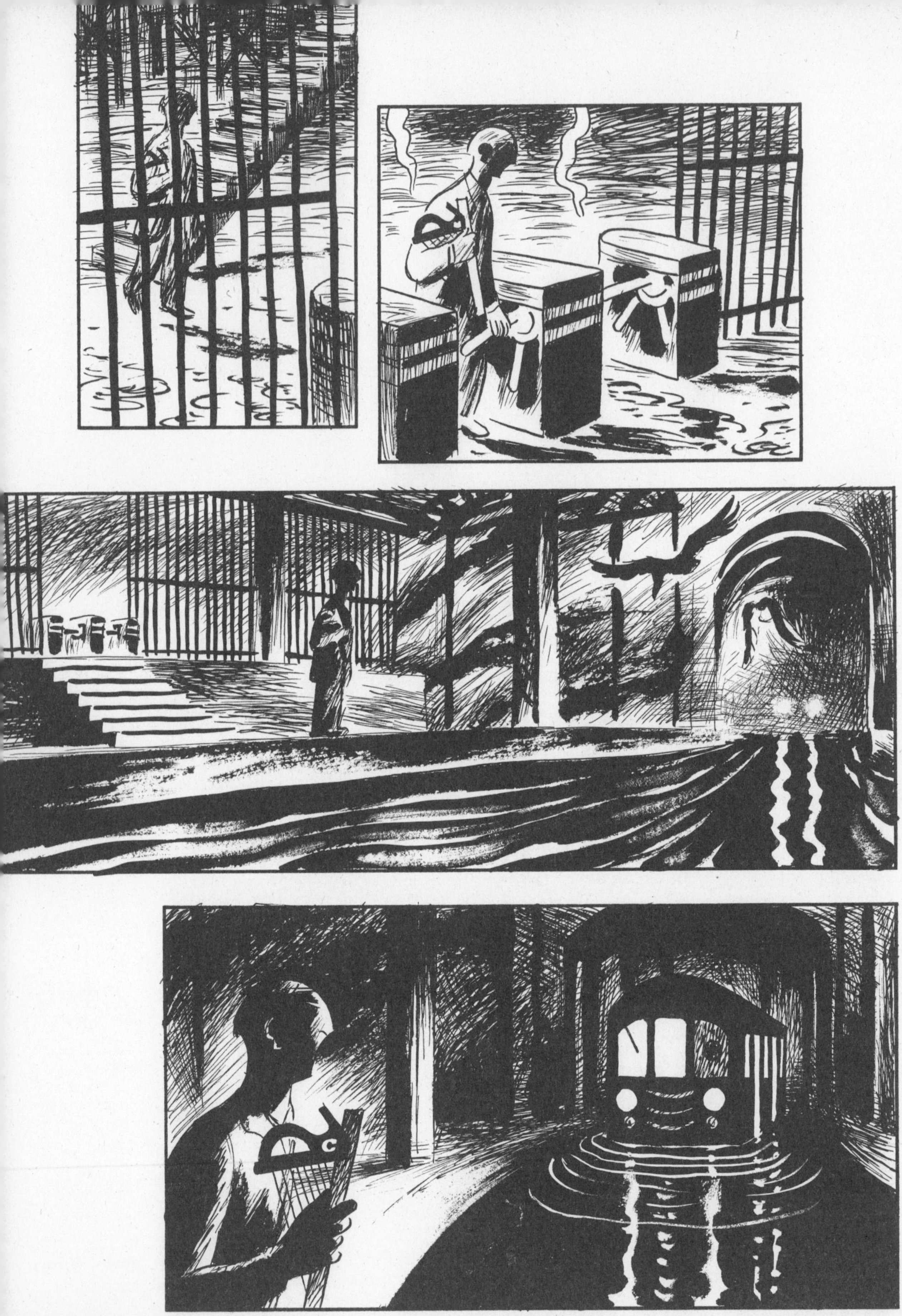

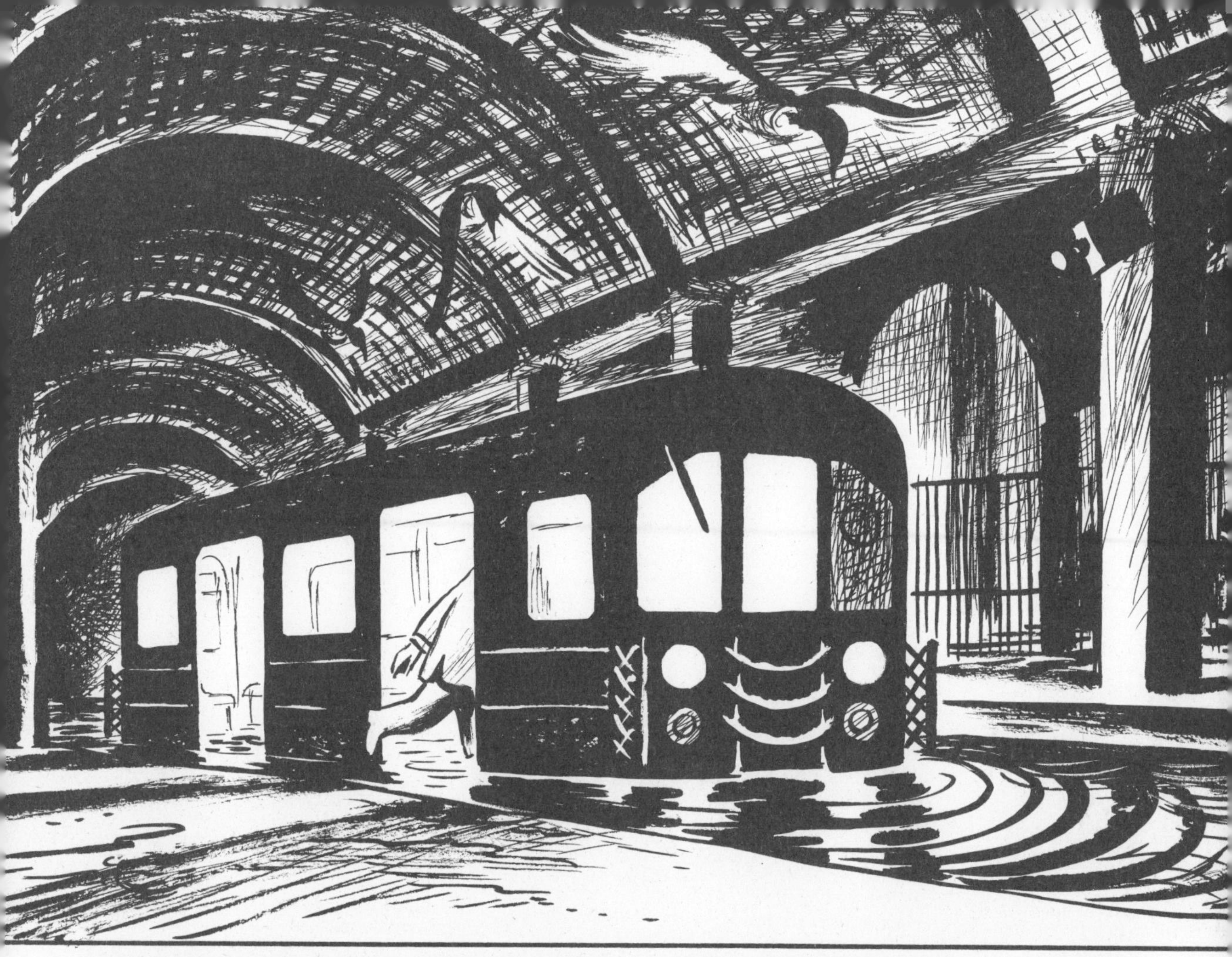

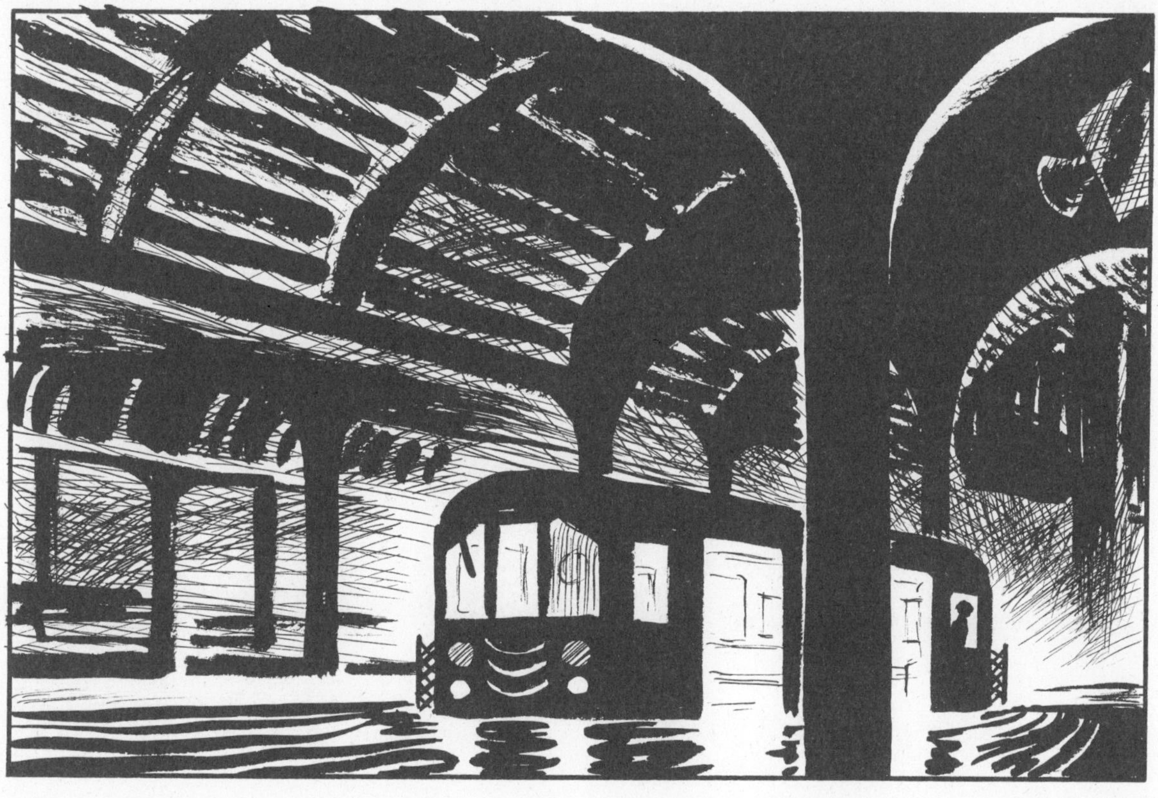

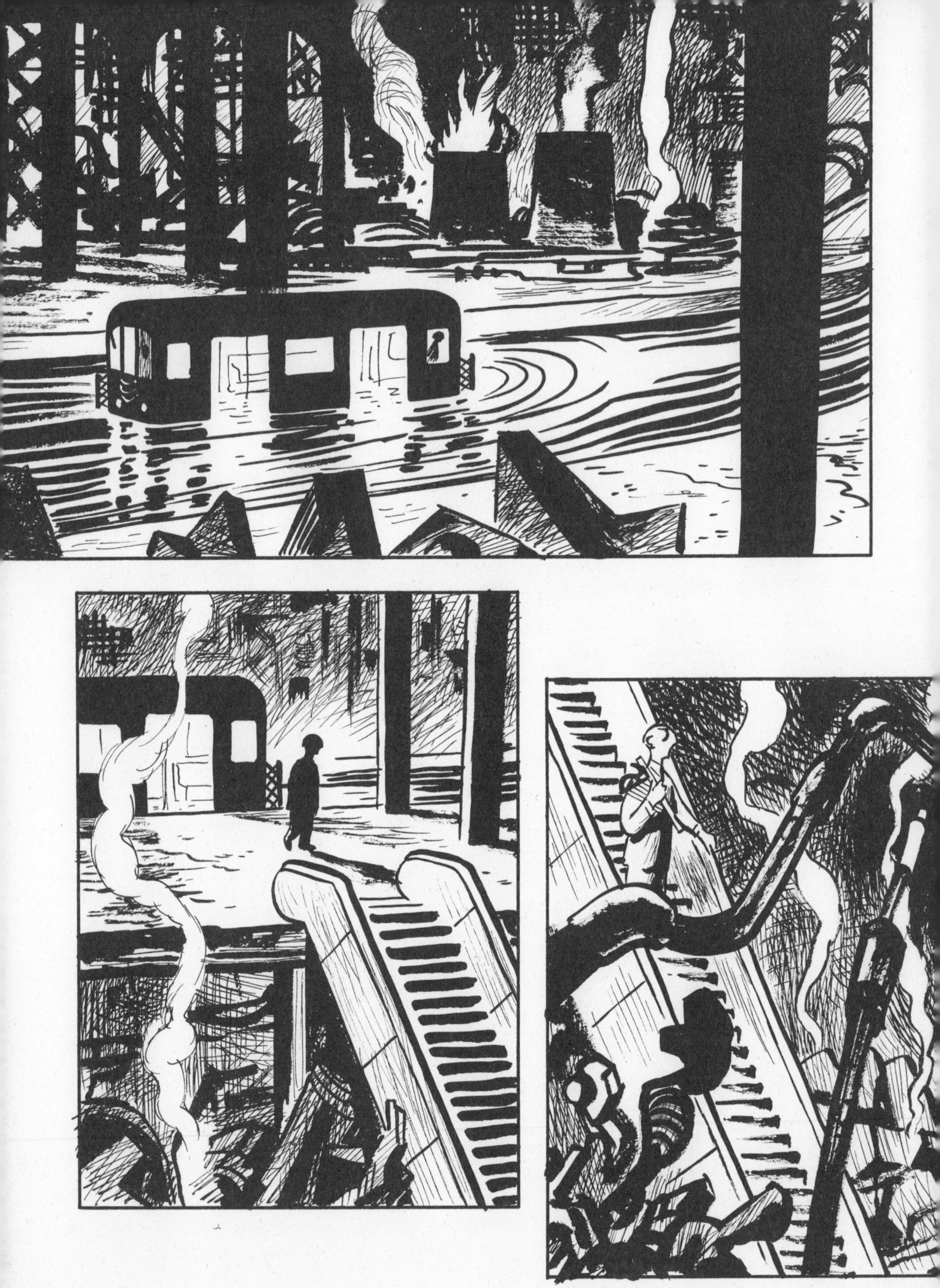

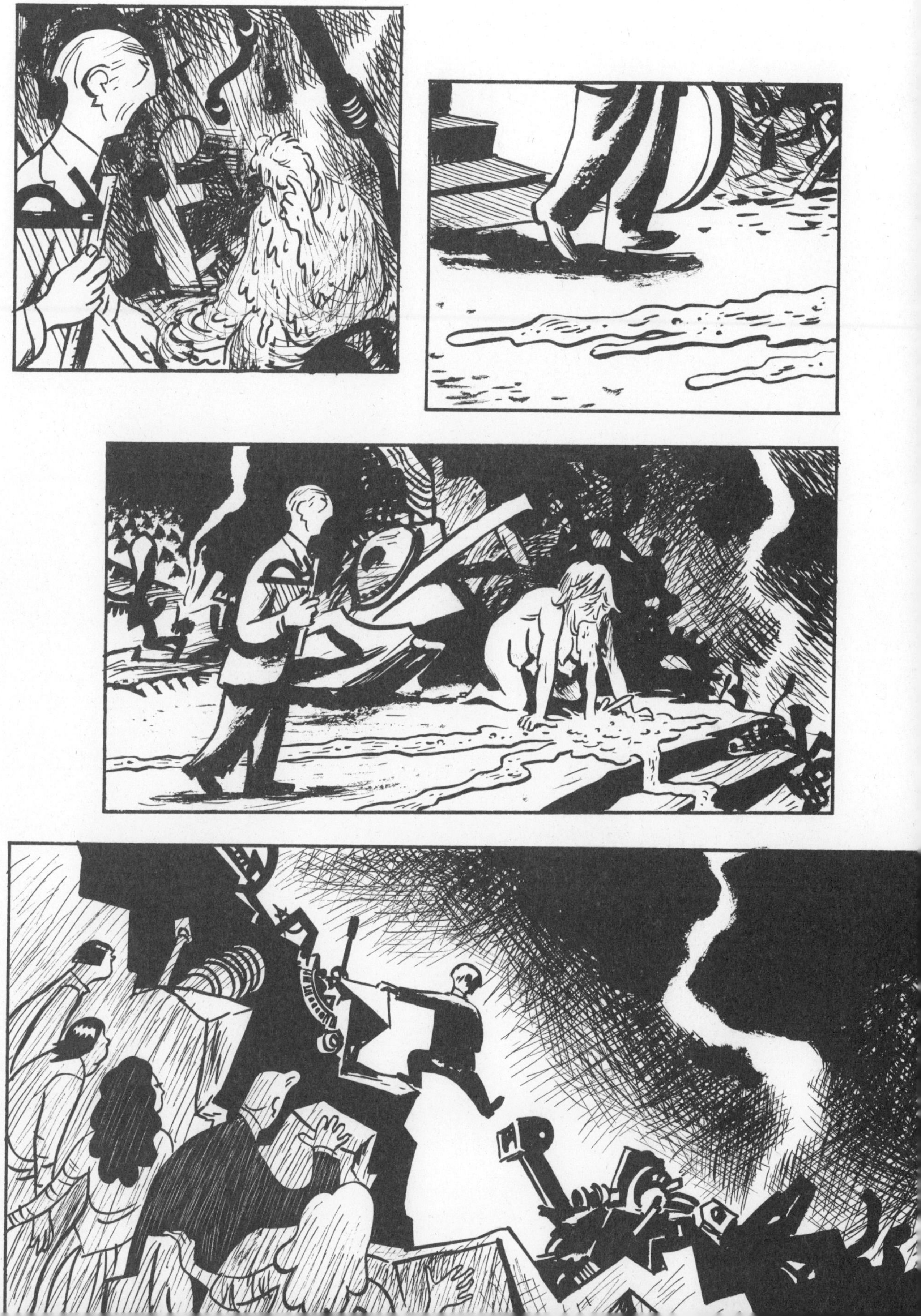

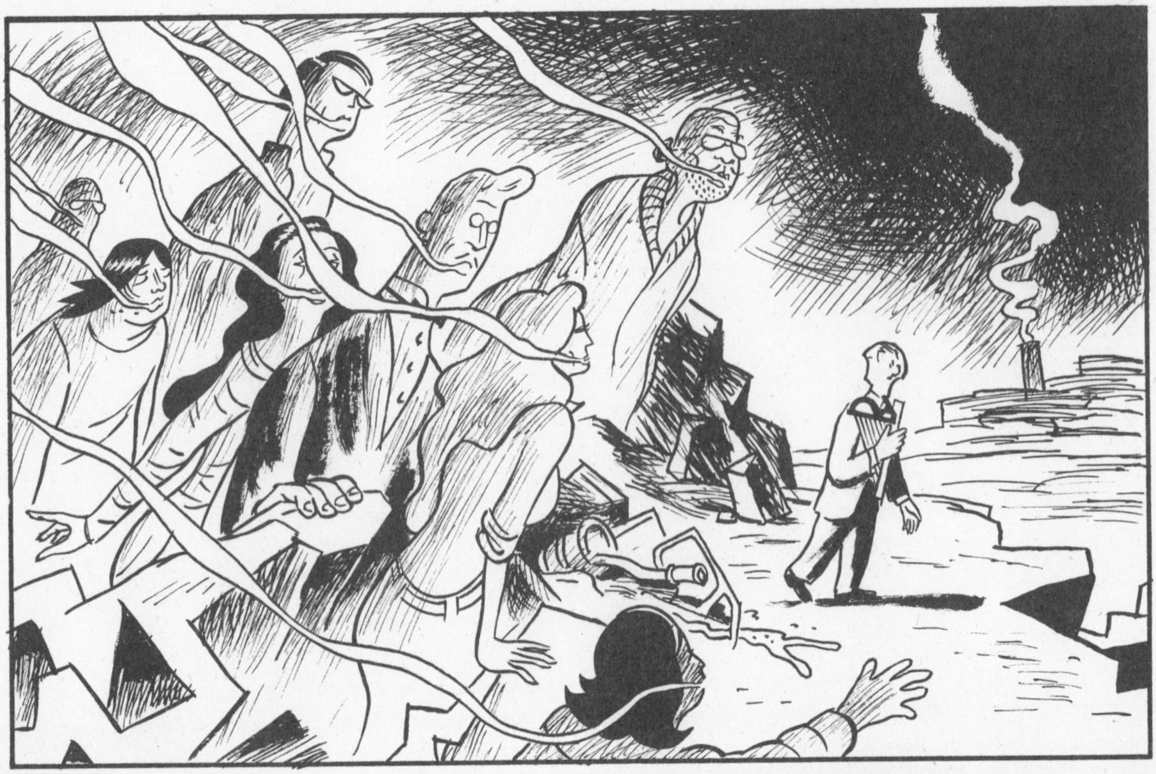
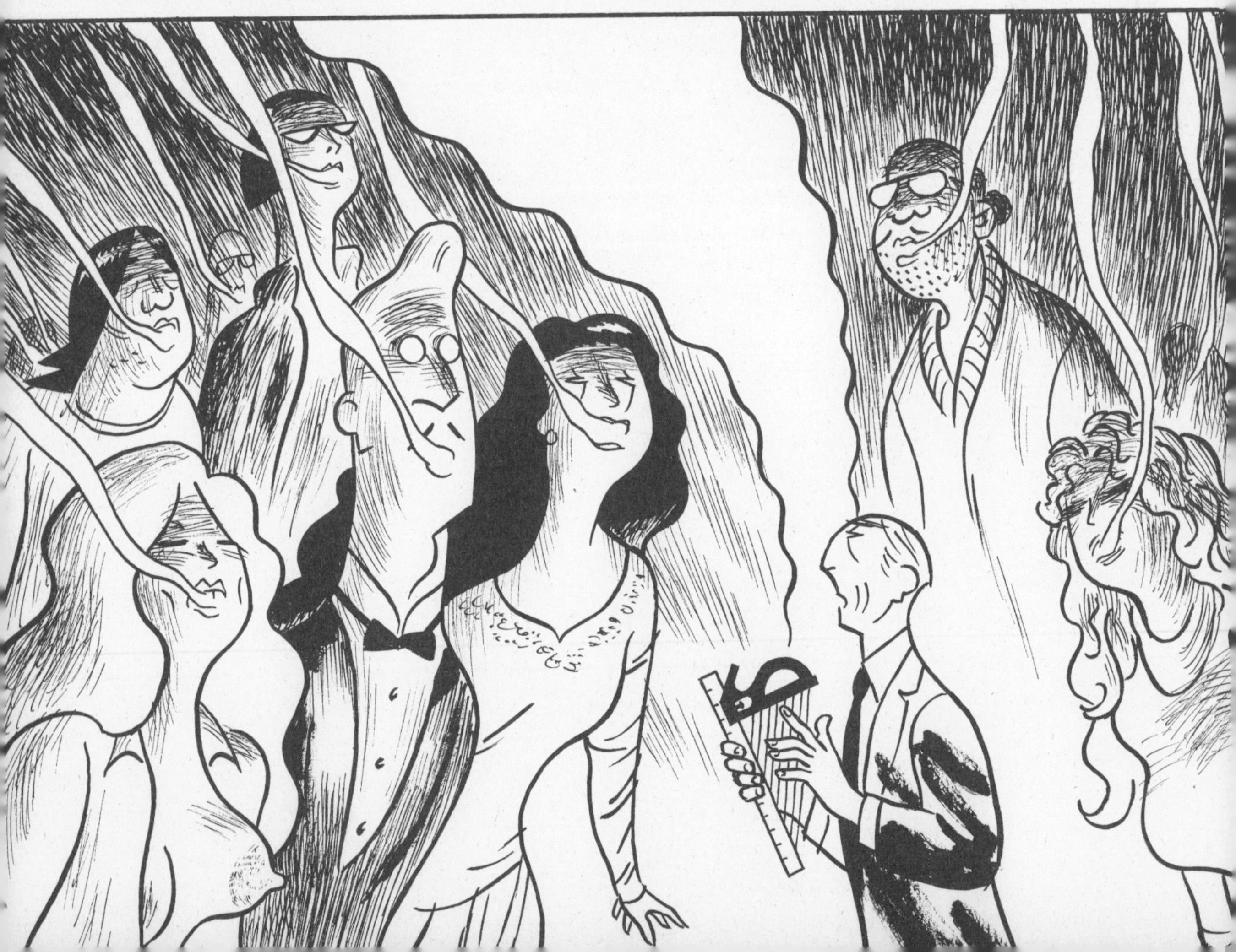

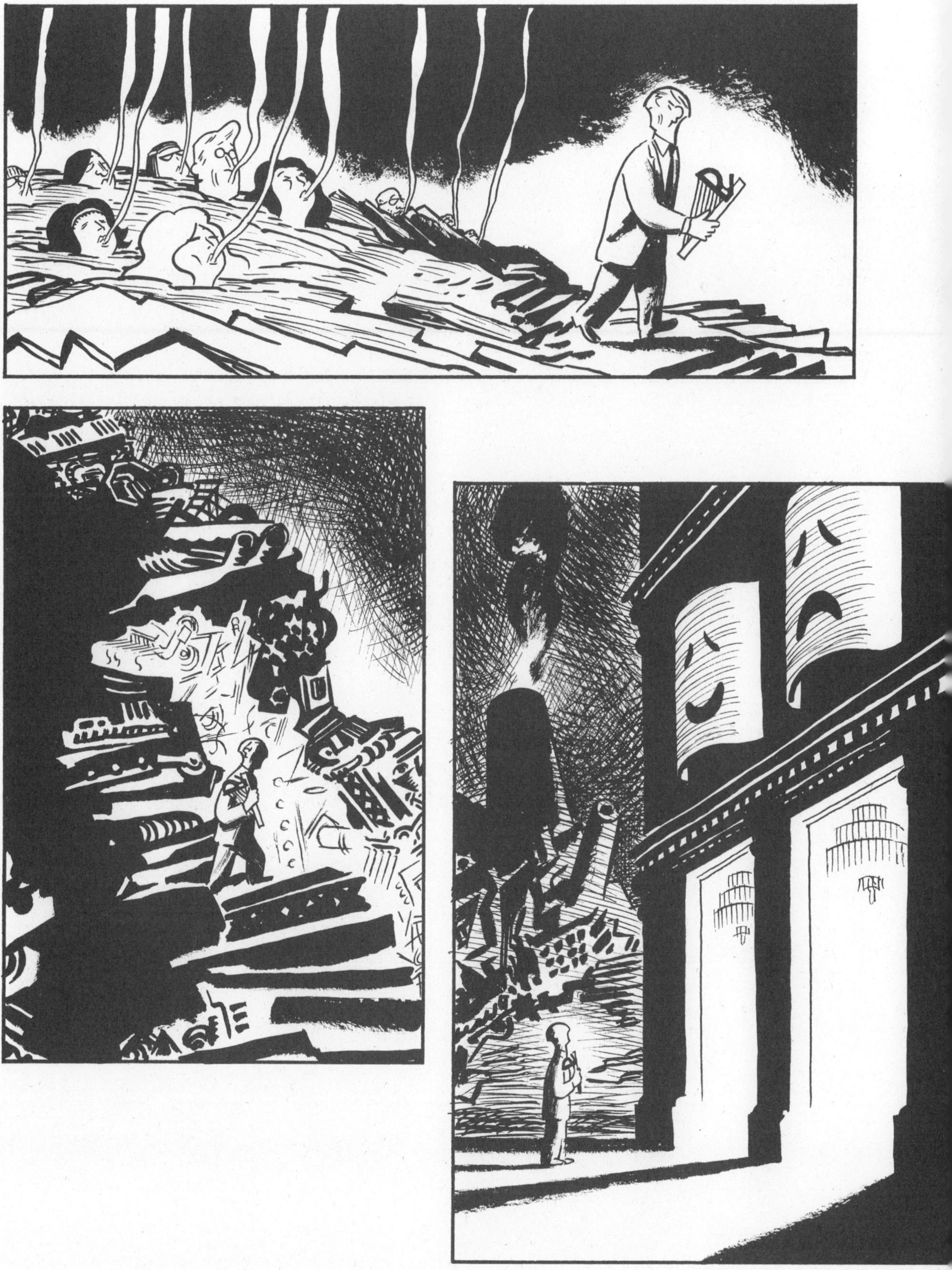

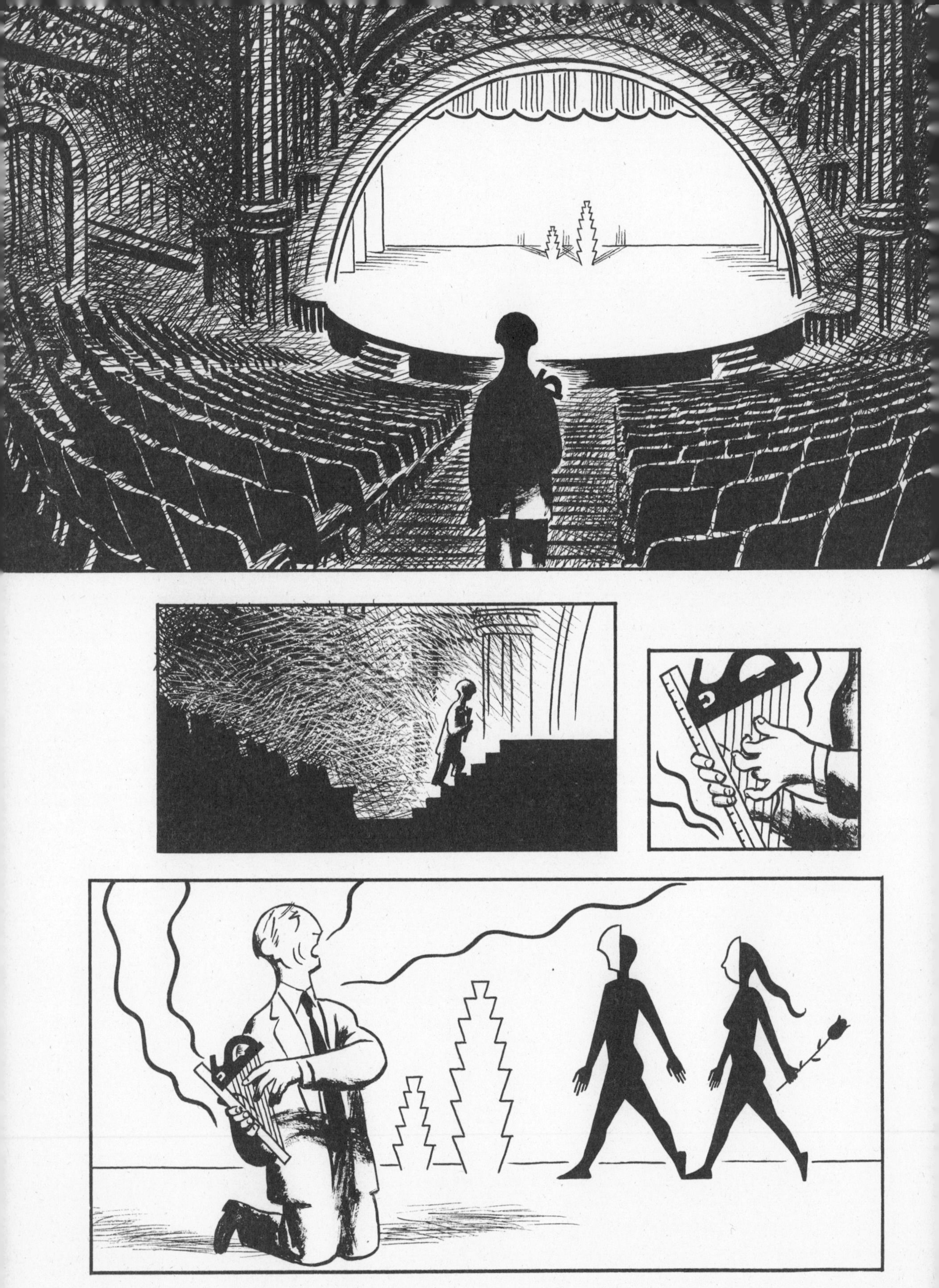

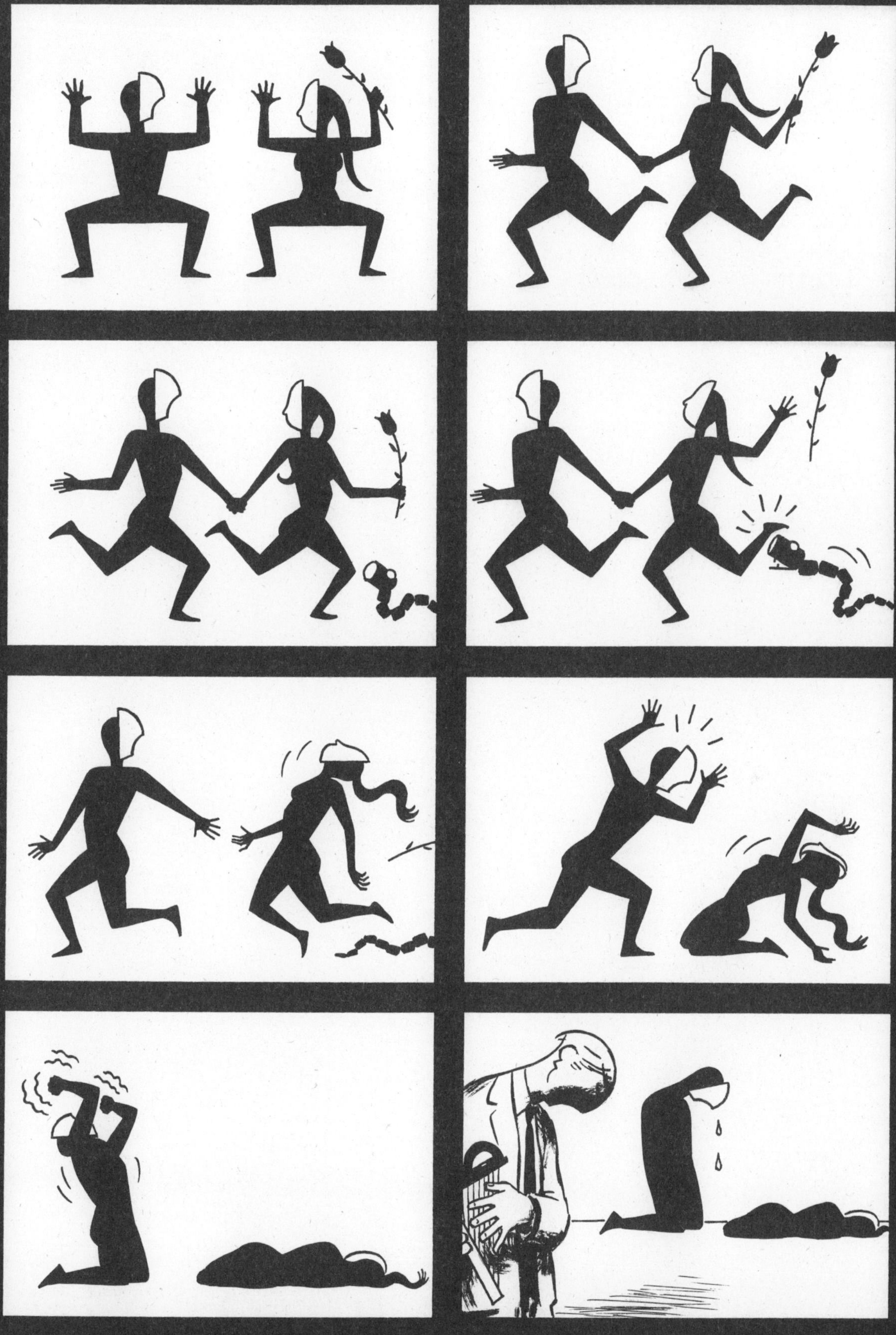

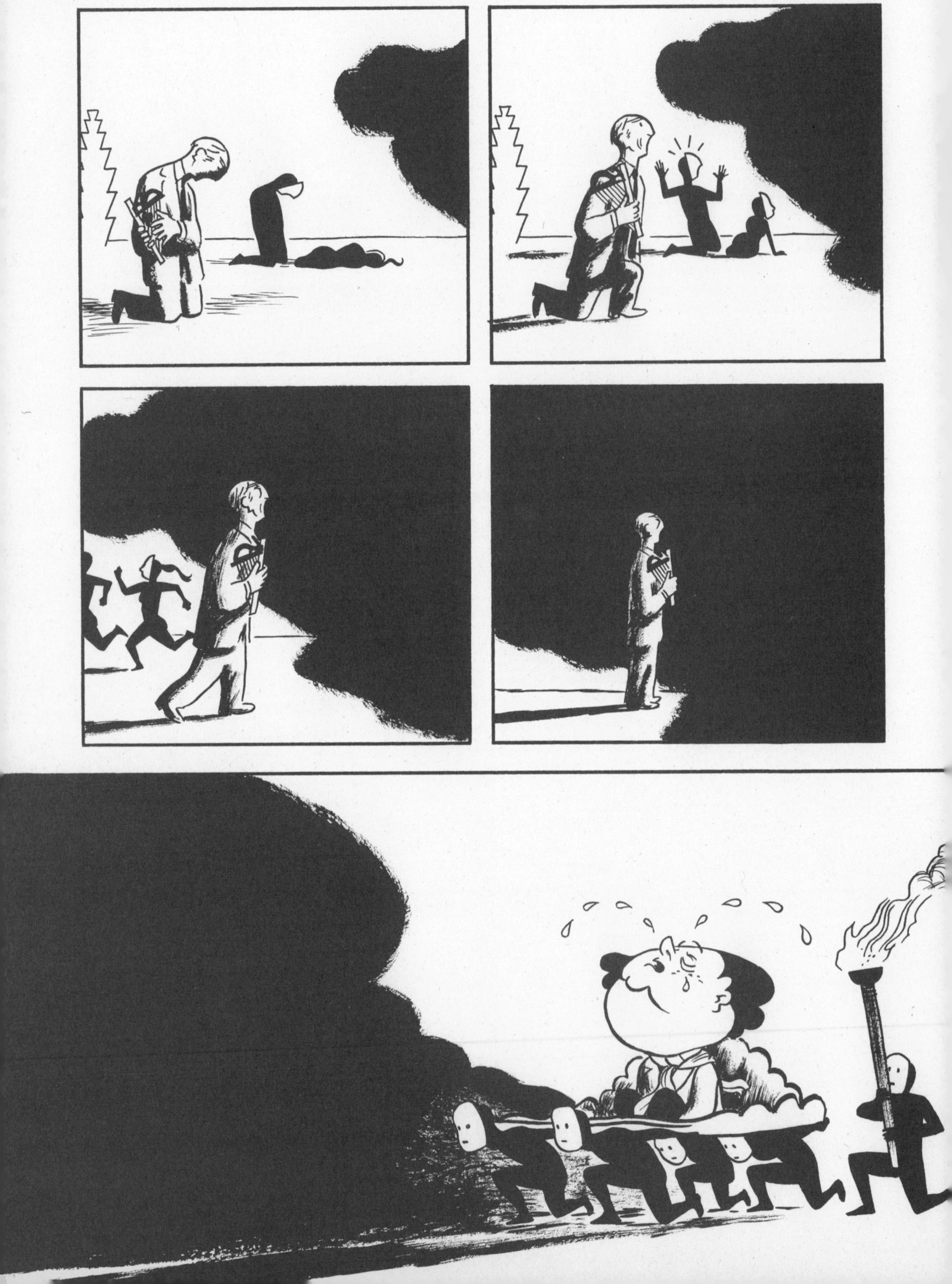

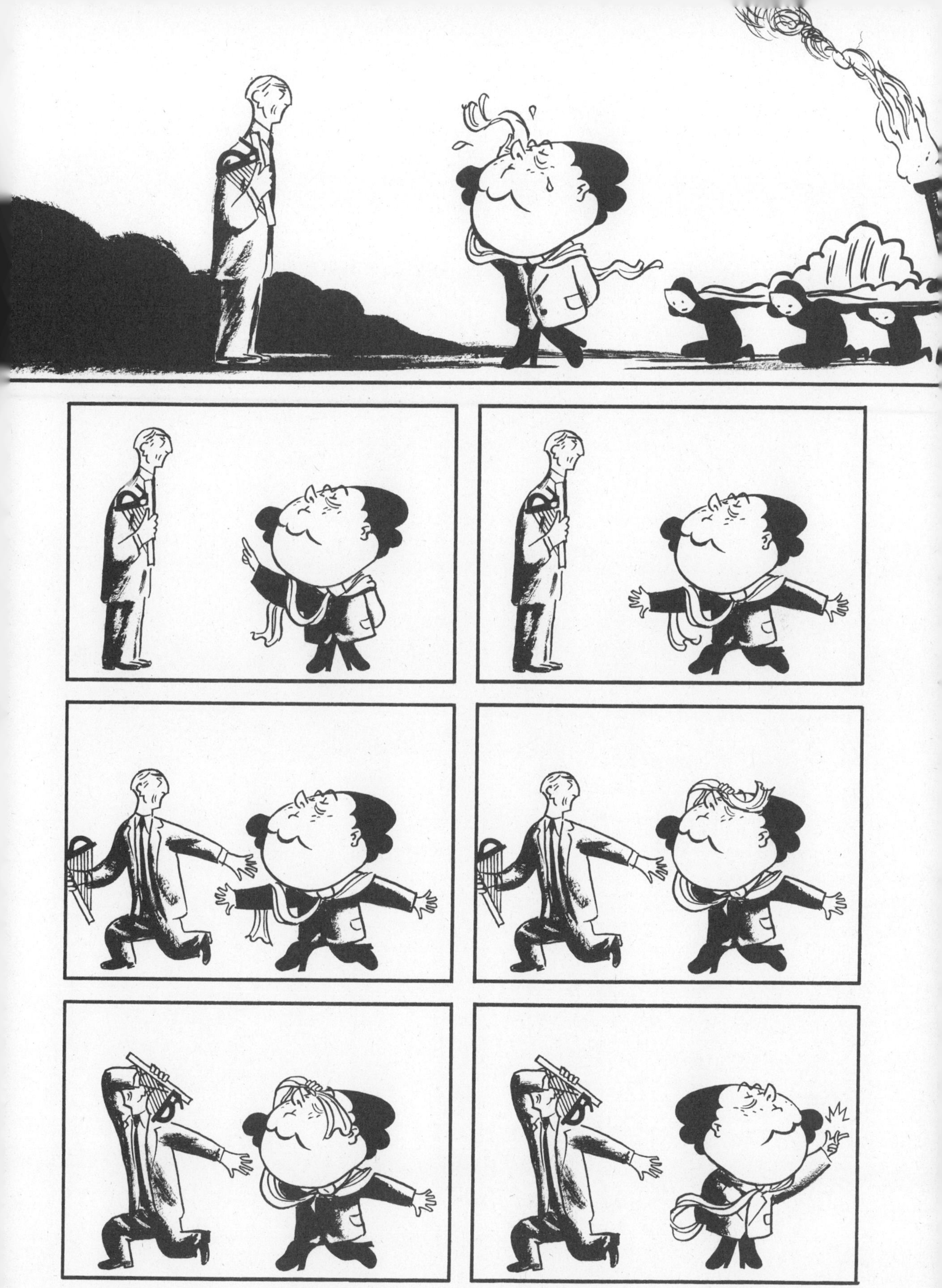

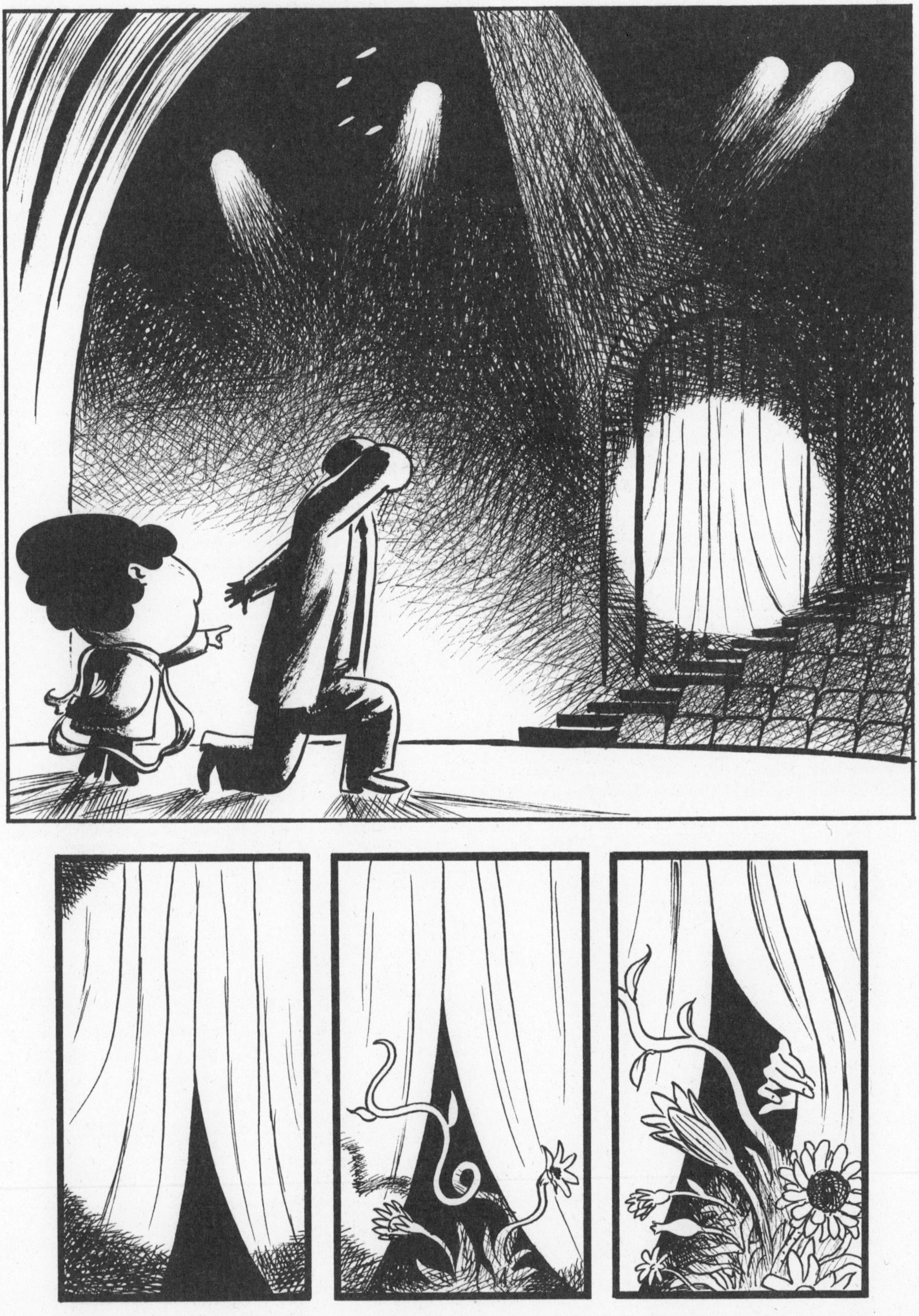

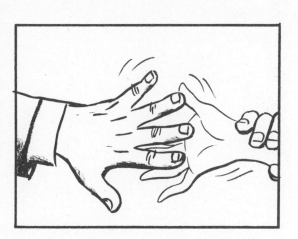

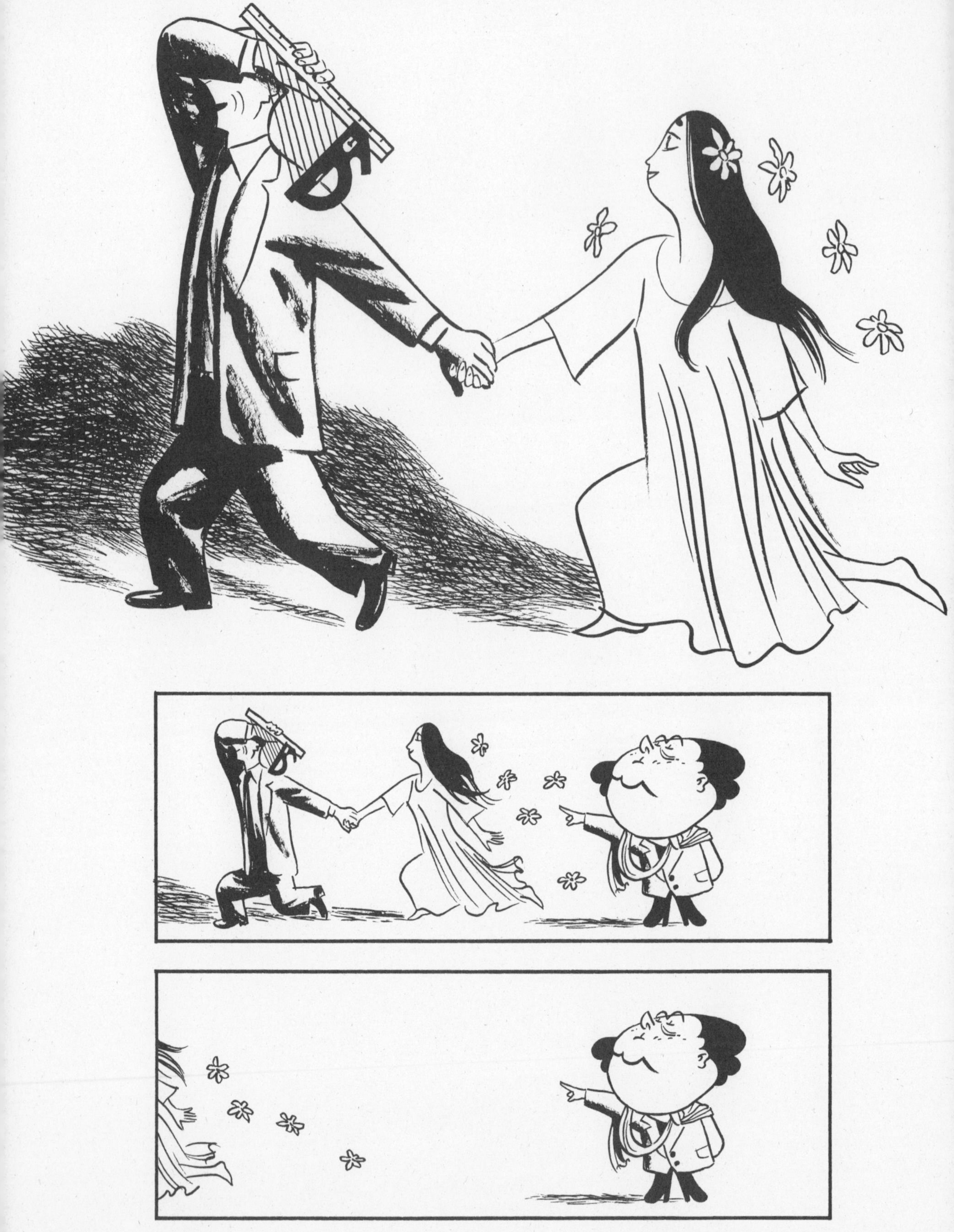

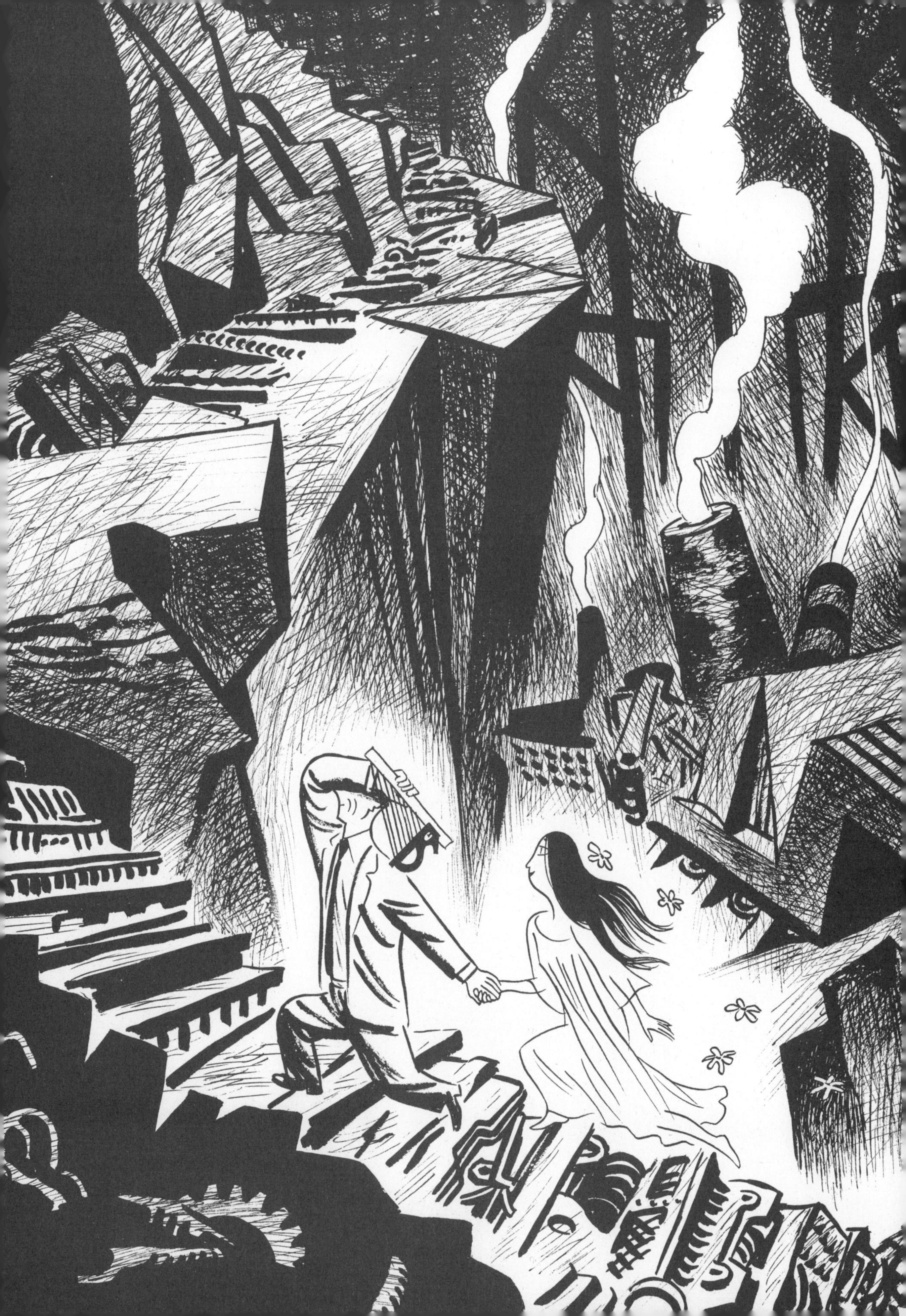

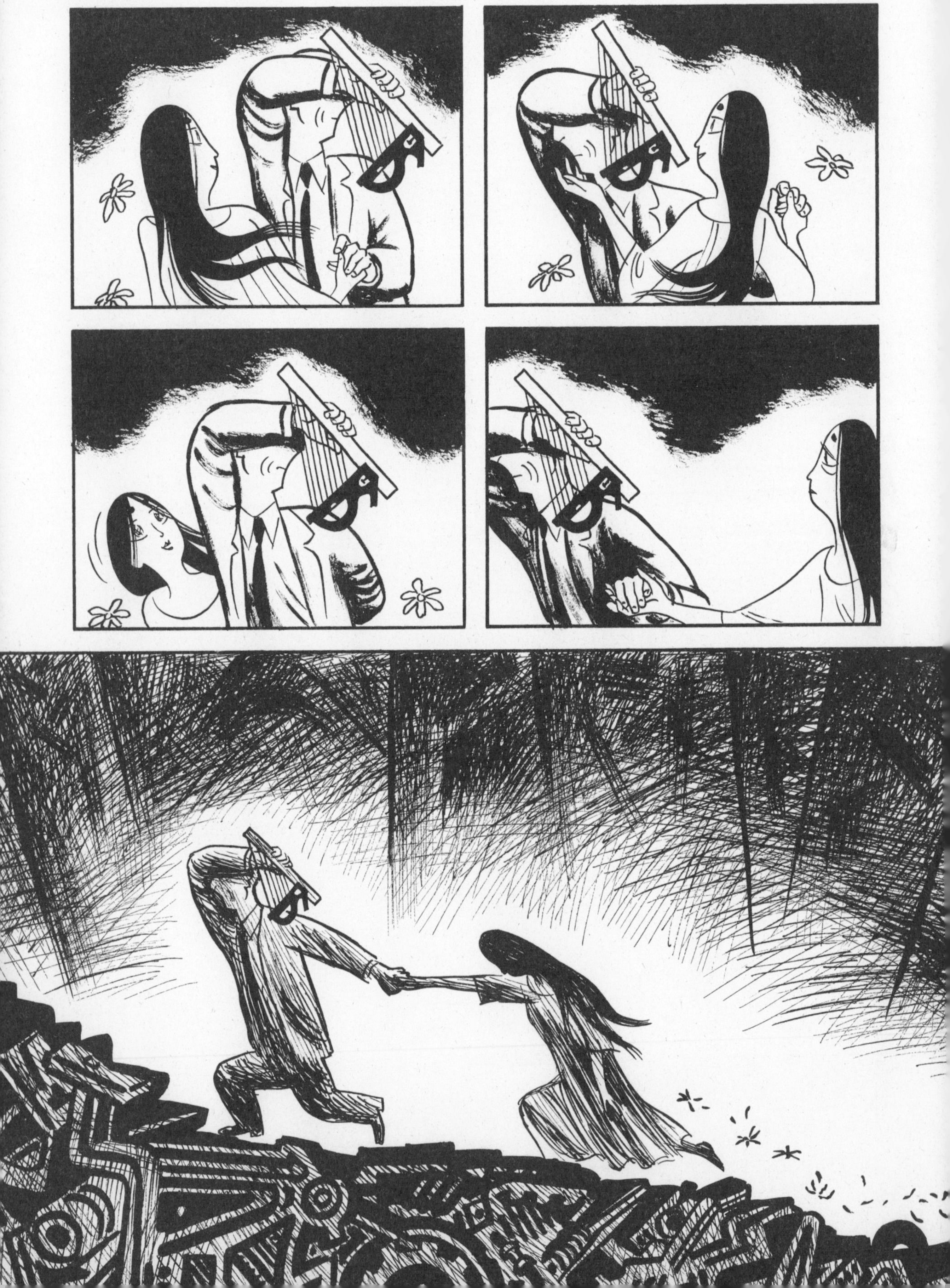

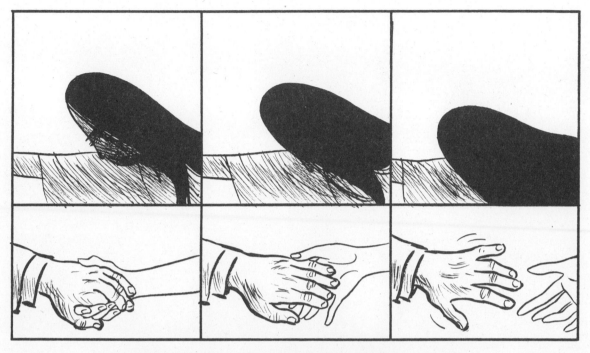

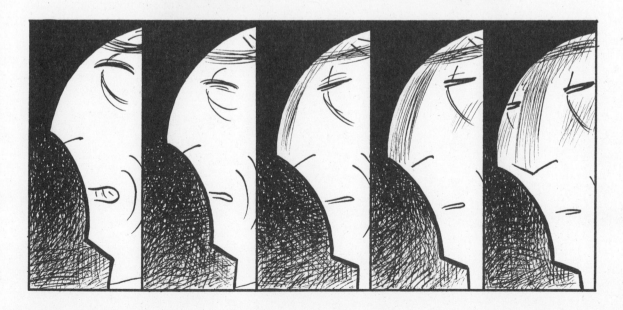

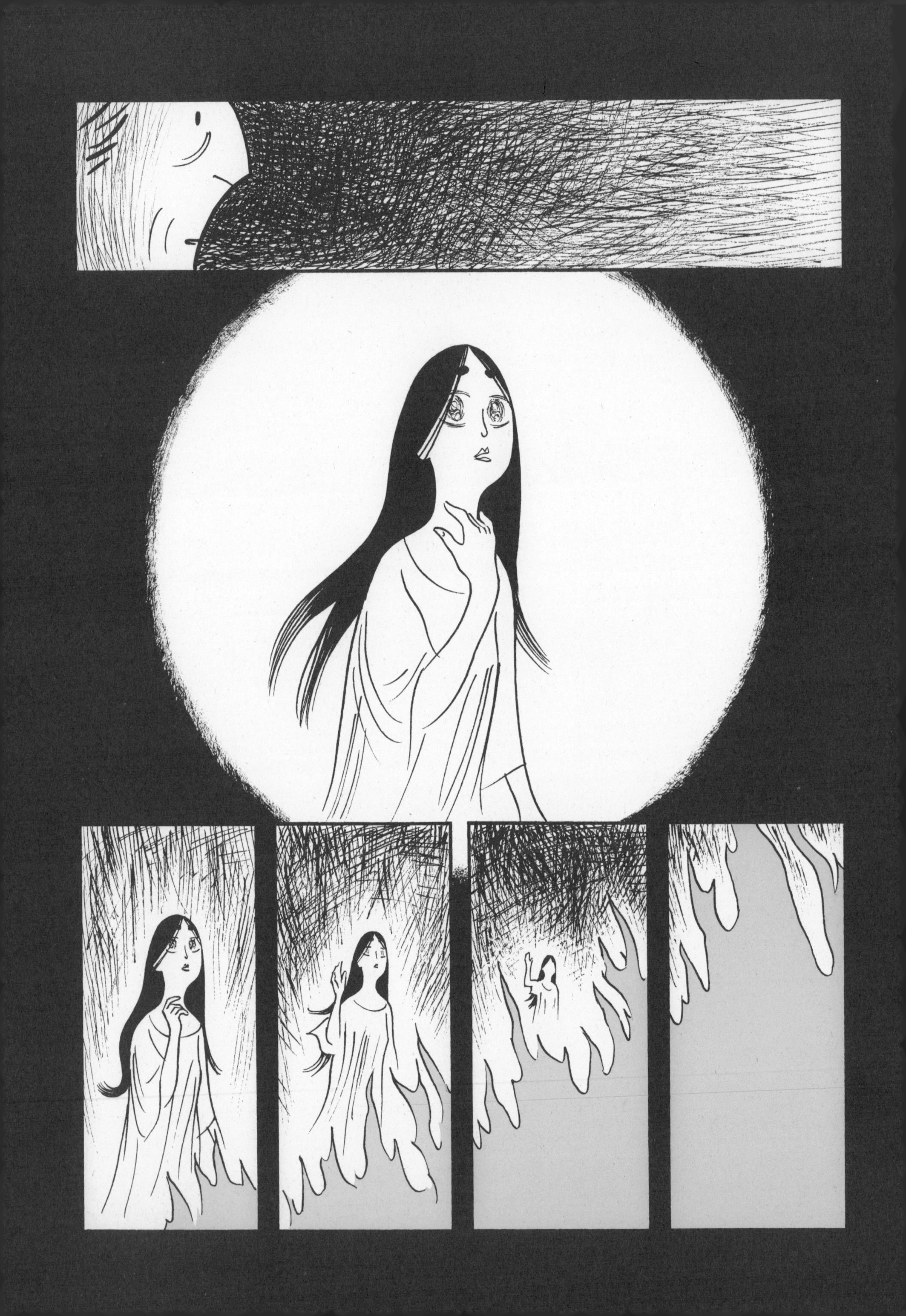

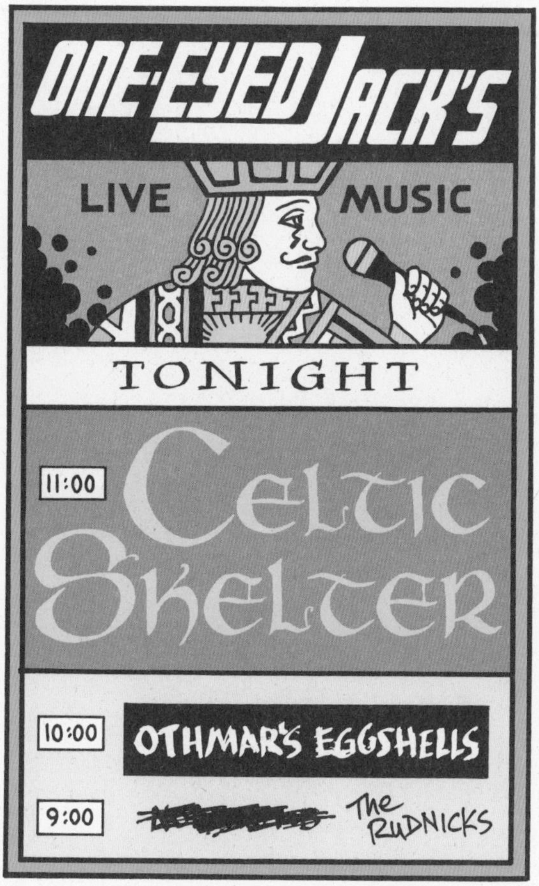
ONE-EYED JACK'S
LIVE MUSIC
TONIGHT
11:00
Celtic Shelter
10:00
OTHMAR'S EGGSHELLS
9:00
The RUDNICKS

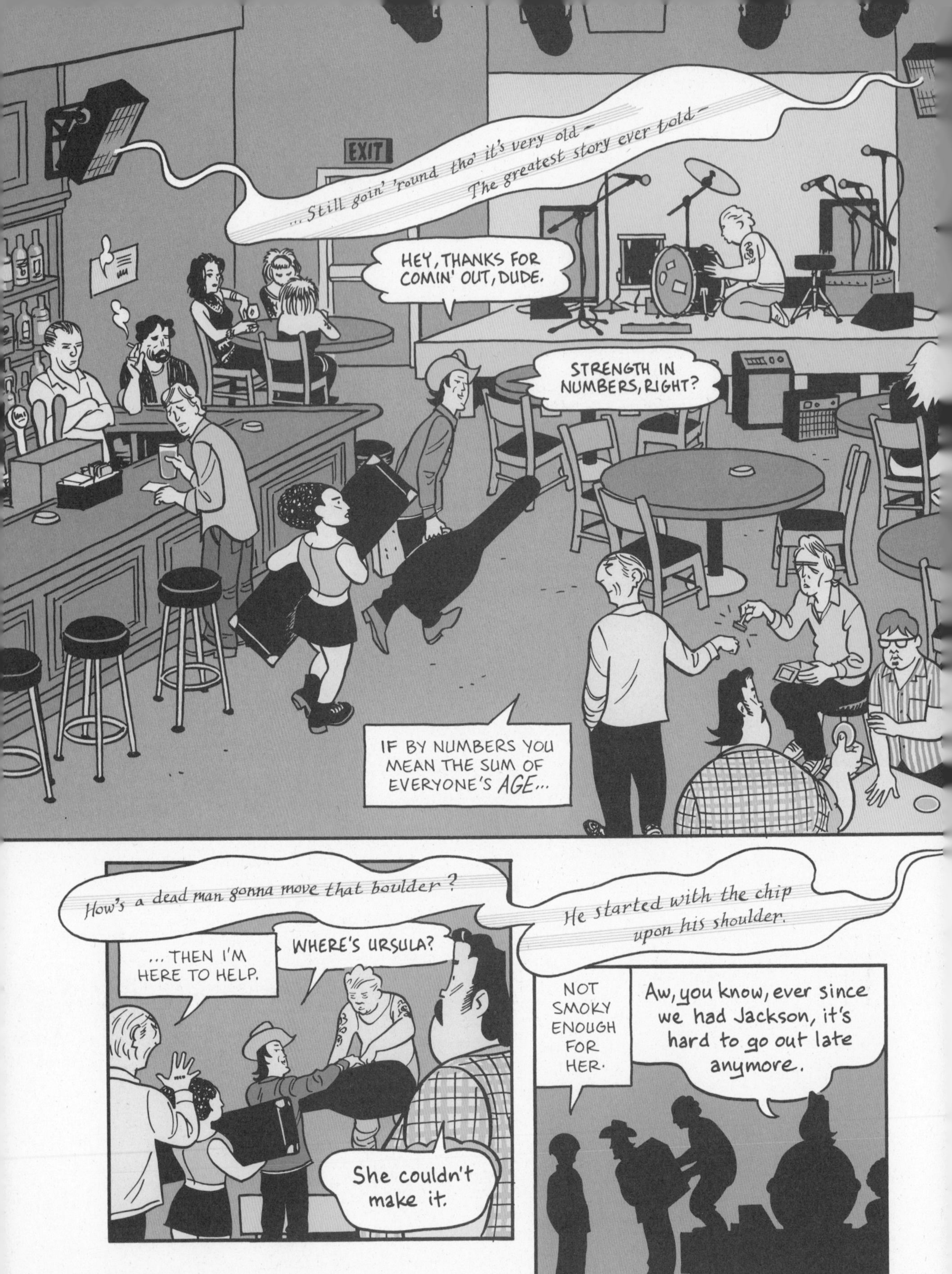

EXIT
...Still goin' 'round tho' it's very old—
The greatest story ever told—
HEY, THANKS FOR COMIN' OUT, DUDE.
STRENGTH IN NUMBERS, RIGHT?
IF BY NUMBERS YOU MEAN THE SUM OF EVERYONE'S *AGE*...
How's a dead man gonna move that boulder?
He started with the chip upon his shoulder.
...THEN I'M HERE TO HELP.
WHERE'S URSULA?
She couldn't make it.
NOT SMOKY ENOUGH FOR HER.
Aw, you know, ever since we had Jackson, it's hard to go out late anymore.

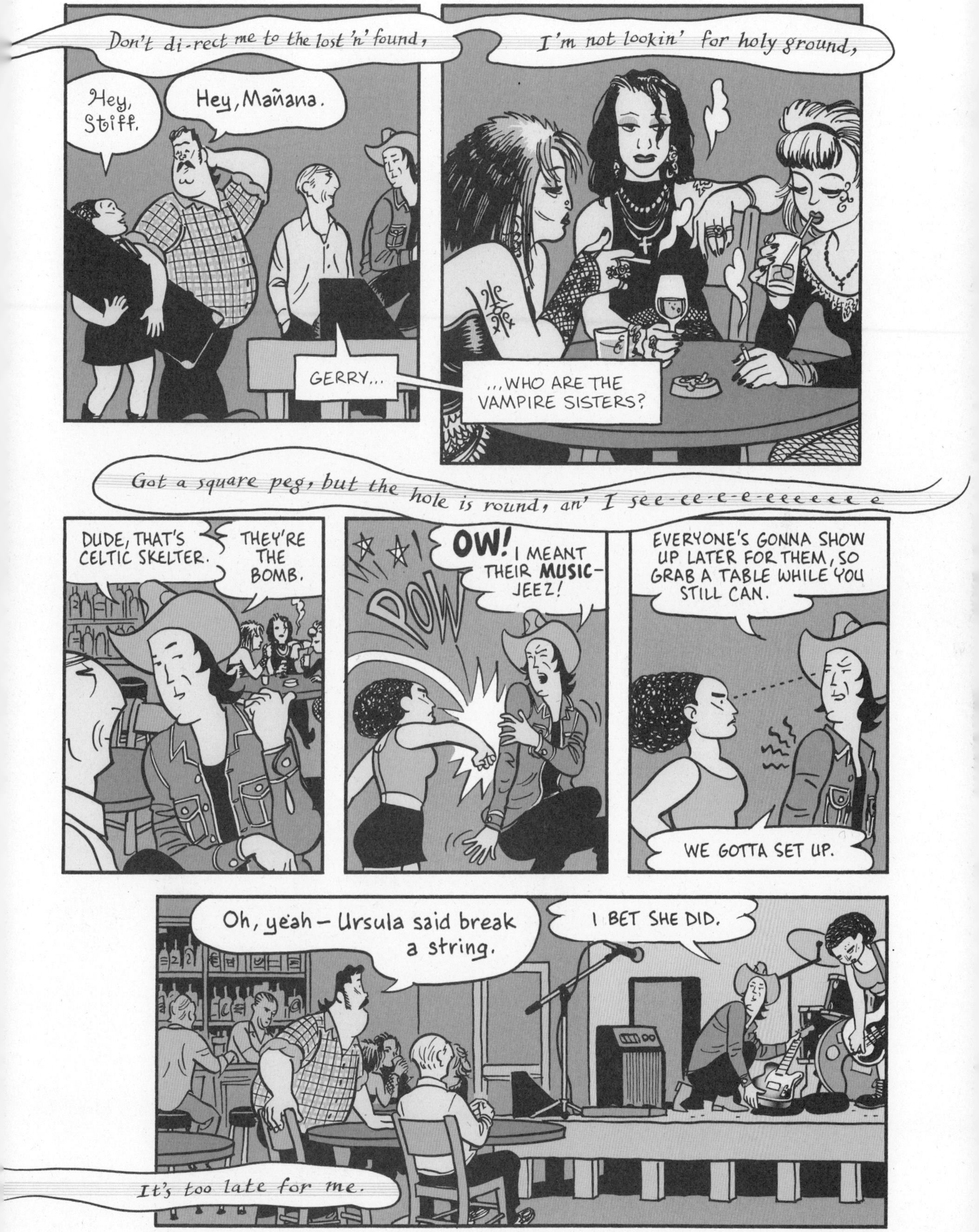

Don't di-rect me to the lost 'n' found,
Hey, Stiff.
Hey, Mañana.
GERRY...
I'm not lookin' for holy ground,
...WHO ARE THE VAMPIRE SISTERS?
Got a square peg, but the hole is round, an' I see-ee-e-e-eeeeee e
DUDE, THAT'S CELTIC SKELTER.
THEY'RE THE BOMB.
POW
OW! I MEANT THEIR MUSIC - JEEZ!
EVERYONE'S GONNA SHOW UP LATER FOR THEM, SO GRAB A TABLE WHILE YOU STILL CAN.
WE GOTTA SET UP.
Oh, yeah - Ursula said break a string.
I BET SHE DID.
It's too late for me.

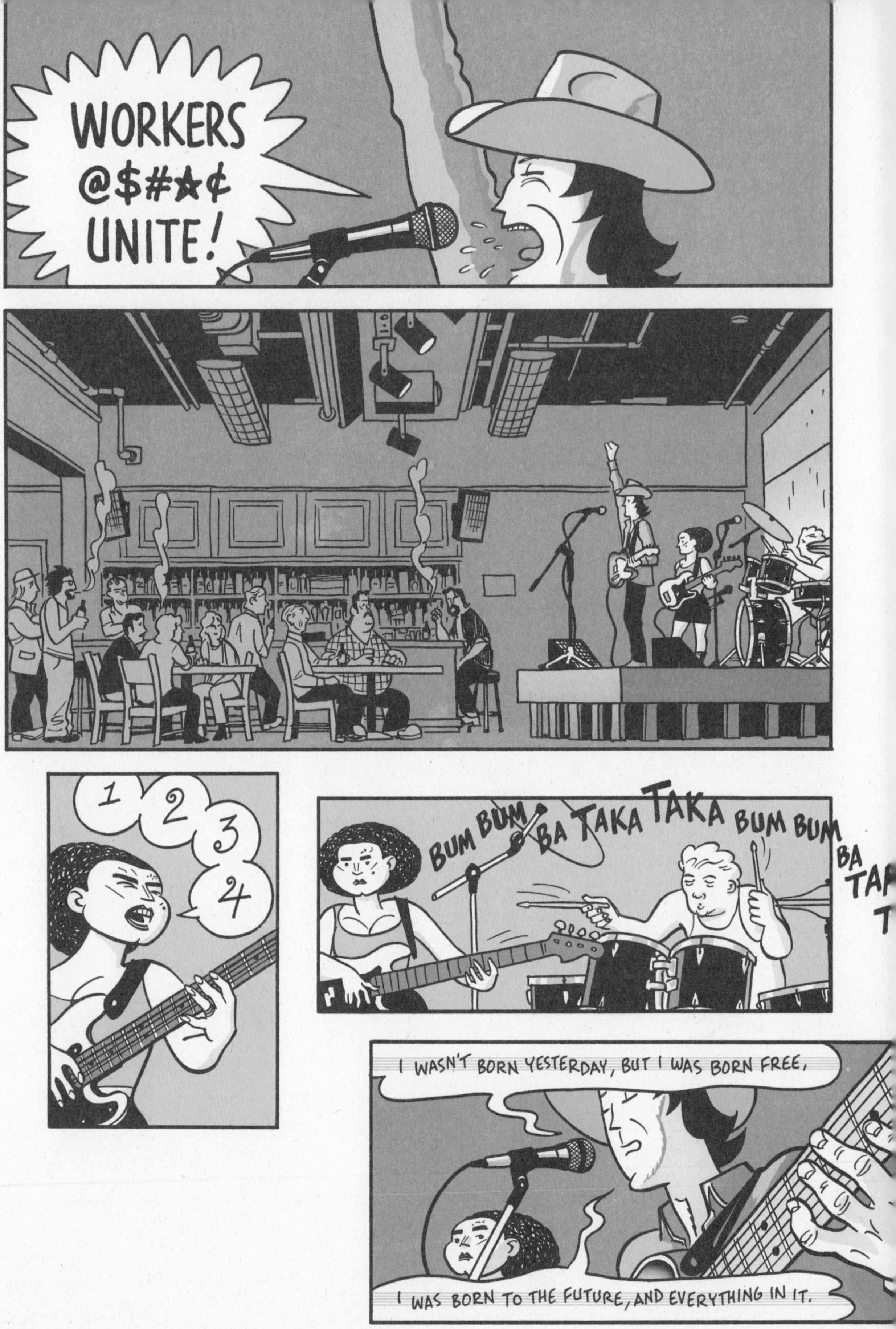
WORKERS @$#★¢ UNITE!
1
2
3
4
BUM BUM BA TAKA TAKA BUM BUM BA
I WASN'T BORN YESTERDAY, BUT I WAS BORN FREE,
I WAS BORN TO THE FUTURE, AND EVERYTHING IN IT.

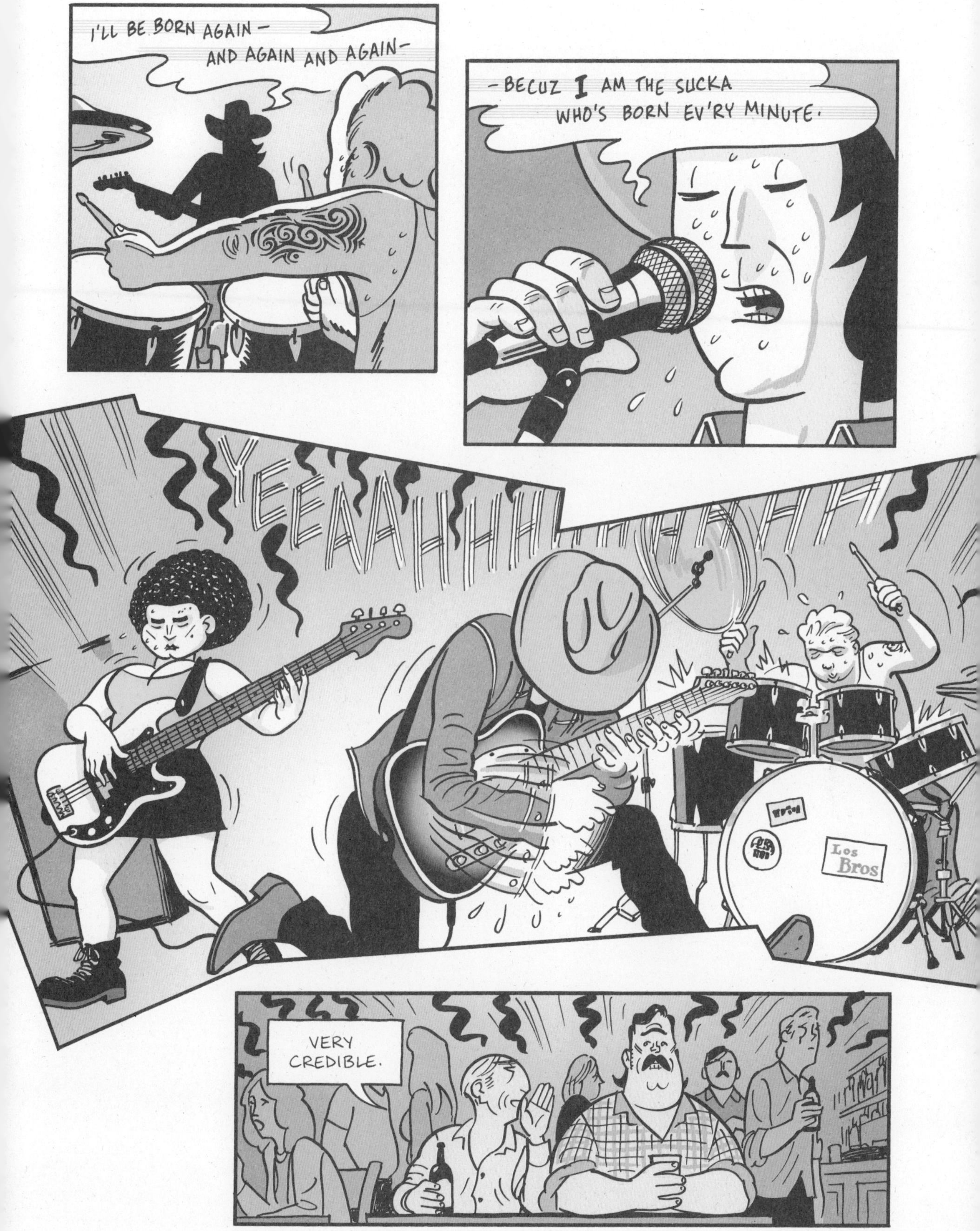
I'LL BE BORN AGAIN— AND AGAIN AND AGAIN—
—BECUZ I AM THE SUCKA WHO'S BORN EV'RY MINUTE.
YEEAAHHHHHHHHH
Los Bros
VERY CREDIBLE.

WELL, I'M NOT SURE YOU MADE ANY CONVERTS, BUT I DID SEE A FEW BOBBING HEADS.

CLINK

S'LIKE I ALWAYS SAY, MAN: FREE YOUR ASS AND YOUR MIND WILL FOLLOW.

Just you be careful where you let that ass roam free, boy.

SHE'S ALL UPSET 'CAUSE NATHAN TOLD HER HIS @$#&¢ THEORY.

THE DRUMMER HAS A THEORY?

MOVE OVER, DARWIN!

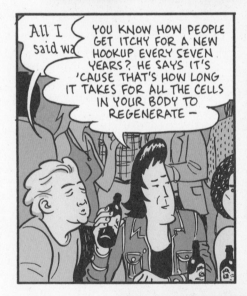

All I said wa

YOU KNOW HOW PEOPLE GET ITCHY FOR A NEW HOOKUP EVERY SEVEN YEARS? HE SAYS IT'S 'CAUSE THAT'S HOW LONG IT TAKES FOR ALL THE CELLS IN YOUR BODY TO REGENERATE —

— SO, IT'S LIKE, EVERY SEVEN YEARS YOU'RE A TOTALLY NEW PERSON.

Yeah, but with the same **mind**, stoopid!

I ALWAYS BELIEVED THAT WHAT KEPT TWO PEOPLE TOGETHER WAS A COMBINATION OF PHYSICAL AND MENTAL ATTRACTION...

...BUT YOU TWO, STIFF—YOU AND URSULA—YOU SEEM TO HAVE NOTHING IN COMMON.

Aw, Ursula says me an' her a' been together since the crack of time.

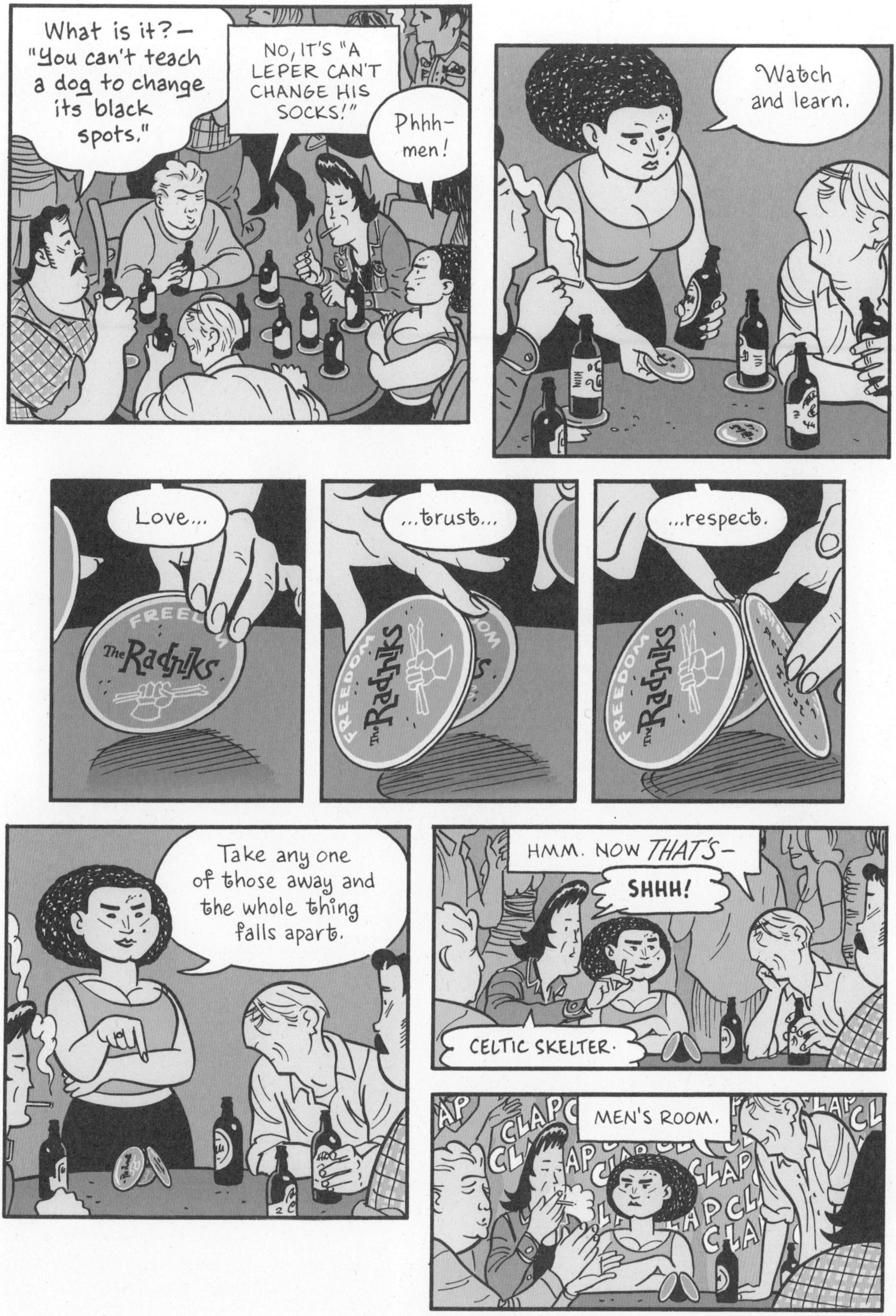
What is it?— "You can't teach a dog to change its black spots."
NO, IT'S "A LEPER CAN'T CHANGE HIS SOCKS!"
Phhh-men!
Watch and learn.
Love...
...trust...
...respect.
FREEDOM
The Radniks
Take any one of those away and the whole thing falls apart.
HMM. NOW THAT'S—
SHHH!
CELTIC SKELTER.
MEN'S ROOM.
CLAP
CLAP
CLAP
CLAP

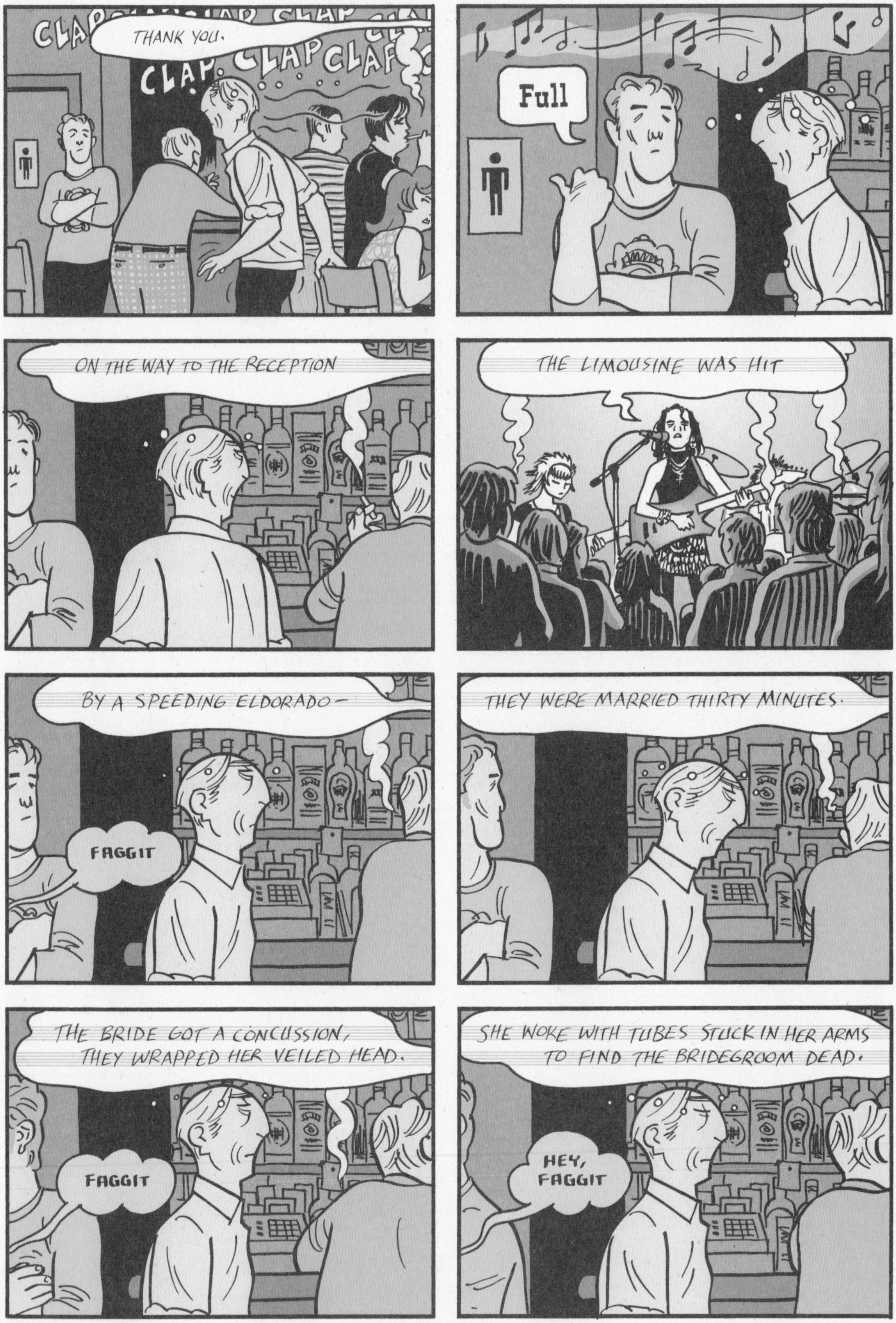
CLAP CLAP CLAP CLAP
THANK YOU.
CLAP CLAP CLAP CLAP
Full
ON THE WAY TO THE RECEPTION
THE LIMOUSINE WAS HIT
BY A SPEEDING ELDORADO—
FAGGIT
THEY WERE MARRIED THIRTY MINUTES.
THE BRIDE GOT A CONCUSSION,
THEY WRAPPED HER VEILED HEAD.
FAGGIT
SHE WOKE WITH TUBES STUCK IN HER ARMS
TO FIND THE BRIDEGROOM DEAD.
HEY, FAGGIT

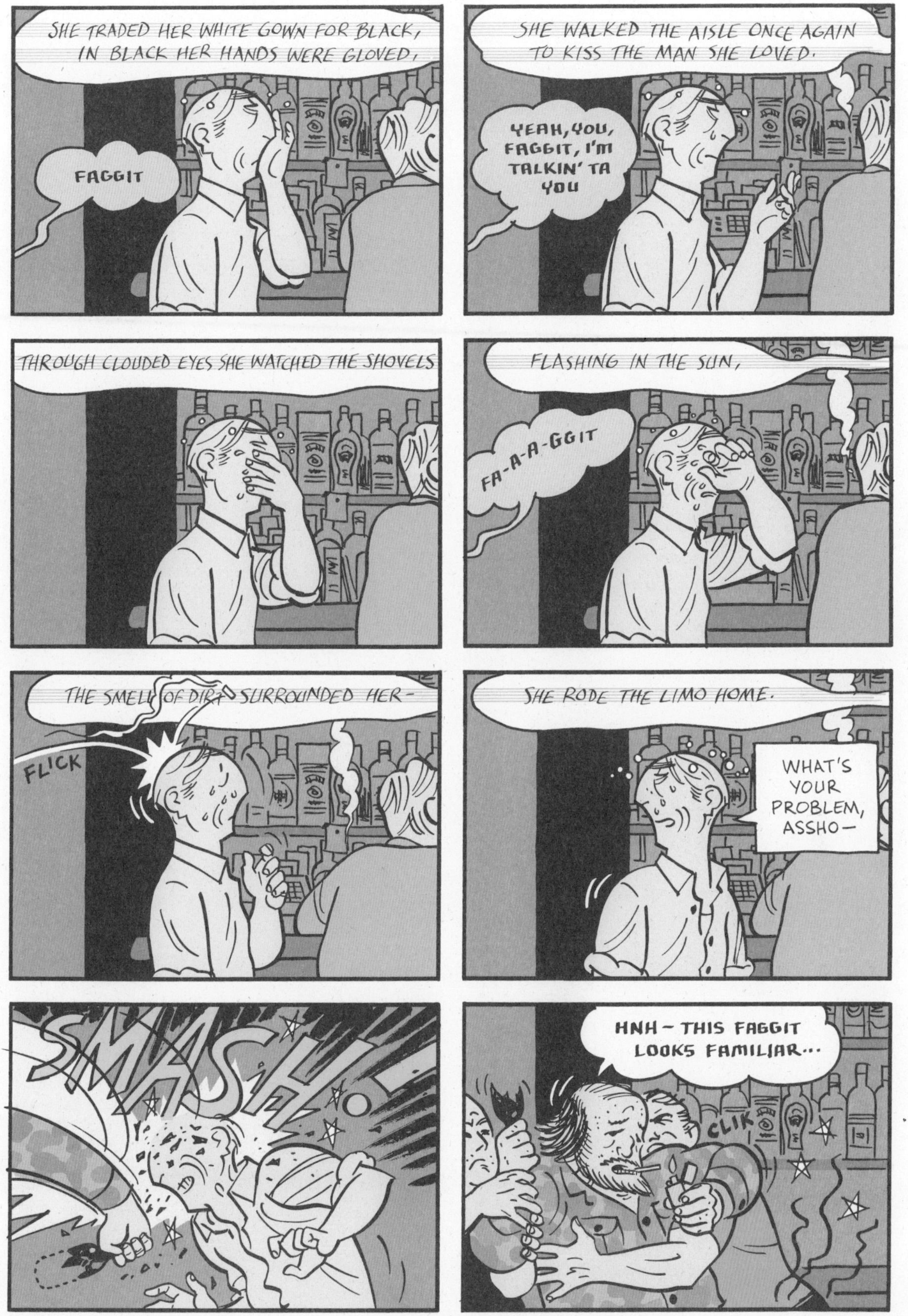
SHE TRADED HER WHITE GOWN FOR BLACK, IN BLACK HER HANDS WERE GLOVED,
FAGGIT
SHE WALKED THE AISLE ONCE AGAIN TO KISS THE MAN SHE LOVED.
YEAH, YOU, FAGGIT, I'M TALKIN' TA YOU
THROUGH CLOUDED EYES SHE WATCHED THE SHOVELS
FLASHING IN THE SUN,
FA-A-A-GGIT
THE SMELL OF DIRT SURROUNDED HER-
FLICK
SHE RODE THE LIMO HOME.
WHAT'S YOUR PROBLEM, ASSHO-
SMASH
HNH - THIS FAGGIT LOOKS FAMILIAR...
CLIK

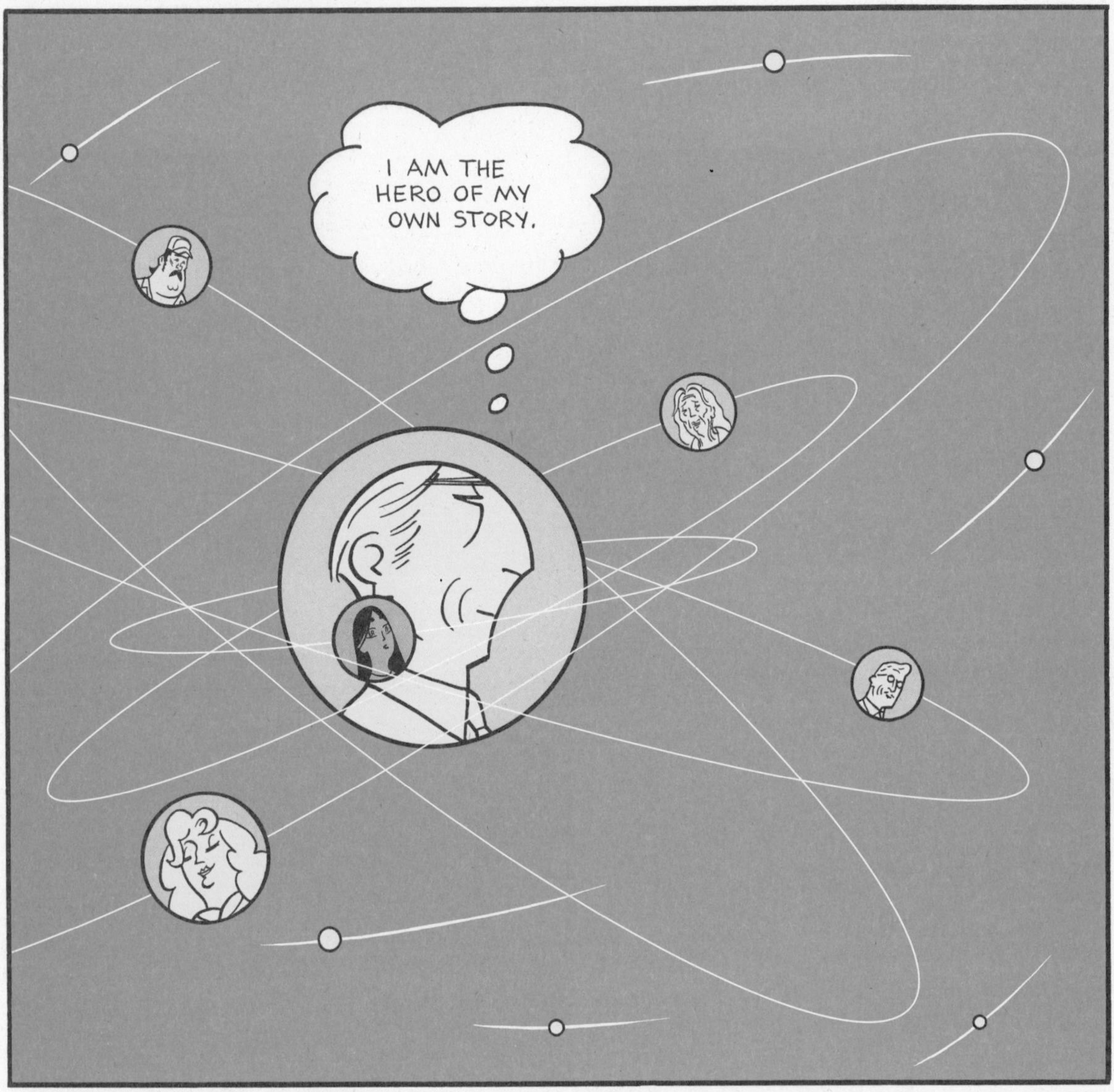
I AM THE HERO OF MY OWN STORY.

ASTERIOS THOUGHT HE UNDERSTOOD WHY PEOPLE BELIEVE IN A SOLITARY, OMNISCIENT GOD.

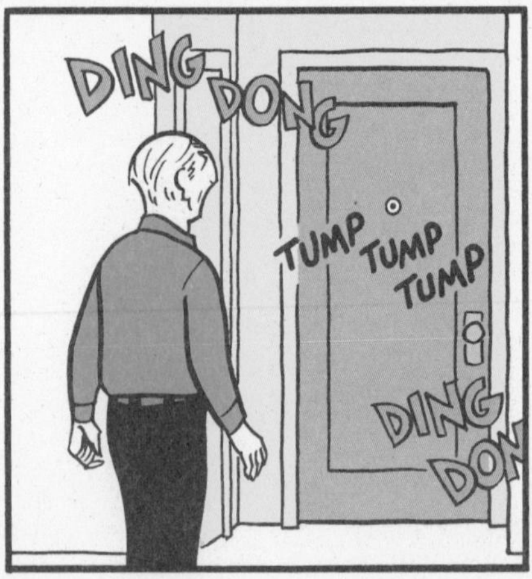
DING DONG
TUMP TUMP TUMP
DING DON

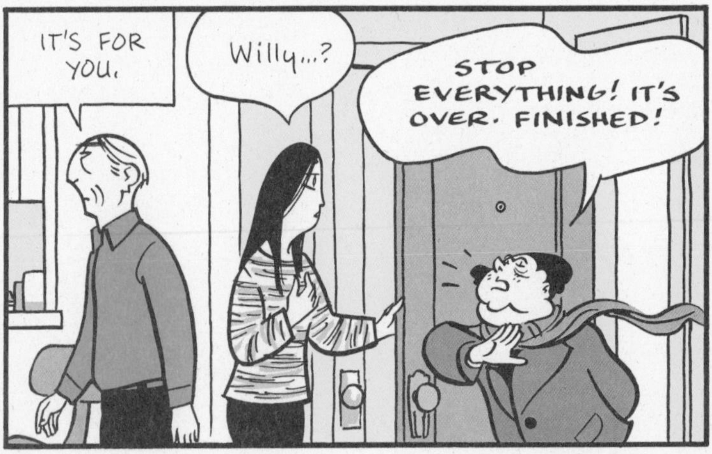
IT'S FOR YOU.
Willy...?
STOP EVERYTHING! IT'S OVER. FINISHED!

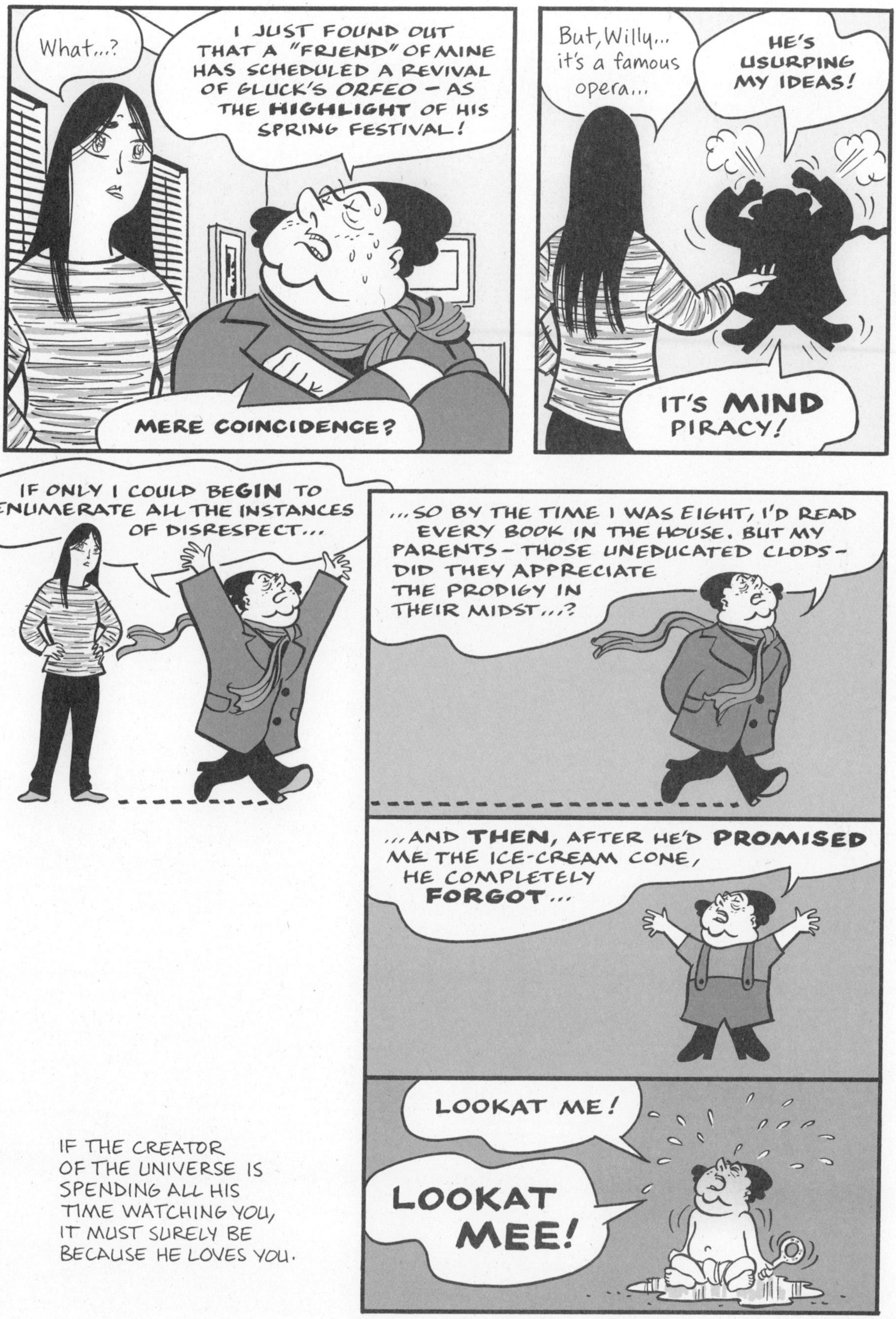
What...?
I JUST FOUND OUT THAT A "FRIEND" OF MINE HAS SCHEDULED A REVIVAL OF GLUCK'S ORFEO – AS THE HIGHLIGHT OF HIS SPRING FESTIVAL!
MERE COINCIDENCE?
But, Willy... it's a famous opera...
HE'S USURPING MY IDEAS!
IT'S MIND PIRACY!
IF ONLY I COULD BEGIN TO ENUMERATE ALL THE INSTANCES OF DISRESPECT...
...SO BY THE TIME I WAS EIGHT, I'D READ EVERY BOOK IN THE HOUSE. BUT MY PARENTS – THOSE UNEDUCATED CLODS – DID THEY APPRECIATE THE PRODIGY IN THEIR MIDST...?
...AND THEN, AFTER HE'D PROMISED ME THE ICE-CREAM CONE, HE COMPLETELY FORGOT...
LOOKAT ME!
LOOKAT MEE!
IF THE CREATOR OF THE UNIVERSE IS SPENDING ALL HIS TIME WATCHING YOU, IT MUST SURELY BE BECAUSE HE LOVES YOU.

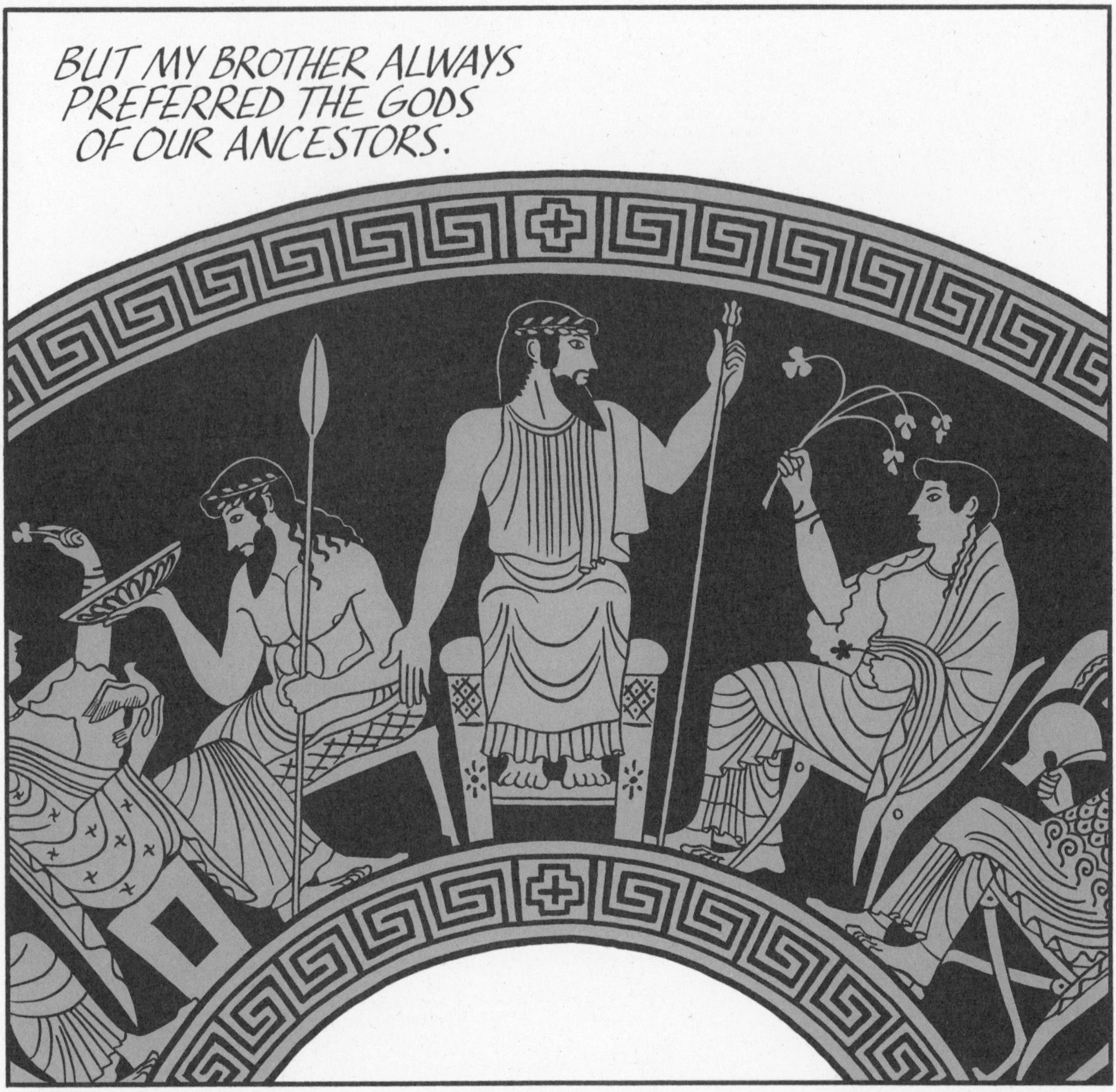
BUT MY BROTHER ALWAYS PREFERRED THE GODS OF OUR ANCESTORS.

BY GIVING THEM HUMAN PERSONALITIES, THE ANCIENT GREEKS COULD FEEL THAT THE WORLD MADE SENSE...

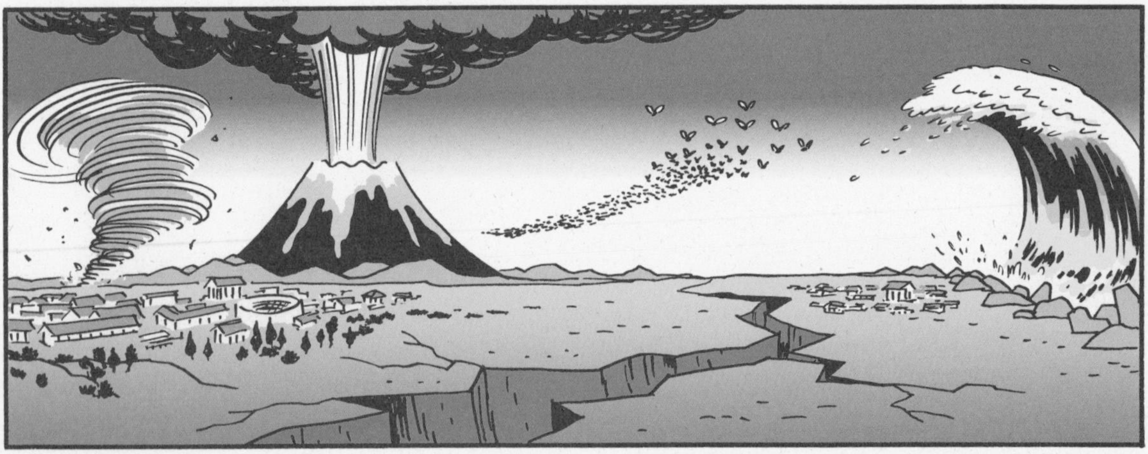

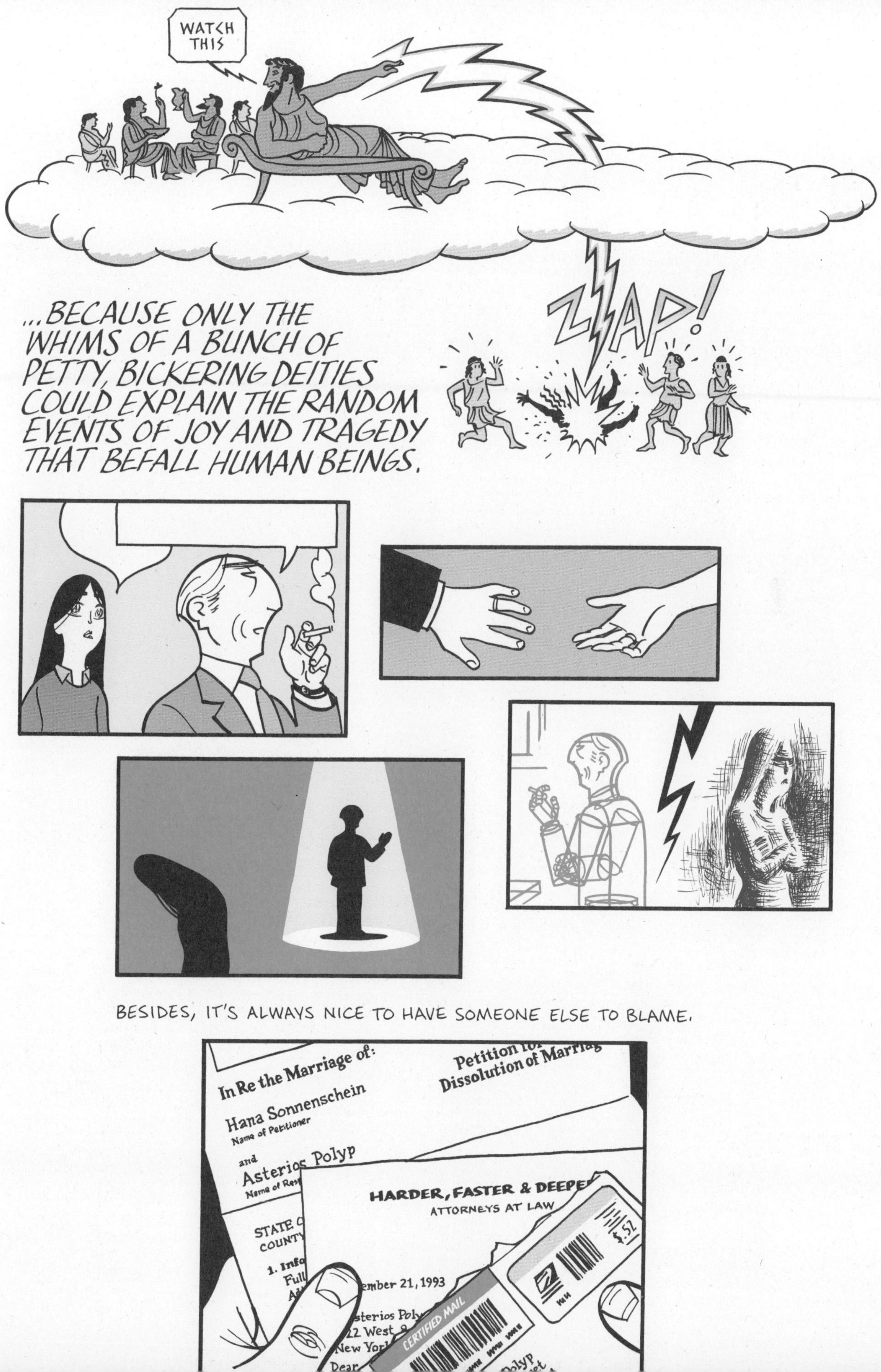

WATCH THIS
...BECAUSE ONLY THE WHIMS OF A BUNCH OF PETTY, BICKERING DEITIES COULD EXPLAIN THE RANDOM EVENTS OF JOY AND TRAGEDY THAT BEFALL HUMAN BEINGS.
ZZAP!
BESIDES, IT'S ALWAYS NICE TO HAVE SOMEONE ELSE TO BLAME.
In Re the Marriage of:
Petition for
Dissolution of Marriag
Hana Sonnenschein
Name of Petitioner
and
Asterios Polyp
HARDER, FASTER & DEEPE
ATTORNEYS AT LAW
ember 21, 1993
CERTIFIED MAIL
$.52

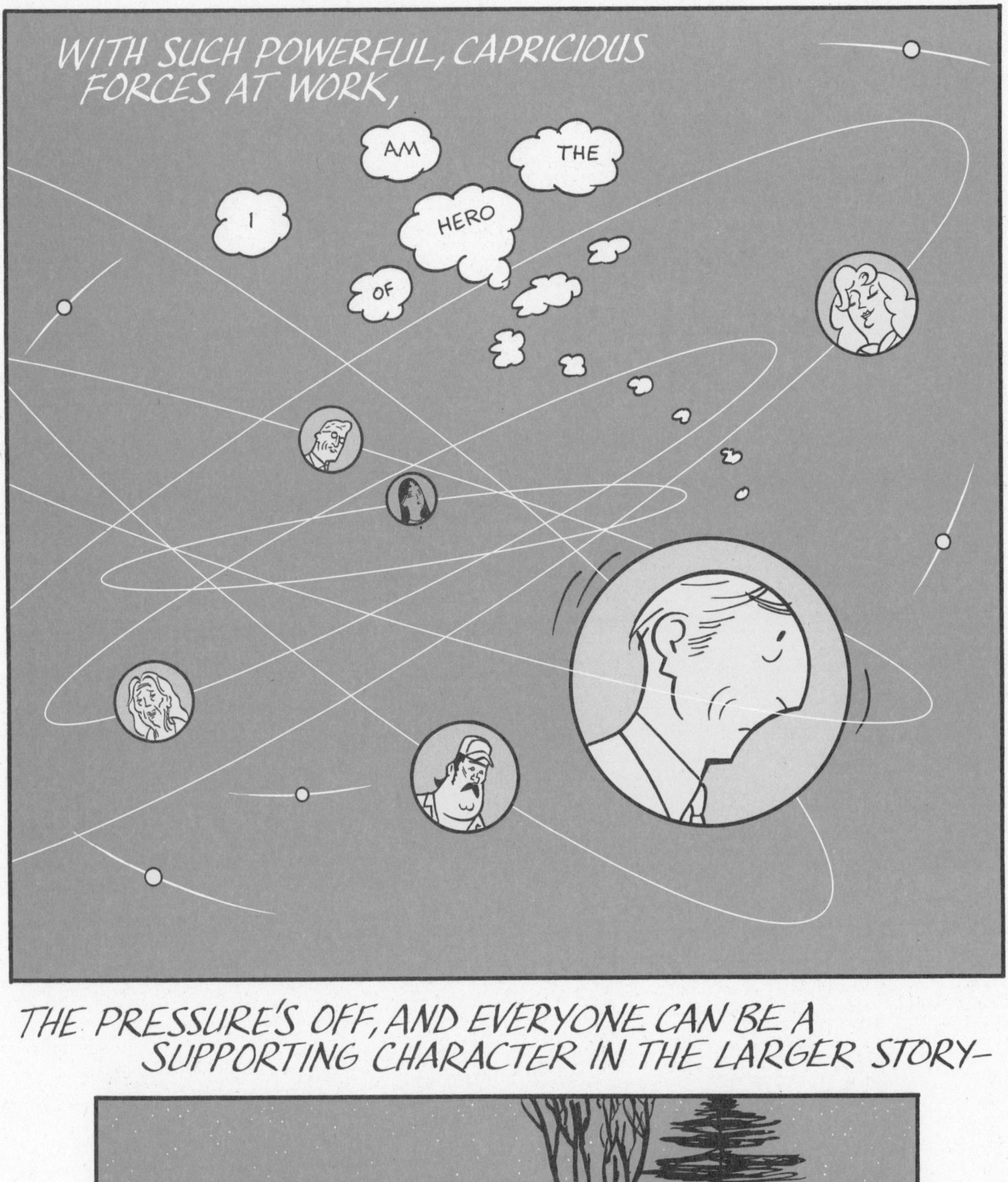
WITH SUCH POWERFUL, CAPRICIOUS FORCES AT WORK,
I
AM
THE
HERO
OF

THE PRESSURE'S OFF, AND EVERYONE CAN BE A SUPPORTING CHARACTER IN THE LARGER STORY-

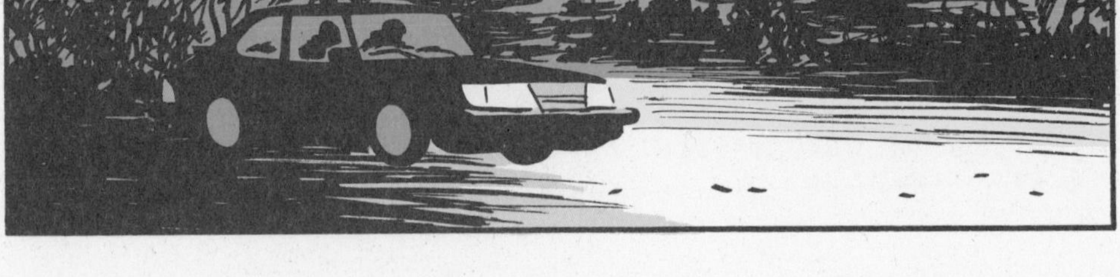

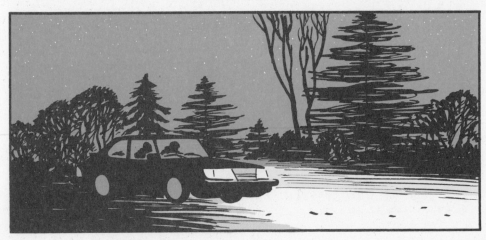

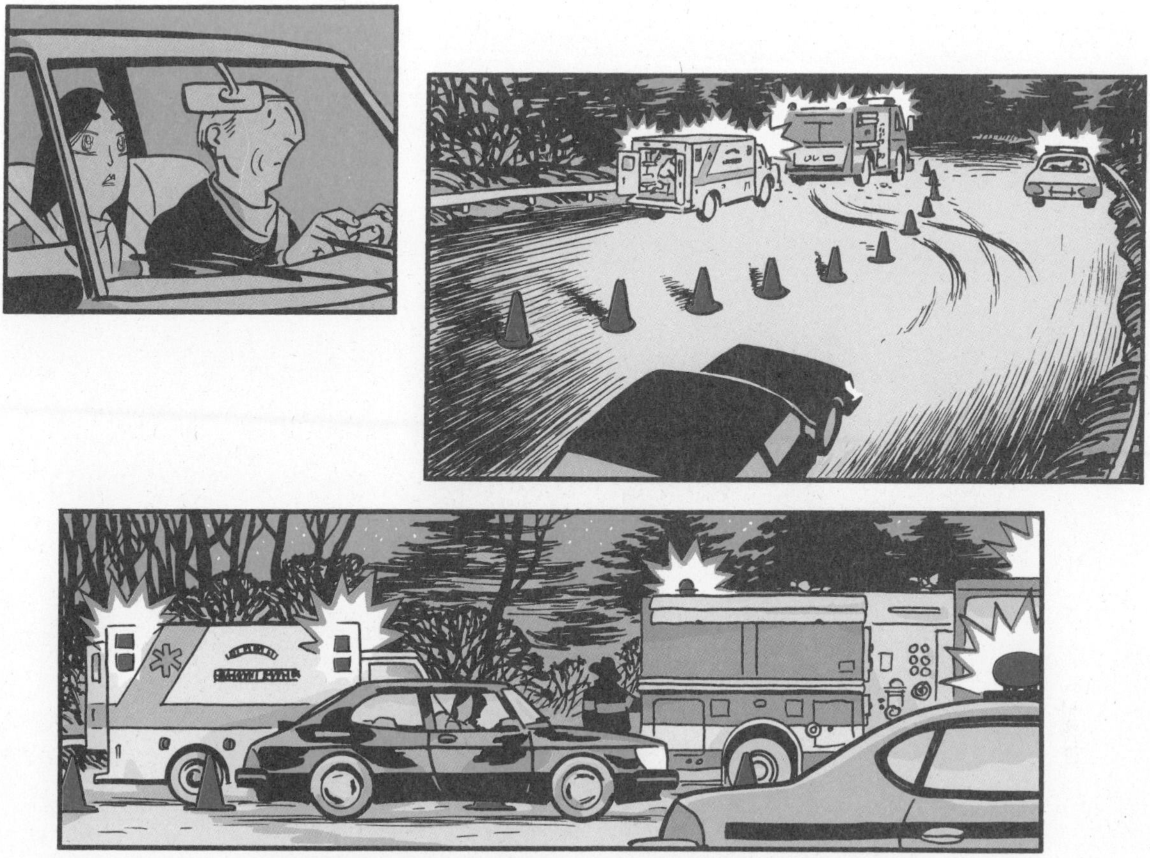

–HOWEVER BRIEF OR COLLATERAL
THAT ROLE MAY BE.

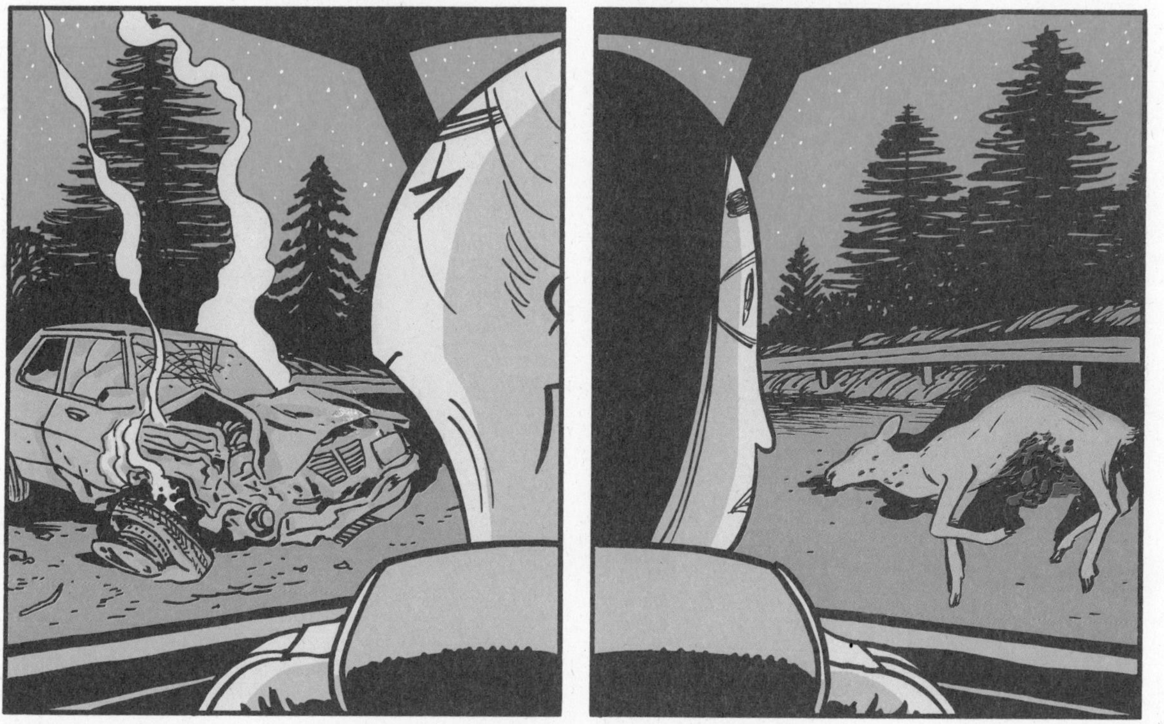

THE FIRST EMPEROR OF CHINA, QIN SHIHUANG, PREPARED FOR ETERNITY BY ORDERING THAT A REPLICA OF HIS VAST ARMY BE BURIED WITH HIM WHEN HE DIED.

THIS WAS CERTAINLY AN IMPROVEMENT ON THE LOCAL RULERS' TRADITION OF INTERRING AN ENTIRE RETINUE ALIVE.

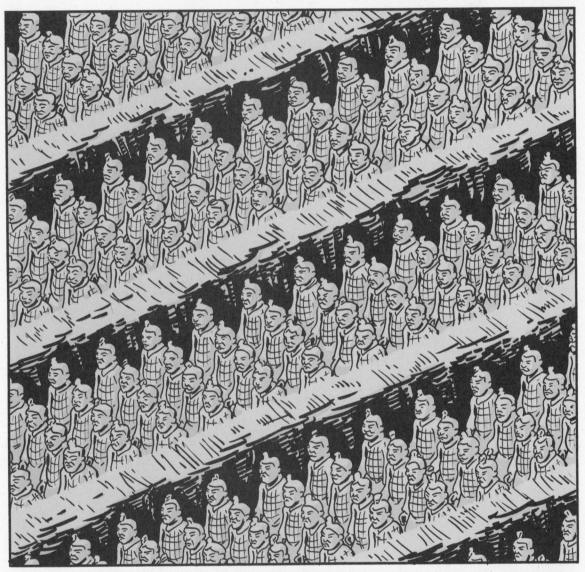

SEVEN THOUSAND TERRA-COTTA SOLDIERS STOOD WATCH IN HIS TOMB, UNDISTURBED, FOR TWO MILLENNIA.

THE EMPEROR, BORN IN 259 B.C., EXPIRED IN 210 B.C., BEFORE HE COULD CELEBRATE HIS FIFTIETH BIRTHDAY.

FROM THE VANTAGE OF TWO THOUSAND YEARS, THE SPAN BETWEEN 259 B.C. AND 210 B.C. MAY SEEM NEGLIGIBLE TO SOMEONE LIVING TODAY,

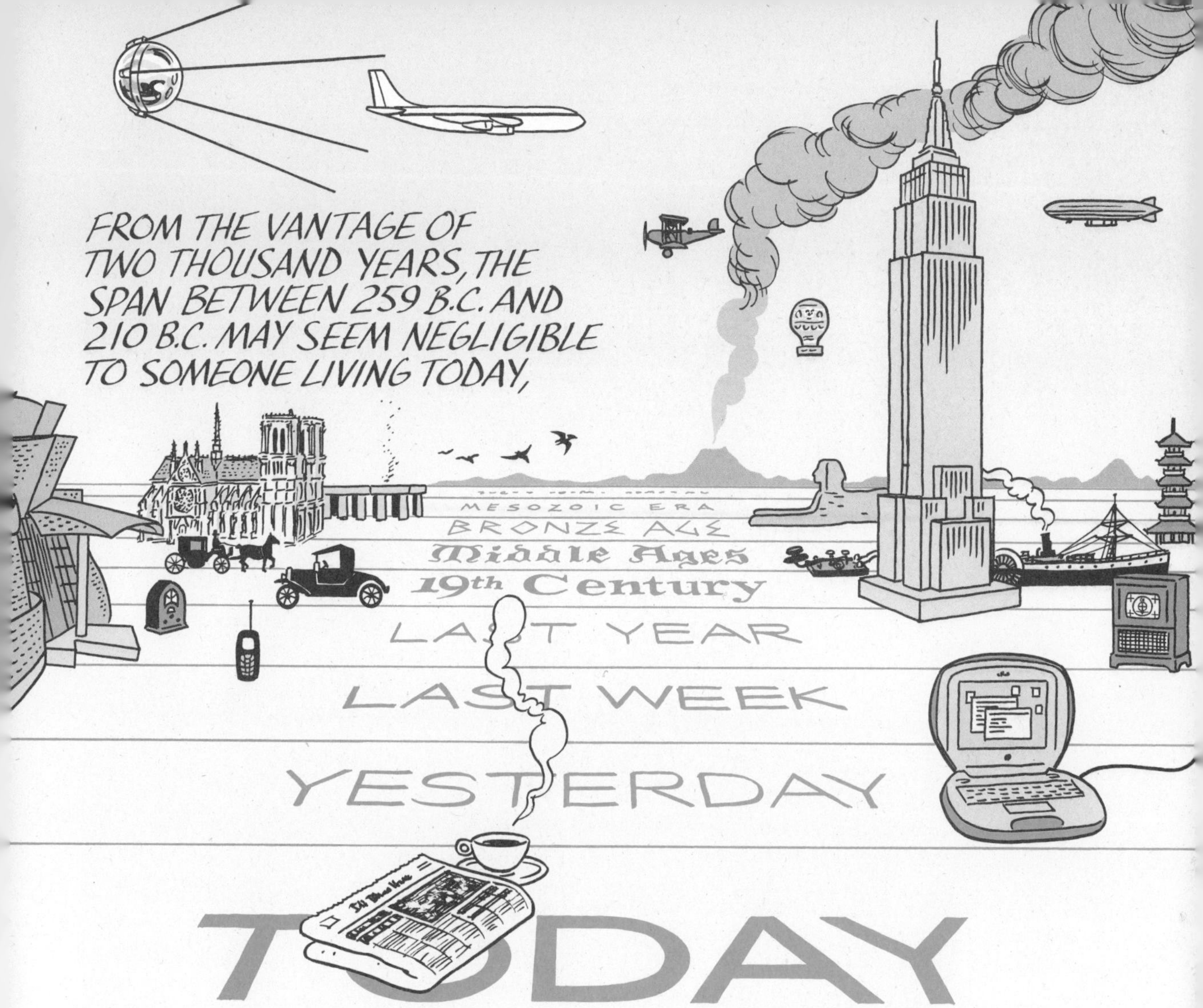

MESOZOIC ERA
BRONZE AGE
Middle Ages
19th Century
LAST YEAR
LAST WEEK
YESTERDAY
TODAY

BUT (ASTERIOS COULD TELL YOU BETTER THAN I) EACH OF THOSE EIGHTEEN THOUSAND DAYS MUST HAVE BEEN AS PRECIOUS AND UNPREDICTABLE AS THIS ONE.

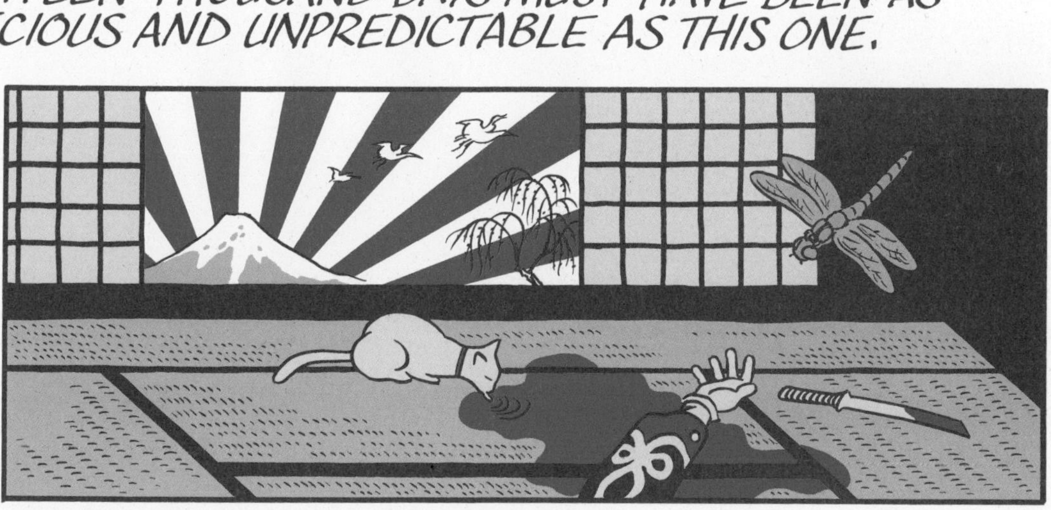

AFTER ALL, WHO KNOWS WHICH DAY WILL BE HIS LAST?

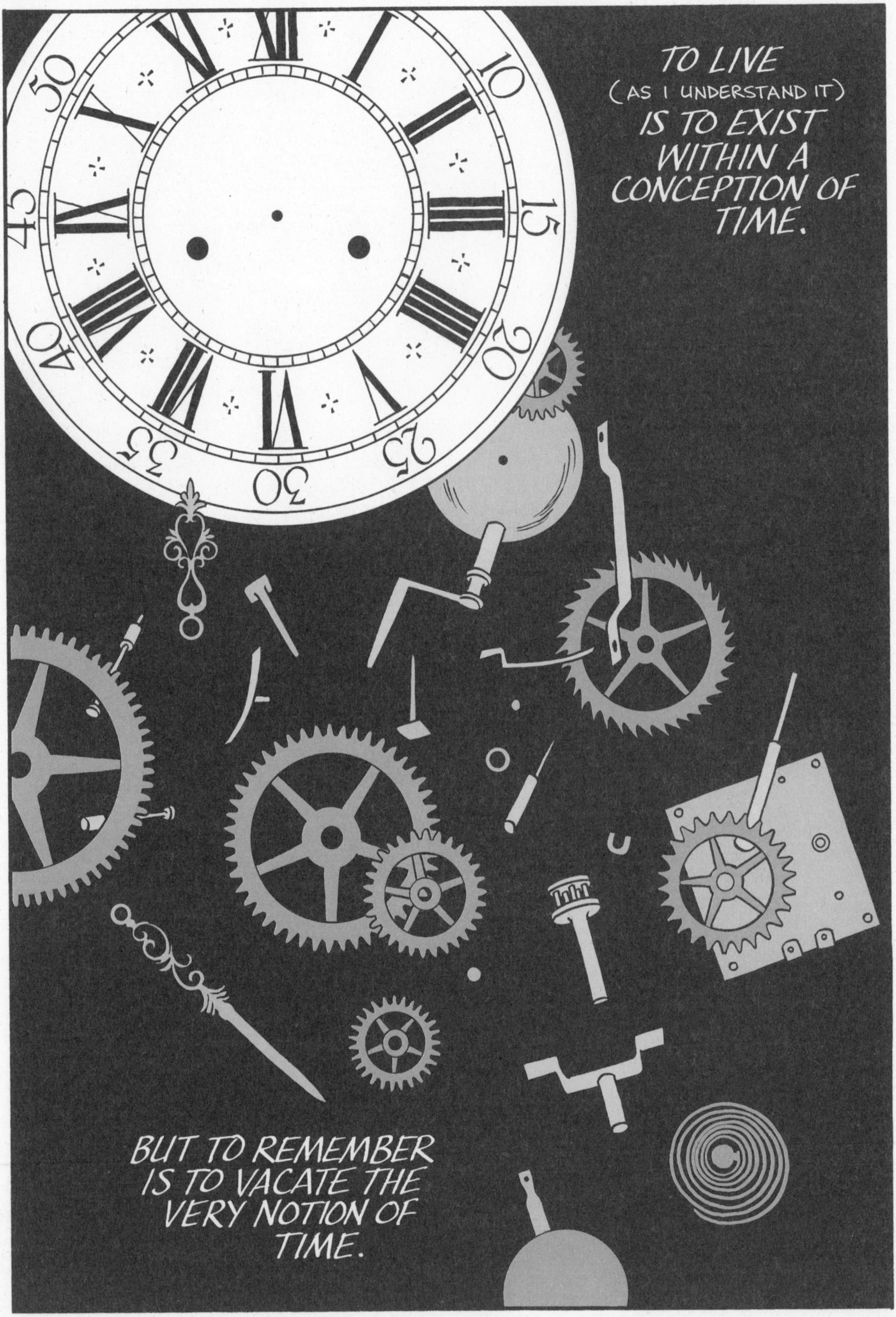
TO LIVE (AS I UNDERSTAND IT) IS TO EXIST WITHIN A CONCEPTION OF TIME.
BUT TO REMEMBER IS TO VACATE THE VERY NOTION OF TIME.

EVERY MEMORY, NO MATTER HOW REMOTE ITS SUBJECT, TAKES PLACE "NOW," AT THE MOMENT IT'S CALLED UP IN THE MIND.

Life is stressful. That's why they say "rest in peace".
REMEMBER, ASTERIOS, STRONG TEA MAKES YOU WEAK, WEAK TEA MAKES YOU STRONG.

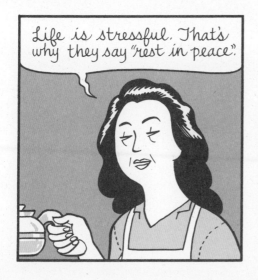

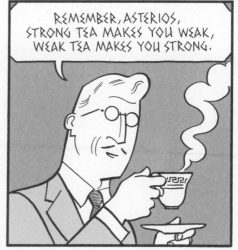

THE MORE SOMETHING IS RECALLED, THE MORE THE BRAIN HAS A CHANCE TO REFINE THE ORIGINAL EXPERIENCE,

It's just a matter of paying attention.
It's just a matter of paying more attention.
You just have to pay more attention.
You just don't pay enough attention.

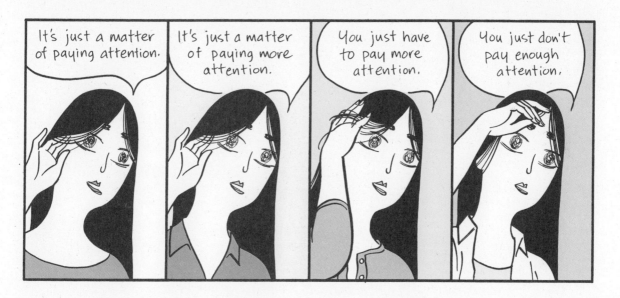

BECAUSE EVERY MEMORY
IS A RE-CREATION,
NOT A PLAYBACK.

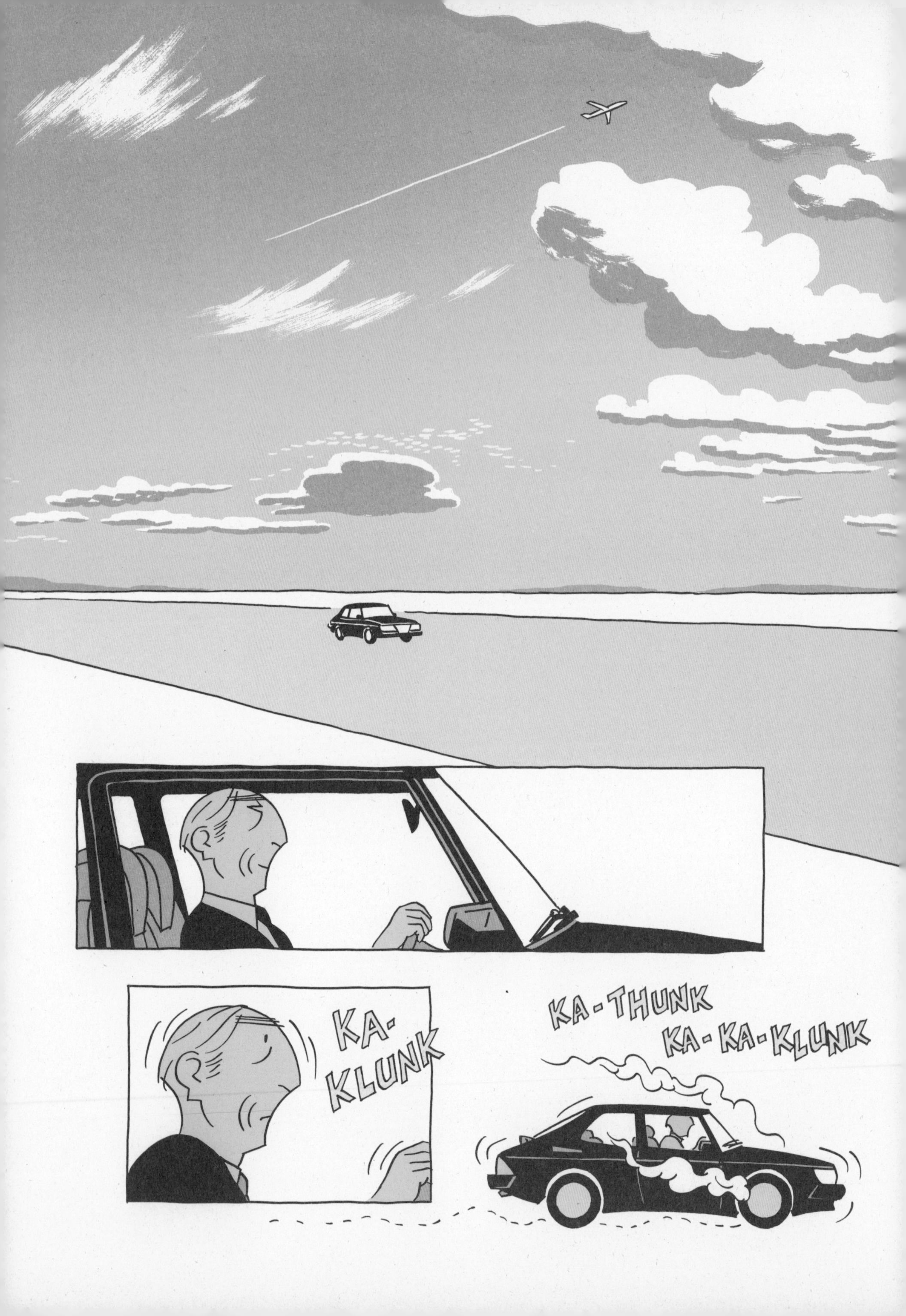
KA-
KLUNK
KA-THUNK
KA-KA-KLUNK

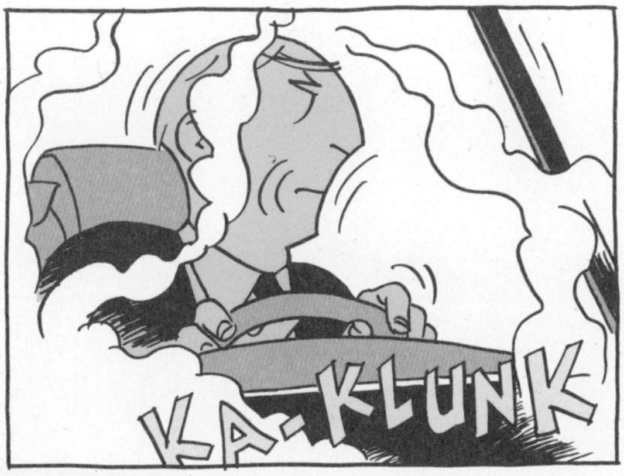
KA-KLUNK

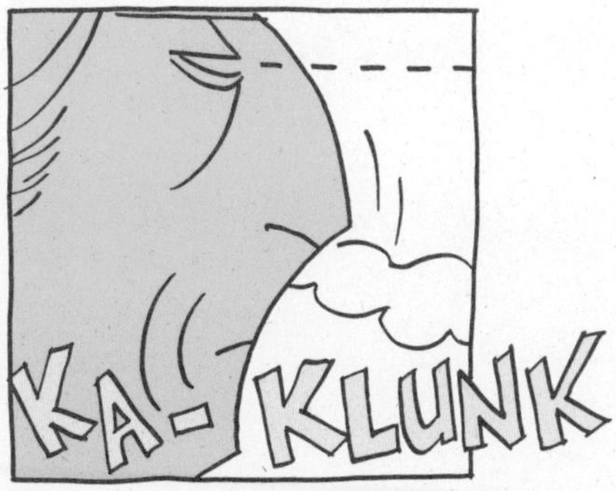
KA-KLUNK

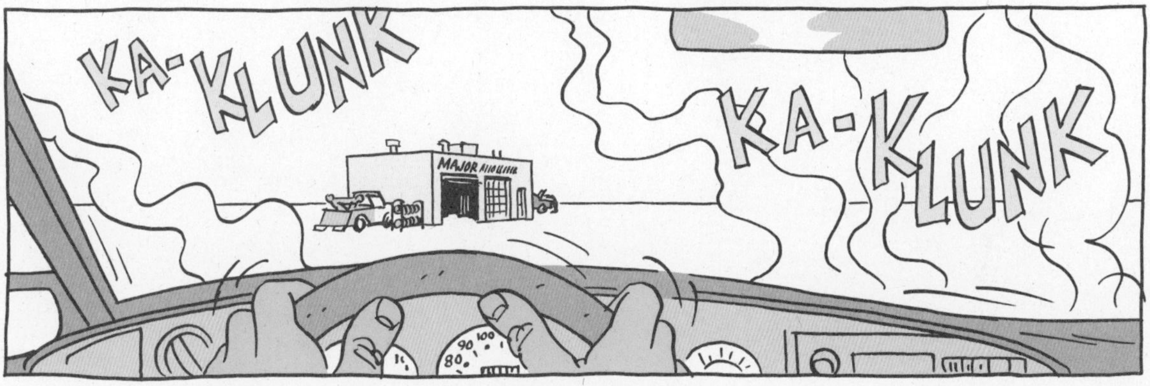
KA-KLUNK
KA-KLUNK

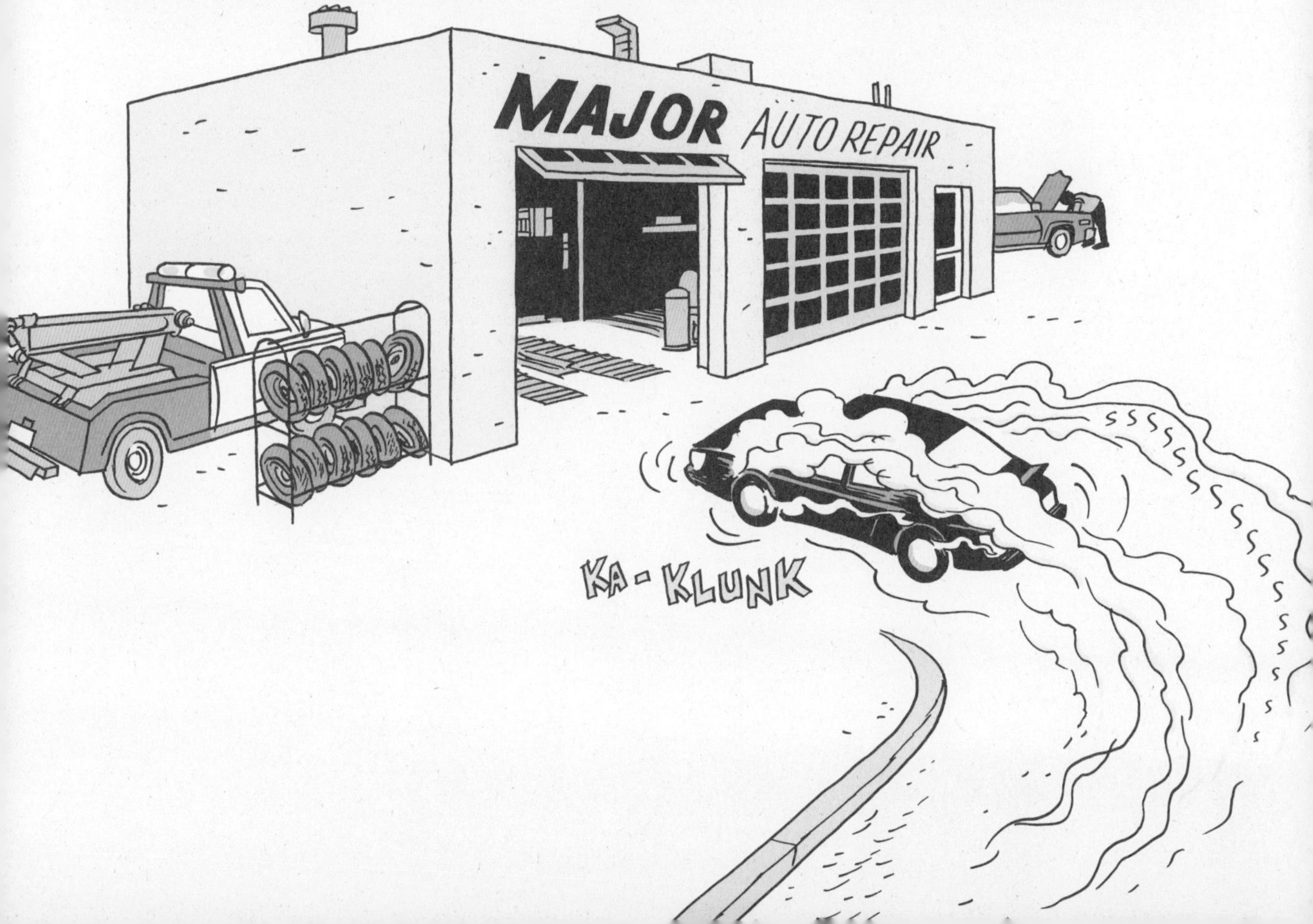
MAJOR AUTO REPAIR
KA-KLUNK

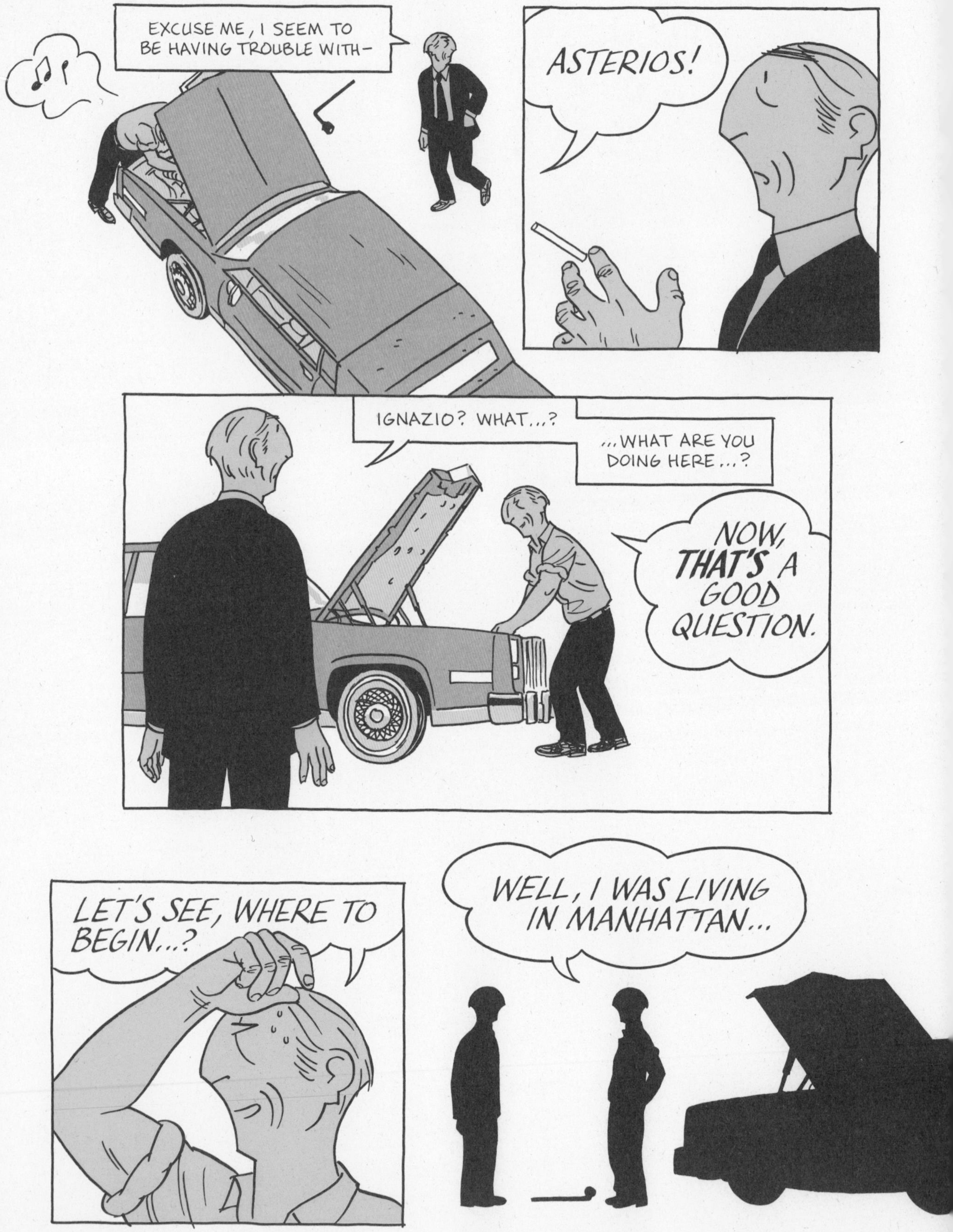
EXCUSE ME, I SEEM TO BE HAVING TROUBLE WITH-
ASTERIOS!
IGNAZIO? WHAT...?
...WHAT ARE YOU DOING HERE...?
NOW, THAT'S A GOOD QUESTION.
LET'S SEE, WHERE TO BEGIN...?
WELL, I WAS LIVING IN MANHATTAN...

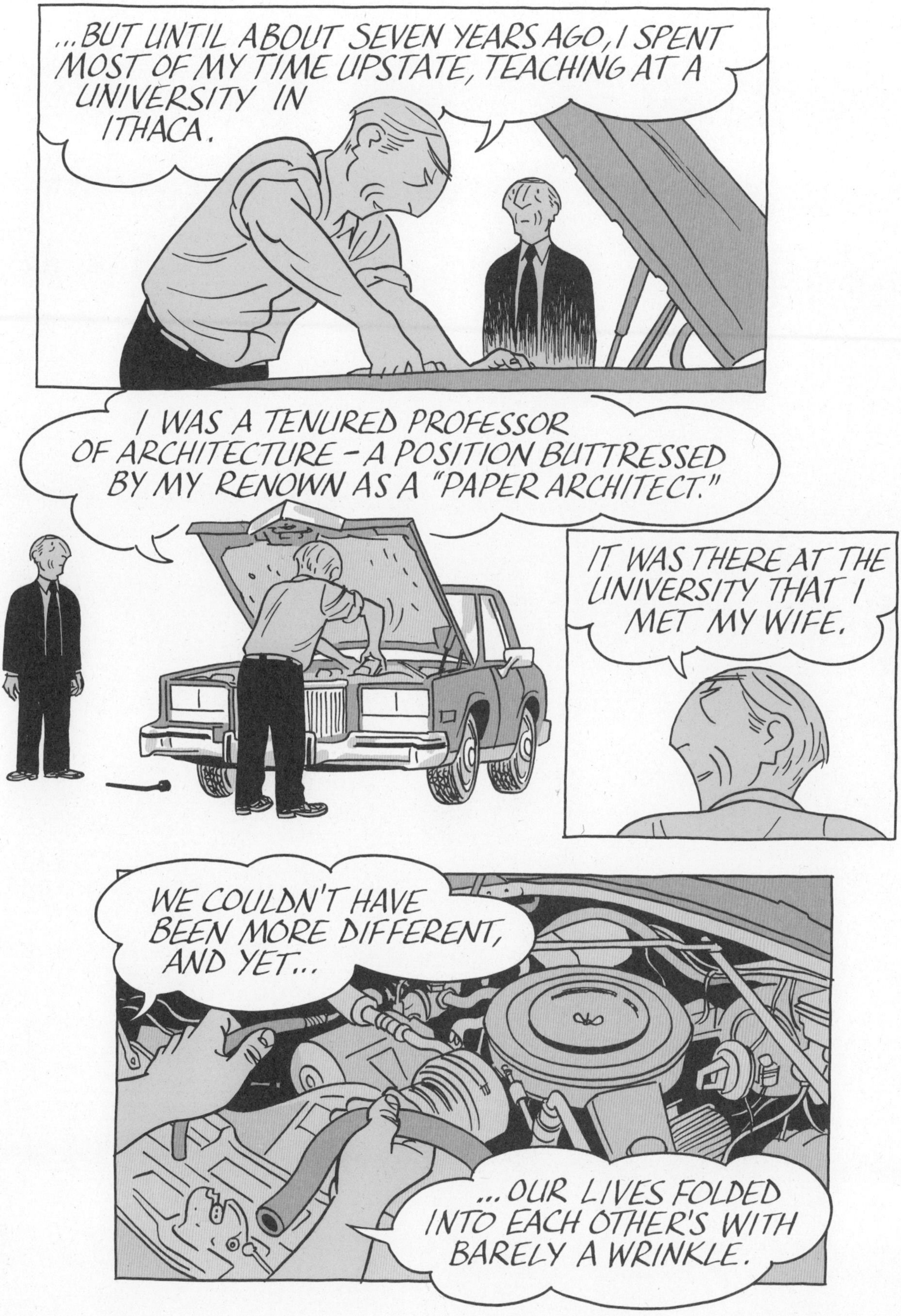
...BUT UNTIL ABOUT SEVEN YEARS AGO, I SPENT MOST OF MY TIME UPSTATE, TEACHING AT A UNIVERSITY IN ITHACA.
I WAS A TENURED PROFESSOR OF ARCHITECTURE - A POSITION BUTTRESSED BY MY RENOWN AS A "PAPER ARCHITECT."
IT WAS THERE AT THE UNIVERSITY THAT I MET MY WIFE.
WE COULDN'T HAVE BEEN MORE DIFFERENT, AND YET...
...OUR LIVES FOLDED INTO EACH OTHER'S WITH BARELY A WRINKLE.

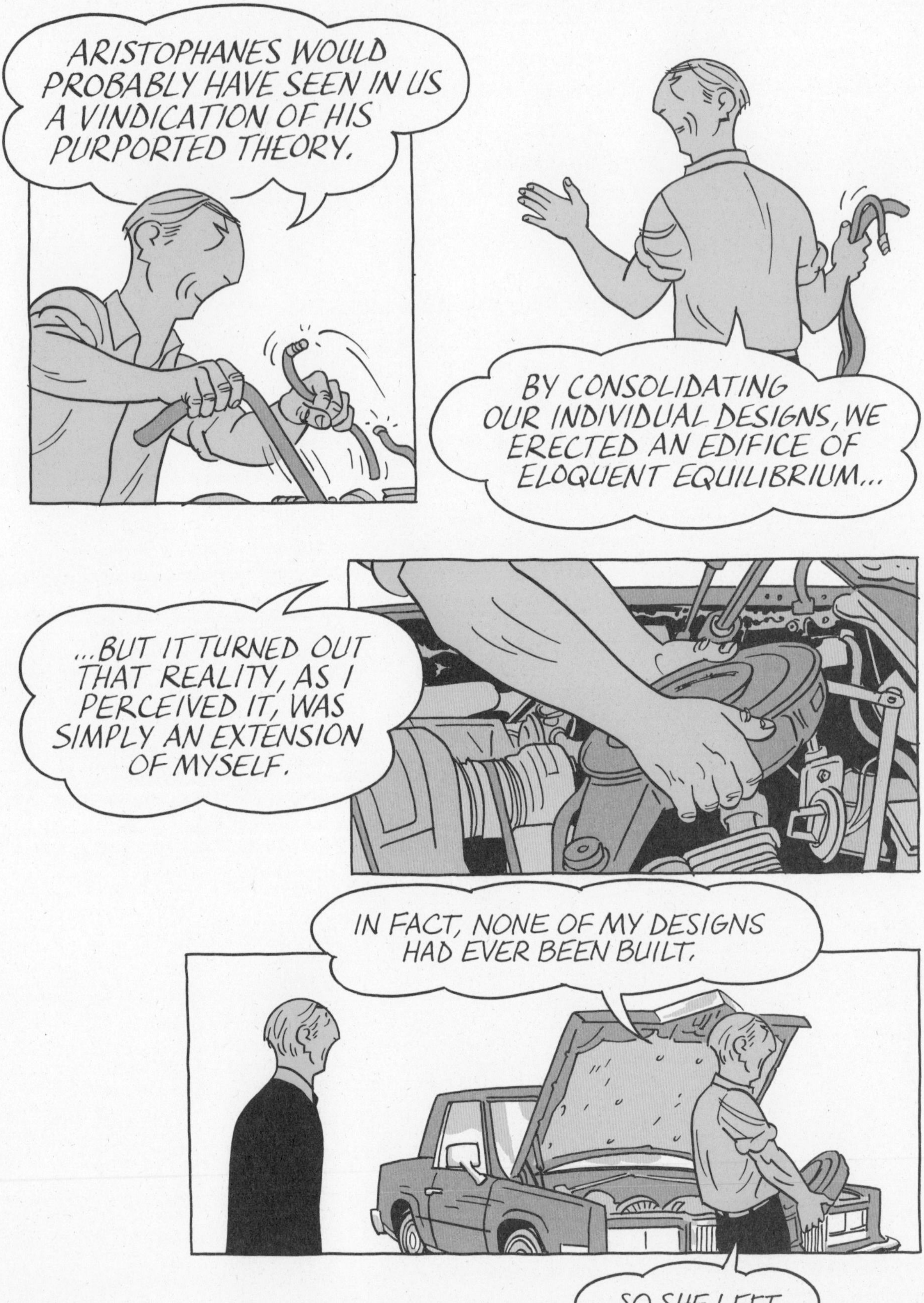
ARISTOPHANES WOULD PROBABLY HAVE SEEN IN US A VINDICATION OF HIS PURPORTED THEORY.
BY CONSOLIDATING OUR INDIVIDUAL DESIGNS, WE ERECTED AN EDIFICE OF ELOQUENT EQUILIBRIUM...
...BUT IT TURNED OUT THAT REALITY, AS I PERCEIVED IT, WAS SIMPLY AN EXTENSION OF MYSELF.
IN FACT, NONE OF MY DESIGNS HAD EVER BEEN BUILT.
SO SHE LEFT.

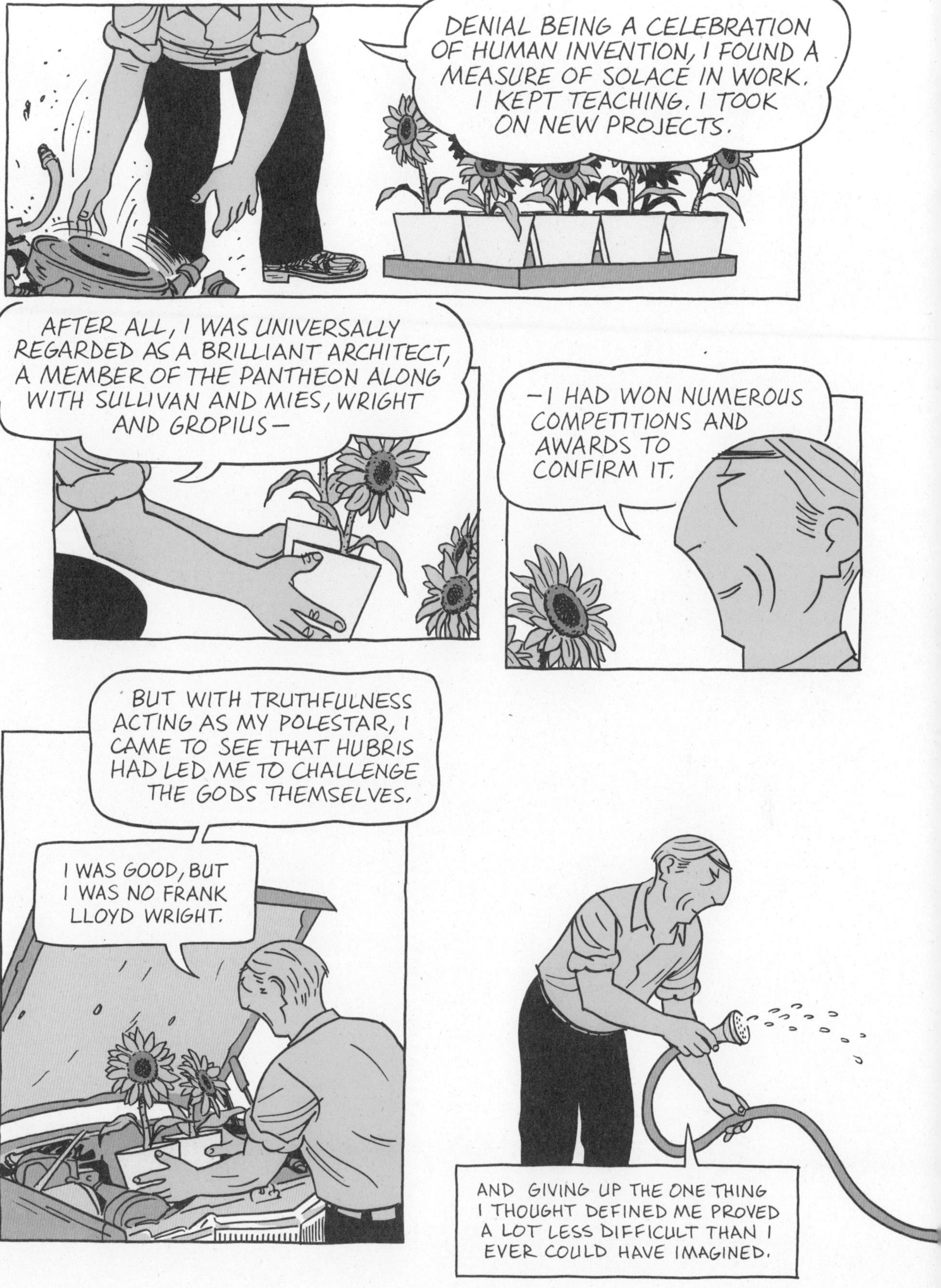
DENIAL BEING A CELEBRATION OF HUMAN INVENTION, I FOUND A MEASURE OF SOLACE IN WORK. I KEPT TEACHING. I TOOK ON NEW PROJECTS.
AFTER ALL, I WAS UNIVERSALLY REGARDED AS A BRILLIANT ARCHITECT, A MEMBER OF THE PANTHEON ALONG WITH SULLIVAN AND MIES, WRIGHT AND GROPIUS—
—I HAD WON NUMEROUS COMPETITIONS AND AWARDS TO CONFIRM IT.
BUT WITH TRUTHFULNESS ACTING AS MY POLESTAR, I CAME TO SEE THAT HUBRIS HAD LED ME TO CHALLENGE THE GODS THEMSELVES.
I WAS GOOD, BUT I WAS NO FRANK LLOYD WRIGHT.
AND GIVING UP THE ONE THING I THOUGHT DEFINED ME PROVED A LOT LESS DIFFICULT THAN I EVER COULD HAVE IMAGINED.

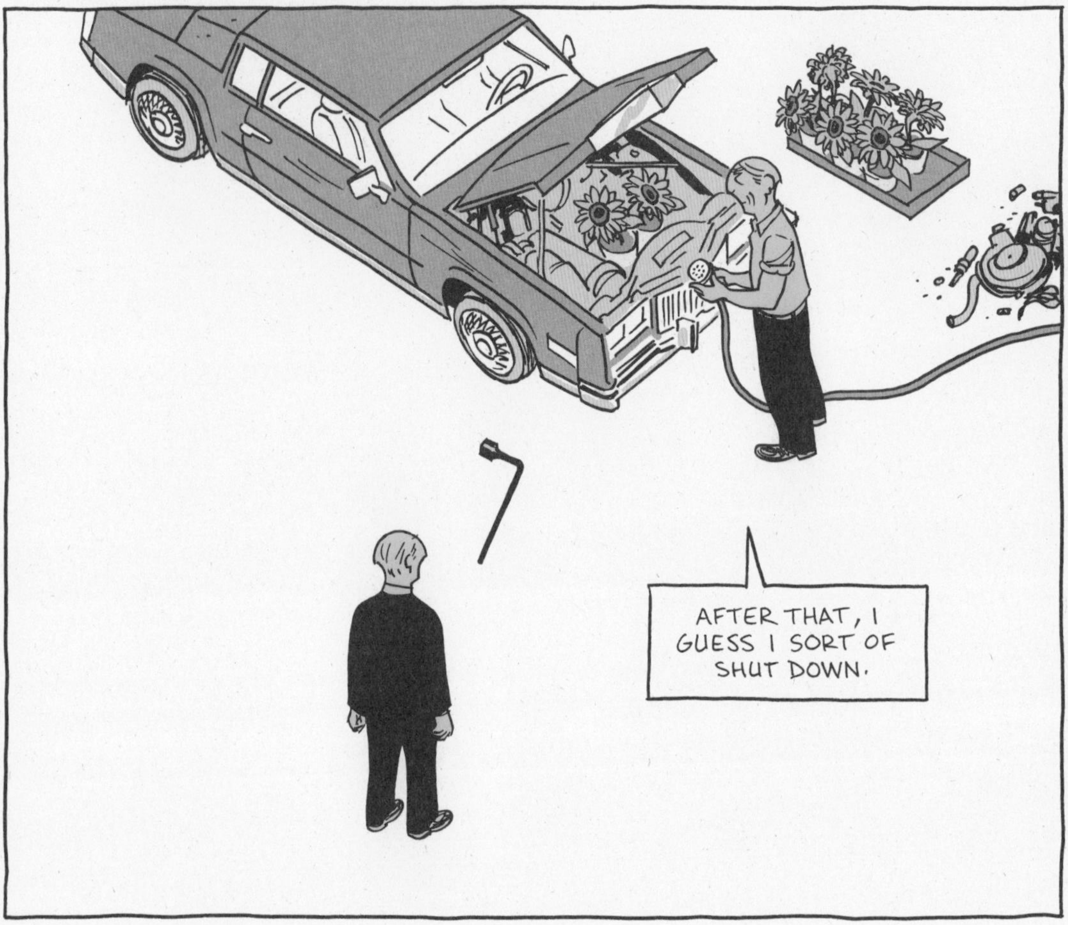
AFTER THAT, I GUESS I SORT OF SHUT DOWN.

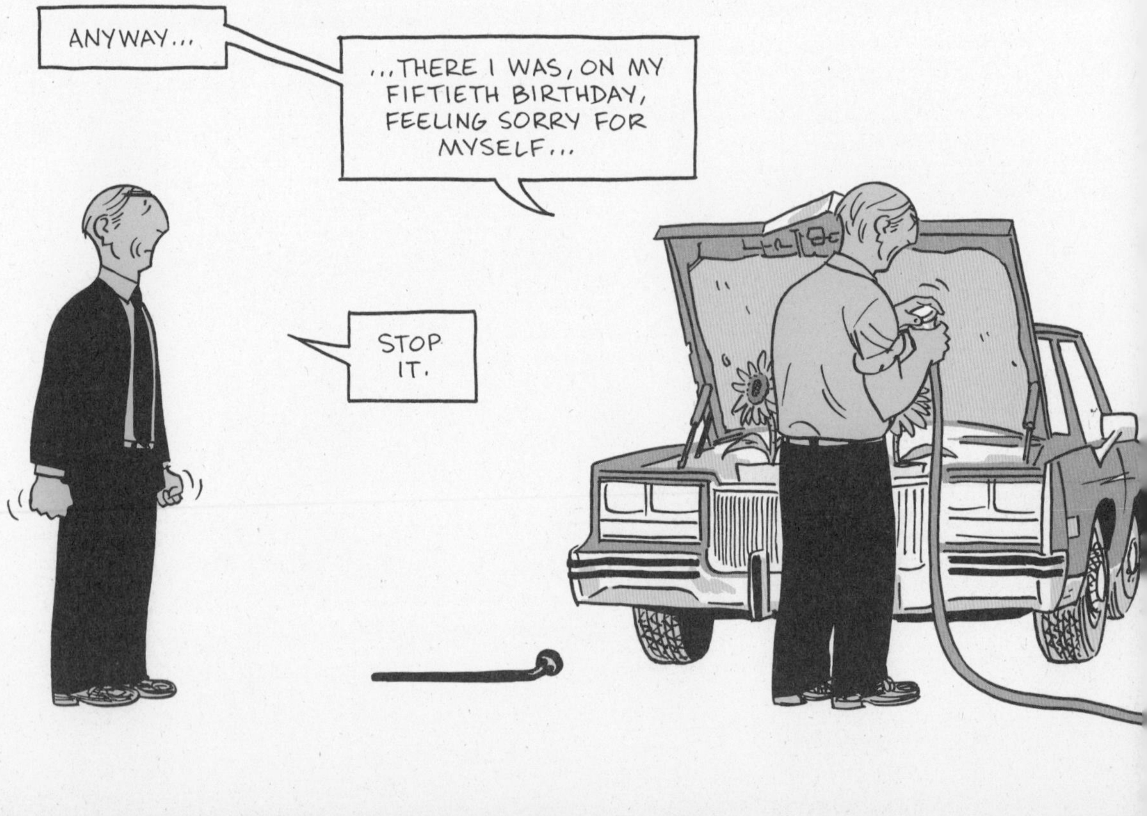
ANYWAY...
...THERE I WAS, ON MY FIFTIETH BIRTHDAY, FEELING SORRY FOR MYSELF...
STOP IT.

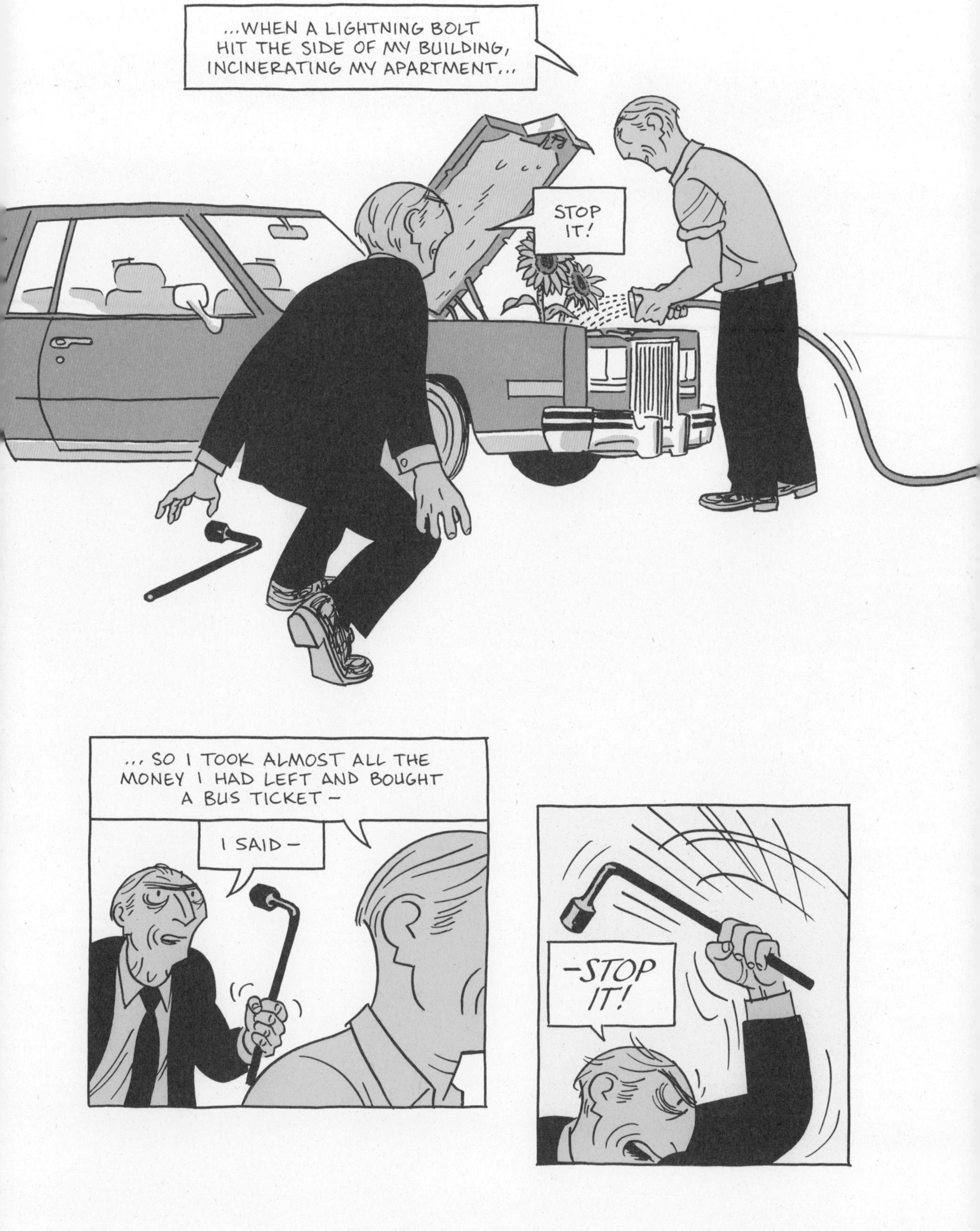
...WHEN A LIGHTNING BOLT HIT THE SIDE OF MY BUILDING, INCINERATING MY APARTMENT...
STOP IT!
... SO I TOOK ALMOST ALL THE MONEY I HAD LEFT AND BOUGHT A BUS TICKET –
I SAID –
–STOP IT!

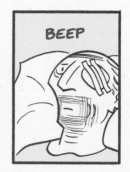

Hey, Sterio—
you're awake!

...HEY,
STIFF...

BEEP BEEP BEEP BEEP BEE

How you
feelin'?

...I'VE BEEN
BETTER.

WHAT ARE YOU
DOING HERE?

Aw, Ursula's always tellin' me I gotta
do more male bondage stuff.

WELL... I
APPRECIATE IT.

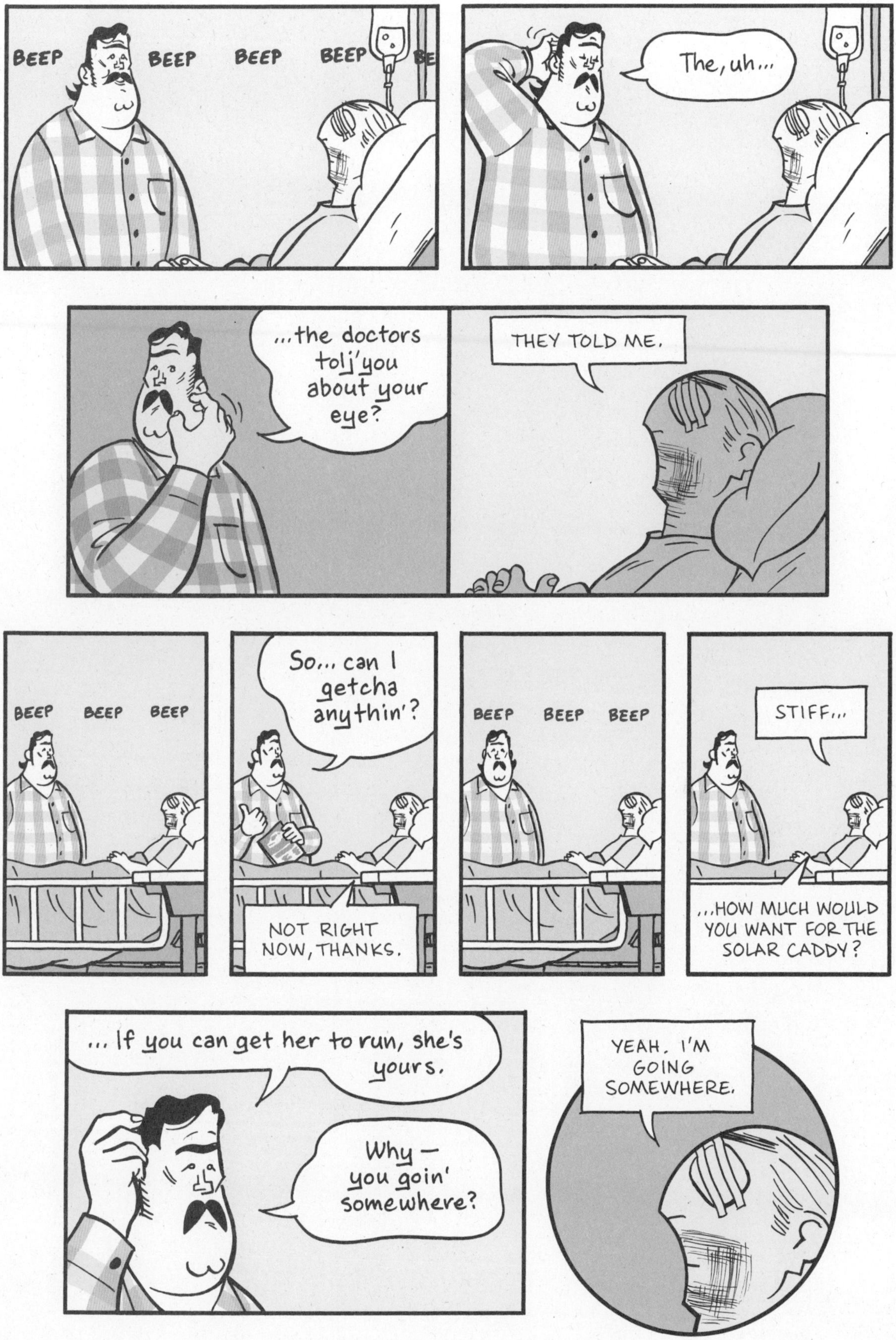

BEEP BEEP BEEP BEEP BE
The, uh...
...the doctors tolj'you about your eye?
THEY TOLD ME.
BEEP BEEP BEEP
So... can I getcha anythin'?
NOT RIGHT NOW, THANKS.
BEEP BEEP BEEP
STIFF...
...HOW MUCH WOULD YOU WANT FOR THE SOLAR CADDY?
... If you can get her to run, she's yours.
Why — you goin' somewhere?
YEAH. I'M GOING SOMEWHERE.

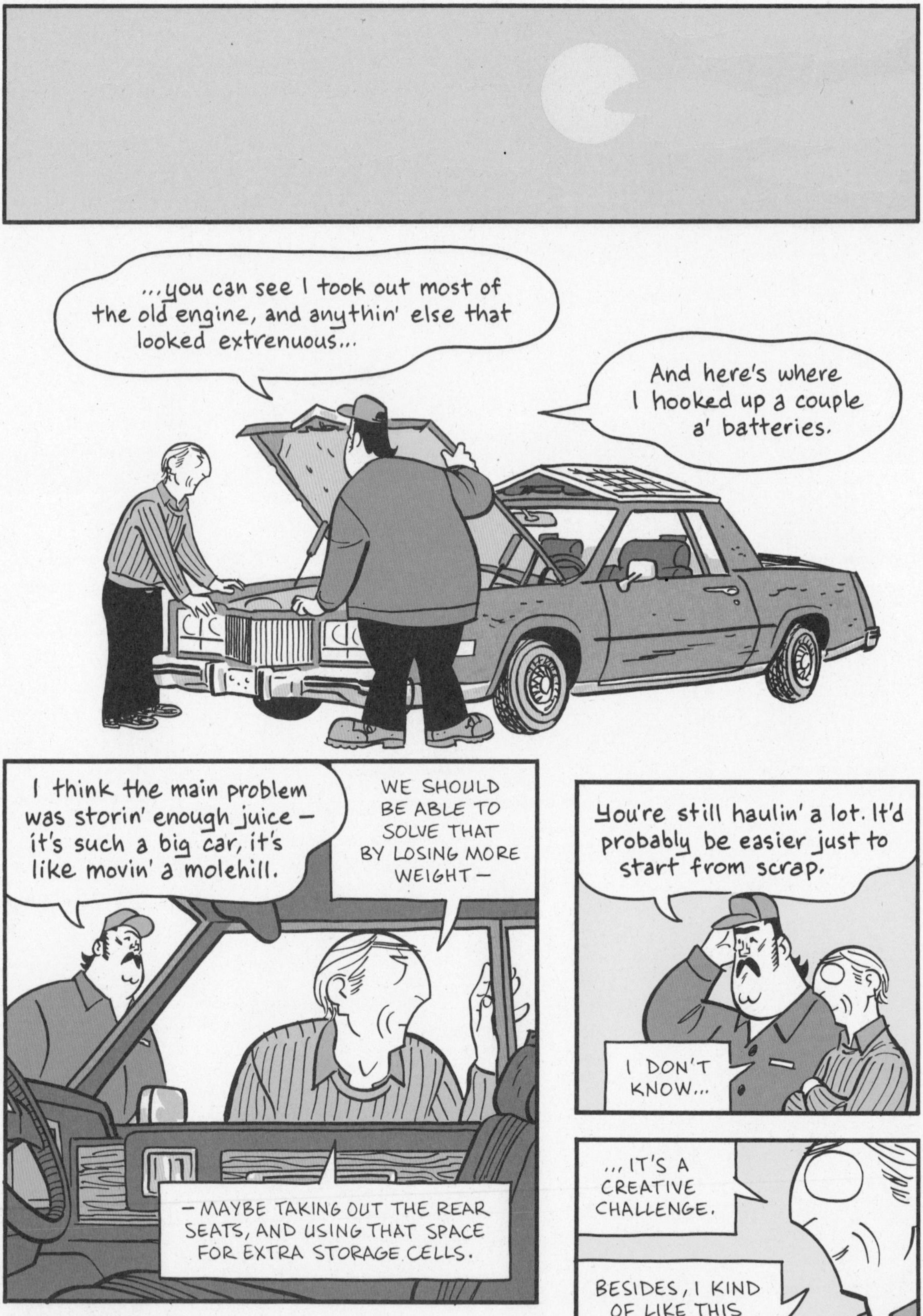

...you can see I took out most of the old engine, and anythin' else that looked extrenuous...
And here's where I hooked up a couple a' batteries.
I think the main problem was storin' enough juice — it's such a big car, it's like movin' a molehill.
WE SHOULD BE ABLE TO SOLVE THAT BY LOSING MORE WEIGHT—
—MAYBE TAKING OUT THE REAR SEATS, AND USING THAT SPACE FOR EXTRA STORAGE CELLS.
You're still haulin' a lot. It'd probably be easier just to start from scrap.
I DON'T KNOW...
...IT'S A CREATIVE CHALLENGE.
BESIDES, I KIND OF LIKE THIS OLD BOAT.

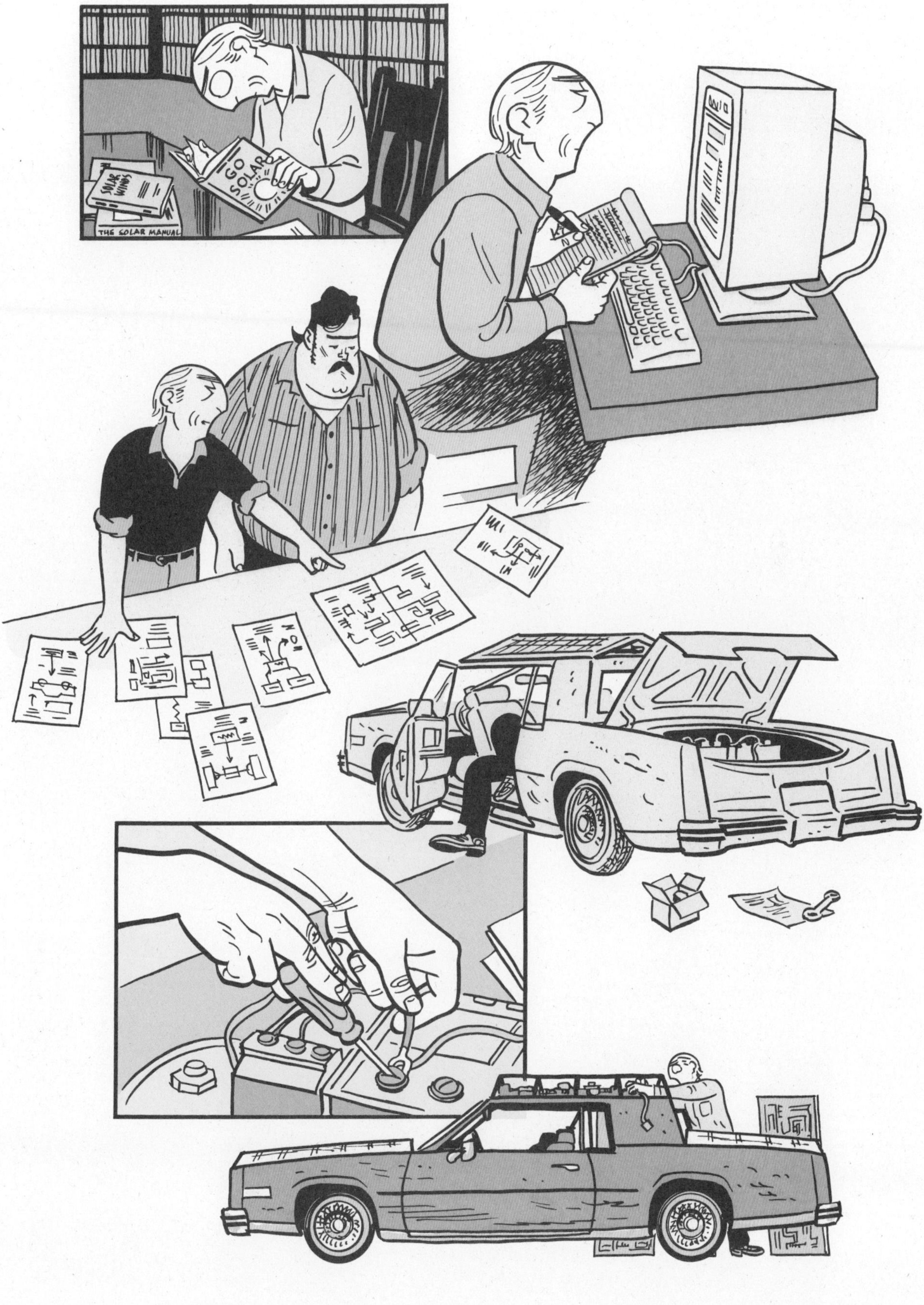
GO SOLAR
SOLAR WINDS
THE SOLAR MANUAL

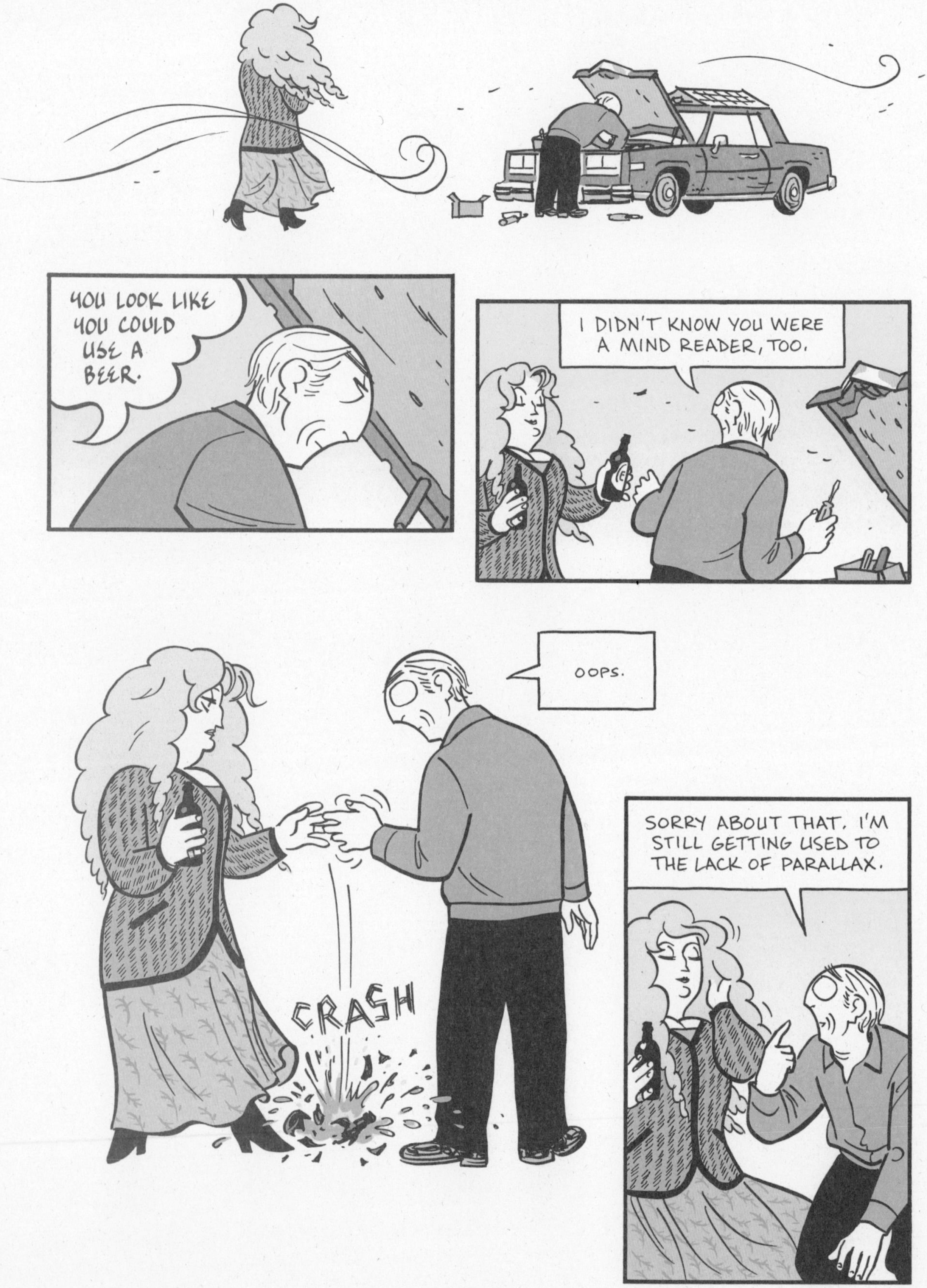
YOU LOOK LIKE YOU COULD USE A BEER.
I DIDN'T KNOW YOU WERE A MIND READER, TOO.
OOPS.
CRASH
SORRY ABOUT THAT. I'M STILL GETTING USED TO THE LACK OF PARALLAX.

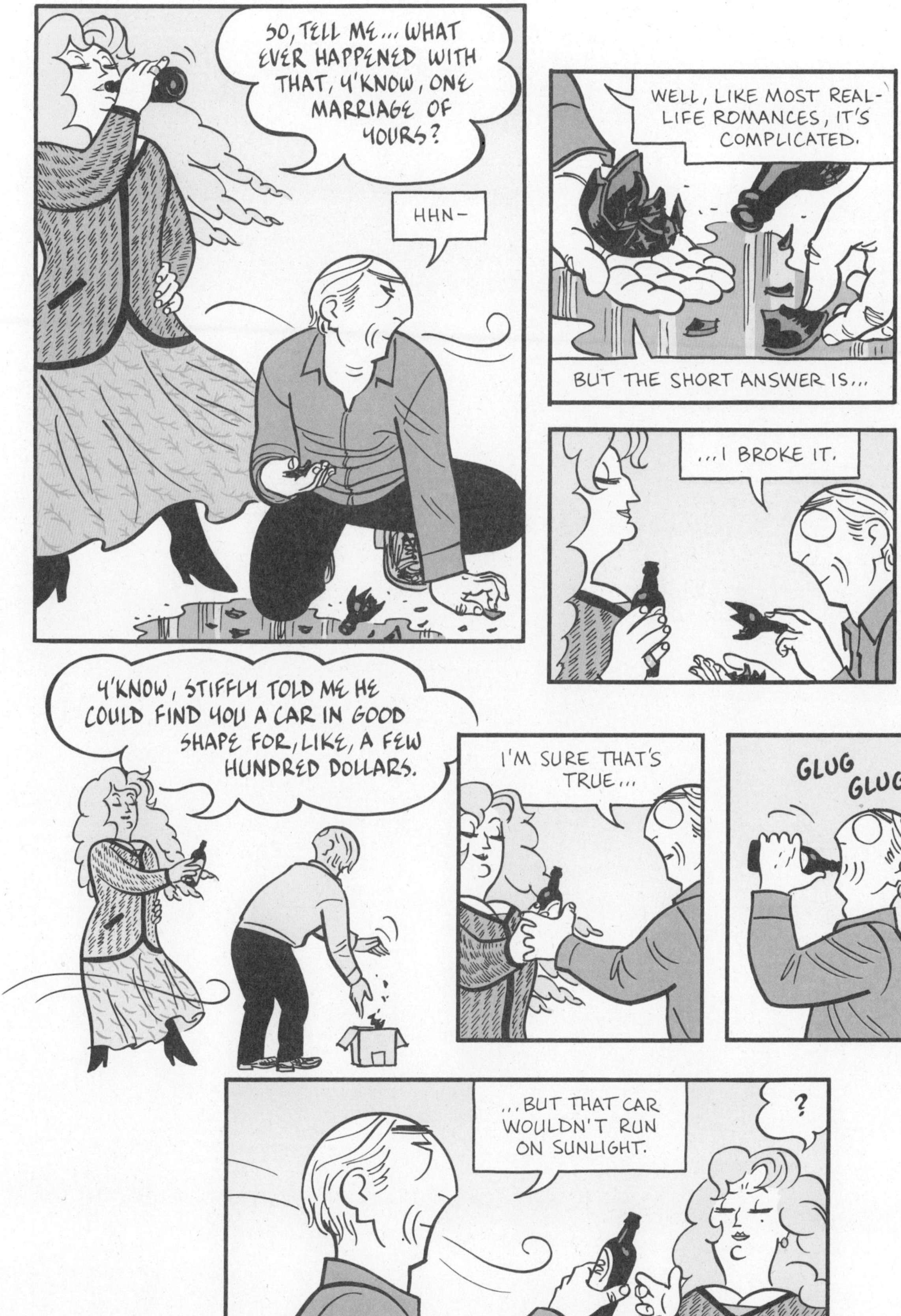
SO, TELL ME... WHAT EVER HAPPENED WITH THAT, Y'KNOW, ONE MARRIAGE OF YOURS?
HHN-
WELL, LIKE MOST REAL-LIFE ROMANCES, IT'S COMPLICATED.
BUT THE SHORT ANSWER IS...
...I BROKE IT.
Y'KNOW, STIFFLY TOLD ME HE COULD FIND YOU A CAR IN GOOD SHAPE FOR, LIKE, A FEW HUNDRED DOLLARS.
I'M SURE THAT'S TRUE...
GLUG
GLUG
...BUT THAT CAR WOULDN'T RUN ON SUNLIGHT.
?

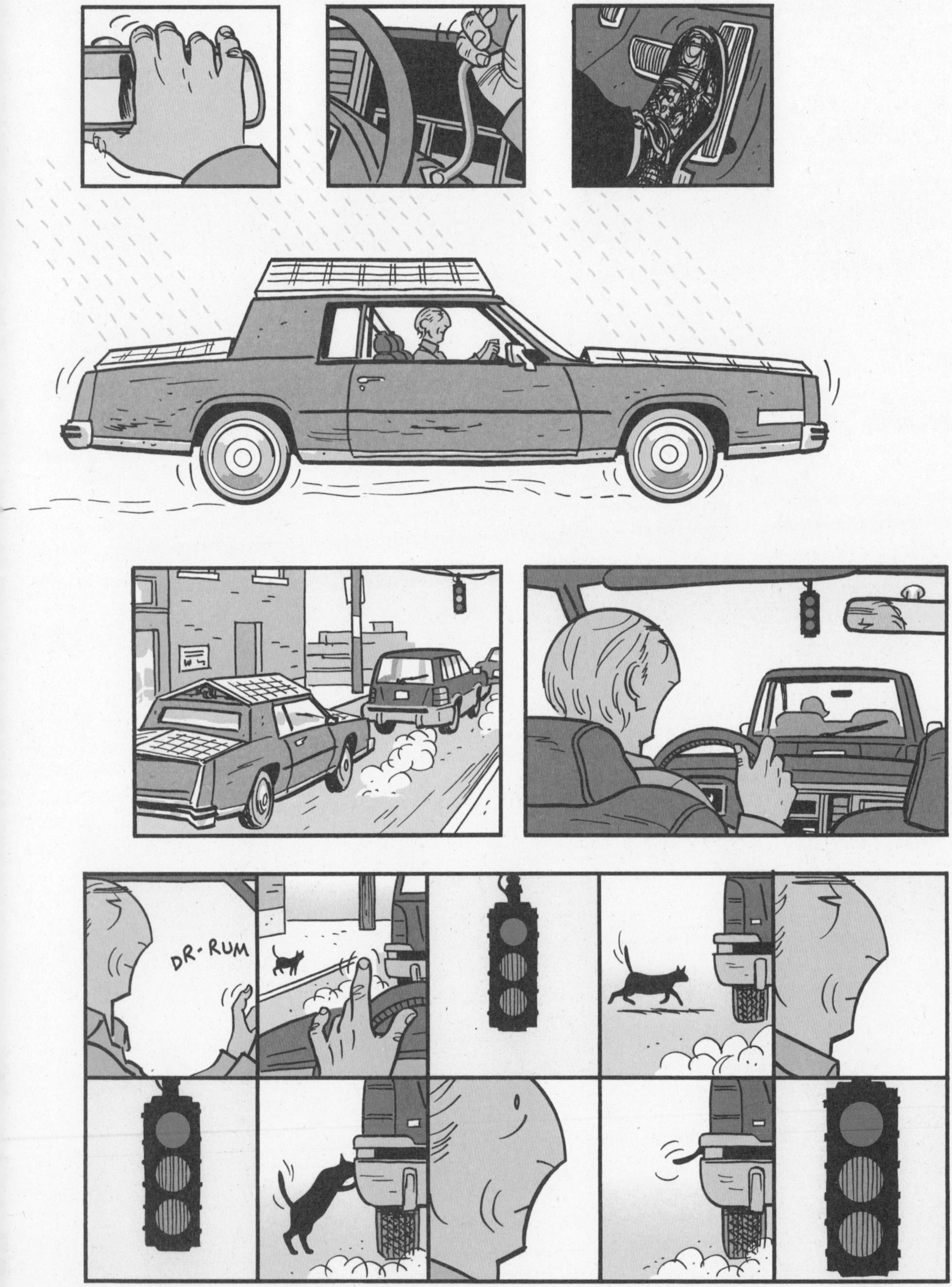
DR-RUM

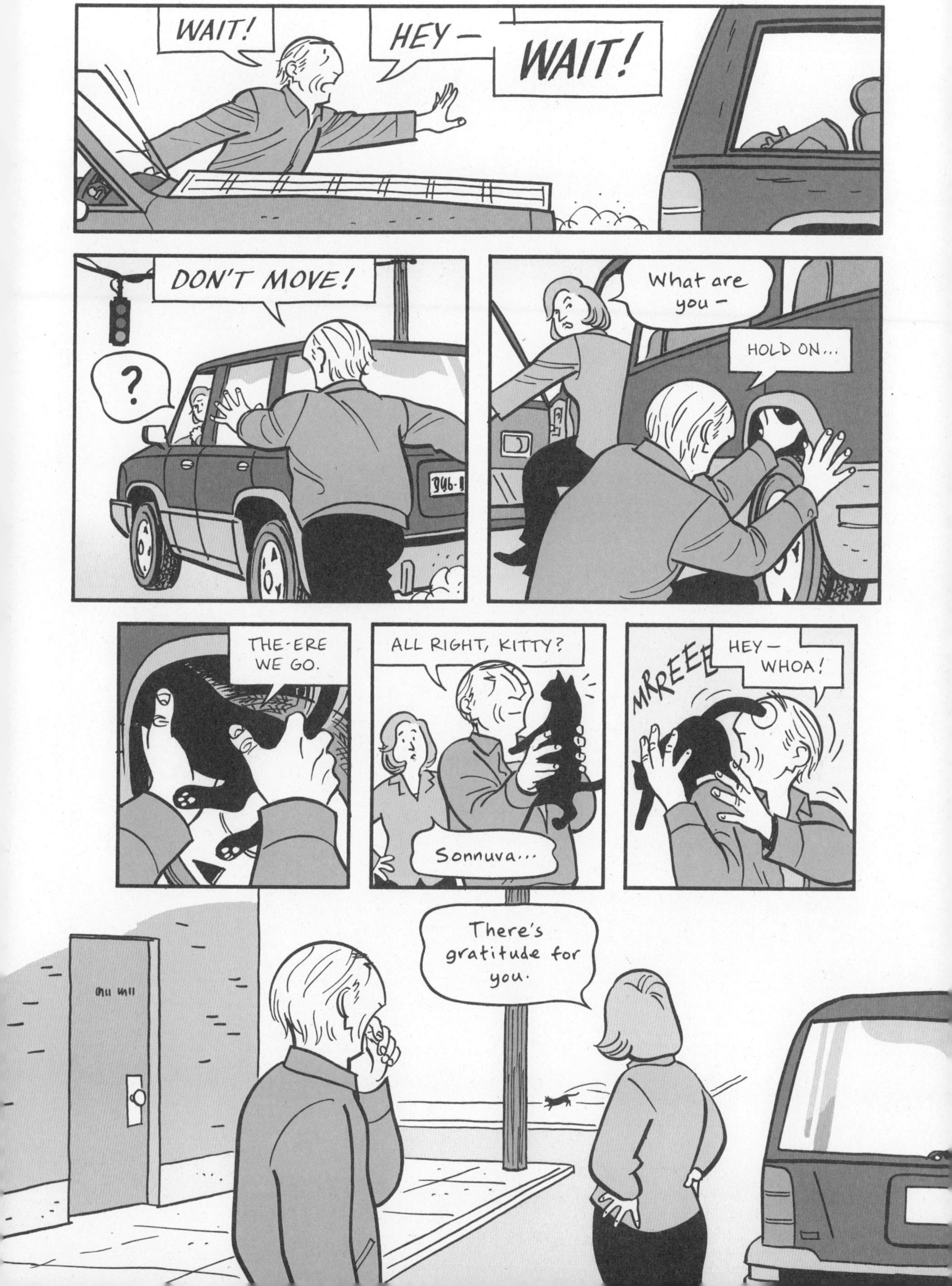
WAIT!
HEY—
WAIT!
DON'T MOVE!
?
What are you—
HOLD ON...
THE-ERE WE GO.
ALL RIGHT, KITTY?
Sonnuva...
MRREEE
HEY— WHOA!
There's gratitude for you.

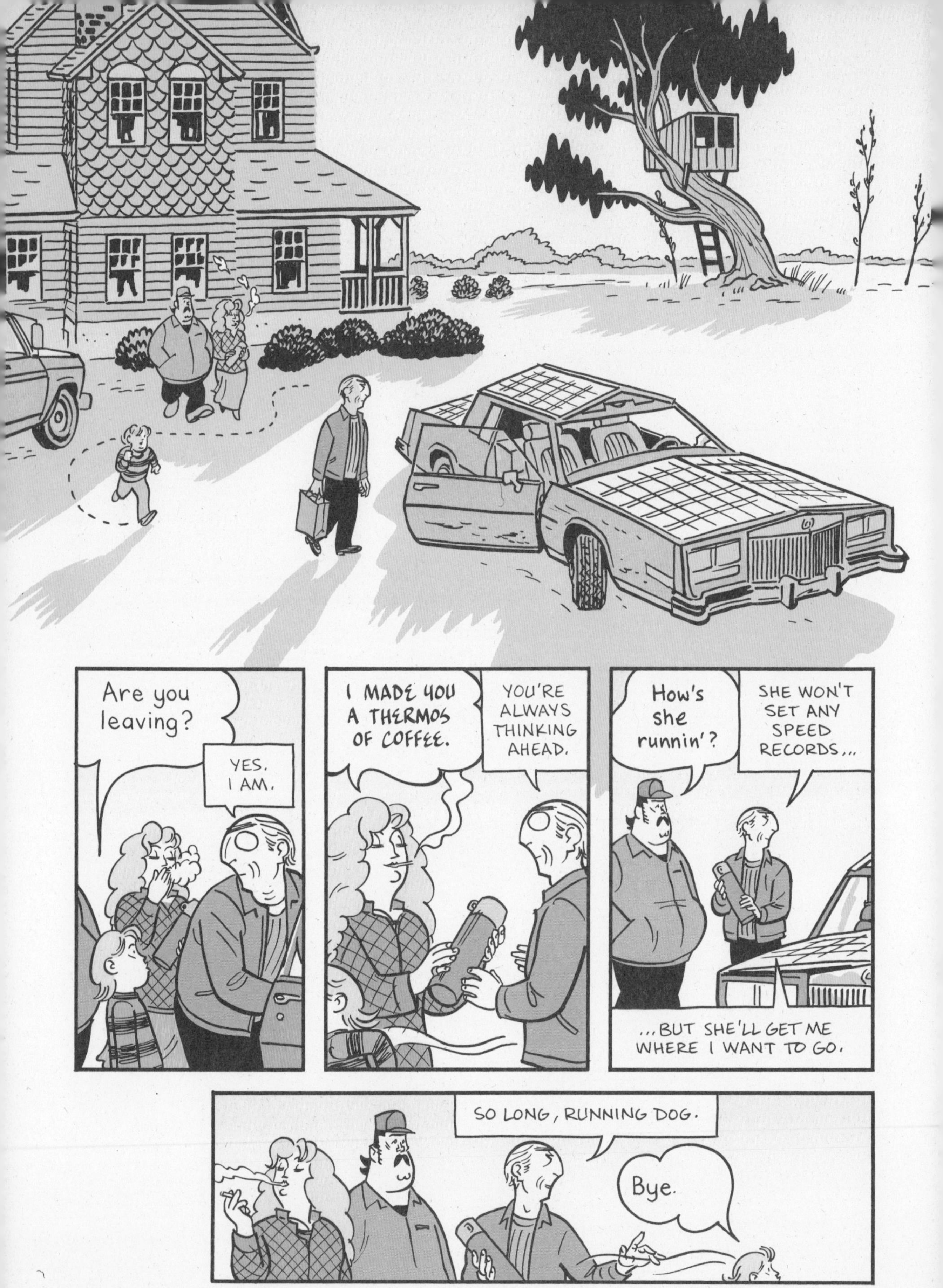
Are you leaving?
YES. I AM.
I MADE YOU A THERMOS OF COFFEE.
YOU'RE ALWAYS THINKING AHEAD.
How's she runnin'?
SHE WON'T SET ANY SPEED RECORDS...
...BUT SHE'LL GET ME WHERE I WANT TO GO.
SO LONG, RUNNING DOG.
Bye.

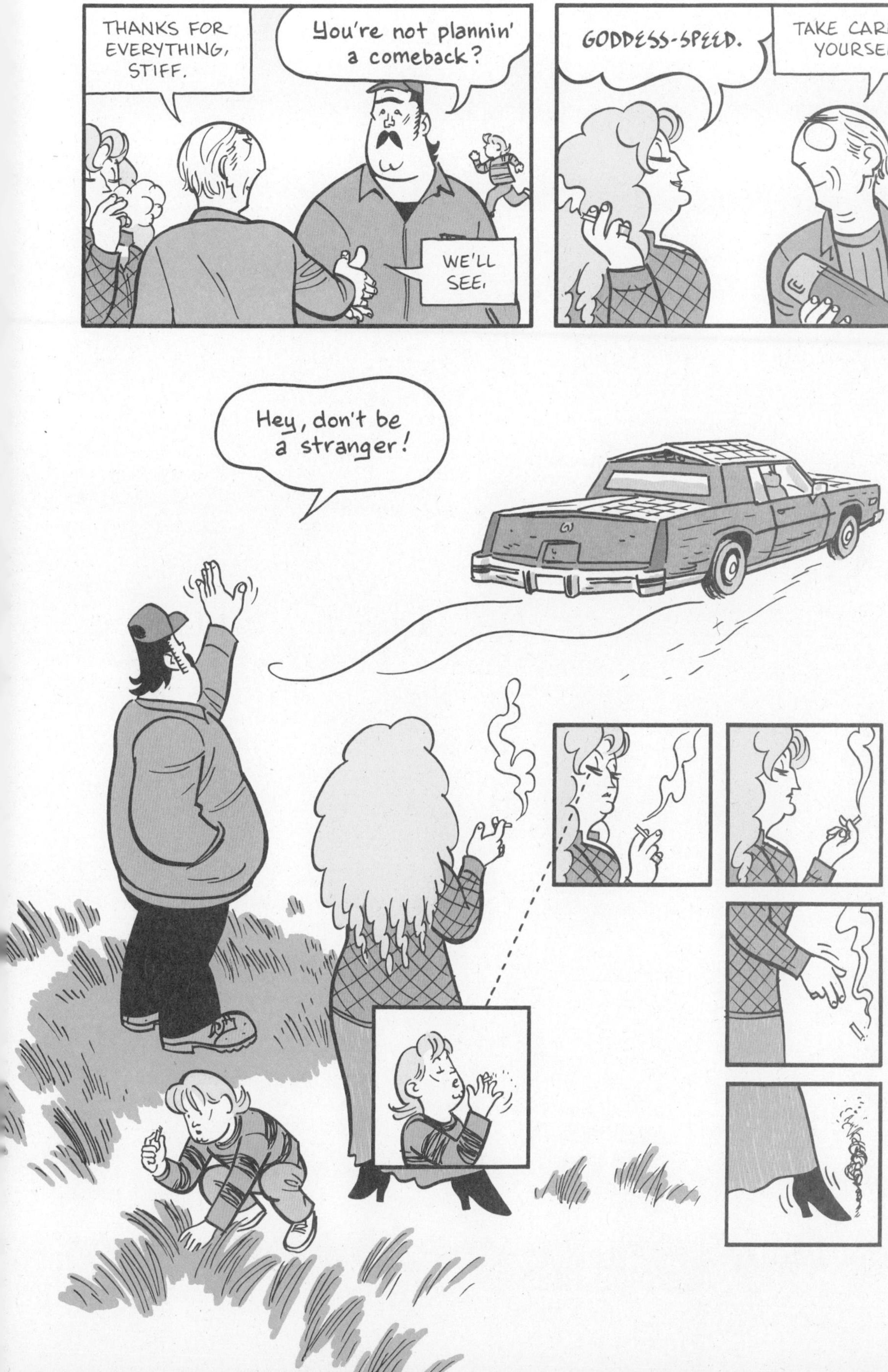
THANKS FOR EVERYTHING, STIFF.
You're not plannin' a comeback?
WE'LL SEE.
GODDESS-SPEED.
TAKE CARE OF YOURSELF.
Hey, don't be a stranger!

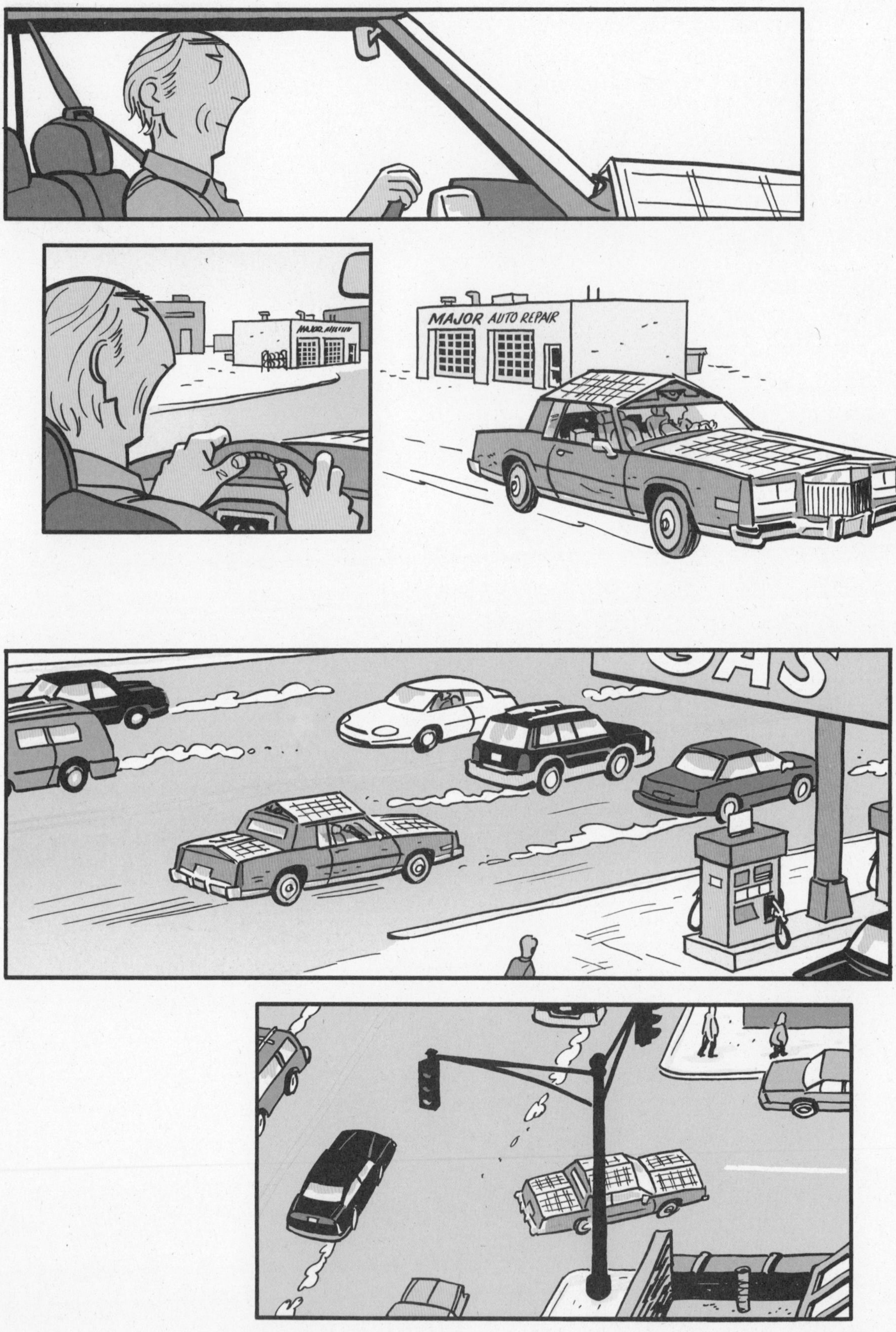
MAJOR AUTO REPAIR
GAS

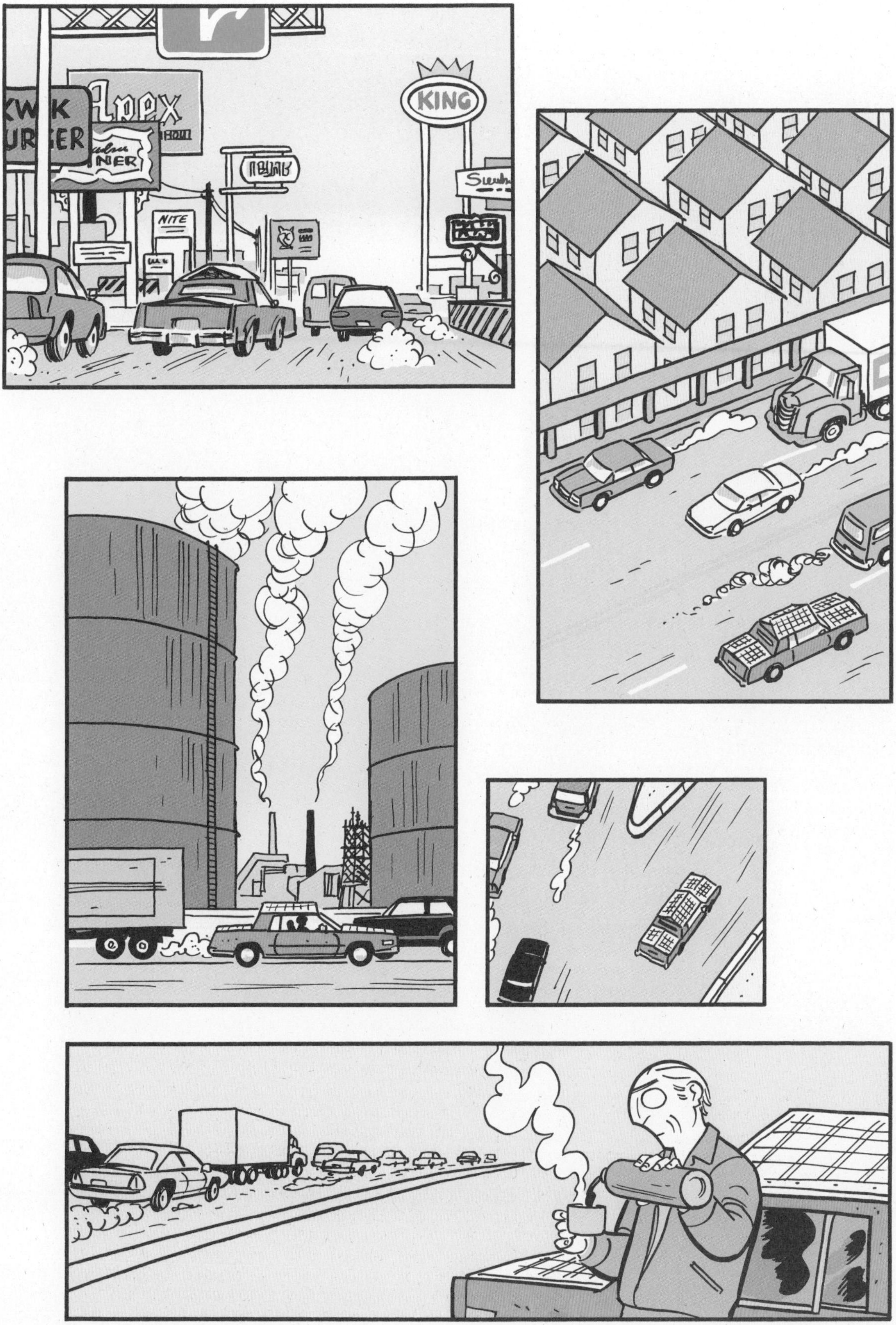
Apex
KING
NITE

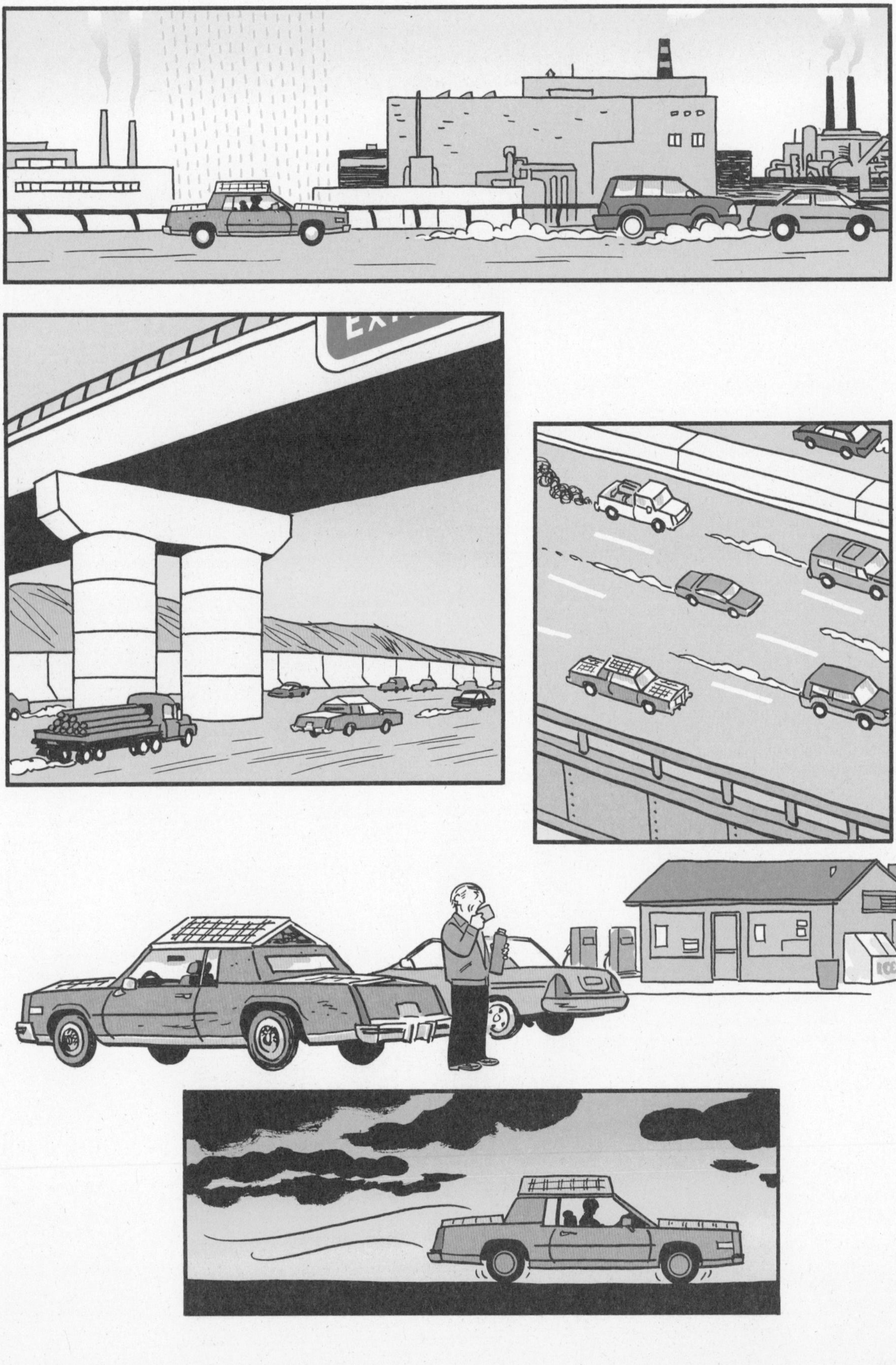
ICE

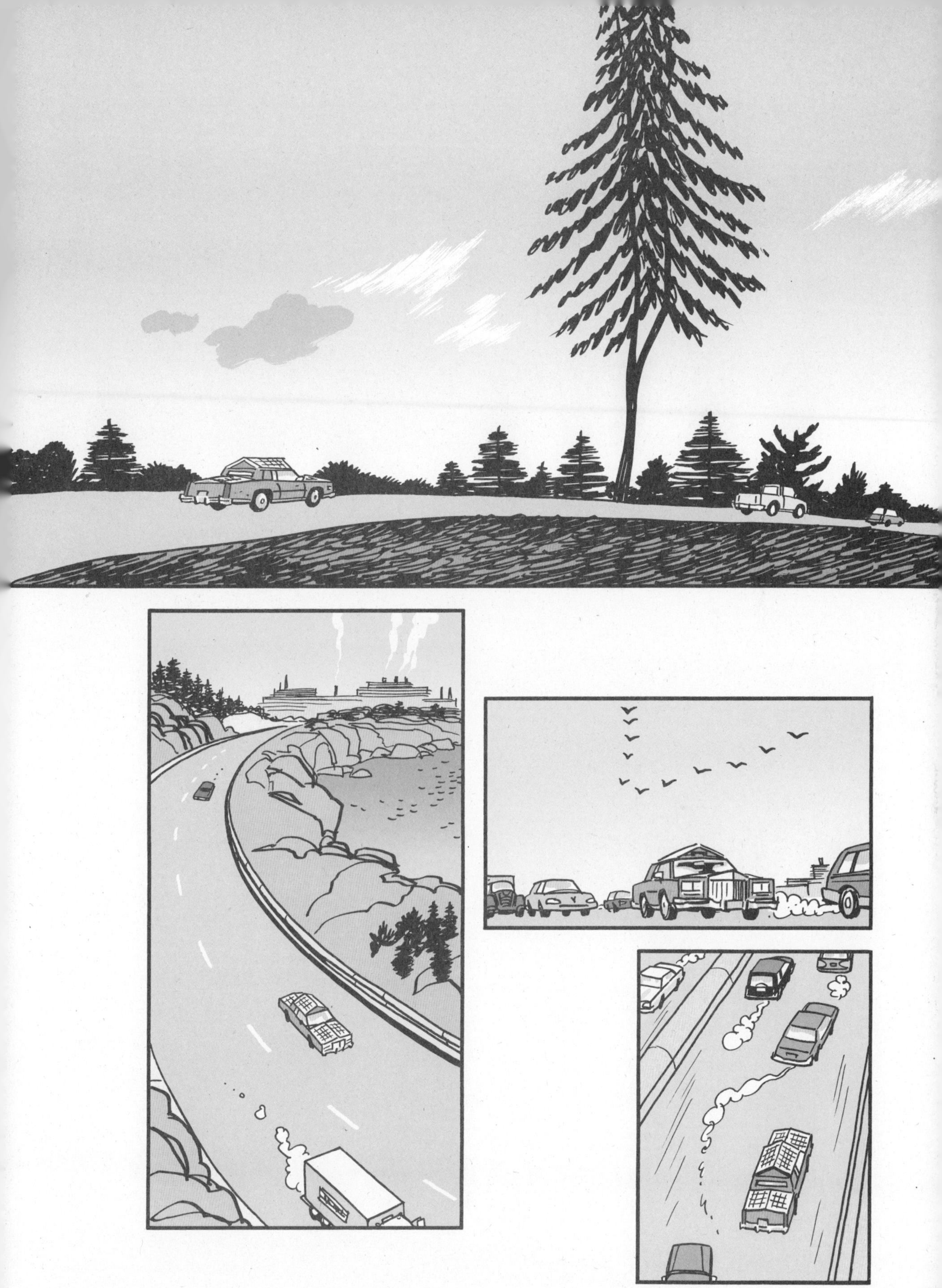

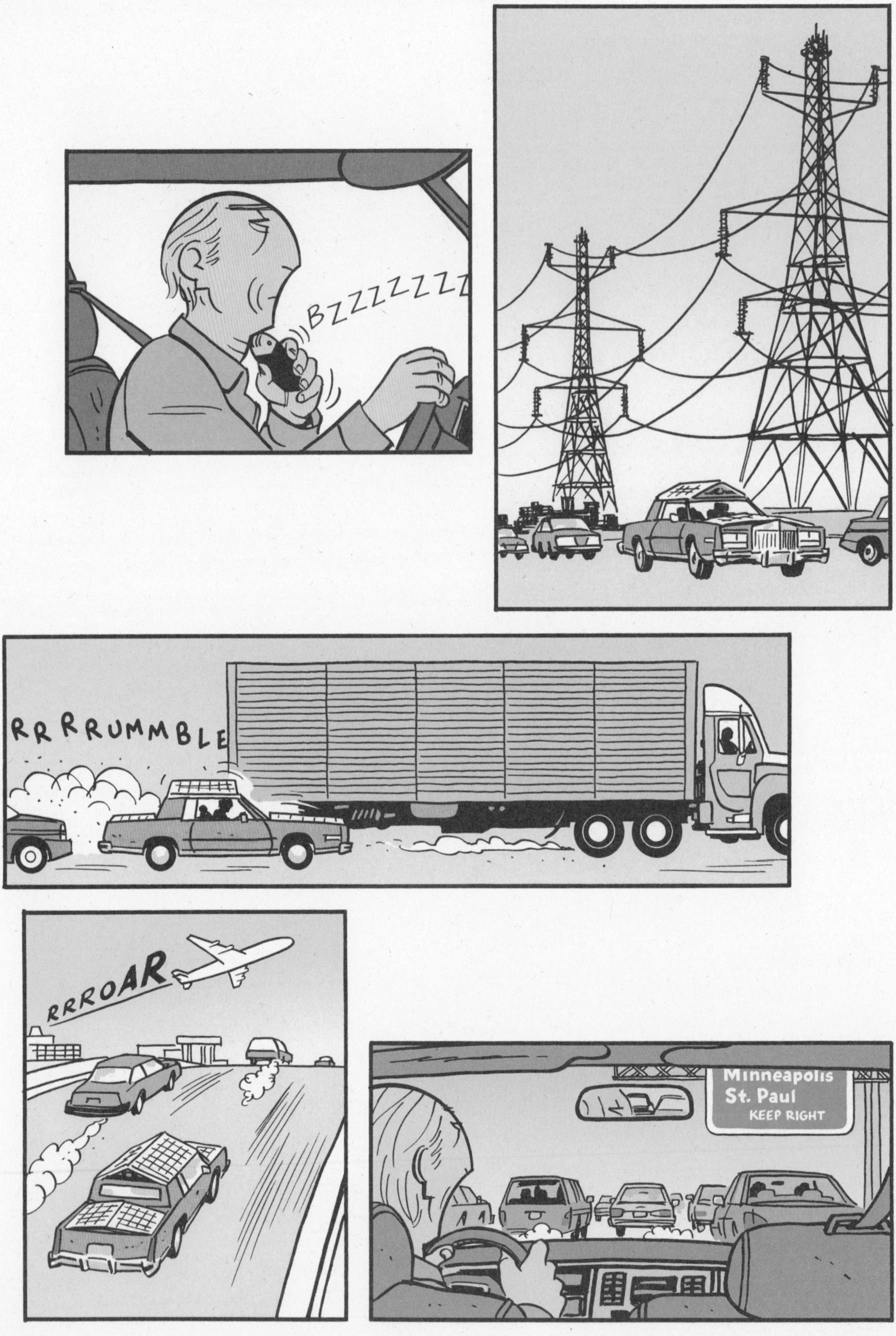
BZZZZZZZ
RRRRUMMBLE
RRROAR
Minneapolis
St. Paul
KEEP RIGHT

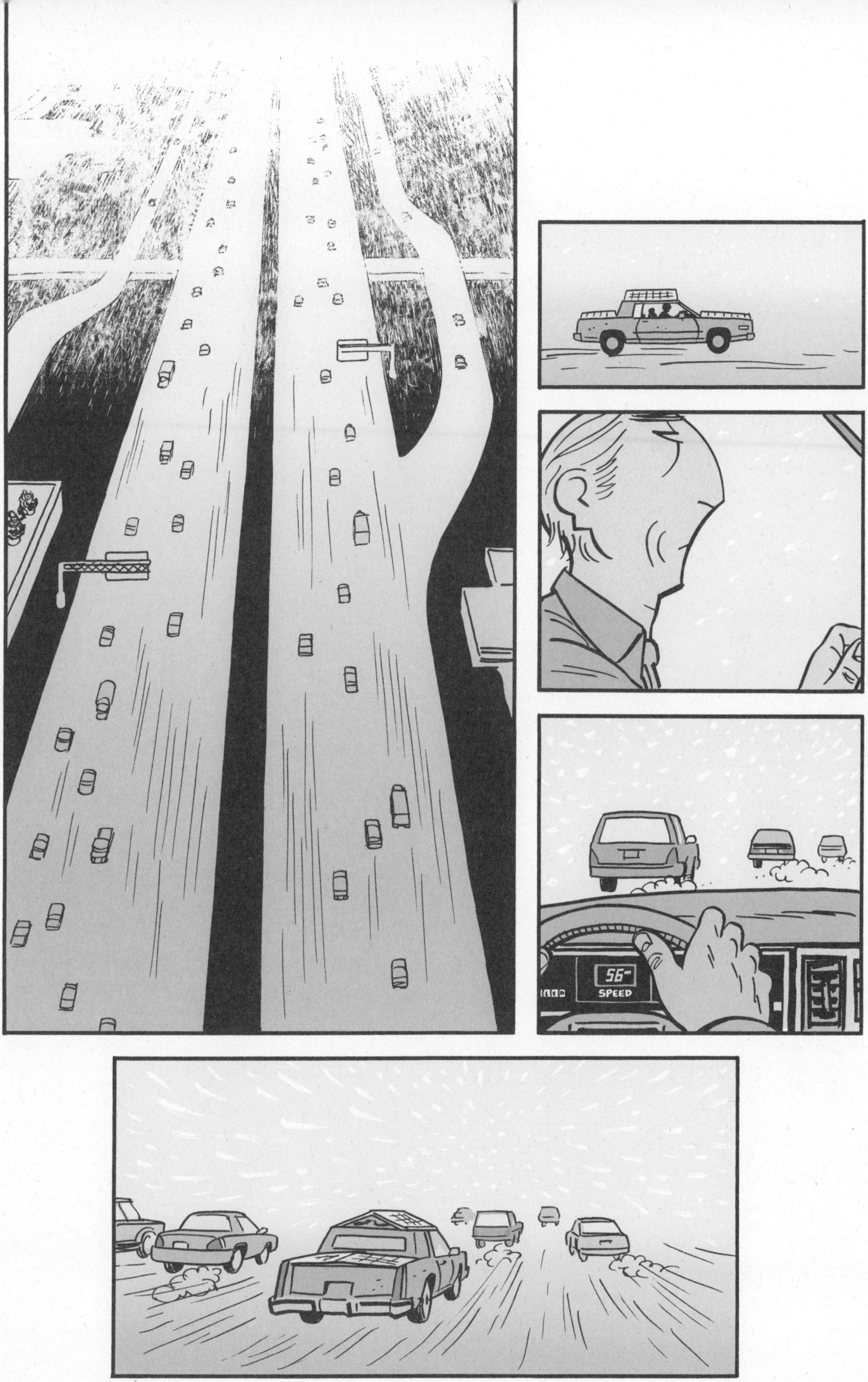
56
SPEED

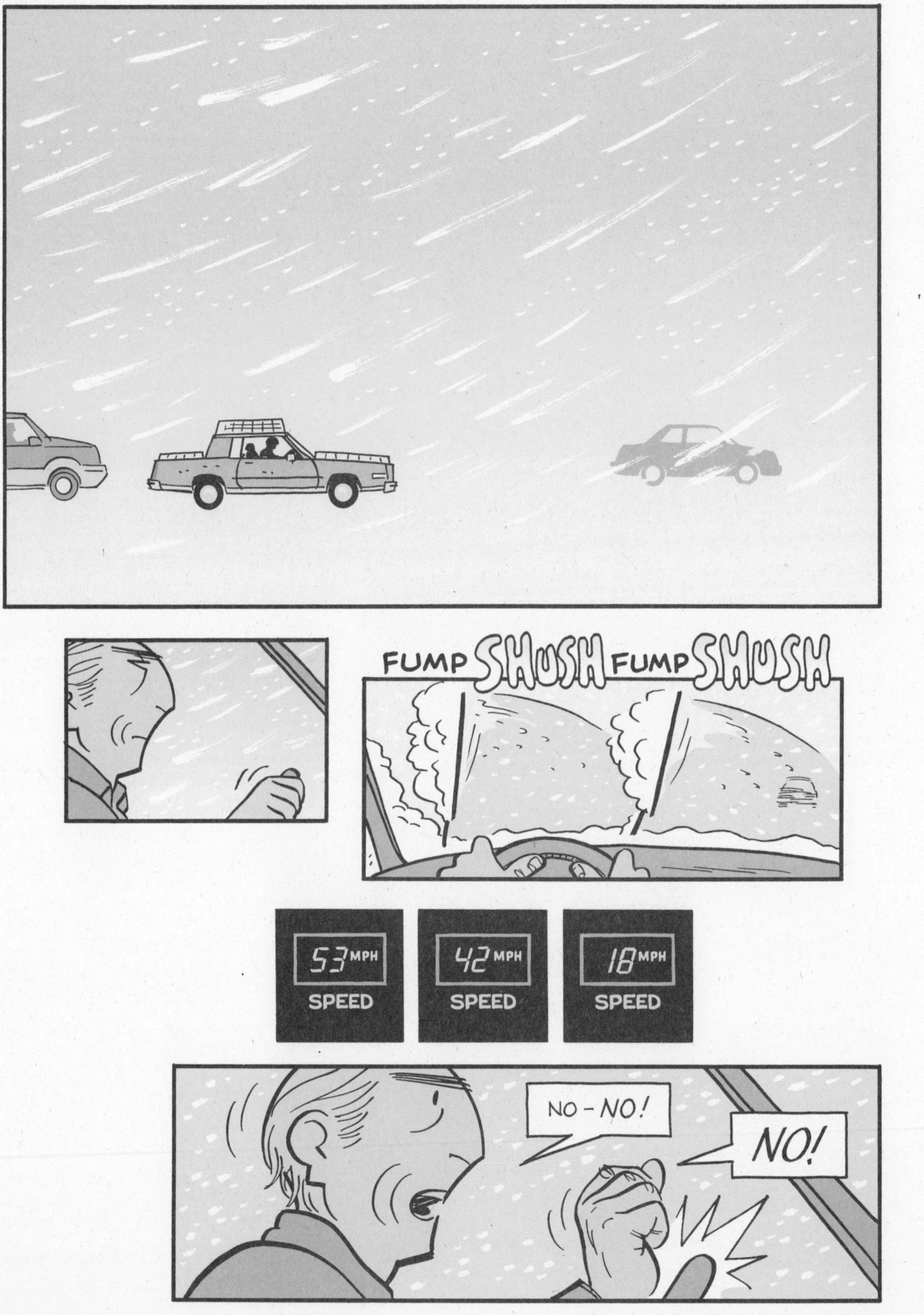
FUMP SHUSH FUMP SHUSH
53 MPH
SPEED
42 MPH
SPEED
18 MPH
SPEED
NO-NO!
NO!

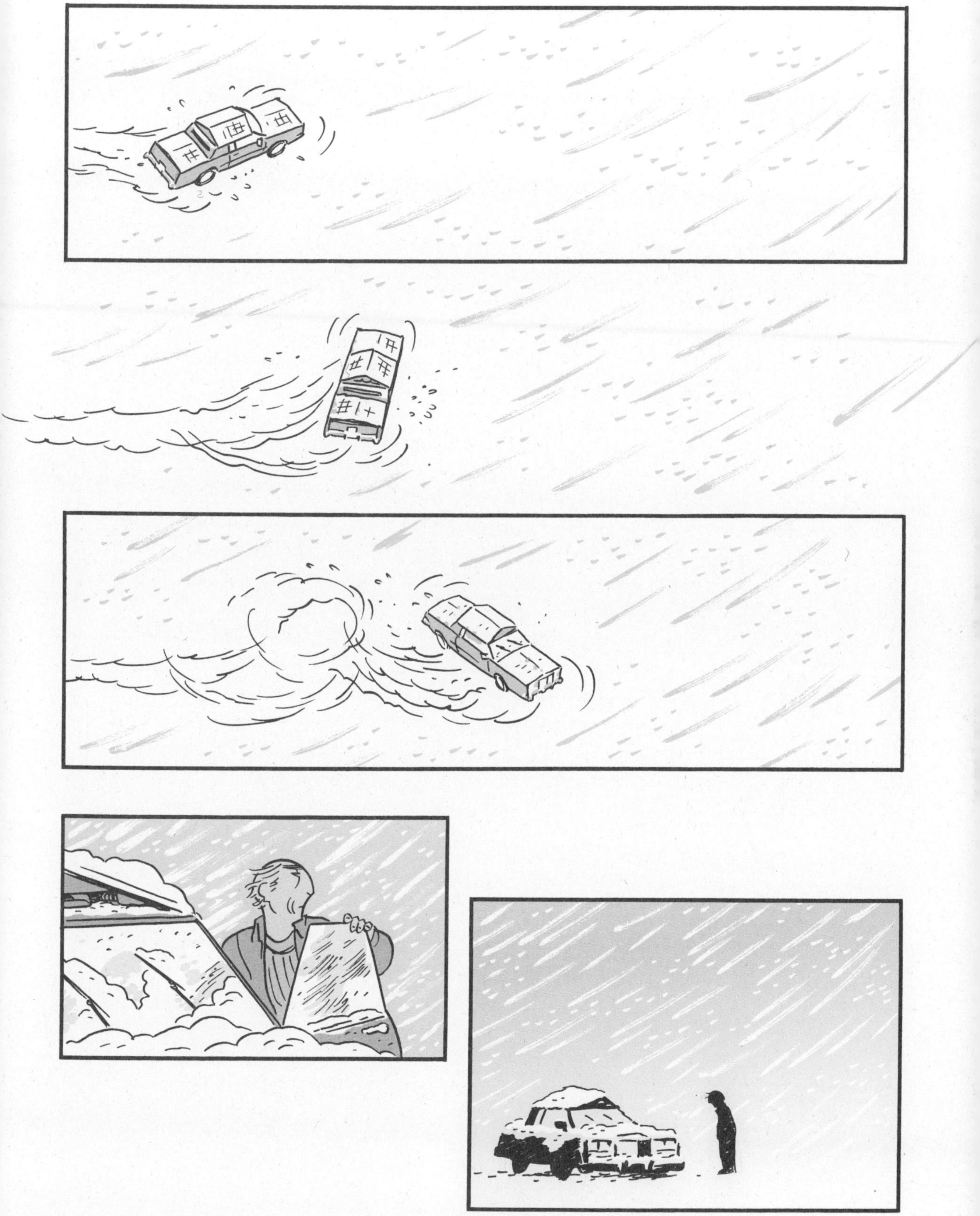

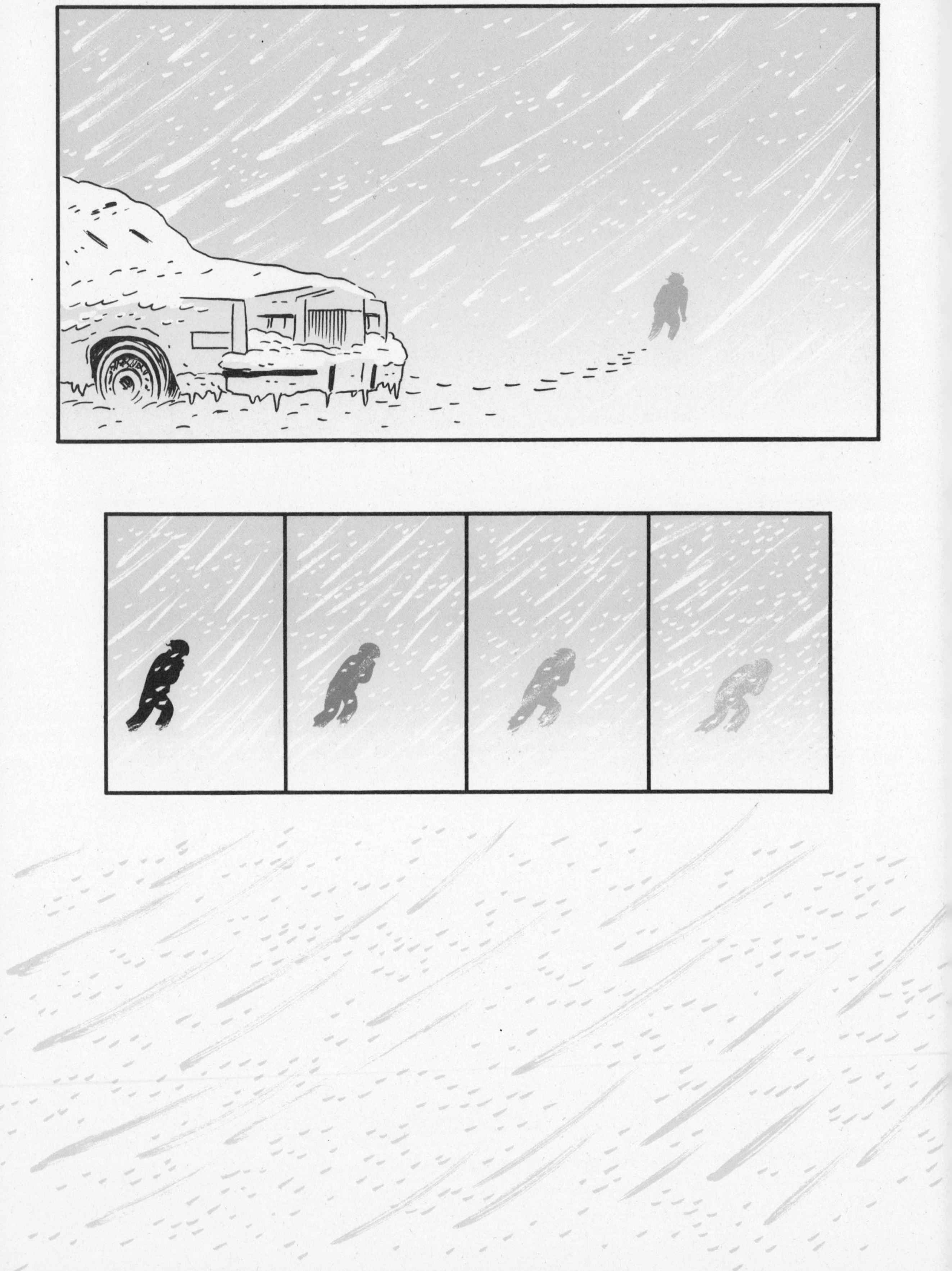

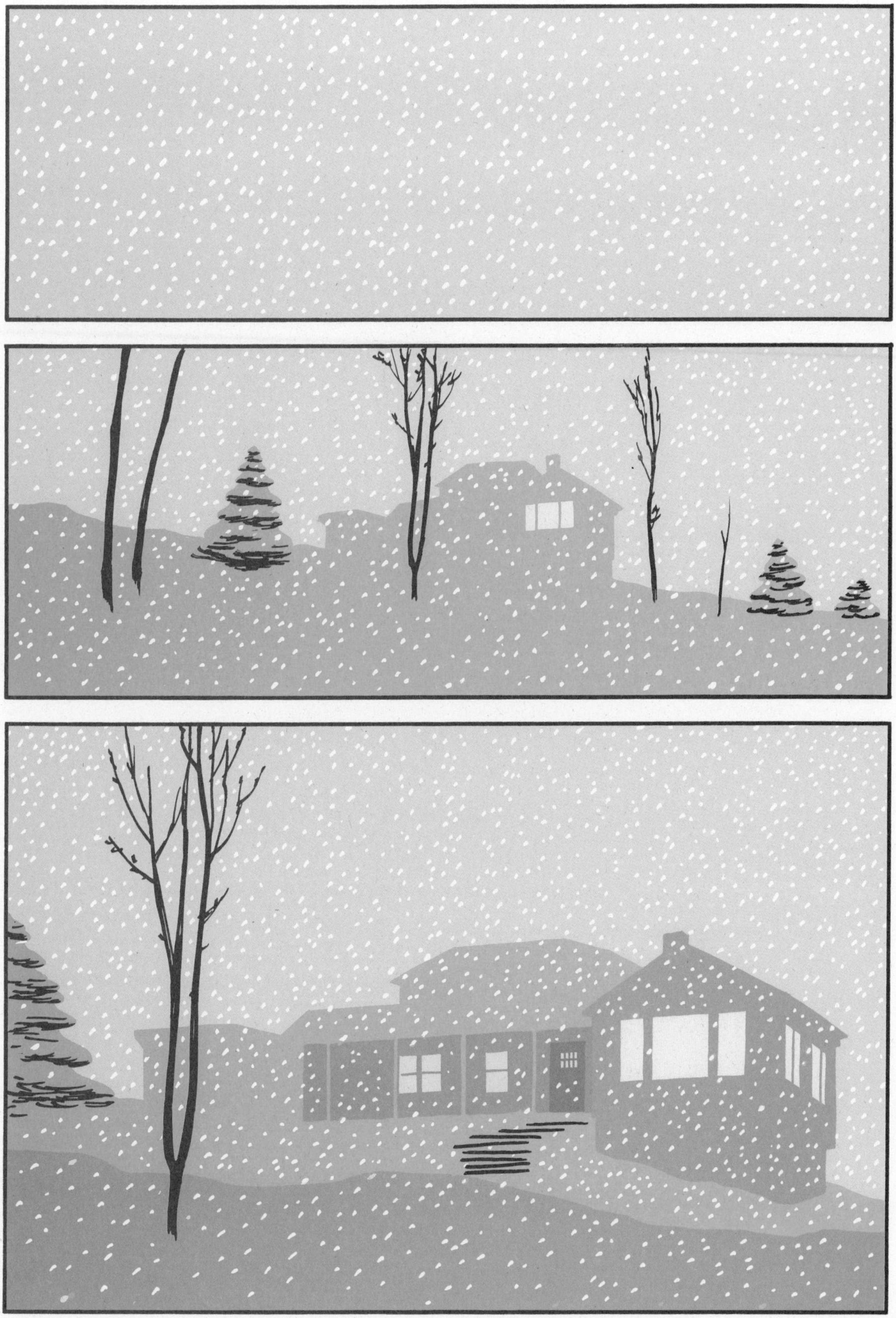

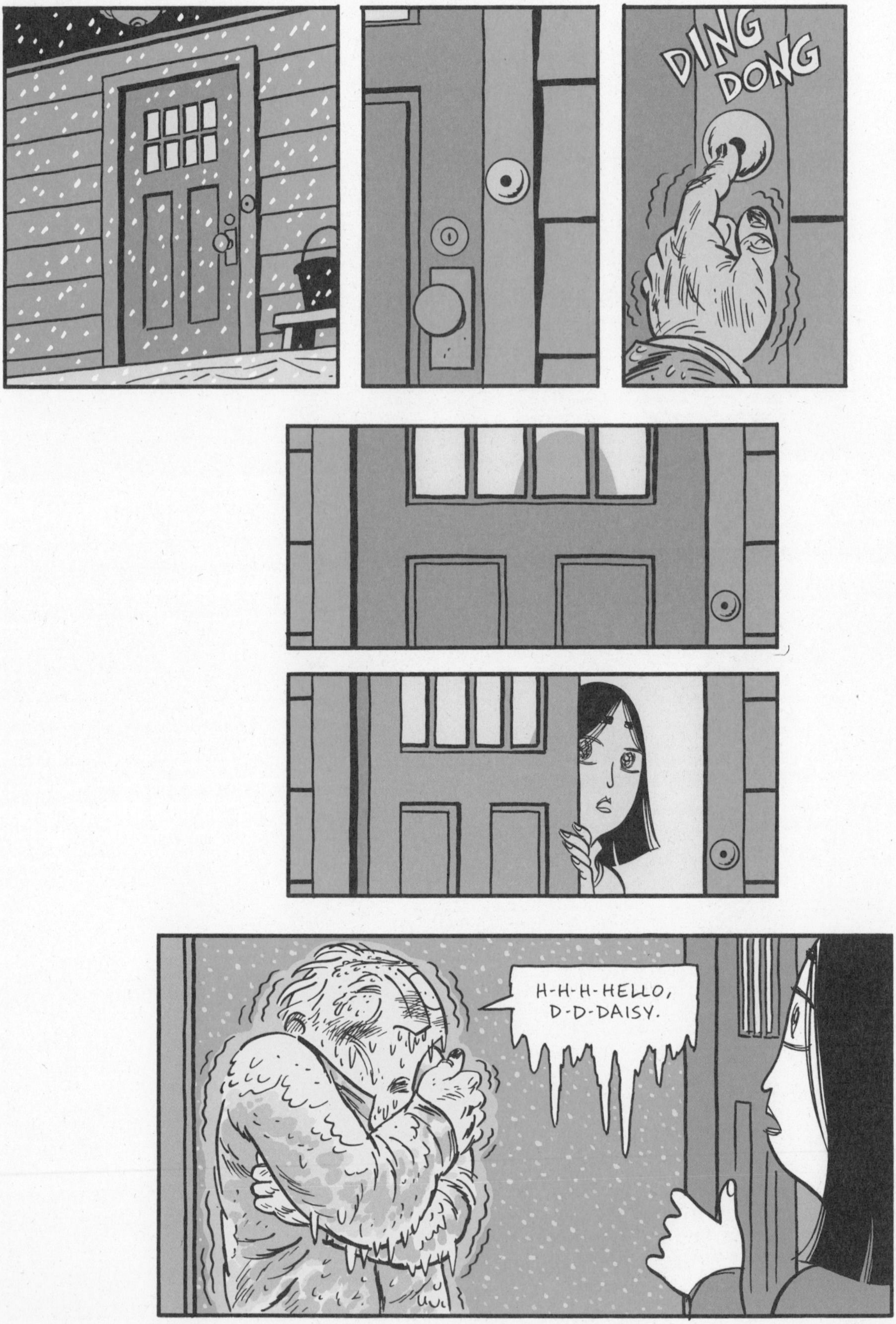
DING DONG
H-H-H-HELLO, D-D-DAISY.

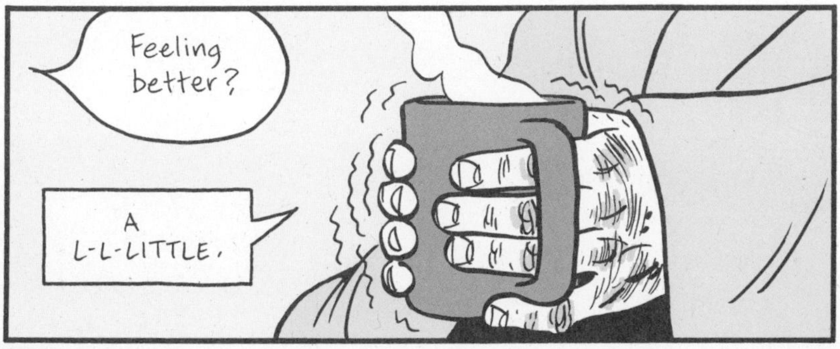
Feeling better?
A L-L-LITTLE.

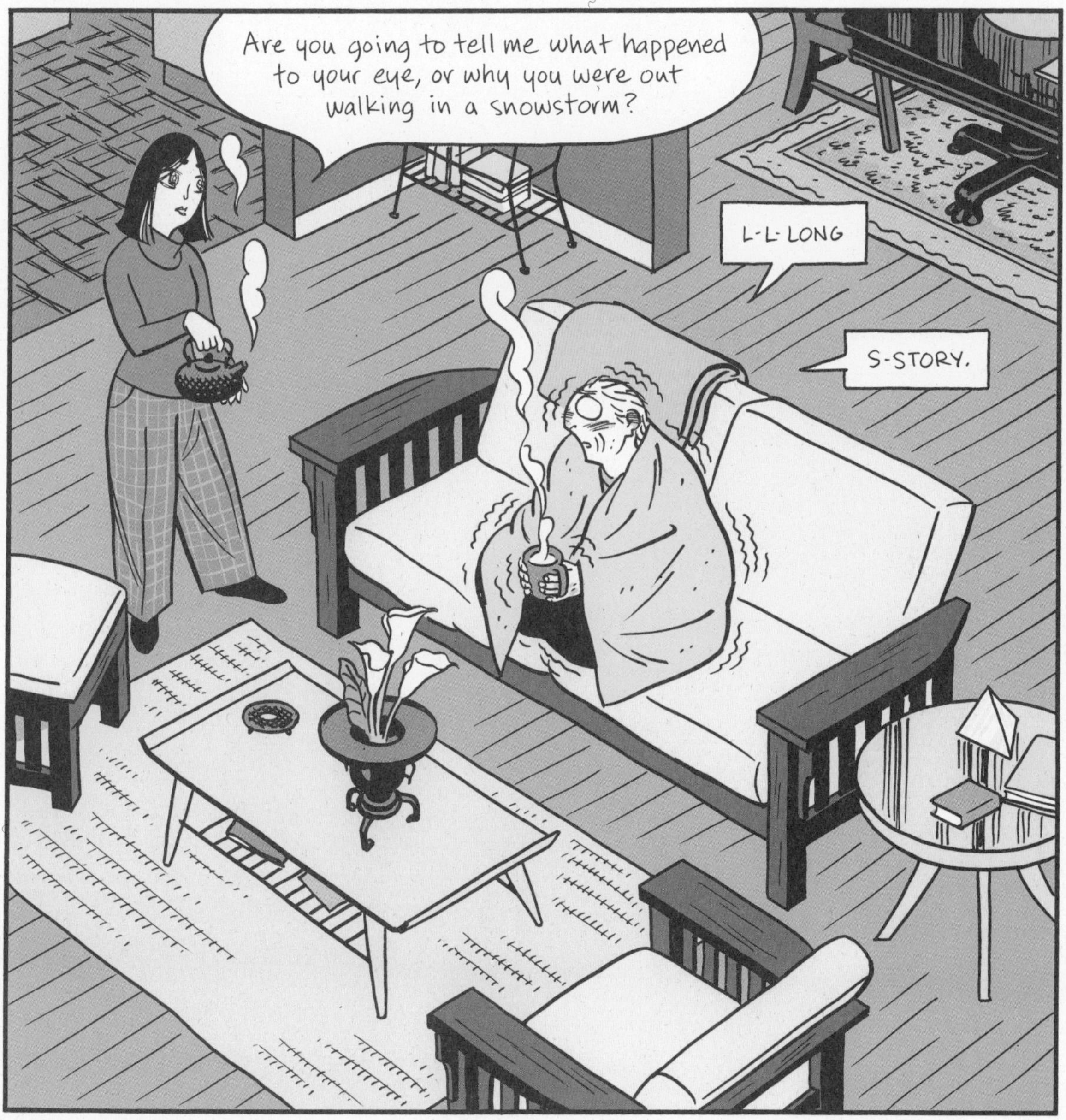
Are you going to tell me what happened to your eye, or why you were out walking in a snowstorm?
L-L-LONG
S-STORY.

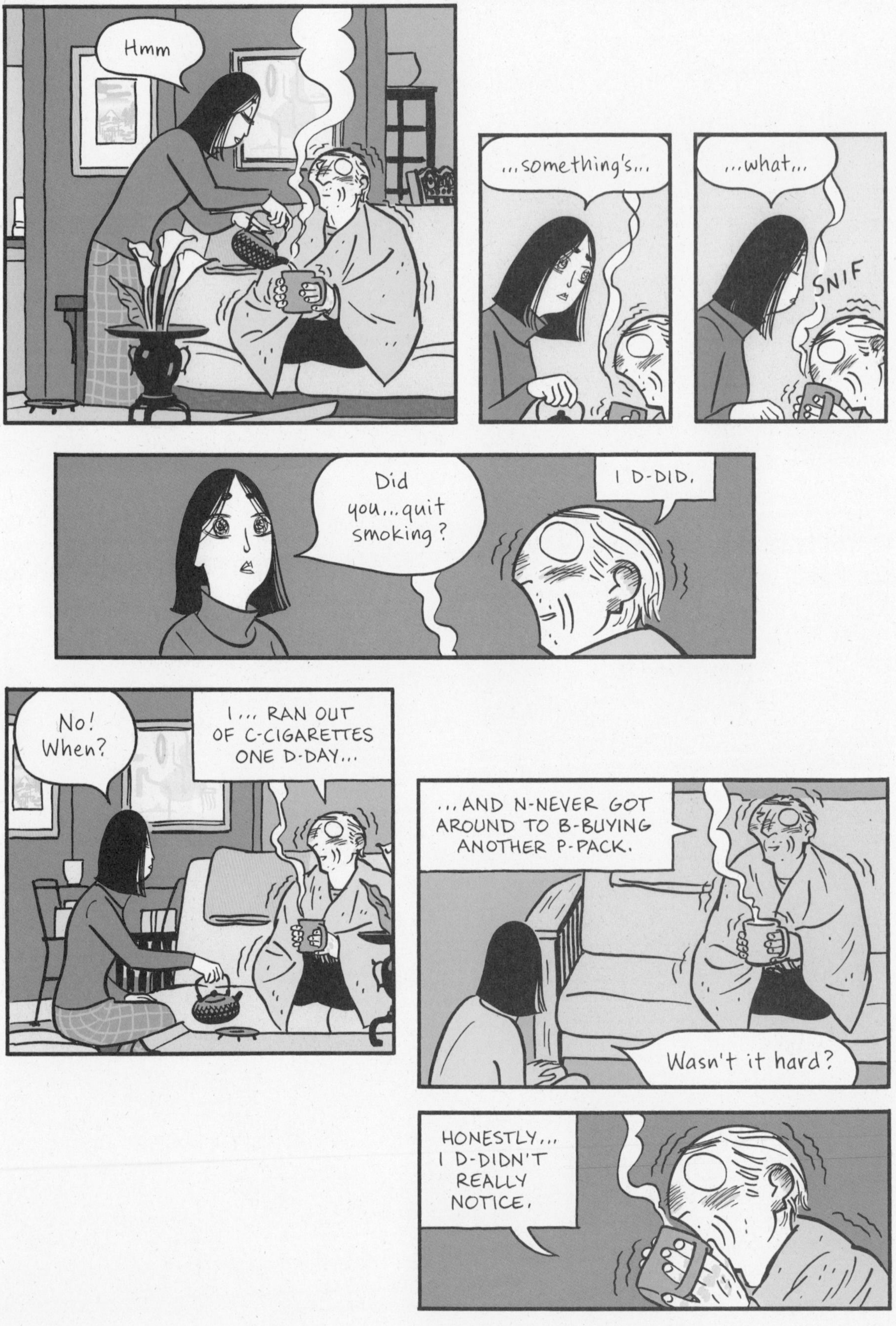
Hmm
...something's...
...what...
SNIF
Did you...quit smoking?
I D-DID.
No! When?
I... RAN OUT OF C-CIGARETTES ONE D-DAY...
...AND N-NEVER GOT AROUND TO B-BUYING ANOTHER P-PACK.
Wasn't it hard?
HONESTLY... I D-DIDN'T REALLY NOTICE.

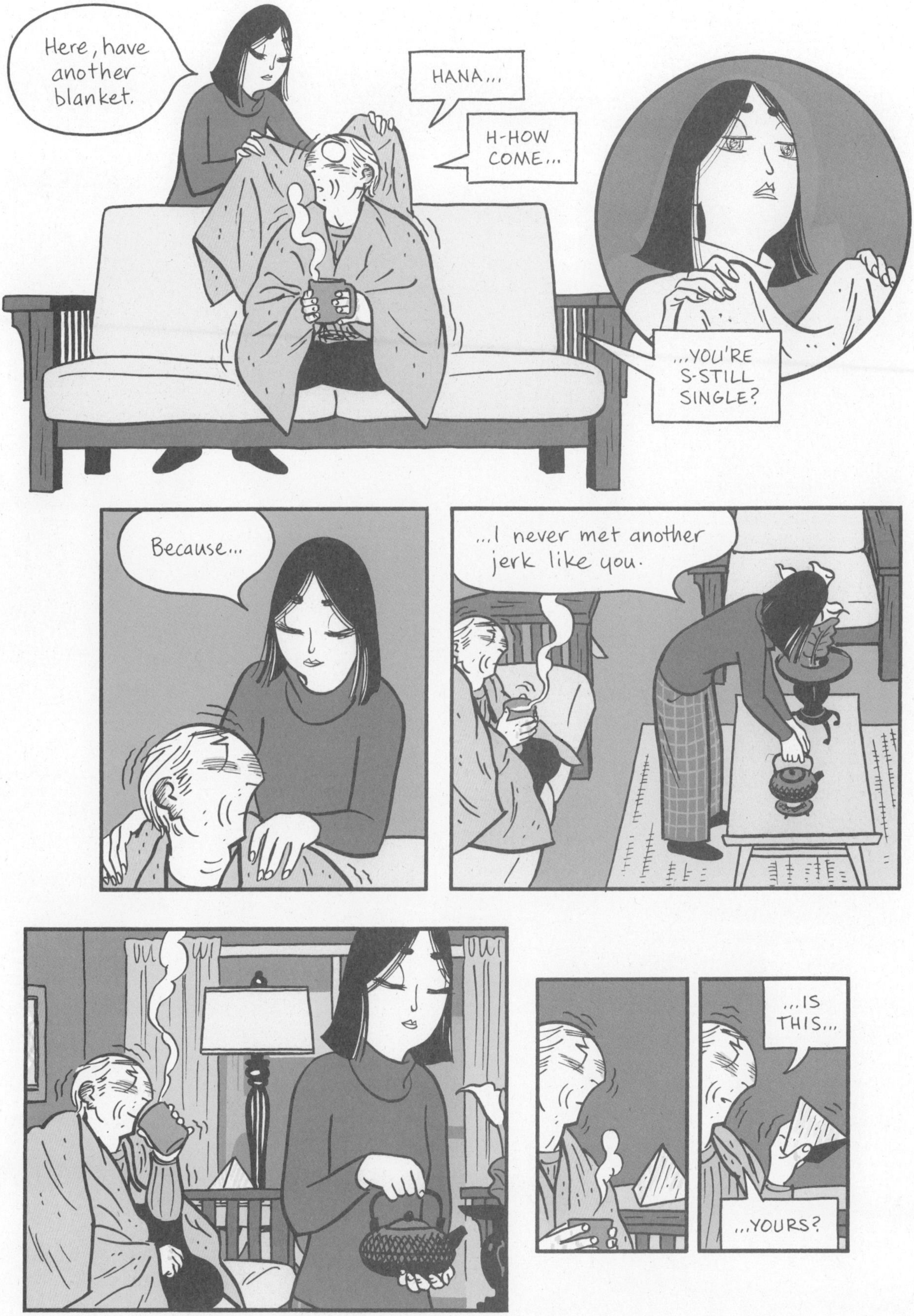
Here, have another blanket.
HANA...
H-HOW COME...
...YOU'RE S-STILL SINGLE?
Because...
...I never met another jerk like you.
...IS THIS...
...YOURS?

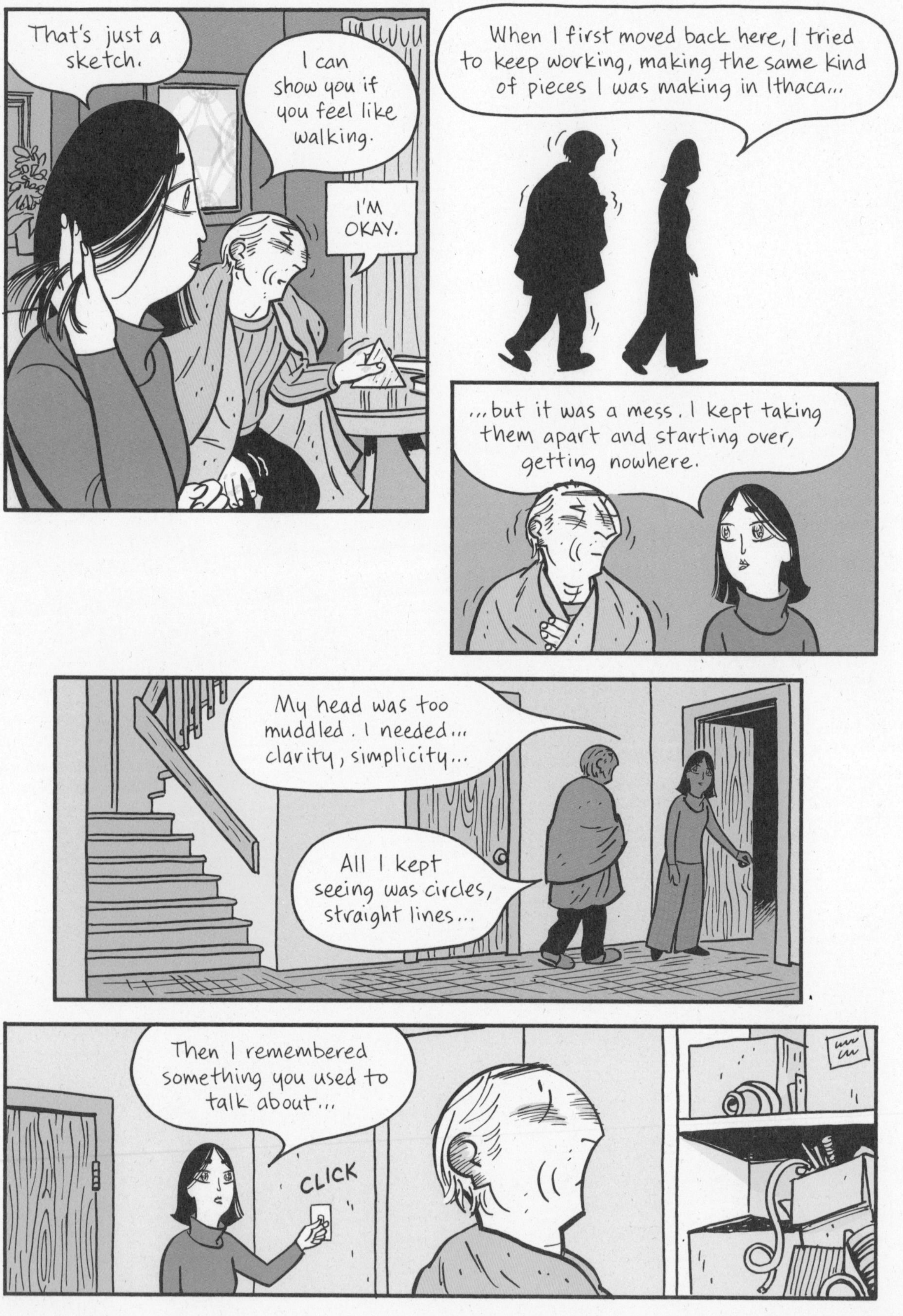
That's just a sketch.
I can show you if you feel like walking.
I'M OKAY.
When I first moved back here, I tried to keep working, making the same kind of pieces I was making in Ithaca...
...but it was a mess. I kept taking them apart and starting over, getting nowhere.
My head was too muddled. I needed... clarity, simplicity...
All I kept seeing was circles, straight lines...
Then I remembered something you used to talk about...
CLICK

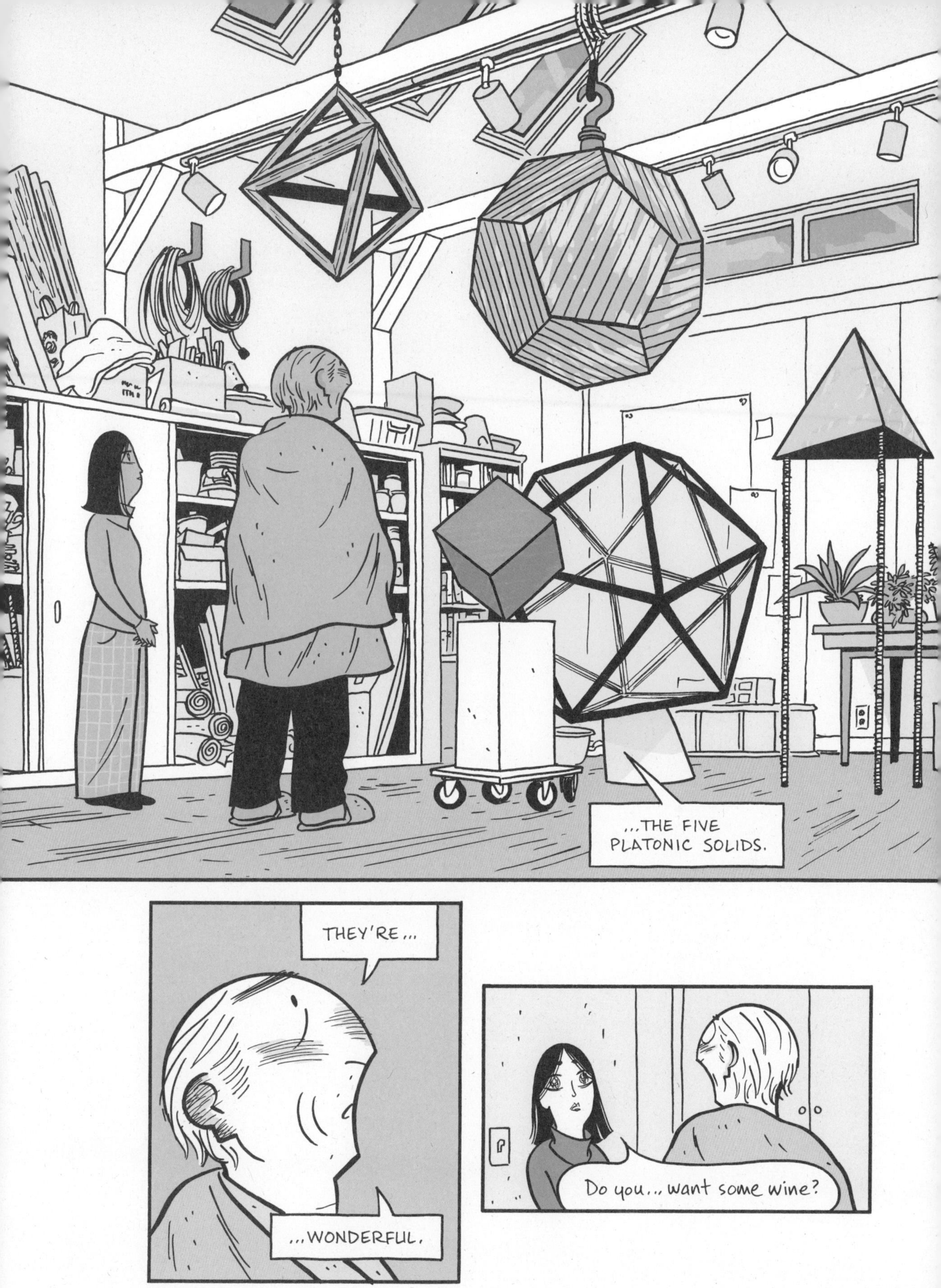
...THE FIVE PLATONIC SOLIDS.
THEY'RE...
...WONDERFUL.
Do you... want some wine?

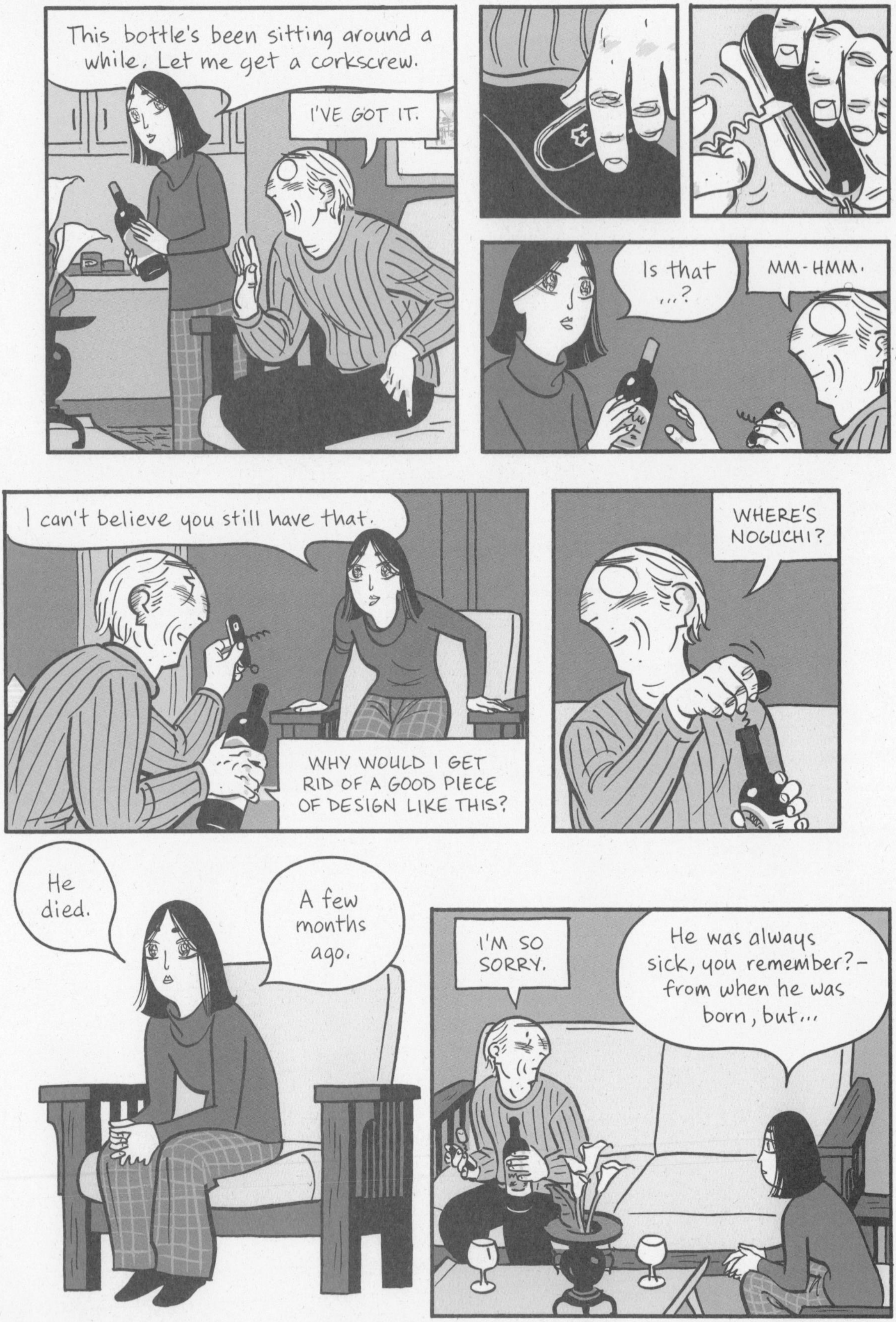
This bottle's been sitting around a while. Let me get a corkscrew.
I'VE GOT IT.
Is that ...?
MM-HMM.
I can't believe you still have that.
WHY WOULD I GET RID OF A GOOD PIECE OF DESIGN LIKE THIS?
WHERE'S NOGUCHI?
He died.
A few months ago.
I'M SO SORRY.
He was always sick, you remember?– from when he was born, but...

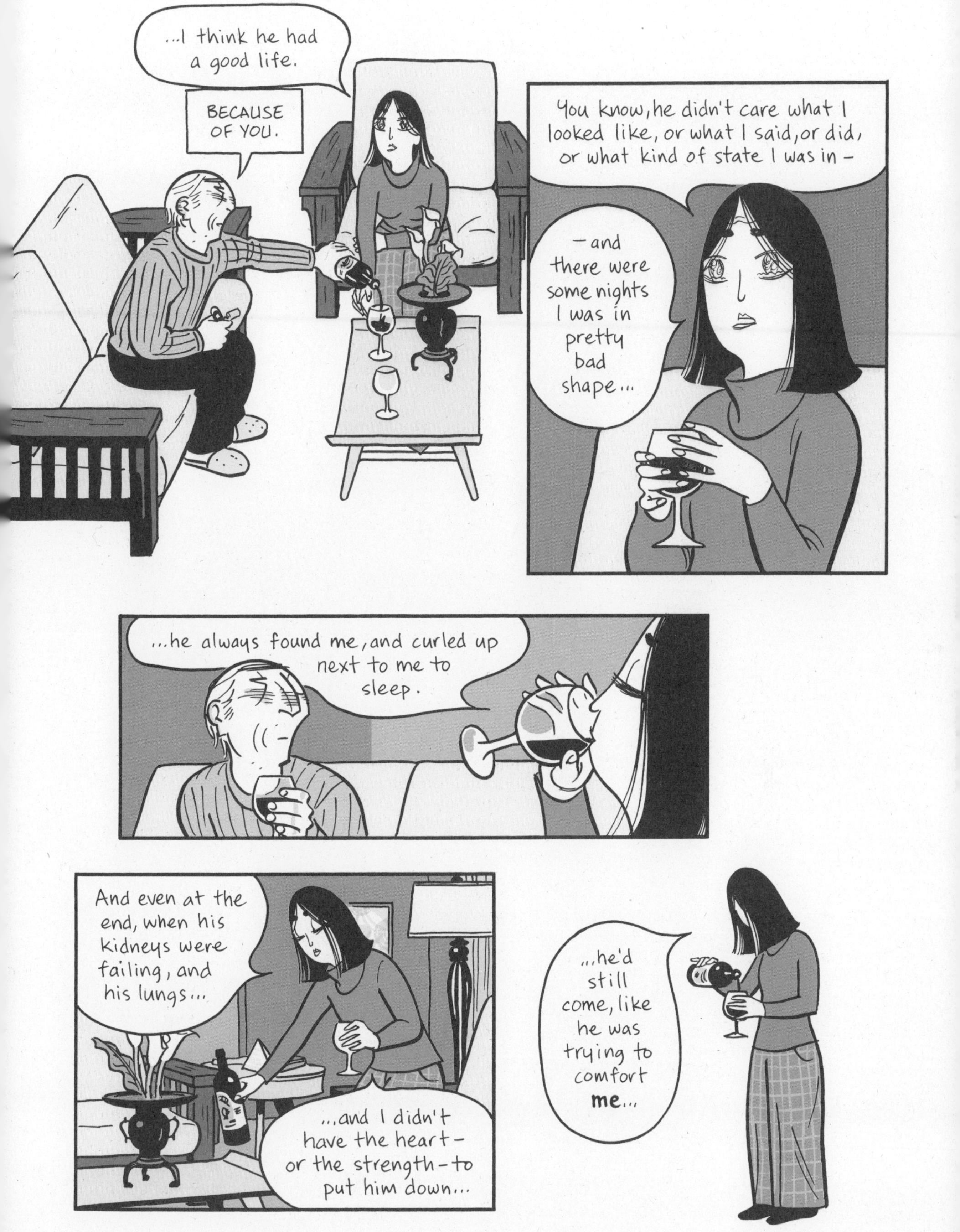

...I think he had a good life.
BECAUSE OF YOU.
You know, he didn't care what I looked like, or what I said, or did, or what kind of state I was in –
– and there were some nights I was in pretty bad shape...
...he always found me, and curled up next to me to sleep.
And even at the end, when his kidneys were failing, and his lungs...
...and I didn't have the heart – or the strength – to put him down...
...he'd still come, like he was trying to comfort **me**...

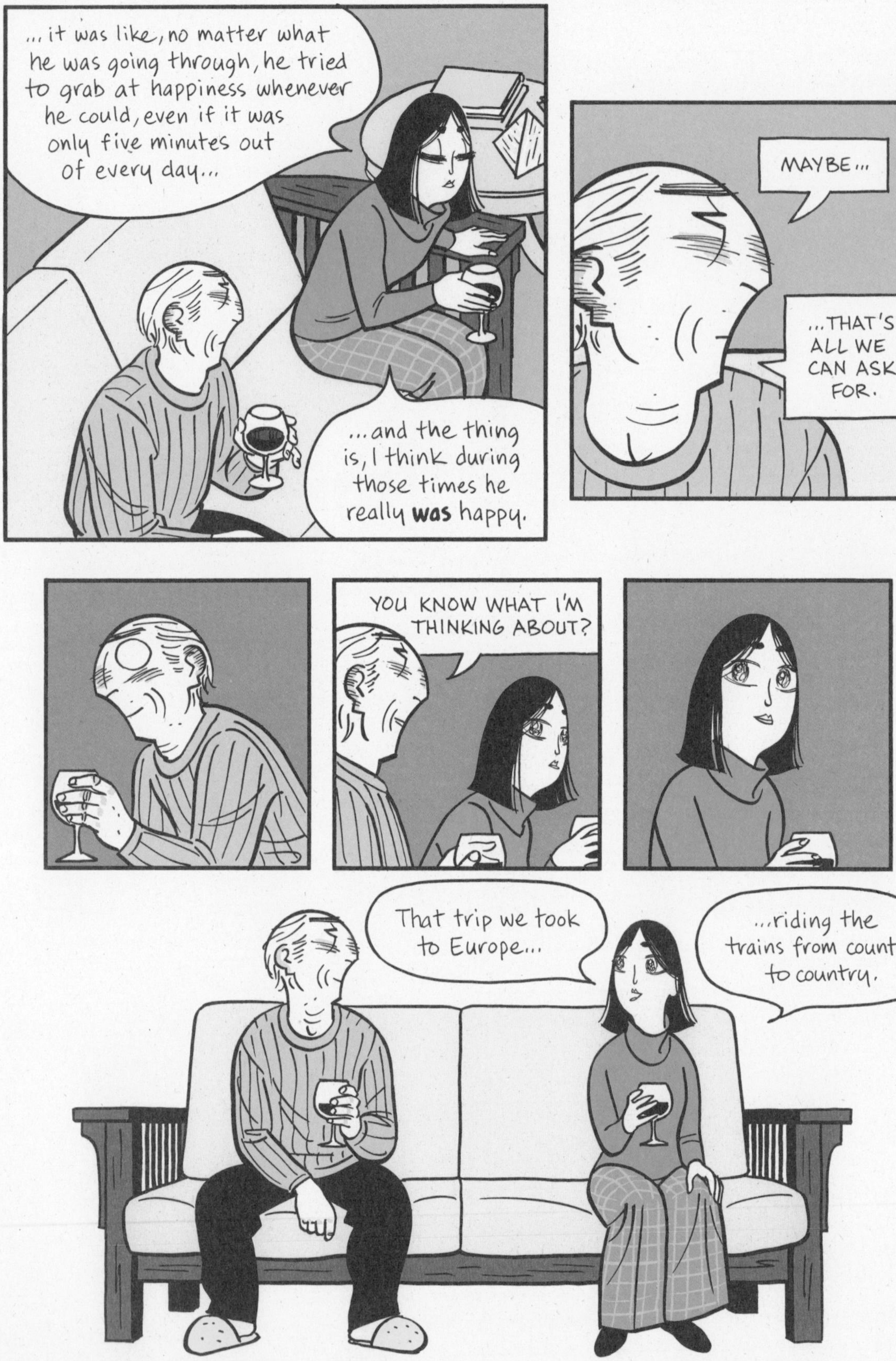
...it was like, no matter what he was going through, he tried to grab at happiness whenever he could, even if it was only five minutes out of every day...
...and the thing is, I think during those times he really **was** happy.
MAYBE...
...THAT'S ALL WE CAN ASK FOR.
YOU KNOW WHAT I'M THINKING ABOUT?
That trip we took to Europe...
...riding the trains from country to country.

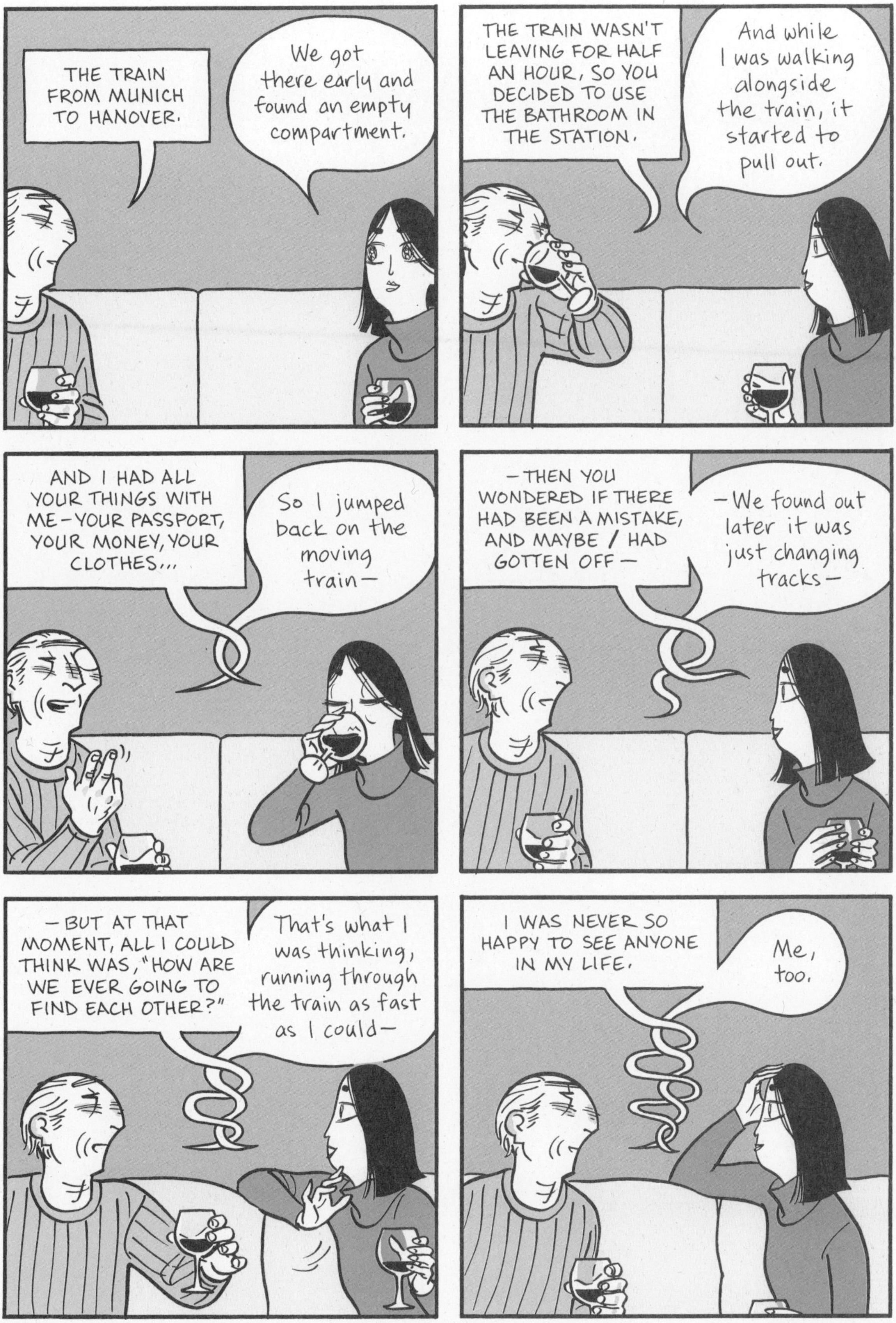
THE TRAIN FROM MUNICH TO HANOVER.
We got there early and found an empty compartment.
THE TRAIN WASN'T LEAVING FOR HALF AN HOUR, SO YOU DECIDED TO USE THE BATHROOM IN THE STATION.
And while I was walking alongside the train, it started to pull out.
AND I HAD ALL YOUR THINGS WITH ME—YOUR PASSPORT, YOUR MONEY, YOUR CLOTHES...
So I jumped back on the moving train—
—THEN YOU WONDERED IF THERE HAD BEEN A MISTAKE, AND MAYBE I HAD GOTTEN OFF—
—We found out later it was just changing tracks—
—BUT AT THAT MOMENT, ALL I COULD THINK WAS, "HOW ARE WE EVER GOING TO FIND EACH OTHER?"
That's what I was thinking, running through the train as fast as I could—
I WAS NEVER SO HAPPY TO SEE ANYONE IN MY LIFE.
Me, too.

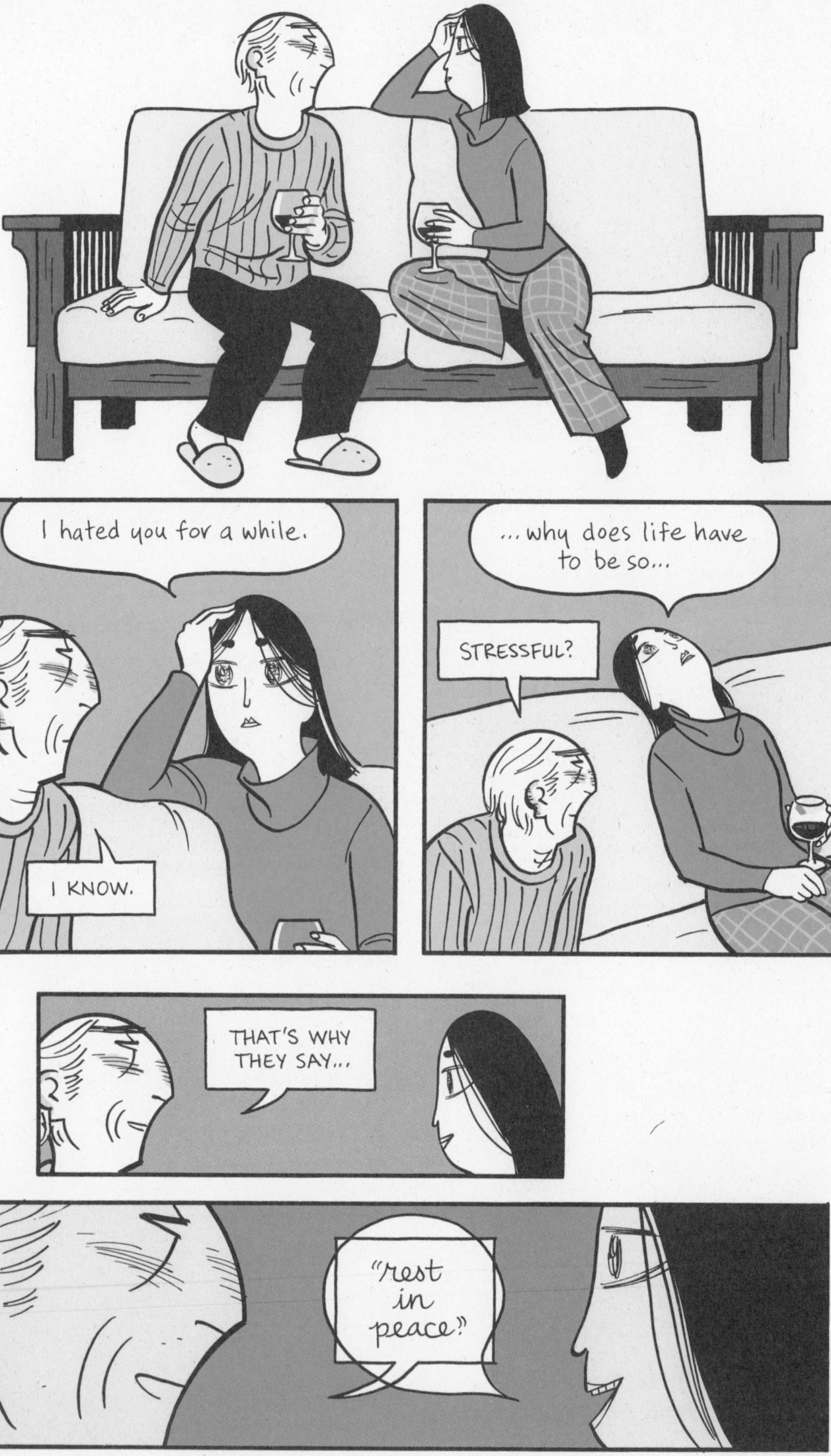
I hated you for a while.
I KNOW.
...why does life have to be so...
STRESSFUL?
THAT'S WHY THEY SAY...
"rest in peace."

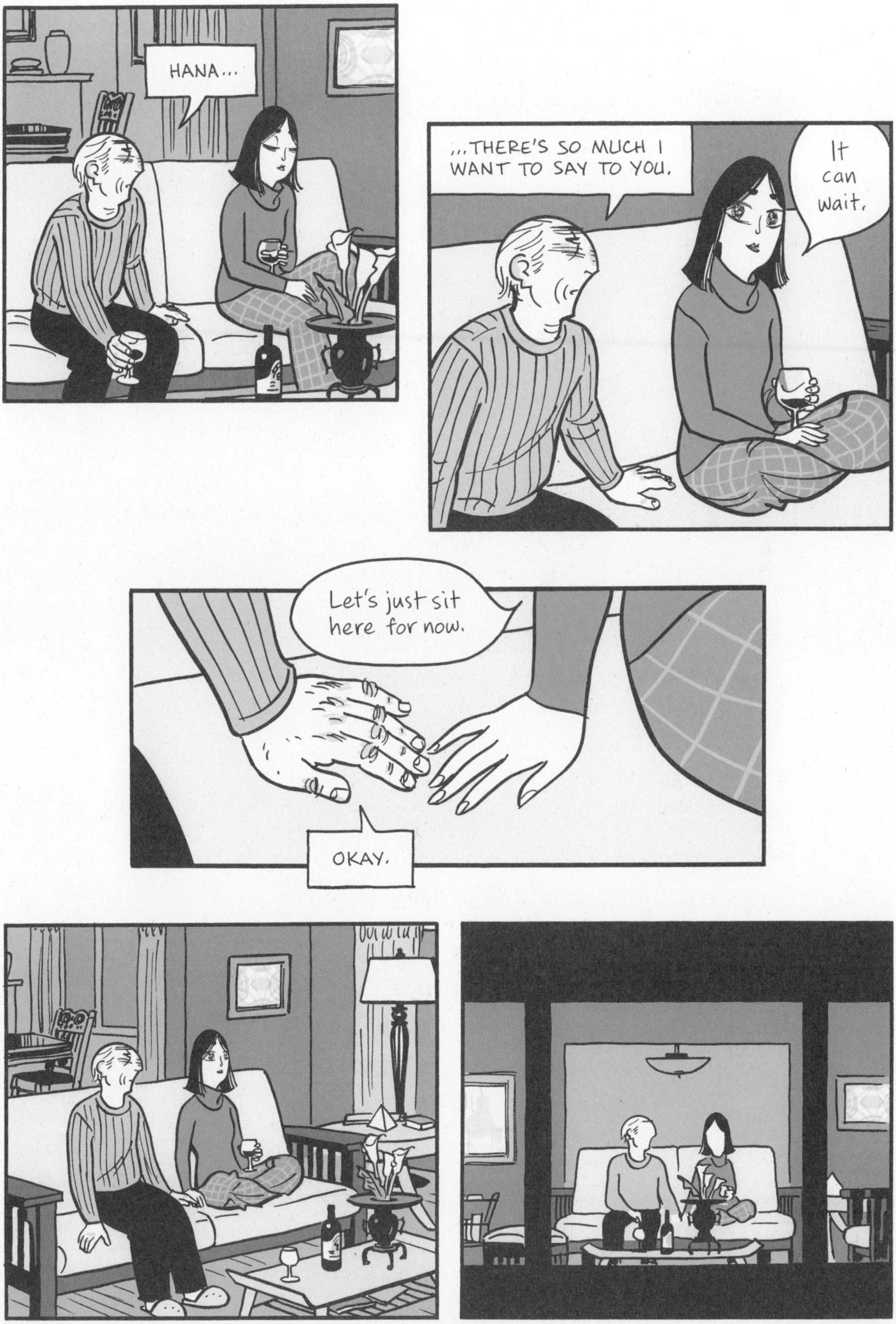
HANA...
...THERE'S SO MUCH I WANT TO SAY TO YOU.
It can wait.
Let's just sit here for now.
OKAY.

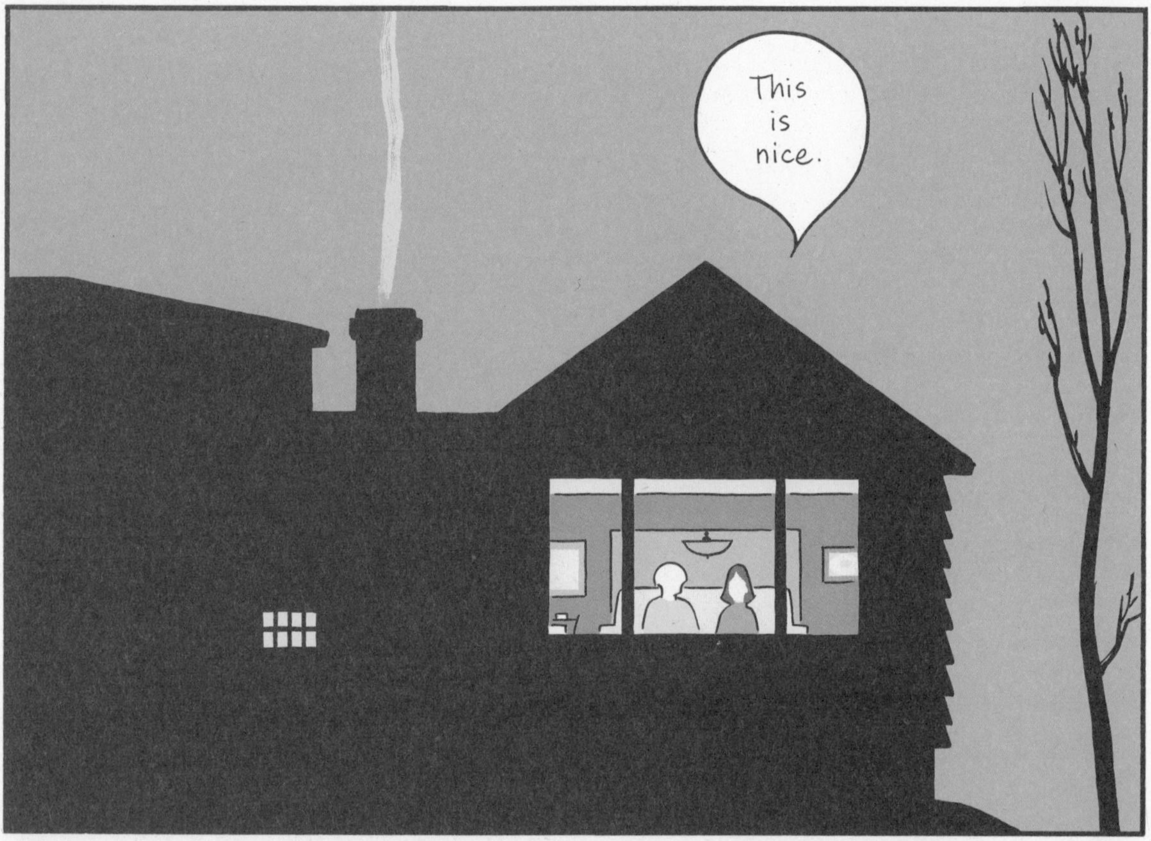
This is nice.

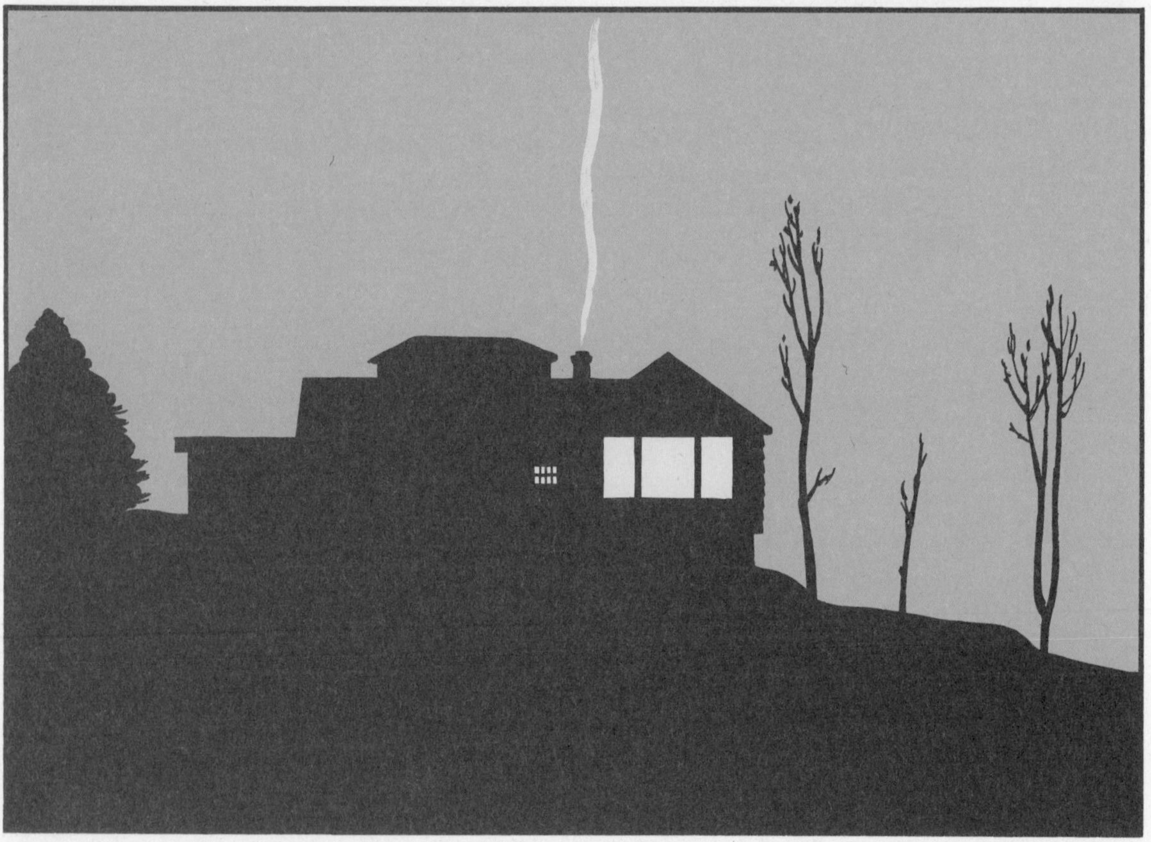

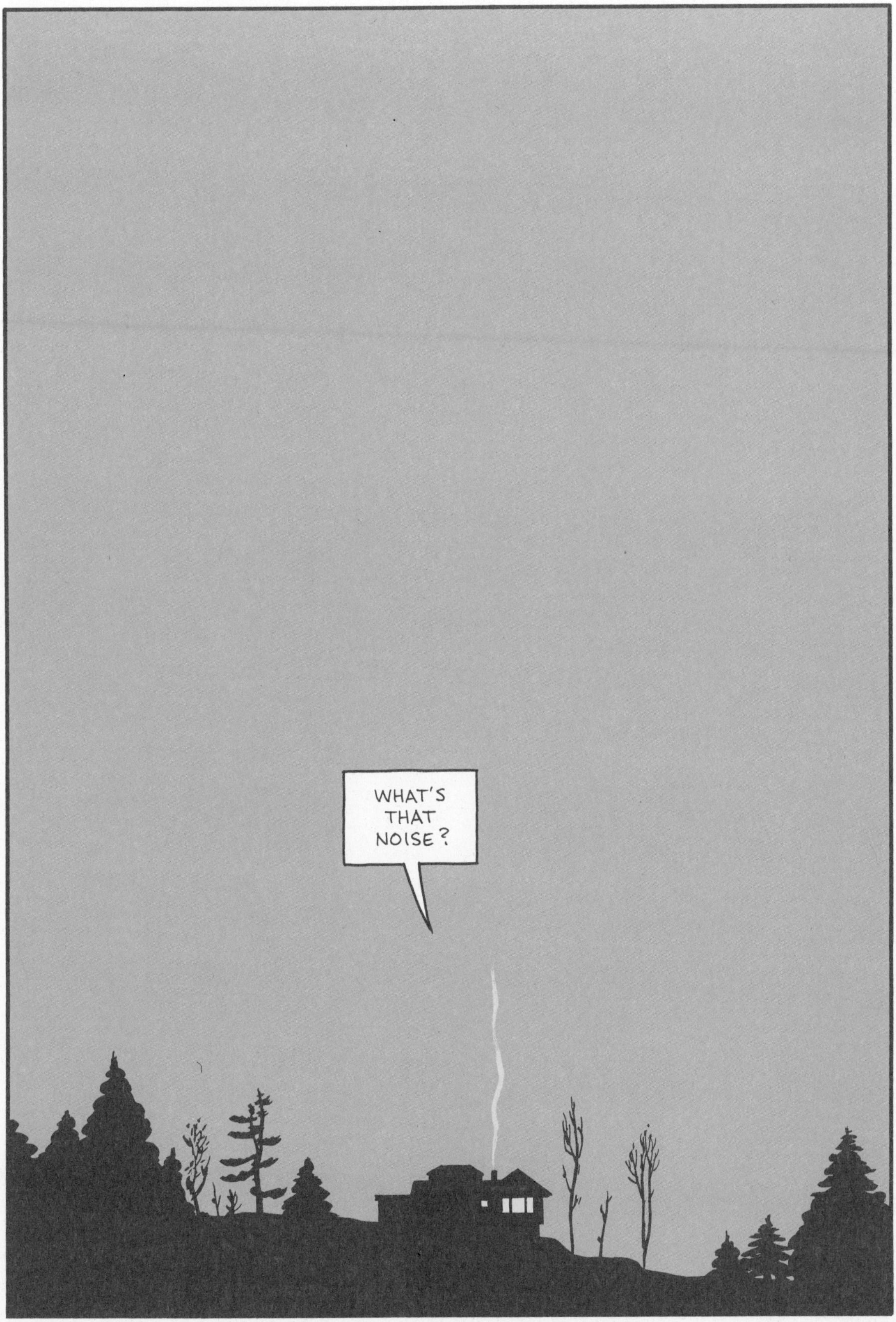
WHAT'S THAT NOISE?

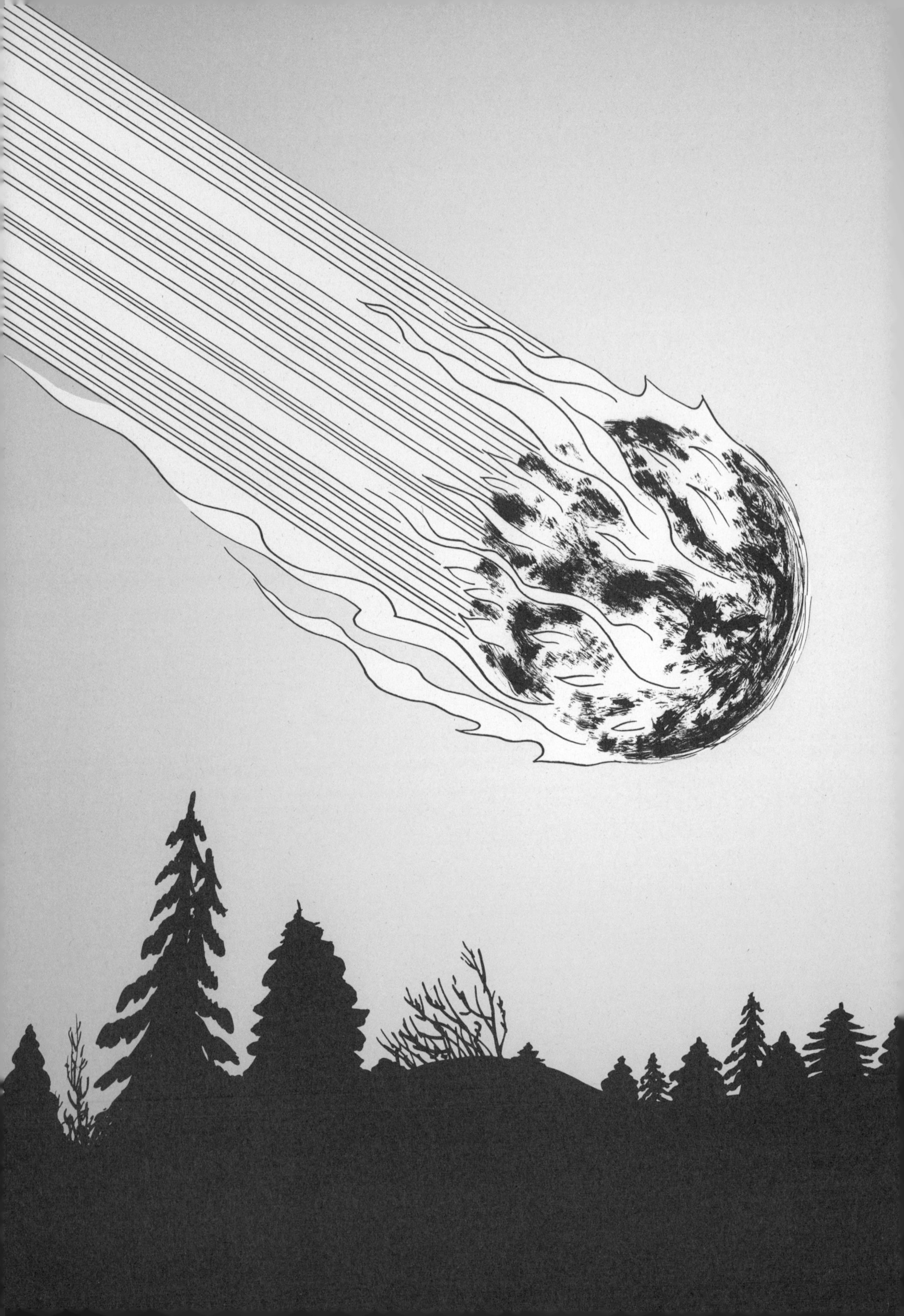

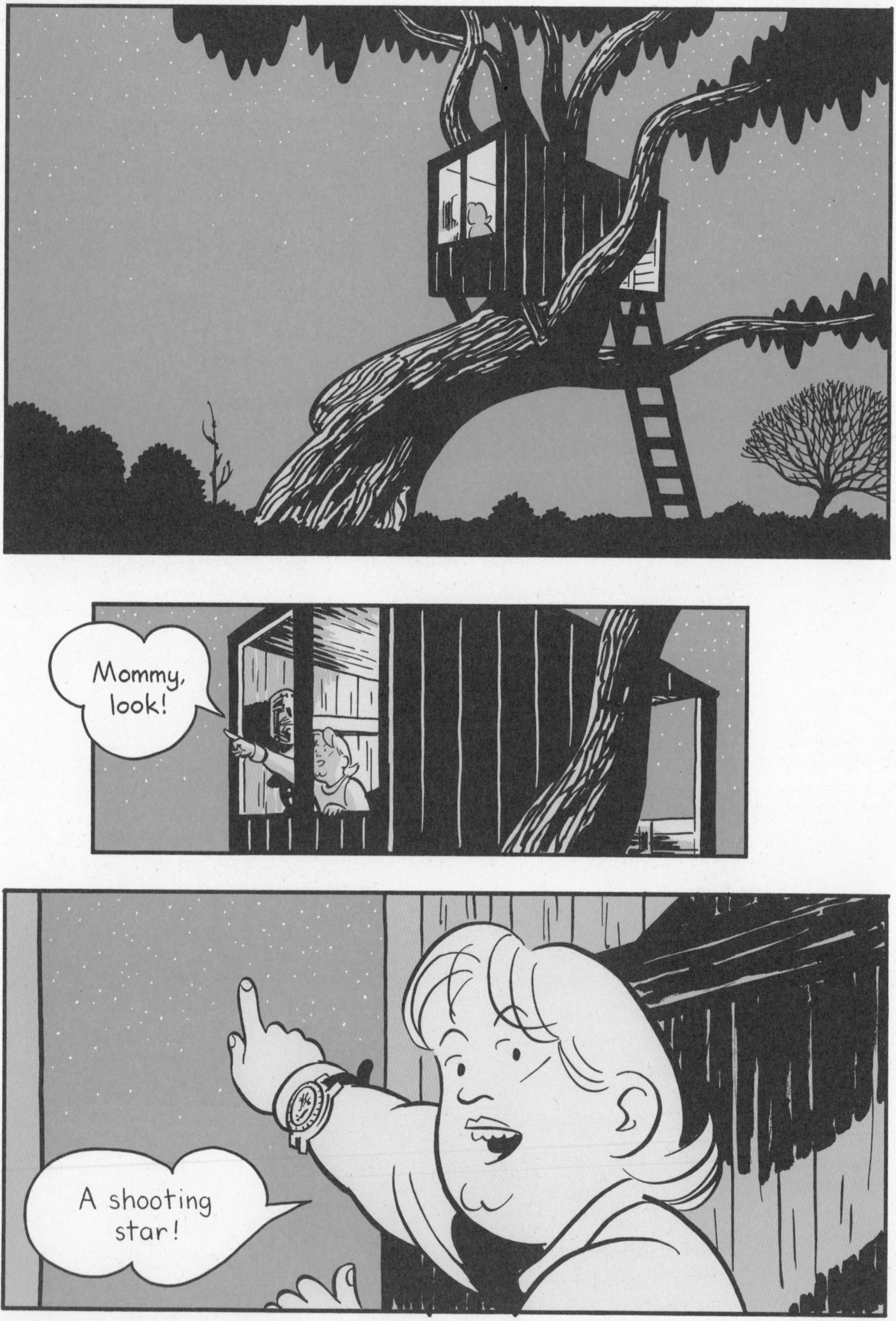
Mommy, look!
A shooting star!

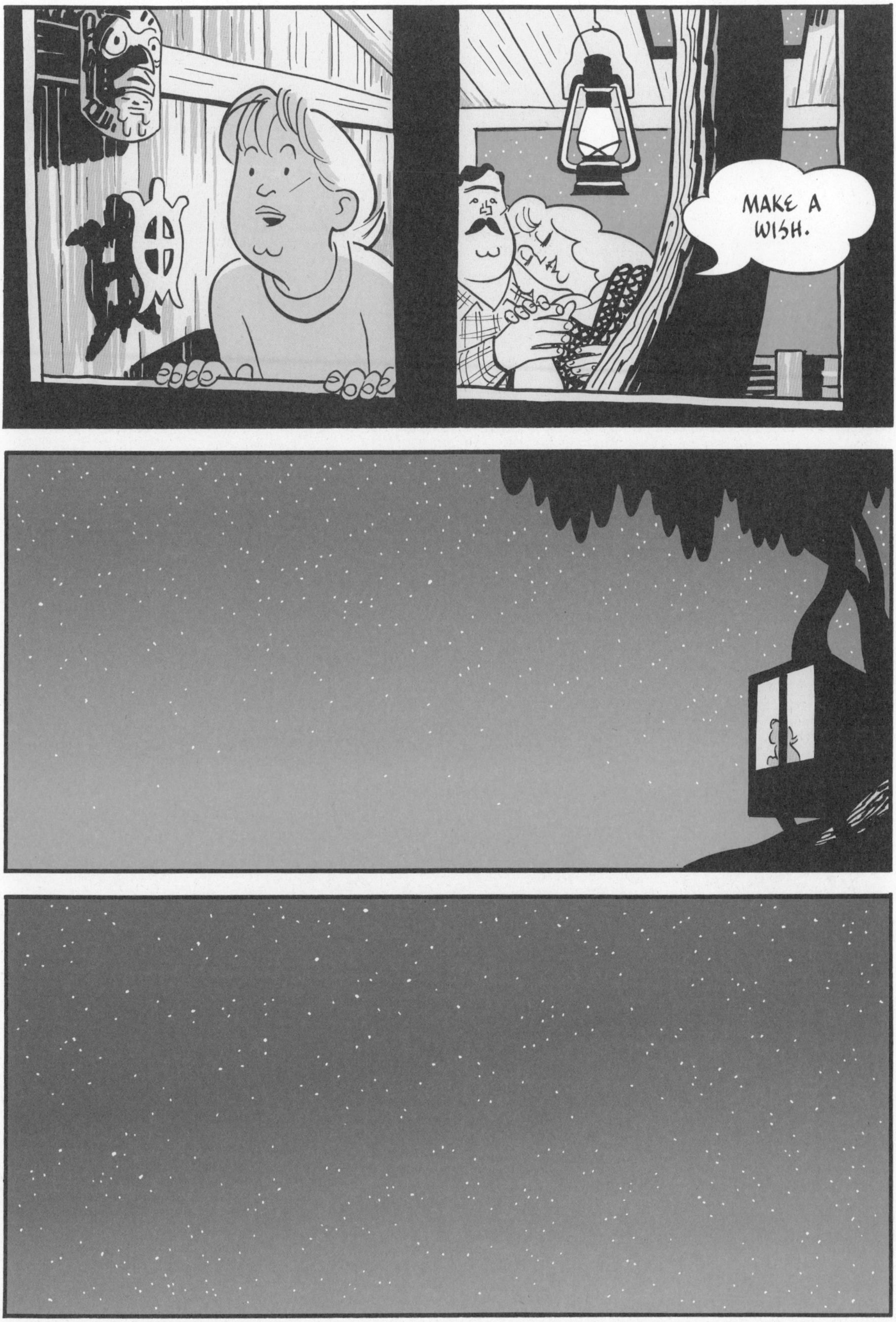
MAKE A WISH.